The Collected Works of Boris Sidis

Volume One

Table of Contents

Foreword

"They wouldn't do this for me...If they call me a genius, what superlative have they reserved for your husband?"

-William James to Sara Sidis after Harvard's waiver of multiple PhD requirements, including an oral exam, for Boris.

Boris Sidis, one of William James's personal friends and favorite pupils, is a pivotal but, for reasons that will be enumerated here, forgotten figure. A touching tribute to the doctor was published in the Journal of Abnormal Psychology:

"Sidis was one of the first to undertake a really scientific exploration of the subconscious region of the mind, and his findings therein were both varied and of practical importance. His formulation of the law of reserve energy and of the principal factors in suggestion, his demonstration of the value of the hypnoidal method as a means of gaining access to the subconscious, his exposition of the part played by the self-regarding instinct and by over-development of the fear instinct in the causation of psychopathic maladies, would alone suffice to give him a conspicuous place in the history both of psychology and of scientific psychotherapy. (Bruce, 1910)"

For defying the Tsarist decree against teaching peasants Boris was sentenced to two years in a cell that could not accommodate the length of an ordinary man's body. Instead of breaking his spirit, it only fueled his hatred for tyranny and his determination to combat it whenever it reared its head. Later he credited this period of solitary confinement with his immense capacity for concentration. After fleeing to America, Boris went through a series of menial jobs to support his independent reading at the Boston library, the first sight of which he likened to "the gates of heaven" (Wallace, 1989). During this time he met a young woman whose family had fled the Russian pogroms. Sara, who aspired to become a medical doctor, needed to pass her entrance exam. Boris tutored her. She would eventually become his wife. In line with other accounts, one colleague described him as a man who "had a very active and forceful mentality…and possessed a genial and kindly nature, but was apt to express his opposition to what he considered fraudulent or dishonest with abruptness and vigor. He was of a retiring disposition, and did not seek a following of pupils. He made few contacts with his colleagues, but the few friends he did make, among them Morton Prince [q.v.], were his loyal admirers" (Linenthal, 1923).

The four works selected for this volume cover the breadth of his thought while remaining accessible to the layperson. *The Psychology of Suggestion* is as engaging and provocative as any modern work on hypnosis, from its detailed investigations into the subconscious to its closing chapters about the historical, sociological, and economic consequences of our "subwaking selves." It is important to note that Sidis was not just writing as a theorist, but as an esteemed clinician who had treated droves of patients, some quite disturbed, with stunning success (Bruce, 1910). Compared to the permissive, varied, and occasionally bizarre techniques employed by Ericksonians (Battino and South, 2005) some hypnotists may find his inductions - which involved asking patients to follow a monotonous sound like a metronome or letting them guide themselves into trance by narrating their thoughts - boring or primitive. They nevertheless, for the most part, served his purposes.

Nervous Ills: Their Causes and Cure is a stirring counterpoint to the prevailing psychoanalytic prescriptions for anxiety, depression, and related maladies. Although it was published long before the first DSM, the sorts of neurotic ailments described in it should be immediately recognizable (he was, like any good medical professional, an astute observer). Near the outset Sidis calls psychoanalysis "a sort of Astrology, full of superstitious symbolizations, dream vagaries, and idle interpretations, foisted on the credulous, on those obsessed by sexual inclinations, and on those suffering from sexual perversions...psychoanalysts care for nothing else but the fulfillment of sexual wishes. It is useless to argue with psychoanalysts, who as a rule possess no more critical sense than Mormon saints." Earlier in an academic journal he'd written "some of Freud's admirers, with a metaphysical proclivity, are delighted over the theory of repressed wishes. The wish is fundamental and prior to all mental states. This piece of metaphysical psychologism is supposed to be based on clinical experience. If wishes were horses, beggars would ride. The Freudist manages to ride such horses (Sidis, 1911)."

An enraged Ernest Jones promptly sent a letter to James Putnam: "Sidis' remark is of course unpardonable, and Prince should not have allowed it to be printed; one will be bound to ignore him in the future." Psychiatry was not the only area where Boris confronted implacable dogmas and unapologetic dogmatists. At this time *Philistine and Genius* is his most widely read book, perhaps because it is brief and requires no specialized knowledge to understand. Its popularity may also attributable to its continued relevance as a critique of American culture and its connection to the controversial child-rearing methods he and Sara famously applied to their own son. Its excoriation of public schools, the American obsession with athletics, and the then accepted forms of parenting struck several nerves at once. Its tone, which occasionally veers into indignation, did not resonate with most readers. The overriding belief in the tremendous potential of *every* person the piece extolled was ignored; he'd condemned himself to being forever pilfered as an elitist for attacking the baser (and, in his opinion, perfectly remediable) parts of commonness.

His accomplishments were not limited to pedagogy or psychiatry. Dr. Bruce did not recognize (being without a crystal ball, how could he?) the significance of *The Theory of Moment Consciousness*. While James's influence is undeniable, the piece contains its share of original insights. Moreover its contentions, particularly those about hierarchical processing, seem to preempt those made later by Newell, Baars, DeHaene, and other proponents of Global Workspace Theory (Baars and Alonzi, 2018) as well as "dynamic core" models (Damasio, 1999). His work was expunged from the records by the moratorium placed upon the use of words like cognition, memory, and scores of other terms he, his teachers, and hundreds of generations of men and women have used for thousands of years to describe the subjective states all sentient beings experience. Because mental states could not be directly observed, they were deemed unworthy of serious inquiry, or formal recognition, by Watson, Skinner, and their followers (Baars, 1989). Even with the advent of advanced neuroimaging techniques the scientific study of consciousness remains woefully - or delightfully - interdisciplinary. Sidis saw the inextricable interconnectedness of all fields of knowledge. This is one of his strengths. It consistently shows in his writing.

His atheism, Jewish ancestry, fervent rejection of Freudian psychoanalysis, isolationist position towards American intervention in the First World War, opposition to eugenics, and obvious theoretical and methodological irreconcilability with the rising tide of Behaviorism in research psychology all conspired to ensure his alienation from society in his lifetime as well as the posthumous interment of his achievements. We must count his son, arguably the greatest child prodigy in recorded history, among them. However, Billy was another contributing factor to his father's fall from grace. Worse was that after graduating from Harvard William James Sidis, who had been a regular source of sensationalized stories for the press, led an adult life that did not seem to meet the expectations set by his boyhood feats.

Maybe the lad cracked under pressure? Likely not. Boris had more in common with a modern Montessori instructor than James Mill. Long before William entered his teens the newspapers had decided he was bound to have a nervous breakdown. Before he was of grade school age they decided Boris's methods would ruin his son's health. A significant portion of the claims made by the Yellow Press were either exaggerated or, even more often, completely fabricated (Wallace, 1986). Had they bothered to acquaint themselves with Sidis senior's views on education they would have known he did not just discourage cramming, but "study" itself. Learning was best, he claimed, when it was effortless; genius begins when instruction becomes indistinguishable from play. A precocious polyglot, an astounding mathematician, and a Harvard freshman by the age of 11, Billy's IQ is estimated to have been between 250 and 300. This amused his father, who dismissed intelligence tests as "silly, pedantic, absurd, and grossly misleading (Sidis, 1914)."

Extant photographs present us with a severe man standing in the stalwart fashion of someone who has spent their life upholding an ideal, a Hercules at once fatigued and emboldened by his labors. Perhaps he was too ready defend himself, too uncompromising in his commitments. The search for truth sometimes has to give up its seat to diplomacy. Although Boris disliked organized religion, he had an impressive command of the scriptures of more than one religion. He read the Hebrew Bible, the New Testament in Koine Greek, and the Sanskrit epics of India. He also regularly spoke with holy men of different faiths. Like any serious student of history or crowd psychology he was acutely aware of the darker features of the human mind, but there are few proponents of human potential as optimistic as Boris Sidis. Thus he differed from Freud not just in his picture of the subconscious, but in his very conception of human nature. In this respect, if no other, there are few who could be considered a more worthy successor to the aims and spirit of the psychology propounded by his cherished friend and mentor, William James. One wonders how psychiatry and psychology in the twentieth century would have developed had their torrents been tempered more by Boris Sidis.

Adam Alonzi

November 3, 2018

References and Suggested Reading

Baars, Bernard J. *The cognitive revolution in psychology.* Vol. 157. New York: Guilford Press, 1986.

Baars, Bernard, and Adam Alonzi. "Global Workspace Theory." *The Routledge Handbook of Consciousness* 2018, pp. 122–137.

Battino, Rubin, and Thomas L. South. *Ericksonian Approaches-: A Comprehensive Manual*. Crown House Publishing, 2005.

Bruce, H. Addington. "Masters of the mind." *American Magazine* 71 (1910): 71-81.

Damasio, Antonio. "The feeling of what happens." *Body and Emotion in the Making of Consciousness* (1999).

Linenthal, Harry. *Who's Who in America, 1022-23; Harvard Coll. Class of 1894*, 1923.

Jones, Ernest. "The Controversy over Psychoanalysis." Received by James Putnam, 6 Mar. 1911.

Mahony, Dan. The Sidis Archives, www.sidis.net

Sidis, Boris. *The foundations of normal and abnormal psychology*. RG Badger, 1914.

Sidis, Boris. "Fundamental states in psychoneurosis." *The Journal of Abnormal Psychology* 5.6 (1911): 320.

Wallace, Amy. *The Prodigy*. E.P. Dutton, 1986.

The Psychology of Suggestion

By Boris Sidis

DEDICATED TO DAVID GORDON LYON, PH.D.
HOLLIS PROFESSOR OF DIVINITY AT HARVARD UNIVERSITY.

INTRODUCTION

I AM glad to contribute to this book of Dr. Boris Sidis a few words of introduction, which may possibly gain for it a prompter recognition by the world of readers who are interested in the things of which it treats. Much of the experimental part of the work, although planned entirely by Dr. Sidis, was done in the Harvard Psychological Laboratory, and I have been more or less in his confidence while his theoretic conclusions, based on his later work in the Pathological Institute of the New York State Hospitals, were taking shape.

The meaning of personality, with its limits and its laws, forms a problem which until quite recently had to be discussed almost exclusively by logical and metaphysical methods. Within the past dozen years, however, an immense amount of new empirical material had been injected into the question by the observations which the "recognition" by science of the hypnotic state set in motion. Many of these observations are pathological: fixed ideas, hysteric attacks, insane delusions, mediumistic phenomena, etc. And altogether, although they are far from having solved the problem of personality, they must be admitted to have transformed its outward shape. What are the limits of the consciousness of a human being ?

Is self -consciousness only a part of the whole consciousness ? Are there many "selves "dissociated from one another ? What is the medium of synthesis in a group of associated ideas? How can certain systems of ideas be cut off and forgotten ? Is personality a product, and not a principle ? Such are the questions now being forced to the front — questions now asked for the first time with some sense of their concrete import, and questions which it will require a great amount of further work, both of observation and of analysis, to answer adequately.

Meanwhile many writers are seeking to fill the gap, and several books have been published seeking to popularize the new observations and ideas and present them in connected form. Dr. Sidis' work distinguishes itself from some of these by its originality, and from others by the width of its scope.

It is divided into three parts: Suggestibility; the Self; Man as One of a Crowd. Under all these heads the author is original. He tries by ingenious experiments to show that the suggestibility of waking persons follows an opposite law to that of hypnotic subjects. Suggestions must be veiled, in the former case, to be effective ; in the latter case, the more direct and open they are the better. By other ingenious experiments Dr. Sidis tries to show that the "subliminal"or "ultra-marginal "portions of the mind may in normal persons distinguish objects which the attentive senses find it impossible to name. These latter experiments are incomplete, but they open the way to a highly important psychological investigation.

In Part II, on "The Self,"a very full account is given of "double personality,"subliminal consciousness, etc. The author is led to adopt as an explanation of the dissociations which lie at the root of all these conditions the physiological theory of retraction of the processes of the brain cells, which in other quarters also seems coming to the front. He makes an elaborate classification of the different degrees of dissociation or amnesia, and, on the basis of a highly interesting and important pathological case, suggests definite methods of diagnosis and cure. This portion of the book well deserves the attention of neurologists.

In Part III the very important matter of "crowd psychology"is discussed, almost for the first time in English. There is probably no more practically important topic to the student of public affairs. Dr. Sidis illustrates it by fresh examples, and his treatment is highly suggestive.

I am not convinced of all of Dr. Sidis' positions, but I can cordially recommend the volume to all classes of readers as a treatise both interesting and instructive, and original in a high degree, on a branch of research whose importance is daily growing greater.

WILLIAM JAMES. HARVARD UNIVERSITY, November 1, 1897. •

TABLE OF CONTENTS

PART III. SOCIETY.

CHAPTER XXVII.
SOCIAL SUGGESTIBILITY.

CHAPTER XXVIII.
SOCIETY AND EPIDEMICS.

CHAPTER XXIX.
STAMPEDES.

CHAPTER XXX.
MEDIEVAL MENTAL EPIDEMICS.

CHAPTER XXXI.
DEMONOPHOBIA.

CHAPTER XXXII.
FINANCIAL CRAZES.

CHAPTER XXXIII.
AMERICAN MENTAL EPIDEMICS.

THE PSYCHOLOGY OF SUGGESTION

THE study of the subconscious is becoming of more and more absorbing interest. The phenomena of hysteria and of hypnosis are now studied by the French psychologists with remarkable acumen and with an unrivalled fertility of ingenious devices, and the results obtained thus far form almost an epoch in the history of psychology. Although the French psychologists work independently of one another and disagree among themselves on many important points, still their method and general line of investigation are pretty nearly the same. They all care for clinical cases more than for minute, detailed laboratory experiments—the present hobby of the Germans—and their chief work falls within the domain of the subconscious. The French psychologists seem to be on the track of a rich gold vein. Without closely formulating their method, they have all, as if by a mutual tacit understanding, chosen the right way that leads to a better and deeper insight into the nature of mind. For the mechanism of consciousness is hidden deep down in the depths of the subconscious, and it is thither we have to. descend in order to get a clear understanding of the phenomena that appear in the broad daylight of consciousness.

The German school, with "Wundt at its head, at first started out on similar lines, but they could not make any use of the subconscious, and their speculations ran wild in the fancies of Hartmann. The reason of this failure is due to the fact that the concept of the subconscious as conceived by the German school was extremely vague, and had rather the character of a mechanical than that of a psychical process. An unconscious consciousness that was their concept of the subconscious. In such a form as this the subconscious was certainly meaningless—mere nonsense—and had to be given up. The German psychological investigations are now confined to the content of consciousness in so far as the individual is immediately conscious of it. But as this form of consciousness is extremely narrow and circumscribed, the results arrived at, though remarkable for their thoroughness, are after all of a rather trivial nature. It is what Prof. James aptly characterizes "the elaboration of the obvious."We may therefore, with full right, assert that it was the French psychologists who made proper use of the subconscious and arrived at results that are of the utmost importance to psychology, although it were well if the French were to conduct their investigations with German thoroughness.

It is not, however, the French alone who work along the lines of the subconscious, but the English and Americans, too, have a large share in the work. Gourney, James, Myers, and others, have done much toward the elucidation of the obscure phenomena of the subconscious. Psychology is especially indebted to the genius of Myers for his wide and comprehensive study

of the phenomena of the subconscious, or of what he calls the manifestations of the subliminal self. The only drawback in Myers's concept of the subliminal self is that he conceives it as a metaphysical entity, as a kind of a cosmic self. Now, while Myers may be right in his belief, the phenomena under investigation do not warrant the hypothesis of metaphysical entities. I have therefore avoided the use of the term "subliminal self,"however excellent it might be in itself, in order not to entangle the reader in the metaphysical considerations that cluster round that concept, and also because my point of view of the subconscious widely differs from that of Myers.

The study of subconscious phenomena is of great interest from a purely practical standpoint, because of the use that can be made of it in the state of health and disease. A knowledge of the laws of the subconscious is of momentous import in education, in the reformation of juvenile criminals and offenders, and one can hardly realize the great benefit that suffering humanity will derive from a proper methodical use of the subconscious within the province of therapeutics.

The study of the subconscious is especially of great value to sociology, because nowhere else does the subconscious work on such a grand, stupendous scale as it does in the popular mind; and the sociologist who ignores the subconscious lacks a deep insight into the nature of social forces. For the practical man who takes part in social affairs, in so far as they concern his own interests, the knowledge of the subconscious can hardly be overestimated; and this knowledge becomes an imperative necessity to him who lives in a democracy. The object of this book is the study of the sujb -

conscious, normal or abnormal, individual or social, in its relation to suggestion and suggestibility; and let me hope that the thoughtful reader will find my work not only interesting, but stimulating to thought and useful in practical life.

PATHOLOGICAL INSTITUTE, OF THE NEW YORK STATE HOSPITALS, NEW YORK, 1897 .

CHAPTER I:
SUGGESTION AND SUGGESTIBILITY

PSYCHOLOGICAL investigators employ the term "suggestion "in such a careless and loose fashion that the reader is often puzzled as to its actual meaning. Suggestion is sometimes used for an idea bringing in its train another idea, and is thus identified with association. Some extend the province of suggestion, and make it so broad as to coincide with any influence man exerts on his fellow-beings. Others narrow down suggestion and suggestibility to mere symptoms of hysterical neurosis. This is done by the adherents of the Salpetriere school. Suggestion, again, is used by the Nancy school to indicate the cause which produces that peculiar state of mind in which the phenomena of suggestibility become especially prominent.

This vague and hazy condition of the subject of suggestion causes much confusion in psychological discussions. To free the subject from this confusion of tongues, we must endeavour in some way or other to give a strict definition of suggestion, and rigorously study the phenomena contained within the limited field of our investigation. "We must not follow in the way of those writers who employ the terms suggestion and suggestibility in all possible meanings. Such carelessness can not but lead into a tangle of words. In order to give a full description of suggestion and make its boundary lines clear, distinct, and definite, let us take a few concrete cases and inspect them closely.

I hold a newspaper in my hands and begin to roll it up; soon I find that my friend sitting opposite me rolled up his in a similar way. This, we say, is a case of suggestion.

My friend Mr. A. is absent-minded; he sits near the table, thinking of some abstruse mathematical problem that baffles all his efforts to solve it. Absorbed in the solution of that intractable problem, he is blind and deaf to what is going on around him. His eyes are directed on the table, but he appears not to see any of the objects there. I put two glasses of water on the table, and at short intervals make passes in the direction of the glasses—passes which he seems not to perceive; then I resolutely stretch out my hand, take one of the glasses, and begin to drink. My friend follows suit—dreamily he raises his hand, takes the glass, and begins to sip, awakening fully to consciousness when a good part of the tumbler is emptied.

To take an interesting and amusing case given by Ochorowitz in his book Mental Suggestion:

"My friend P., a man no less absent-minded than he is keen of intellect, was playing chess in a neighbouring room. Others of us were talking near the door. I had made the remark that it was my friend's habit when he paid the closest attention to the game to whistle an air from Madame Angot. I was about to accompany him by beating time on the table. But this time he whistled something else-—a march from Le Prophete.

'Listen,' said I to my associates; ' we are going to play a trick upon P. We will (mentally) order him to pass from Le Prophete to La Fille de Madame Angot.'

First I began to drum the march; then, profiting by some notes common to both, I passed quickly to the quicker and more staccato measure of my friend's favourite air. P. on his part suddenly changed the air and began to whistle Madame Angot. Everyone burst out laughing. My friend was too much absorbed in a check to the queen to notice anything.

'Let us begin again,' said I, ' and go back to Le Prophete.' And straightway we had Meyerbeer once more with a special fugue. My friend knew that he had whistled something, but that was all he knew.

A huckster stations himself in the middle of the street, on some public square, or on a sidewalk, and begins to pour forth volumes of gibberish intended both as a compliment to the people and a praise of his ware. The curiosity of the passers-by is awakened. They stop. Soon our hero forms the centre of a crowd that stupidly gazes at the 'wonderful' objects held out to its view for admiration. A few moments more, and the crowd begins to buy the things the huckster suggests as grand, beautiful, and cheap."

A stump orator mounts a log or a car and begins to harangue the crowd. In the grossest way he praises the great intelligence, the brave spirit of the people, the virtue of the citizens, glibly telling his audience that with such genius as they possess they must clearly see that the prosperity of the country depends on the politics he favours, on the party whose valiant champion he now is. His argumentation is absurd, his motive is contemptible, and still, as a rule, he carries the body of the crowd, unless another stump orator interferes and turns the stream of sentiment in another direction. The speech of Antony in Julius Caesar is an excellent example of suggestion.

All these examples undoubtedly belong to the province of suggestion. Now what are their characteristic traits? What are the elements common to all these cases of suggestion? We find in all these instances a stream of consciousness that goes on flowing in its peculiar, individual, idiosyncratic way; suddenly from the depths of the stream a wave rises to the surface, swamps the rest of the waves, overflows the banks, deflects for a while the course of the current, and then suddenly subsides, disappears, and the stream resumes its natural course, flowing once more in its former bed. On tracing the cause of this disturbance, we invariably find that it is due to some external source, to some other stream running alongside the one disturbed. Stating the same in the language of Baldwin, we may say that "by suggestion is meant a great class of phenomena typified by the abrupt entrance from without into consciousness— of an idea or image which becomes a part of the stream of thought, and tends to produce the muscular and volitional efforts which ordinarily follow upon its presence."*

Is this the final word on suggestion ? Far from being the case. On closer inspection of our examples we find some more traits which are of the utmost importance. The subject accepts uncritically the idea suggested to him, and carries it out almost automatically. This can be easily detected in nearly every instance of suggestion, but it stands out especially clear and sharp in its outline in cases of hypnosis.

I hypnotized Mr. F., * and commanded that, after awakening, when he would hear me cough, he should take three oranges on the table and give them to my friends who were present at the seance. I woke him up. A few minutes later I coughed; he snatched from the table the oranges, which were, in fact, nothing but ordinary potatoes, and distributed them among my friends. While carrying out this post-hypnotic suggestion he appeared to be in a peculiar automatic condition. His movements were hurried, as if some spring was loosened in his ideo-motor mechanism; his eyes were dull and glassy; it was plain he was in a semiconscious state. On my asking him afterward how the oranges appeared to him he replied:

"They seemed to me rather queer; they were too small and heavy for oranges. I thought they were lemons, but I did not attempt to examine them; something impelled me to carry out the order and be done with it."

To take a still better example from the store of my hypnotic experiments: I hypnotized Mr. F., and suggested to him that after awakening, on hearing me cough, he should take the umbrella, open it, and promenade in the room three times. I woke him up. A few minutes later I coughed; up went his legs, but he remained sitting in the chair. I coughed again; once more up went his legs, but he did not carry out my commands. I rehypnotized him, and this time I strongly and authoritatively commanded him he should carry out my post-hypnotic suggestion, taking care to suggest to him he should forget everything that passed during the hypnotic trance. He was awakened, felt well, conversed with his friends. While he was engaged in conversation I went behind his chair and coughed. Up he jumped, opened the umbrella, and walked in the room three times. When he was through with the suggested promenade the umbrella dropped from his hands on the floor, and, without picking it up, he sat down on a chair and smiled. He remembered very clearly the umbrella affair, and it seemed to him queer and comical. I asked him whether he knew what he was going to do when he heard me cough. "Yes, I knew I must do something—in a general way, though. When I took the umbrella, I do not know how it happened, but I opened it and began to walk."I asked him whether he knew how many times he had to walk, to which he answered : "No, I did not know, but I kept on walking; and when it came to the end of the third turn, the umbrella dropped from my hands."

I could easily bring many more instances of the same type, but I think that those given will suffice for our purpose. What we find in all these cases is the uncritical acceptance of the ideas or actions suggested, and also the motor automatism with which these ideas or actions are realized. In short, mental and motor automatism constitute the prominent elements of suggestion.

There is, however, one more element in suggestion—an element which must be taken into account, and without which our definition of suggestion will be incomplete. This factor, or element, is the overcoming or circumventing of the subject's opposition. The suggested idea is forced on the stream of consciousness; it is a stranger, an unwelcome guest, a parasite, which the subject's consciousness seeks to get rid of. The stream of the individual's consciousness combats suggested ideas as the organism does bacteria and bacilli that tend to disturb the stability of its equilibrium. It is this opposition element that Dr. J. Grossmann has in mind when he defines suggestion as "der Vorgang, bei dem eine Yorstellung sich einem Gehirn aufzuzwin-gen versucht."*

My friend would not have rolled up his paper, nor would Mr. A. have taken the glass and sipped the water, nor would Mr. P. have whistled his airs, nor would the crowd have bought the articles of the huckster or voted for certain political candidates had they been openly commanded to do so. They would have opposed strenuously the suggestion given to them. It was required to devise means in order to circumvent this opposition. The same necessity for circumvention of opposition we find in post-hypnotic suggestion. At first the subject F. opposed the idea of walking with the umbrella. When I rehypnotized him I asked him, "Why did you not carry out my command ?"The reply was, "I wanted to see whether I could resist."That this was actually the case we can see from the fact that, while his legs started at the signal and went up to fulfil the order, Mr. F. exclaimed, "I know what you want me to do, but I will not do it."This opposition was overcome only after repeated and insistent injunctions that he must obey my command.

The first stages of hypnosis are especially characterized by this spirit of opposition, which, however, gradually slackens as the subject falls into a deeper state of hypnosis, and completely disappears with the advent of somnambulism. To watch the struggle of the mind in its opposition to the engrafted suggested idea is of intense interest to the psychologist, and of great value to a clearer comprehension of suggestion itself.

I hypnotized Mr. J. F. With one resolute command I made him cataleptic. "Rise!"I commanded him. He rose. "Walk!"He walked. "You can not walk forward!"He tried to walk, but he could not. "You can only walk backward!"He began to move backward. At the very first sitting he seemed to have fallen completely under my control and to carry out without any opposition all the motor suggestions given to him. This, however, was not really the case. Opposition was there, only it was ineffective. As we continued our sittings (and we had many of them) Mr. J. F. became more and more intractable, my control over him grew less and less, and now it is only after great exertion and repeated imperative commands that I am enabled to bring him into any cataleptic condition at all. The opposition or inhibition kept in abeyance during the first seance asserted itself as the subject became more familiar with the hypnotic condition.

The following experiments are still more interesting, as revealing to us in the clearest way possible the internal struggle—the great opposition which the consciousness of the subject shows to the parasitic suggested idea :

Mr. L. falls into a slight hypnotic condition—into the first degree of hypnosis; he can open his eyes if I challenge him that he is unable to do it. Although his hypnosis is but slight, I still tried on him post-hypnotic suggestions. While he was in the hypnotic condition I suggested to him that after awakening, when he will hear a knock, he will go to the table, take a cigarette, and light it. I suggested to him he should forget everything that passed during the hypnosis.

On awakening he remembered everything. I gave a few knocks in quick succession. He rose from his chair, but immediately sat down again, and laughingly exclaimed, "No, I shall not do it!""Do what ?"I asked. "Light the cigarette—nonsense!""Had you a strong desire to do it?"I asked him, putting the desire in the past, although it was plain he was still struggling with it. He did not answer. "Did you wish very much to do it ?"I asked again. "Not very much,"he answered curtly and evasively.

On another occasion I hypnotized Mr. L. by the method of fascination.* He seemed to have fallen into a slightly deeper hypnotic condition than usual. The post-hypnotic suggestion was to light the gas, and also complete amnesia. On awakening he remembered everything that passed during hypnosis. He ridiculed the post-hypnotic suggestions I gave him. After a few minutes' conversation, without my giving the suggestion signal, which was to be a knock, I left the room for a few moments—for five or ten seconds. When I returned I found him lighting the gas. "What are you doing that for, Mr. L. ?"I asked.

'Ordinarily I use the method of Nancy; it is the most convenient and pleasant way of hypnotization, as it requires no strain on the side of the subject .

"To feel easier,"he answered; "I felt somewhat uneasy."Evidently the post-hypnotic suggestion took deep root in his mind. He struggled hard against it, to put it down, to suppress it; and it was due to this fact that he attempted to counteract the suggested idea by ridiculing it. As long as I was in the room he wanted to show the energy of his will, and he struggled hard against the insistent idea, keeping it at bay; but when I left the room one of the motives of resisting the suggestion was removed, and the struggle became an unequal one. The insistent parasitic idea asserted itself with greater force than before, and this time, not meeting with such a strenuous opposition, it gained the upper hand and realized itself completely.

To take one more instance of the many sittings I had with Mr. L. I hypnotized him once in the presence of two acquaintances of mine, and gave him a post-hypnotic suggestion to take from the table a box of matches and light the gas. This he had to do when hearing me cough. I woke him up, and as soon as he heard me cough he started up from his chair, looked hard at the box of matches, but did not take it. He went up to the window, put his head against the window pane, and seemed to be engaged in a severe struggle against the insistent suggested idea. Now and then one could perceive a slight shudder passing over his entire body, thus making almost palpably evident the inner, restless, contentious state of his consciousness.

Again and again the suggested idea cropped up in his mind, and again and again it was suppressed; now the suggestion gained ground, and now once more it was beaten and driven back into the obscure regions from which it came. I then rehypnotized him, strongly emphasized my suggestion, and then awakened him. I slightly coughed. This time the suggested idea got a stronger hold of his mind. Mr. L. rose from his chair, took the box of matches, kept it in his hand for a second or two, and threw it resolutely on the table. "No,"he exclaimed, "I will not do it!"

Such cases might be multiplied by the hundreds, but I think that the hypnotic experiments made on my subjects L. and J. F. will suffice for our purpose. They show most clearly that the trait of opposition is an ingredient of suggestion. This opposition element varies with the state of mind of the individual. What the nature of this variation is we shall see later on; meanwhile the present stage of our discussion fully enables us to formulate a definition of suggestion and suggestibility.

By suggestion is meant the intrusion into the mind of an idea; met with more or less opposition by the person; accepted uncritically at last; and realized un-reflectively, almost automatically.

By suggestibility is meant that peculiar state of mind which is favourable to suggestion.* [1]

CHAPTER II.
THE CLASSIFICATION OF SUGGESTION AND SUGGESTIBILITY.

ONCE the subject-matter under investigation is defined, we must proceed to a further subdivision of it; we must define and classify the different species of suggestion and suggestibility. Already in our last chapter, in adducing different cases of suggestion, suggestibility in the normal state was tacitly implied. We have now reached a stage in our discussion in which we must state this fact more explicitly. The soil favourable for the seeds of suggestion exists also in what we call the normal individual. Suggestibility is present in what we call the normal state, and in order to reveal it we must only know how to tap it. The suggestible element is a constituent of our nature; it never leaves us; it is always present in us. Before Janet, Binet, and many other investigators undertook the study of hysterical subjects, no one suspected the existence of those remarkable phenomena of double consciousness that opened for us new regions in the psychical life of man.

These phenomena were merely not noticed, although present all the while; and when at times they rose from their obscurity, came to light, and obtrude themselves on the attention of people, they were either put down as sorcery, witchcraft, or classed contemptuously with lying, cheating, and deception. The same is true with regard to normal suggestibility. It rarely attracts our attention, as it manifests itself in but trifling things. When, however, it rises to the surface and with the savage fury of a hurricane cripples and maims on its way everything it can not destroy, menaces life, and throws social order into the wildest confusion possible, we put it down as mobs. We do not in the least suspect that the awful, destructive, automatic spirit of the mob moves in the bosom of the peaceful crowd, reposes in the heart of the quiet assembly, and slumbers in the breast of the law-abiding citizen.

"We do not suspect that the spirit of suggestibility lies hidden even in the best of men; like the evil jinnee of the Arabian tales is corked up in the innocent-looking bottle. Deep down in the nature of man we find hidden the spirit of suggestibility. Every one of us is more or less suggestible. Man is often defined as a social animal. This definition is no doubt true, but it conveys little information as to the psychical state of each individual within society. There exists another definition which claims to give an insight into the nature of man, and that is the well-known ancient view that man is a rational animal; but this definition breaks down as soon as we come-to test it by facts of life, for it scarcely holds true of the vast multitudes of mankind. Not sociality, not rationality, but suggestibility is what characterizes the average- specimen of humanity, for man is a suggestible animal. The fact of suggestibility existing in the normal individual is of the highest importance in the theoretical field of knowledge, in psychology, sociology, ethics, history, as well as in practical life, in education, politics, and economics; and since this fact of suggestibility may be subject to doubt on account of its seeming paradoxicality, it must therefore be established on a firm basis by a rigorous experimentation, and I have taken great pains to prove this fact satisfactorily.

The evidence for the existence of normal suggestibility I shall adduce later on in our discussion; meanwhile I ask the reader to take it on trust, sincerely hoping that he will at the end be perfectly satisfied with the demonstration of its truth. The presence of suggestibility in such states as the hysterical and the hypnotic is a fact well proved and attested, and I think there is no need to say a word in its defence. Since the hysterical, the hypnotic, the somnambulic states do not belong to the routine of our experience; since they are but rare and occur under special peculiar conditions; since they unfit one for social life, disable in the struggle for existence, I think the reader will hot quarrel with me for naming such states abnormal.

Thus it becomes quite clear that suggestibility must be classed under two heads: (1) Suggestibility in the normal state, or normal suggestibility, and (2) suggestibility in the abnormal state, or abnormal suggestibility.

Turning now to suggestion, we find that it can be easily subdivided and classified according to the mode it is effected in consciousness. Concrete examples will best illustrate my meaning. The hypnotizer commands his subject to walk; the latter walks. He raises the hand of the patient, and it remains uplifted in a contracted cataleptic condition. The hypnotizer tells the subject that after awakening, when he will hear a knock, he will take off his coat and dance a polka, and the subject, on awakening and perceiving the signal, fulfils the order most faithfully. In cases like these the experimenter gives his orders or suggestions directly, without beating around the bush, without any circumlocution, without any evasions. In a plain and brusque manner

does the hypnotizer give his suggestion, so much so that it partakes of the nature of an imperative command issued by the order of the highest authority from which there is no appeal. The essential feature here, however, is not so much the authoritativeness, for in many cases it may be totally absent, and a courteous, bland way of expression may be used; not so much the authoritativeness, I say, as the plainness, the directness with which the suggestion is given. Such a suggestion we may designate as direct suggestion.

Suggestions may also be given in quite a different way. Instead of openly telling the subject what he should do, the experimenter produces some object, or makes a movement, a gesture, which in their own silent fashion tell the subject what to do. To illustrate it by a few examples, so as to make my meaning clearer: I stretch out the hand of the hypnotic subject and make it rigid, and while doing this I press his arm with an iron rod. In the next seance as soon as the iron, rod touches the arm the hand becomes rigid. I tell the subject to spell the word "Napoleon,"and when he comes to "p "I stretch out my hand and make it stiff; the subject begins to stammer; the muscles of his lips spasmodically contract and stiffen. Dr. Tuckey brings a case of suggestion given by him unintentionally in such an indirect way. He hypnotized a physician and ordered him to wake up in a quarter of an hour. He then left the room for about half an hour, being sure that in the meantime the subject would come back to himself. "When he returned he was surprised to find the patient still sitting in the chair, and in the most distressed condition possible. The patient could not recover his speech ; his jaws were firmly shut. Dr. Tuckey thinks that while hypnotizing he inadvertently passed his hand over the mouth of the subject, and this was taken as a suggestion to keep the mouth firmly shut. My friend who drank the glass of water on account of my suggestive movements; Mr. P., whom Prof. Ochorowitz suggested to whistle certain airs; the crowd that was induced by the politician by means of flattery and talk of business prosperity to vote for the party whose cause he advocated—all these are good cases of this type of suggestion.

This mode of influencing the mind plays a great part in the history of humanity, and is therefore of great importance in sociology. Such a kind of suggestion may be properly designated as indirect suggestion. Suggestion partakes of the nature of reflex action. This truth was implied in our discussion of the last chapter, and in the definition of suggestion we finally arrived at. And authorities are not lacking who go to support the same view. "Eine sorgfaltige Beobach-tung,"writes Prof. Forel, "der Bedingungen der Sug-gestibilitat bringt uns immer wieder auf die relativ Ruhe des Gehirns zuriick, auf einen plastischen Zustand des-selben oder wenigstens eines Theiles desselben, worin die Vorstellungen eine schwachere Kraft oder Tendenz haben sich zu associiren und deshalb leichter dem von aussen commenden Impuls folgen."Der Mechanismus (der Suggestion),"writes Dr. Bernheim, "ist ein physiologischer Mechanismus dessen Realisation sich mit den Eigenschaften unseres Hirn ganz gut vereinbarn lasst. [2] What Dr. Bernheim means to say here is that suggestion partakes of the nature of the reflex and automatic activity that characterizes the physiological mechanism in general. He makes himself more explicit in another place. "The mechanism of suggestion,"lie writes in his book Suggestive Therapeutics, "may be summed up in the following formula: Increase of the reflex ideo-motor, ideo-sensitive, and ideo-sensorial excitability."

Goumey tells us in his simple straightforward way that the mechanism of "suggestion is conscious reflex action."* As reflex action of consciousness, suggestion has a double aspect: afferent, centripetal, or sensory, and efferent, centrifugal, or motor. This is perfectly obvious, for in suggestion we deal, on the one hand, with the impression of the suggested idea on the mind and its acceptance by consciousness; this is the afferent, sensory side of suggestion; and, on the other hand, with the realization of the accepted idea; this is the efferent, motor side of suggestion. The process of suggestion may therefore be represented in the form of an arc, which may be called the suggestion arc. It is quite clear that in classifying suggestion as direct and indirect, we had solely in view the afferent, the sensory aspect of suggestion. If now we regard suggestion from the other aspect, from the efferent or motor aspect, we find that suggestion is subject to another subdivision. Concrete instances will bring out this subdivision most clearly.

The experimenter suggests to the subject to turn over the chair and sit down near it on the floor. This is faithfully and immediately carried out by the subject. The experimenter raises the patient's arm and bends it; immediately the arm becomes stiff, rigid, cataleptic. The suggested idea impressed on the brain is immediately discharged into the motor tracts. The same holds true of post-hypnotic or deferred suggestion. The idea suggested or the order given is present

in the mind, only there is present a suggested obstacle to its motor discharge; but as soon as some kind of suggested signal is perceived, the obstacle is removed and the idea immediately discharges itself along the motor tracts. I hypnotized one of my subjects, Mr. F., and ordered him that on awakening, when he hears me cough, he shall put out the gas. I woke him up. He remained quietly sitting in his chair, waiting, as it seemed, for my signal. He himself, however, was not in the least conscious of it; f of when his brother asked him whether he would like to go home, as it was rather late, he answered in the negative. I then coughed, and Mr. F. immediately rushed for the light and put it out. What we find here is the literal carrying out of the suggested idea. This kind of suggestion the realization of which bears a direct and immediate relation to the suggested object or act is, of course, also present in normal suggestibility, as in the case of the buyer who chooses the goods suggested to him by the salesman or huckster, as in the case of the citizen who votes for the unknown candidate suggested to him by the politician. In short, when there is full and complete realization of the idea or order suggested, directly or indirectly, we have that kind of suggestion which I designate as immediate.

Instead, however, of immediately taking the hint and fully carrying it into execution, the subject may realize something else, either what is closely allied with the idea suggested or what is connected with it by association of contiguity. A suggestion is given to the subject that when he wakes up he will see a tiger. He is awakened, and sees a big cat. The subject is suggested that on awakening he will steal the pocketbook lying on the table. When aroused from the hypnotic state he goes up to the table, does not take the pocketbook, but the pencil that lies close to it. The buyer does not always choose the precise thing which the salesman suggests, but some other thing closely allied to it. In case the suggestion is not successful, it is still, as a rule, realized in some indirect and mediate way. Man is not always doing what has been suggested to him; he sometimes obeys not the suggested idea itself, but some other idea associated with the former by contiguity, similarity, or contrast. Suggestion by contrast is especially Interesting, as it often gives rise to counter-suggestion. Now such kind of suggestion, where not the suggested idea itself but the one associated with it is realized, I designate as mediate.

Thus we have four kinds of suggestion:

(a) Direct. (c) Immediate.

(b) Indirect. (d) Mediate.

CHAPTER III
THE EVIDENCE OF NORMAL SUGGESTIBILITY.

IN our last chapter we ventured to generalize that every man in his full normal waking state is more or less suggestible. I should not wonder if such a seemingly sweeping generalization should startle many a cautious reader, and should call forth strenuous opposition. We must therefore rigorously demonstrate the fact of the universality of normal suggestibility. Such a proof is of the more importance, as the generalization which it establishes supplies a new principle to sociology, furnishes a key to the comprehension of many a great historical event, gives a deeper insight into the phenomena of political and economical life, and might possibly be of use in education. Is there such a thing as suggestibility in the normal waking condition ? The Nancy school, with Bernheim and Liebault at its head, gives an affirmative answer. "Jemanden hypnotisiren,"says Bernheim, "heisstnur: seine Suggestibilitat kiinst-lich erhohen."In fact, the hypnotic state itself is induced by suggestion. "Es giebt keinen Hypnotismus: es giebt nur Phanomene der Suggestion,"exclaims the Nancy professor. "Als etwas pathologisches, als eine kiinstliche Neurose betrachtet existirt ein Hypnotismus nicht. Wir schaffen im eigentlichen Sinne mit ilim keinen besonderen Zustand des Gehirns oder des Nervensystems; wir machen uns ganz einfach nur eine physiologische Eigenthumlichkeit des Gehirns —die Sugges-tibilitat—zu Nutze und schaffen die zur Entfaltung dieser Suggestibility giinstigen Vorbedingungen."On closer inspection, however, we find that the great authority of the Nancy school stretches too wide and far the conception of suggestion, for, according to him, "Jede Yorstellung ist eine Suggestion."This, I say, is too far-fetched; for it is to identify the whole field of mental activity with but a part of it, namely, suggestibility. This is, in fact, the obliteration of all traces of the problem itself. If now we turn and ask for facts that go to support his view, we find that Bernheim does not sustain his cause. He limits his instances to but a small class of persons who are easily suggestible in their waking state, but he offers no proof that suggestibility is present in all men. "Es giebt Menschen bei denen...die einfache Affirmation, ohne Schlaf und ohne vorhergehende ihn begunstigende Manipulationen bei ihnen alle sogenannten hypnotischen Phenomena hervorruft. Durch das einfache Wort schafft man bei ihnen Anasthesia, Contractur, Hallucinationen, Impuls, die verschiedensten Handlungen." [3]

Although the instances Prof. Bernheim adduces do not certainly establish the fact of the universality of normal suggestibility, they are still interesting for us as they show the presence of normal suggestibility in some particular cases at least.

"Many subjects,"writes Bernheim in his Suggestive Therapeutics, "who have previously been hypnotized may manifest susceptibility to the same suggestive phenomena in the waking state, without being again hypnotized, however slightly might have been the influence of a small number of previous seances. Here, for example, is the case of K., one of my patients who is accustomed to being hypnotized, and is subject to light somnambulism. Without putting him to sleep, I say directly : ' Close your hand. You can not open it again.' He keeps his hand closed and contracted, and makes fruitless efforts to open it. I make him hold out his other arm, with his hand open, and say, ' You can not shut it.' He tries in vain to do BO ; brings the phalanges into semiflexion, but can do no more in spite of every effort. There is in my service a young hysterical girl afflicted with sensitivo-sensorial hemiansesthesia of the left side, and capable of being hypnotized into deep sleep. In the waking condition she is susceptible to catalepsy or suggestive contraction.

I can affect transfer of the hemianaesthesia from the left to the right side without hypnotizing and without touching her. In one of my somnambulistic cases I can obtain all possible modifications of sensibility in the waking condition. It suffices to say,' Your left side is insensible '; then if I prick his left arm with a pin, stick the pin into his nostril, touch the mucous membrane of his eye, or tickle his throat, he does not move. The other side of his body reacts. I transfer the anaesthesia from the left to the right side. I produce total anaesthesia, which was on one occasion so profound that my chef de clinique pulled out the roots of five teeth which were deeply embedded in the gums, twisting them round in their sockets for more than ten minutes. I simply said to the patient, ' You will have no feeling whatever.' He laughed as he spat out the blood, and did not show the least symptom of pain."

Here, as we see, the experiments were carried on with somnambulic and hysterical subjects; the result, therefore, cannot prove the facts of suggestibility in normal and perfectly healthy people. Some of my own experiments might possibly prove more conclusive. Mr. W., an acquaintance of mine, who was never hypnotized by anyone, readily took suggestions in his waking state. I told him he could not write his name. He tried, and he did write it. I stretched out my arm, opened my hand and stiffened the fingers, and said, "Try now."He could not write—his hand became cataleptic. I made a whole series of experiments of this kind,'but as they interested me from quite a different point of view I shall give a detailed account of them later on. Meanwhile this one instance will suffice for our present purpose to show the power of suggestion in the waking state. The fact, however, of its rarity 'and singularity makes it unfit to prove the universality of normal suggestibility.

In the Zeitschrift fiir Hypnotismus * [4] Prof. J. Del-boeuf brings cases of suggestibility in normal condition. Thus he made a patient anaesthetic who was not and could not be hypnotized. He told the patient: "Rei-chen Sie mir Ihren Arm, sehen Sie mich fest an und zeigen Sie mir durch Ihren Blick, dass Sie entschlossen sind, nichts zu f uhlen, und Sie werden thatsachlich nichts fiihlen."The patient did it. Prof. Delboeuf severely pricked the subject's arm, and the latter felt no pain.

To take another case. An old man of seventy suf-ered great pain from facial neuralgia for more than fifteen years. "Ich komme zu ihm,"says Prof. Delboeuf; "ziehe ihn heftig am Bart und erklare ihm, dass er keine Schmerzen mehr hat, dass er auch ferner keine Schmer-zen haben wird, und meine Prophezeihung erfiillt sich."

These cases, like the preceding one, are subject to the same objections; they do not prove the universality of normal suggestibility on account of their rarity and singularity. Not everyone can so easily be made cataleptic or anaesthetic in his waking condition. With most people such suggestions are failures even in hypnosis. The only way, then, to test the verity of normal suggestibility is to lay aside all experimentation on hysterical, somnambulic, hypnotic, and extraordinarily suggestible subjects, and start a series of experiments on perfectly healthy and normal individuals. Thanks to Prof. H. Minsterberg and to the admirable facilities afforded by the Psychological Laboratory of Harvard University and the Pathological Institute of the New York State Hospitals, I was enabled to carry out more than eight thousand experiments relating to the subject of suggestion.

The order of experiments taken up first was suggestion of letters and figures. The mechanism of this class of experiments was as follows : A successive series of letters or of figures was introduced through a slit on a white screen, each letter or figure being pasted on a separate slip of cardboard which in colour and position coincided with the background of the screen. Each experiment consisted of a series of nine slips. Each slip was kept on the background for two or three seconds. The interval between the slip and its successor was also two or three seconds. Time was measured by a metronome enclosed within a felt box, with a rubber tube passing close to the ear of the experimenter, so that the subjects should not be disturbed by the ticking of the metronome. For the same reason the experimenter and his movements of inserting the slips into the white screen were all carefully hidden by screens. The ring of a bell indicated that the series came to an end, and it also served as a signal for the subjects to write down immediately on paper which they kept ready in their hands anything that came into their mind at that particular moment —letters, numerals, words, phrases, etc.

While looking for evidence for normal suggestibility, an opportunity was also taken to arrange the experiments according to different factors, so that should it be proved that suggestion in the normal state is an indubitable fact, we should be enabled to know what kind of factors are the more impressive and suggestive.

The seizes of letters and figures were arranged according to the following factors and their combinations :

1. Repetition.

2. Frequency.

3. Coexistence.

4. Last impression.

Great care, of course, was taken not to repeat the same series of letters or figures. As I had many slips at my disposal the series could be easily changed both by permutation and insertion of new slips. The subjects did not and could not possibly suspect the suggested letter or figure, first, because there were so many of them in each series; second, because the factors studied were constantly varied; and, third, because sham series, such as inverted or coloured letters, etc., were introduced so as to baffle the subjects.

I had twelve subjects at my disposal, and experimented with three or four at a time. Recently I made experiments of this kind with thirteen subjects more, so that the total number of subjects is twenty-five. The results are as follows :

1. REPETITION. — In the middle of the series a letter or numeral was shown three times in succession — e. g.:

B 3

E 6

K 8

M 5

M or 5

M 5

K 7

O 2

P 9

Of 300 experiments made, 53 succeeded—that is, the subject wrote the letter or numeral suggested by the factor of repetition. The factor of repetition gives a suggestibility of IT'6 per cent.

2. FREQUENCY. — A letter or numeral was shown three times in the series, and each time with an interruption— e. g. :

B 5

K 3

E 7

K 3

M or 9

K 3

C 4

E 8

D 6

Of 300 experiments made, 128 succeeded. The factor of frequency gives a suggestibility of 42.6 per cent.

3. COEXISTENCE. — A letter or numeral was shown repeatedly; not, however, in succession, as it was in the case of the factor of repetition, also not with interruptions as it was in the case of frequency, but at the same time—e. g.:

B 4

E 1

C 2

L 6

E E E, or 7 7 T

M 5

L 3

A 9

F 8

Of 300 experiments made, only 20 succeeded. The factor of coexistence gives as its power of suggestion 6.6 percent.

4. LAST IMPRESSION. —Here was studied the suggestibility affected by the last impression, by the last letter or figure. In all our experiments unnecessary repetition was carefully avoided. It is plain that the nature of these experiments of last impression required that not one letter or figure should be repeated twice in the series—e. g.:

A 7

K 9

F 5

L 8

D or' 6

E 2

B 4

E 1

M 3

Of 300 experiments made, 190 succeeded. The factor of last impression gives a suggestibility of 63.3 per cent .

5. COEXISTENCE AND LAST IMPRESSION. —In these experiments a slip with three identical characters pasted on it appeared at the end of the series, thus combining in one the factor of coexistence with that of last impression—e. g.:

E 2

N 5

C 7

K 1

B or 9

M 8

Q 4

Z 6

A A A 333

Of 300 experiments made, 55 succeeded. The combined effect of coexistence and last impression gives a suggestibility of 18.3 per cent.

6. FREQUENCY AND LAST IMPRESSION. —The letter or numeral repeated with interruptions was also shown at the end of the series—e. g.:

M 5

C 2

B 8

C 2

K or 4

C 2

P 9

N 6

C 2

Of 150 experiments made, 113 succeeded. The combined effect of the two factors gives a suggestibility of 75.2 per cent. Arranging now the factors in the order of their rate of effected suggestibility, we have the following table :

Frequency and last impression 75.2

Last impression 63.3

Frequency 42.6

Coexistence and last impression... 18.3

Repetition 17.6

Coexistence 6.6

Comparing now the suggestibility affected by different factors,[5] that of the last impression stands out most prominently. The "last impression "is the most impressive. Our daily life teems with facts that illustrate this rule: The child is influenced by the last impression it receives. In a debate he, as a rule, gains the victory in the eyes of the public who has the last word. In a crowd he moves and stirs the citizens to action who makes the last inciting speech. In a mob he who last sets an example becomes the hero and the leader.

Frequency comes next to last impression and precedes repetition. This may be explained by the fact that in repetition the suggestion is too grossly obvious, lying almost on the surface; the mind, therefore, is aroused to opposition, and a counter-suggestion is formed; while in frequency the suggestion, on account of the interruption, is not so tangibly obvious, the opposition therefore is considerably less, and the suggestion is left to run its course.

Coexistence is a still poorer mode of suggestion than repetition; it only arouses opposition. Coexistence is in reality of the nature of repetition, for it is repetition in space; it is a poor form of repetition. On the whole, we may say that in the normal state temporal or spatial repetition is the most unfortunate mode of suggestion, while the best, the most successful of all the particular factors, is that of the last impression—that is, the mode of bringing the idea intended for suggestion at the very end. This rule is observed by influential orators and widely read popular writers ; it is known in rhetoric as bringing the composition to a climax. Of all the modes of suggestion, however, the most powerful, the most effective, and the most successful is a skilful combination of frequency and last impression. This rule is observed by Shakespeare in the speech of Antony. Be these rules of the particular factors what they may, one thing is clear and sure: these experiments unquestionably prove the reality of normal suggestibility; they prove the presence of suggestibility in the average normal individual.

From suggestion of ideas I turned to suggestion of movements, of acts. The first set of experiments was rather crude in form, but not without its peculiar interest and value. The experiments were carried on in the following way: On a little table I put a few objects, screened from the subject by a sheet of white cardboard. The subject was asked to concentrate his attention on a certain spot of the screen for about twenty seconds. On the sudden removal of the screen the subject had immediately to do something—anything he liked. It was, of course, also understood that the subject should keep his mind a blank as much as it was in his power, and, at any rate, that he should not beforehand make up his mind what to do. The subjects, I must add, were perfectly trustworthy people—coworkers in the Psychological Laboratory.

Now, while the screen was removed I at the same time loudly suggested some action—such as "Read!""Write!""Cut!""Strike!""Ring! "etc. On the table were objects appropriate to such actions—a book, a pen, a knife, a hammer, a bell. The subjects very frequently carried out the commands, the suggestions given to them. Of five hundred experiments made, about one half succeeded; that is, the subject carried out the suggestion given to him during the removal of the screen. Allowing ten per cent for chance, there remains about forty percent in favour of suggestibility.

On interrogating the subjects of their state of mind at the moment of action, many of them told me that they felt no desire nor any particular impulse to carry out the act suggested, but that they complied with my order out of sheer politeness. (I should say, though, that the fact of the order being realized so many times, be it even from mere politeness, indicates the presence of suggestibility). Some of the subjects became totally unfitted to do anything at all. It seemed as if all activity was for the time being under some powerful inhibition.

In the case of one subject—Mr. S., one of the ablest men in the Psychological Laboratory—I found that my order was carried out in a reflex way; so much so that a few times, when I called out "Strike!""Hammer !"the hand went down on the table instantaneously and with such violence that the table was nearly shattered. Mr. S. felt pain in his hand for some minutes. On one occasion I called out, "Look there!"Quick as lightning Mr. S. turned round and looked hard. On another occasion I commanded, "Rise ! "Back moved the chair and up went Mr. S .

Now this set of experiments, if regarded alone, certainly does not carry conviction as to the presence of suggestibility in all perfectly normal and healthy persons; but along with other experiments—with those that relate to suggestion of ideas, and with those in relation to choice suggestion, of which I shall soon give a detailed account—this last set of movements' and acts' suggestion certainly contributes its mite of evidence. It is not, however, on account of their positive side that I value these movement experiments, but on account of their negative side. I shall resume this subject further on in its proper place. Interesting as that last line of investigation was, I still had to abandon it, because the experiments could not possibly be expressed in precise quantitative terms. Except in the case of Mr. S., I could not precisely know how far the experiment succeeded and how far it failed. The different factors remained unanalyzed, and the whole mechanism was extremely crude and primitive. Thanks to the advice of Prof. H. Munsterberg, I was enabled to continue my research further and penetrate deeper into one of the most obscure, most mysterious, but also most promising regions of human nature.

The experiments which I am about to describe were carried out with great care and minuteness of detail. The new factors studied were carefully analyzed and separated. I must confess that at first I did not fully realize the import and value of these experiments ; I saw in them nothing else than a further test and affirmation of the fact of normal suggestibility, especially on its efferent or motor side. The highest I thought of their value was that along with the preceding experiments they would carry to the mind conviction—perfect certitude as to the universality of normal suggestibility. But later on, when I summed up the results and thought the matter over, I was glad to discover that the results had a profounder meaning than the one I put on them; that they pointed to something beyond, to something deeper and wider than the problem they were intended to solve.

To pass now to the experiments themselves. The experiments were carried on in the following way : Six small squares (30x30 mm.) of different colours were placed on a white background. The white background with the six squares on it was again covered by a black cardboard. The subject was told to fix his attention on the black cardboard for five seconds (time being measured by the metronome). At the end of five seconds the black cover was removed, and the subject had immediately to take one of the coloured squares, whichever he liked.

The subjects were nineteen in number. No subject was allowed to take part in these experiments more than one hour a week. Precautions were also taken that the same series of colours should not be repeated in the experiments with the same subject. For this purpose Bradley's colours were used, which give an endless combination of different colours. At the beginning of each week the colours were rearranged in new series of six squares each; no series containing the same colour, the squares were all of different colours. Precaution was also taken to hide the arrangement of the experiments from the subjects.*

* As the squares were rather small in size they could with equal facility be reached with either hand, and there was, therefore, no tendency to prefer the squares of one side more than those of the other side. Besides, control-experiments with black squares were made by me; and these experiments still further confirmed th

In these experiments on suggestion of choice the following six factors were studied:

    1. Abnormal position.

2. Colored cover.

3. Strange shape.

4. Colour verbally suggested.

5. Place verbally suggested.

6. Environment.

1. ABNORMAL POSITION. —One of the coloured squares was placed in some abnormal way, thus:

2. COLOURED COVER. —Instead of the usual black cover a coloured cover was used in these experiments. A square of the same colour as that of the cover was placed in the series of squares.

3. STRANGE SHAPE. —One of the coloured squares was here of some peculiar shape, of the form of a triangle, oblong rectangle, rhomboid, pentagon, star, etc., thus:

A

view that this factor of preference by convenience was totally absent .

4. COLOUR VERBALLY SUGGESTED. —One of the coloured squares was shown to the subject, who had to determine its colour. This was not an easy task, as the subject had to tell the constituents of the colour, and give the precise name of it. The subject usually kept the coloured square in his hand, and spoke about it for more than a minute. In case he did not succeed, I told him the name of the colour. Then the square was replaced in the series, and the experiment proper began.

5. PLACE VERBALLY SUGGESTED. —The place of one of the coloured squares was suggested by calling out a number during the removal of the cover and the set of choice, as, for instance, "Three!" meaning the third in the row beginning from the left hand. In order that the subject should understand the number suggested and get used to this mode of counting, I asked of him in other suggestion experiments that, after having chosen a coloured square, he should also tell its place, counting from left to right.

C. ENVIRONMENT. —One of the six coloured squares was put on a larger square of differently coloured paper. A fringe environing the square was thus formed.

Special care was taken not to leave in the same place the square suggested, but to shift it with each subsequent experiment. The differently coloured squares suggested were each time put in different places, so that the subject should not form a habit of choosing from one place more than from another. To counteract all expectation as to what the nature of the experiment was, the experiments were constantly changed as to the nature of the factor, and, to be the more sure of completely eliminating expectation, sham experiments were introduced. Instead of the usual coloured squares, the subject frequently found a row of black squares, looking like a funeral march. These black squares were often screened by a cover of gay colour.

Before I proceed to give a detailed account of the experiments, I think it would be well to give the precise meaning in which I here employ the terms of mediate and immediate suggestion and suggestibility. By immediate suggestion I mean to indicate the full realization of the suggestion given to the subject — the fact of his taking the square suggested to him in a direct or indirect way. By mediate suggestion I mean to indicate the fact of incomplete realization of the suggestion — the fact of taking a square next to the one suggested by the experiment — e. g. :

d, Immediate suggestion. c or 6, Mediate suggestion. The results are as follows : *

1. ABNORMAL POSITION.

Per cent.

Immediate suggestion 47.85

Mediate suggestion 53.7

Total suggestion 53-22

* See Appendix A .

2. COLOURED COVER.

Per cent.

Immediate suggestion 38-16

Mediate suggestion 5-83

Total suggestion 43-99

3. STRANGE SHAPE.

i Immediate suggestion 43

Mediate suggestion 13

Total suggestion 56

4. COLOUR VERBALLY SUGGESTED.

3. MAKE TABLES

Immediate suggestion 28*89

Mediate suggestion 4*44

Total suggestion 33-33

5. PLACE VERBALLY SUGGESTED.

Immediate suggestion 19-41

Mediate suggestion 0-58

Total suggestion 19*99

6. ENVIRONMENT.

Immediate suggestion 30-44

Mediate suggestion 22-22

Total suggestion 52-66

Making now a table of the factors and arranging them in the order suggestibility effected, we have the following :

TABLE OF IMMEDIATE SUGGESTIBILITY.

Per cent.

Abnormal position 47.8

Strange shape 43.0

Coloured Cover 38.1

Environment 3O.4

Colour verbally suggested 28.8

Place verbally suggested 19.4

Mediate suggestibility necessitates a rearrangement of the factors:

TABLE OF MEDIATE SUGGESTIBILITY.

Per cent.

Environment 22'2

Strange shape 13.0

Coloured cover 5.8

Abnormal position 5.3

Colour verbally suggested 4.4

Place verbally suggested 0.5

A scrutiny of the table of immediate suggestibility shows that the factors of abnormal position and of abnormal or strange shape give the strongest suggestion. A familiar thing in a strange abnormal position or shape produces the most effective suggestion. Nothing speaks so much to the childish or popular mind as a caricature, monstrosity, a grotesque figure. A distorted picture of a familiar scene or person will at once attract the attention of the child, and powerfully affect its conduct in case the picture is intended to show the fate of bad children. The angelical happiness of saints, the pure, holy bliss of martyrs, the intolerable torments suffered by the wicked in hell, speak volumes to the vulgar religious mind. When Vladimir, the Russian Kniase (king), intended to abandon paganism and accept a monotheistic religion, missionaries came to him from the Jews, Mohammedans, and Christians.

No argument could affect the barbarian. The cunning Greeks then showed him a picture representing the day of judgment. The righteous enjoy eternal bliss in the company of beautiful maidenlike angels, while the wicked, with distorted faces, writhe and wriggle in agonies of pain. The infidels are cooked in enormous kettles containing a hellish soup of hot, seething oil and bubbling sulphur and pitch. The sinners, the blasphemers, are mercilessly fried and roasted by horned, tailed, cloven-hoofed, grinning, hideous-looking devils. Vladimir was deeply affected by the picture of the Christian hell, and at once accepted the Greek faith. This Russian tradition may serve as a good illustration of the great power of suggestion possessed by the two factors of abnormal position and strange shape.

Turning now to the table of mediate suggestibility, we find that the factor of environment gives us as high a rate as 22.2 per cent, almost twice .the rate of the mediate suggestibility possessed by the factor of strange shape, and more than five times the rate of the mediate suggestibility possessed by the factor colour verbally suggested. This can possibly be explained by the fact that one of the conditions of the environment factor was to put one of the squares on a differently coloured background. The fringed square looked somewhat prettier than its fellows, and it was this prettiness that enhanced the mediate suggestibility. An adorned, beautiful object sheds glory on its homely neighbours and makes them more eligible.

But however the case may he with the relative suggestibility of the particular factors studied, these last experiments on choice suggestion, together with the other suggestion experiments, establish the fact of normal suggestibility on a firm and unshakable basis. MAN

CHAPTER IV.
THE CONDITIONS OF NORMAL SUGGESTIBILITY.

1. THE first and general condition of normal suggestibility is fixation of the attention.

In all my experiments the one indispensable condition was to fix the attention on some spot and thus to prepare the subject for the acceptance of the suggestion. I asked the subject to look on some particular point chosen by me, the time of fixation usually varying from two to five seconds. In my experiments with letters and figures the attention of the subject was fixed on the white surface of the screen for about two seconds before the first character of the series appeared; then, again, between each figure or letter and the next following there was an interval of two or three seconds during which the subject had to look fixedly at the uniformly white screen. In my experiments with coloured squares, or on choice suggestion, the condition of fixation of attention was scrupulously observed; the subject had to fix his attention on a particular point for five seconds. The same condition was observed in my experiments on suggestion of movements and of acts. The fixation of attention, as I said, was usually not continued longer than five seconds. Thus, out of 4,487 experiments made on suggestion, only 500 experiments (those dealing with suggestion of movements) had a fixation time higher than five seconds .

Fixation of attention is one of the most important conditions of normal suggestibility — so much so that when this condition was absent the experiments were unsuccessful, the suggestion given invariably failed. The subject declared he was disturbed, mixed up, that he was not in the mood, that he could not make up his mind to write anything, to execute movements, or to choose squares.

2. The next condition of normal suggestibility is distraction of the attention. The subject had to fix his attention on some irrelevant point, spot, thing that had no connection with the material of the experiments, no resemblance to the objects employed for suggestion. Usually I asked my subjects to fix their attention on some minute dot, because a large spot or a big object might have interfered with the suggestion, on account of form, size, etc. The attention had to be diverted from the objects of the experiments. I found that when this condition of distraction of attention was absent the experiments, as a rule, failed. A. Binet, in his valuable article on Double Consciousness,[6] the results of which we will discuss later on, tells us that the suggestion of movements brought about in healthy, normal persons when in their waking condition required one "necessary condition: that attention should not be fixed on the hand and what is taking place there."Now Binet made his suggestion experiments on the hand movements of the subject; the condition, then, he requires is that of distraction of the attention from the objects of the experiments.

3. In all the experiments I had to guard against variety of impressions. Slight noises coming from the adjoining rooms in the laboratory, a new man coming into the room where the experiments were being carried on, a book dropping, an Italian playing on the street organ, and many other kindred impressions, were distinctly unfavourable to the experiments, and had to be avoided as much as possible. The subjects had to accustom themselves to the conditions and objects in the room, and any new impressions strongly interfered with the success of the suggestion. A fresh, new impression, however slight, proved always a disturbance. When the impression was a strong one, or when many impressions came together, the experiments were interrupted and the whole work came to a standstill. The experiments could be carried on only in a monotonous environment, otherwise they failed. Thus we find that 'monotony is an indispensable condition of normal suggestibility.

4. While fixing their attention the subjects had to keep as quiet as possible; for otherwise the subject became disturbed, his attention began to wander, and the suggestion failed. Before the experiments began the subjects were asked to make themselves as comfortable as possible, so that they should not have to change their position during the experiments. We find, then, that normal suggestibility requires as one of its conditions a limitation of voluntary movements.

5. Limitation of the field of consciousness may be also considered as one of the principal conditions of normal suggestibility. This condition, however, is in fact a result of the former ones—namely, fixation of attention, monotony, and limitation of voluntary movements ; for when these last conditions are present the field of consciousness is contracted, closed to any new incoming impressions, limited only to a certain set of sensations, fixed, riveted to only a certain point.

Contraction of the field of consciousness may, however, be effected where the other conditions are absent. A sudden, violent impression may instantly effect an enormous shrinkage of the field of consciousness, and then the other conditions will naturally follow, or rather coexist; for consciousness will reverberate with this one violent sense impression and will thus attend to only the latter. There will also be monotony, since this one sudden and violent sense impression tolerates few neighbours and drives out fresh incomers. Voluntary movements will then certainly be limited, since the stream of consciousness is narrowed, and along with it its ideomotor side. The fact that limitation or contraction of the field of consciousness may occur by itself without having been preceded by the conditions mentioned above led me to consider it a separate condition of normal suggestibility.

6. The experiments, again, could not be carried on without the condition of inhibition. I asked the subject that, when he concentrated his attention and fixed a particular dot pointed out to him, he should try as much as it was in his power to banish all ideas—images that had no connection with the experiments in hand ; that he should not even think of the experiments themselves; in short, that he should make his mind a, perfect blank, and voluntarily inhibit ideas, associations that might arise before his mind's eye and claim attention. Of course, this condition was rather a hard task for the subject to comply with, still it was observed as far as it was possible. When this condition was neglected by the subject the experiments invariably failed. Inhibition, then, is a necessary condition of normal suggestibility.

7. The very last condition, but at the same time the principal one, the most fundamental condition sine qua non experiments in normal suggestion, was immediate execution. The subject was told that as soon as he perceived the signal he should immediately write, act, or choose. To make a synopsis of the conditions of normal suggestibility:

   1. Fixation of attention.

2. Distraction of attention.

3. Monotony.

4. Limitation of voluntary movements.

5. Limitation of the field of consciousness.

6. Inhibition .

CHAPTER V.
THE LAW OF NORMAL SUGGESTIBILITY.

WE must turn again to our experiments and give a close study to the results obtained. We take choice suggestion first. Now, out of the six factors studied, four belong to direct suggestion and two to indirect suggestion. The factors of abnormal position, strange shape, coloured cover, environment, are of one type, while the factors of colour verbally suggested and place verbally suggested are of the other opposite type of suggestion. Is there any difference in the rate of suggestibility of the two types of suggestion ? Yes, and a very good one, too. For even a superficial glance at the two tables of immediate and mediate suggestibility,* if the latter are only inspected from the standpoint of the two types of suggestion, will at once disclose this radical difference. The average immediate suggestibility of the four factors belonging to the first type—to indirect suggestion—amounts to 39.8 percent, whereas the average rate of immediate suggestibility of the two last factors belonging to the second type—to direct suggestion—amounts only to 2.1 percent.

And if we inspect the table of mediate suggestibility, we find again a similar difference; for the average mediate suggestibility of the first four factors belonging to the type of indirect suggestion gives a rate of 11.5 percent.[7] Whereas the average rate of mediate suggestibility of the last two factors belonging to the type of direct suggestion amounts-to only 2.4 per cent.

The difference between the two types of suggestion becomes very striking indeed if we make a table of total suggestibility—that is, if we add together the mediate and immediate suggestibility of each factor. Making thus the table and arranging the factors in the order of their respective rates of total suggestibility, we have the following results: *

TABLE OF TOTAL SUGGESTIBILITY.

Per cent.

Strange shape 56

Abnormal position 53.2

Environment 52.6

Coloured cover 43.9

Colour verbally suggested 33.3

Place verbally suggested 19.9

A mere glance at this table shows the great difference of the two types of suggestion; and tins difference becomes yet more evident, still more striking, if we take the rate of the average total suggestibility of the first type of factors and compare it with that of the second. For the average total suggestibility of the first four factors amounts to as much as 51.4 per cent, while that of the last two amounts only to 26.6 percent. The one rate is about twice the other. The conclusion is obvious, as it lies now before us clear and distinct in its outlines. In the case of normal suggestibility indirect suggestion is far more effective than direct suggestion.[8]

If we examine closer the nature of the last two factors, colour verbally suggested and place verbally suggested, factors which we classed in the type of direct suggestion, we find that they are only relatively direct; for, after all, the subject was not explicitly and directly told to take that colour. What we really must say of them is, that they far more approach the type of direct suggestion than the other four factors do.

If now we inquire as to the rate of suggestibility when the factor is of the actual explicit type of direct suggestion, the answer is, naught. The experiments on suggestion of movements bring out clearly this answer. The suggestion employed there was that of the most direct and explicit kind, and, with the exception of Mr. S., the experiments proved a total failure. The subjects ironically complied with my command. The results were negative—zero. Direct suggestion is at the freezing point of normal suggestibility. It is only in proportion as a given factor becomes more indirect that it rises in the scale of suggestibility. In other words, the more indirect a factor is the higher is the rate of its suggestibility.

Should we like to have still further proofs we can easily get them ; for a close scrutiny of the tables of immediate, mediate, and total suggestibility most clearly shows the truth of my position, namely, that in the normal state a suggestion is more effective the more indirect it is, and in proportion as it becomes direct it loses its efficacy. Abnormal position, strange shape, and environment are the most indirect, and they give the highest suggestibility (environment in mediate suggestibility gives a slightly higher rate because of the additional factor of attractiveness). Abnormal position and abnormal shape have about the same rate; for, on the whole, it makes no difference for man whether a familiar thing is put into an abnormal position or whether it appears in a strange garb: he is equally impressed and moved. As we come to the factor of coloured cover we find a slight decrease in the rate of suggestibility.

For if we take the average immediate suggestibility of abnormal position and strange shape we have 45.4 per cent, while that of coloured cover is 38.1 percent; the difference is 7.3 percent; and we find a difference between the same factors in the case of total suggestibility, the difference being 10.6 percent. Now the suggestion of coloured cover is somewhat more direct than that of abnormal position, or strange shape; for in spreading a coloured cover over the squares, the subject, on seeing and fixing his attention on it, could not help suspecting that it was a square of the same colour that I wanted him to choose: opposition was aroused and the suggestion failed. [9] Although I repeatedly baffled and disappointed the expectation of the subject by putting black squares under the coloured cover, or spreading one over a row of squares totally different in colour from that of the cover, still I could not completely dislodge the suspicion from the subject's mind; it was always lurking in the background of his consciousness.

Of the two factors, colour verbally suggested and place verbally suggested, the former is more indirect than the latter. In the one I merely showed a square to the subject and asked him to determine the colour, without hinting my intention (the subject very frequently being absorbingly interested in guessing the name) ; while in the other the number of the place of the suggested square was called out during the removal of the cover—the hint, therefore, was more direct. If now we look at the tables of immediate, mediate, and total suggestibility of the two factors we find a great difference in their rates of efficiency.

The immediate suggestibility of the factor colour verbally suggested is 28.8 percent, while that of place verbally suggested is 19.4 "the difference amounting to 9.4 "The mediate suggestibility of the factor colour verbally suggested is 4.4 "while that of place verbally suggested is but 0-5 "

the difference amounting to 3.9 "The total suggestibility of colour, etc., is 33.3 "while that of place, etc., is 19.9 the difference being 13.4."

If again we turn to our very first study with letters and figures, we find the results pointing to the same truth. The factors of frequency and last impression are far more indirect than those of coexistence and repetition, and we correspondingly find a great difference in their rates of suggestibility. Thus the average rate of frequency and of last impression is (63*3 -f 42'6) -f-2 — 52.9 per cent; while the average rate of suggestibility of repetition and of coexistence is (1T'6 + 6.6) -r-2 — 12.1 percent, the difference being 40*8 per cent. The factor of last impression, again, is relatively more indirect than that of frequency, and correspondingly we find a difference in their rates of suggestibility .

The factor of last impression gives 63.3 percent, while that of frequency gives 42*6 "

the difference being 20.7 The factor of repetition is relatively more indirect than that of coexistence, in the latter the suggestion being almost grossly obvious, and once more we find a corresponding difference in their rates of suggestibility. Repetition gives 1.6 percent, while the factor of coexistence gives 6.6 - the difference being 11.

Furthermore, the factor of last impression came with as high a rate as 63.3 percent, but when the same factor of last impression enters into combination with that of coexistence, forming one factor of coexistence and last impression, the rate falls as low as 18'3 per cent, thus strongly contrasting the efficacy of direct with that of indirect suggestion. What is the outcome of this whole discussion? Nothing less than the law of normal suggestibility—a law which we shall find later on of the utmost importance. Normal suggestibility varies as indirect suggestion, and inversely as direct suggestion .

CHAPTER VI.
THE CONDITIONS OF ABNORMAL SUGGESTIBILITY.

THE great type of abnormal suggestibility is the hypnotic state; so much so that the Nancy school defines hypnosis as a state of heightened suggestibility. The conditions of abnormal suggestibility are, in fact, those of hypnosis. What are they ?

1. The first and foremost is that of fixation of the attention. Thus Braid used to hypnotize his subjects by fixing their attention on some brilliant object or point. He considered a steady attention indispensable if hypnosis were to be attained ; the subject must look steadily at the object, he must only think of the thing he was fixing, and must not allow his attention to be diverted from it. Of such permanent importance is fixation of attention that, according to Braid, if only this condition is observed one can hypnotize even in the dark. The ability to direct one's thoughts in any particular direction is very favourable to hypnosis. Those who can by no possibility fix their attention, who suffer from continual absence of mind, or those who are helplessly stupid and lacking the power of concentration, are not hypnotizable. I find in my notes the case of an extremely stupid young boy of sixteen who, on account of lack of concentration of mind, is unable to solve the most elementary arithmetical problem. I foretold that he would be unhypnotizable (of course I did not tell that to him). Although I hypnotized in his presence three good subjects, he remained refractory. I tried all kinds of methods I could think of ; the last one was that of Braid. For more than twenty minutes he fixed an object, his eyes being converged in the most orthodox fashion, inward and upward ; tears were trickling down his cheeks, but he remained unaffected, and for the simple reason that his attention was not kept steady—it was roving and wandering all the while. All methods of hypnotization require fixation of attention as their indispensable condition. The adherents of the Salpetriere school frequently hypnotize by fixing the subject's attention on the expectation of some sudden brilliant ray of light meant to induce the hypnotic state. The followers of the Nancy school fix the attention of the subject on the two fingers held before his eyes and on the sounds of suggestion given by the operator. "I hold two fingers,"says Bernheim,* "before the patient's eyes and ask him to concentrate his attention on the idea of sleep."The efficacy of mesmeric passes is also due to the fixation of attention, for by those means the whole attention of the subject is directed to the particular place where the passes are made. "Let anyone,"says Dr. Moll,f "allow his arm or his leg to be mesmerized by passes, and he will find that his whole attention is directed to this part of his body, and much more strongly than if his attention was concentrated on the limb in another manner.""Die Hauptsache ist,"Lehmann tells us, "dass in der Hypnose die Aufmerksamkeit in einer bestimmten Bichtung gebunden ist." [10] This is not exactly true of the hypnotic state itself, but it holds true with regard to the induction of hypnosis. "Children under three and four and insane persons, especially idiots, are unusually hard to hypnotize,"says Prof. James.* "This seems due to the

impossibility of getting them to fix their attention continually on the idea of the coming trance."Prof. James seems to me to have hit the mark when he tells us that the concentration of attention on the coming trance induces hypnosis. In short, fixation of attention is an indispensable condition of hypnosis. [11]

2. Monotony of impressions is another condition of the hypnotic state. If you want to hypnotize a subject, especially if it is for the first time, you must put him into a monotonous environment. You must prevent fresh, new impressions from reaching the sensorium of the subject. Whatever your mode of hypnotization may be, it must always be of the same kind. This might be affected by a strong stimulus acting for a moment or two, or, what is far more often the case, by a prolonged monotonous series of slight stimuli. Thus Binet tells us that "slight and prolonged stimuli of the same nature "constitute one of the modes of producing the hypnotic state. Bernheim expresses himself on this point more clearly: "Let us add,"he says, "that in the majority of the passes the monotonous, wearying, and continuous impression of one of the senses produce a certain intellectual drowsiness, the prelude of sleep. The mind, entirely absorbed by a quiet, uniform, and incessant perception, becomes foreign to all other impressions ; it is too feebly stimulated, and allows itself to become dull."This condition of monotony is very clearly seen in the case of the Nancy method of hypnotization. The operator suggests in so many words the same idea of going to sleep : "Your eyelids are heavy ; your eyes are tired ; they begin to wink; you feel a sort of drowsiness; your arms and legs are motionless ; sleep is coming; sleep."My mode of hypnotization consists in forming a monotonous environment; the light is lowered, and a profound silence reigns in the room; then gently and monotonously stroking the skin of the subject's forehead, and in a low, muffled, monotonous voice, as if rocking a baby to sleep, I go on repeating, "Sleep, sleep, sleep,"etc., until the subject falls into the hypnotic state.

3. Limitation of voluntary movements is also one of the conditions of inducing hypnosis. The subject sits down on a chair in a comfortable position, and is asked to relax his muscles and make as few movements as possible — to keep as quiet as a mouse. This condition is, in fact, supplementary to that of fixation of attention, for many different movements strongly interfere with the steadiness of the attention. The attention changes, oscillates in different directions, and the induction of hypnosis is rendered impossible. Dr. Moll says that "fascination is induced by limitation of voluntary movements."This is no doubt perfectly true, only Dr. Moll ought not to limit it to "fascination "alone, for limitation of voluntary movements is one of the principal conditions of inducing hypnosis in general.

4. Limitation of the field of consciousness must certainly be included among the conditions of inducing hypnosis. The consciousness of the subject must be narrowed to one idea of sleep. "I endeavour,"says Braid in his Neurypnology, "to rid the mind at once of all ideas but one"Wundt defines the very nature of hypnosis as limitation of the field of consciousness, and to a certain extent he is justified in his assertion, seeing that all the methods of hypnotization turn on it as on a pivot. Thus the method of Braid narrows the field of consciousness to a brilliant point, that of mesmerism to the passes, that of the Nancy school to the tips of the fingers held out before the subject, or to the one idea of expectation of sleep. To induce hypnosis we must in some way or another induce such a limitation.

We know that a strange emotion narrows down the field of consciousness. We often find that people under the emotion of intense excitement lose, so to say, their senses; their mind seems to be paralyzed, or rather, so to say, the one idea that produces the excitement banishes all other ideas, and a state of monoideism, or concentration of the consciousness, is thus effected. People are frequently run over by carriages, cars, or trains on account of the sudden great fright caused. The one idea of danger reverberates in the mind like a sudden powerful clap of thunder, confusing and stunning all other ideas ; the mind is brought into a contracted cataleptic condition, and the field of consciousness is narrowed down to that one idea, to a single point. We find that the hypnotic trance can also be induced by a strong and sudden stimulus acting on the sense organ. "Hypnotization,"says Binet, "can be produced by strong and sudden excitement of the senses."This mode of hypnotization may be successful with people of an intensely emotional nature or with hysterical subjects. A strong, sudden stimulus acts on them like a thunderclap, contracts their field of consciousness, and throws them into a hypnotic state. On the whole, we may say that limitation of the field of consciousness is one of the most important conditions of hypnotic trance.

5. The hypnotic trance, again, can not be induced without the condition of inhibition. The subject must inhibit all ideas, all images that come up before his mind. He must only think of the brilliant point, of the tips of the hypnotizer's fingers, of the passes, of the idea of going to sleep. "Look at me and think of nothing but sleep,"tells Bernheim to his patients. "Make your mind a blank,"is one of the conditions required by the hypnotizer of his subjects. Concentration of attention and limitation of the field of consciousness are, in fact, impossible without the presence of this condition of inhibition. The case of the boy mentioned above, who could not be hypnotized because his attention was roaming, because he was unable to concentrate his mind, was in reality due to the fact of lacking the power of inhibition. Inhibition, voluntary or involuntary, is an indispensable condition of hypnosis.

To make a synopsis of the conditions of hypnosis, or, what is the same, of abnormal suggestibility :

1. Fixation of attention.

2. Monotony.

3. Limitation of voluntary movements.

4. Limitation of the field of consciousness .

CHAPTER VII.
THE NATURE OF ABNORMAL SUGGESTIBILITY.

FROM the condition of hypnosis we turn now to an inquiry into its nature. To do this I think it would be best to examine from a purely empirical standpoint the general states into which the hypnotic subject may fall.

Bernheim finds that there are not less than nine states or stages:

1. Drowsiness.

2. Drowsiness, with inability to open the ey«s.

3. Suggestive catalepsy slightly present.

4. Suggestive catalepsy more pronounced.

5. Suggestive contractures fully induced.

6. Automatic obedience.

7. Loss of memory on waking. Hallucinations not possible.

8. Loss of memory. Slight possibility of producing hallucinations, but not post-hypnotically.

9. Loss of memory. Hypnotic and post-hypnotic hallucinations possible.

Dr. Liebault finds that there are only six of them :

1. Drowsiness.

2. Drowsiness. Suggestive catalepsy inducible.

3. Light sleep. Automatic movements possible.

4. Deep sleep. Phenomena rapport manifested.

5. Light somnambulism. Memory hazy on waking .

6. Deep somnambulism. Total amnesia.

Phenomena of post-hypnotic suggestion possible. Prof. August Forel reduces them to three :

1. Drowsiness.

2. Inability to open the eyes. Obedience to suggestion.

3. Somnambulism. Amnesia.

Dr. Lloyd-Tukey gives the following states:

1. Light sleep.

2. Profound sleep.

3. Somnambulism.

Max Dessoir reduces them to two:

1. Voluntary movements show changes.

2. Abnormalities in the functions of the sense organs are added.

Edmund Gurney, the most philosophical of all the writers and investigators on the subject of hypnotism, gives the following two states:

1. The alert state.

2. The deep state.

As a matter of fact, however, the subjects little respect all those quasi-scientific classifications of hypnotic states. Dr. Kingsbury is no doubt right in his remark that "patients vary as much in hypnosis as they do in their features."No doubt there are as many hypnotic states as there are persons; no doubt that it is utterly impossible to give cut-and-dried definitions for the infinite variety of hypnotic stages. Although all this is perfectly true, we still assert that there is a line of subdivision—a boundary line that separates one region of hypnotic phenomena from that of another. This boundary line is, in fact, implied in nearly all the classifications of hypnosis.

To find this boundary line, let us examine the state of mind of the subject when he is in a light hypnotic trance. The subject is in a passive condition. If during hypnotization he was sitting in a chair, there he will remain until roused, his limbs relaxed, his features placid, making as few movements as possible, occasionally changing his position if it becomes very uncomfortable. If his eyes are closed, he will continue to keep them in that condition. Try now to make a direct suggestion that might in the least interfere with what he considers as his voluntary life, with his freedom of action; challenge him, for instance, by raising his hand and telling him that he can not lower it, that he can not open his eyes ; down goes the hand and up goes the eyelid, thus showing us that, passive as he appears to be, he does have control over his limbs.

The controlling consciousness is there, only it is inactive, passive, and it requires a special external stimulus to set it going, to put it into activity. My friend Mr. L. told me once he wondered greatly at the passivity in which he was when in a state of hypnosis. He told me he firmly made up his mind that when hypnotized again he would start a conversation on different topics. A few minutes later I hypnotized him, but he remained as passive as usual. To start him into activity an impulse from without was first required. Mark now the peculiarity. The activity set going does not continue longer than the challenged act. I raise the subject's arm and challenge him to lower it ; he does lower the arm, but keeps it down there in a passive condition. I tell the subject he is unable to walk; the challenge is accepted; he makes a step, very rarely two, showing me that he can walk, that he possesses full control over his legs, but remains passively in one place. He makes another step if you challenge him again.

The controlling consciousness is in a passive state, and reasserts itself at every single challenge to act. The act done, and the controlling consciousness falls back into its former state—the subject relapses into his passive condition. Hypnotization produces a deep cleft in the mind of the subject, a cleft by which the waking, controlling consciousness is separated from the great stream of conscious life.

Now when the cleft is not deep enough we have the different slight hypnotic states, but as the cleft becomes deeper and deeper the hypnosis grows more profound, and when the controlling consciousness is fully cut off from the rest of conscious life we have a state of full hypnosis which is commonly called somnambulism, and in which there is complete amnesia on awakening. That is why we have the strange accounts of hypnotic subjects, especially of those who are on the verge of somnambulism, that during hypnosis they were indifferent to the actions of their body—the latter acted by itself; that they were mere spectators of all the experiments performed on them, of all the strange actions, dramas, that transpired during the trance; that it seemed to them as if they themselves, their personality, retreated far, far away. We have not to wonder that on the question "Where are you ?"the subject sometimes gives the seemingly absurd reply of Krafft-Ebing's patient— "In your eye."

There are pathological cases on record which are analogous to this state. The conscious controlling "I"seems to retreat far, far away from the worM. Dr. Krishaber brings the case of a patient who gives the following account of himself: "I myself was immeasurably far away. I looked about me with terror astonishment; the world was escaping from me. I remarked at the same time that my voice was extremely far away from me, that it sounded no longer as if mine. Constantly it seemed to me as if my legs did not belong to me. It was almost as bad with my arms. I appeared to myself to act automatically, by an impulsion foreign to myself. It was certainly another who had taken my form and assumed my functions. I hated, I despised this other; he was perfectly odious to me."

To return, however, to hypnosis. In the superficial stages, when the subject is not in a very deep trance, we frequently meet with curious phenomena of the following kind: I raise the hand of the subject and put it in some uncomfortable position and let it remain there; there it stays all the while. I challenge him to lower his hand. He does not answer. I repeat again the challenge. No reply. "Answer me: Why don't you lower the hand?""I do not care to,"comes the slow answer. I keep on challenging him for some seconds. At last the stimuli get summated, the controlling consciousness is stimulated, makes strenuous efforts, and the hand, shaking and in jerks, slowly descends.

I tell the subject that he forgot his name, that he can by no means remember it. He keeps silent. "You forgot your name, you do not remember it,"I assert firmly and positively. "Yes, I do,"comes in a low voice the slow and tardy reply. "But you do not know your name.""Yes, I do.""No, you don't.""Yes, I do."And so he wrangles with me for about three or five minutes, until at last he seems to brace himself up and tells me his name. "But why did you not tell it to me before ? ""I really do not care to tell my name."The cleft in the mind is here of some depth, and it requires a strong challenge, an intense stimulus, to set the controlling consciousness into activity.

When the patient sinks into a deeper and deeper hypnotic condition, when the hypnosis is so profound as to verge on somnambulism, the waking, controlling consciousness hangs, so to say, on a thread to the rest of organic life; and when that thread, too, is cut off by suggestion, or by some other means, the waking, guiding consciousness loses all contact with the stream of life.

We can easily state our theory in terms of physiological psychology. The nervous centres of man's nervous system, if classified as to function, may be divided into inferior and superior. The inferior centres are characterized by reflex and autonomic activity. A stimulus excites the peripheral nerve endings of some sense organ; at once a nervous current is set up in the afferent nerves. This current in its turn stimulates a plexus of central ganglia, the nervous energy of which is set free and is propagated along the efferent nerves toward glands or muscles; secretions, excretions, muscular contractions, or relaxations are the final result. Ingoing and outgoing nervous currents may be modified by the nervous centres ; nervous currents may be intensified, decreased in energy, or even entirely inhibited by mutual interaction, according to the law derived by Prof. Ziehen from the general physiology of the nerves—namely: "

If an excitation of definite intensity (m) take place in one cortical clement (i), and another excitation of a different intensity (n) take place at the same time in another cortical element (c), which is connected by a path of conduction with 5, the two intensities of excitation may reciprocally modify each other."Although such a modification may frequently occur, still it remains true that the inferior centres are of a reflex nature. No sooner is the nervous energy of a lower centre set free than at once it tends to discharge itself into some kind of action, of movement. The physiological process of setting free the nervous energy in a central ganglion, or in a system of central ganglia, is accompanied in the simpler but more integrated, more organized centres by sentience, sensitiveness, sensibility,[12] and in the more complex but less integrated, less organized centres by consciousness, sensations, perceptions, images, and ideas.

Turning now to the superior or the highest nervous centres, we find that they possess the function of choice and will. A number of impressions, of sensations, of ideas reach those will-centres, and a sifting, a selecting, an inhibitory process at once begins. Some of the impressions are rejected, inhibited; others are permitted to work themselves out within certain limits, and others again are given full, free play. Psychologically, this process expresses itself in the fiat, in the "I will"or the "I will not."Everyone is well acquainted with the will-effort, especially when having to make some momentous resolution. These superior choice and will-centres, localized by Ferrier, Bianchi, and others in the frontal lobes, and by other writers in the upper layers of the cortex—these centres, on account of their selective and inhibitory function, may be characterized as inhibitory centres par excellence.

Now, parallel to the double system of nervous centres, the inferior and the superior, we also have a double consciousness, the inferior, the organic, the reflex consciousness, and the superior, the controlling, the choice, and will consciousness. The controlling consciousness may be characterized as the guardian consciousness of the species. And from an evolutionary teleological standpoint we can well see of what use this guardian consciousness is to the life of the species. The external world bombards, so to say, the living organism with innumerable stimuli; from all sides thousands of impressions come on, crowding upon the senses of the individual. Each impression has a motor tendency which, if not counteracted by other impressions, must fatally result in some action. It is not, however, of advantage to the organism always to act, and to act immediately on all stimuli reaching it; hence that organism will succeed in the struggle for life that possesses some inhibitory choice and will-centres. The choice and will-centres permit only a certain number of impressions to take effect; the rest are inhibited. Only those impressions that are advantageous to the life existence of the organism are allowed to take their course; the others are nipped in their bud. The guardian consciousness wards off as far as it is able all the harmful blows with which the environment incessantly assails the organic life of the individual.

Having all this in mind, we can now understand the nature of hypnosis. In the normal condition of man the superior and the inferior centres work in perfect harmony; the upper and the lower consciousness are for all practical purposes blended into a unity forming one conscious personality. In hypnosis the two systems of nervous centres are dissociated, the superior centres and the upper consciousness are inhibited, or, better, cut off, split off from the rest of the nervous system with its organic consciousness, which is thus laid bare, open to the influence of external stimuli or suggestions. Physiologically, hypnosis is an inhibition of the inhibitory centres, or, in other words, hypnosis is a disaggregation of the superior from the inferior centres necessarily followed, as is the removal of inhibition in general, by an increase of the idea-motor and ideo-sensory reflex excitability. Psychologically, hypnosis is the split-off disaggregated organic reflex consciousness, pure and simple.

This theory of hypnosis is, in fact, a generalization in which the views of the two schools, the Salpetriere and the Nancy, are included. With the Nancy school, we agree that suggestion is all-powerful in hypnotic trance ; the hypnotic trance is, in fact, a state of heightened suggestibility, or, rather of pure reflex consciousness ; but with the Paris school we agree, that a changed physiological state is a prerequisite to hypnosis, and this modification consists in the disaggregation of the superior from the inferior centres, in the segregation of the controlling consciousness from the reflex consciousness. In hypnotic trance the upper inhibiting, resisting consciousness being absent, we have direct access to man's organic consciousness, and through it to organic life itself.

Strong, persistent impressions or suggestions made on the reflex organic consciousness of the inferior centres may modify their functional disposition, induce trophic changes, and even change organic structures. But whatever the case may be with regard to psycho-therapeutics, this, it seems, may be fairly granted, that the process of hypnotization consists in the separation of the higher inhibitory cortical ganglion cells from the rest of the cerebro-spinal and sympathetic nervous systems. Hypnosis, we may say, is the more or less effected disaggregation of the controlling inhibitory centres from the rest of the nervous system; along with this disaggregation there goes a dissociation of the controlling guardian consciousness from the reflex organic consciousness. Dissociation is the secret of hypnosis, and amnesia is the ripe fruit. The magnitude of this disaggregation greatly varies. If it is at its minimum, the hypnosis is light; if at its maximum, the hypnosis is deep, and is known as somnambulism. From our standpoint of hypnosis we may say that there are only two great distinct classes of hypnotic states:

1. Incomplete dissociation of the waking, controlling consciousness.

2. Complete dissociation of the waking consciousness.

Stating the same somewhat differently, we may say that there are two states :

1. Incomplete hypnosis accompanied by a greater or lesser degree of memory.

2. Complete hypnosis with no memory. In other words, hypnosis has two states:

1. The mnesic state.

2. The amnesic state.

Amnesia is the boundary line that separates two different hypnotic regions. This view of the matter is, in fact, taken by Edmund Gourney; for he tells us that "we might without incorrectness describe the higher hypnotic phenomena as reflex action, in respect of the certainty with which particular movements follow on particular stimuli ; but they are, and their peculiarity consists in their being, conscious reflex action."[13] "The heart of the problem [of hypnotism] "he says in another place, "lies not in CONSCIOUSNESS, but in WILL."In his paper on The Stages of Hypnotising E. Gourney distinguishes two states of hypnosis — the alert and the deep state. "The question then presents itself,"he writes, "Is there any distinction of kind between the two states? I believe that there is such a distinction, and that the phenomena needed to establish it are to be found in the domain of memory."Gurney, however, thinks that not only is the deep, but the hypnotic state as a whole, that is, the alert one, too, is separated from the normal state by amnesia—a proposition which is not borne out by facts. On the whole, however, I may say that Gurney was on the right track; he cast a searching glance deep into the nature of hypnosis.

If we turn now to the classifications reviewed by us we find that they have a change of memory, amnesia, as their fundamentum divisionis. Max Dessoir's forms the only exception, but his classification sins against the truth of facts. For there are cases of subjects who fall into deep hypnosis and still there can be induced no abnormal changes in the sense organs. I myself have a somnambule, Mr. F., who can be led through a series of imaginary scenes and changes of personalities, but whose sense organs remain almost normal, perfectly free from suggestion ; by no means can I make him see a picture on a blank paper, or feel the taste of sugar on eating salt, or take a glass of water for a glass of wine— phenomena which I easily induce in another somnambule, Mr. W. There are again other cases on record where the sense organs are deeply affected, but no abnormalities can be induced in the voluntary movements. Bernheim brings a few cases of this kind. Amnesia is the only boundary line in hypnosis, and degeneration of consciousness is its source.

Suggestion is at present the shibboleth of many a "scientific" psychologist. Suggestion is the magic key that opens all secrets and discloses all mysteries. Suggestion explains everything. To any question as to hypnosis asked of the suggestionist, he, like a parrot, has but one answer : "Suggestion!""Well may Binet say: "It is insufficient to explain everything that takes place in hypnotized subjects by invoking the hackneyed term 'Suggestion!' And that suffices for all purposes; that explains everything, and, like the panacea of the ancients, it cures everything. As a matter of fact, theories of suggestion thus invoked amount to nothing less than makeshifts to save people the trouble of serious and delicate investigation."Suggestionists make of suggestion a kind of metaphysical absolute, a Spinozistic *causa sui*, for, according to this trance-philosophy, hypnosis is nothing but suggestion ; and by what is it induced ? Why, by suggestion! Suggestion is thus its own cause. Absurd as this trance-philosophy of suggestionism is, it is none the less the current view of many a "scientific"psychologist. Still the authorities on the subject do not always talk the suggestion jargon; in their more lucid states they use quite a different language. The pity only is that they do not grasp the full import and meaning of their own propositions; they do not see the far-reaching consequences of their own statements.

Dr. Moll, in his remarkable book on Hypnotism, sums up his theory of hypnosis thus: ""We may, then, consider every hypnosis as a state in which the normal course of the ideas is inhibited. It matters not whether the ideas have to do with movements or with sense impressions. Their normal course is always inhibited. The idea of a movement called up in a subject in or out of hypnosis has a tendency to induce the movement. But in waking life this idea is made ineffectual by the voluntary idea of the subject that he will prevent the suggested movement ; the hypnotized subject can not do this* The same is the case with suggested paralysis. Sense delusions can be explained in a similar way. We tell the hypnotic subject, ' Here is a dog,' and he realizes it, and sees the dog. The limitation of the normal course of the ideas allows the idea of the dog to become a perception.

The subject is unable to control the external ideas, or to put forward his own ; the external ones dominate his consciousness. Psychologically speaking, what we mean by attention is the power of fixing certain ideas in the mind and of working with them. Consequently we may say that there is an alteration of attention in hypnosis. But attention may be either spontaneous or reflex. When by any act of will we choose one of several ideas and fix our attention upon it, this is spontaneous attention ; but when one idea among several gets the upper hand through its intensity or for some other reason, and thus suppresses other ideas and draws exclusive attention upon itself, this is reflex attention. Now it is only spontaneous attention which is altered in hypnosis — i. e., the subject's ability voluntarily to prefer one idea to another is interfered with, while reflex attention is undisturbed, and it is through this last that a suggested idea, the choice of which has not, however, been left to the subject, comes into prominence.

"Many investigators,"continues Dr. Moll, "conceive hypnotism in this way. The works of Durand de Gros, Liebault, and more lately of Beard, Kichet, Schneider, Wundt, and Bentivegni, are in the main direct to this point."

It is truly amusing to see how people concede the main substance to their opponents and still cling to the empty shell of their old creeds. Accepting inhibition of spontaneous attention as the source, as the nature of hypnosis, the psychologist of the suggestion school fully abandons his medical charm, his all-powerful magic suggestion. Inhibition of spontaneous attention, of voluntary control, leaving a residue of reflex attention, what is it, if not the full admission that the hypnotic state is a mental disaggregation, a dissociation of the controlling from the reflex consciousness?

Turning now to one of the leaders of the Nancy school, to the greatest popularizer of suggestionism— Prof. Bernheim—we find him to be still more explicit on this point. I humbly ask the reader's pardon for the lengthy quotation I am going to offer him. I find it will give additional confirmation to my view of the nature of hypnosis. In his book, "Suggestive Therapeutics,"Bernheim gives us the following account of hypnosis, an account that practically amounts to a complete abandonment of his omnipotent deity—suggestion: "The one thing certain is that a peculiar aptitude for transforming the idea received into an act exists in hypnotized subjects who are susceptible to suggestion. In the normal consciousness every formulated idea is questioned by the mind.

After being perceived by the cortical centres, the impression extends to the cells of the adjacent convolutions; their peculiar activity is excited ; the diverse faculties generated by the gray substance of the brain come into play ; the impression is elaborated, registered, and analyzed by means of a complex mental process which ends in its acceptation or neutralization; if there is cause, the mind vetoes it. In the hypnotized subject, on the contrary, the transformation of thought into action, sensation, movement, or vision is so quickly and so actively accomplished that the intellectual inhibition has not time to act.

When the mind interposes, it is already an accomplished fact, which is often registered with surprise, and which is confirmed by the fact that it proves to be real, and no intervention can hamper it further. If I say to the hypnotized subject, ' Tour hand remained closed,' the brain carries out the idea as soon as it is formulated; reflex is immediately transmitted from the cortical centre, where the idea induced by the auditory nerve is perceived, to the motor centre, corresponding to the central origin of the nerves subserving flexion of the hand ; contracture occurs hi flexion. There is then exaltation of the ideo-motor reflex excitability, which effects the unconscious (subconscious?) transformation of the thought into movement unknown to the will. The same thing occurs when I say to the hypnotized subject, 'You have a tickling sensation in your nose.' The thought induced through hearing is reflected upon the centre of olfactory sensibility, where it awakens the sensitive memory image of the nasal itching as former impressions have created it and left it imprinted and latent. This memory sensation thus resuscitated may be intense enough to cause the reflex action of sneezing. There is also, then, exaltation of the ideo-sensorial reflex excitability, which affects the unconscious transformation of the thought into sensation, or into a sensory image. In the same way the visual, acoustic, and gustatory images succeed the suggested idea.

Negative suggestions are more difficult to explain. If I say to the hypnotized subject, ' Your body is insensible, your eye is blind,' the impression transmitted by the auditory nerve to the centre of tactile or visual anaesthesia is that retinal vision exists, but the cerebral perception no longer exists. It seems as if it might be a reflex paralysis of a cortical centre, which the suggested idea has produced in this case. The mechanism of suggestion in general may then be summed up in the following formula: Increase of the reflex ideo-motor, ideo-sensorial excitability. In the same way through the effect of some influence —strychnine, for example—the sensitive-motor excitability is increased in the spinal cord, so that the least impression at the periphery of a nerve is immediately transformed into contracture without the moderating influence of the brain being able to prevent this transformation. In the same way in hypnotization the ideo-reflex excitability is increased in the brain, so that any idea received is immediately transformed into an act, without the controlling portion of the brain, the higher centres, being able to prevent the transformation."

Thus we clearly see that when the suggestionist comes to discuss the nature of hypnosis, he abandons his position and admits that a split in the brain cutting off the higher controlling centres from the lower ones is at the basis of hypnosis. The very conditions of hypnosis proclaim this fact, for they are but keen psychical scalpels and have the power to effect a deep incision in the semifluid stream of consciousness. Fixation of attention, monotony, limitation of the field of consciousness, limitation of voluntary movements, inhibition — all of them are calculated to pare, to split off the controlling from the reflex consciousness. The nature of hypnosis, of abnormal suggestibility, is a disaggregation of consciousness .

CHAPTER VIII.
THE LAW OF ABNORMAL SUGGESTIBILITY.

A CLOSE examination of the facts of hypnotic suggestion will readily yield us the law of abnormal suggestibility.

I hypnotize Mr. N., and tell him that on awakening, when he will hear me cough, he will go to the table, take the Bible, open it on the first page, and read aloud the first verse of the first chapter. He is then awakened. I cough. He rises, walks up to the table, but stops there and does not budge. I rehypnotize him. He tells me he did not want to carry out the suggestion. "But you must do it! "I insist. "You must go to the table, open the Bible on the first page, and read the first verse of the first chapter. You must do it ! you can not help doing it !"He is then awakened, and this time the post-hypnotic suggestion is fully carried out.

I hypnotize Mr. L. "Rise!"I command. He rises. "Walk! "He walks.""You are unable to walk !"He makes a step or two, showing me that he can easily do it. "But it is impossible for you to walk; you can not walk ; you are utterly unable to walk; you must not, and you can not walk ; you lost all power of moving; no matter how you try, you find it impossible to take a step ; you can not move your legs; you have lost all control over them; they are stiff, rigid, and firmly fixed to the ground. Oh, no, you can not walk; it is a physical impossibility for you to walk."I go on in this way, pouring forth a torrent of suggestions; and this time my suggestion takes full. effect. The subject tries hard to move; he can not do it, his legs are rigid, cataleptic.

I hypnotize Mr. J. F., a strong, powerful, healthy, burly fellow. "Rise!"I command. He rises. "Walk!"He walks. "You can not move! "I command again in a somewhat louder voice. The subject makes a step forward. "But you can not move!"I insist in a still louder voice than before, laying more stress on "can not."He makes a step hesitatingly and with great difficulty, like one dragging a heavy burden on his legs. "You can not move!"I call out in a louder and more commanding tone, putting still more emphasis on the suggestion "can not."The subject comes to a complete standstill. He is fully paralyzed ; by no effort of will can he take a step forward.

We may put it down as a rule, that when the suggestion is not taken there is a far higher probability of bringing it into effect by repeating the suggestion over and over again in a louder key and in a more commanding voice. The rule of hypnotic suggestion is, The more direct we make our suggestion the greater the chance of its success. If we examine the facts of suggestion in the deeper states of hypnosis we find that the same rule holds true. The hypnotizer must make himself perfectly understood by the subject, by the reflex consciousness of the patient.

I hypnotize Mr. L., make passes over his hand, and suggest that it is rigid, stiff. It becomes cataleptic. On a second occasion, when I make the passes, his hand becomes rigid; he knows from previous experiments what it is I want of him. [14]

The experiments of Braid, Heidenhein, etc., and the controversy between the Nancy and Salpetriere school beautifully bring out this general rule of hypnosis. Thus Braid, in his Neurypnology, tells us of some phreno-hypnotic experiments he made with a subject. "This patient,"he writes, "being pressed over the phrenologist organ of time, always expressed a desire * to write' a letter to her mother or her brother; over the organ of tune, ' to sing'; between this and wit, * to be judicious'; the boundary between wit and causality, ' to be clever'; causality, ' to have knowledge,' and so on."

Heidenhein found that in pressing certain regions of the subject's body certain abnormal phenomena appeared ; that in pressing the neck echolalia resulted— the patient repeated everything that was said before him with the exactness of a phonograph ; that the stimulation of the neck produced vocal sounds, as in Goltz's experiments. Silva, Binet, Fere, and Heidenhein believe that they can move single limbs of the somnambule by stimulating the parts of the head which correspond to the motor centres of the limbs concerned. Chalan-der even proposed to study the physiology of the brain in this way. Charcot, Dumontpallier, Berillon, Lepine, Strahl, Griitzner, and Heidenhein regard hemihypnosis —that is, hypnosis of one side of the body—as a physiological condition induced by the closing of one eye. I must add here that Braid, in his later investigations in hypnosis, became fully aware of the real source of the phenomena. By friction of one half of the crown of the head. Binet and Fere claim that a magnet can affect a transfer of anaesthesia, etc., to the opposite side of the body.

Now such experiments invariably fail when made by other observers and on other subjects. Braid himself tells us: "I also very soon ascertained that the same points of the cranium when thus excited did not excite the *same ideas or emotions i*n the minds of different patients, which I considered ought to have been the case."He hastens, however, to add: "I have since discovered the cause of this — namely, not having operated at the proper stage of the hypnotic condition"The Italics are his own, although Braid meant in quite a different sense from that implied by me. You may press a.bump on the head of a fresh subject, and press it as much and as long as you like, and nothing particular will result, or anything might follow. And the reason is, the subject does not know what to expect ; he has no suspicion of what the experimenter wants him to do. Charcot and his school maintain that there are three states of what they name "le grand e hypnotisme."These states are induced physiologically.

1. The lethargic state is induced by fixation upon an object, or by passing lightly upon the eyeball through the closed eyelids. In this stage suggestion is impossible, but we find in it anaesthesia, a certain muscular hyperexcitability; any muscle excited by pressure or light friction contracts; pressure upon the ulnar nerve provokes the ulnar attitude; and pressure upon the facial nerve is followed by distortion of the features of the corresponding side of the face.

2. A subject in the lethargic condition can be made to pass into the second or cataleptic state by raising his eyelids. If one eye only is opened the corresponding side of the body alone passes into the cataleptic condition, the other side remaining lethargic. Suggestions can be induced through the muscular sense. If the subject's hand is put into a condition as if to give a kiss, his face assumes a smiling expression ; if his hands are joined as in prayer, the face becomes grave and the subject kneels down. This condition of catalepsy can also be induced at. once without having the subject pass through lethargy, and that is caused by some nervous shock produced by a brilliant point or a violent noise.

3. Lethargy and catalepsy can be transformed into somnambulism by light or repeated friction of the top of the subject's head. Anaesthesia, hyperacute sensibility, and susceptibility to all kinds of suggestion characterize this state.

Now when other observers came to verify these three states they invariably failed to reproduce them without the agency of suggestion. Wetterstrand never found them at all among 3,589 different persons. "I have been as little able,"writes Dr. Moll, "as have many others, to observe the stages of Charcot in my experiments. I have, besides, often experimented on several hystero-epileptics, but have failed to observe the stages, in spite of Bichet's opinion that every one who experiments on such persons will obtain the same results as the school of Charcot did."Bernheim finds that these three stages can not be induced without suggestion. Continued suggestion alone has been able to produce them. Liebault, who hypnotized more than six thousand persons, never observed anything that should go to confirm the hypnotic stages as described by Charcot.

"I have never been able,"writes Bernheim, "to determine without suggestion any phenomena by pressure exercised upon certain points of the cranium. For example, here is one of my somnambulistic cases. I press upon the different points of the cranium; no result. I say, ' Now I am going to touch that part of the cranium which corresponds to the movement of the left arm, and this arm will go into convulsions.' Having said this, I touch an arbitrary part of the head; immediately the left arm is convulsed. I state that I am going to induce aphasia by touching the region corresponding to speech. I touch any part of the head, and the subject no longer replies to my questions. Then I state that I shall touch the head in such a way that irritation of the centres of speech will result. The person then answers my questions in the following manner: ' What is your name ?' ' Marie, Marie, Marie.' ' How are you ? ' ' Well, well, well.' ' You have no pain ?' * None at all, none at all, none at all.' "

I myself made similar experiments on my subjects and with similar results. I pressed different regions of the head of my subject and nothing resulted. I then said, "I am going to press your shoulder and you will be unable to speak."I pressed it, and he could not speak. In my following seances, whenever I pressed that subject's shoulder he lost the power of speech.

I pressed the head of Mr. W. in different places and no result followed. I then said, "I will press the centre of speech and you will be unable to speak."I firmly pressed an arbitrary part of the head, and the subject was unable to speak. Without suggestion, by mere physiological means, we are unable to induce any particular changes in the hypnotic subject. The subject must know what we require of him.

It is not necessary to make suggestions to each subject separately. If a hypnotizable person is present at a seance, he takes the hint at once, and when he is hypnotized he manifests phenomena similar to the one he has witnessed. He knows exactly what the hypnotizer wants of him.

"Here is an experiment,"writes Bernheim,* "which I made with M. Beaunis. We hypnotized a nurse in our service who was susceptible to somnambulism. She had never been present either as witness or as subject of the kind of experiment which I wanted to try on her. I put the upper left limb into the cataleptic condition in the horizontal position, the thumb and index fingers stretched out, the other fingers bent; the right arm remained relaxed. I applied the magnet to it for eight minutes. Nothing occurred. Then turning to M. Beaunis, I said: ' Now I am going to try an experiment. I shall apply the magnet to the right hand (on the unaffected hand), and in a minute you will see this arm lifted and take the exact attitude of the left one, while the latter relaxes and falls.' I placed the magnet just where it was at first, and in a minute the suggested transfer was realized with perfect precision. If, then, without saying anything more, I put the magnet back against the left hand at the end of a minute the transfer occurred in inverse order, and so on consecutively. Afterward I said, ' I shall change the direction of the magnet, and the transfer will take place from the arm to the leg.'

At the end of a minute the arm fell and the leg was raised. I put the magnet against the leg without saying anything, and the transfer took place from the leg to the arm. If, without saying anything to the subject, I replace the magnet by a knife, a pencil, a bottle, a piece of paper, or use anything in its place, the same phenomenon occurs. The next day I repeated these experiments on another somnambulist who had been present the day before, and without saying anything to her, or to any of the persons present, they succeeded marvellously / the idea of the transfer had been suggested to her mind by the circumstances of which she had been a witness"

In deep hypnosis, on account of the hypersesthesia of the subject's senses, the slightest hint suffices. But here, too, the subject must be trained by previous experiments as to the interpretation of the hint. In short, we may fully assert that in hypnosis the subject must know what the hypnotizer wants of him, so that the more precise, exact, and frank the suggestion is, the surer will be its success. We may put it down as a rule for practitioners who intend to use hypnotism for therapeutic purposes, In giving the suggestion to the patient, make your language plain, precise, and direct to the point.

The following cases will show the necessity of observing this last rule:

Prof. W. James gave to one of his patients a post-hypnotic suggestion to smoke only one pipe of tobacco a day. When the patient came again Prof. James asked him how many pipes he smoked a day ? The answer was, "One only."On being hypnotized the patient confessed that he bought a pipe with a bowl of large dimensions, and that it was this one pipe he was smoking the whole day.

Mr. F. suffered from attacks of acute headache. On account of the violent pain he had to discontinue his work. He came to me to be cured by hypnotism. I have hypnotized him several times and greatly relieved his headache. He could continue his occupation without any inconvenience. At the eighth sitting he told me he had no more violent attacks, but was only suffering from occasional slight headaches. I suggested that he will have no more slight headaches. Next day he came to me complaining of a severe attack.

All the facts discussed in this chapter prove in the clearest way the truth that in hypnosis, in the state of abnormal suggestibility, the more direct a suggestion is the greater is the chance of its being realized, the stronger is its efficacy ; and vice versa, the more indirect a suggestion is the less is the chance of having it realized, the less is its efficacy. The law of abnormal suggestibility may be stated as follows :

Abnormal suggestibility varies as direct suggestion. and inversely as indirect suggestion.

PLATE I shows the influence of suggestion in the production of catalepsy. The subject was put into a state of hypnosis and a sphygmographic record was taken of him. In the middle of the record the subject was thrown into a cataleptic state. At once the record changed; the characteristic pulse-wave disappeared and was replaced either by a curve full of fine minute vibrations (A and D), or by a series of broken lines (B and E) —traces of the pulse-waves—r.nd sometimes by one rapidly descending straight line passing over into a series of fine minute vibrations as the suggestion of rigidity was more and more enforced (C). Now, at the height of the cataleptic state the subject was suggested that he was "well "again, and immediately the characteristic pulse-wave appeared once more, and very often in a better condition, the ascending limb on the upward stroke was higher, and the secondary or dicrotic wave on the descending limb became more emphasized.

The arrow »-> indicates the direction in which the record runs.

CHAPTER IX.
SUGGESTIBILITY AND THE WAKING CONSCIOUSNESS.

IT is now high time to gather up the threads of our discussion and weave them into one organic, living whole; to bring the stray rays of light that reached us in the course of our research together into one focus, and illuminate the dark, mysterious regions we undertook to explore. To do this we must retrace our steps and inspect closer the conditions that admit one into that strange land of puzzles, wonders, and prodigies. A comparison of the conditions of normal and abnormal suggestibility will, I think, prove interesting and valuable, as it might give us a glimpse deep into the nature of suggestibility in general.

To facilitate this comparison, it would be best to make a table in which the conditions of normal and abnormal suggestibility should run parallel to each other.

TABLE OF CONDITIONS OF NORMAL AND ABNORMAL SUGGESTIBILITY.

Normal Suggestibility. Abnormal Suggestibility.

   1. Fixation of attention. 1. Fixation of attention.

   2. Distraction. 2.

   3. Monotony. 3. Monotony.

   4. Limitation of voluntary 4. Limitation of voluntary movements. movements.

   5. Limitation of the field of 5. Limitation of the field of consciousness. consciousness.

   6. Inhibition. 6. Inhibition.

   7. Immediate execution. 7.

A glance at our last table will show at once that the conditions in both cases are essentially the same, with the only difference that in abnormal suggestibility two conditions are wanting—namely, distraction and immediate execution. This sameness of conditions clearly indicates that both normal and abnormal suggestibility flow from some one common source, that they are of like nature, and that they are due to similar causes. Now a previous study led us to the conclusion that the nature of abnormal suggestibility is a disaggregation of consciousness, a slit, a scar produced in the mind, a crack that may extend wider and deeper, ending at last in a total disjunction of the waking, guiding, controlling consciousness from the reflex consciousness, from the rest of the stream of life. Normal suggestibility is of like nature—it is a cleft in the mind; only here the cleft is not so deep, not so lasting as it is in hypnosis, or in the state of abnormal suggestibility; the split is here but momentary, evanescent, fleeting, disappearing at the very moment of its appearance.

This fleeting, evanescent character of the split gives the reason why suggestion in the normal state, why normal suggestibility requires immediate execution as one of its most indispensable conditions. We must take the opportunity of the momentary ebb of the controlling consciousness and hastily plant our suggestion in the soil of reflex consciousness. "We must watch for this favourable moment; not let it slip by, otherwise the suggestion is a failure. Furthermore, we must be careful to keep in abeyance, for the moment, though, the ever-active, ever-restless waves of the controlling consciousness; we must find for them work in some other direction; we must divert, we must distract them. That is why normal suggestibility requires the additional conditions of distraction and of immediate execution.

For in the normal state the waking, controlling consciousness is always on its guard, and when enticed, leaves its ground only a single step, and that only for but a moment. In normal suggestibility the psychical scar is faint; the lesion affected in the body of consciousness is superficial, transitory, fleeting. In abnormal suggestibility, on the contrary, the slit is deep and lasting—it is a severe gash. In both cases, however, we have a removal, a dissociation of the waking from the subwaking, reflex consciousness, and suggestion being effected only through the latter. It is the subwaking, the reflex, not the waking, the controlling, consciousness that is suggestible. Suggestibility is the attribute, the very essence of the subwaking, reflex consciousness. That our suggestions should take root and bring forth fruit, that they should become fully realized, we must address them to the subwaking consciousness directly, and in order to do that a disaggregation of consciousness must be effected.

If we turn to the laws of normal and abnormal suggestibility, we find still further evidence in support of our view as to the nature of suggestibility and its relation to the subwaking, reflex consciousness. A mere comparison of the two laws reveals the truth of our position:

Abnormal suggestibility varies Normal suggestibility varies as as direct suggestion, and in- indirect suggestion, and inversely as indirect sugges- versely as direct suggestion, tion.

The two laws are the reverse of each other, thus clearly indicating the presence of a controlling, inhibitorj conscious element in the one case, and its absence in the other. In the normal state we must guard against the inhibitory waking consciousness, and we must therefore make our suggestion as indirect as possible. In the abnormal state, on the contrary, no circumspection is needed; the controlling, inhibitory waking consciousness is more or less absent, the subwaking reflex consciousness is exposed to external stimuli, and our suggestions, therefore, are the more effective the more direct we make them. With full right may we now assert that suggestibility is a disaggnegation of consciousness — a disaggregation in which the subwaking, reflex consciousness enters into direct communication with the external world.

The general law of suggestibility is now plainly obvious:

SUGGESTIBILITY VARIES AS THE AMOUNT OF DISAGGREGATION, AND INVERSELY AS THE UNIFICATION OF CONSCIOUSNESS.

CHAPTER X.
THE SECONDARY SELF.

THE law of suggestibility in general, and those of normal and abnormal suggestibility in particular, indicate a coexistence of two streams of consciousness, of two selves within the frame of the individual; the one, the waking consciousness, the waking self; the other, the subwaking consciousness, the subwaking self. But although the conditions and laws of suggestibility clearly point to a double self as constituting human individuality, still the proof, strong as it appears to me to be, is rather of an indirect nature. We must therefore look for facts that should directly and explicitly prove the same truth. We do not lack such facts. We turn first to those of hysteria.

If we put a pencil or scissors into the anaesthetic hand of the hysterical person without his seeing it, the insensible hand makes adaptive movements. The fingers seize the pencil and place it in a position as if the hand were going to write. Quite differently does the hand possess itself of the scissors: the hand gets hold of the instrument in the proper way, and seems ready for work, for cutting. Now all the while the subject is totally unconscious of what is happening there to his hand, since it is insensible, and he can not possibly see it, as his face is concealed by a screen. It is obvious that in order for such movements of adaptation to occur that there must be recognition of the object kept by the anaesthetic hand.

But recognition requires a complex mental operation: it requires that the object should be perceived, should be remembered, and should be classed with objects of a certain kind and order. The very fact of the adaptation movements indicate the presence of some kind of embryonic will. Simple as these experiments are, they none the less strongly indicate the presence of a hidden agency that works through the anaesthetic hand; an agency that possesses perception, memory, judgment, and even will. Since these last operations are essentially characteristics of consciousness, of a self, we must necessarily conclude that it is a conscious agency that acts through the insensible hand of the hysterical person. Since the activity of this intelligence, simple and elementary as it is, is unknown to the subject, it is quite clear that there is present within him a secondary consciousness standing in no connection with the primary stream of personal consciousness, and somehow coming in possession of the person's hand.

As we advance in our research and make the conditions more and more complicated, all doubt as to the presence of a conscious being, behind the veil of the subject's primary consciousness, completely disappears. "We put a pen," says Binet,[15] "into the anaesthetic hand and we make it write a word; left to itself, the hand preserves its attitude, and at the expiration of a short space of time repeats the words often five or ten times. Having arrived at this fact, we again seize the anaesthetic hand and cause it to write some familiar word—for example, the patient's own name—but in so doing we intentionally commit an error in spelling. In its turn the anaesthetic hand repeats the word, but, oddly enough, the hand betrays a momentary hesitation when it reaches the letter at which the error in orthography was committed. If a superfluous letter happens to have been added, sometimes the hand will hesitatingly rewrite the name along with the supplementary letter; again, it will retrace only a part of the letter in question; and again, finally, entirely suppress it." It is quite evident that we have here to deal with a conscious agent hesitating about mistakes and able to correct them; we can not possibly ascribe such activity to mere unconscious cerebration.

If again we take the anaesthetic hand and trace on the dorsal side of it a letter or a figure, the hand traces this figure or letter. Evidently the secondary consciousness is in full possession of these perceptions, although the primary consciousness of the subject is totally ignorant of them.

Furthermore, insensible as the anaesthetic hand is, since no pinching, pricking, burning, or faradization of it are perceived by the subject, still we can show that there exists a hidden sensibility in the hand ; this can easily be proved by the aesthesiometer. If we prick the insensible hand with one of the points of a pair of compasses, the hand automatically traces a single point. Apply both points, and the automatic writing will trace two points, thus informing us of its degree of insensibility .

The amaurotic or hysterical eye gives us still stronger evidence of the existence of a secondary being perceiving things which lie outside the visual distance of the subject's waking consciousness. Hysterical subjects often complain of the loss of sight. As a matter of fact, when we come to test it we find that the subject does see what he claims not to see. This is detected by the so-called "box of Flees."This box is so skilfully arranged that the patient sees with his right eye the picture or the figure situated to the left, and with his left eye what is situated to the right. The hysterical person blind in the right eye, when put to such a test, declares that he sees the picture to the left side but not that to the right. He sees with the blind eye.

Amaurosis may also be tested in a somewhat different way. A pair of spectacles in which one glass is red and the other green is put on the patient's eye, and he is made to read six letters on a blank frame, alternately covered with red and green glass. When one eye is closed only three letters can be seen through the spectacles—namely, the ones corresponding in color to the spectacle glass through which the eye is looking; the other three can not be seen on account of the two complementary colors forming black. The patient, then, blind in one eye (say the right), ought to see only three letters when he has the spectacles on. When, however, put to this test the patient promptly reads the six letters. The right eye undoubtedly sees, only the image is retained by the secondary self, and a special arrangement of conditions is required to force that hidden self to surrender the image it stole.

To reveal the presence of this secondary self that perceives and knows facts hidden from the upper conciousness or primary self, I frequently employ the following simple but sure method, which may be characterized as the method of "guessing”: Impressions are made on the anaesthetic limb, and the subject who does not perceive any of the applied stimuli is asked just to make a "wild guess "as to the nature and number of the stimuli, if there were any. Now the interest is that nearly all the guesses are found to be correct. Dr. William A. White, of Binghamton State Hospital, finds that this method works well in his cases. "In the case of D. F./' Dr. White writes to me, "whose field of vision I sent you, I find by experiment, taking a hint from you, that, by introducing fingers between the limit of her field of vision (which is very contracted) and the limit of the normal field, she could guess each time and tell which finger was held up."

To bring out still more clearly and decisively the presence of a secondary consciousness that perceives the image which the hysterical person does not see, A. Binet performed the following experiment: "We place,"he says,[16] "the hysterical subject before a scale of printed letters, and tentatively seek the maximum distance from the board at which the subject is able to read the largest letters. After having experimentally determined the maximum distance at which the subject can read the largest letters of the series, we invite him to read certain small letters that are placed below the former. Naturally enough, the subject is unable to do so; but if at this instant we slip a pencil into the anaesthetic hand, we are able by the agency of the hand to induce automatic writing, and this writing will reproduce precisely the letters which the subject is in vain trying to read. It is highly interesting to observe that during the very time the subject is repeatedly declaring that he does not see the letters, the anaesthetic hand, unknown to him, writes out the letters one after another. If, interrupting the experiments, we ask the subject to write of his own free will the letters of the printed series, he will not be able to do so; and when asked simply to draw what he sees, he will only produce a few zigzag marks that have no meaning."

These experiments plainly prove that the secondary consciousness sees the letters or words, and directs the anaesthetic hand it possesses to write what it perceives. Furthermore, if we remove the subject at too great a distance, so that the letters are altogether out of the range of vision of the secondary consciousness, the automatic writing begins to make errors—writing, for instance, "Lucien "instead of "Louise"; it tries to guess. Now if anything plainly shows the presence of a hidden intelligence, it is surely this guessing of which the subject himself is totally unconscious, for guessing is essentially a characteristic of consciousness. "An automaton,"truly remarks Binet, "does not mistake; the secondary consciousness, on the contrary, is subject to errors because it is a consciousness, because it is a thing that reasons and combines thoughts."This last conclusion is still further proved by the following experiments: "There are patients,"writes Binet* "(St. Am., for example), whose hand spontaneously finishes the word they are made to trace. Thus I cause the letter ' d' to be written; the hand continues and writes 'don.' I write 'pa,' and the hand continues andwrites 'pavilion.' I write 'Sal,' and the hand writes ' Salpetriere.' Here it is still more obvious that we are in the presence of a hidden agency that can take hints and develop them intelligently.'

We saw above that distraction of attention is one of the indispensable conditions of suggestibility in the normal waking state. Now, M. Janet, in his experiments on hysterical persons, used chiefly this condition, or (as it may be called) "method of distraction,"as a means for coming into direct oral communication with the secondary suggestible self. In hysterical persons it is easier to bring about the conditions of suggestibility, because, as a rule, they possess a contracted field of consciousness, and when engaged in one thing they are oblivious to all else. "When Lucie [the subject] talked directly with anyone,"says M. Janet, "she ceased to be able to hear any other person. You may stand behind her, call her by name, shout abuse in her ear, without making her turn round; or place yourself before her, show her objects, touch her, etc., without attracting her notice. When finally she becomes aware of you she thinks you have just come into the room again, and greets you accordingly."M. Janet [17] availed himself of these already existent conditions of suggestibility, and began to give her suggestions while she was in the waking state. When the subject's attention was fully fixed on a conversation with a third party M. Janet came up behind her, whispered in her ear some simple commands, which she instantly obeyed. He made her reply by signs to his questions, and even made her answer in writing if a pencil were placed in her hands. The subject's primary consciousness was entirely ignorant of what was going on. In some cases the patient was made to pass through a series of awkward bodily positions without the least spark of knowledge on his side. The following is a very interesting and striking case:

P., a man of forty, was received at the hospital at Havre for delirium tremens. He improved and became quite rational during the daytime. The hospital doctor observed that the patient was highly suggestible, and invited M. Janet to experiment on him. "While the doctor was talking to the patient on some interesting subject,"writes M. Janet,' 55 ' "I placed myself behind P., and told him to raise his arm. On the first trial I had to touch his arm in order to provoke the desired act; afterward his unconscious obedience followed my order without difficulty. I made him walk, sit down, kneel—all without his knowing it. I even told him to lie down on his stomach, and he fell down at once, but his head still raised itself to answer at once the doctor's questions. The doctor asked him, 'In what position are you while I am talking to you ?' ' Why, I am standing by my bed ; I am not moving."1 The secondary self accepted motor suggestions of which the primary self was totally unaware.

As the orders thus whispered to the secondary, subwaking self become more complicated the latter rises to the surface, pushes the waking self into the background and carries out the suggested commands. "M. Binet had been kind enough," writes M. Janet, "to show me one of the subjects on whom he was in the habit of studying acts rendered unconscious by anaesthesia, and I had asked his permission to produce on this subject the phenomenon of suggestion by distraction. Everything took place just as I expected. The subject (Hab.), fully awake, talked to M. Binet. Placing myself behind her, I caused her to move her hand unconsciously, to write a few words, to answer my questions by signs, etc. Suddenly Hab. ceased to speak to M. Binet, and, turning toward me, continued correctly by the voice the conversation she had begun with me by unconscious signs. On the other hand, she no longer spoke to M. Binet, and could no longer hear him speak; in a word, she had fallen into elective somnambulism (rapport). It was necessary to wake her up, and when awakened she had naturally forgotten everything. Now Hab. had no previous knowledge of me at all; it was not, therefore, my presence which had sent her to sleep. The sleep was in this case manifestly the result of the development of unconscious actions, which had invaded and finally effaced the normal consciousness. This explanation, indeed, is easily verified.

My subject, Madame. B , remains wide awake in my neighbourhood so long as I do not provoke unconscious phenomena, but when the unconscious phenomena become too numerous and too complicated she goes to sleep." We have here clear and direct proof as to the presence of a conscious agency lying buried below the upper stratum of personal life, and also as to the identity of this hidden, mysterious self with the hypnotic self. The self of normal and that of abnormal suggestibility are one and the same. Turning now to hypnosis, we find that the classical experiments of P. Janet and Gourney on deferred or post-hypnotic suggestion furnish clear, valid, and direct evidence of the reality of a secondary consciousness, of an intelligent, subwaking, hypnotic self concealed behind the curtain of personal consciousness.

"When Lucie was in a state of genuine somnambulism,"writes P. Janet, "I said to her, in the tone used for giving suggestions, 'When I clap my hand twelve times you will go to sleep again.' Then I talked to her of other things, and five or six minutes later I woke her completely. The forgetfulness of all that had happened during the hypnotic state, and of my suggestion in particular, was complete. I was assured of this forgetfulness, which was an important thing here, first, by the preceding state of sleep, which was genuine somnambulism with all its characteristic symptoms; by the agreement of all those who have been engaged upon these questions, and who have all proved the forgetfulness of similar suggestions after waking; and, finally, by the results of all the preceding experiments made upon this subject, in which I have always found this unconsciousness.

Other people surrounded Lucie and talked to her about different things; and then, drawing back a few steps, I struck my hand five blows at rather long intervals and rather faintly, noticing at the same time that the subject paid no attention to me, but still talked on briskly. I came nearer and said to her, 'Did you hear what I just did ?' ' What did you do ?' said she, ' I was not paying attention.' ' This' (I clapped my hands). ' You just clapped your hands.' ' How many times ?' ' Once.' I drew back and continued to clap more faintly every now and then. Lucie, whose attention was distracted, no longer listened to me, and seemed to have completely forgotten my existence. When I had clapped six times more in this way, which with the preceding ones made twelve, Lucie stopped talking immediately, closed her eyes, and fell back asleep. ' Why do you go to sleep ?' I said to her. ' I do not know anything about it; it came upon me all at once,' she said.

"The somnambulist must have counted, for I endeavoured to make the blows just alike, and the twelfth could not be distinguished from the preceding ones. She must have heard them and counted them, but without knowing it; therefore, unconsciously (subconsciously). The experiment was easy to repeat, and I repeated it in many ways. In this way Lucie counted unconsciously (subconsciously) up to forty-three, the blows being sometimes regular and sometimes irregular, with never a mistake in the result. The most striking of these experiments was this: I gave the order, ' At the third blow you will raise your hands, at the fifth you will lower them, at the sixth you will look foolish, at the ninth you will walk about the room, and at the sixteenth you will go to sleep in an easy-chair.' She remembered nothing at all of this on waking, but all these actions were performed in the order desired, although during the whole time Lucie replied to questions that were put to her, and was not aware that she counted the noises, that she looked foolish, or that she walked about.

"After repeating the experiment I cast about for some means of varying it, in order to obtain very simple unconscious judgments. The experiment was always arranged in the same way. Suggestions were made during a well-established hypnotic sleep, then the subject was thoroughly wakened, and the signals and the actions took place in the waking state. 'When I repeat the same letter in succession you will become rigid.' After she awoke I whispered the

letters, 'a,' 'c,' 'd,' 'e,' 'a,' 'a.' Lucie became motionless and perfectly rigid. That shows an unconscious judgment of resemblance. I may also cite some examples of judgments of difference: ' You will go to sleep when I pronounce an uneven number,' or ' Your hands will revolve around each other when I pronounce a woman's name.' The result is the same; as long as I whisper even numbers or names of men nothing happens, but the suggestion is carried out when I give the proper signal. Lucie has therefore listened unconsciously (subconsciously), compared, and appreciated the differences.

"I next tried to complicate the experiment in order to see to what lengths this faculty of an unconscious (subconscious) judgment would go. 'When the sum of the number which I shall pronounce amounts to ten you will throw kisses.' The same precautions were taken. She was awakened, forgetfulness established, and while she was chatting with other people who disturbed her as much as possible, I whispered, at quite a distance from her, 'Two, three, one, four,' and she made the movement. Then I tried more complicated numbers and other operations. 'When the numbers that I shall pronounce two by two, subtracted from one another, leave six, you will make a certain gesture'—or multiplication, and even very simple divisions. The whole thing was carried out with almost no errors, except when the calculation became too complicated and could not be done in her head. There was no new faculty there, only the usual processes were operating unconsciously (subconsciously).

"It seems to me that these experiments are quite directly connected with the problem of the intelligent performance of suggestion that appears to be forgotten. The facts mentioned are perfectly accurate. Somnambulists are able to count the days and hours that intervene between the present time and the performance of a suggestion, although they have no memory whatever of the suggestion itself. Outside of their consciousness there is a memory that persists, an attention always on the alert, and a judgment perfectly capable of counting the days, as is shown by its being able to make these multiplications and divisions."

The experiments of E. Gourney confirm the same truth—that behind the primary upper consciousness a secondary lower consciousness is present.

"P 11," writes E. Gourney, "was told on March

26th that on the one hundred and twenty-third day from then he was to put a blank sheet of paper in an envelope and send it to a friend of mine whose name and residence he knew, but whom he had never seen. The subject was not referred to again till April 18th, when he was hypnotized and asked if he remembered anything in connection with this gentleman. He at once repeated the order, and said, ' This is the twenty-third day—a hundred more.'

(hypnotizer). How do you know ? Have you noted each day ?

P U. No; it seemed natural.

S. Have you thought of it often ?

P II. It generally strikes me early in the

morning. Something tells me, 'You have got to count.'

S. Does that happen every day ?

P U. No, not every day—perhaps more likely

every other day. It goes from my mind. I never think of it during the day. I only know it has to be

done. "He was questioned again on April 20th, and at once said, ' That is going on all right—twenty-five days'; and on April 22d, when in the trance, he spontaneously recalled the subject and added ' Twenty-seven days.' After he was awakened (April 18th), I asked him if he knew the gentleman in question or had been thinking about him. He was clearly surprised at the question."The hypnotic self knew he had to do something, knew the particular act and the precise day when he had to perform it; watched the flow of time, counted the days and all that was going on, without the least intimation to the consciousness of the waking personal self.

E. Gourney then conceived the happy idea of further tapping the intelligence and knowledge of this subwaking hypnotic self by means of automatic writing.

"I showed P 11,"says E. Gourney, [18]"a planchette—he had never seen or touched one before—and got him to write his name with it. He was then hypnotized, and told that it had been as dark as night in London on the previous day, and that he would be able to write what he had heard. He was awakened, and as usual was offered a sovereign to say what it was he had been told, and as usual without impunity to my purse. He was then placed with his hand on the planchette, a large screen being held in the front of his face, so that it was impossible for him to see the paper or instrument. In less than a minute the writing began. The words were, ' It was a dark day in London."

"When asked what he had written, he did not know. He was given a post-hypnotic suggestion to poke the fire in six minutes, and that he should inform us how the time was going, without any direction as to writing. He wrote soon after waking "will you poke the fire in six minutes ?"'To prove decisively the intelligence of the secondary, subwaking, hypnotic self, Gourney gave the entranced subject arithmetical problems to solve, and immediately had him awakened. When put to the planchette the subject gave the solution of the problem, without being conscious as to what he was doing. It was the hypnotic self who made the calculation, who solved the arithmetical problem.

W was told to add together 5, 6, 8, 9, and had just time to say "5,"when he was awakened in the fraction of a second with the words on his lips. The planchette immediately produced "28."P 11 was told during trance to add all the digits from 1 to 9; the first result was 39, the second 45 (right). Rehypnotized, and asked by S. what he had been writing, he said, "You told me to add the figures from 1 to 9 = 45.""Did you write it ?""Yes, I wrote it down."

W s was hypnotized and told that in six minutes he was to blow a candle out, and that he would be required at the same time before this to write the number of minutes that had passed and the number that had still to elapse. He was awakened, laughed and talked as usual, and, of course, knew nothing of the order. In about three and a half minutes (he was taken by surprise, so to say) he was set down to the planchette, which wrote, "Four and a half— one more."

About a minute passed, and W s was rehypnotized, but just as his eyes were beginning to close, he raised himself and blew out the candle, saying, "It is beginning to smell."Hypnotized and questioned, he remembered all that lie had done; and when it was pointed out to him that four and a half and one do not make six, he explained the discrepancy by saying, "It took half a minute for you to tell me ; I reckoned from the end of your telling me."

S 1 was told in the trance that he was to look out of the window seven minutes after waking, and that he was to write how the time was going. He was then awakened. This was 7:34 P.M. I set him to the planchette, and the writing began at 7:36. I did not watch the process, but when I stood holding the screen in front of his eyes I was so close to his hand that I could not help becoming aware that the writing was being produced at distinct intervals. I remarked that he was going by fits and starts, and seemed to have to pause to get up steam. Immediately on the conclusion of the writing at 7.40 he got up and drew aside the blind, and looked out. Examining the paper, I found "25, 34, 43, 52, 61, 7."

Clearly he had aimed at recording at each moment when he began the number that had passed and the number that remained. The subwaking, suggestible, hypnotic being seems to be not a physiological automaton, but a self, possessing consciousness, memory, and even a rudimentary intelligence.Sphygmographic or tracings of the radial artery seem to point to the same conclusion. Thus in the normal state, on the application of agreeable stimuli, such as perfumes, the curves become broader, the pulse slower, indicating a muscular relaxation of the heart; while on the other hand, if disagreeable or painful stimuli are applied, such as pricking, faradic or galvanic currents, ammonia, acetic acid, formaline, etc., the pulse becomes rapid, the "Rickstoss elevation,"or the

PLATE II. A, B, C and D are sphygmographic or pulse tracings in the fully waking normal state. The first part of each tracing in A, C and D shows the normal pulse of the subject; the rest ia under the influence of pain stimuli, such as ammonia or acetic acid. B, in the first part of the record, ia normal, with no stimulus ; the second part of the record shows the influence of the pleasant stimulus of vanilla ; the third part of B shows the effect of acetic acid.

Tracings B and C are of the same subject whose characteristic normal (rather abnormal) pulse was that of C normal. Under the influence of pleasant stimuli (B, "vanilla ") the abnormal (normal to this subject) characteristics of this pulse became more manifest. Under the influence of painful stimuli (acetic acid, ammonia, etc.) the abnormal characteristic (normal pulse of this subject) disappeared, and the pulse became a typical normal pulse.

Tracing E, in the first part of the record, shows the pulse in hypnosis, but with no application of any stimuli; the second part of the record shows the influence of pain stimuli in hypnosis with suggestive analgesia.

dicrotic wave, becomes accentuated, and even rises in height (in cases where the dicrotic wave is absent it reappears under pain), the heart beats increase, indicating a more frequent muscular contraction.

If now the subject is hypnotized and made anaesthetic and analgesic, and agreeable and disagreeable stimuli are applied, although the subject feels no pain whatever, still the characteristics of the pain and pleasure curves are strangely marked, indicating the presence of a diffused subconscious feeling.

Kecords of respiration and of the radial artery, or what is called pneumographic and sphygmographic tracings, bring out clearly the real nature of the subconscious. This is done in the following way: A simultaneous pneumographic and sphygmographic record is first taken of the subject while he is in his normal waking state. A second record is then taken, with the only difference that disagreeable and painful stimuli, such as faradic current or odours of ammonia or acetic acid, are introduced. The tracings will at once show the painful sensations of the subject.

The curves will suddenly rise, revealing the violent reactions to the unwelcome stimuli. If now the subject is thrown into a hypnotic trance and a third record is taken, we shall then have the following curious results: If disagreeable and painful stimuli are applied, and if analgesia is suggested, the subject claims that he feels no pain whatever. In his normal waking state the subject will strongly react, he will scream from pain, but now he keeps quiet. Is there no reaction ? Does the subject actually feel no pain ? Far from being the case. If we look at the pneumographic tracings we find the waves uniformly deep and broad, the respiration is hard and laboured; a similar change we find in the tracings of the radial artery. The pain feeling is there, only it is not concentrated ; it is diffused. The upper consciousness does not feel the pain, but the subconsciousness does. The painful or uneasy feeling is diffused all over the organic consciousness of the secondary self.

PLATE III. A A are sphygmographic and pneu-mographic tracings of the subject in the normal state. B B are tracings of normal state with pain stimuli, and the reaction of the subject is shown in the abruptly ascending waves. 0 C are tracings of the subject in a state of hypnosis, with suggested analgesia or loss of pain sensibility, and under the uninterrupted application of pain stimuli (acetic acid, ammonia, electricity, pricking, etc.).

(The upper tracing of each couplet is sphygmographic ; the lower is pneumographic.)

<-

PLATE IV. A A are sphygmographic and pneumographic records in normal state under the influence of pain stimuli (acetic acid, ammonia, electricity, etc.). B B and C C are tracings under the continuous application of pain stimuli in the state of hypnosis with suggestive analgesia. In C C the suggestion of analgesia was in one place annulled, the reaction became very powerful, and the curve rose; with the renewed suggestion of analgesia the reaction disappeared and the curve immediately fell.

(The upper tracing of each couplet is sphygmographic ; the lower is pneumographic.)

CHAPTER XI
THE SUBCONSCIOUS SELF AND UNCONSCIOUS CEREBRATION.

THE facts of post-hypnotic negative hallucinations or of systematized anaesthesia still further reveal the presence of a subconscious self below the upper waking consciousness. The following interesting experiments made by Bernheim and M. Liegeois, and quoted by Binet in his remarkable book, The Alternations of Personality, may serve as good illustrations:

"Elise B., eighteen years old, a servant, suffering from sciatica. She was a respectable young girl, steady, of average intelligence, and, with the exception of her sciatica, presenting no neuropathic manifestations, symptoms, nor hereditary tendencies.

"It was very easy, after her first sitting, to bring on somnambulism coupled with a. state in which she was sensitive to hallucinations both hypnotic and post-hypnotic, and to amnesia on awaking. I easily developed negative hallucinations with her. During her sleep I said to her, 'When you wake you will no longer see me: I shall have gone.' "When she awoke she looked about for me, and did not seem to see me. I talked to her in vain, shouted in her ear, stuck a pin in her skin, her nostrils, under the nails, and thrust the point of the pin in the mucous membrane of the eye. She did not move a muscle. As far as she was concerned, I had ceased to exist, and all the acoustic, visual, tactile, and other impressions emanating from myself did not make the slightest impression upon her ; she ignored them all. As soon, however, as another person, unknown to her, touched her with the pin, she perceived it quickly, and drew back the member that had been pricked.

"I may add, in passing, that this experiment is not equally successful with all somnambulists. Many patients do not realize negative sensorial suggestions, and others only partially. Some, for example, when I declare that they shall not see me on awaking, do not see me, indeed, but they do hear my voice and feel my touch. Some are astonished to hear me and feel the pricks without seeing me, others do not attempt to understand it, and, finally, others believe that the voice and the sensation come from another person who is present. Sometimes the negative hallucination is made complete for all their sensations when the suggestion is given in this way: ' When you wake, if I touch you and prick you you will not feel it; if I speak to you you will not hear me. Moreover, you will not see me: I shall have gone.' Some subjects' sensations are quite neutralized after this detailed suggestion; with others, only the visual sensation is neutralized, all the other negative sensorial suggestions remaining ineffectual.

"The somnambulist of whom I speak realized everything to perfection. Logical in her delusive conception, she apparently did not perceive me with any of her senses. It was useless to tell her that I was there and that I was talking to her. She was convinced that they were simply making fun at her expense. I gazed at her obstinately, and said: ' You see me well enough, but you act as if you did not see me. You are a humbug; you are playing a part.' She did not stir, and continued to talk to other people. I added with a confident manner: ' However, I know all about it. You can not deceive me. It is only two years since you had a child, and you made away with it. Is that true? I have been told so.' She did not move; her face remained peaceful. Wishing to see, on account of its medico-legal bearing, whether a serious offence might be committed under cover of a negative hallucination, I roughly raised her dress and skirt. Although naturally very modest, she allowed this without a blush. I pinched the calf of her leg and thigh. She made absolutely no sign whatever. I am convinced that she might have been assaulted in this state without the slightest resistance.

"That established, I asked the head of the clinic to put her to sleep again and suggest to her that I should again be there when she awoke. This she realized. She saw me again, and remembered nothing that had happened in the interval. I said to her: 'You have just seen me. I talked with you.' She was astonished, and said, ' Why, no, you were not there.' ' I was there, and I did talk with you. Ask these gentlemen if I didn't.' 'I saw these gentlemen very well. M. P. tried to persuade me that you were there. But that was only a joke. You were not there.' ' Very well,' I said, 'but you remember everything that happened while I was not there—all that I said and did to you.' ' But how could you say and do anything to me when you were not there ?' I insisted. Speaking seriously,-and looking her in the face, I laid stress on every word: ' It is true, I was not there, but you remember just the same.' l put my hand on her forehead and declared, ' You remember everything, absolutely everything. There—speak out: what did I say to you? '

After a moment's concentrated thought, she blushed, and said, ' Oh, no, it is impossible; I must have dreamed it.' ' Very well; what did I say to you in this dream ?' She was ashamed, and did not want to say. I insisted. At last she said, ' You said that I had had a child.' ' And what did I do to you ?' ' You pricked me with a pin.' ' And then ?' After a few minutes she said, ' Oh, no, I would not have allowed you to do it; it is a dream.' ' What did you dream ?' ' That you exposed me,' etc.

"In this way I was able to call up the memory of all that had been said and done by me while she supposed that she did not see me. Therefore, in reality she both saw and heard me, notwithstanding her apparent obtuseness—she neither saw nor heard me. She saw me with her bodily (subconscious) eyes, but she did not see me with the eyes of the mind (upper consciousness). She was smitten with blindness, deafness, and psychical anaesthesia as far as I was concerned. All sensorial impressions emanating from me were distinctly perceived, but remained unconscious for her (upper consciousness).

"Similar experiments were performed by M. Liegeois. ' I no longer existed,' writes M. Liegeois, ' as far as Madame M. was concerned, to whom M. Liebault had, at my request, suggested that when she woke she would no longer see or hear me. I spoke to her: she did not reply. I stood before her: she did not see me. I pricked her with a pin: she felt no pain. She was asked where I was: she said she did not know—that I had undoubtedly gone, etc.

"I then conceived the idea of making some suggestions in loud tones to this person, for whom I had seemed to become an entire stranger; and, what was very singular, she obeyed these suggestions,

"I told her to rise: she rose. To sit down: she seated herself. To make her hands revolve round one another: she did so. I suggested a toothache to her, and she had a toothache; sneezing, and she sneezed. I said that she was cold, and she shivered ; that she ought to go to the stove—in which there was no fire—and there she went; until I told her that she was warm, and then she was all right. During all this time she was, as far as all the assistants were concerned, as fully awake as they were. When questioned by them, she replied that I was absent, she did not know why; perhaps I would soon come back, etc. Questioned by me with the use of the first personal pronoun, all my questions remained unanswered. She only realized the ideas I expressed impersonally, if I may use such an expression, and as if she drew from her own thought. It is her unconscious (subconscious) ego that causes her to act, and the conscious ego has not the slightest idea of the impulse that she receives from without.

The experiment seemed to me sufficiently interesting to bear repeating on another subject, Camille S., and here is a concise resume of the proofs and verifications secured some days later from this girl:

"Camille S. is eighteen years old, and a very good somnambulist. M. Liebault and I have known her for nearly four years. We have often put her to sleep. We always found her to be perfectly sincere, and we came to have entire confidence in her. This statement is necessary, as we shall see, to give weight to the singular results obtained which confirmed absolutely the first observation made on Madame M.

M. Liebault put Camille to sleep, and at my request suggested to her that she would no longer see or hear me; then he left me to experiment in my own way. When she awoke the subject was in communication with everybody, except that I no longer existed for her. Yet, as I am about to show, that is not quite accurate. It was as if there were two personalities within her— one that saw me when the other did not see me, and that heard me when the other paid no attention to what I was saying.

In the first place, I assured myself of the state of her sensibility. And it was very curious that this existed for all the assistants, but did not exist for anything emanating from me. If any one else pricked her she quickly drew her arm back. If I pricked her she did not feel it. I stuck pins in her that remained hanging from her arms and cheek. She complained of no sensation, not feeling them at all. This fact of anaesthesia, not real, but in a measure personal, is certainly very singular. It is quite new, if I am not mistaken. In the same way, if I held a bottle of ammonia under her nose she did not push it away, but she turned away from it when it was presented to her by a strange hand.

While she was in this condition, neither seeing nor hearing me — apparently, at least —almost all the suggestions are carried out that may be made in the waking state. I sum them up in the order in which they follow, from my notes taken at the time, June 14th, 1888. I need not repeat that if I speak directly to Camille S. —if I ask her, for example, how she is, how long it is since she stopped growing, etc. —her countenance remains impassive. She neither sees nor hears me—at least she is not conscious of so doing. I then proceed, as I said above, impersonally, talking not in my own name, but as if an internal voice of her own was speaking, and expressing such ideas as the subject would be likely to get from her own private thought. Then somnambulistic automatism shows itself in this new and unexpected guise as complete as any of the other forms already known.

I said aloud, 'Camille is thirsty; she is going to the kitchen for a glass of water, that she will bring back and set on this table.' She did not seem to have heard me, and yet in a few minutes she acted as I had said, and carried out the suggestion with that brisk and impetuous manner which has already been frequently noticed in somnambulists. She was asked why she brought the glass that she put on the table. She did not know what was meant. She had not moved. There was no glass there.

I said, 'Camille sees the glass, but there is no water in it, as they are trying to make her believe; it is wine, and very good wine, too; she is going to drink it, and it will do her good.' She promptly performed the order thus given to her, then immediately forgot all about it.

I made her say some words in succession that were scarcely proper. * Devil take it!' ' Confound it!' ' Con— -' and she repeated all that I suggested to her, but instantly losing the memory of what she had just said.

A certain M. F., astonished at this, upbraided her for using these unseemly expressions. She said : ' I did not say those vulgar words. What do you take me for ? You are dreaming; you must have gone mad.'

She saw me without seeing me, as this shows. I said, ' Camille is going to sit on M. L.'s knee.' She immediately jumped violently on my knee, and, on being questioned, declared that she had not moved from the bench where she was seated a moment before .

M. Liebault spoke to me. As she neither saw nor heard me consciously, she was astonished, and then began a conversation with him in which I played the part of a prompter who dwelt in her own brain. I suggested all the following words to her, and she uttered them, thinking that she was expressing her own thought:

'M. Liebault, aren't you talking to the wall ? I must put you to sleep to cure you. We will change roles,' etc.

M. F., how is your bronchitis ?

M. F. asked her how and why she said all this. She replied, after I had whispered to her: ' How do you think it comes to me ? Just as it comes to everyone. How do your own thoughts come ?' and she continued to enlarge upon the theme given her by me. She seemed to be in a perfectly normal state, and held her own with all the assistants with great presence of mind. Only in the midst of her conversation she inserted the phrases that I created in her mind, unconsciously making them her own.

Thus, while she was arguing with M. F., whom she told that she would take to Mareville, [19] her interlocutor having objected, ' I am not insane,' she replied : ' All insane people say that they are not insane. You say that you are not insane, therefore you must be insane.' She was very proud of her syllogism, and never suspected that she had just got it from me.

"Wishing to make sure, once more, that she saw me without being conscious of it, I said : ' Camille is going to take a bottle of cologne out of M. L.'s vest pocket; she will uncork it and enjoy its delightful odour.' She rose, came directly to me, looked first in the left, then in the right pocket, took out a bottle of ammonia, uncorked it, and inhaled it with pleasure. I was obliged to take it away from her. Then, still under the influence of suggestion, she took off my right shoe. M. F. said to her: ' What are you doing there ? You are taking off one of M. L.'s shoes!' She was offended. * What are you talking about ? M. L. is not here, so it is not possible for me to take off his shoe. You are still more insane than you were just now !' And when M. F. raised both arms while he was talking to me, Camille cried: ' Absolutely, I must take you to Mare-ville. It is too bad! Poor M. F.!' He did not seem to be cast down by her remark. ' But what shoe is that that you are holding ? what is it ?' I came to my subject's assistance, and said: 'It is a shoe that Camille must try on; she was not able to do it this morning at home, because the shoemaker did not keep his appointment. He was drunk, and he has only just brought it. She is going to try it on right here.'

"All that was accepted, repeated exactly, and promptly performed as if by spontaneous inspiration. For propriety's sake she turned toward the wall to try on my shoe. She found it a little large, and returned it to me, because I said she ought to return it to me.

"Finally, at my suggestion, she took the glass back lo the kitchen. When she returned, questioned by M. F., she declared that she had not left the room, that she had not drunk anything, and that she had not had a glass in her hands. It was of no use to show her the wet ring that the bottom of the glass had left on the table. She did not see any ring; there was none; they were trying to fool her. And then, in order to prove what she said, she passed her hand over the table several times, making the leaves fly on which I took my notes, and which shared in my privilege of being invisible, witliout seeing them. If there had been an inkstand there, it too would undoubtedly have been thrown to the floor.

"In order to bring this series of tests to an end, I said aloud: 'Camille,you arc going to see and hear me, I will open your eyes. You are now all right.' I was three metres from her, but the suggestion openiled. Camille passed without any apparent transition stage from the state of negative ballucinatioD into which M. Libault had thrown her into the, normal style, which in her case wan, as usual, accompanied by complete, amnesia. She had no idea of all that bad just happened the numerous experiments, varied in every conceivable way, the hallucinations, the words, the actions in which she played the principal part— all this was forgotten; it was all, as far as she was concerned, as if it had not been. 11

I can not do better than to bring M. Liegeois own interpretation of his experiments, an interpretation with which I fully agree:

"During the negative hallucinations,"says M. Liegeois, "the subject sees what IK; does not seem to and hears what he docs not seem to hear. Two penOfl alities (selves) exist within him an unconscious (subconscious) ego that sees and hears, and a conscious that does not fee nor hear."And I may add that not only do the two egos exist within the state of negative hallucination, but also within the normal state. The facts of hypnotic, memory alone strongly indicate the intelligent nature of the subconscious, ('and the theory of unconscious cerebration explain, for instance, the fact of suggested amnesia during hypnosis ? I hypnotise Mr. V. F., and make him pass through many lively scenes and actions, I give him hypnotic and post-hypnotic suggestions. The subject is wakened and hypnotized time and again. At last he is put into a hypnotic state, and is suggested that on awaking he shall not remember anything of what had happened in the state of hypnosis. The subject, on emerging from his trance, remembers nothing of what he has passed through.

I then put my hand on his forehead and tell him in a commanding voice, u You remember now thing!"As if touched by the wand of a magician, the suppressed memories become endowed with life and movement and invade the consciousness of the subject Everything is now clearly remembered, and the subject is able to relate the tale of his adventures without the omission of the least incident, So detailed is the account that one can not help wondering at the extraordinary memory displayed by the subject. How is the theory of unconscious cerebration to account for this strange fact Prof. Ziehen, in his Physiological Psychology, tells us that "it is still a matter of doubt whether, despite their completeness, all the facts of the hypnotized individual are not motions accomplished without any concomitant psychical processes,"and that "even the recollection of the hypnotic psychical processes do not necessarily argue of their existence during hypnotic trance."This extreme view is earth only wrong; for the subject during hypnosis not only acts, moves, but he also speaks, answers questions intelligently, reasons, discusses; and if such an individual may still be regarded as a mere machine, on the same grounds we may as well consider any rational man as a mere unconscious automaton.

The advocates of unconscious cerebration must admit at least this much, that hypnosis is a conscious state. How, on the theory of unconscious cerebration it is truly inconceivable how psychical states can be suppressed, the accompanying unconscious physiological processes alone being left, and all that done by a mere word of the experimenter. The restoration of memory is still more incomprehensible than even the suggested amnesia. A command by the experimenter, "Now you can remember!"brings into consciousness a flood of ideas and images. It is not that the experimenter gives the subject a clew which starts trains of particular images and ideas, but the mere general, abstract suggestion, "You can remember! "is sufficient to restore memories which to all appearances have completely vanished from the mind of the subject. Are the unconscious physiological nervous modifications so intelligent as to understand suggestions and follow them ? Does unconscious cerebration understand the command of the experimenter, and does it oblige him to become conscious ?

On closer examination, we find the term unconscious cerebration to be of so loose a nature that under its head are often recorded facts that clearly indicate the working of an intelligence. Thus Mr. Charles M. Child brings the following fact as a specimen of unconscious cerebration: f

"I had earnestly been trying,"a gentleman writes Besides, posthypnotic amnesia is rarely spontaneous ; as a rule, it is induced by suggestion to Mr. Child [20], "to make a trial balance, and at last left off working, the summary of the Dr. and Or. sides of the account showing a difference of £2.10s., the Dr. side being so much smaller. The error I had not found on Saturday night when I left the counting house. On this same Saturday night I retired feeling nervous, and angry with myself. Some time in the night I dreamed thus: I was seated at my desk in the counting house and in a good light; everything was orderly and natural, the ledger lying before me. I was looking over the balance of the accounts and comparing them with the sums in the trial-balance sheet. Soon I came to a debit balance of £2.10. I looked at it, called myself sundry names, spoke to myself in a deprecating manner of my own eyes, and at last put the £2 10. to its proper side of the trial-balance sheet and went home. I arose at the usual Sunday time, dressed carefully, breakfasted, went to call on some . . . friends to go to church. Suddenly the dream flashed on my memory. I went for the keys, opened the office, also the safe, got the ledger, and turned to the folio my dream had indicated. There was the account whose balance was the sum wanted which I had omitted to put in the balance sheet, where it was put now, and my year's posting proved correct."

The adherents of unconscious cerebration tacitly include under this term not only unconscious physiological processes, or nerve modifications, but also psychical states. Keeping clearly in mind the real meaning of unconscious cerebration as referring to physiological processes or nerve modifications with no psychical accompaniment, the difficulties of unconscious cerebration to account for the phenomena of hypnotic memory become truly insurmountable. For if the physiological processes subsumed under the category of unconscious cerebration are completely lacking any psychical element whatever, how can a general abstract negative phrase suppress particular psychical states, and how can a similar positive phrase bring the forgotten memories back to consciousness ? It is simply incomprehensible.

Furthermore, while the subject is in a hypnotic condition we can suggest to him that on awaking he shall not remember anything, but that when put to the automatic recorder he shall be able to write everything that has taken place in the state of hypnosis. The subject is then awakened; he remembers nothing at all of what he had passed through while in the state of hypnotic trance. As soon, however, as he is put to the automatic recorder the hand gives a full, rational account of all the events. If now you ask the subject what it is he has written, he stares at you in confusion ; he knows nothing at all of the writing. How shall we account for this fact on the theory of unconscious cerebration ? Can unconscious physiological processes write rational discourses ? It is simply wonderful, incomprehensible.

These, however, are not the only difficulties which the theory of unconscious cerebration has to encounter. Take the following experiment: I gave Mr. Y. F. the suggestion that on awaking he should put my coat on three times, take it off, and put it on again; that he should do it when he should hear a signal which should be a knock ; amnesia was suggested, and also the possibility of writing the suggestion. The subject was then roused from his trance. There was not the slightest recollection of what had been suggested, but when he was put to the automatic recorder the hand at once proceeded to write in full everything. In the middle of the writing, "When a signal will be given..."I stopped the subject's hand and asked him what he was writing about. "I do not know,"he answered. "How is it,"I asked again, "you write, and you do not know what you write ?""I do not know; I think it was something about a coat""What was it you were writing about a coat ?""I do not know; maybe about the make of a coat."Then when the signal came he rose and put on the coat three times. To take another experiment of the same kind: I give the subject the suggestion that he should bow to the gas whenever the door should be opened; again amnesia is suggested, with the possibility of writing. The subject is stopped when he finished his account. "What was it you wrote ?"I ask. The subject looks surprised. I repeat my question. "I do not know; I think something about a door ? ""What was it about a door?""I do not know."I have made many similar experiments, and all of them with the same results. It is evident that the writing is not an unconscious automatic process, for the subject possesses a general knowledge of what he has written, or even of what he is going to write. Now, on the theory of unconscious cerebration this general knowledge ought to be entirely lacking, since the physiological processes of the suppressed memory have no psychical accompaniment. It would not do to say that the subject knows each word as he writes it, but becomes unconscious of it, forgets it, as soon as it is written down; because the subject is able to tell the central idea— that is, he has a general knowledge of it; and, what is more, he is able to tell us this general central idea even before he finishes the writing—in "fact, he can do it"when stopped in the middle of the phrase. On the theory of secondary consciousness, however, the experiments could not possibly give other results. The secondary consciousness understands the suggestions given by the experimenter, accepts them, obeys the commands, keeps the suppressed memories, and sends up a general knowledge of them to the upper consciousness, [21] and, if commanded, communicates the suppressed particular suggestions in all their details.

The advocates of unconscious cerebration assume too much: they assume that normal memory, or recollection in the normal state, can be fully accounted for by unconscious physiological processes, and the only thing required is to apply this theory to the phenomena of hypnotic memory. It would be well to examine this theory and see how strong its claims are in the case of normal memory.

Many a modern psycho-physiologist no doubt smiles at the crude, ancient psycho-physiological theory of perception. Images or copies of objects emanate from objects, get deposited in the mind ; hence perception, cognition, memory. The modern psycho-physiological speculations, however — the speculations of Maudsley, Carpenter, Ziehen, Ribot, etc.—are no less crude. Thus Ziehen, for instance, conceives that each sensation deposits a copy of itself—an image, an idea—in some one of the memory ganglion cells, and memory consists in the reproduction of this copy—the hen lays an egg from which another hen may come out. Maudsley expresses the same thing in slightly different terms ; instead of "deposits of images in memory ganglion cells,"he uses "modifications of nerve elements.""It may be supposed,"says Maudsley, "that the first activity did leave behind it, when it subsided, some after-effect, some modification of the nerve element, whereby the nerve circuit was disposed to fall again readily into the same action, such disposition (unconscious) appearing in consciousness as recognition or memory."Bibot and many other psychologists, with slight variations in minor points, follow the same beaten track. All of them agree that it is the nerve modifications produced by the physiological processes of sensations, emotions, etc., that constitute the basis, nay, the very essence, of memory itself. It does not require a close examination to find the deficiencies of this theory. A mere modification left behind as a trace can not possibly explain memory, recollection, the fact of referring a particular bit of experience to an experience felt before. The retention of a trace or of a nervous modification, and the reproduction of that trace or modification, can not in the least account for the fact that a series of sensations, ideas, images, emotions, felt at different times, should become combined, brought into a unity, felt like being similar, like being one and the same, like being repetitions, copies of one original experience. It is not retention or reproduction, but it is the recognition element that constitutes the essentials of memory.

The rose of to-day reminds me of the rose seen yesterday, of the same rose seen the day before yesterday. Now, the image of the rose may be retained, may even be reproduced, but if it is not recognised as having happened in my past, there can be no recollection; in short, without recognition there is no memory. As Prof. James strongly puts it, "the gutter is worn deeper by each successive shower, but not for that reason brought into contact with previous showers."Does the theory of unconscious physiological processes, of material brain traces, of nerve modifications— does this theory take into account this element of recognition ? Can the theory of unconscious cerebration offer the faintest suggestion as to how that element of recognition is brought about ? What is that something added to the unconscious physiological trace or nerve modification that effects a conscious recognition ?

Furthermore, first impressions can be localized in the past, but so can also each subsequent revival. How shall we explain, on the theory of unconscious physiological nerve registration, that the original, the primitive sense experience, as well as each subsequent revival, can be referred to as distinct psychical facts ? For if the structural nerve elements are slightly modified with every revival, how shall we account for this psychical distinction of the original sense experience as well as of the modified revivals ? The remembered experience leaves its own individual trace, then a trace of its being a copy of a former original impression, and also a trace of its being a member in a series of similar traces, each trace being both a copy of one another and a copy of the original impression. How this is done is a mystery.

The difficulties of the unconscious registration theory increase still more if we consider that the account of memory as usually given by psychologists is rather inadequate. Memory is the recurrence or reproduction in consciousness of a former experience. "We saw a certain object yesterday, and to-day, when we happen to think of that object, we say that the image or idea is the reproduction and recognition in memory of the previous perception. This, however, is but a partial account of what actually takes place in the process of recollection. Psychologically speaking, when we remember something we have not a reproduction of some past experience, but an actual present experience with the quality of pastness about it. I remember the rose I saw and smelled the day before; what I have here is simply a present experience in the moment content of consciousness, and this experience is projected into the past of my subjective time. The image of the rose I have now turns out to be a rose of yesterday, and the yesterday itself is a part in the content of the present moment consciousness; in other words, my present experience is projected into my present subjective yesterday.

The present image is the primary fact, and the projection of it into the past is but a secondary effect; but, then, the process is reversed—the present experience is regarded as secondary, and the secondary as primary. Subjectively considered, memory is the reproduction of the present into the past. It is only if regarded from an objective standpoint that memory becomes the reproduction of the past into the present. In short, in memory, there is a double process going on : the projection of the subjective present into the subjective past, and then, again, the projection of the objective past into the objective present.

Does the physiological registration theory account for this double process ? It certainly does not. If now the theory of unconscious physiological traces or nerve modifications is found inadequate to explain the most elementary act of conscious memory, can we rely upon it, when offered to us in the garb of unconscious cerebration, to account for such complex psychical phenomena as hypnotic memory?

Unconscious cerebration failing, we must fall back on the psychical interpretation of hypnosis in general, and of hypnotic memory in particular. The subconsciousness is not an unconscious physiological automatism; it is a secondary consciousness, a secondary self .

CHAPTER XII.
THE DOUBLE SELF.

IN the last chapter we came to the conclusion that the subconsciousness is not a mere unconscious physiological automatism, but a consciousness, a self in possession of memory, and even intelligence. Experiments and observations, however, go further to prove that this hidden intelligence may be of still higher organization; it may possess even some degree of self-consciousness, which may grow and develop. By means of the so-called method of distraction Prof. Janet entered into direct communication with the secondary self of his subject, Louise.

"Do you hear me ?"asked Prof. Janet.

Ans. No.

J. But, in order to answer, one must hear.

Ans. Certainly.

J. Then how do you manage ?

Ans. I do not know.

J. There must be somebody who hears me.

Ans. Yes.

J. Who is it ?

Ans. Not Louise.

J. Oh, someone else. Shall we call her Blanche ?

Ans. Yes, Blanche.

J. Well, then, Blanche, do you hear me ?

Am. Yes.

This name, however, had soon to be given up, as it happened to have very disagreeable associations in Louise's mind; and when Louise was shown the paper with the name Blanche, which she had unconsciously written, she was angry and wanted to tear it up. Another name had to be chosen.

J. What name will you have ?

Ans. No name.

J. You must; it will be more convenient.

Ans. Well, then, Adrienne.

Now it proved that Adrienne knew of things of which Louise was entirely ignorant. Louise's special terror, which recurred hi wild exclamation in her hysterical fits, was somehow connected with hidden men. She could not, however, recollect the incident. But Adrienne, when questioned, was able to describe all the details.

Louise was thrown into catalepsy; then M. Janet clinched her left hand (she began at once to strike out), put a pencil in her right hand, and said, "Adrienne, what are you doing ?"The left hand continued to strike and the face to bear the look of rage, while the right hand wrote, "I am furious!""With whom ?""With F.""Why?""I do not know, but I am very angry."M. Janet then unclinched the subject's left hand and put it gently to her lips. It began "to blow kisses,"and the face smiled. "Adrienne, are you still angry ?""No, that is over.""And now ?""Oh, I am happy.""And Louise?""She knows nothing; she is asleep."

This case is extremely interesting as indicating at first the lack of self-consciousness in the hypnotic subwaking self, but acquiring it in the course of communication with the external world. Under favourable conditions the subwaking self wakes from the deep trance in which it is immersed, raises its head, becomes completely conscious, and rises at times even to the plane of personality.

When Leonie B. (a subject of M. Janet) is hypnotized her personal character undergoes a radical change. She assumes a different name, that of Leontine. Now Leontine (that is Leonie hypnotized) was told by Prof. Janet that after the trance was over and Leonie had resumed her ordinary life she, Leontine, was to take off her apron and then to tie it on again. Leonie was then awakened and conducted by Prof. Janet to the door, talking with her usual respectful gravity. Meantime her hands untied the apron and took it off. Prof. Janet called Leonie's attention to the loosened apron. "Why, my apron is coming off!" Leonie exclaimed, and with full consciousness (waking consciousness) she tied the apron on again. She then continued the talk. At Leontine's prompting the hands once more began their work, and the apron was taken off again, and again replaced, this time without Leonie's attention having been directed to the matter at all. Only then Leon-tine was fully satisfied and became quiet. Next day Prof. Bichet hypnotized Leonie again, and presently Leontine as usual emerged. "Well," she said, "I did what you told me yesterday. How stupid the other one looked while I took off her apron! Why did you tell her that the apron was falling off ? I was obliged to begin the job all over again."

Once this secondary self attains self-consciousness and gets crystallized into a new and independent personality, it now and then rises to the surface and assumes control over the current of life. The secondary personality may blame, dislike, ridicule, the primary personality. Thus Leontine calls Leonie "that stupid woman." Sometimes the secondary personality may treat the primary with great animosity, and may even threaten to destroy it. Prof. Janet received from Madame B. a very curious letter. "On the first page," he says, "was a short note, written in a serious and respectful style. She was unwell, she said—worse on some days than on others—and she signed her true name, Madame B. But over the page began another in a quite different style. ' My dear sir,' thus the letter ran, ' I must tell you that B. really makes me suffer much; she can not sleep; she spits blood; she hurts me; I am going to demolish her; she bores me; I am ill also. This is from your devoted Leontine."

Dr. Osgood Mason reports the following interesting case: Alma Z. has been under my observation during the past ten years. In childhood she was remarkable for her intelligence and unusual endowments. Up to her eighteenth year she was in robust health, excelling all her companions not only in intellectual attainments but also in physical culture, being expert in gymnastic exercises, skating, and athletic sports generally. At that time, owing to overwork in school, . . . peculiar psychical conditions made their appearance. Instead of the educated, thoughtful, dignified, womanly personality, worn with illness and pain, there appeared a bright, sprightly child personality, with a limited vocabulary, ungrammatical and peculiar dialect, decidedly Indian in character, but, as used by her, most fascinating and amusing. The intellect was bright and shrewd, her manner lively and good-natured, and her intuitions were remarkably correct and quick; but, strangest of all, she was free from pain, could take food, and had comparatively a good degree of strength. She called herself 'Twoey,' and the normal or usual personality she always referred to as ' 'No. 1.' She possessed none of the acquired knowledge of the primary personality, but was bright and greatly interested in matters going on about her —in family affairs, and everything which pertained to the comfort and well-being of No. 1.

"The new personality would usually remain only a few hours, but, occasionally, her stay was prolonged to several days; and then the normal self—the No. 1 of ' Twoey'—returned with all her intelligence, patience, and womanly qualities, but also with the weakness and suffering which characterized her illness. No. 1 and No. 2 were apparently in every respect separate and distinct personalities. Each had her own distinct consciousness and distinct train of thought and memories. When No. 1 was absent and ' Twoey' took her place, on resuming her consciousness she commenced at the place where her own personality had been interrupted and resumed her ordinary life exactly at that point. To No. 1 the existence of any second personality was entirely unknown by any conscious experience, and the time which ' Twoey' occupied was to her a blank. If 'Twoey' appeared at noon on Tuesday and remained until Thursday night, when she disappeared and No. 1 resumed her own consciousness and life, she would commence at Tuesday noon where that consciousness was interrupted. The intervening time to her was a blank. No. 2, however, while having her own distinct life, knew also the life of No. 1, but only as a distinct personality, entirely separate from herself. No. 1 also came to know ' Twoey ' by the description given by others, and by the change in her own personal belongings and affairs which she saw had been affected during her absence.

The two personalities became great friends. No. 2 admired No. 1 for her superior knowledge, her patience in suffering, and the lovely qualities which she recognised, and she willingly took her place in order to give her rest, and, as it seemed, the possibility of living at all. No. 1 also became fond of Twoey on account of the loving care which she bestowed upon her and her affairs, and for the witty sayings and sprightly and pertinent conversations which were reported to her, and which she greatly enjoyed. Twoey seemed to have the power of going and coming at will. She often left communications to No. 1, mostly written (for she became able to write in her peculiar dialect—very difficult to decipher), telling her what had been done in her absence, where she would find certain things, or advising her when she deemed it necessary; and her advice was always sound and to the point.

"Under an entire change in medical treatment— change of scene and air and the use of animal magnetism and hypnotism—health and normal conditions were restored, and Twoey's visits became only occasional, under circumstances of extreme fatigue or mental excitement, when they were welcome to the patient and enjoyed by her friends. Two years later the patient married, and became a most admirable wife and intelligent and efficient mistress of the household.

"Later on, however, the No. 2 condition or personality began to return with greater frequency, but at length one night ' Twoey' announced that she would soon take her departure, but that another visitor would come to take her place. Presently an alarming attack of syncope occurred, lasting several hours; and when consciousness did at last return, it was represented by a third personality, entirely new and entirely distinct, both from the primary self and also from the ' Twoey' with whom we were so well acquainted. The new personality at once announced itself as 'The Boy,' and that it had come in the place of ' Twoey ' for the special aid of No. 1; and for several weeks, whenever this third personality was present, all its behaviour was entirely consistent with that announcement.

"Gradually, however, she became accustomed and reconciled to her new role and new surroundings, and adapted herself with most astonishing grace to the duties of wife, mother, and mistress of the house, though always when closely questioned she persisted seriously in her original declaration that she was ' The Boy.' The personality was of much more broad and serious type than that of the frolicsome ' Twoey,' and while entirely separate in consciousness and personality from No. 1, she was much nearer to her in general outline of character. The acquired book knowledge of No. 1—the Latin, mathematics, and philosophy acquired at school—were entirely wanting in the new personality; the extensive knowledge of general literature—the whole poems of Tennyson, Browning, and Scott which No. 1 could repeat by heart, also her perfect familiarity with the most beautiful and poetic portions of the Bible—all these were entirely lacking in this personality. In a general knowledge of affairs, however, in the news of the day from all over the world, and in current literature, she at once became thoroughly interested and thoroughly intelligent, and the judgment was keen and sound. She took the greatest delight in every kind of amusement—the theater and literary and musical entertainments—and her criticisms of performances and of books were independent, acute, and reliable. At the same time her household affairs and her interest in them and all subjects pertaining to the family were conspicuous.

"Of the preceding personalities she was fully cognizant, and had great admiration and affection for them both. She would listen to no disparaging remarks concerning 'Twoey,' and her admiration for No. 1 was unbounded. Neither Twoey nor No. 3 ever seemed anxious to continue and prolong their visits, but, on the contrary, were always desirous that No. 1 should regain her health sufficiently to get on without them ; and they referred with much feeling to the causes which prevented it.

The peculiar and interesting incidents which diversified these different states of consciousness would fill a volume. No. 1, when in her condition of greatest weakness, would occasionally astonish her listeners by announcing to them some event which they had kept profoundly secret from her. For instance: * You need not be so quiet about it; I have seen it all. Mrs. C. died the day before yesterday. She is to be buried to-morrow'; or, ' There has been a death over in such and such a street. Who is it that died ?' ' Twoey's sagacity, amounting almost to prevision, was often noticed, and many a time the neglect to be guided by her premonitions was deeply regretted. 'The Boy,' or No. 3, frequently exhibited peculiar perceptive powers. At times the sense of hearing would be entirely lost, so that the most violent noises close to her ears and when perfectly unexpected failed to startle or disturb her in the slightest degree, although usually she was easily startled by even a slight, sudden, or unexpected noise. Under these circumstances she had a peculiar faculty of perceiving what was said by watching the lips of the speaker, though ordinarily neither she nor the primitive self had any such faculty.

In this condition she had often carried on conversations with entire strangers, and entertained guests at table without having it once suspected that all the while she could not hear a sound of any sort. I have myself seen her sit and attend to the reading of a new book simply by watching the lips of the reader, taking in every word and sentiment, and laughing heartily at the funny passages, when I am perfectly sure she could not have heard a pistol shot from her head.

When the No. 3 personality had persisted for a considerable period—weeks, for instance, at a time, as it has sometimes done—the temporary return of No. 1 under the influence of some soothing condition or pleasing sentiment or emotion has been beautiful to witness. I saw this transformation once while sitting with her in a box at the Metropolitan Opera House. Beethoven's concerto in C Major was on the programme; in the midst of the performance I saw the expression of her countenance change; a clear, calm, softened look came into the face as she leaned back in her chair and listened to the music with the most intense enjoyment. I spoke a few words to her at the close of the number, and she replied in the soft and musical tones peculiar to her own normal condition, and I recognised without the slightest doubt the presence of No. 1. A few minutes later her eyes closed; presently she drew two or three short, quick respirations •; again her countenance changed, and No. 3 was back again. She turned to me and said, 'So No. 1 came to hear her favourite concerto ?' I replied, ' Yes ; how did you know it ?' ' Oh, I was here and listened to it too.' ' Where were you ?' I asked. ' I sat on the front of the box. I saw you speaking to her. How greatly she enjoyed the music! ' and then she went on listening to the music and commenting upon the programme in the usual discriminating manner of No. 3."In this interesting case, communicated by Dr. Osgood Mason, we find a weakening by disease of the upper controlling personality, the subconscious self gained mastery, rose to the plane of conscious individuality and became a person, a "Twoey."The "Twoey "personality, however, seemed to have been unstable, and a new personality, that of "The Boy,"emerged. Both "Twoey "and "The Boy "were but two different expressions, two different particular, individualized manifestations of the same underlying reality—the subconsciousness. It was from the depth of the subconscious self that those bubble personalities rose to the surface of conscious life.

As a rule, the stream of subwaking consciousness is broader than that of waking consciousness, so that the submerged subwaking self knows the life of the upper, primary, waking self, but the latter does not know the former. There are, however, cases on record that show that the two streams may flow in two separate channels, that the two selves may be totally ignorant of each other. The subwaking self, in attaining self-consciousness, personality, may become so much individualized as to lead a perfectly independent life from that of the waking self. And when the lower new person rises to the surface and assumes control of the current of life, he shows no signs of having once known the old master, the old person. An interesting case of this kind is given by Prof. W. James in his Psychology, and fully described by Mr. Hodgson in the Proceedings of the Society for Psychical Research for the year 1891. I quote from Prof. "W. James's book: *

"On January 17, 1887, Rev. Ansel Bourne, of Greene, R. I., an itinerant preacher, drew five hundred and fifty-one dollars from a bank in Providence with which to 1 pay for a certain lot of land in Greene, paid certain bills, and got into a Pawtucket horse car. This is the last incident which he remembers. He did not return home that day. He was published in the papers as missing, and, foul play being suspected, the police sought in vain his whereabouts. On the morning of March 14th, however, at Korristown, Pa., a man calling himself A. J. Brown, who had rented a small shop six weeks previously, stocked it with stationery, confectionery, fruit, and small articles, and carried on this quiet trade without seeming to anyone unnatural or eccentric, woke up in a fright and called in the people of the house to tell him where he w.as. He said that his name was Ansel Bourne, that he was entirely ignorant of Norristown, that he knew nothing of shopkeeping, and that the last thing he remembered—it seemed only yesterday—was drawing money from the bank in Providence. He would not believe that two months had elapsed. The people of the house thought him insane. Soon his nephew came and took him home. He had such a horror of the candy store that he refused to set foot in it again.

The first two weeks of the period remained unaccounted for, as he had no memory, after he had resumed his normal personality, of any part of the time, and no one who knew him seems to have seen him after he left home. The remarkable part of the change is, of course, the peculiar occupation which the so-called Brown indulged in. Mr. Bourne has never in his life had the slightest contact with trade. Brown was described by the neighbours as taciturn, orderly in his habits, and in no way queer. He went to Philadelphia several times; replenished his stock; cooked for himself in the back shop, where he also slept; went regularly to church; and once at a prayer-meeting made what was considered by the hearers a good address, in the course of which he relates an incident he had witnessed in his natural state of Bourne.

"This was all that was known of the case up to June 1, 1890, when I induced Mr. Bourne to submit to hypnotism, so as to see whether in the hypnotic trance his Brown memory (Brown self-consciousness) would not come back. It did so with surprising readiness—so much so, indeed, that it proved quite impossible to make Mm while in hypnosis remember any of the facts of his normal life. He had heard of Ansel Bourne, ' but did not know as he had ever met the man.' When confronted with Mrs. Bourne, he said that he had never seen the woman before. On the other hand, he told us of his peregrinations during the last fortnight, and gave all sorts of details during the Norristown episode. ... I had hoped by suggestion to run the two personalities into one, and make the memories continuous, but no artifice would avail to accomplish this, and Mr. Bournds skull to-day still covers two distinct personal selves."

CHAPTER XIII.
THE INTERRELATION OF THE TWO SELVES.

THE phenomena of abnormal states reviewed by us clearly reveal the presence of a subwaking self below the threshold of the waking self-consciousness. Turning now to a different class of phenomena, we find still further confirmation of the same truth. There is a great class of phenomena in which the sub-waking self is brought to the light of day, but so as not to suppress the primary self. The two streams of consciousness run parallel to each other, the two selves coexist. The primary personality enters into direct intercourse with the risen lower, subwaking self. The phenomena I mean here are those of automatic writing.

Usually, as the automatic writer begins his practice on the planchette, the pencil brings out but mere scrawls and scratches; but as the practice continues, letters, figures, words, phrases, and even whole discourses, flow from under the automatic pencil. It takes some time before there occurs a cleavage between the subwaking self and the waking personality. Gradually the subwaking self rouses itself from its trance, begins to bring out latent memories, starts to lisp, attempts to think coherently, gathers more intelligence and reason, attains even some degree of self-consciousness, gives itself a name, becomes at times eloquent, pouring forth flat discourses on metaphysics and religion.

To induce the first stages of automatic writing the same conditions are requisite as those of normal suggestibility. The subject starting his first lesson in automatic writing must strongly concentrate his attention on some letter, figure, or word; he must distract his attention from what is going on in his hand ; he must be in a monotonous environment; he must not be disturbed by a variety of incoming sense impressions ; he must keep quiet, thus limiting his voluntary movements / his field of consciousness must be contracted • no other ideas but the requisite ones should be present in the mind; and if other ideas and images do enter his mind, they must be inhibited. These conditions, as we know, are favourable to dissociation, disaggregation of consciousness. In the phenomena of automatic writing we have a disaggregation of consciousness—the secondary subwaking consciousness is severed from the primary, waking self-consciousness. Both selves coexist; one does not interfere with the freedom of the other. Once the cleavage is accomplished the further observance of the conditions is, of course, superfluous —the phenomena of automatic writing manifest themselves freely, the subwaking self cheerfully discourses on all sorts of subjects whenever it is in the mood, and as long as it continues its independent life.

There are, of course, different stages of cleavage. The incipient stage of automatic writing is described by Mr. P. Myers in the Proceedings of the Society for Psychical Research.* The account is given by Mr. H. Arthur Smith: "I think I have observed that when my hand was on it [on the planchette], the wrist being grasped by the other hand, a word on which I concentrated rny attention was written without any conscious volitional effort. I am doubtful as to this, as it is a difficult thing to be sure of the absence of volition, but such is my decided impression."The cleavage here between the two selves was faint, shadowy; nothing further occurred.

Then, again, we have the case (given by Mr. F. Myers in the Proceedings of the Society for Psychical Research, November, 1884) of Mr. A., who can write words by mere attention (fixation), without any muscular effort whatever. He fixes his mind on a word, and his hand writes it with an involuntary spasm, while he is studiously avoiding all intentional impulse. A case of a more advanced stage of automatic writing is given in the Psychological Review for July, 1895. The subject knows beforehand what the hand is going to write, and he is not quite sure from whom the writing proceeds, whether from himself or from some "other."The cleavage is incomplete, partial.

The highest stage of cleavage, when the subwaking self gathers round its being masses of intelligence and discourses on philosophical and religious questions, may be well illustrated by a very interesting and very instructive case of automatic writing given by Prof. W. James in his Psychology:

"Some of it [automatic writing],"writes Mr. Sidney Dean to Prof. "W. James, "is in hieroglyph or strange compounded arbitrary characters, each series possessing a seeming unity in general design or character, followed by what purports to be a translation or rendering into mother English. I never attempted the seemingly impossible feat of copying the characters .

They were cut with the precision of a graver's tool, and generally with a single rapid stroke of the pencil…when the work is in progress I am in the normal condition, and seemingly two minds, intelligences, persons, are practically engaged. The writing is in my own hand, but the dictation not of my own mind and will, but that of another, upon subjects of which I can have no knowledge, and hardly a theory; and I myself consciously criticise the thought, fact, mode of expressing it, etc., while the hand is recording the subject-matter, and even the words impressed to be written…"Sentences are commenced without knowledge of mine as to their subject or ending.

There is in progress now at uncertain times, not subject to my will, a series of twenty-four chapters upon the scientific features of life, moral, spiritual, eternal. Seven have already been written in the manner indicated. These were preceded by twenty-four chapters relating generally to the life beyond material death, its characteristics, etc. Each chapter is signed by the name of some person who has lived on earth, some with whom I have been personally acquainted, others known in history. ... I know nothing of the alleged authorship of any chapter until it is completed and the name impressed and appended. I am interested not only in the reputed authorship—of which I have nothing corroborative—but in the philosophy, thought, of which I was in ignorance until these chapters appeared. It is an intelligent ego that writes, or else the influence assumes individuality, which practically makes the influence a personality. It is not myself; of that I am conscious at every step of the process."

When the cleavage of the two selves from each other occurs, and the subwaking self begins to express himself and gets into possession of some organ which was before under the control of the waking personality, this organ becomes anaesthetic. The upper waking self does not get any more the peripheral sense impressions coming from that organ. It is now the subwaking self who possesses himself of these sense impressions and becomes conscious of them. The secondary self may extend its range of activity in its intercourse with the external world; it may go on enriching itself with the spoils got by plundering the waking self. Amaurosis, hysterical anaesthesia, and analgesia are facts in point. Anaesthesia is found not only in hysteria, but also in such cases in which the cleavage is but transitory, and the possession of the organ into which the subwaking self comes is but momentary. Such anaesthesia is, of course, fugitive, and lasts only as long as the organ is possessed or obsessed by the subwaking self. Prof. W. James [22] beautifully demonstrated this truth in the case of automatic writing:

"William L. Smith, student at the Massachusetts Institute of Technology, aged twenty-one, perfectly healthy and exceptionally intelligent, sat with Mr. Hodgson and myself, January 24, 1889, with his right hand extended on the instrument [planchette], and his face averted and buried in the hollow of his left arm, which lay along the table. Care was taken not to suggest to him the aim of the inquiry (i. e., to test for anaesthesia induced in healthy subjects by the mere act of automatic writing). The planchette began by illegible scrawling. After ten minutes I pricked the back of the right hand several times with a pin; no indication of feeling. Two pricks on the left hand were followed by withdrawal, and the question, ' What did you do that for ?' to which I replied, ' To find whether you were going to sleep.' The first legible words which were written after this were ' You hurt me.' . . . After some more or less illegible writing I pricked the right wrist and fingers several times again quite severely, with no sign of reaction on S.'s part. After an interval, however, the pencil wrote, ' Don't you prick me any more.' S. then said, 'My right hand is pretty well asleep.' I tested the two hands immediately by pinching and pricking, but found no difference between them, both apparently normal. S. then said that what he meant by ' asleep ' was the feeling of ' pins and needles' which an insensible limb has when ' waking up.'

"The last written sentence was then deciphered aloud. S. laughed, having become conscious only of the pricks on his left hand, and said, 'It is working those two pin pricks for all they are worth.' I then asked,

"' What have I been excited about to-day ? '

"'May be correct, do not know, possibly sleeping.'

'What do you mean by sleeping ?'

I do not know. You (the subject's right hand made this figure evidently to indicate pricking) me 19, and think I'll write for you. We find here local anaesthesia induced in the hand possessed or obsessed temporarily by the subpersonal self. And when, on a later day, the pencil was placed in the left hand instead of the right, the left hand took up the memories of the right hand's previous pains. No wonder the memory was the same, for it was the same subwaking self possessed or obsessed of different organs. The last experiment may be regarded as an experimentum crucis of the significant truth that what the sub waking self obsesses of that the waking self is deprived. The latter may, however, be informed of the particular experience by reading the automatic writing, or by gazing into a crystal. Once the cleavage occurred, we may say that, as a rule, the growth, the development of the individualized subwakiny self is i/n inverse ratio to that of the waking consciousness .

CHAPTER XIV.
SUBCONSCIOUS SENSE-PERCEPTION IN THE WAKING STATE.

THUS far we have dealt with such uncanny abnormal states as hysteria, hypnosis, automatism. "We saw in them the manifestation of the split-off secondary self, and we also hinted at the relation the latter bears to the waking self.

Is there any direct evidence of the presence of the subwaking self in the normal state of perfectly healthy individuals? Yes, there is, and very strong evidence, too. Once more I turn to hypnosis, but this time not as showing the cleavage that occurs in that state, but rather as pointing out the plane of cleavage, the presence of a subwaking self when the individual is in his normal state.

The subwaking hypnotic self surpasses the waking self in its sensitiveness; its range of sensibility extends farther than that of the upper personality. The senses of touch, pressure, and temperature • are much more delicate in the hypnotic condition. The sesthesiometer showed in Mr. J. F., one of my subjects, when in normal state, the sensibility of the skin on the forehead to be eighteen millimetres, while the same in hypnosis (slight degree) was but fourteen millimetres. The sensibility of Mr. A. F. in normal state was fourteen millimetres, while in hypnosis (falls into the deepest state) it was eight millimetres. Mr. D. W. showed a sensibility in the normal state fourteen millimetres, but when in hypnosis (falls into the deepest state) it was eight millimetres.

"It is quite certain,"writes Braid, "that some patients can tell the shape of what is held an inch and a half from the skin on the back of the neck, crown of the head, arm, or hand, or other parts of the body, the extremely exalted sensibility of the skin enabling them to discern the shape of the object so presented from its tendency to emit or absorb caloric. A patient could feel and obey the motion of a glass funnel passed through the air at a distance of fifteen feet." [23]

The entranced subject is able to walk freely about the room with bandaged eyes or in absolute darkness without striking against anything, because, as Moll, Braid, Poirault, and Drjevetzky point out, he recognises objects by the resistance of the air and by the alteration of temperature. We find in the hypnotic subject hypersesthesia of vision, of hearing, and of smell. One cannot help being struck by the great acuteness of the sense of hearing in hypnotic trance. To give an example. While Mr. W.' was in a state of hypnosis Mr. G. whispered in my ear, "Six o'clock."I scarcely could hear the whisper. I then turned to Mr. W. and asked him whether he heard what Mr. G. said. "Yes,"he answered, "Mr. G. said ' Six o'clock.'

To prove visual hyperaesthesia in my subject, A. F., I gave him a book to read while he was in hypnotic trance and his eyes were closed. "Head!"I commanded. "I can not,"he answered. "Yes, you can; you must read. Try!"He began to read. So miraculous seemed this experiment that one of the gentlemen present exclaimed, "Now I believe in hypnotism!"The fact, however, really was that Mr. A. F. raised his eyelids, but so slightly, so imperceptibly, that no one of the people present could notice it, and even I myself am not quite sure I saw it clearly ; I only suspected it was so. However the case might have been, it was altogether impossible for any one in his normal state to read under similar conditions of closure of the eyelids.

An extraordinary example of visual hypersesthesia is brought by Bergson, whose subject could read the image of a page reflected in the experimenter's cornea. The same subject could discriminate with the naked eye details in a microscopic preparation. "The ordinary test of visual hyperacuteness in hypnotism," [24] writes Prof. W. James, "is the favourite trick of giving a subject the hallucination of a picture on a blank sheet of cardboard and then mixing the latter with a lot of similar sheets. The subject will always find the picture on the original sheet again and recognise infallibly if it has been turned over or upside down, although the bystanders have to resort to artifice to identify it again. The subject notes peculiarities on the card too small for waking observation to detect."The experiment may be made in a far simpler manner: A blank sheet of cardboard is given to the subject, and instead of giving him a hallucination, a thing not very easy to do with many subjects, as they often do not realize the suggested hallucination, the subject is simply asked to take good notice of the card. The card is then mixed with other similar sheets. The subject invariably picks out the sheet shown to him. I have repeatedly made these experiments on my subjects.

The same holds true in the case of smell. There is an exaltation of this sense in hypnosis. Braid's subject restored articles to the rightful owners, finding the latter out by mere smell. "They [the subjects],"writes Braid,* "began sniffing, and traced out the parties robbed and restored it [the article] to them. On being asked, ' How do you know the person ? ' the answer was, ' I smell them [or him].' Every time the experiment was tried the result was the same and the answer the same."

Carpenter, in his Mental Physiology, tells of a youth who in hypnosis could "find out by the sense of smell the owner of a glove which was placed in his hand from among a party of more than sixty persons, scenting at each of them, one after the other, until he came to the right individual. In another case the owner of a ring was unhesitatingly found from among a company of twelve, the ring having been withdrawn before the somnambule was introduced."

In short, the range of sensibility of the hypnotic sub-waking consciousness is wider than that of the waking self. Now, if this subpersonal, subwaking hypnotic self is present in the normal state, we ought to find that sensory impressions, which on account of their faintness or indistinctness did not reach the waking self, were still perceived by the subwaking self. With this view in hand I made the following experiment:

I placed Mr. L. and Mr. P. at such a distance that they could not hear my whisper. Although Mr. L. is an intimate friend of mine, on whose honesty I can fully rely, .still, for the sake of having the experiment carried out in a rigorous fashion, I placed near him Mr. P., whose ear was far more acute than that of Mr. L., in order to testify that nothing could be heard at such a distance. I then whispered in the ear of Mr. G. the following words: "The Subliminal Consciousness, by Mr. Myers."I repeated this phrase five times in succession in the same whisper, asking each time of Mr. L. and Mr. P. whether they had heard anything. The reply was "No; nothing."They strained their ears, but could not perceive any words except an indistinct whisper. I then hypnotized Mr. L., who fell into a slight hypnosis (Mr. P. could not be hypnotized; it was the first seance in which he took part), and asked him to tell what he had heard. "I did not hear anything.""Try hard, and you will be able to tell,"I commanded him. "I heard only a certain rhythm in your whisper, and that was all.""Well, then, guess! ""I can not.""But you must!""I think you said

* My ""What more ? Go on ! "I urged him. "I

think you said ' consciousness.' ""Go on ! ""I think you said 'sub."

"Several friends,"writes Max Dessoir, "were in my room, one of whom, Mr. W., was reading to himself, while the rest of us were talking with one another. Someone happening to mention the name of Mr. X., •in whom Mr. W. is much interested, Mr. W. raised his head and asked, ' What was that about Mr. X. ?' He knew nothing he told us about our previous conversation ; he had only heard the familiar name, as often happens. I then hypnotized him, with his consent, and when he was pretty deeply entranced I asked him again as to the conversation. To our great astonishment, he now repeated to us the substance of our whole conversation during the time that he was reading to himself."

Similar experiments I performed on A. Fingold. The subject, when in the state of hypnosis, gave me details of a conversation which he could not have possibly overheard consciously, and of which he knew nothing at all in his previous waking state. The subwaking self, not being occupied with the work that engaged the attention of the upper consciousness, was on the alert, and listened to the conversation, which escaped the fixed and distracted attention of the waking personality. It is clear, then, that the subwaking hypnotic self is present in the normal state and can hear and guess that of which the waking self has no inkling .

CHAPTER XV.
THE SUBCONSCIOUS SELF AND HALLUCINATIONS.

TURNING now to the interesting phenomena of crystal-gazing we meet with facts of like nature proving the same truth.

"I find in the crystal,"writes a crystal-gazer,* "a bit of dark wall covered with jessamine, and I ask myself, Where have I walked to-day ? I have no recollection of such a sight—not a common one in the London streets; but to-morrow I repeat my walk of this morning, with a careful regard for the creeper-covered walls. Tomorrow solves the mystery. I find the very spot, and the sight brings with it the further recollection that at the moment we passed the spot I was engaged in absorbing conversation with my companion, and my voluntary attention was preoccupied.

"On March 9 I saw in the crystal a rocky coast, a rough sea, an expanse of sand in the foreground. As I watched, the picture was nearly effaced by that of a mouse. . . . Two days later I was reading a volume of poetry which I remembered having cut open, talking the while, certainly not consciously reading. As I turned over the leaves a couple of lines struck me: Only the sea intoning, Only the wainscot mouse." [25]

The same automatic writer looked in the crystal and saw a "newspaper announcement. It reported the death of a lady at one time a very frequent visitor in my circle and very intimate with some of my nearest friends ; an announcement, therefore, which, had I consciously seen it, would have interested me considerably. I related my vision at breakfast, quoting name, date, place, and an allusion to ' a long period of suffering ' borne by the deceased lady, and added that I was sure that I had not heard any report of her illness, or even for some months any mention of her likely to suggest such an hallucination. I was, however, aware that I had the day before taken the first sheet of the Times, but was interrupted before I had consciously read any announcement of death. Mrs. H. Sidgwick immediately sought for the paper, when we discovered the paragraph almost exactly as I had seen it."

In his article, Some Experiments in Crystal Yision, Prof. James H. Hyslop, of Columbia College,* reports the case of Mrs. D., "who used to have a visual hallucination (in the crystal) of a bright-blue sky overhead, a garden with a high-walled fence, and a peculiar chain pump in the garden situated at the back of a house. She attached no significance to it, but took it for one of the many automatisms in her experience which were without assignable meaning to her. But two summers ago she had gone West, to her old home in D., Ohio, and made the acquaintance of a lady whom she had never known before, and by chance was invited to take tea with her one evening. She went, and after tea remarked that she would like to have a drink of water. The lady of the house remarked: 'All right; let us go out into the garden and get a fresh drink from the well.'[26] They went, and, behold, there was the identical blue sky, high fence, and chain pump which she had so often seen in her vision! After going home in the evening Mrs. D. told her mother of her experience, remarking how strange it was. Her mother replied that when Mrs. D. was a little girl about two or three years old she used to visit this house very frequently with her mother."

Prof. James relates the case of a Cambridge lady who happened to misplace a valuable set of silver knives. She searched everywhere, but could not discover its whereabouts. Having heard of crystal-gazing, the lady thought she might as well try it. She procured a crystal and looked into it for a few minutes. Something appeared at the bottom of the crystal; gradually the image took the shape of a box with straight objects lying in it diagonally. The image had the following shape: Presently she found herself taking a chair, mounting it, and reaching out her hand for a top closet. There was the realization of her visual hallucination—there was the box, and inside it the set of knives placed diagonally.

"I saw in the crystal," writes another crystal-gazer," [27] a young girl, an intimate friend, waving to me from her carriage. I observed that her hair, which had hung down her back when I last saw her, was now put up in young-lady fashion. Most certainly I had not consciously seen even the carriage. Next day I called on my friend, was reproached by her for not observing her as she passed, and perceived that she had altered her hair in the way which the crystal had shown.

"I was writing at an open window and became aware that an elderly relative inside the room had said something to me; but the noise of the street prevented my asking what had been said. My ink began to run low, and I took up the inkstand to tip it. Looking into the ink I saw a white florist's parcel as though reflected on its surface. Going into another room, I there found the parcel in question, of which I had had no knowledge. I returned carrying it, and was greeted with the remark: ' I told you half an hour ago to attend to those flowers ; they will all be dead.'

"I looked across the room this morning to a distant table, where I expected to see a book I wanted. It was not there, but my eye was caught by another book, which I saw was strange to me. I tried, but could not read the title at that distance (I have since proved that, even now I know it, this is impossible), and turned away to resume my writing. On my blank paper, as in a crystal scene, I read ' The Yalley of Lilies,' which I found to be the title of the book. I have no recollection of ever seeing the book before."

The phenomena of shell-hearing belong to the same class of facts with those of crystal-gazing. The shell often reports to its listener facts and conversations that have escaped the latter's attention. "The shell,"writes a shell-hearer, "is more likely after a dinner party to repeat the conversation of my neighbour on the right than that of my lawful interlocutor on the left."*

Now all these facts of crystal-gazing and shell-hearing clearly reveal the presence of a secondary, submerged, hyperaesthetic consciousness that sees, hears, and perceives what lies outside the range of perception of the primary personal self.

CHAPTER XVI.
THE SUBWAKING SELF AND THE NORMAL INDIVIDUAL.

THE subwaking self gets manifested in automatic writing, crystal-gazing, and hypnosis, but these phenomena do not occur in everyone. To prove, therefore, fully our proposition that the secondary self is part and parcel of our normal state, we must make experiments on perfectly healthy and normal subjects who never dealt in crystal-gazing, shell-hearing, automatic writing, nor were they ever put into the state of hypnosis. I made three thousand laboratory experiments, eight hundred of which I made on myself and two thousand two hundred on fifty subjects, and the results gave direct and conclusive proof of the presence of the sub-waking, subpersonal, hyperaesthetic self in our normal state. Since the results of my experiments tell us of the subwaking consciousness something more than its mere bare presence, I reserve the account of them for the next chapter, where the discussion of them will be more appropriate. Meanwhile the experiments of Binet will fully suffice for our present purpose. Binet set himself the task to find out "whether the phenomena of the duplication of consciousness are to be met with in healthy, nonhysterical individuals,"or, in other words, whether there can be detected the presence of another self in perfectly healthy and normal subjects. He conducted the experiments in the following way :

"I requested my subjects,"says Binet,* "to whom, • of course, no explanation was given of what was going to be done, to seat themselves before a table and leave their right hands to me, while I gave them something interesting to read. One of the experiments it appeared to me easiest to effect was that of the repetition of passive movements. A pencil being placed in the hand of the subject, who was attentively reading a journal, I made the hand trace a uniform movement, choosing that which it executes with most facility—for example, shadings, or curls, or little dots. Having communicated these movements for some minutes, I left the hand to itself quite gently ; the hand continued the movement a little. After three or four experiments the repetition of the movement became more perfect, and with Mile. G. at the fourth sitting the repetition was so distinct that the hand traced as many as eighty curls without stopping."Furthermore, there was a rudimentary memory of the movements imparted. "When the hand had been successfully habituated to repeating a certain kind of movement—for example, curls—it was to this kind of movement that it had a tendency to return. If it was made to trace the figure 1 a hundred times and was afterward left to itself, the stroke of the figure became rapidly modified, and turned into a curl."This subwaking self, like a child, learned to use the hand and to write, and showed that it remembered what it once learned, and that it was easier for it to perform the acts once acquired.

"When any kind of movement had been well repeated it could be reproduced without solicitation every time a pen was put in the subject's hand and she fixed her attention on reading. But if the subject thought attentively of her hand the movement stopped. With a slight pressure I was able to 'make the hand go obediently in all directions, carrying the pen with it. This is not a simple mechanical compulsion, for a very feeble and very short contact is sufficient to bring a very long movement of the hand. The phenomena, I believe, can be approximated to a rudimentary suggestion by the sense of touch. Nothing is more curious than to see the hand of a person who is awake and thinks she is in full possession of herself implicitly obey the experimenter's orders."

Thus we find that by distracting the attention of the waking self we may gain access to the subwaking self of the normal individual and teach it to use the bodily organs which we place at its disposal to express itself. It can not attain, however, to any degree of efficiency, because the disaggregation effected is but slight and transitory—the controlling consciousness is wide awake. Meanwhile, during the time the secondary self takes its exercises in writing slight anaesthesia supervenes. Pain is not as well perceived, the aesthesiometer shows diminished sensibility.

Furthermore, Binet finds that "the more the subject is distracted (by reading, mental calculation, etc.) the more irregular become the voluntary movements of the hand, and if the distraction is very intense these movements may cease completely. On the contrary, the more distracted the subject is, the more regular and considerable become the automatic movements of the hand. The contrast is striking."Here once more we strike upon the truth, and this time in the case of perfectly normal people, that the growth and expansion of the subwaking consciousness is in inverse ratio to that of the waking self-consciousness.

However the case may be with this last proposition, one central truth remains firm, valid, unshaken, and that is the presence of a subpersonal self in normal life. The results of laboratory experiments on perfectly healthy people in their normal waking state, the phenomena of hypnosis, of automatic writing, of crystal-gazing, and of shell-hearing—all go to form a strong, irrefragable chain of evidence in support of the truth that behind the primary self a secondary consciousness lies hidden.

CHAPTER XVII.
THE INTERCOMMUNICATION OF THE TWO SELVES.

THE two selves in normal man are so co-ordinated that they blend into one. For all practical purposes a unity, the conscious individual is still a duality. The self-conscious personality, although apparently blended with the subwaking self, is still not of the latter. The life of the waking self -consciousness flows within the larger life of the subwaking self like a warm equatorial current within the cold bosom of the ocean. The swiftly coursing current and the deep ocean seem to form one body, but they really do not. The one is the bed in which the other circulates. The two do not mingle their waters ; and still, separate and different as the two are, they nevertheless intercommunicate. The warmth of the Gulf Stream is conducted to the ocean, and the agitation of the ocean is transmitted to the Gulf Stream. So is it with the two selves. Apparently one, they are, in fact, two—the warm stream of waking self-consciousness does not mingle its intelligence with that of the subwaking self. But though flowing apart, they still intercommunicate. Messages come from the one to the other ; and since the range of sensibility—life— is wider and deeper in the case of the subwaking self, the messages, as a rule, come not from the waking to the subwaking, but, on the contrary, from the subwaking or secondary to the waking or primary self. The two streams of consciousness and their intercommunication may be represented thus :

We find such messages in the case of hysteria. Ask the hysterical patient to think of a number, and if he holds a pen or a pencil in the anaesthetic hand he will write down the number, or if he has a dynamometer in his hand he will press distinctly as many times as there are units in the number, not being aware of what he is doing. In these cases the message is transmitted from the primary to the secondary self.

"A hysterical patient totally anaesthetic,"says Binet, "gazed fixedly at a blue cross; the position and arrangement of the cross by simultaneous contrast caused the production of a yellow colour about the cross. During this time the right hand, into which, without the patient's knowledge, a pen had been slipped, did not cease to write, ' Blue, yellow, blue, yellow, etc." : Here once more we have the message transmitted from the primary to the secondary self.

On the other hand, "let us seize the anaesthetic hand,"says Binet "and let us cause it to trace behind a screen the word ' Paris.' We know that this word will be repeated several times. Then, upon addressing ourselves to the principal subject (that is, to the waking self-consciousness) we will ask him to write the word ' London.' The subject, entirely ignorant of what has just taken place, eagerly seizes the pen with the intention to carry out our wish, but to his utter astonishment the indocile pen, instead of writing ' London,' writes ' Paris.'"Here we have a motor message transmitted from the secondary to the primary self.

The following experiments, also made by Binet on hysterical subjects, are still more striking :

"Let us make ten punctures in the anaesthetic hand, and thereupon let us ask the subject, who, as a matter of course, has not seen his hand, which is hidden behind a screen, to think of some number and to name it; frequently the subject will answer that he is thinking of the number ten. In the same manner let us put a key, a coin, a needle, a watch, into the anaesthetic hand, and let us ask the subject to think of any object whatsoever; it will very often happen that the subject is thinking of the precise object that has been put into his insensible hand."

If we turn to hypnosis, we find again the frequent occurrence of such messages.

I hypnotized Mr. A. F., and told him two stories; then I suggested to him that when he wakes up he shall remember nothing at all of what I had told him—that is, the memory shall remain only in possession of the sub-waking self. I then awakened him. My friends who were present at the seance asked him if he knew what I told him. He was surprised at the question ; he could not remember anything. A few minutes later I went up to him, put my hand on his brow, and said : "You can remember now everything that passed during hypnosis. Try hard; you can ! "He thought some time, and at once, as if he received sudden information, told us the two stories in detail. Another time I made him pass through a series of actions, again giving the suggestion of oblivion, and again with the same results. He thought he slept deeply for about half an hour. As soon as I put my hand to his forehead the subwaking self sent at once a despatch of the detained information to the waking consciousness. Once I made Mr. A. F. pass through a series of scenes and different complicated events of life. The suggestion of oblivion was again enforced. When he was awakened he remarked that he slept very long—for about an hour and a half; he could not remember anything. I put my hand to his brow, gave the suggestion of recollection, and the hypnotic self at once sent up the intelligence.

Now, if the hyperaesthetic, subwaking self and the waking self-consciousness, their interrelations and intercommunications, subsist also in normal life, as they most certainly do in the states of hypnosis, automatic \v riting, and crystal-gazing—if they subsist, I say, also in the life of every man, we ought to find it out by experiments. We ought to find that sensory impressions that lie outside the range of sensibility of the waking self, but within the range of the subwaking self, that such sensory impressions will still be transmitted to the primary self. The guesses of the subject must rise far above the dead level of chance—probability. And such is actually the case.

The first set of experiments I made on myself. My right eye is amblyopic; it sees very imperfectly; for it, things are enshrouded in a mist. When the left eye is closed and a book is opened before me I am unable to tell letter from figure; I see only dots, rows of them ,

all indistinct, hazy, oscillating, appearing and disappearing from my field of. vision. When a single letter or figure is presented to my right eye, I see only a black dot, as a kernel surrounded by a film of mist.

I asked Mr. B. to make twenty-five slips and write down on each slip four characters—letters, figures, or both—in different combinations, but so that in all the twenty-five slips the number of letters should equal the number of figures. When a slip was presented to my right eye, the other being closed, I had to guess which of the characters was letter and which was figure. When the first series of twenty-five was ended the slips were shuffled, and a second series began. Later on, the same slips were used for two more series. I made two groups of experiments with two series in each group. Each series consisted of a hundred experiments, so that there were, four hundred experiments in all.

In this class of experiments, named Class A, the results are as follows: In the first series of the first group, out of one hundred characters sixty-eight were correctly guessed. Since there were only two guesses —letter or figure— fifty percent must be subtracted, as so much might have been due to mere chance (we shall find, however, from our other experiments that the percentage subtracted is too high) ; eighteen per cent thus remains in favour of messages coming from the secondary self— in other words, eighteen per cent is left in favour of secondary sight.

In the second series of the first group, out of one hundred characters seventy-two were guessed aright; here again we must subtract fifty per cent which might have been due to chance; thus twenty-two per cent remains in favour of secondary sight. In the first series of the second group, seventy characters were guessed out of one hundred shown; subtracting fifty, we have twenty per cent in favour of secondary sight.

In the second series of the second group, out of one hundred characters shown seventy-six were guessed rightly; subtracting fifty, we have twenty-six per cent in favour of secondary sight.

Out of four hundred experiments made, the general character was guessed two hundred and eighty-six times, which gives 71.5 per cent; subtracting fifty per cent, we have 21.5 per cent in favour of secondary sight.

Figures often speak more eloquently, more convincingly, than volumes. The results of the correct answers as to the general nature of the character due to secondary sight are far below the actual one, for in subtracting fifty per cent we subtracted too much, as our experiments will show farther on; still they were so striking that I communicated them to Prof. James, and he was kind enough to encourage me in my work, and advised me to pursue the inquiry further in the same direction.

The experiments were now somewhat modified. Five different letters, and as many different figures, were chosen. The letters were A, B, E, N, T; the figures, 2, 4, 5, 7, 9. Each capital or figure was written on a separate card. I knew the characters, and had to guess none but these. I had not to name merely letter or figure, thus having only two guesses, as the case was in the experiments of Class A, but I had to name one of the ten characters shewn; in short, I had always to give the particular name. Now here each guess could

either be general, or both particular and general, or fail altogether. When I took letter as letter, or figure as figure, but gave the wrong name—for instance, I took 5 for 7, or E for N—I guessed rightly the general nature only of the character shown. When I gave the correct name, I guessed, of course, both the particular and the general nature. When, however, I mistook a letter for a figure or a figure for a letter, I failed, and failed completely. As the series of ten was finished the cards were shuffled and a new series was started. But few experiments were made at a time, as I had to keep my left eye closed, and looked only with my right eye, which soon became extremely fatigued.

These experiments, named Class B, give the following results:

Out of four hundred experiments made, the general character was guessed correctly two hundred and seventy-three times, of which the particular character was guessed correctly one hundred and eighty-eight times.

The remarkable success of these last experiments led me to try the same on people with normal vision. The experiments were carried on in the following way: Ten cards were taken; on each one was put down in faint outlines a small capital or figure, the number of figures being equal to that of the letters, so that there were five cards with a different letter on each, and again five cards with a different figure on each. The subject in these experiments was put at such a distance that the character was outside his range of vision; he saw nothing but a mere dot, blurred, and often disappearing altogether. The subject was told that there were ten cards in the pack, that the number of letter cards was equal to that of the figure cards, but he was not told the particular names of the characters. Each time a card was shown the subject had to give some particular name of character he took that dot to be. "They are all alike, mere blurred dots,"complained the subjects. "No matter,"I answered; "just give any letter or figure that rises in your mind on seeing that dot."

The number of subjects was eight. I worked with each separately, giving five rounds to each subject, making the number of experiments fifty, and four hundred in all. In this class of experiments, named Class C, the results are as follows: Out of four hundred experiments two hundred and fifty-five correct guesses were as to general character, of which ninety-two were also correct as to the particular character.

In the last experiments of Class C the characters were written in print; still I could not succeed to have the letters well formed: the characters were not made of exactly the same thickness and size. I therefore made other sets of experiments, and this time with twenty quite different subjects. I took ten cards and pasted on them letters and numerals of the same size. Each card

had a different letter or figure of the following size: The number of figure cards being equal to that of letter cards (five figure cards and five letter cards), I told the subject that I had a series of ten cards, a letter or a numeral on each, and that the number of figure cards equalled that of the letter cards, but I did not tell him the particular names of the characters.

I worked with each subject separately, making only two series with ten experiments in each. The subject was placed at such a distance from the card that the character shown was far out of his range of vision. He saw nothing but a dim, blurred spot or dot. The subject had to name some character which that particular dot shown might possibly be. "It is nothing but mere guess,"commented the subjects.

At the end of the first series the cards were shuffled and the second series was given. Each subject saw the same card but twice. The number of the subjects being twenty, all the first series form a group of two hundred experiments, and so do the second series.

The results in Class D are as follows:

In the first group, out of two hundred characters, one hundred and thirty were guessed as to their general character, of which the particular gave forty-nine.

In the second group, out of two hundred, one hundred and forty were of a general character, of which the particular as fifty-four.

I then made with the same number of subjects another set of experiments that should correspond to Class B, made on myself — namely, to tell the subjects the particular characters used, which were:

Letters B, Z, K, U, H.

Figures 2, 4, 5, 7, 9.

The characters were all of the same size, printed, and the letters were all capitals. The subject had to name only one of these characters. Only two series of ten each were made with each subject, thus giving two groups of two hundred experiments each.

The results in Class E are as follows :

In the first group, out of two hundred characters, one hundred and forty were guessed correctly as to their general character, of which sixty-eight were correct particular guesses.

In the second group, out of two hundred, one hundred and fifty-one were guessed correctly as to the general character, of which seventy-one were particular guesses.*

As I remarked above, the subjects often complained that they could not see anything at all; that even the black, blurred, dim spot often disappeared from their field of vision ; that it was mere "guessing "; that they might as well shut their eyes and guess. How surprised were they when, after the experiments were over, I showed them how many characters they guessed correctly in a general way, and how many times they gave the full name of the particular character shown !

Now all these experiments tend to prove the presence within us of a secondary subwaking self that perceives things which the primary waking self is unable to get at. The experiments indicate the interrelation of the two selves. They show that messages are sent up by the secondary to the primary self.

Furthermore, the results seem to show that, in case the particular message fails, some abstract general account of it still reaches the upper consciousness. An inhibited particular idea still reaches the primary self as an abstract idea. An abstract general idea in the consciousness of the waking self has a particular idea as its basis in the subwaking self.

The great contention of nominalism and conceptualism over the nature of abstract general ideas thus may find here its solution. The conceptualists are no doubt right in asserting that a general abstract idea may exist in consciousness apart from the particular idea or perception perceived, but they do not say that this consciousness is that of the waking self. The nominalists, again, are right in asserting that a general abstract idea or concept has a particular idea or percept as its basis ; but they do not add that this percept may be totally absent from the waking consciousness and only present in the subwaking consciousness. No general abstract idea without some particular percept as basis.

To return, however, to my work in hand. While the above-mentioned experiments on secondary sight were under way another set of experiments was carried out by me, the purpose of which was to tap directly the suggestibility of the secondary self, and to find out the influence the subconscious has on the primary consciousness.

The mechanism of the experiments was as follows: On slips of paper I made a series of complicated drawings. Each slip had a different pattern. The subject had to look at the pattern of the drawing for ten seconds, and then the slip was withdrawn and he had to reproduce the drawing from memory—a task extremely difficult. It took him about fifteen seconds and more before he could make anything bearing the slightest resemblance to the drawing shown. When he finished the drawing an elongated cardboard with eight digits pasted in a row was shown to him and the subject had to choose whichever digit he pleased. Now, on the margin of each slip was written a digit contained in the number of digits on the cardboard from which the subject had to choose.

The subject, not having the slightest suspicion of the real purpose of the experiments, being perfectly sure that the whole matter was concerning imitation of the drawings, and being assured by me that the choosing of the digits on the cardboard was nothing but a device "to break up the attention "in passing from one drawing to another, and being besides intensely absorbed in the contemplation and reproduction of the drawing, which was extremely complicated—the subject, I say, wholly disregarded the figure on the margin— he did not even notice it. I so fully succeeded in allaying all suspicions and distracting the attention of the subjects that when Prof. James interrogated one of them, an intelligent man, he was amazed at the latter's complete ignorance as to what was actually going on.

The purpose of these experiments, as I said, was to address myself directly to the subwaking consciousness, and to see whether it sent up suggestion-messages to the primary consciousness, which by the very mechanism of the experiments was thrown off its guard. In the previous suggestion-experiments, in spite of all precautions taken, the subject was more or less conscious of what was going on. I could not completely banish all suspicions, and success, therefore, could only be assured by the many conditions favourable to normal suggestibility, and especially that of immediate execution^ so that no time was given to the upper self to inhibit the carrying out of the suggestion. In the present experiments, on thc other hand, the suggestion was addressed directly (of course, as far as this was possible in the normal waking state) to the subwaking self. The upper primary self, being completely absorbed with the drawing, did not notice the figure, or, if it did, it soon learned to disregard it, because h e

thought it insignificant, and because it would only distract his attention. But although the figure was not noticed and fully disregarded (a fact I was careful to find out from the subjects in an indirect way), it still impressed the sense organ, reached the secondary self, which took it as a suggestion, sending it up as a message to the primary self or personality and influencing the latter's choice.

This choice suggestion is strikingly analogous to post-hypnotic suggestion. I hypnotized, for example, Mr. J. F., and told him that ten minutes after awakening he will put out the gas. He was awakened, and ten minutes later he put out the gas. On my asking him why he did it, he answered he did not know why, but somehow the idea came into his mind, and he enacted it and did put out the gas. The post-hypnotic suggestion rises up from the depths of the secondary self as a fixed, insistent idea. A similar state of mind it was of interest to find in the case of the subjects in the present experiments under consideration. The suggestion given was to be carried out only after the imitation of the drawing—that is, some fifteen, twenty, or twenty-five seconds later. Now, when the suggestion was eight, and the subjects chose eight, they very often told me that they did not know why, but that number came at once into their mind on being presented with the cardboard of figures. We have not to wonder at it, for the same psychical elements are here at work as in the state of post-hypnosis. In hypnosis the suggestion is taken up by the secondary, subwaking, suggestible self, and then afterward this suggestion breaks through the stream of the waking consciousness, coming up as an insistent idea; so here, too, in these choice experiments the suggestion was impressed on the subwaking self directly and firmly, and this suggestion was then sent up to the waking consciousness. And just as we find in the case of post-hypnotic suggestion, that not always and not all suggestions given during hypnosis are sue. cessful in being carried out, so here, too, in our experiments, the suggestions —messages from the subconscious regions—were not always taken by the upper consciousness of the subject. We cannot possibly expect invariably success in a state when the waking self is in full swing and possesses all the power of inhibition. Still the success was remarkable.

Before giving the results let me say a few words as to the classification of the experiments. When I started my first experiments of this kind a suspicion crept into my mind that it might be fully possible that in case a suggestion given did not succeed it might still succeed partially as mediate suggestion, by arousing some association which will be obeyed. For instance, in giving 6 as a suggestion, 6 itself might not be chosen, but some number that succeeds or precedes it, such as 5 or Y, or possibly a numeral next to the suggested one in place, say 1 or 2, for I arranged my figures on the cardboard in such a way as to break up the natural succession of the digits. I was therefore careful to make two separate classes for these two kinds of association suggestions—namely, suggestion ly locality and suggestion by numbers, which we may term as locality and number suggestions. The results of my experiments showed me the mediate suggestion was here of but little importance.

I made one thousand experiments and operated with twenty subjects, of which sixteen were fresh ones, not having taken part in any of my other experiments .

The figures on the cardboard were arranged thus: 26471538

In suggesting number 6 the subject could have taken by number suggestion—that is, either 5 or 7; or by locality suggestion—that is, either 4 or 2.

SUGGESTION

The results are as follows: *

Per cent.

Immediate suggestion 32'1

, r ,. I locality 6*2

Mediate suggestion <

(number 3*3

How shall we explain the fact that in our experiments the percentage of correct guesses is far above the one due to chance alone ? Two theories are on the field to account for this fact: one is the well-known unconscious cerebration, and the other is my own point of view, or what I may call the psycho-physiological theory.

On the theory of unconscious cerebration, each figure shown outside the range of vision made an impression on the retina. This impression was transmitted to the sensorium, to the central ganglia of the brain, the occipital lobes, exciting there physiological .processes that are not strong enough to rise above the threshold of consciousness. In short, each figure stimulated the peripheral sense organ, giving rise to a central but unconscious physiological process. Now, according to the theory of unconscious cerebration, it was this unconscious physiological process that helped the subject to form correct guesses.

The psycho-physiological theory, while agreeing with the theory of unconscious cerebration as to the physiological account, makes a step further. Each figure certainly made an impression on the peripheral sense organ and induced central physiological processes, but these processes had their psychical accompaniments. Far from being mere mechanical, unconscious work, these physiological processes were accompanied by consciousness ; only this consciousness was present not to the upper, but to the lower subconscious self.

If we analyze the theory of unconscious cerebration we find it deficient in giving a full account of the matter. No doubt each figure started some central physiological process, but a physiological process without any psychical accompaniment can not possibly serve as a clew to the psychical process of correct guessing; for as long as a material process remains material, it is from a psychical standpoint as well as nonexistent — that is, it can not possibly be taken cognizance of by an already existing consciousness, but, by hypothesis itself, it does not and it can not give rise to a consciousness. It is only in so far as physiological processes have psychical accompaniments that they can serve at all as a clew for correct guessing. In short, the percentage of correct guesses in our experiments can not be accounted for on the theory of unconscious cerebration ; there must therefore have been conscious perception.

Furthermore, to have a correct general idea of a scarcely perceptible dot as being letter or figure, there must evidently be some perception of the particular traits of the dot; there must be a subconscious perception of the particular letter or figure. Moreover, to be still more sure that subconscious perception is a vera causa in correct guessing, I made the following experiments:

On five cards were put five proper names, one name on each card. The cards were then shown to the subjects, who were put at such a distance that they could see only some faint dots. The subject was told that there were five cards, and that on each card there was some proper name — the name of a river, of a city, of a bird, of a man, and of a woman — but he was not told the proper name itself. Now each time a card was shown the subject had to guess which is city, river, bird, man, or woman. The number of subjects was ten. The total number of experiments made was five hundred.

Of these five hundred experiments, three hundred and six were wrong guesses and one hundred and ninety-four were correct guesses. Since there were five names to guess, one fifth, or twenty per cent, of the total number of guesses might have been due to chance —that is, one hundred guesses may be put down to chance, but there still remains a residuum of ninety-four guesses, or 18.8 percent of the total number of experiments.

This residuum must be explained by something other than chance. Now, on the theory of unconscious cerebration the fact of this residuum is almost incomprehensible. How can one guess correctly what one does not see— that it looks like man, river, or city — unless one actually perceives the proper name shown?

On the psycho-physiological or on the subconscious perception theory we can fully see the reason of this residuum. The names were actually perceived. The lower, secondary self, or the subconsciousness, perceived the proper names, but only some of them could be communicated to the upper consciousness.

The facts and experiments discussed above seem to point, by mere force of cumulative evidence, to the presence within us of a secondary, reflex, subwaking consciousness—the highway of suggestion —and also to the interrelation and communication that subsist between the two selves .

CHAPTER XVIII.
THE SUBCONSCIOUS SELF IN THE WAKING STATE.

THE results of our experiments prove the secondary self to be the highway of suggestion. Suggestibility is the very essence of the sub waking self; and since this is also the essential characteristic of the hypnotic self, we may therefore conclude that the subwaking self of the normal individual is identical with the hypnotic self. We arrived already at this conclusion in a former chapter, when we were discussing The Double Self; and now, having started from quite a different point, we once more come to the same truth. The proof therefore seems to be complete. Still, in order to elucidate thoroughly the subject under investigation, I bring here one more proof as to the identity of the normal sub-consciousness and the hypnotic self.

An acquaintance of mine, Mr. W., a highly suggestible young man, came to visit me. For the sake of amusement, without expecting any definite result, I tried upon him the following experiment: I took an umbrella, put it on the ground, and asked him to pass it. He did it easily. "Well,"I said, "but this is not the way I want you to go about it."I put myself opposite him. "I will count slowly, one, two, three, four, and each time you make a step."I counted ; he passed the umbrella. "Now, once more!"I counted with great solemnity, with great emphasis, and laid particular stress on number four. He passed the umbrella, but, it seemed to me, with some hesitation and difficulty. "Without giving him time to rest, I exclaimed, "And now, once more!"I counted slower than before, with greater emphasis and laid still more stress on four, and while pronouncing it I stretched out my arm and made my hand as rigid as possible. To my great surprise, and to that of those present, Mr. W could not pass the charmed umbrella. His legs became rigid, and his feet were as if fastened to the ground. He was suspected of simulation. The gentlemen who witnessed the experiment could not conceive how a strong, sane young man, in the full possession of his consciousness, should not be able to pass such an innocent object as an umbrella. Mr. W. really could not accomplish this ordinary feat, which a child of two can easily do; he tried hard; his face became red and bathed in perspiration on account of the muscular strain, but all his efforts were futile. "No,"he exclaimed at last in great dismay, "I can not do it!"

Later on, in the presence of two Boston High School instructors, I repeated again the same experiment on Mr. W., and with the same result: Mr. W. exerted himself to the utmost, but all his efforts were in vain; he could not pass the charmed line. By this time he became accustomed to this strange phenomenon, and he sat down with a smile, acknowledging that he could not step over the umbrella.

I then tried on Mr. W. another experiment. Pronounce "Boston."—"Boston,"and he said it easily enough. "And now again."I stretched out my hand and made it perfectly rigid. "P-p-p-p-oston!"he ejaculated with great difficulty. "Again."I mad my hand still stiffer, and pointed it almost. directly in his face. No sound. "Don't look at me,"he said at last, "and I'll be able to say it."

Fig. 1, normal writing; Figs. 2, 3, and 4, writing under suggestion that the hand is becoming rigid.

"Well, then,"I said, "try the following sentence: ' Peter Piper picked a peck of pickled peppers.' "He began to say it, but when he came to "peck of"I raised my hand and stiffened it. "P-p-p-e-ec-k "cam e

from his lips; he began to stammer and could not continue.

"Well, then,"I said, "let me see if you are able to pronounce your name."He pronounced it. "Try again."I stiffened my hand, and again the same result—he was unable to pronounce his own name.

"Is it possible,"asked Mr. "W. of me, "that if you meet me on the street you could make me of a sud-

Fig. 1, normal signature; Figs. 2, 3, 4, and 5, signature under suggestion of the hand being rigid. 1 3

den dumb and paralytic ?"I gave him an evasive answer.

"Try now to write ' Boston,' "I requested Mr. "W". He did it, and wrote with great ease. "Again."1 stiffened my hand, loudly and authoritatively suggesting a like rigidity of his hand. His hand grew more and more rigid; "Boston"became more and more broken; the hand went in jerks and jumps, breaking at last the point of the pencil.

"And now let me see whether you are able to write your name."Again the same result. He could not write his own name.

Specimens of his writings will be found on pages 182 and 183.

Afterward I hypnotized Mr. W., and found he fell into the very last stage of somnambulism.

Now these last experiments, together with others of the kind adduced by Bernheim, Delboeuf, etc., and mentioned by me in a previous chapter, certainly do give strong evidence of the presence of the hypnotic self in the normal waking state. We have here a young man who in his normal waking condition takes suggestions characteristic of the hypnotic state. The hypnotic self is present in the waking state of man as the subwaking self. The case adduced by me is certainly rare, unique, but it serves to bring out the truth of our contention clearly before the mind of the reader.

We saw above that all kinds of suggestibility, whether normal or abnormal, must have as their prerequisite some disaggregation of consciousness, a disaggregation of the two selves, of the waking and of the hypnotic subwaking self. Now such a disaggregation could easily be effected in Mr. W., and this was proved by the fact of his subsequent falling into the deepest somnambulic condition on being hypnotized. For, as we have shown above, the difference between normal and abnormal suggestibility is only a difference of degree of disaggregation. In the hypnotic state this disaggregation is comparatively more complete, far more permanent, than in that of normal suggestibility. In the normal state, even when the subject is highly suggestible, the disaggregation is transitory, fleeting; it occurs only during the time of the suggestion, and the equilibrium is restored on the suggestion being over; but this is not the case in the state of abnormal suggestibility. In the waking state, however suggestible the individual may be—that is, however easy it is to dissociate momentarily the one self from the other—still the waking self does not lose its hold on the subwaking self; the waking self can still control; his authority, although somewhat impaired, has nevertheless power and commands obedience. This is beautifully shown by the experiments I made on Mr. W. the day after.

Next day Mr. "W. came to me again. Again I tried on him the same experiments so successfully carried out the day before, but this time the results were quite different.

I put the umbrella on the ground and asked him to step over it. He did it without the slightest inconvenience. I counted slowly, stiffened my hand, but of no avail. He stepped over the umbrella, although occasionally with some slight difficulty.

"Just try to write your name,"I said. He wrote it. "Again."He wrote it once more. I asked him to write slowly ; meanwhile I raised my hand, stiffened it, kept it before his very eyes. The results were now extremely interesting. His hand became cataleptic ; he could not manage it. In a loud voice he began to give suggestions to himself. "I am able to write my name; I can write my name; I will and shall write it; yes, I can; I can write my name ;"etc. Each time as he caught sight of my raised hand and listened to the torrent of suggestions I poured forth his hand became slightly cataleptic and the letters became broken, but each time as he repeated his suggestions the hand went on writing. The waking self of Mr. W. and I were contending for the possession of Mr. W.'s secondary self; and Mr. W. succeeded at last in gaining full control over his secondary self. My suggestions were completely disregarded.

These last experiments and observations bring out clearly the fact that the hypnotic consciousness is present in the waking state as the subconscious self.

CHAPTER XIX.
THE PROBLEM OF PERSONALITY.

IT is certainly of great interest to know whether the subconscious revealed behind the upper consciousness is a personality or not. To answer this question we must first turn to the problem of personality. What is personality? Omitting the metaphysical hypotheses of the soul and of the transcendental ego, we find on the field of empirical psychology two contending theories of personality : the one is the association theory of the English and of the Herbartians, the other is the "wave theory "of Prof. James.

The personal self is regarded by the associationists as a train of ideas of which memory declares the first to be continuously connected with the last. The successive associated ideas run, as it were, into a single point. Memory and personality are identified. Personality is considered as a series of independent ideas so closely associated as to form in memory one conscious series. "The phenomena of self [28] and that of memory,"says J. S. Mill, "are merely two sides of the same fact. . . . My memory of having ascended Skiddaw on a given day and my consciousness of being the same person who ascended Skiddaw on that day are two modes of stating the same fact. ... I am aware of a long and uninterrupted succession of past feelings, going back as far as memory reaches, and terminating with the sensations I have at the present moment, all of which are connected by an inexplicable tie. . . . This succession of feelings which I call my memory of the past is that by which I distinguish myself (personality)."Mill's identification of memory and personality is rather unfortunate, for brutes have memory,* but it is certainly questionable whether they have personality. We shall, however, soon see that not only Mill, but psychologists who seem to take the opposite view, fall into the same fallacy of identifying personality with memory. In another place J. S. Mill expresses himself clearer as to his meaning of personality : "If we speak of the mind as a series of feelings, we are obliged to complete the statement by calling it a series of feelings which is aware of itself as past and future."Mill, however, clearly sees the difficulty of his position—namely, "the paradox that something which, ex hypothesi, is but a series of feelings can be aware of itself as a series."He endeavours to extricate himself from this difficulty by saying "that we are here face to face with that final inexplicability at which, as Sir W. Hamilton observes, 'we inevitably arrive when we reach ultimate facts.' "

Now Prof. James takes Mill to task, and points out that Mill himself, when "speaking of what may rightly be demanded of a theorist [29], says: He is not entitled to frame a theory from one class of phenomena, extend to another class which it does not fit, and excuse himself by saying that if we can not make it fit it is because ultimate facts are inexplicable.'"The class of phenomena which the associationist school takes to frame its theory of the ego are feelings unaware of each other. The class of phenomena the ego presents are feelings of which the latter are intensely aware of those that went before. The two classes do not "fit,"and no exercise of ingenuity can ever make them fit. No shuffling of unaware feelings can make them aware. In another place Prof. James says : "This inexplicable tie which connects the feelings, this ' something in common ' by which they are linked and which is not the passing feelings themselves, but something ' permanent ' of which we can ' affirm nothing ' save its attributes and phenomena, what is it but the metaphysical substance come again to life?"

Prof. James's criticism of associationism is certainly just and acute, and one can not help agreeing with him. But now, what is Prof. James's own theory of personality ? The passing thought, according to Prof. James, is the thinker. Each passing wave of consciousness, each passing thought, is aware of all that has preceded in consciousness ; each pulse of thought as it dies away transmits its title of ownership of its mental content to the succeeding thought. To put it in his own words:

"Each thought out of a multitude of other thoughts of which it may think is able to distinguish those which belong to its own ego from those which do not. The former have a warmth and intimacy about them of which the latter are completely devoid. ... Each pulse of cognitive consciousness, each thought, dies away and is replaced by another. The other, among the things it knows, knows its own predecessor, and finding it ' warm,' greets it, saying, ' Thou art mine and part of the same self with me.' Each later thought, knowing and including thus the thoughts which went before, is the final receptacle, and, appropriating them, is the final owner of all they contain and own. Each thought is thus born an owner, and dies owned, transmitting whatever it realizes as itself to its own later proprietor. As Kant says, it is as if elastic balls were to have not only motion but knowledge of it, and a first ball were to transmit both its motion and its consciousness to a second, which took both up into its consciousness and passed them to a third, until the last ball held all that the other balls had held, and realized it as its own. It is this trick which the nascent thought has of immediately taking up the expiring thought and adopting it which is the foundation of the appropriation of most of the remoter constituents of the self. Who owns the last self owns the self before the last, for what possesses the possessor possesses the possessed. A thing,"Prof. James goes on to say, "can not appropriate itself—it is itself; and still less can it disown itself. There must be an agent of the appropriating and disowning ; but that agent we have already named. It is the thought to whom the various " constituents' are known. That thought is a vehicle of choice as well as of cognition, and among the choices it makes are those appropriations or repudiations of its own. But the thought never is an object in its own hands. It ... is the hook from which the chain of past selves dangles, planted firmly in the present. . . . Anon the hook itself will drop into the past with all it carries and then be treated as an object and appropriated by a new thought in the new present, which will serve as a living hook in its turn.

Like the associationists, Prof. James looks for personality in the function of memory; like them, he regards personality as a series, with the only difference that he postulates a synthesis of that series in each passing thought. Each thought has the title to the content of previous thoughts, but this momentary thought does not know itself. The thought can only be known when dead, when it has become a content of a succeeding wave of consciousness. In short, Prof. James seems to think that personality is a synthesis of a series, and that this synthesis is not conscious of itself. We see at once that although Prof. James attacks so valiantly and justly the association theory, he himself falls into an error no less flagrant—he omits from his account of personality the fact of self-consciousness.

Mill, in starting with a disconnected series of sensations and ideas, could not see how that series could possibly become synthetized and conscious of itself as such, as a series, and he was compelled to fall back in that refuge of ignorance, the unknowable, placing this synthetic conscious activity into a noumenal world, but he at least clearly saw that personality requires self-consciousness. Prof. James, however, while accounting for the synthetic side of the "pure ego,"totally omits the self-conscious side of personality. He even emphasizes this lack of self-consciousness in the passing thought, the present personal thinker. "All appropriations,"he says, "may be made to it, ~by a thought not at the moment immediately cognised by itself."If, then, the passing thought can be known only as content, can there possibly be self-consciousness at all ? According to Prof. James the passing thought with its synthesized series of contents can be known only as object, but then the consciousness of an object is not self-consciousness. Where, then, does the fact of self-consciousness come in? Self-consciousness can not be in the mere object-consciousness, for in it the object occupies the whole field of mental vision, and, besides, the object content is but the material, the inheritance of former dead owners. Self-consciousness, again, is not present in the passing thought, for the passing thought, according to Prof. James, "can not own itself"; nor can self-consciousness be in the succeeding thought, for then the previous thought has already perished, and it is now another thought that is conscious of the thought gone—a state that can in no wise be self-consciousness; it is rather other-consciousness. How, then, is self-consciousness possible ? Prof. James attempts to escape from the difficulties by making the thoughts feel "warm,"but surely "animal warmth"advances us very little toward a clear comprehension of the "pure ego."A warm thought, whatever it may mean to Prof. James, is as much an object as a cold thought.

The fact is that Prof. James, in asserting that the present passing thought or the present moment of consciousness lacks knowledge of itself, seems to have forgotten his own distinction of the two kinds of knowledge—knowledge about and knowledge of acquaintance .

The blind man who knows the theory and laws of light has knowledge about, but he sadly lacks the most essential knowledge—knowledge of acquaintance; he does not know what the sensation of light is hi itself—that is, he has mediate but not immediate knowledge. Now the most that Prof. James can claim is that the present thought lacks knowledge about, but it nevertheless does possess knowledge—knowledge of acquaintance. Prof. James, however, is not altogether unaware of it, for in asserting that "the present moment is the darkest in the whole series,"he also tells us that "it may feel its own immediate existence,"but he hastens to qualify this last statement of his by adding, "hard as it is by direct introspection to ascertain the fact."Even if it be granted that Prof. James did keep in mind the two kinds of knowledge, and denied to the passing thought only knowledge about, he is still in the wrong; for self-consciousness partakes of the two kinds of knowledge: it is both knowledge about and knowledge of acquaintance.

A close examination of the two theories shows that neither the bundle of associationism nor Prof. James's passing thought gives us a true account of personality. The "pure ego "or personality is not a series, for a disconnected series can not possibly make a unity a person; nor is personality a mere synthesis of passing thoughts, for there may be synthesis or memory in each passing wave of consciousness and still no personality. The consciousness of a dog, of a cat, may fully answer Prof. James's description of the "pure ego."The central point of the ego or of personality lies in the fact of the thought knowing and critically controlling itself in the very process of thinking, in the very moment of that thought's existence.

Prof. James is certainly wrong in asserting that in personality the passing thought does not know itself in the moment of thinking. He seems to assume that the knowledge of an object and the knowledge of that knowledge require two distinct pulses of consciousness, two distinct thoughts; but, as we pointed out above in our discussion, if this were the case self-consciousness would have been an impossibility. The fact is that the knowledge of an object and the knowledge of that knowledge do not require two distinct moments, but only one and the same moment. Once a thought has come to assert "I feel,"the knowledge and the feeling constitute one and the same thought. The pure ego, the "I,"taken by itself means consciousness of consciousness. What the "I"asserts is that there is present consciousness of consciousness. "I feel"means that there is consciousness of a feeling along with consciousness of that consciousness. The "I know, and I know that I know,"and the "I know that I know that I know,"and so on, do not require so many separate thought-moments, but only one and the same moment of self-consciousness.

Prof. James's defective analysis of personality seems to be the result of his imperfect discrimination between the present moment of consciousness and the present time-moment. It is this want' of discrimination between the two moments that underlies the ideal structure of Hegelianism; and although Prof. James kicks vigorously against Hegel, he still can not free himself from the influence of that great dialectician. Prof. James, in fact, is a Hegelian at heart.

Moments, Hegel [30] tell us, f are in a continuous flux; the now and the here, the this and the that, change with each coming moment. No sooner does the moment of consciousness posit its now, than the moment is changed and the now turns out to be something different. The negation lies on the very face of the moment's affirmation. The moment of consciousness taken in its immediacy cannot know itself, because it negates itself in the very act of its affirmation. "Le moment ou je parle est déjà loin de m,oi"It is partly this consideration that Prof. James has in mind when he declares that "the present moment of consciousness is the darkest in the whole series."

Before we proceed further with our discussion it would not be amiss to point out the fact that Prof. James is also guilty of confounding two widely different moments : the present moment of consciousness and the present moment of self-consciousness. This is, in fact, implied by his whole theory of the passing thought with no self-consciousness to back it; and this confusion of the two moments is especially clearly revealed in the "darkness of the present moment of consciousness."Prof. James means by the present moment of consciousness the present thought, the present thinker—that is, the present moment of self-consciousness. Now, even if it be granted that the present moment of consciousness be "the darkest in the whole series,"the present moment of self-consciousness is certainly the brightest of all.

Turning now to the Hegelian flux fallacy—a fallacy committed by many a philosopher and psychologist—we find that two qualitatively different moments are lumped together into one, namely, the present time moment and the present moment of consciousness. While in the schema of objective time the present moments are in a continuous flux, the present moments of consciousness are far from being in a parallel incessant change. The moments in the schema of time may go on flowing, but the present moment of consciousness may still remain unchanged ; nay, it is even fully conceivable that a present moment of consciousness should fill a whole eternity. The radical difference of those two moments is well illustrated in the popular story of the monk, who happened to listen to the song of a bird from paradise for but a single moment and found that meanwhile a thousand years had passed away.

The present moment of consciousness does not change with the change of the present time moment; the two moments are totally different in their nature. Now the moment of consciousness not being a time moment, not being in a continuous flux as the latter is, may include as well its own consciousness, and thus be a moment of self-consciousness; and as a matter of fact a present moment of self-consciousness does include the knowledge of the present moment of consciousness within the selfsame present moment.

Prof. James passes a severe criticism on Hume for not making his ego-bundle a little more of a decent whole; he censures Hume for denying the synthetic unity of the pure ego. On similar grounds may Prof. James be criticised for not making his evanescent thinker a little more of a decent person; he may be censured for not seeing that knowledge of the conscious moment within the very present moment of consciousness ; in other words, that self-consciousness is of the very essence of the pure ego.

The central point of personality is self-consciousness. A series of moments-consciousness cognized as a unity or synthesis of many moments in one thought, or by one thought, is not at all an indispensable prerequisite of personality. We can fully conceive an eternal moment of self-consciousness with no preceding moments to synthetize, and still such a moment of self-consciousness is no doubt a personality. An ego of such a type is not constituted of a series of moments, and has therefore neither memory nor personal identity ; and still such an ego is a person, and possibly the most perfect of persons, since the personality, independent of all time, is completely synthetized by the very nature of its self-conscious being. "We can again conceive a being with distinct pulses in each moment of self-consciousness. Each pulse of consciousness, however, being a moment of self-consciousness, is certainly of the nature of personality. "We have here an objective series of moments of self-consciousness, originating from the primitive life consciousness, but each moment remaining distinct in itself, not owned, not synthetized by the succeeding moment, of self-consciousness.

This type of self-consciousness has a series, but no synthesis, no memory, no personal identity. On the other hand, there may be a series of pulses of consciousness, there may be memory, there may be a synthesis of all the preceding moments in each passing moment of consciousness, and still if there is no self-consciousness such a consciousness is certainly no personality. Neither a connected series of moments nor their synthesis is of the essence of personality; it is only consciousness of consciousness, the knowledge of consciousness within the same moment of consciousness; in short, it is only the moment of self-consciousness that makes of a consciousness a personality.

Consciousness and self-consciousness may hypothetically be arranged in the following series of stages or types :

I. Desultory consciousness. In this type of consciousness there is no connection, no association, between one moment of consciousness and another; there is certainly no synthesis of moments, and consequently no memory, no recognition, no self-consciousness, no personality. This type of consciousness may have its representatives in the psychic life of the lowest invertebrates.

II. Synthetic consciousness. In this type of consciousness there is synthesis of the preceding moments in each passing moment, but there is no recognition. Former experiences are reinstated in consciousness, but they are not recognised as such. Instinctive consciousness falls naturally under this type of mental activity. Memory is certainly present, but it is objective in its nature ; it exists only for the observer, not for the individual consciousness itself. The subjective side of memory, the projection of the present experience into the subjective past of the present moment consciousness, is wanting; and, of course, it goes without saying that the synthetic consciousness has no self-consciousness, no personality.

III. Recogniti/ue consciousness. In this type of consciousness there is not only an objective synthesis of the preceding moments in each moment of consciousness, but there is also present a subjective synthesis.[31] Former experiences are not only simply reinstated in consciousness, but they are also recognised as such. This type of mental activity may be represented by the consciousness of the higher vertebrate animals. There is here memory, there is the projection of the present into the subjective past, there is recognition, but there is no self-consciousness, no personality.

IV. Desultory self-consciousness. This type of self-consciousness has no synthesis in each present moment of the preceding past moments of self-consciousness. Such a form of consciousness may be regarded as a series of independent, instable personalities coming like bubbles to the surface of consciousness and bursting without leaving any marked trace behind them. It is evident that this type of personality, although it has a series of moments, has no memory of that series, nor has it any personal identity.

V. Synthetic self-consciousness. This form of self-consciousness has a series of moments, and all the moments in the series can be included in and owned by each present moment of self-consciousness. The moments in the series are intimately linked and intertwined. -Each moment synthetizes, owns, knows, and controls the preceding ones. This type of consciousness possesses synthesis, reproduction, recognition, personality, personal identity, and is represented by man's mental activity.

VI. The eternal moment of self -consciousness. In this form of self -consciousness there is no series; it is but one moment. Memory and personal identity are not present because they are superfluous, since there is no preceding series to synthetize. This type of personality may transcend the synthetic personality, as the former may contain the whole content of all complete lines of series in one eternal moment of self-consciousness. This form of self-consciousness may be considered as the pure type of personality; it is the perfect person.*

CHAPTER XX.
THE ELEMENTS AND STAGES OF SUBCONSCIOUSNESS.

FROM the standpoint gained in our discussion on personality or the "pure ego "we can once more turn to the study of the secondary self. The secondary or subconscious self must not be regarded as an individual; it is only a form of mental life, and as such may belong to one of the three types of consciousness. It may be desultory, synthetic, or recognitive. The secondary consciousness is recognitive at its highest, desultory at its lowest.

The subconscious self is a coordination of many series of moments-consciousness. In the subconscious-ness series of moments-consciousness form groups, systems, communities, clusters, constellations. This coordination of series, however, can be dissolved; each separate series again can be broken up into its constituent moments, which may be endowed with a conscious tendency to reunite at a stated interval. The content of the isolated moment is not any more represented in the moments of the other series, and is not therefore known or cognized by them. The inhibited content knowledge or object consciousness has not disappeared; it is still present in the dissociated moments, and can be revealed by different methods.

Synthesis and catalysis of moments-consciousness are at the heart of th# subconscious .

The catalysis of moments-consciousness is often brought about by psychic stimuli under the conditions of suggestibility—conditions that favour a dissociation of the primary from the secondary consciousness. Once this dissociation is effected, a catalysis of the constellations of moments-consciousness constituting the sub-consciousness may be produced by suggestion and by other means. A dissociation of consciousness may be effected by the impression of a very powerful stimulus, such as a strong shock. The conditions of suggestibility—conditions that favour disaggregation of the upper from the lower consciousness, conditions that lay bare the subconscious self to the influence of external stimuli—are here brought about by the overpowering intensity of the stimulus. An intense, overpowering shock limits the activity of the voluntary muscles— frequently paralyzes them momentarily, and sometimes for an appreciable period of time fixes the attention on the impression to the exclusion of all else, strongly inhibits all other mental activity, and narrows the field of the upper consciousness— in fact, very often totally removes it. The subconscious self thus emerges.

If the stimulus is too strong even for the secondary self, the disaggregation goes still further, the subconsciousness becomes disaggregated in its turn, and falls from the plane of recognitive to that of synthetic consciousness. With a further increase of the stimulus the dissolution goes on further, the disaggregation becomes deeper, and the subconsciousness falls from the level of synthetic to that of desultory consciousness.

Now, if such a disaggregation of moments consciousness occurs, whatever may be the cause of it, if the moments can not get synthetized, and if new combinations with different psychic contents are formed, then the result is amnesia —amnesia for that particular state of moment-consciousness.

We must discriminate between the psychic content that may be characterized as the moment-content of consciousness and the synthesis of that content. It is this synthesis of the content that constitutes the nature of a moment-consciousness. In short, a moment-consciousness is content plus synthesis.

Psychic or moment-contents may be represented in the synthesis of different moments-consciousness, so that while certain moments-consciousness may be entirely cut off from given psychic contents, other moments may be in full possession of all that material. Thus there may be loss of mental experience and amnesia for certain states of consciousness, and at the same time full presence of that mental experience as well as recollection of it in other states of consciousness.

Synthetic moments are merely reproduced, but they are not recognised as former, as past. It is only an external observer who occupies a higher plane than that of the synthetic consciousness, it is only such an observer who can notice the reproduction in the synthetic moment. There is, then, a higher plane of consciousness where a new synthesis is affected—that of recognition. This synthesis of recognition is the highest stage that mere consciousness, which takes as yet no recognizance of itself, can attain.

The stages of consciousness and their interconnections in relation to the nature and range of growth of the subconscious self are graphically represented in the diagram at the bottom of the preceding page.

CHAPTER XXI.
THE PHYSIOLOGY AND PATHOLOGY OF SUBCONSCIOUSNESS.

THE mental processes of association and aggregation of psychic contents in the synthesis of moment-consciousness and the including of the moments-consciousness in synthesis of higher and higher unities can be expressed in physiological terms of cellular activity. The structure of the cell and its morphological relation to other cells can give us a glimpse into the physiological processes that run parallel to mental synthesis and dissociation.

The nerve-cell, as the reader knows, is a nucleated mass of protoplasm highly complicated in its structure and organization. The nerve-cell possesses many filaments or "processes,"all of which, called dendrons, branch repeatedly and terminate in a network of multitudes of fibre-processes representing a greater volume than the cell body itself, with the exception of a single process termed neuraxon, which remains comparatively unchanged in its diameter along its whole course and sends out but a few branches called collaterals. The terminals of collaterals and neuro-axons are in their turn split into a comparatively small number of branches called the terminal arborization!

If we inquire as to the connection of nerve-cells with one another, we find that no nerve-cell is anatomically connected with other cells. Every nerve-cell with all its processes forms a distinct and isolated morphological individual. Every nerve-cell anatomically considered is a complete unit. The processes coming out from different nerve-cells do not fuse with processes coming out from other nerve-cells, but rather interlace and come in contact, like the electrodes of a battery in forming the electric circuit. Thus neurological investigations point to the highly significant fact that the connections among the nerve-cells are not of an anatomical but of a physiological nature. The association of nerve-cells is not organic, but functional.

Nerve-cells with concomitant psychic moments-content come into contact with other nerve-cells accompanied by psychic content by means of their fine terminal processes. This association of cells forms a group whose Nerve . cell of cortex: dr., den-physiological function has dendrons, neuraxons, collaterals; arb., terminal concomitant mental activity arborization. resulting in some form of psychic synthesis. By means of association fibres the groups are organized into systems, the systems into communities, the communities into clusters, the clusters into constellations, and each of the higher, more complex aggregates is more feebly organized by less stable association fibres. The combination of groups into systems and of these systems into clusters and constellations by means of association fibres have as their psychic concomitants higher and higher forms of mental syntheses. Thus moments-content are synthesized in the unity of moments-consciousness, and the latter are synthesized in their turn in higher and higher unities.

The simpler, the less complicated a group of nerve-cells is, and the longer and more frequent their fine processes come in contact, the greater is the tendency of that group to form permanent relations; and the same holds true of systems of cells in communities, clusters, and constellations. We may therefore say that the organization of a system or constellation of cells is in proportion to the duration and frequency of their associative activity.

Groups of nerve-cells with a more or less stable function become gradually organized and form a stable organization. The more complex, however, a system of nerve-cells is, the greater is its instability, and in the very highest systems or constellations of clusters the instability reaches its maximum. The instability of a system is in proportion to its complexity. In the very highest constellations the instability is extreme, and there is going on a continuous process of variation. Under the action of the slightest external or internal stimuli, such unstable systems or constellations lose their equilibrium, dissolve and form new systems, or enter into combination with other constellations. On the psychical side we have the continuous fluctuation of the content of attention. The characteristic trait of the highest type of psycho-physical life under the ordinary stimuli of the environment is a continuous process of association and dissociation of constellations.

As the stimuli increase in their intensity, be they of an external or internal nature — be they toxic, such as the influence of a poison, or purely mechanical, such as the action of a blow, or be they of a purely internal psycho-physiological character, such as a strong emotion—a process of dissolution sets in, and the highest, the most unstable, the least organized constellations of clusters are the first to dissolve. With the further increase of the intensity of the stimulus the dissolution goes deeper and extends further—the simpler, the more stable, the more organized systems become dissolved. The psycho-physical content, however, does not disappear with the dissolution of the system; the content exists in the less complex forms of cell-associations, and psychically in the simpler forms of mental synthesis.

The same result may be effected by stimuli of less intensity but of longer duration. A durable hurtful stimulus is in fact by far the more detrimental to the life of cell-aggregation. The pathological process of dissociation and disaggregation may be regarded as a function of two factors— of duration and intensity.

Such a dissociation is not of an organic but of a functional character. The association fibres that connect groups into systems, communities, clusters, constellations contract. The fine processes of the nerve cells , the dendrons, or the terminal arborization, or the collaterals that touch these dendrons, thus forming the elementary group, retract and cease to come in contact*

Association fibres combining the highest constellations are the first to give way; they are the latest to arise in the course of psycho-physical evolution, they are the most unstable, the least organized, and are also the first to succumb to the process of dissolution. The instability of association fibres is proportionate to the complexity and instability of the joined clusters and constellations.

At the first onslaught of inimical stimuli the cell-communities combined into clusters and constellations by association fibres become dissociated and independent of one another. Cell-communities, being more firmly organized than clusters and constellations, of which they are a part, and acting as a more organized whole, resist longer the action of hurtful stimuli. The association-cells that connect different clustered cell-communities contract or retract their fine terminal processes, and the cluster is dissolved. As the hurtful stimuli become more intense, the systems within the cell-community,[32] though more firmly organized by association-fibres than the clusters, withdraw in their turn from the action of the hurtful stimuli. The association-cells that combine systems into communities retract their terminal processes, and the result is the dissolution of the cell-community into its constituent systems, which have more power of resistance than communities of cells, because systems are far more stable, far better organized. As the stimuli rise in intensity the process of disaggregation reaches the systems and they fall asunder into groups. With the further increase of the intensity of the hurtful stimuli the process of disaggregation affects the group itself, the fine processes of the nerve-cell, the dendrons or collaterals and the terminal arborization of the neuraxon contract, withdraw from the hurtful stimuli, as the monocellular organism retracts its pseudopodia from the influence of noxious stimuli. Thus the groups themselves become dissociated, and are dissolved into a number of simple and isolated nerve-cells. For plan of the organization of brain-cells, see Plate Y.

The following experiment, made at my request by Mr. R. Floyd, at the Pathological Institute of the New York State Hospitals, tends to confirm the theory of retractility of the extensions of the ganglion cell protoplasm. The fibrillse of the dendrons, and perhaps of the axon also, which are continuous with the fibrillar network in the cell-body, may become correspondingly retracted. The dendrons are not shown in the preparation, but the root of the axon with its parallel fibrils continuous with the cell-body network is shown at the right-hand side.

This whole process of dissolution is functional, for the disaggregation occurs only in the different forms of cell combinations. The cell itself, however, with all its processes remains intact and organically sound. With the removal, therefore, of the hurtful stimuli, there is once more a tendency, on account of the habit acquired from previous combination, to form old associations, and the old relations and functions are gradually restored. In.short, until the process of dissolution reaches the individual cell, the process is not of an organic out of a functional character.

All functional diseases are cases of psycho-physiological disaggregation, and the gravity of the disease is proportional to the amount of dissociation. A functional disease or functional change is a disaggregation of clusters and systems of nerve-cells with their concomitant moments-consciousness and moments-contents. This disaggregation consists in the withdrawal of the simpler and better organized cell-colonies* from the more complex systems, and, lastly, in the withdrawal of individual cells from the group or cell-colony. The whole process of dissociation or disaggregation is one of contraction, of shrinkage, from the influence of hurtful stimuli. First, the most unstable association-fibres are loosened, and communication is interrupted in the clusters forming the highest and most complex constellations, and then, as the intensity of the stimuli increases, the more stable association-fibres are loosened from the systems they connect. "With the further increase of the stimuli the process of disaggregation descends still lower, to the elementary group formed of individual cells; the cells withdraw the terminal processes by which they come in contact with those of other cells in the same group.

In post-hypnotic states, in cases that go under the name of hysteria, in many forms of aphasia, in many obscure mental diseases, in many psychic states subsequent to great mental shocks, in many mental maladies known as the "psychic equivalent of epilepsy,"* we meet with cases of different degrees of cell-disaggregation, accompanied by all shades and forms of mental dissociation or amnesia, forms and types which I shall discuss further on. These forms may be spontaneous, as in cases of diseases, or they may be artificial, as in the case of hypnosis. One psycho-pathological process, however, underlies all the various forms of functional diseases, and that is the process of cell-disaggregation, with its concomitant dissociation of moments-consciousness.

I wish here to express my acknowledgment and sincere thanks to Dr. Ira Van Gieson, Director of the Pathological Institute of the New York State Hospitals, for his kind assistance afforded me in the preparation of the accompanying plate
.

CHAPTER XXII.
THE CASE OF THE REV. THOMAS CARSON HANNA.

IMPORTANT as the problem of amnesia is for psychology and psychiatry, no case of amnesia has been studied carefully and experimented on, so as to bring out the inner nature of the subconscious self. Fortunately, a very important case of amnesia recently fell under my care and observation. Dr. S. P. Goodhart, of New York, in making a clinical examination of a case of amnesia and not finding any external signs of organic lesion, had the kindness to refer the case to me for psychological investigation. Thanks to the scientific spirit and excellent facilities for research work at the Pathological Institute of the New York State Hospitals, I was enabled to undertake the work. Dr. Goodhart was so much interested in the case that he gave up much of his time to assist me in my psychological investigations of the intricacies of this case.

This case of amnesia is certainly unique in the annals of psychiatry, because it presents such a rich store of manifold phenomena bearing an intimate relation to many important problems in the science of psychology, and especially because no other case within my knowledge has been so closely and vigilantly watched, so carefully experimented upon, and so many momentous results elicited concerning the nature of the subconscious. From a clinical standpoint, too, this case of amnesia is of the utmost consequence, on account of the methods worked out for the diagnosis of different types of amnesia. From a practical therapeutic standpoint the case can not but be of the highest interest, because of the psychotherapeutic methods first worked out and applied by me to this case in order to effect a complete cure.

I give here but a very brief outline of this extremely interesting case, since a full account of it, together with a discussion of the methods used and the results arrived at, will appear in the State Hospitals' Bulletin, published by the New York State Hospitals. For our purpose, meanwhile, a short account of the case will suffice to reveal the presence and the nature of the secondary self, to work out the different forms of subconscious states, and to classify the different types of amnesia to which these states may give rise.

The following is a brief statement of the case: The patient, Rev. Thomas C. Hanna, of Plantsville, Conn., twenty-five years of age, is a man of extraordinary abilities and high aspirations. He has an excellent university education. He has a good family history, free from any taint of degeneration. He is possessed of a vigorous, healthy constitution and of a strong power of will. On April 15, 189Y, Mr. Hanna met with an accident; he fell from a carriage, and was picked up in a state of unconsciousness. When the patient came to himself he was like one just born. He lost all knowledge acquired by him from the date of his birth up to the time of the accident. He lost all power of voluntary activity, knew nothing of his own personality, and could not recognise persons or objects. He had, in fact, no idea whatever of an external world. Objects, distance, time did not exist for him. Move -

ments alone attracted his involuntary attention, and these he liked to have repeated. Nothing remained of his past life, not even a meaningless word, syllable, or articulate sound. He was totally deprived of speech. He had lost all comprehension of language. The conversation of the people around him was to him nothing but sounds, without any meaning. He had lost all sense of orderliness in his responses to the calls of Nature. The patient was smitten with full mental blindness, with the malady of complete oblivion. Impressions coming to him from the external world had lost their meaning; the patient did not know how to interpret them. He was like a newborn babe. The patient opened his eyes on a fresh world. Impressions received by his sense organs kept his attention busy in the elaboration of his new world of experience. He did not know, could not recognise anything from his former life. No object, no person, however intimate and near, awakened in him even the vaguest sense of familiarity.

The patient had to learn all over again. He soon regained the use of his voluntary muscles from involuntary movements and instruction. He learned to use his arms and legs in walking and working, and acquired a knowledge of objects and their distance; he no longer attempted to seize his own image in the mirror, no longer stretched out his hand to grasp distant trees or far-off shining lights. He learned to know different articles of food; he no longer ate apple, core, and stem, nor did he any more attempt to devour cakes of soap given to him. With a strong intelligence left entirely intact the patient learned things very quickly. His progress in the acquirement of knowledge was such a rapid one that in a few weeks he was fairly able to comprehend his environment and to communicate with people. At first he imitated words and phrases heard, thinking that this would help him to make his wants known to others ; then he dropped this method, and by systematic imitation of words in connection with the objects they indicated the patient learned to speak. He also gained a knowledge of reading and writing, in a very imperfect way, though. In reading, he asked for the meaning of nearly every third word, and his writing was like that of a child who had just begun to learn the formation of letters. His reading was extremely slow, hesitating, and his handwriting awkward. He was ambidextrous; he could write equally well with both hands, something the patient could not achieve before the accident.

All knowledge of his life before the accident was totally gone; all his scholarly attainments, all his higher scientific and linguistic acquirements, all the memories of his former experience, seemed to have been wiped out by the destructive violence of the catastrophe. Persons whom he once knew intimately had to be introduced to him again. He could not recognise his parents, nor the young lady to whom he was attached. From a later inquiry it was found that the patient lost his sexual instincts. He had no idea of the sexual functions and of the difference between men and women. The only life experience known to him dated from the time of the accident. He was practically but a few weeks old, and in this brief period of time he rapidly passed in his development through all the stages an infant passes in its slow growth of years.

When I first met the patient I found him in a state of complete amnesia. To quote from my notes taken at that time:

"H. has absolutely no recollection of any experience previous to the accident. His former life is completely gone from his memory. He has recollections only for such events of his life as have occurred since the injury. The patient is like one just born, a being that had just entered into life. Patient says ' I know ' of events that have occurred since the accident; of experiences previous to that time he knows from reports, of what ' others tell him.' He regards the history of his life before the accident as an experience that had occurred within the life of quite a different person.

"He is but a few weeks old, and no memory of his previous life spontaneously occurs to him. The accident may be considered as the boundary line separating two distinct lives of the same individual. What had occurred in his former life before the accident is unknown to the personality formed after the accident. Two selves seem to dwell within H. One seems to be deadened, crushed in the accident, and the other is a living self whose knowledge and experience are but of yesterday. It seems to be a case of double consciousness, and the patient is now in a secondary state."

Such was the cursory diagnosis of the case the very first time I met the Rev. Th. C. Hanna, and I was glad to find that the diagnosis was fully verified by the results.

The patient was then examined and tested in different ways and was found perfectly normal in all other respects. No lesion was found anywhere; no abnormality could be discovered in his organic or psycho-motor life. He was well and healthy. There was not the least disturbance in his sense organs, no sign of peripheral or central injury. His sensibility and reactions to sense stimuli were fully normal.

His intelligence, his power of inference, his acuteness for distinguishing fine points, his persistence in carrying on a long and complicated train of reasoning, were truly remarkable. His sense of number and his perception of form and symmetry were admirable. He showed the superiority of his mind by his inquisitive-ness and his great anxiety to learn new things. Although he had not yet learned (in this state) his fractions, nor did he know anything of geometry, he still could solve very complicated problems in a simple way, making the best use of the knowledge he acquired.

The tenacity with which he retained the knowledge once acquired was truly astounding. His memory was extraordinary, and whatever was mentioned to him once was retained by him down to the least detail ever after. His appreciation of the beautiful was keen; his disgust for the ugly was extreme; he shivered and turned away at the sight of deformity. He was extremely sensitive to the harmonious. In his morality he was as pure and innocent as a child. What struck me especially was his patience, and the total absence of any angry moods. The only flaw was the incompleteness of his acquired material. He asked the meaning of the simplest words, did not know the spelling of the most commonplace names, and wondered at trite things of ordinary life, as if witnessing something unusual, something he had "never seen before,"to use the patient's own words.

His keen sense of the proportionate, the harmonious, and the musical, his delicate appreciation of the good and the beautiful, his remarkable logical acumen, his great power of carrying on a long train of reasoning, the extraordinary rapidity and facility with which he acquired new knowledge, the immediate use to which he put it, the significant fact that in the course of a few weeks he learned to speak English correctly, pronouncing well and making no mistakes—all that, taken as a whole, confirmed me in the conclusion that the old personality was not crushed to death, that it was only dissociated from the rest of conscious life, and that from the subconscious depth into which it sunk it still exerted a great influence on the newly formed personality of the patient.

To tap the subconscious self and find whether or not the seemingly dead experiences are present there, the patient was asked to relate his dreams.

"I have two kinds of dreams,"he answered. "In the one kind the pictures are not clear; I can recall, but I can not see them well. In the other kind of dreams it is so clear that even now I can see them well."The first kind of dreams, the indistinct ones, were those commonplace dreams of everyday life. They were all experiences coming from the patient's life after the accident. The second kind of dreams, however, proved to be of the highest importance ; they were rifts through which one could catch a glimpse into the darkness of the subconscious life.

It turned out that the dreams related by the patient, and characterized by him as "clear picture dreams,"and afterward as "visions,"and which we may term "vivid experiences,"in contradistinction to dreams being "faint experiences"if compared to those of the waking life, it turned out that these dreams were real occurrences of the patient's former life now lapsed from his memory. The patient, however, did not recognise them as past experiences. To him they were extraordinarily vivid dreams, strange visions, having taken place within his present life experience and without the least hint as to their qualitative pastness. The meaning of these visions was beyond the patient's ken.

In these visions, incidents, names of persons, of objects, of places, were arising from the depths of the patient's split-off subconscious life, and, reaching the surface of the upper consciousness, were synthesized within the narrowed circle of the patient's waking self. This synthesis in memory, however, lacked the element of recognition in so far as the life previous to the accident was concerned. The patient did remember well the "visions,"but he did not refer them to his previous life history; he regarded them as "lively dreams."The different proper names brought up to his memory by the "visions "were to him meaningless, so many empty sounds which could only be understood by the experienced observer, or by his parents, who were acquainted with all the details of his life. Thus, in one of his dreams the patient saw a house on which there was a sign with the following letters (he spelled them out): N-E-W B-O-S-T-O-N J-TJ-N-C. He could now make out what N-E-W meant, as he had since learned the word "new,"but the meaning of the rest of the letters was to him entirely unintelligible and unfamiliar.

The patient's father, who was present at the recounting of the dreams, identified the places described by his son, and found that all the names of the places, persons, and objects were perfectly correct. Mr. Hanna not having heard of all that since the accident, regarded these experiences as "strange dreams "which he could not understand, because he saw in them places, persons, and objects which, according to his own statements, he had "never seen before."The patient greatly wondered at the comments and amplifications the father was making on "the visions."When the father accidentally happened to mention the name "Martinoe,"the patient's amazement knew no bounds .

"That is the name of a place I passed in my dream (vision),"the patient exclaimed, "but how do you know it ? It is only a dream! "

The subconscious memories of the patient were then tested by different methods, especially by the method which I.term "hypnoidization."This method consists in the following procedure: The patient is asked to close his eyes and keep as quiet as possible, without, however, making any special effort to put himself in such a state. He is then asked to attend to some stimulus, such as reading or singing. When the reading is over, the patient, with his eyes still shut, is asked to repeat it, and tell what came into his mind during the reading, during the repetition, or after it. Sometimes, as when the song-stimulus is used, the patient is simply asked to tell the nature of ideas and images that entered into liis mind at that time or soon after. This method, simple as it is, I find to work wonders, especially in cases of amnesia.

In the case of our patient the hypnoidization brought forth phenomena of the utmost interest and value. Events, names of persons, of places, sentences, phrases, whole paragraphs of books totally lapsed from memory, and in languages the very words of which sounded bizarre to his ears and the meaning of which was to him inscrutable—all that flashed lightninglike on the patient's mind. So successful was this method, that on one occasion the patient was frightened by the flood of memories that rose suddenly from the obscure subconscious regions, deluged his mind, and were expressed aloud, only to be forgotten the next moment. To the patient himself it appeared as if another being took possession of his tongue.

The probing of the patient's subconscious self made it perfectly clear that his old and forgotten memories did not perish, that they were present to the secondary consciousness. To be still more sure of my conclusion, I arranged with Dr. Goodhart, who assisted me in my psychological examination and investigation of the case, to watch for the appearance of "the vision."After having watched in vain a whole night, we were at last amply rewarded for our vigilance ; we were fortunate enough to be present at the visitation of one of those "visions."Dr. Goodhart was taking notes, while I was trying to insinuate myself by means of questioning into the patient's mind, and lead him on so as to reveal the inner working of his subconscious mental states.

The patient acted out and Jived through experiences long forgotten and buried. He was in what may be called a "hypnoidic "state. In these hypnoidic states moments-consciousness not synthesized within the focus of the ego, moments-consciousness dissociated from the main stream of personal life, but present to the less organized and less focalized life of the subconsciousness, emerge from the obscure depths of the mind in focalized clusters, in synthesized systems of moments-consciousness. Outlived personalities with these moments-consciousness come to life again, run through in a short period the whole cycle of events and actions they had once worked through. These outlived personalities with their moments-content of consciousness become infused with new life activity, only once more to merge into the ocean of disaggregated consciousness and to give place to new focalization, to new resurrected personalities seemingly dead years ago.

By leading questions, without his least knowledge of it, the patient, as if answering to his own thoughts, was induced to tell of his life forgotten in the waking state. Thus the rich store of the subconscious self was laid bare. The amnesia was only for the self-conscious waking personality, but not for the aggregated totality of moments-consciousness of the subconscious life.

A week later the patient was transferred, for the sake of further investigation, to the Pathological Institute of the New York State Hospitals, and under the influence of psychic and physiological stimuli [33] fell into a state of double consciousness or double personality. The old memories, instead of rising in the form of hypnoidic and hypnoidal states, rose to the full light of the upper consciousness. The "primary state "included the patient's whole life up to the time of the accident; the "secondary state"dated from the accident, and included all the knowledge and experience acquired in that state. In the primary state the patient was discussing metaphysics, philosophy, theology, and even once wrote for me a concise statement on the science of pathology; in the secondary state he did not even know the meaning of these terms. In the primary state his handwriting was fine and delicate; in the secondary state it was awkward and childish, and he could only print capitals, as he had not yet learned to write them. "Whatever he did in one state he could remember only when he again passed into that state. The events of one state were not known to the patient when in the other state. Complete amnesia separated the two states.

In the artificially induced persistent alternations between the two states, [34] all the primary entered into one synthetic unity of consciousness, and so also all the secondary states. By means of the psychic and physiological stimuli used by me, two personalities were crystallized in the depths of his subconsciousness and kept alternating in the upper consciousness. A short interval of complete unconsciousness or of a low desultory consciousness with full anaesthesia and analgesia intervened between the two states. This interval lasted from one to about three minutes. This intermediate state was an attack; it was sudden in its onset, and may be termed hypnoleptic.

By means of a method used by me—a method the value of which seems to me to be inestimable for theoretical and practical purposes—the two alternating personalities were finally run together into one.f The patient is now perfectly well and healthy, and has resumed his former vocation.

CHAPTER XXIII.
FORMS OF SUBCONSCIOUS STATES AND TYPES OF AMNESIA.

WITH the case of H. before us, we return once more to the discussion of subconscious states and types of amnesia. In our analysis of consciousness we arrived at the conclusion that consciousness consists of moments-consciousness. A moment-consciousness contains as much psychic matter or moments-content as is present within one given synthesis of consciousness. Now, the subconscious includes within it the sum total of all the moments-content and also of all the moments-consciousness in a condition of indifferent association and dissociation.

The subconscious is not a selective activity; it simply stands for the sum total of all the moments-consciousness. In the moment-consciousness, again, selection is absent; it is simply a matter of chance what psychic matter shall enter into the synthesis of the moment-consciousness. It is only as we reach the higher plane of psychic life characteristic of the primary self, it is only then that we for the first time meet with selective activity. The primary self, being an active self-conscious synthesis, is selective in its nature. Out of a number of sensations, ideas, and feelings the activity of the primary self selects only some, and leaves the rest in the background of consciousness. The primary sel f

has its more or less definite, determinate outlines that constitute its personal character. Only material of a certain kind and quality, only moments-content and moments-consciousness of a definite character fitting into the form activity of the self, only such material is taken up within the circle of its experience; the rest of the material is simply ignored. This leaving out, this ignoring of many moments, ranges through all degrees of synthetic activity, from the laying up of the moments with a view to further use, from the possibility of synthetizing the rejected material up to the total ignoring of it, when the material is entirely resigned, never to be used again because of its total incongruence with the character of the selective activity or because of the weakness within the energy of the synthetic agency. Many mental diseases, and especially those that go under the collective name of hysteria, have as their psychic cause some of those conditions or all of them in different combination and in various degrees of intensity.

This ignoring of mental material, ranging through all shades and degrees, and also the selective synthetic agency, having different degrees of weakness in the energy of its intensive and extensive "activity, give rise to dissociation of mental states, to disaggregation of synthetized moments from those that were not taken up in that particular synthesis that constitutes for the time being the patient's principal individuality. All the types and degrees of amnesia depend on the nature and degree of such dissociation or disintegration. Where the dissociation is incomplete the amnesia will also be incomplete.

Moments-consciousness as well as moments-content may drop out from the unity of the synthetic consciousness and produce forgetfulness or amnesia. In such a kind of amnesia, however, the gap formed is felt and appreciated by consciousness as a gap. Glimpses of memory come back and disappear again; the forgotten moments tend to recur times and again. The range of such an amnesia varies greatly, from simple forgetfulness of some few details to the oblivion of many important events. This type of amnesia may be characterized as reproductive or recurrent.

Where the dissociation, however, is complete, the amnesia in regard to the disaggregated new synthetized material is total. Under conditions that bring about a disruption in consciousness the whole moment of synthetic self-consciousness may in a disaggregated form fall into the region of desultory moments-consciousness, and very frequently with a tendency to combine and emerge at the first favorable opportunity to the surface of the primary consciousness. Meanwhile, another series of moments-content and of moments-consciousness rise to the level of the upper consciousness and become synthetized in another different moment. that takes the place of the disaggregated one. Between the two moments there is a break, a gap ; fragmentary reproduction of the one by the other is not impossible; if induced by certain methods, the recognition element may be present, but may also be totally lacking. This form of amnesia may be termed irretraceable.

Many of the former moments consciousness and moments content may come up in this newly formed moment consciousness, still the moment, on the whole, is a new and different synthesis. Hence we may say that irretraceable amnesia is the possible manifestation of the phenomena of double consciousness.

We may put it down as a law, that the degree of amnesia is proportional to the amount of psycho-physiological disaggregation. The psycho-physiological process of dissolution may extend still further and deeper. From a disaggregation of systems of moments-consciousness the process may pass into a disintegration of the moments-content themselves, and the amnesia then is absolute ; for a disintegration of the moment content itself practically means a total loss of that psychic content and the impossibility of its reinstatement in the synthesis of moment consciousness.

The physiological side of amnesia is to be found in the disaggregation of clusters of cells into their constituent systems and groups. This disaggregation is due to the violent, hurtful impressions of strong stimuli that effect a contraction of these systems and groups joined by association fibres into clusters. Under the influence of some strong injurious stimulus a whole system or group may withdraw from a constellation of coordinate systems of cells, but in such a way that the contraction is effected only in relation to some of the systems—that is, only some of the association paths get interrupted, while through other paths the system still stands in connection with the cluster .or constellation. There will, of course, be amnesia, but it will be of a vacillating, unstable character, because the connection of the disaggregated system can be effected in an indirect way through other systems. Such amnesia will be reproductive. The easiness with which this reproduction can be brought about is in inverse proportion to the extent of disaggregation effected, in inverse proportion to the number of interrupted association paths.

If, however, the system has contracted completely, and has fully withdrawn from the cluster of systems so that all association paths are interrupted, the result is complete irretraceable amnesia. In irretraceable amnesia the system that has withdrawn is perfectly sound, only it possesses groups of cells of a less complex nature, and the former connections can be again reinstated under favorable circumstances. Should, however, the hurtful stimulus be of such a nature as to destroy a whole system of cells, then the amnesia effected is absolute. The connections can not any more be reinstated, because the system itself is destroyed.

The process of disaggregation setting in under the action of strong and hurtful stimuli is not something new and different in kind from the usual; it is a continuation of the process of association and dissociation normally going on in the higher constellations. The one process gradually passes into the other with the increase of the intensity or duration of the hurtful stimulus. Both processes are of one and the same nature. A further continuation of the process of disaggregation passes into that of cell destruction, which, accepting Dr. Ira Yan Gieson's terminology of cell disintegration, may be characterized as cytoclasis.*

The process may be represented as follows:

Association and Dissociation I Disaggregation I Cytoclasis Normal _^-^^ Dissolution ___ —"^

Psychologically, we find that different degrees of amnesia shade into each other imperceptibly, and that between the two extremes—namely, that of normal forgetfulness and that of absolute amnesia. In reproductive or recurrent amnesia the patient must make a special effort to bring out the dissociated experiences, and the strength of the effort is proportional to the amount of dissociation. In irretraceable amnesia the patient can by no effort of will bring back the lost memories, but they emerge under artificial conditions, such as in the state of hypnosis -or in the induction of slight hypnoidal states, when isolated ideas and sensations, fragments of experiences, without being recognised as past, emerge to the surface of consciousness ; also in hypnoidic states, when all the memories are found to be present. The case of Hanna is a fair example. In the hypnoidic states, as the "vision dreams,"the patient proved to know everything he had forgotten in his seemingly normal waking state.

In absolute amnesia, however, there are no means by which the lost memories may be restored ; no psychic condition can reinstate them in consciousness. They are gone and lost, never to return; they are utterly destroyed.

From a practical clinical standpoint it is of vital importance to make a differential diagnosis as to the kind of amnesia. In a case of amnesia with no possibility on the side of the patient, no matter how strong the efforts are, to bring up the lost memories, it is of the utmost importance to find out whether it is a case of irretraceable or a case of absolute amnesia, as the prognosis and treatment in each one of the two maladies are totally different. To make such a diagnosis, the subconscious must be tapped by means of different methods.

The clinician, the alienist, must bear in mind that a case of amnesia, where tfie lost memories lie beyond the control of the patient, may be irretraceable, disaggregative, and therefore curable, or absolute, cytoclastic, and therefore completely incurable.

Turning now to irretraceable or disaggregative amnesia, we find that hypnotic, hypnoid,* hypnoidic, and hypnoidal states reveal the presence of lost memories in the depths of the subconscious self. Memories which the upper personality is unable to recall, and which seem to be altogether obliterated, suddenly emerge to the surface of consciousness with the removal of the upper layers of mental activity. In hypnosis the removal of the waking consciousness is followed by a state of high reflex suggestibility characteristic of the indefinite nature of the secondary self. In the hypnoidic state such suggestibility is absent, because another quasi-personality emerges with a more or less definite character, a personality that is inaccessible to direct suggestion. The hypnoidic state, however, is amenable to indirect suggestion. By means of indirect suggestion it is even possible entirely to remove this hypnoidic personality, and have it replaced by another one, which in its turn may be treated in like manner.

The character of the hypnoidic individuality is some outlived phase of the patient's personal life. Such states may also be induced in hypnosis, but then the hypnoidic state is vague and ill defined. More frequently the hypnoidic state may be fully brought about in post-hypnotic or what may be termed hypnonergic states. I could effect such an analogous state in my somnambulic subjects by post-hypnotic suggestion. The difference between the post-hypnotic or hypnonergic and the true spontaneous hypnoidic state consists in the relation of the subject to external impressions. In the hypnonergic state the subject receives external impressions directly and refers them to some external source. He hears, sees, feels, perceives things that happen around him, and frequently carries on very animated conversations on different topics. Even in the case of post-hypnotic negative hallucinations, the patient is still fully alive to other not inhibited sense impressions that reach him from all sides. Quite different is the true hypnoidic state. The sense organs of the patient are closed to the impressions of external stimuli. He does not perceive anything that takes place around him. His environment is that of the past, and in it he lives and moves. Shut up within one of his past lives, he remains insensible to the world of his objective present. If by chance any impressions do reach the subject, they are at once worked into his present hallucinatory life experience. If the patient is touched, squeezed, pricked, he feels nothing at all; he is totally anaesthesic and analgesic, and still within his "vision "he may be extremely sensitive to pain, shiver from cold, complain of fatigue, and undergo tortures of pricking sensations caused by a strong gale blowing icicles into his face. Of such a nature were the visions in the case of Hanna.

The patient hears none of the conversation carried on in his presence. When the patient is spoken to on subjects not directly related to his resurrected life experience, he makes no reply; he simply does not hear. Only when he is addressed on something relating to the experience he is passing through, it is only then that he makes a reply. He does not realize, however, that it is some one else who speaks to him ; his replies to questions are to him either answers to his own thoughts, or sometimes—a case very rare—he seems to converse with some imaginary person within his hypnoidic state.

No suggestions are taken by the hypnoidic personality. It is fully rational in relation to the environment in which it lives. Thus, in one of his hypnoidic states Kev. Thomas C. Hanna lived through a terrible accident that happened to him once. He was on Mount Jewett, Pa. The wind blew high. Lightning lit the sky, thunder crashed overhead. The gale gained strength and became a tempest. Broken branches and trees were falling on all sides. "There is an old woman with a child! "he exclaimed. "Oh, it is terrible ! it is terrible!"he moaned. ""We must run! we must run! I must drag the woman. Thunder! It is terrible! Save the woman ! I am so cold! My heart is so weak! Oh, it is terrible! We must run ! we must run!"To my question whether he knew Miss C., the answer of the hypnoidic personality was highly interesting and instructive. "Don't know her yet —acquainted with her a year later. From Mount Jewett to her is a year."(This was found to be correct.) "When I suggested to him that his friend S. was with him, he laughed me to scorn. "That is impossible !"he exclaimed; "S, is many miles away from here."I asked for the date. He gave the date in which the event took place. "It is August now,"he said. "When I insisted that it was May (the actual time when the vision occurred), the hypnoidic personality became impatient, raised its hand, struck the bed with great force, and exclaimed: "I am sure it is now August. You can not make me crazy! "

All that time the patient was sitting up in his bed, with his eyes firmly shut, blind and deaf to all impressions that had no relation to the "vision."By indirect leading questions this particular personality gradually dwindled away, and lo! a new personality appeared on the scene—a boy personality.

The Rev. Thomas C. Hanna became a boy of thirteen. The scenery changed completely. He was on Umbrella Island. It was sunset, it was "beautiful."He was expected for supper, but he was on the water, rowing and fishing.

On awakening from his hypnoidic state the patient remembered the "vision "very clearly; he could reproduce it, as if it were impressed on his mind in images of fire. He could not recognise the experiences of his vision as events that had taken place in his past life; he did not know that I or any one else conversed with him and led him to give answers ; nor did he remember any of the many statements to my indirect questioning he had made in his hypnoidic state. He could not remember the answers he gave me on the suggestion that his friend S. was with him; he did not know anything of the quarrel we had about the date; nor did he remember anything of the interesting information he gave me about the events of his life, such as the date of his acquaintance with Miss C. He could only remember, and that with extraordinary clearness and distinctness, everything that directly related to the "vision "itself.

Left to itself the hypnoidic personality tends to disappear, to fall back into the undifferentiated mass of moments-consciousness of the subconscious self, for the hypnoidic personality is unstable in its nature. Unstable, however, as the hypnoidic personality is, it is in closer contact with the subconscious life than is the waking self. The hypnoidic personality is in possession of facts, experiences, memories, of which the upper central consciousness is entirely ignorant. Absolute amnesia, where there is full destruction of psychic experience, is the only type of amnesia that may touch the hypnoidic personality; all other forms of amnesia are maladies of the upper self.

The hypnoidal states are of an entirely different nature. They are sudden intrusions of isolated moments-consciousness into the upper regions of the waking personality, and can be induced by post-hypnotic suggestion, as well as by methods of hypnoidization. Like the hypnoidic, the hypnoidal states are outlived experiences, but, unlike the hypnoidic state, they are not outlived personalities. The hypnoidal states are bits, mere fragments of past experiences.

In hypnoidal states past, outlived experiences heave up into the upper consciousness from the depths of the subject's subconscious life. The subject does not welcome these experiences as his own; he does not recognise them as belonging to the stream of his conscious life once lived through; they are volcanic eruptions from the subconscious life.

The hypnoidal differ from the hypnoidic states in four very important points :

1. They can be and usually are artificially induced by the method of hypnoidization. The hypnoidic can not be artificially induced ; they are always spontaneous.

2. The upper consciousness takes direct cognizance of the hypnoidal states in the moment of their appearance. The hypnoidic states are not directly cognized by the upper consciousness; the latter is always absent when the hypnoidic states are present.

3. The experience of hypnoidal states is vague, and tends to disappear from the upper consciousness the next moment after its occurrence. The experience of the hypnoidic state is inscribed on the mnemonic tables of the upper consciousness in letters of fire.

4. While the hypnoidic states form complete systems of experiences, whole personalities, the hypnoidal states are mere bits, chips of past experiences.

In both states, hypnoidic and hypnoidal, we find, however, one common trait, and that is the emergence of moments-consciousness that may be known and recalled, whether directly or indirectly, by the primary self. These experiences, as we pointed out, are not remembered as past; they are not regarded as experiences that had taken place within the former life history of the patient.

The most important element of memory—namely, recognition—is here totally absent; for memory is the reproduction and recognition of one's past conscious experience. Hence, where this recognition element is lacking, there true memory is also absent. The reproduction of past experience without the element of recognition, a condition of mind characteristic of hypnoidic and hypnoidal states in their relations to the upper consciousness, may be termed recognitive amnesia.

In contradistinction to this type of amnesia, there is another one where not only recognition but even the synthesis of reproduction is absent. Such a type may be termed synthetic amnesia.

Irretraceable amnesia may be recognitive or synthetic. The dissociated moment may come and go, may suddenly emerge, to the surprise of the patient, to the upper stream of consciousness, be synthetized, sometimes even recognised, and then be lost again. Such a lapse of memory may be termed simple amnesia.

Where the loss of memory is for events of a certain period, as an hour, a day, a month, or even several years, and where all events before and after that gap can be recalled, then we have that type of amnesia which is characterized as localized amnesia.

If the loss of memory is only for certain systems of events, while other events that happened at the same time can be fully recalled, such a loss is termed systematized amnesia.

When the lost content remains unaltered during the whole course of the disease, the amnesia is stable.

If the amnesia sets on at intervals, it is periodic. If psychic states keep on alternating, each one being completely amnesic for the other, such as is the case in double-consciousness, then the amnesia is alternating.

When the content of memory is continually decreasing, ending at last in a more or less total loss of it, such as we find in general paralysis, then the amnesia \& progressive.

The dissociation in consciousness may be in relation to sensations. The patient experiences the sensation but does not comprehend its meaning. Tliis may be termed sensory or perceptual amnesia. This form of amnesia may be limited to one or two classes of sensations, or may extend to all of them.

If the amnesia is of one sense, it may be called local; if of all of them, total sensory amnesia. Where the dissociation occurs in the motor consciousness or motor centres, the amnesia is motor. This type may be again local or total. If the amnesia is of the whole life experience, as it is in the case of Th. C. H., it may be termed general. If, however, the amnesia is of but a part of life experience, as, for instance, in cases of aphasia, or of localized amnesia, it may be termed special. If the cause of the amnesic state is some intense mechanical stimulus, such as a fall or a blow on the head, the amnesia is traumatic.

Amnesia is toxic when the cause is some extrinsic poison absorbed by the organism, as, for instance, in the case of alcoholic intoxication. Amnesia is autotoxic when the poison that cause the disease is periodically developed by the organism itself, on account of its defective working and imperfect elimination of waste products. Such cases of amnesia may occur in the status epilepticus, in the states of mind that go under the name of psychic equivalent of epilepsy, which are found interspersed in the series of typical epileptic motor attacks that are accompanied by a mental activity that can rise no higher than the most elementary desultory moment-consciousness.

If amnesia is the result of fatigue, of nervous exhaustion, or of the instability of central organization, it may be termed asthenic. Amnesia is emotional or pathematic when the cause of it is an intense emotion. These types of amnesia occur spontaneously in many mental diseases, and can also be produced artificially by hypnotic suggestion. Whether artificial or spontaneous, the mechanism of these types is at bottom the same—it is a disaggregation or disintegration of moments-consciousness.

Thus there are three types of amnesia, if regarded from the standpoint of extensiveness:

1. Reproductive.

2. Irretraceable or disaggregative.

3. Absolute or cytoclastic.

According to intensiveness, there are three types of amnesia:

1. Simple.

2. Recognitive.

3. Synthetic.

According to the lost content, amnesia has six types:

1. General.

2. Special.

3. Localized .

4. Systematized.

5. Sensory location

According to stability or fluctuation of content amnesia has four types:

1. Stable.

2. Periodic.

3. Alternating.

4. Progressive.

Etiologically, or according to cause, there are five types of amnesia:

1. Traumatic.

2. Toxic.

3. Autotoxic.

4. Asthenic.

5. Emotional or pathematic.

A summary of all the principal forms of subconscious states and of all the types of amnesia gives the following table:

Forms of subconscious states:

1. Hypnotic.

2. Somnambulic.

3. Hypnonergic.

4. Hypnoid.

5. Hypnoidic.

6. Hypnoidal.

7. Hypnoleptic. Types of amnesia:

1. Reproductive or recurrent.

2. Irretraceable or disaggregative.

3. Absolute or cytoclastic.

4. Simple .

5. Recognitive.

6. Synthetic.

7. Localized.

8. Systematized.

9. Sensory

11. General.

12. Special.

13. Stable.

14. Periodic.

15. Alternating.

16. Progressive.

17. Traumatic.

18. Toxic.

19. Autotoxic.

20. Asthenic.

21. Emotional

CHAPTER XXIV.
THE CHARACTER OF THE SUBCONSCIOUS SELF.

THE problem that interested me most was to come into closer contact with the subwaking self. What is its fundamental nature ? What are the main traits of its character ? Since in hypnosis the subwaking self is freed from its chains, untrammelled by the shackles of the upper controlling self; since in hypnosis the underground self is more or less exposed to our view, it is plain that experimentation on the hypnotic self will introduce us into the secret life of the subwaking self; for, as we pointed out above, the two are identical. Now I have made all kinds of experiments, bringing subjects into catalepsy, somnambulisms, giving illusions, hallucinations, post-hypnotic suggestions, etc. As a result of my work one central truth stands out clear before my mind, and that is the extraordinary plasticity of the subwaking self. If you can only in some way or other succeed in separating the primary controlling consciousness from the lower one, the waking from the subwaking self, so that they should no longer keep company, you can do anything you please with the subwaking self. You can make its legs, hands, any limb you like, perfectly rigid; you can make it eat pepper for sugar; you can make it drink water for wine ;

feel cold or warm; hear delightful music; feel pain or pleasure; see oranges where there is nothing; nay, you can make it even eat them and feel their taste. In short, you can do with the subwaking self anything you like. The subwaking consciousness is in your power like clay in the hands of the potter. The nature of its plasticity is revealed by its complete suggestibility. Unlike clay, however, it can not be hardened into any permanent and durable form.

I wanted to get an insight into the very nature of the subwaking self; I wanted to make personal acquaintance with it. "What is its personal character?"I asked. How surprised was I when, after close interrogation, the answer came to me that there could possibly be no personal acquaintance with it, for the sub-waking self lacks personality. Under certain conditions a cleavage may occur between the two selves, and then the subwaking self may rapidly grow, develop, and attain the plane of self-consciousness, get crystallized into a person, and give itself a name, imaginary or borrowed from history. But this newly crystallized personality is, as a rule, extremely unstable, ephemeral, shadowy in its outlines, tends to subside, to become amorphous, again and again gets formed, rising to the surface of life, then sinks and disappears for evermore. The two selves blend, and once more form one conscious individuality.

The following account by an automatic writer [35] is extremely interesting from our point of view. I bring the account in full, as I find it of great value.

"The experiment,"writes Mr. A., "was made Easter, 1883, on one day, and, after an interval of a week, continued on three consecutive days. Upon the first day I became seriously interested; on the second puzzled; on the third I seemed to be entering upon entirely novel experiences, half awful, half romantic; upon the fourth the sublime ended painfully in the ridiculous.

"FIRST DAY.

"Ques. Upon what conditions may I learn from the unseen ?

"Ans. My hand immediately moved, though not to a very satisfying issue.

"Q. What is it that now moves my pen ?

"A. Religion.

"Q- What moves my pen to write that answer ?

"A. Conscience.

"Q, What is religion ?

"A. Worship.

"Q- What is worship ?

"A. Wbwbwbwb.

"Q. What is the meaning of w b ?

"A. Win, buy.

"Q. What?

"A. Knowledge). .

"Here I knew the letters which were to follow, and the pen made a sudden jerk, as if it were useless to continue.

"Q. How ?

"A. - — "

We find here the secondary self emerging from its prison, giving unintelligent and unintelligible answers, as one dazzled by the light of day .

"SECOND DAY.

"Ques. "What is man ?

"Ans. Flise.

"Q. What does F stand for ?

"A. Fesi.

« Q. 1 ?

"A. le.

"<?. it

"A Ivy.

"Q. s?

"J.. sir.

"Q. e? "-4. eye.

"' Fesi le ivy sir eye/ "Q. Is this an anagram ? « JL. Yes.

"Q. How many words in the answer ? 11 A. 4. "This was made out as:

* Every life is yes.'"

The secondary self could not stand long the midday light of the waking consciousness, and plunged once more into the depths of the obscure regions, whence it came.

"THIRD DAY.

"Ques. What is man ?

"Ans. Sefi Haslesbli lies.

"Q. Is this an anagram ?

"A. Yes.

"Q. How many words in the answer ?

"A. v (5).

"Q. What is the first word ?

"A. See .

"Q. What is the second word ?

"A. e e e.

"Q. Must I interpret it myself ?

"A. Try.

"Presently I got out:

' Life is the less able.'

"I do not know whether any other interpretation can be given to the letters, but these fulfil the requirements; and the action of the pen, assisting in the process of interpretation, pointing to the letters, accepting these and rejecting those combinations, left no doubt in my mind that I had hit the meaning.

"But now I was so astonished at the apparently independent will and intellect manifested in forming the above anagrams that it was not without something of awe that I put:

"Q. Who art thou ?

"A. Clelia.

"Q. Thou art a woman ?

"A. Yes.

"Q. Hast thou ever lived upon the earth ?

"A. No.

"Q. Wilt thou ?

"A. Yes.

"Q. When ?

"A. Six years.

"Q- Wherefore dost thou then speak with me ?

"A. E if Clelia el.

"I made out, < I Clelia feel.'

"But upon my asking whether this was right Clelia wrote again, thus,

<Eif Clelia el. 20. '

"Q. Is 20 your age ? "A. GO (She was eternal). "Q. Then 20 what ? "A. Words. .
. .

"FOURTH DAY.

"Ques. Wherefore dost thou speak with me ?

"Ans. (Wavy line. Repetition and emphasis): Wherefore dost thou speak with me f

"Q- Wherefore dost thou answer me ?

"A. (Wavy line) Wherefore dost thou answer me f

"Q. Do I answer myself ?

"A. Yes.

"Q. IsCleliahere?

"A. No.

"Q. Who is, then, now here ?

"A. Nobody.

"Q. Does Clelia exist ?

"A. No.

"Q. With whom did I speak yesterday ?

"A. No one.

"#. Why didst thou lie ?

"A. (Wavy line) Why didst thou lie ?

"Q. Do souls exist in another world ?

"jl. M b.

"Q. What does M b mean ?

"A. May be.

"Q' What was the last answer of yesterday again ?

"A. Eif Clelia o el.

"I. e., ' I feel no Clelia.'

"Or the original may have been : ' I Clelia flee.'

"And the 20 meant no, negativing my interpretation .

"My pen now became altogether wild, sometimes affirming and sometimes denying the existence of Cle-lia, and finally performed as follows :

"I wrote ce. and u. c., and placed my pen in the middle. It refused to point to either, but upon my writing 'partly each' above, my pen underlined my words."

This case beautifully illustrates the evolution and dissolution—the birth, life, and death—of the personality acquired by the subwaking self. At first the secondary subwaking self lacked rationality in its answers; soon it gathered round itself more consciousness, intelligence, rationality, and even rose for an instant into the high plane of self-consciousness ; but there it could not maintain itself long, and once more it subsided into the obscure regions of subpersonal life, whence it emerged possessing none the less memory of what had passed before. The subwaking self- of the fourth day is fully justified in saying that Clelia does not exist. Who, then, speaks ? Nobody—that is, no personality, no independent self-conscious being, but only the sub-personal, secondary, subwaking self, an unconscious cerebration, if you please.

And still Clelia did speak, Clelia did exist, there was a self-conscious being that communicated with Mr. A.; but how could the subpersonal self convey the idea that Clelia, the personal being, is not anything apart from itself, from the subwaking self? The sub -

waking self exists, but Clelia—what is she by herself? Nobody, nothing. The subwaking self in the darkness of its impersonality could not grapple with the puzzling problem. Clelia is a reality and still she has no being. Clelia is the subconscious self, and yet the subconscious self which is still in existence is not Clelia. How solve this intricate, perplexing problem? The subpersonal self, by its very nature, could not grasp the situation, and it grew bewildered, and became agitated, and the pen ran riot, now affirming, now denying the existence of Clelia, at last assenting to the significant suggestion "ce. and u. c. —partly each."The subwaking self was helped out from its seemingly insurmountable difficulty.

The subwaking self is devoid of all personal character ; it is both subpersonal and impersonal. And when it attains the plane of self-consciousness and the conditions are favourable to its remaining there it is always roaming about, passing through the most fantastic metamorphoses, assuming with equal ease all kinds of personalities without regard to time, station, sex, or age. In automatic writing and kindred phenomena the subwaking, subpersonal self is now Luther, now Mme. Pompadour, now Mozart, now Charlemagne, now Aristotle, Plato, and now an Indian brave or squaw. With marvellous plasticity, with an unequalled placidity, it assumes indifferently all kinds of character and of person, for it has no individuality. This impersonality of the hypnotic self is clearly revealed in the following hypnotic experiments performed by me in the Pathological Institute of the New York State Hospitals:

Mr. Y. F. was brought by me into a deep hypnotic condition, and a post-hypnotic suggestion of personality metamorphosis was given to him.

Experimenter. I will wake you up and you must write by the aid of the automatic recorder, "I am to become Sidis, and Miss B. (the librarian of the Institute, who was then present at the experiments) will be yourself, Y. F."You will ask her how her health is, how she is getting on with her work. Then you will hypnotize her. You must tell her to sit down in the hypnotic chair, and if she does not want to you must compel her. You must carry out my commands. On awakening, you will forget everything. (Wakes up.)

A few seconds later a sudden change passed over his all being, and he abruptly turned to Miss B. with

"How do you do ? How are you getting on with your work ?"

B. Pretty well.

Subject. Sleep well ?

E. Yes.

Sub. Have dreams ?

B. No.

Sub. Get up early ?

B. Yes.

Sub. How early ?

B. About seven.

Sub. Well, that is better than you used to do. You used to get up at ten.

I then walked up to the subject and addressed him by his name, Y. F. With a wave of his hand and with a half-humourous, half-ironical smile of the man who knows better, he pointed to Miss B., saying, "This is Y. F."

Exp. Pardon me, what is your name ?

Sub. (with a smile). My name is Dr. Sidis,'and —let me see—your name is Miss B. Will you sit down, Miss B. ?

. I did not tell the subject to take me for Miss B., but it seems that by the process of exclusion he had to take me for that lady.

Sub. (turns to Miss B.). Now I am going to hypnotize you.

He leads Miss B. over to the hypnotic chair, but as she does not want to sit down he pushes her down by force. Miss B. laughs and puts her hands over her face.

Sub. Now put your hands down and compose yourself.

Miss B. laughs.

Sub. (impatiently). What are you laughing at? Just concentrate your mind on sleep.

Miss B. continues laughing.

Sub. Now what is the matter ?

Exp. I think Mr. Y. F. does not want to be hypnotized.

Sub. (angrily). I have him under my control; possibly your standing there might interfere and affect him. (Turns to Miss B.) Here, now, don't purse your mouth up like that. (Miss B. still continues laughing.) What is the cause of all this ? You must not allow yourself to get worked up. Sleep, sleep, sleep. (Then suddenly raises her hand to see whether it is cataleptic.)

As the lady began to feel rather uncomfortable, I went up to the subject, passed my hand over his face, and he at once passed into the usual passive somnambulic trance.

Exp. What is your name ?

Sub. Dr. Sidis.

Exp. No, your name is not Sidis, but Y. F. What is your name ?

Sub. Y. F .

Later on, when I asked the subject how he could take me for Miss B., Miss B. for himself, and himself for Sidis, he simply answered : "I felt like being Dr. Sidis, and there I saw Y. F., for some reason or other, dressed in female attire. I took you for Miss B. I did not and could not question myself. I was very angry when you interfered and suggested that Mr. Y. F. did not want to be hypnotized. I felt like showing you out of the room, asking you to mind your own business there in the library room, but then I changed my mind and simply asked you to step aside."

Dr. H. Deady, Chief Associate in Pathology at the Pathological Institute of the New York State Hospital, gives the following account of an experiment in personality metamorphosis performed by me in his presence :

"Mr. Y. F., the subject, a man as to whose health and good character I can fully testify, was hypnotized by Dr. B. Sidis in my presence. Dr. Sidis gave the subject a suggestion that on awakening and hearing four raps he should become myself, Dr. Deady, and that he should take me for himself, for Y. F. The subject was then awakened. For a few minutes he looked perfectly normal; for more than four or five minutes the subject kept up an animated conversation, smoked and joked freely. When the conversation reached its height of animation and interest, Dr. Sidis gave the signal. So faint and indistinct were the raps that they would have entirely escaped my notice had I not known of the suggestion. It seemed to me that the subject did not hear the raps, but he did hear them after all. A moment later a profound change suddenly passed over his face; something was struggling up into his mind. At first Mr. Y. F. looked as if dazed ; his eyes lost their natural lustre and expression, a s

if darkness set on them, as if the mind became enshrouded by a dense cloud. A few seconds later and everything was clear again. The subject looked at me fixedly and smiled. He was myself, Dr. Deady. He assumed my role completely. He began to besiege me with questions—questions which I had put to him when he was in his waking state. Perfectly oblivious to the presence of other people in the room, his whole attention was engrossed by me, whom he evidently took for himself, for Y. F. A few minutes later he excused himself for leaving the room, pleading urgent work in the office. Without attracting his attention, I followed him at a distance. He entered my office, sat down at my desk, but was at a loss what to do. A letter was lying on my desk; he took it, opened it, read it through carefully, was lost in thought for a second or two, as if trying to remember something, but, not succeeding, put the letter back in the envelope. At this turn Dr. Sidis came into the office, and I returned to the Pyschological Laboratory where the experiments were made. Through a telephone that connects this laboratory with the office I had the following conversation with Mr. Y. F.:

"Deady. I wish you would order an ounce of tan-nic acid for me.

"Subject. Who is that ?

"Z. Dr. Y.

"Sub. Who is Dr. Y?

"D. One of the men working in the institute.

"Sub. Who is going to pay for it ?

"D. The office, I suppose.

"Sub. Well, I do not know about that; I'll have to see about it. Where shall I get it ?

"D. Send to any of the druggists.

"Sub. Well, I'll see about that.

"D. Say, there is a man out here—says his name is V. F.—wants to see you.

"Sub. What does he want ?

"D. I do not know.

"Sub. I have no time to bother with him. Tell him to come some other time; tell him to go paint pictures. (The subject is an artist.)

"D. He can't paint.

"Sub. I know that, but I would not tell him so. Tell him to stay where he is, or to go to Jericho. I am busy.

"D. All right. Good-bye.

"Dr. Sidis then induced the subject to return to the room; a young lady was waiting there to make Dr. Deady's (that is, the subject's) acquaintance. When in the room he acted Dr. Deady to life. I say 'acted,' but it was not that; he seemed to feel like Dr. Deady, he was Dr. Deady, and as such he introduced himself to Miss S., who had entered the room during his hypnotic sleep, and whom he had never met nor heard of before. When asked about the institute, the subject began to enlarge on the scope and purpose of the institution, of the pathological work on sunstroke cases done by Dr. Yan Gieson and his associates, and of the knowledge the medical profession really needs. When asked about Mr. V. F. (myself), whose presence he seemed totally to ignore, he gave a merciless and cutting but truthful account of himself, an account which he would otherwise not have given in the presence of a strange young lady. The conversation then turned on hypnotism, and the subject related two of my cases as happening within his medical experience. So true to life, so complete was the subject's mimicry of my per -

sonality, that he almost expressed my inmost thoughts. . . . As the subject happens to live in the same house with me, I availed myself of the opportunity to watch the after-effects of the experiments. Dr. Sidis, it seemed, did not sufficiently remove the suggestions given to the subject during hypnosis. Mr. Y. F. evidently was not in his normal state; something was working in him. When left alone he began to converse with himself; he wanted to know ' who he was not.' Next day the subject was hypnotized again by Dr. Sidis, and the after-effects entirely vanished. Mr. V. F. felt better and happier than ever."

I may add to Dr. Deady's account that before de-hypnotizing the subject I suggested to him that he was Mr. V. F., but that on awakening he would not remember what had transpired during hypnosis. The suggested amnesia did not remove the Deady personality, but simply suppressed it into the region of the subconscious. Hence the after-effects, hence the fact of double personality.

The phenomena of personality-metamorphosis are still clearer revealed in the following experiments :

I hypnotized Mr. A. Fingold and brought him into a deep somnambulic state. I gave him a pencil and paper and asked him to sign his name. He signed it in English. "You are ten years old,"I suggested. The subwaking self instantaneously changed and became a boy of ten. "Sign your name,"I commanded. My friends present at the experiments, and myself, were surprised to see the hand changing its direction, and instead of writing from left to right, started from right to left. The subject signed his name not in English but in the modern rabbinical script used by the Eastern Jews ; the subject knew no other alphabet when he was of that age. His brother, Mr. J. F., who was also present at the seance, wondered at the writing, as it curiously-resembled the actual childish handwriting of the subject.*

"You are a boy of seven. "Write a letter to your father."

This means:

"Papa I want you to come to me. Chaim wants to lick me. AB. FINGOLD."

The following is a faithful reproduction of the subject's writing:

He wrote, instead of "father,"the word "tate "(a word mostly used by Russian Jewish children).

A name in common use among the Russian Jews .

10 years old.

Normal.

The same kind of experiments I repeated on Mr. F. at another seance.

"You are twelve years old. "Write a letter to your father."

The translation of it is:

"DEAR FATHER :

"I ask of you to send me money.

"A. FINGOLD."

And now began a metamorphosis of personalities.

Experimenter. What is your name ?

Subject. Ab. Fingold.

Exp. No, no. Your name is not Fingold. Your name is Sam Finestein. Who are you ? What is your name ?

Sub. Ab. Fingold.

Exp. (in a commanding voice). You are Sam Fine-stein, and you are thirty years old. Who are you ?

Sub. Sam Finestein.

Exp. How old are you ?

Sub. I am thirty years old.

Exp. What is your occupation ?

Sub. I have none for the present. I live on interest.

Exp. Are you married ?

Sub. No.

Exp. (hesitatingly). But I heard you were married.

Sub. No, I am not, and shall never court one unless she be rich.

Exp. (hesitatingly). But, Mr. Finestein, I was told you had two children. Are you a widower ?

Sub. (in an angry tone). I want you to understand that I am not married and never was.

Exp. Have you ever met a man by name of Ab. Fingold ?

Sub. Yes, I think I did.

Exp. Can you tell me anything about him?

Sub. Yery little; I met him but once. If I am no t

mistaken, he is a cigar-maker. He complains of headaches (the subject's disease).

Exp. And how are you?

Sub. Oh, I am well.

Exp. Can you tell me anything more about Ab. Fingold?

Sub. I told you I met him but once.

Exp. Have you met a man by name J. Fingold? (The subject's brother.)

Sub. Yes, I did. Is he not Mr. Ab. Fingold's brother?

Exp. Yes. Can you tell me anything about him?

Sub. People say he is an honest man, but that is all I know of him. He is to me a stranger.

Exp. From what country do you come?

Sub. From Russia.

Exp. How long are you from Russia?

Sub. Fifteen years. (Correct. He came here when he was fifteen years old, and being now thirty, he was just fifteen years from Russia.)

Exp. What is the name of the city you came from?

Sub. Brest-Litovsk. (Correct.)

Exp. Where do you live now?

Sub. 37 Main St., Allston. (A fictitious address. The subject lives in Boston.)

Exp. You are Jacob Aaronson, and you are sixty years old. Who are you?

Sub. Jacob Finestein.

Exp. (emphatically). You are Jacob Aaronson, and you are sixty years old. Who are you?

Sub. Jacob Aaronson.

Exp. How old are you?

Sub. Sixty years .

Exp. What is your business ?

Sub. I retired from business.

Exp. (hesitatingly). Have you any money of your own ?

Sub. You are too inquisitive.

Exp. Are you married ?

Sub. Oh, no, I would not marry again.

Exp. Again ? Have you been married once ?

Sul>. Yes; that' was about forty years ago, but my wife died two years after marriage, and I made up my mind not to marry again. She was a loving wife. I shall go to my grave a widower.

Exp. Would not you like to make your will ?

Sub. I do not expect to die so soon. Although my hairs are gray, still I am strong enough.

Exp. Have you met a man by name Sam Finestein ?

Sub. I think I met him about thirty years ago. (Subject was now sixty, and as Sam Finestein he was but thirty.)

Exp. What do you think of Sam Finestein ? He says he does not want to court any girl unless she is rich.

Sub. You know we have not much to think of such a fellow.

Exp. Have you met one by name Ab. Fingold ?

Sub. Let me see—let me see—let me see (trying hard to recollect). It is a long while since I saw him last—about forty years. (The subject is twenty years of age.)

Exp. Can not you tell me anything about him ?

Sub. I can not tell you anything about him; it is a long while since I met him last. I had no business with him. I met him but once. He did me no harm, nor has he done me any good. 1 8

Exp. Where do you come from ?

Sub. From Russia.

Exp. How long are you from Russia ?

Sub. Forty-five years. (45 -\- 15 = 60.)

Exp. Would you like to tell me the amount of money you possess ?

Sub. What for do you want to know it ?

Exp. It is good to know for the sake of reference— for the sake of business.

Sub. But I do no business.

Exp. (hesitatingly). Still I should like to know.

Sub. (decisively). I shall not tell you. It is rather suspicious. What do you want to know it for ? It is suspicious.

I made him then pass through a whole series of events. I suggested to him he had a poor nephew. He promised to start "the poor fellow "into business—to give him five hundred dollars. He was, however, better than his word, and gave the nephew one thousand dollars. "What can one do with five hundred dollars,"he said.

Exp. (hesitatingly). Would not you like to sign a check on one thousand dollars ?

Sub. (decisively). I shall sign no checks. I give cash money. (He produced from his pocket imaginary money.)

Exp. Would not you like to enter into business, Mr. Aaronson ?

Sub. I worked enough in my life. Let young people do the work.

During the time of his being J. Aaronson he behaved like an old invalid, rocking himself slowly and comfortably, speaking in a low, drawling tone, and assuming an air of superior knowledge and experience in his conversation with his nephew, telling the latter, "You talk like a young man."

Exp. What is your name ? Who are you ?

Sub. Jacob Aaronson.

Exp. (authoritatively). No, you are not Aaronson! Who are you ?

Sub. Sam Finestein.

Exp. (authoritatively). No, you are not Finestein! Who are you ?

Sub. Ab. Fingold.

I gave him now a post-hypnotic suggestion that after awakening, when he will see me rub my hands, he will become Sidis and take me for Fingold. I woke him up. He felt all right; spoke to his brother. I began to rub my hands. Something began to struggle within him. He looked at me hard, fixedly. I went on rubbing my hands. He rose from his chair and became Sidis, addressing me as Fingold. It would take up too much space to describe all he did and said; I can only say that he mimicked me to perfection. My friends could not restrain themselves from laughing. He then proceeded to hypnotize me, doing it in a careful and guarded way. He rubbed my head, telling me: "You have no headaches—the pain is gone. I took away the pain. You feel well, comfortable, cheerful,"and so on. He then took a chair, placed it near mine, sat down, took my hand in his, and said : "I give you five minutes to sleep. The sleep will refresh you, and you will wake up strong, healthy, and in good spirits."He took out his watch and looked at the time. At the end of the five minutes he gave me again the suggestion of feeling well, etc., arid commanded me to count till five, and wake up. I did not count. He raised his voice, and in a tone full of authority commanded ,

"Count till five, and wake up!"I counted till five, but did not open my eyes. "Wake up! wake up fully!"he urged. I kept my eyes closed. He felt my pulse; put his ear to my chest. "Be quiet! Be quiet! "he soothed me. Then suddenly in a loud, impressive voice, emphasizing each word, he authoritatively commanded, "Count till five, and wake up!"I counted, and opened my eyes. All the time I watched him closely from the corner of my eye; his face bore an air of unrivalled gravity. Mr. Fingold's subwaking self assumed the Sidis-personality, and for the time being it was Sidis.

I went behind his chair, passed my hand over his face, and simply said, "Sleep!"He closed his eyes and passed into a passive state.

Exp. What is your name ? Who are you ?

Sub. Dr. Sidis.

Exp. No, you are not Dr. Sidis ! Who are you ?

Sub. Jacob Aaronson.

Exp. No, you are not Jacob Aaronson! Who are you ?

/Sub. Sam Finestein.

Exp. No, you are not Sam Finestein! Who are you ?

Sub. Ab. Fingold.

When Mr. Fingold awoke he did not remember anything. "I slept a long time,"he remarked. I then put my hand to his forehead and told him, "Try hard, you can remember everything."A flood of facts and items poured into his consciousness.

In the presence of two Boston High School instructors, Mr. S. and Mr. E., I made similar experiments on their former pupil Mr. W. Mr. W. was now a boy of six; now a boy of twelve; now a Mr. Thomas Davis, a labourer in a sugar factory, thirty .years of age, married, and having two children; now a teacher of rhetoric; now Mr. E. The change from one personality to the other was instantaneous, and the acting was lifelike. The subwaking self actually passed through the experience of each personality it assumed; it lived that particular life, it was that personality.

When Mr. W. awoke he remembered everything. It was a dream. He remembered how he worked nights in the sugar factory, remembered the looks of the factory. He did work there. He remembered the house in which he lived with his wife and the two "kids,"as he named his children. He remembered he was a teacher of rhetoric examining and censuring his idle class, and that he was Mr. E.

The dreaming, subpersonal, subwaking self is chameleon in its nature ; it is almost absolutely plastic ; it can get metamorphosed into all kinds' of .beings, it can assume indifferently and instantaneously all sorts of characters and personalities, for it has no personality of its own. Once a personality is assumed, the sub-waking self mimics it to perfection. Quick as lightning, like an evil genius, the subwaking self gets into possession of all ideas and clusters of associations that relate to that assumed personality, embodies, incarnates itself in them, and struts about a different person.

Subpersonal and impersonal as the subwaking self is, it has a rich store of memories, and as it gets crystallized into a new person it takes up memories adapted to that assumed personality. Thus, Mr. F. was Sam Finestein, thirty years of age; he was fifteen years fcom Russia, because he left that country when he was about fifteen years old. As Jacob Aaronson he was sixty years of age ; he was forty-five years from Russia, and again for the same reason.

Recently I suggested to A. Fingold a fictitious personality of a Thomas McYane. He told me he was Irish; came from Dublin; was a bricklayer; was a devout Catholic; went to church every Sunday; spoke of the "Holy Pope "in terms of reverence and awe; upbraided his sons for being great drunkards. The subwaking self is impersonal, and still it possesses memory of all the personalities it has assumed. In the case of Mr. F., as well as in the case of my other subjects, the emphatic denial of each subsequent personality brings immediately to light the precedent one. The personalities lived through form a chain of contiguous memories. The subwaking self seems to know only one kind of association—that of contiguity .

CHAPTER XXV.
SUBCONSCIOUSNESS AND INSANITY.

BEFORE we proceed to sum up the characteristics of the subconscious self I think it would be well to show of what importance the phenomenon of posthypnotic suggestion in general, and those of transformation of personality in particular, are in relation to many forms of insanity. There is, for instance, a form of mental alienation known under the name of "insistent ideas." From some source unknown to the patient an idea rises into consciousness with a persistency that can not be overcome. The idea haunts the patient like a ghost. A concrete case will bring this disease clearly before the mind of the reader.

A young man of intelligence, of good education, and free from hereditary tendency to neurotic affections, was pursuing his studies at college, when one day he heard his companions talking of the mysterious fatality connected with the number thirteen. An absurd idea took possession of his mind. "If the number thirteen is fatal," he thought to himself, "it would be deplorable if God were thirteen." "Without attaching any importance to this conception, he could not prevent himself from thinking of it continually, and at each instant he accomplished mentally an act which consisted in repeating to himself "God thirteen." He began to attach a certain cabalistic value to this formula, and attributed to it a preservative influence. "1 know perfectly well," he said, "that it is ridiculous that I should think myself obliged to imagine ' God thirteen ' in order to save myself from being thirteen," but nevertheless the intellectual act was repeated without ceasing. Very soon he began to apply the same mysterious word to eternity, to the infinite, and similar ideas. His life was thus passed in mentally saying, "God thirteen ! The infinite thirteen! Eternity thirteen ! "The patient was fully aware of the absurdity of the idea, but still that idea continued to rise from the depth of his mind and insert itself into all his mental operations.

In impulsive insanity we meet with a similar state of mind. A seemingly unaccountable impulse suddenly seizes on the mind of the patient, an impulse which is sometimes so overwhelming that restraint is simply unthinkable. No sooner does the impulse come into consciousness than it works itself out with fatal necessity. It is a kind of emotional automatism. A young man, for instance, at the sight of a black silk dress is suddenly possessed by an impulse to ruin silk dresses, and he is bound to carry out his work of destruction whenever he is confronted with a dress of that material. "I was altogether excited by the sight of that handsome silk dress, and it was impossible for me to resist. I do not know why the idea ever came into my mind."A young lady at the sight of a bare shoulder is suddenly seized by the impulse to bite, and she straightway sinks her teeth into the flesh of her victim. [36]

"E. D.,"writes Dr. Stearns, "lias been insane for several months. . . . He appeared to improve, when on one occasion, while he was standing in his room, his attendant advanced toward him with the intention of passing, when the patient suddenly drew back and struck the attendant a blow which brought the latter to the floor. Immediately after it was over the patient apologized, and said he was very sorry and quite ashamed of himself; he could not tell what had led him to strike, especially his attendant, with whom he was in the most pleasant relations, but the concept suddenly flashed upon and filled his mind as he saw him approach, and the impulse to strike became irresistible."*

Pyromania, or the impulse to incendiarism, kleptomania, or the impulse to steal, homicidal or suicidal impulses—all of them belong to that peculiar form of mental alienation that may be characterized as impulsive insanity.

Whence rise those insistent ideas, those imperative conceptions, those mysterious, unaccountable impulses ? We can not ascribe these phenomena to the mechanism of associative processes ; we can not say that some of the links in the chain of association became abnormally predominant, because those impulses are felt emphatically as having no connection with the association process going on in the consciousness of the patient. Those impulses are psychical parasites on the patient's consciousness. Ideas, impressions implanted in the subconscious self, when accidentally dissociated from ike upper personality, rise to the periphery of consciousness as insistent ideas, imperative concepts, and uncontrollable impulses of all sorts and descriptions. In hypnotic, and especially in post-hypnotic, suggestion we hold the key to all forms of conceptual and impulsive insanity.

When my subject, Mr. A. Fingold, was in a deep hypnosis and his subconsciousness was laid bare, I suggested to him that when he will wake up and hear a knock he shall drive away his brother and Mr. H. L. from the sofa on which they were sitting and lie down there. When Mr. Fingold woke up and the signal was given, he rushed to the sofa with such impetuosity that his brother was frightened and left the place at once. Mr. H. L. was rather tardy in his retreat. The subject angrily caught hold of his arm and pushed him away with such violence that poor Mr. H. L. flew to the opposite wall. The subject then stretched himself out on the sofa and felt satisfied. As in the case of impulsive insanity, the suggested impulse set on suddenly and was enacted with a like emotional automatism.

Experiments of like nature I have also performed on other subjects, and « with like results. The suggested ideas buried in the depths of the subconsciousness frequently rise to the surface of the subject's active life, and are realized with all the vehemence and fatality of an irresistible insane impulse. The post-hypnotic suggestion may manifest itself in a different form. Instead of a sudden onset it may develop slowly, grow, and finally become uncontrollable. I hypnotized Mr. Y. F., and suggested to him that a few minutes after awakening he should sit down on Miss B.'s chair ; that if she would not like to leave he should make her go. A few minutes after awakening Mr. Y. F. turns to Miss B., whose acquaintance he made at the beginning of the experiments, with the following request :

F". F. May I sit on your chair ?

B. Why do you want my chair ? There are other chairs in the room; can't you take one of them ?

V. "Well, you take this one, will you ?

B. No; I am very well satisfied with this one. Won't that one do you just as well ?

V. No. I wish you would give it to me—won't you?

B. No.

V. I think that one over there will be much more comfortable. I would rather have this one.

B. Why can't you let me sit here ?

V. I can, but I would like to have the chair. I could throw you out, but that would not be exactly square ; but at the same time I want that chair.

B. Won't any other chair answer ?

V. Yes, any other chair would answer my purpose just as well.

B. Have you any claim to it ?

V. No, no claim or right, but I want it. Let me have it, won't you ? You just like to tease me.

B. Why do you think so ? To keep one's chair is not teasing.

V. You see, it works this way : you don't want the chair, and you know I want it, but you won't let me have it, and that amounts to teasing.

B. Why do you want it ?

V. No reason. I simply want it.

B. That is very little reason.

V. Yes, very little. You don't simply want to keep what you have; you don't want to give it to me. That is your reason, is it not ?

B. I am more comfortable here.

V. You are only teasing me. I can see your eye s

twinkle. You look at Dr. Sidis and see what he thinks about it.

JS. I won't give you this chair.

V. Is that your only reason ?

B. What is your reason ?

V. I have no reason. I have only a sneaking sort of desire to sit down in the chair.

The desire kept on growing. The subject pleaded for a seat in the chair with more and more urgency. He must have this particular chair, happen what may. The desire became an irresistible impulse. Mr. V. F. took a piece of cord, tied it round the much-longed-for chair, and exclaimed: "Now I will show you a modern Stonewall Jackson. If you don't get up I shall pull you down. I'll count three."He counted one, two, and when he came to three he gave a strong pull, and pulled out the chair from under Miss B. and sat down on it in great haste.

The evolution of the impulse was here a gradual one. Each rebuff served only to increase the intensity of the impulse, until at last the impulse became irresistible and the craved-for object was taken by main force. Thus we see that insistent ideas, imperative conceptions, and insane impulses in general work through the mechanism of the subconscious. An idea sunk into the disaggregated subconsciousness, like a post-hypnotic suggestion, struggles up as an insane impulse.

The phenomena of the subconscious give us an insight into the nature of paramnesia. Paramnesia, or illusions of memory, may be divided into positive or additive and negative or subtractive. In positive or additive paramnesia the patient recognises a new perception as having taken place within his former experience. The patient meets strangers as old familiar acquaintances. Thus Jensen reports the case of a patient complaining to him: "Doctor, I feel so very strange to-day. When I stand like this and look at you, then it seems to me as if you had stood there once before, and as if everything had been just the same, and as if I knew what was coming."

An interesting case of paramnesia is reported by Dr. Arnold Pick in the Archiv fur Psychiatric for 1876. An educated man who seems to have understood his disease, and who himself gave a written description of it, was seized at the age of thirty-two with a singular mental affection. If he was present at a social gathering, if he visited any place whatever, if he met a stranger, the incident with all the attendant circumstances appeared so familiar that he was convinced of having received the same impression before, of having been surrounded by the same persons or the same objects, under the same sky and the same state of weather. If he undertook any new occupation, he seemed to have gone through with it at some previous time and under the same conditions. The feeling sometimes appeared the same day, at the end of a few moments or hours, sometimes not till the following day, but always with perfect [37] distinctness.

Sander brings the case of an invalid who, upon learning of the death of a person whom he knew, was seized with an indefinable terror, because it seemed to him that he knew of the event before. "It seemed to me that at some time previous, while I was lying here in this same bed, X. came to me and said, ' Miiller is dead.' I replied, ' Miiller has been dead for some time.'"

Similar cases of paramnesia occur also in normal life. Prof. Royce, in an interesting article, Hallucinations of Memory and Telepathy, * called attention to "a not yet recognised type of instantaneous hallucination of memory, consisting in the fancy at the very moment of some exciting experience that one has expected it before its coming."According to Prof. Royce, many facts of telepathy recorded by Gourney in his book The Phantasms of the Living belong to this last type of paramnesia.

In subtractive paramnesia, on the contrary, the patient has a false memory as to an event that had actually taken place in his experience. He is sure that the event has never occurred to him. Thus Wernicke brings the case of a patient who assaulted a public official and afterward could not be convinced that he had ever done anything like it, although he remembered well everything that happened at that time.

How shall we explain these interesting phenomena of paramnesia ? We can not possibly agree with Ribot, who thinks that paramnesia is due to the fact that the memorial image evoked by the present perception is more vivid than the perception itself, and the result is that the present experience as the weaker and fainter one is considered a copy of the more vivid memorial image.

It does not require a deep insight to see the weakness of such a forced explanation. First of all, Ribot is wrong in identifying pastness with faintness. A faint perception is not a past perception. Second, even if we accept the proposition that faintness gives the feeling of pastness, Ribot is still wrong in his explanation.

He simply did not analyze well the phenomena of paramnesia. In paramnesia the present perception has about it all the vivid feeling of present-ness ; what is added to it is the feeling that the perception has been experienced formerly. Were Ribot's account the true one, the present perception would not have been felt as present, but as past, and the evoked memorial image instead would have been felt as present, which is not the case. Besides, such a process would give rise not to paramnesia but to mere illusion. The phenomena of paramnesia are due to a disaggregation effected within the consciousness of the patient.

The disaggregated subconsciousness, on account of its wider range of sensibility, or on account of the temporary inhibition of the upper consciousness, gets the perception first, and after some appreciable interval it is transmitted with a feeling of pastness to the upper consciousness, which by this time already has its own direct perception. The present perception of the upper consciousness is then recognised — recognised as familiar, as having already been before within the experience of the patient. This transmitted message coming from the secondary to the primary self may be more or less instantaneous, or it may come some time after, as in the interesting case of the patient reported by Dr. Pick.

Subtractive paramnesia admits of still easier explanation if regarded from the standpoint of the subconscious. The disaggregated secondary consciousness possesses itself of certain details in experience that never reached the primary consciousness. The patient therefore with full right asserts that he is sure that the given details had never occurred within his self-conscious experience .

Subtractive paramnesia is analogous to the phenomenon of negative hallucination which occur in post-hypnotic or hypnonergic states. Turning now to demonomania and paranoia, we once more encounter the underground working of the subconscious self. In paranoia we find that an insistent idea or an imperative concept, often accompanied by illusions and hallucinations, and detached from the main stream of consciousness, gets inserted into the associative processes of the primary self. The idea soon gathers round itself clusters of other ideas and forms a system tinged with emotional colour. The insistency and uncontrollableness of this slowly evolving disaggregated cluster give it all the characteristics of an external reality. Hence we have a more or less stable delusion of a systematized order. Ideas and impulses coming from the disaggregated subconscious self are projected outward, and ascribed to the activity of an external agency. Hence the ideas of persecution by hidden, mysterious enemies.

With the evolution of that subconscious cluster the primary self is weakened, a new specious personality is formed within the depths of the subconscious, a personality which rises to the surface of consciousness and occupies the whole field of mental vision, the old self existing in the background as memory. Hence we have the last stage of paranoia, known as the stage of transformation of personality.

To give the reader an idea of the mental malady known as paranoia, I select two cases from the reports sent to me for the Pathological Institute of the

* Subtractive paramnesia is a form of amnesia. For a fuller discussion of amnesia see Chapters XXI-XXIII .

York State Hospitals by Dr. Spellman, of Manhattan Hospital, Ward's Island, New York :

"Patient, B. F. Hunter, was admitted in 1895, aged thirty-seven. Memory perfect. He gives a full account of himself up to the year 1892. 'In 1892,' says the patient, ' I lived with Mr. C. Mr. C. went to the country, and I was to look after the place. One hot summer day when I was asleep a sharp, distinct voice called me. I went to look for the caller, but there was none outside. There was a man who lived in the house and who took care of the property. He would leave in the morning and come back at night. I asked him if he had called during the day, and he said he had not. At night I went down to my house and said to my wife: "Something very queer has happened. I heard a sharp, distinct voice call me, and when I looked out of the window I saw no one."Another time, about half past twelve in the night, I heard again a sharp, distinct voice call me, "Ben! Ben!"and when I looked out of the window I could see no one. This was the third time I had been called.

"'During Cleveland's second term, in 1892, one night while I lay in bed I saw Grover Cleveland in the Executive Mansion. Some other party stood behind me and said to me, "What do you see ?"I said, "I see Grover Cleveland.""Go and tell him,"said the person behind me, "that he will be the next President of the United States."About the 8th of March I sent a long letter to Mr. Cleveland. I don't know exactly what I said, but here are a few of the words: "On a certain day of the month God notified me to tell you that you would be the next President of the United States, and so you are. When God tells his servant to tell a man such things as I have told 1 9

you there is something behind it unknown to human beings."

"' The next year, 1894, I wrote letters to all the governors of the States to the following effect: "It is hereby known to all nations, people, and things that there is a prophet among the people with bad tidings from God. Yery respectfully, B. F. Hunter."

"* Last June, 1896, it was revealed to me that I was the prophet Nebuchadnezzar.' "

The other case reported by Dr. Spellman is also characteristic of paranoia, and points to the subconscious source whence the delusion originates.

"Solomon Monroe. Admitted January 6, 1897, aged thirty-four; nativity, Germany ; salesman; Protestant ; single ; temperate. No hereditary tendencies are known to exist. The cause of attack is supposed to be lack of food. The patient states emphatically that he is Jesus Christ, and his general demeanour corresponds to his statement. He states as follows: ' I have told you that I am Jesus Christ. I have been Jesus Christ since my birth. I have not always known it, but found it out about six weeks before I came here. I received my proper enlightenment. I was educated in the common schools of Germany. Since coming to New York, about four and a half years ago, I have followed out a religious train of thought, teaching Bible classes, etc. I had hope; birthmarks on my body-viz., scars on my face and sign of a cross on my forehead and hands— confirmed my belief. I was anointed on my head. This anointment came during the night. Later the revelations came through insight and ears. I have them now days and nights. God my Father holds constant communication with me. I am the same Christ treated of in the Holy Word, and this is my second coming. Father, Father, the Holy Spirit has always been within me.' The patient eats and sleeps well, and aside from his general exaltation of demeanour appears as other people."

The phenomena of personality-metamorphosis in hypnotic and post-hypnotic or hypnonergic states reproduce on a smaller scale the condition of paranoia. We find in them the growth of systematized delusions culminating in the phenomenon of personality-metamorphosis. The reader is already acquainted with these facts from our previous experiments, and there is no use for me to bring here more of them. One thing is clear from the experiments, and that is the fact that the phenomena of personality metamorphosis are due to a specious parasitic personality formed within the depth of the disaggregated, whether by hypnotization or by disease—subconscious self. Dissociation of the subconscious is a requisite of paranoia *

Prof. Josiah Royce, in his remarkable paper on Some Observations on the Anomalies of Self -Consciousness, f maintains that self-consciousness is social consciousness, and whenever the derangement is in the mass of ideas involving social relationship there necessarily happens a transformation of personality. That may be. But Prof. Royce must still explain the fact why this change in the social consciousness should be. [38]

The theory of Ribot, that metamorphosis of personality is due to a fundamental change in common sensibility, is more fanciful than it is commonly supposed, for that fundamental change remains yet to be proved. There may be a change in common sensibility without a transformation of personality, and also a transformation of personality without a change in common sensibility. Besides, Ribot's theory can not account for the phenomena of coexistent double or multiple personality.

felt as induced by mysterious revelations, uncontrollable, heavenly inspirations, and the activity of hidden agencies. How does it happen that an uncontrollable element, a "sort of non-ego,"is formed within "the ego "of the patient ? How do insistent ideas, imperative conceptions, irresistible impulses, seize on the consciousness of the patient ? What is the source of the strange elements out of which paranoia evolves ? This source is the disaggregated subconsciousness. [39]

When my work was already complete Prof. James called my attention to the recent work of Wernicke, Grundriss der Psychiatric, f in which the author discusses the phenomena of paranoia. It is interesting to observe that Dr. C. Wernicke is so near to the solution of the problem and still he does not see it in its full light. He characterizes paranoia as a "sejunction "of consciousness; he tells us that in the state of paranoia the patient is vexed by what Wernicke calls "autochthonic ideas "—ideas that arise from the depth of the patient's "sejuncted "mind, and which the patient projects outside him. I heartily agree with Dr. Wernicke, and I am glad to find that the work of such a great physiologist and psychiatrist falls in the same line with my own investigations. What, however, Dr. Wernicke does not see is the full meaning of "sejuncted consciousness,"the fact that paranoia is essentially a diseased hypnoidic state, a pathological condition of the subconscious self. The subconscious self must not be conceived as any distinct being; it is rather a diffused consciousness of any strength of intensity with a content rich and varied.

The subconscious, as we have pointed out, is impersonal. Occasionally, however, it reaches the plane of self-consciousness, but then soon subsides again into its former impersonal obscurity. The subconscious self may become crystallized into a personality, but this personality is ephemeral, transient in its nature. Suppose, now, that the subconscious or secondary self is easily dissociated from the primary self or conscious personality ; suppose, further, that within the bosom of the subconscious a new personality is in the process of formation— a personality no longer of an evanescent character, but of a stable nature—we shall then have a case of decomposition of personality. The newly forming parasitic personality will again and again obtrude itself on the primary consciousness, and time and again it will be beaten back into its subconscious obscurity. The patient will then consider himself as having a devil within him, a demon that fights and tempts his honest personality. If the parasitic personality grows in strength or the primary personality is weakened the patient may regard himself as double—the two personalities are of equal rank. It is not, however, only one personality, but two, three, and even more coexistent personalities may be formed within the womb of the subconscious. "We have, then, the cases of the mental malady known under the name of demonoinania.

Demonomania is a special form of paranoia; it is a decomposition of personality; it is the formation of new personalities within the depths of the subconscious. The patient claims to be possessed by a demon. The evil spirit sometimes recounts what he did on earth, and what he has done since he left it for the infernal regions. The attack throws the patient into a fury of excitement, into violent convulsions. In the presence of a stranger, especially of a priest, the violence of the convulsions is greatly increased. When the crisis is over the patient looks about with a somewhat astonished air, and returns to the work in which he was engaged at the beginning of the fit. The patient does not remember what he had said or done during the attack. In very rare cases, where there is memory, the patient asserts: "I know well that he (the devil) has said so, or done so and so, but it was not I. If my mouth has spoken, if my hand has struck, it was he who made me speak and caused the blows."The patient is sometimes possessed not by one demon, but by many demons. The patient feels and hears them moving in his body.

S., forty years of age, is devoured by two demons who have taken up their abode in her haunches and come forth through her ears. Devils have made several marks upon her person, and her heart is daily displaced. She shall never die, though the devil may tell her to go and drown herself. She has seen the two devils by which she is possessed. They are cats, one of which is yellow and white, and the other black. She puts tobacco, wine, and particularly grease, upon her head and in her ears, to exorcise the devil. She walks constantly with naked feet in fair and rainy weather, and while walking picks up whatever comes in her way. She mislays her clothing ; eats largely. She sleeps not; is filthy, emaciated, and her skin very, much sunburnt. There is no coherence in the system of ideas that constantly occupies her mind.

A young man at Charenton has a dracq in his abdomen. The dracq or destiny enters his head, tortures him in a thousand ways during the day,'and particularly in the night addresses and threatens him. If I ask this unfortunate young man what this dracq may be, "I know nothing about it,"he replies, "but it is a destiny that has been imposed upon me, and everything has been done to deliver me from it, but without success."*

Prof. James, in his article, Notes on Automatic Writing, f brings, a very interesting case of personality or ego decomposition akin to demonomania, or demoniacal possession. The case is reported by Dr. Ira Barrows, of Providence. The record begins in the nineteenth year of the patient's age, and continues for several years. It runs as follows:

"September 17, I860.—Wild with delirium. Tears her hair, pillow-cases, bedclothes, bath sheets, nightdress, all to pieces. Her right hand prevents her left hand, by seizing and holding it, from tearing out her hair, but she tears her clothes with her left hand and teeth.

"29th. —Complains of great pain in right arm, more and more intense when suddenly it falls down by her side. She looks at it in amazement. Thinks it belongs to someone else; positive it is not hers. Sees her right arm drawn around her spine. Cut it, prick it, do what you please to it, she takes no notice of it. Complains of great pain in the neck and back, which she now calls her shoulder and arm; no process of reasoning can convince her to the contrary. To the present time, now nearly five years, the hallucination remains firm. She believes her spine is her right arm, and that her right arm is a foreign object and a nuisance. She believes it to be an arm and a hand, but treats it as if it had intelligence, and might keep away from her. She bites it, pounds it, pricks it, and in many ways seeks to drive it from her. She calls it ' Stump,' ' Old Stump.' Sometimes she is in great excitement and tears, pounding Old Stump. Says Stump has got this or the other that belongs to her. The history of September is her daily and nightly history till October 25th.

"November 12th. —From eleven to twelve at night sits up, apparently asleep, and writes with her paper against the wall. After she wakes seems to be unconscious of what she has written.

"From November 20th to January 1, 1861, raving delirium; pulls her hair nearly all out from the top of her head. The right hand protects her against the left as much as possible.

"February 1st to 11th. —Under the influence of magnetism writes poetry ; personates different persons, mostly those who have long since passed away. When in the magnetic state, whatever she does and says is not remembered when she comes out of it. Commences a series of drawings with her right paralyzed hand, Old Stump. Also writes poetry with it. Whatever Stump writes, or draws, or does, she appears to take no interest in; says it is none of hers, and that she wants nothing to do with Stump or Stump's. I have sat by her bed and engaged her in conversation, and drawn her attention in various ways, while the writing and drawing has been uninterrupted.

"March, 1861. —She became blind.

"January 4,1862. —Is still blind; sees as well with eyes closed as open ; keeps them closed much of the time. Draws in the dark as well as in the light. Writes poetry chiefly with the right hand, and often while it is dark. The handwriting differs greatly in different pieces.

"January 10th. —When her delirium is at it height, as well as at all other times, her right hand is rational, asking and answering questions in writing; giving directions ; trying to prevent her tearing her clothes; when she pulls out her hair it seizes and holds her left hand. When she is asleep it carries on conversation; writes poetry; never sleeps; acts the part of a nurse as far as it can; pulls the bedclothes over the patient, if it can reach them, when uncovered; raps on the headboard to awaken her mother (who always sleeps in the room) if anything occurs, as spasms, etc.

"January, 1863. — At night and during her sleep Stump writes letters, some of them very amusing; writes poetry, some pieces original. Writes Hasty Pudding, by Barlow, in several cantos, which she had never read ; all correctly written, but queerly arranged —e. g., one line belonging in one canto would be transposed with another line in another canto. She has no knowledge of Latin or French, yet Stump produces the following lines:

"Sed tempus recessit, and this was all over, Cum illi successit, another gay rover; Nam cum navigaret in his own cutter, Portentum apparet, which made them all flutter.

"Et horrid us anguis which they behold, Haud dubio sanguis within them ran-cold; Tringinta pedes his head was upraised, Et corporis sedes in secret was placed.

"Sic serpens manebat, so says the same joker, Et sese ferebat as stiff as a poker; Tergum fricabat against the old lighthouse, Et sese liberabat of scaly detritus.

"Tune plumbo percussit thinking he hath him, At serpens exsiluit full thirty fathoms, Exsiluit mare with pain and affright, Conatus abnare as fast as he might .

"Neque ille secuti ? no, nothing so rash, Terrore sunt muti he'd made such a splash; Sed mine adierunt the place to inspect, Et squamas viderunt, the which they collect.

"Quicumque non credat and doubtfully rails, Adlocum accedat, they'll show him the scales; Quas, sola trophea, they brought to the shore; Et causa est ea, they couldn't get more.

"Stump writes both asleep and awake, and the writing goes on while she is occupied with her left hand in other matters. Ask her what she is writing:

she replies, ' I am not writing; that is Stump writing. I don't know what he is writing. I don't trouble myself with Stump's doings.' Reads with her book upside down, and sometimes when covered with the sheet. Stump produces two bills of fare in French.

"Upon this one subject of her right arm she is a monomaniac. Her right hand and arm are not hers. Attempt to reason with her, and she holds up her left arm and says: ' This is my left arm. I see and feel my right arm drawn behind me. You say this Stump is my right arm. Then I have three arms and hands.' In this arm the nerves of sensation are paralyzed, but the nerves of motion preserved. She has no will to move it. She has no knowledge of its motion. This arm appears to have a separate intelligence. When she sleeps, it writes or converses by signs. It never sleeps ; watches over her when she sleeps ; endeavours to prevent her from injuring herself or her clothing when she is raving. It seems to possess an independent life."

Prof. James, -who is in possession of the full record, adds "that Old Stump used to write to Miss W. in the third person as Anna. "

Instead of being possessed by an evil spirit, as is usually the rule in Catholic countries, this patient was possessed by a good spirit, who took care of the patient and watched over her, and who, like spirits in general, claimed to be clairvoyant. This good spirit was probably a peculiarly crystallized personality formed of the sane remnants of the patient's subconscious self.

In the Journal of Nervous and Mental Diseases * Dr. Irving C. Rosse describes the following interesting case of triple personality :

"M. L., age thirty-five; brasier ; single ; nativity, Connecticut; education, common school ; religion, Roman Catholic. No hereditary or atavistic antecedents of note. His habits from earliest manhood have been of a kind that it would be charitable to designate simply as irregular. Alcoholic, nicotinic, and venereal excesses have been followed by persistent masturbation and constant erotic tendency.

"Nothing unusual occurred in his life until about 1884, when he got to drinking, became nervous, sleepless, and finally had mania a potu, with a series of epileptiform convulsions. His physicians prescribed more whisky and a hypodermic of morphine, which did not quiet him altogether, and while lying on the bed a ' picture form' appeared on the wall and gradually assumed the form of Lucifer, whose voice issued forth, saying, 'Who has hold of your blood — God, or the devil ?' (the beginning of the delusional state as near as can be ascertained). Leaping from the bed, he ran to a priest's house for protection from the Evil One. Subsequently was sent to a private asylum for four weeks; afterward under asylum treatment on three different occasions, about three years in all; finally, escaping and getting drunk, was arrested for using profane language on the street, and spent four weeks in jail. Regaining his liberty, worked as porter, Lucifer still pursuing him, but not so troublesome as formerly. On speaking to a priest about the delusion, the patient was advised to stop drink. Shortly after went to New York, where he kept up his bad habits.

At length returned to his home in Connecticut, insulted his mother, sister, and a young woman visitor, owing to which erotic conduct he was compelled to quit the paternal roof, ultimately bringing up in Boston, where he enlisted in the Marine Corps. This last act was voluntary, and not the outcome of Lucifer's instigation as were the preceding acts, especially those of a criminal or sinful nature; but when asked by an examining officer if there had been anything the matter with him that would tend to disqualify him for military sendee, Lucifer spoke up and said ' No.' After enlisting he kept up his bad habits. He was transferred to "Washington, where his erotic habits and eccentric conduct, particularly his speaking aloud to himself and gesticulating wildly while communing with Lucifer, attracted the attention of officers and men, and led to his being sent to a hospital.

"M. L. speaks of himself as an innocent person who is controlled by a spirit whom he calls ' the young man,' and who in his turn is under the influence of Lucifer, or, at any rate, is engaged in a continual struggle with the latter for supremacy in controlling the actions of L. The young man abuses himself sexually at times, but L. is not responsible for these actions. He does not see Lucifer, but hears him talking and roaring like a lion when opposed and angered. Lucifer tell s

him to kill the writer or other person finding out L.'s business, but he resists that advice.

"The patient is generally well conducted, and when not assisting at work about the ward will go to a secluded place, where he can be heard upbraiding Lucifer in a loud tone for attempting to control his speech and actions against his will, and tempting him to do things that he knows to be improper. The patient dwells a great deal on the importance of religious duties, earnestly wishes to comply with the rules of the Church, and believes that Lucifer can finally be expelled or chased out by a species of exorcism.

"Patient's memory is fair as regards dates, but he is indifferent to surroundings and to recent occurrences, political or other. Knew when Mr. Cleveland was President; don't know who is now and don't care, his only concern being to get his personality out of trouble, as he feels that he has to answer to God for being the cause of them. For the past six years he has been in league with Lucifer to ' down' L., but for the last six months he has endeavoured to give up his dealings with Lucifer and to assist L. to return to God. He, as the 'young man,' wants to become L.'s good angel. Formerly he was L.'s bad angel or evil counsellor, owing to some sinful act which placed him in Lucifer's power. At each attempt to emancipate himself from the power of Lucifer the latter tantalizes him in every conceivable way. He says Lucifer is afraid of God, but tries to bluff L. into the belief that God does not know and see all things. The patient keeps religious souvenirs about him, which displease Lucifer and induce * kicking' on his part."

The phenomena of insistent concepts, of imperative ideas, of impulsive mania, of paramnesia, of paranoia and demonomania, can be fully reproduced in our laboratories. From the way we induce the phenomena artificially we can learn how they originate spontaneously. To bring about insistent concepts, irresistible impulses, and all kinds of changes of the ego, we must dissociate the secondary subconscious self from the primary controlling consciousness ; we must then inoculate the subconscious self with the idea, impulse, or specious personality, and make a deep cleft between the two selves by enforcing amnesia, otherwise the suggestion will simply rise as a memory. Once, however, disaggregation is enforced, we can easily induce all kinds of insistent ideas, imperative concepts, all forms of irresistible impulses, all sorts of changes of personality ; and we may assert that all these forms of insanity have at their basis a disaggregation of consciousness, a dissociation of the primary and secondary subconscious selves
.

CHAPTER XXVI.
THE TRAITS OF THE SUBCONSCIOUS SELF.

WE are now in a position to characterize the underground self.

The subwaking self is stupid; it lacks all critical sense. A thing must be told to it plainly in all details, and even then it follows more the letter than the spirit of the suggestion. I remind the reader of Prof. W. James's subject who smoked but "one "pipe the whole day, and also of my own subject, who, on being suggested not to have any slight headache, next day came complaining of violent pain. The lack of critical sense is well brought out in the following experiment:

Mr. Y. F. is hypnotized and is suggested to be Sam Smith, a bootblack, ten years of age.

Exp. What is your name ?

Sub. Sam Smith.

Exp. Your occupation ?

Sub. A bootblack.

Exp. How old are you ?

Sub. Ten years.

Exp. What is your father's name ?

Sub. (Gives his father's correct name.)

Exp. How is it that your name is Sam Smith and your father's is different ?

Sub. I do not know .

On another occasion I made the following experi* ment on the same subject:

Exp. Are you alive ?

Sub. Yes.

Exp. No, you are dead.

Sub. Yes, I think I am dead.

Exp. How long is it since you died ?

Sub. A few days ago.

Exp. From what disease ?

Sub. I do not know; just died.

Exp. Can you hear and feel me ?

Sub. Yes.

Exp. But how can you feel if you are dead ?

Sub. I do not know.

The subwaking self is ready to take any suggestion, no matter how ridiculous or painful the suggestion is.

Mr. Y. F. is hypnotized and is suggested that on awakening he should light the gas and bow to the light whenever the door is opened. On awakening he at once rushes to light the gas, and is at last satisfied when he sees the flame.

Exp. "What did you light the gas for ?

Sub. I do not know, unless I wanted to light my pipe.

Exp. But you have no pipe.

Sub. That is true, but then I can light a cigarette. (Takes a cigarette from my table, lights it, and begins to puff.)

The reason here given by the subject is extremely stupid, because he could far easier light directly the cigarette with the match, and, besides, the gas jet was so high up that he had to give a good jump to reach it.

I then opened the door. The subject bowed to the light. I opened the door again; again the subject bowed to the gas jet. Each opening of the door was followed by a polite bow to the fire.

Exp. Why do you bow to the fire ?

Sub. I do not know. I suppose I am practising. I do not know. I feel like a chump while I am doing it.

Exp. Why are you doing it ? Can you give any reason ?

Sub. None, except that I want to.

Exp. Have you any desire to do it ?

Sub. Yes, I think it is a nice thing to do.

I take the hand of the subject, put it on the table, and tell the hypnotic self that the pencil is a lighted candle, the flames issuing from the point. When I now touch any part of the subject's body with the point of the pencil the self screams from great pain. I tell the self, "You have a toothache,"and he does get the ache.

The subwaking self is extremely credulous; it lacks all sense of the true and rational. "Two and two make five.""Yes."Anything is accepted if sufficiently emphasized by the hypnotizer. The suggestibility and imitativeness of the subwaking self was discussed by me at great length. What I should like to point out here is the extreme servility and cowardliness of that self. Show hesitation, and it will show fight; command authoritatively, and it will obey slavishly.*

The subwaking self is devoid of all morality; it will steal without the least scruple; it will poison; it will stab; it will assassinate its best friends without the least scruple. When completely cut off from the waking person it is precluded from conscience.The subwaking self dresses to fashion, gossips in company, runs riot in business panics, revels in the crowd, storms in the mob, and prays in the camp meeting. Its senses are acute, but its sense is nil. Association by contiguity, the mental mechanism of the brute, is the only one that it possesses.

The subwaking self lacks all personality and individuality; it is absolutely servile; it works according to no maxims; it has no moral law, no law at all. To be a law unto one's self, the chief and essential characteristic of personality, is just the very trait the subwaking self so glaringly lacks. The subwaking self has no will; it is blown hither and thither by all sorts of incoming suggestions. It is essentially a brutal self.

The primary self alone possesses true personality, will, and self-control. The primary self alone is a law unto itself—a person having the power to investigate his own nature, to discover faults, to create ideals, to strive after them, to struggle for them, and by continuous, strenuous efforts of will to attain higher and higher stages of personality.

"Zwei Seelen wohnen, ach! in meiner Brust, Die eine will sich von der andern trennen : Die eine halt, in derber Liebeslust, Sich an die Welt, mit klammernden Organen ; Die andre hebt gewaltsam sich von Dust Zu den Gefilden hoher Ahnen."— FAUST.

PART III. SOCIETY.

CHAPTER XXVII.
SOCIAL SUGGESTIBILITY.

SUGGESTIBILITY is a fundamental attribute of man's nature. We must therefore expect that man, in his social capacity, will display this general property; and so do we actually find the case to be. What is required is only the condition to bring about a disaggregation in the social consciousness. This disaggregation may either be fleeting, unstable—then the type of suggestibility is that of the normal one; or it may become stable —then the suggestibility is of the abnormal type. The one is the suggestibility of the crowd, the other that of the mob. In the mob direct suggestion is effective, in the crowd indirect suggestion. The clever stump orator, the politician, the preacher, fix the attention of their listeners on themselves, interesting them in the "subject."They as a rule distract the attention of the crowd by their stories, frequently giving the suggestion in some indirect and striking way, winding up the long yarn by a climax requiring the immediate execution of the suggested act. Out of the infinite number of cases, I take the first that comes to my hand. In August 11, 1895, at Old Orchard, Me., a camp meeting was held. The purpose was to raise a collection for the evangelization of the world. The preacher gave his suggestions in the following way:

"The most impressive memory I have of foreign iands is the crowds, the billows of lost humanity dashing ceaselessly on the shores of eternity. . . . How desperate and unloved they are—no joy, no spring, no song in their religion ! I once heard a Chinaman tell why he was a Christian. It seemed to him that he was down in a deep pit, with no means to get out. [Story.] Have you wept on a lost world as Jesus wept ? If not, woe unto you. Your religion is but a dream and a fancy. We find Christ testing his disciples. Shall he make them his partners? Beloved, he is testing you to-day. [Indirect suggestion.] He could convert one thousand millionaires, but he is giving us a chance. [Suggestion more direct than before.] Have we faith enough ? [A discourse on faith follows here.] God can not bring about great things without faith. I believe the coming of Jesus will be brought about by one who believes strongly in it. . . . Beloved, if you are going to give grandly for God you have got faith. [The suggestion is still more direct.] The lad with the five loaves and the two small fishes [story] —when it was over the little fellow did not lose his buns; there were twelve baskets over. . . . Oh, beloved, how it will come back! . . . Some day the King of kings will call you and give you a kingdom of glory, and just for trusting him a little ! What you give to-day is a great investment. . . . Some day God will let us know how much better he can invest our treasures than we ourselves."The suggestion was effective. Money poured in from all sides, contributions ran from hundreds into thousands, into tens of thousands. The crowd contributed as much as seventy thousand dollars.

A disaggregation of consciousness is easily effected in the crowd. Some of the conditions of suggestibility work in the crowd with great power and on a large scale. The social psychical scalpels are big, powerful; their edges are extremely keen, and they cut sure and deep. If anything gives us a strong sense of our individuality, it is surely our voluntary movements. "We may say that the individual self grows and expands with the increase of variety and intensity of its voluntary activity; and conversely, the life of the individual self sinks, shrinks with the decrease of variety and intensity of voluntary movements. We find, accordingly, that the condition of limitation of voluntary movements is of great importance in suggestibility in general, and this condition is of the more importance since it, in fact, can bring about a narrowing down of the field of consciousness with the conditions consequent on that contraction—all favourable to suggestibility.

Now nowhere else, except perhaps in solitary confinement, are the voluntary movements of men so limited as they are in the crowd; and the larger the crowd is the greater is this limitation, the lower sinks the individual self. Intensity of personality is in inverse proportion to the number of aggregated men. This law holds true not only in the case of crowds, but also in the case of highly organized masses. Large, massive social organisms produce, as a rule, very small persons. Great men are not to be found in ancient Egypt, Babylon, Assyria, Persia, but rather in the diminutive communities of ancient Greece and Judea.

This condition of limitation of voluntary movements is one of the prime conditions that help to bring about a deep; a more or less lasting dissociation in the consciousness of the crowd—the crowd passes into the mob-state. A large gathering on account of the cramping of voluntary movements easily falls into a state of abnormal suggestibility, and is easily moved by a ringleader or hero. Large assemblies carry within themselves the germs of the possible mob. The crowd contains within itself all the elements and conditions favourable to a disaggregation of consciousness. What is required is only that an interesting object, or that some sudden violent impressions should strongly fix the attention of the crowd, and plunge it into that state in which the waking personality is shorn of its dignity and power, and the naked subwaking self alone remains face to face with the external environment.

Besides limitation of voluntary movements and contraction of the field of consciousness, there are also present in the crowd, the matrix of the mob, the conditions of monotony and inhibition. When the preacher, the politician, the stump orator, the ringleader, the hero, gains the ear of the crowd, an ominous silence sets in, a silence frequently characterized as "awful."The crowd is in a state of overstrained expectation; with suspended breath it watches the hero or the interesting, all-absorbing object. Disturbing impressions are excluded, put down, driven away by main force. So great is the silence induced in the fascinated crowd, that very frequently the buzzing of a fly, or even the drop of a pin, can be distinctly heard. All interfering impressions and ideas are inhibited. The crowd is entranced, and rapidly merges into the mob-state.

The great novelist Count Tolstoy gives the following characteristic description of a crowd passing into the entranced condition of the mob:

"The crowd remained silent, and pressed on one another closer and closer. To bear the pressure of one another, to breathe in this stifling, contagious atmosphere, not to have the power to stir, and to expect something unknown, incomprehensible, and terrible, became intolerable. Those who were in the front, who saw and heard everything that took place, all those stood with eyes full of fright, widely dilated, with open mouths; and straining their whole strength, they kept on their backs the pressure of those behind them."

The following concrete cases taken from American life will perhaps show clearly the factors that work in the entrancement of the crowd, and will also disclose the disaggregation of consciousness effected in the popular mind. One of the American newspapers gives the following sensational but interesting account of feminine crowds entranced by Paderewski: "There is a chatter, a rustling of programmes, a waving of fans, a nodding of feathers, a general air of expectancy, and the lights are lowered. A hush. All eyes are turned to a small door leading on to the stage; it is opened. Paderewski enters. ... A storm of applause greets him, . . . but after it comes a tremulous hush- and a prolonged sigh, . . . created by the long, deep inhalation of upward of three thousand women. . . . Paderewski is at the piano. . . . Thousands of eyes watch every commonplace movement [of his] through opera glasses with an intensity painful to observe. He the idol, they the idolators. . . . Toward the end of the performance the most decorous women seem to abandon themselves to the influence. . . . There are sighs, sobs, the tight clinching of the palms, the bowing of the head. Fervid exclamations: ' He is my master !' are heard in the feminine mob."In this highly sensational report the paper unconsciously describes all the conditions requisite to effect a disaggregation of consciousness.

The conditions of crowd entrancement are clearly revealed in the following case :

In 1895 a "modern Messiah,"a "Man-Christ"by name of Francis Schlatter, appeared in this country. He worked miracles. People believed in his divine, supernatural power. Men, women, and children flocked to him from all sides, and Schlatter did cure many of them of "the ills of the flesh "by "mere laying on of hands,"as the hypnotizer treats the entranced subject or the one he intends to entrance. A disaggregation of consciousness was easily effected in the manipulated crowd of believers, the subwaking reflex self emerged, and Schlatter's suggestions took effect. A reporter describes the scene as follows:

"Men, women, and children with the imprint of mental illness upon their faces were on all sides. . . . Every moment the crowd was augmented, . . . and soon the place was a sea of heads as far as the eye could see. [Limitation of voluntary movements.] . . . Then a sudden movement went through the assemblage, and even the faintest whisper was hushed. [Monotony, inhibition.] . . . Schlatter had come."[Concentration of attention]. The reporter, as the individual of the crowd, fell into the trance condition characteristic of the person in the mob. "As I approached him,"writes the reporter, "I became possessed of a certain supernatural fear, which it was difficult to analyze. My faith in the man grew in spite of my reason, "

The waking, controlling, thinking, reasoning self began to waver, to lose its power, and the reflex, subwaking consciousness began to assert itself. "As he released my hands my soul acknowledged some power in this man that my mind and my brain (?) seemed to fight against. When he unclasped my hands I felt as though I could kneel at his feet and call him master"

The suggestion given to the entranced crowd by the "master "spreads like wildfire. The given suggestion reverberates from individual to individual, gathers strength, and becomes so overwhelming as to drive the crowd into a fury of activity, into a frenzy of excitement. As the suggestions are taken by the mob and executed the wave of excitement rises higher and higher. Each fulfilled suggestion increases the emotion of the mob in volume and intensity. Each new attack is followed by a more violent paroxysm of furious demoniac frenzy. The mob is like an avalanche: the more it rolls the more menacing and dangerous it grows. The suggestion given by the hero, by the ringleader, by the master of the moment, is taken up by the crowd and is reflected and reverberated from man to man, until every soul is dizzied and every person is stunned. In the entranced crowd, in the mob; every one influences and is influenced in his turn; every one suggests and is suggested to, and the surging billow of suggestion swells and rises until it reaches a formidable height.

Suppose that the number of individuals in the crowd Is 1,000, that the energy of the suggested idea in the "master "himself be represented by 50, and that only one half of it can be awakened in others; then the hero awakens an energy of 25 in every individual, who again in his or her turn awakens in everyone an energy of 12.5. The total energy aroused by the hero is equal to 25 X 1,000 = 25,000. The total energy of suggestion awakened by each individual in the crowd is equal to 12'5 X 1,000, or 12,500 (the hero being included, as he is, after all, but a part of the crowd). Since the number of individuals in the crowd is 1,000, we have the energy rising to as much as 12,500 X 1,000; adding to it the 25,000 produced by the ringleader, we have the total energy of suggestion amounting to 12,-525,000!

The mob energy grows faster than the increase of numbers. The mob spirit grows and expands with each fresh human increment. Like a cannibal it feeds on human beings. In my article A Study of the Mob f I point out that the mob has a self of its own; that the personal self is suppressed, swallowed up by it, so much so that when the latter comes once more to the light of day it is frequently horrified at the work, the crime, the mob self had committed; and that once the mob self is generated, or, truer to say, brought to the surface, it possesses a strong attractive power and a great capacity of assimilation. It attracts fresh individuals, breaks down their personal life, and quickly assimilates them; it effects in them a disaggregation of consciousness and assimilates the subwaking selves. Out of the subwaking selves the mob-self springs into being. The assimilated individual expresses nothing but the energy suggestion, the will of the entranced crowd; he enters fully into the spirit of the mob. This can be well illustrated by a curious incident describing the riots of the military colonists in Russia in 1831, taken from the memoirs of Panaev:

"While Sokolov was fighting hard for his life I saw a corporal lying on the piazza and crying bitterly. On my question, ' Why do you cry ?' he pointed in the direction of the mob and exclaimed, ' Oh, they do not kill a commander, but a father ! ' I told him that instead of it he should rather go to Sokolov's aid. He rose at once and ran to the help of his commander. A little later when I came with a few soldiers to Sokolov's help, I found the same corporal striking Sokolov with a club. f Wretch, what are you doing ? Have you not told me he was to you like a father ?' To which he answered : ' It is such a time, your honor ; all the people strike him ; why should I keep quiet ?'

To take another interesting example: During the Russian anti-Jewish riots in 1881 the city of Berditchev, consisting mainly of Jewish inhabitants, suffered from Jewish mobs. One day a Jewish mob of about fifteen thousand men, armed with clubs, butchers' knives, and revolvers, marched through the streets to the railway station to meet the Katzapi.[40] To the surprise of intelligent observers, many Christians were found to participate in this Jewish mob.An interesting case of this kind is brought by the Rev. H. C. Fish in his Handbook of Revivals:

"While a revival was in progress in a certain village a profane tavern keeper swore he would never be found among the fools who were running to the meetings. On hearing, however, of the pleasing mode of singing his curiosity was excited, and he said he did not know but he might go and hear the singing, but with an imprecation that he would never hear a word of the sermon. As soon as the hymn before the sermon was sung he leaned forward and secured both ears against the sermon with his forefingers. Happening to withdraw one of his forefingers, the words, ' He that hath ears to hear let him hear,' pronounced with great solemnity, entered the ear that was open and struck him with irresistible force. He kept his hand from returning to the ear, and, feeling an impression he had never"known before, presently withdrew the other finger and hearkened with deep attention to the discourse which followed."The tavern keeper was fascinated, drawn into the mob of true believers, was converted, and, in the words of the Rev. H. C. Fish, "became truly pious."

The power of suggestion possessed by the revival meeting is well brought out in another case related by the Rev. H. C. Fish in his Handbook of Revivals:

"An actress in one of the English provincial theatres was one day passing through the streets of the town when her attention was attracted by the sound of voices. Curiosity prompted her to look in at an open door. It was a social (revival) meeting, and at the moment of her observation they were singing:

Depth of mercy ! can there be Mercy still reserved for me ?

She stood motionless during a prayer which was offered. . . . The words of the hymn followed her. . . . The manager of the theatre called upon her one morning and requested her to sustain the principal character in a new play which was to be performed the next week. . . . She promised to appear. The character she assumed required her on her first entrance to sing a song, and when the curtain was drawn up the orchestra immediately began the accompaniment. But \ she stood as if lost in thought (she seemed to have fallen into a trance), and as one forgetting all around her and her own situation. The music ceased, but she did not sing, and, supposing her to be overcome by embarrassment, the band again commenced. A second time they paused for her to begin, but still she did not open her lips. A third time the air was played, and then with clasped hand and eyes suffused with tears she sang not the words of the song,"but the verses suggested to her at the revival meeting :

Depth of mercy ! can there be Mercy still reserved for me ?

"The performance,"the Rev. H. C. Fish naively adds, "was suddenly ended."

The extreme impulsiveness of the mob self is notorious. No sooner is a suggestion accepted, no matter how criminal, how inhuman it might be, than it is immediately realized, unless another suggestion more in accord with the general nature of suggestions in which the mob self was trained, interferes and deflects the energy of the mob in another direction. The following interesting case will perhaps best illustrate my meaning:

On February 26, 1896, at Wichita Falls, Texas, a mob of several thousand men attacked the jail where two bank robbers were confined. The mob battered the jail doors and forcibly took possession of the two prisoners. The two men were taken to the bank - which they attempted to rob the day before. An improvised scaffold was erected. The first impulse of the mob was to burn the prisoners. Roasting was the programme. This inquisitorial mode of execution "without shedding human blood "was by suggestion changed to hanging, the way of execution commonly in use in this country to inflict capital punishment, the way of murder common to all American lynching mobs.

The consciousness of the mob is reflex in its nature. In the entranced crowd, in the mob, social consciousness is disaggregated, thus exposing to the direct influence of the environment the reflex consciousness of the social subwaking self. The subwaking mob self slumbers within the bosom of society.

CHAPTER XXVIII.
SOCIETY AND EPIDEMICS.

WHEN animals, on account of the great dangers that threaten them, begin to rove about in groups, in companies, in herds, and thus become social, such animals, on pain of extinction, must vary in the direction of suggestibility ; they must become more and more susceptible to the emotional expression of their comrades, and reproduce it instantaneously at the first impression. When danger is drawing near, and one of the herd detects it and gives vent to his muscular expression of fear, attempting to escape, those of his comrades who are most susceptible reproduce the movements, experience the same emotions that agitate their companion, and are thus alone able to survive in the struggle for existence. A delicate susceptibility to the movements of his fellows is a question of life and death to the individual in the herd. Suggestibility is of vital importance to the group, to society, for it is the only way of rapid communication social brutes can possibly possess. Natural selection seizes on this variation and develops it to its highest degree.

Individuals having a more delicate susceptibility to suggestions survive, and leave a greater progeny which more or less inherit the characteristics of their parents. In the new generation, again, natural selection resumes its merciless work, making the useful trait of suggestibility still more prominent, and the sifting process goes on thus for generations, endlessly. A highly developed suggestibility, an extreme, keen susceptibility to the sensorimotor suggestions, coming from its companions, and immediately realizing those suggestions by passing through the motor processes it witnesses, is the only way by which the social brute can become conscious of the emotions that agitate its fellows. The sentinel posted by the wasps becomes agitated at the sight of danger, flies into the interior of the nest buzzing violently, the whole nestful of wasps raises a buzzing, and is thus put into the same state of emotion which the sentinel experiences.

Suggestibility is the cement of the herd, the very soul of the primitive social group. A herd of sheep stands packed close together, looking abstractedly, stupidly, into vacant space. . Frighten one of them ; if the animal begins to run, frantic with terror, a stampede ensues. Each sheep passes through the movements of its neighbour. The herd acts like one body animated by one soul. Social life presupposes suggestion. No society without suggestibility. Man is a social animal, no doubt ; but he is social because he is suggestible. Suggestibility, however, requires disaggregation of consciousness ; hence, society presupposes a cleavage of the mind, it presupposes a plane of cleavage between the differentiated individuality and the undifferentiated reflex consciousness, the indifferent subwaking self. Society and mental epidemics are intimately related / for flie social gregarious self is the suggestible subconscious self. The very organization of society keeps up the disaggregation of consciousness. The rules, the customs, the laws of society are categorical, imperative, absolute .

One must obey them on pain of death. Blind obedience is a social virtue. [41] But blind obedience is the very essence of suggestibility, the constitution of the disaggregated subwaking self. Society by its nature, by its organization, tends to run riot in mobs, manias, crazes, and all kinds of mental epidemics. With the development of society the economical, political, and religious institutions become more and more differentiated; their rules, laws, by-laws, and regulations become more and more detailed, and tend to cramp the individual, to limit, to constrain his voluntary movements, to contract his field of consciousness, to inhibit all extraneous ideas — in short, to create conditions requisite for a disaggregation of consciousness. If, now, something striking fixes the attention of the public—a brilliant campaign, a glittering holy image, or a bright "silver dollar "— the subwaking social self, the demon of the demos, emerges, and society is agitated with crazes, manias, panics, and mental plagues of all sorts.

With the growth and civilization of society, institutions become more stable, laws more rigid, individuality is more and more crushed out, and the poor, barren subwaking self is exposed in all its nakedness to the vicissitudes of the external world. In civilized society laws and regulations press on the individual from all sides. Whenever one attempts to rise above the dead level of commonplace life, instantly the social screw begins to work, and down is brought upon him the tremendous weight of the socio-static press, and it squeezes him back into the mire of mediocrity, frequently crushing him to death for his bold attempt. Man's relations in life are determined and fixed for him; he is told how he must put on his tie, and the way he must wear his coat; such should be the fashion of his dress on this particular occasion, and such should be the form of his hat; here must he nod his head, put on a solemn air ; and there take off his hat, make a profound bow, and display a smile full of delight. Personality is suppressed by the rigidity of social organization ; the cultivated, civilized individual is an automaton, a mere puppet.

Under the enormous weight of the socio-static press, under the crushing pressure of economical, political, and religious regulations there is no possibility for the individual to determine his own relations in life; there is no possibility for him to move, live, and think freely; the personal self sinks, the suggestible, subconscious, social, impersonal self rises to the surface, gets trained and cultivated, and becomes the hysterical actor in all the tragedies of historical life.

Laws and mobs, society and epidemics—are they not antagonistic ? In point of fact they are intimately, vitally interrelated, they are two sides of the same shield. Under normal conditions social activity no doubt works wonders; it elaborates such marvellous products as language, folklore, mythology, tribal organization, etc.—products that can only be studied and admired by the intellect of the scientist. When, however, the social conditions are of such a nature as to charge society with strong emotional excitement, or when the institutions dwarf individuality, when they arrest personal growth, when they hinder the free development and exercise of the personal controlling consciousness, then society falls into a hypnoid condition, the social mind gets disaggregated. The gregarious self begins to move within the bosom of the crowd and becomes active; the demon of the demos emerges to the surface of social life and throws the body politic into convulsions of demoniac fury.

CHAPTER XXIX.
STAMPEDES.

MENTAL epidemics, panics, stampedes occurring in social animals, are especially interesting from our point of view. In the Journal of Mental Science for January, 1872, Dr. "W. Lauder Lindsay brings a few cases of stampedes among cavalry horses. Of these stampedes four deserve our special attention. Three were English and one was Russian.

On Monday, August 30,1871, a stampede happened among the horses of the First Life Guard, encamped on Cove Common, near Aldershot. The Daily Telegraph of September 1, 1871, gives the following description of the panic: "A sudden noise frightened the horses of two officers and caused them to start from their pickets, followed by six troop horses. A panic then seized on the whole line; three hundred horses broke loose simultaneously, running in all directions, some dragging the cords and pins, and all wearing their saddle cloths. . . . Almost every open route had been taken by the fugitives. ... At one point the troop dashed against the closed toll-gate and smashed it to pieces, while . . . many plunged against stakes or other obstructions, seriously injuring themselves. Several dropped down dead within an hour; some were drowned in the canal, and others were captured in a crippled state." Who could have thought," exclaims the Times, "that horses would go mad, like Goldsmith's dog, to gain some private end of their own ? and yet, what other conclusion can we form ? . . . A sedate and virtuous body of three hundred horses suddenly going mad, running over one another, kicking and fighting among themselves, and committing suicide by all the means in their power. . . . The three hundred horses . . . became frenzied with the same unity of purpose."

On September 2, 1871, a second stampede occurred to the horses of the Second Dragoon Guards, also encamped on Cove Common. This time the stampede was on a somewhat smaller scale than the first one. According to the Daily News of September 4, 1871, "seventy-six horses suddenly broke loose from the right wing of the regiment and galloped madly in all directions. The vast expanse of common ground in the locality is intersected by the Basingstoke Canal and numerous ditches, into which many of the animals plunged or fell, and were with difficulty rescued from drowning or suffocation."

Next day, September 3d, a still smaller stampede of forty only occurred in the same camp to the horses of the Tenth Hussars. The epidemic was rapidly losing ground, and vanished altogether with the third stampede.

If now we inquire after the immediate or exciting cause in all these stampedes, we find it invariably to be some very trivial accident, in itself utterly disproportionate to the effect produced. Thus the first stampede was caused by a flock of geese that disturbed the repose of the chargers, and the second was brought about by "a runaway horse from an adjacent camp."The exciting cause was insignificant; what, then, was the predisposing cause ?— The natural social suggestibility of horsekind.

Compare now these equine stampedes with similar stampedes or panics among men. The following case may serve as a good illustration:

In the year 1761 the citizens of London were alarmed by two shocks of an earthquake, and the prophecy of a third, which was to destroy them altogether. A crack-brained fellow named Bell, a soldier in the Life Guards, was so impressed with the idea that there would be a third earthquake in another month that he lost his senses and ran about the streets predicting the destruction of London on the 5th of April. Thousands confidently believed his prediction and took measures to transport themselves and their families from the scene of the impending calamity. As the awful day approached the excitement became intense, and great numbers of credulous people resorted to all the villages within a circuit of twenty miles, awaiting the doom of London. Islington, Highgate, Hampstead, Harrow, and Blackheath were crowded with panic-stricken fugitives, who paid exorbitant prices for accommodation to the housekeepers of these secure retreats. Such as could not afford to pay for lodgings at any of those places remained in London until two or three days before the time, and then encamped in the surrounding fields, awaiting the tremendous shock which was to lay the- city all level with the dust. The fear became contagious, and hundreds, who had laughed at the prediction a week before, packed up their goods when they saw others doing so and hastened away. The river was thought to be a place of great security, and all the merchant vessels in the port were filled with people, who passed the night between the 4th and 5th on board, expecting every instant to see St. Paul's totter and the towers of Westminster Abbey rock in the wind and fall amid a cloud of dust.

Stampedes have their leaders just as mobs have their instigators, as political parties have their bosses, and as great movements have their saints and heroes. Each great stampede has its political boss, its "runaway horse,"its hero who is obeyed blindly and devotedly followed even to the point of self-destruction. The suggestion of the hero is fatal in its effects. The special correspondent of The Scotsman, in commenting on the English stampedes, truly remarks: "It is always one or two horses which begin the mischief; and if they were quieted at once, the contagion of the panic would be arrested."

If not counteracted, the suggestion given by the boss of the stampede is simply irresistible, and is carried out in a spirit of perfectly blind, slavish obedience. This can be clearly seen in the Russian St. Petersburg stampede of 1871. The Times correspondent gives the following account of it:

"On the second night of the campaign an unlucky accident occurred. ... A regiment of the Empress's Cuirassiers of the Guard, nine hundred strong, . . . had arrived at their cantonments. One of the squadron of horses became alarmed, broke away, was followed by the next squadron, and, a panic seizing them all, in one instant the whole nine hundred fled in wild disorder. . . . Two things were very remarkable in this stampede. In the first place, they unanimously selected one large, powerful horse as their leader, and, with a look at him and a snort at him which they meant and he understood as apres vous, they actually waited until he dashed to the front, and then followed in wild confusion. "When I tell you that some of the horses were not recovered till they had gone one hundred and twenty miles into Finland, you may imagine what the panic was.

"The second remarkable thing is the way that some of them were stopped. In one solid mass they dashed on for miles, and then came directly, at right angles, on a river. In front of them was a bridge, but on the other side of the bridge was a sort of tete du pont and a small picket of cavalry. The horse which led would not face the bridge, seeing the cavalry at the other end, but turned to one side, dashed into the stream, and the whole nine hundred horses swam the river together. As they emerged and flew wildly on, the commander of the picket bethought him of a ruse, and ordered a bugler to blow the appel. This is always blown when the horses are going to be fed. . . . All the old horses pricked up their ears, wavered, stopped, paused, turned round and trotted back. . . . This severed the mass. . . . The rest was broken up."

Those who live in a democracy and have the interests of the country at heart may well ponder on these stampedes. From our standpoint these stampedes are very interesting and highly instructive, because they clearly show the extreme suggestibility to which the social brute is constantly subject .

CHAPTER XXX.
MEDIEVAL MENTAL EPIDEMICS.

THE phenomena of history lie open before us. Looking back to the middle ages, we find them to be times in which abnormal social suggestibility was displayed on a grand scale—times full of mobs, riots, of blind movements of vast human masses, of terrible epidemics ravaging Europe from end to end. They were ages peculiar for the seemingly strange fact that whole cities, extensive provinces, great countries were stricken by one mental disease. Men went mad in packs, in tens of thousands. An obscure individual in some remote country place went off into fits of hysterics, and soon nations were struggling in convulsions of hysterical insanity.

The middle ages appear to us as dark and brutal. We consider ourselves vastly superior to the mediaeval peasant, burgher, and knight, with their superstitions, religious fervor, with their recurrent mental epidemics. But might we not meet with a similar fate at the hands of our descendants ? Might not a future historian look back to our own times with dismay, if not with horror ? He might represent our "modern civilized "times as dark, cruel, brutal; times of the St. Bartholomew butchery and other Protestant massacres ; times of the Thirty Years' War, of the Seven Tears' War, of the terrors of the French Revolution, of the brutal Napoleonic wars ; times of the absurd tulip craze in Holland, of great commercial manias and business bubbles, and of still greater industrial panics and crises; times of Salvation armies, Coxey mobs, of blind religious revivals, of mental epidemics and plagues of all sorts and descriptions.

Different as mediaeval society is from our own, it is still at bottom of like nature. A close inspection of it will therefore help us to see clearer into the nature of our own social life.

The life of the mediaeval individual was regulated down to its least details by rigid laws, orders, and commands. The guild, the order, the commune, and the church all had minute regulations, rules, and prescriptions for the slightest exigencies of life. Nothing was left to individual enterprise ; even love had its rules and customs. Society was divided and subdivided into classes and groups, each having its own fixed rules, each leading its own peculiar, narrow, dwarfish life. The weight of authority was crushing, social pressure was overwhelming, the inhibition of the individual's will was complete, and the suggestible, social, subwaking self was in direct relation with the external environment.

A brief review of the chief mental epidemics of that time will at once show us the extreme suggestibility of mediaeval society. The most striking phenomenon in mediaeval history is that of the Crusades, which agitated European nations for about two centuries, and cost them about seven million men. People were drawn by an irresistible longing toward the Holy Sepulchre, which fascinated their mental gaze, just as the butterfly is blindly drawn toward the candle. This attraction of devout Christians by the Holy Sepulchre manifested itself in pilgrimages, which at first were rare, but gradually spread, and became a universal mania. Bishops abandoned their dioceses, princes their dominions, to visit the tomb of Christ.

At the time of its highest tide, the flood of pilgrims was suddenly stopped by the Seljukian Turks, who conquered Palestine about 1076. As a maniac, when thwarted in his purpose, becomes raving and violent, so did Europe become when the floodgates of the pilgrim torrent were stopped, and only drops were let to trickle through. European humanity fell into a fit of acute mania which expressed itself in the savage ecstasy of the first Crusade.

Peter the Hermit and Pope Urban II were the heroes who first broke the ice, and directed the popular current to the conquest of the Holy Land. The fiery appeals of the emaciated, dwarfish hermit Peter carried everything before them. The frenzy which had unsettled the mind of the hermit was by him communicated to his hearers, and they became enraptured, entranced with the splendid schemes he unfolded.

Meantime Pope Urban II convoked two councils, one after another. At the second council, that of Clermont, the pope addressed a multitude of thousands of people. His speech was at first listened to in solemn silence. Gradually, however, as he proceeded, sobs broke out. "Listen to nothing," he exclaimed, "but the groans of Jerusalem! . . . And remember that the Lord has said, ' He that will not take up his cross and follow me is unworthy of me.' You are the soldiers of the cross ; wear, then, on your breast or on your shoulders the blood-red sign of him who died for the salvation of your soul! "The suggestion was irresistible. Leaving the fields and towns, agricultural serfs and petty traders displayed intense eagerness to reach the Holy City. If a rational individual interfered with a word of warning, their only answer was the suggestion of the pope, "He who will not follow me is unworthy of me."The whole world of Western Christendom fell into a deep somnambulic condition. This state of social somnambulism was naturally accompanied by its usual phenomena, by illusions, hallucinations, and delusions—in other words, by religious visions and miracles.

Heinrich von Sybel, in speaking of the first Crusade, tells us that "we can hardly understand such a state of mind. It was much as if a large army were now to embark in balloons, in order to conquer an island between the earth and the moon, which was also expected to contain the paradise."Swarms of men of different races, with their wives and daughters, with infants taken from the cradle, and grandsires on the verge of the grave, and many sick and dying, came from every direction, all of them ready to be led to the conquest of the Holy Land. Peter the Hermit, Walter the Penniless, and Gottschalk became the heroes, the ringleaders of the mobs, which were cut to pieces before they reached Palestine. Then followed an army led by pilgrim princes, who succeeded in conquering the Holy Land, and founded there a Christian kingdom; but this kingdom was unstable, and it fell again and again into the hands of the unbelievers, and crusade after crusade was organized, each being a weaker copy of the preceding, until 1272, when the crusade epidemic was completely at an end.

During the same period of time there were also western crusades against the Arabians in Spain and against the unfortunate Albigenses in southern France. In the crusade against the Albigenses, according to Albert von Stade, a peculiar religious mania broke out among women ; thousands of them, stark naked arid in deep silence, as if stricken with dumbness, ran frantically about the streets. In Littich many of them fell into convulsions of ecstasy.

The abnormal suggestibility of mediaeval society was most clearly seen in the crusades of children. About 1212, between the fourth and fifth crusades, Stephen, a shepherd boy at Cloyes, in imitation of his elders, began to preach to children of a holy war. Stephen soon became the rage of the day; the shrines were abandoned to listen to his words. He even worked miracles. The appeal of Stephen to the children to save the Holy Sepulchre aroused in the young a longing to join him in the holy pilgrimage.

The crusade epidemic rapidly spread among the little ones. Everywhere there arose children of ten years, and some even as young as eight, who claimed to be prophets sent by Stephen in the name of God. When the "prophets "had gathered sufficient numbers, they began to march through towns and villages. Like a true epidemic, this migration-mania spared neither boys nor girls; according to the statements of the chroniclers, there was a large proportion of little girls in the multitude of hypnotized children.

The king, Philip Augustus, by the advice of the University of Paris, issued an edict commanding the children to return to their homes; but the religious suggestions were stronger than the king's command, and the children continued to assemble unimpeded. Fathers and mothers brought to bear upon the young all the influence they had to check this dangerous migration-mania, but of no avail. Persuasions, threats, punishments were as futile as the king's command. Bolts and bars could not hold the children. If shut up, they broke through doors and windows, and rushed to take their places in the processions which they saw passing by. If the children were forcibly detained, so that escape was impossible, they pined away like migratory birds kept in seclusion.

In a village near Cologne, Nicolas, a boy of ten, began to play at crusade-preaching. Thousands of children flocked to him from all sides. As in France, all opposition was of no avail. Parents, friends, and pastors sought to restrain them by force or appeal; but the young ones pinned so that, as the chroniclers say, their lives were frequently endangered, as by disease, and it was necessary to allow them to depart. Hosts of children assembled in the city of Cologne to start on their pilgrimage to the Holy Land. There they were divided into two armies, one under the leadership of Nicholas, the boy-prophet, the other under some unknown leader. The armies of the little crusaders, like Coxey's army of our own times, were soon reduced in numbers by mere lack of food.

After many tribulations the army led by Nicolas, considerably reduced in size, reached Rome, where the pope, Innocent III, succeeded in diverting this stream of little pilgrims back to Germany. Ruined, degraded, and ridiculed, the poor German children reached their homes; and when asked what they in reality wanted, the children, as if aroused from a narcotic state, answered that they did not know.

The other German army had a worse fate. After untold sufferings and enormous loss of numbers, the y

reached Brindisi, where they were treated with extreme cruelty. The boys were seized by the citizens and sold into slavery, and the girls were maltreated and sold into dens of infamy.

The French little crusaders met with a similar fate. When, after a long and fatiguing journey, they at last reached Marseilles, two pious merchants voluntarily offered to provide vessels to convey the children to Palestine. Half of the vessels suffered shipwreck, and the rest were directed to the shores of Africa, where the little pilgrims were delivered into the hands of the Turks and Arabians. The two pious merchants were slave dealers.

A contemporary chronicler [42] describes the children's crusade epidemic in the following barbaric, doggerel Latin verse:

Hie vide perigrinacionem et qualiter per incantacinnes

sunt decepti,

Illis temporibus stupendum quid crevit. Mundoque mirabilis truffa inolevit. Nam sub boni specie malum sic succrevit. Arte quidem magica ista late sevit.

Talis devocio ante hec non est audito. Aures cunctis pruriunt virgines ornantur. Annos infra sedecim evangelizantur. -Concurrentes pueri certant et sequantur. Et romore viderant casso consolantur. Ungarus Theutunicus Francus sociantur. Boemus Lombardicus Brittoque canantur. Flandria Vestfalia amnes federantur. Friso cum Norwagia cuncti conglobantur Prurit pes et oculus pueros venantur.

Risum luctus occopat digne lamentantur.

No sooner did the crusade epidemic abate than another one took its place, that of the flagellants. In 1260 the flagellants appeared in Italy, and from there spread all over Europe. "An unexampled spirit of remorse,"writes a chronicler, "suddenly seized on the minds of the people. The fear of Christ fell on all; noble and ignoble, old and young, and even children of five, marched on the streets with no covering but a scarf round their waists. They each had a scourge of leather thongSj which they applied to their limbs with sighs and tears with such violence that blood flowed from their wounds."

As the flagellant epidemic was dying away, a terrible plague arose, and this time a deadly one—that of the black death. While the black death was doing its merciless, destructive work, a frenzy of anti-Semitic mania seized on European nations; they brutally burned and slaughtered the unfortunate Jews by thousands, sparing neither sex nor age.

The black death over, the dancing mania began. About the year 1370 thousands of dancers filled the streets of European cities. So virulent was this epidemic that peasants left their ploughs, mechanics their workshops, and housewives their domestic duties, to join the wild revels. Girls and boys quitted their parents, and servants their masters, to look at the dancers, and greedily imbibed the poison of mental infection.

In Italy the dancing mania took a somewhat different form. There a belief spread that he who was bitten by a tarantula (a species of spider whose sting is no more harmful than that of the ordinary wasp) got dangerously sick, and could not be cured unless he danced to the tune of the tarantella. Nothing short o f

death itself was expected from the wound which those insects inflicted; and if those who were bitten escaped with their lives, they were pining away in a desponding state of lassitude. Many became weak-sighted, lost the power of speech, and were insensible to ordinary causes of excitement. At the sounds of musical instruments the patients awoke from their lethargy and started a most passionate dance. Tarantism became the plague of Italy. Crowds of patients thronged the streets of the Italian cities, and danced madly to the merry tune of the tarantella. The epidemic reached such a height and became so widely spread that few persons could claim to be entirely exempt from it. Neither youth nor age was spared. Old men of ninety and children of five were alike attacked by it.

Social suggestibility is individual hypnotization written large. The laws of hypnosis work on a great scale in society. Hypnotic suggestion is especially effective if it accords with the character of the subject. The same holds true in the case of social hypnotization. Each nation has its own bent of mind, and suggestions given in that direction are fatally effective. The Jew is a fair example. Religious emotions are at the basis of his character, and he is also highly susceptible to religious suggestions. The list of Jewish Messiahs is inordinately long. It would take too much space to recount the names of all the "saviours "who appeared among the Jews from the second destruction of the temple down to our own times. A few strong cases, however, will suffice. In the year 1666, on Rosh Hashanah (Jewish New Year), a Jew, by name Sab-bathai Zevi, declared himself publicly as the long-expected Messiah. The Jewish populace was full of glee at hearing such happy news, and in the ardour of its belief, in the insanity of its religious intoxication, shouted fervently, ' ; Long live the Jewish King, our Messiah !"

A maniacal ecstasy took possession of the Jewish mind. Men, women, and children fell into fits of hysterics. Business men left their occupations, workmen their trades, and devoted themselves to prayer and penitence. The synagogues resounded with sighs, cries, and sobs for days and nights together. The religious mania became so furious that all the rabbis who opposed it had to save their lives by flight. Among the Persian Jews the excitement ran so high that all the Jewish husbandmen refused to labour in the fields. Even Christians regarded Sabbathai with awe, for this event took place in the apocalyptic year. The fame of Sabbathai spread throughout the world. In Poland, in Germany, in Holland, and in England, the course of business was interrupted on the exchange by the gravest Jews breaking off to discuss this wonderful event. The Jews of Amsterdam sent inquiries to their commercial agents in the Levant, and received the brief and emphatic reply, "It is He, and no other! "

"Wherever the messages of the Messiah came, there the Jews instituted fast days, according to the cabalistic regulations of Nathan the prophet, and afterward abandoned themselves to gross intemperance. The Jewish communities of Amsterdam and Hamburg were especially conspicuous for their absurd religious extravagances. In Amsterdam the Jews marched through the streets, carrying with them rolls of the torah, singing, leaping, and dancing as if possessed. Scenes still more turbulent, licentious, and wild occurred in Hamburg, Venice, Leghorn, Avignon, and in many other cities of Italy, Germany, France, and Poland. The tide of re -

religious mania rose so high that even such learned men as Isaac Aboab, Moses de Aguilar, Isaac Noar, the rich banker and writer Abraham Pereira, and the Spinozist, Dr. Benjamin Musaphia, became ardent adherents of the Messiah. Spinoza himself seemed to have followed these strange events with great interest.

The tide of religious mania rose higher and higher. In all parts of the world prophets and prophetesses appeared, thus realizing the Jewish belief in the inspired nature of Messianic times. Men and women, boys and girls, wriggled in hysterical convulsions, screaming praises to the new Messiah; many went raving about in prophetic raptures, exclaiming: "Sabbathai Zevi is the true Messiah of the race of David; to him the crown and kingdom are given ! "

The Jews seemed to have gone mad. From all sides rich men came to Sabbathai, putting their wealth at his disposal. Many sold out their houses and all they possessed, and set out for Palestine. So great was the number of pilgrims that the price of passage was considerably raised. Traffic in the greatest commercial centres came to a complete standstill; most of the Jewish merchants and bankers liquidated their affairs. The belief in the divine mission of Sabbathai was made into a religious dogma of equal rank with that of the unity of God. Even when Sabbathai was compelled by the Sultan to accept Mohammedanism the mystico-Messianic epidemic continued to rage with unabated fury. Many stubbornly rejected the fact of his apostasy: it was his shade that had turned Mussulman.

After Sabbathai's death a new prophet appeared, by the name of Michael Cordozo. His doctrine, in spite of its manifest absurdity, spread like wildfire. "The Son of David,"he said, "will not appear until all Israel is either holy or wicked."As the latter was by far the easier process, he recommended all true Israelites to hasten the coming of the Messiah by turning Mohammedans. Great numbers with pious zeal complied with his advice. As an individual man may be foolish and mischievous, but as a social brute he is absurd and dangerous .

CHAPTER XXXI.
DEMONOPHOBIA.

Around the end of the fifteenth century the germs of a fearful epidemic got lodged within the subconscious mind of Western humanity. Demonophobia, the fear of demons, the fear of witchcraft, got possession of the mind of European nations. Whole populations seemed to have been driven crazy with the fear of the devil. For more than a century and a half did the epidemic of demonophobia rage with an overwhelming fury. No one was exempt from this malady of truly infernal origin. The old and the young, the ignorant and the learned, were stricken by it alike.

In all European countries the same absurd opinions and insane ideas prevailed as to the power of impious and malicious people, especially of old. women, to effect supernatural mischief, to fly through space, to change themselves into dogs, cats, wolves, and goats, to kill, worry, or terrify men, women, and children for their pastime, and to feed on the flesh of the latter at horrid banquets presided over by devils. [43]

Europe seemed to have become a vast asylum of paranoiacs, of monomaniacs, possessed with the fear of persecution by infernal agencies. Weak-minded persons, old, helpless, demented men and women, hysterical subjects, and insane patients with a disposition to form delusions were accused, or accused themselves, of having entered into intimate relationship with imps, incubi, succubi, and even of having had direct intercourse with the archfiend himself. So strong were the suspicions of this peculiar acute form of social paranoia persecutoria that neither beauty nor tender age could serve as protection.

The pope, Innocent VIII, in his bull of 1488 made a strong appeal to his Catholic fold to rescue the Church of Christ from the power of Satan. He preached a crusade against the atrocious, unpardonable sin of witchcraft. The land must be purified of this great evil. Those servants of the devil, the sorcerers and witches, commit the horrible crime of having intercourse with impure spirits ; moreover, they delight in mischief and evildoing; they blast the corn of the field, the herbs of the orchard, the grapes of the garden, and the fruits of the trees; they afflict with diseases man and beast. Sorcery must be wiped out from the face of the earth.

The appeal of the pope made a strong impression on the minds of the people, and the malady of demonophobia was fairly under way. On all sides men sprang up who made it their sole business to discover and burn Sorcerers and witches. Sprenger, the author of Malleus Maleficarum, with true German thoroughness, even worked out a whole system of rules by which the inquisitors in other countries might best discover the guilty. The inquisitors, for instance, were required to ask the suspected whether they had midnight meetings with the devil; whether they attended the witches' sabbath ; whether they could raise whirlwinds; whether they had had sexual intercourse with Satan. To elicit affirmative answers, tortures of the most excruciating kinds were employed.

Pious and zealous inquisitors set at once to their deadly work. Cumanus, in Italy, burned forty-one poor women in one province alone ; and Sprenger, in Germany, burned numbers of them ; his victims amounted to as many as nine hundred in a year. The German commissioners appointed by the pope, Innocent VIII, condemned to the stake upward of three thousand victims. The new commissioners for the extermination of witchcraft appointed by each successive pope still further increased the virulence of the epidemic. One was appointed by Alexander VI in 1494, another by Leo X in 1521, and a third by Adrian VI in 1522. The epidemic of demonophobia increased from year to year, and the spirit of persecution grew in vigour and intensity. In Geneva alone five hundred persons were burned in the years 1515 and 1516. Bartholomew de Spina informs us that in the year 1524 no less than a thousand persons suffered death for witchcraft in the district of Como, and that for several years afterward the average number of victims exceeded one hundred annually. One inquisitor, Remigius, took great credit to himself for having during fifteen years convicted and burned nine hundred. The inquisitor of a rural township in Piedmont burned the victims so plentifully and so fast that there was not a family in the place which had not its dead to mourn.

The Reformation helped little to alleviate this witchcraft mania; on the contrary, it only served to intensify this truly demoniacal malady. -The spirit of persecution was even stronger in Protestant than in Catholic countries. In Luther's Table Talk we find the following item :

"August 25, 1538. The conversation fell upon witches, who spoil milk, eggs, and butter in farmyards. Dr. Luther said : ' I should have no compassion on these witches / / would burn aU of them? "

In France, fires for the execution of witches blazed in almost every town. Children were torn away from their parents and wives taken from their husbands and cruelly sacrificed to the Moloch of demonophobia. The people became so strongly possessed with the fear of persecution by infernal agencies that in 1579 a great alarm was raised in the neighbourhood of Melun by the increase of witches, and a council was to devise some measures to stay the evil. A decree was passed that all witches and consultors with witches should be punished with death; and not only those, but also fortune-tellers and conjurers. In the following year the Parliament of Rouen took up the same question, and decreed that the possession of a grimoire, or book of spells, was sufficient evidence of witchcraft, and that all persons on whom such books were found should be burned alive. Three councils were held in different parts of France in the year 1583, all relating to demonophobia.

From the Continent the epidemic spread to England. In 1562 the statute of Elizabeth declared witchcraft as a crime of the highest magnitude. An epidemic terror of witchcraft seized on the English mind, and this epidemic spread and grew in virulence with the growth of Puritanism.

In Scotland the germs of the epidemic were diligently cultivated by the preachers of the Reformation. In 1563 the ninth parliament of Queen Mary passed an act that decreed the punishment of death against witches and consulters of witches. The Scotch nation was smitten with an epidemic fear of the devil and his infernal agents. Sorcerers and witches were hunted out and tortured with a truly demoniacal cruelty. As a fair example of the cruelties and tortures practised on the poor unfortunates convicted of witchcraft may be taken the case of Dr. Fian, a petty schoolmaster of Tranent.

Dr. Fian was accused of sorcery. He was arrested and put on the rack, but he would confess nothing, and held out so long unmoved that the severe tortures of the loots was resolved upon. He fainted away from great pain, but still no confession escaped his lips. Restoratives were then administered to him, and during the first faint gleam of returning consciousness he was prevailed upon to sign a full confession of his crime. He was then remanded to his prison, from which he managed to escape. He was soon recaptured and brought before the Court of Judiciary, James I, the demonologist, being present. Fian denied all the circumstances of the written confession which he had signed; whereupon the king, enraged at his stubborn willfulness, ordered him once more to the torture. Dr. Fian's finger nails were driven out with pincers, and long needles thrust, their entire length, into the quick. He was then consigned again to the boots, in which he continued "so long, and abode so many blows in them that his legs were crushed and beaten together as small as might be, and the bones and flesh so bruised that the blood and marrow spouted forth in great abundance."

The social malady of demonophobia kept on growing among the Scotch, and the spirit of persecution grew in violence from year to year. From the passing of the act of Queen Mary till the accession of James to the throne of England, a period of thirty-nine years, the average number of persecutions for witchcraft in Scotland was two hundred annually, or upward of seventeen thousand victims! Witch-finding in Scotland became a regular trade, and hundreds of ruffians carried on this profession with great profit. It was believed that the devil put his mark on his servants in the shape of an anaesthetic, or rather analgesic, spot—a spot free from pain. Such anaesthetic spots, as we know, exist in hysterical subjects, and can be easily induced by suggestion. The witch-finders, armed with long pins, roamed about the country, pricking the flesh of supposed criminals. Once the anaesthetic spot was found the person was doomed to death. So acute was the social mental malady of demonophobia that no one once accused of relations with the devil was acquitted. To be accused of witchcraft meant to be guilty of it, and to be guilty of witchcraft was certain death.

In the year 1597 King James I published his famous —or infamous—treatise on demonology. "Witches,"says the king, "ought to be put to death, according to the law of God, the civil and imperial law, and the municipal law of all Christian nations: yea, to spare the life, and not strike whom God bids strike, and so severely punish in so odious a treason against God, is not only unlawful, but doubtless as great a sin in the magistrate as was Saul's sparing Agag."He says also that the crime is so abominable that it may be proved by evidence which would not be received against any other offenders—young children who knew not the nature of an oath and persons of an infamous character being sufficient witnesses against them. To be, however, more sure, James gives us well-tried tests for the discov -

ery of witches and sorcerers. "Two good helps,"says James, "may be used: the one is the finding of their mark and the trying of the insensibleness thereof ; the other is their floating on the water; for, as in a secret murther, if the dead carcass be at any time thereafter handled by the murtherer, it will gush out of the blood, as if the blood were crying to Heaven for revenge of the murtherer (God having appointed that secret supernatural sign for trial of that secret unnatural crime); so that it appears that God hath appointed (for a supernatural sign of the monstrous impiety of witches) that the water shall refuse to receive them in her bosom that have shaken off them the sacred water of baptism and wilfully refused the benefit thereof ; no, not so much as their eyes are able to shed tears (threaten and torture them as you please) while first they repent (God not permitting them to dissemble their obstinacy in so horrible a crime); albeit the womankind especially be able otherwise to shed tears at every light occasion when they will, yea, although it were dissembling like the crocodiles."

With the accession of James, the demonologist, to the throne of England the epidemic of demonophobia burst forth among the English with . renewed vigour and with more intense fury than ever. In 1604 the first parliament of King James passed a bill to the effect "that if any person shall use, practise, or exercise any conjuration of any wicked or evil spirit, or shall consult, covenant with, or feed any spirit, the first offence to be imprisonment for a year and standing in the pillory once a quarter; the second offence to be death."

This act of James I against witchcraft was passed when Lord Bacon was a member of the House of Commons and Lord Coke was attorney-general. That act was referred to a committee which had the spiritual guidance of twelve bishops of the Church of England.

As a rule, however, the minor punishment was but rarely inflicted. Nearly all of the records report cases of accused hanged and burned alive and quick. During the long period of social cataclysms from the reign of James I to that of Charles II, the epidemic of deinonophobia continued to rage with unabated fury. Dr. Zachary Grey, in a note to "Hudibras,"informs us that he himself perused a list of three thousand witches executed in the time of the Long Parliament alone. During the first eighty years of the seventeenth century the number executed has been estimated at five hundred annually, making a total of forty thousand.

Among the English inquisitors, Matthew Hopkins, the witch-finder, greatly distinguished himself for his insane passion of witch persecution. He claimed to have a thorough knowledge of "such cattle,"as he called the witches, and soon assumed the title of "Witch-finder Generall."He travelled through the counties of Norfolk, Essex, Huntington, and Sussex for the sole purpose of finding out the servants of the devil. [44] The most favourable test, however, with him was that of swimming. The hands and feet of the suspected persons were tied together crosswise, the thumb of the right hand to the toe of the left foot, and the thumb of the left hand to the toe of the right foot. The unfortunates were then wrapped up in a large blanket and laid upon their backs in a pond or river. If they sank and were drowned, they were innocent; but if they floated, they were guilty of witchcraft and were burned "alive and quick."

Another favourite method of Hopkins, "the Witch-finder Generall,"was to tie the suspected witch in the middle of a room to a chair or table in some uneasy posture. He then placed persons to watch her for four-and-twenty hours, during which time she was kept without food and drink. In this state one of her imps will surely come and visit her and suck her blood. As the imp might come in the shape of a moth or a fly, a hole was made in the door or window to admit it. If any fly escaped from the room, and the watchers could not catch it and kill it, the woman was guilty, and she was sentenced to death. Thus a poor old woman was found guilty, because four flies appeared in the room, and she was made to confess that she had in her employ four imps named "Ilemazar,""Pye-wackett,""Peck-in-the Crown,"and "Grizel-Greedigut."

In the seventeenth century the social malady of demonophobia reached its acme of development. The epidemic was in full swing. "The world seemed to be like a large madhouse for witches and devils to play their antics in."The terror of mysterious evil agencies fell on the spirits of men. The demon of fear seemed to have obsessed the mind of European humanity. Continental Europe, especially France, Germany, and Switzerland, suffered greatly from the epidemic. High and low were attacked by this malady without any discrimination. In fact, the more learned one was the stronger was the malady, the more acute was the fear of inimical mysterious agencies. Social paranoia persecutoria seemed to have become chronic.

The great Bodinus, the highest authority of the seventeenth century, tells us that "the trial of the offence [witchcraft] must not be conducted like other crimes. Whoever adheres to the ordinary course of justice perverts the spirit of the law, both divine and human. He who is accused of sorcery should never be acquitted, unless the malice of the persecutor be clearer than the sun', for it is so difficult to bring full proof of this secret crime, that out of a million of witches not one would be convicted if the usual course were followed!

Thousands upon thousands of victims were cruelly sacrificed to that insane fear of evil spirits. Nuremberg, Geneva, Paris, Toulouse, Lyons, and many other cities, brought on the average an annual sacrifice of two hundred ; Cologne burned three hundred and the district of Bamberg four hundred witches and sorcerers annually.

The list of trials of the city of Wuerzburg for only two years, from 1627 to 1629, may serve as an illustration of the diabolical work done by that insane spirit of demonophobia. Hauber, who has preserved the list in his Acta et Scripta Magica, says, in a note at the end, that it is far from being complete, and that there were a great many other burnings too numerous to specify. This list of executions contains the names of one hundred and fifty-seven persons who were burned in the course of two years in twenty nine burnings, averaging from five to six at a time. It comprises three play actors, four innkeepers, three common councilmen of Wuerzburg, fourteen vicars of the cathedral, the burgomaster's lady, an apothecary's wife and daughter, two choristers of the cathedral, Gobel Babclin, tbe prettiest girl in the town, and the wife, the two little sons, and the daughter of the councillor Stalzenberg. At the seventh of these recorded burnings the victims are described as a wandering boy twelve years of age, and four strange men and women. Thirty of the whole number appear to have been vagrants of both sexes. None escaped. All fell victims to the insane suspicions of religious paranoia persecutoria.

The spirit of persecution did not spare even the little ones. The number of children on the list is great. The thirteenth and the fourteenth burnings comprise a little girl of nine, another child (a younger sister), their mother, and their aunt, a pretty young woman of twenty-four. At the eighteenth burning the victims were two boys of twelve and a girl of fifteen. At the nineteenth, the young heir of Rotenhahn, aged nine, and two other boys, one aged ten and the other twelve. Whoever had the misfortune of falling under the suspicion of practising witchcraft, of dealing with spirits, was lost. Nothing could save him from the homicidal fury of religious demonophobia.

So acute was the malady of demonophobia that nonsensical jargon uttered by poor crazed creatures scared people out of their wits. Thus at Amsterdam a crazy girl confessed that she could cause sterility in cattle and bewitch pigs and poultry by merely repeating the magic words Turius und Shurius Inturius. She was hanged and burned. One insane person was condemned to the stake by the magistrate of Wuerzburg for uttering the following formula:

Lalle, Bachera, Magatte, Baphia, Dajam, Vagath Heneche Ammi Nagaz, Adamator,

Raphael Immanuel Christus, Tetragrammaton,

Agra Jad Loi. Konig ! Konig !

People were condemned to the flames for pronouncing meaningless words, such as

Anion, Lalle, Sabalos, Aado, Pater, Aziel, Adonai Sado Vagoth Agra, Jad, Baphra ! Komm ! Komm ![45]

It was considered an unpardonable sin, a heinous crime that could only be expiated by the auto-da-fe, to repeat the following gibberish :

Zellianelle Heotti Bonus Vagotha, Plisos Sother osech unicus Beelzebub, Dox ! Comm ! Comm !

The wave of the epidemic ran so high that even little children who in their play happened to repeat those awful incantations were seized by the authorities, tried for witchcraft, found guilty, and condemned to the flames. On American ground we find the same malady of demonophobia blazing up in the celebrated trials of Salem witchcraft. On the accusation of a few hysterical girls, f twenty innocent people were condemned to death. Some were hanged, and others suffered a horrible end under the crushing pressure of heavy weights.

One can hardly find on the records of human crimes anything more disgusting, more infamous, than this insane systematic persecution of feeble women and tender children.

CHAPTER XXXII.
FINANCIAL CRAZES.

IF from the horrors of demonophobia we turn to the marketplace, to the world of business and finances, we are once more impressed by the extreme suggestibility characteristic of the social spirit. The enthusiasm of speculative mania and the abject fear of financial panics are epidemical. Men think in crowds, and go mad in herds. The tulipomania of the Dutch, the Mississippi scheme of the French, the South Sea bubble of the English, the financial epidemics and business panics of our own time, may serve as good illustrations.

About the year 1634 the Dutch became suddenly possessed with a mania for tulips. The ordinary industry of the country was neglected, and the population, even to its lowest dregs, embarked in the tulip trade. The tulip rapidly rose in value, and when the mania was in full swing some daring speculators invested as much as 100,000 florins in the purchase of forty roots. The bulbs were as precious as diamonds; they were sold by their weight in perits, a weight less than a grain. A tulip of the species called Admiral Liefken weighing 400 perits was worth 4,400 florins ; an Admiral Von der Eyck weighing 446 perits was worth 1,260 florins; a Childer of 106 perits was worth 1,615 florins; a Viceroy of 400 perits, 3,000 florins ; and 23 34 3 a Semper Augustus weighing 200 perils was thought to be very cheap at 5,500 florins.

An insane mania of speculating in tulips seized upon the minds of the Dutch. Regular marts for the sale of roots were established in all the large towns of Holland—in Amsterdam, Rotterdam, Haarlem, Leyden, Alkmaar. The stock jobbers dealt largely in tulips, and their profits were enormous. Many speculators grew suddenly rich. The epidemic of tulipomania raged with intense fury, the enthusiasm of speculation filled every heart, and confidence was at its height. A golden bait hung temptingly out before the people, and one after the other they rushed to the tulip marts, like flies around a honey pot. Every one imagined that the passion for tulips would last forever, and that the wealthy from every part of the world would send to Holland and pay whatever prices were asked for them. The riches of Europe would be concentrated on the shores of the Zuyder Zee. Nobles, citizens, farmers, mechanics, seamen, footmen, maid servants, chimneysweeps, and old-clothes women dabbled in tulips. Houses and lands were offered for sale at ruinously low prices, or assigned in payment of bargains made at the tulip market. So contagious was the epidemic that foreigners became smitten with the same frenzy and money poured into Holland from all directions.

This speculative mania did not last long; social suggestion began to work in the opposite direction, and a universal panic suddenly seized on the minds of the Dutch. Instead of buying, everyone was trying to sell. Tulips fell below their normal value. Thousands of merchants were utterly ruined, and a cry of lamentation rose in the land. About the year 1717 a maniacal enthusiasm of speculation seized on the French mind. John Law, a sharp Scotchman, was authorized by the Regent of France to establish a company with the exclusive privilege of trading on the western bank of the Mississippi. Expectation rose on all sides, and thousands of people hastened to invest their capital, which was to be raised with unheard-of profits on the water of that great river. With a large fund in hand and with prospects of getting an unlimited supply of money, the Mississippi Company extended the range of its visionary speculation.

In the year 1719 an edict was published granting to the Mississippi Company the exclusive privilege of trading to the East Indies and the South Seas. The prospects of profit were glorious. John Law, the projector, the ringleader of the epidemic, promised a profit of about one hundred and twenty per cent! The enthusiasm of the French nation knew no bounds. Three hundred thousand applications were made for the fifty thousand new shares issued by the company, and Law's house was beset from morning to night by mobs of applicants.

The eagerness to be on the list of the stockholders rose to a pitch of frenzy. Dukes, marquises, counts, with their duchesses, marchionesses, and countesses, waited in the streets for hours every day to know the result. Every day the value of the shares increased, and fresh applications became so numerous that it was deemed advisable to create no less than three hundred thousand new shares at five thousand livres each, in order that the regent might take advantage of the popular enthusiasm to pay off the national debt. For this purpose the sum of fifteen hundred million livres was necessary. Such was the eagerness of the nation that thrice the sum would have been subscribed if the Government had authorized it.

The tide of speculative mania rose higher and higher. The French were seized with an insatiable greed for speculation. There was not a person of note among the aristocracy who was not engaged in buying and selling stock. People of every age and sex and condition in life speculated in the rise and fall of Mississippi bonds. The street where the jobbers met was thronged with multitudes of people, and accidents frequently occurred there on account of the great pressure of the crowd. Houses round the resort of speculation —houses worth in ordinary times a thousand livres of yearly rent—yielded as much as twelve or sixteen thousand. A cobbler who had a stall in that street gained about two hundred livres a day by letting it out and furnishing writing materials to brokers and their clients. The story goes that a hunchback who stood in the street gained considerable sums by lending his hump as a writing desk to the eager speculators.*

A spirit of furious speculation took possession of the French mind to such a degree that thousands abandoned resorts of pleasure to join the orgies of gambling in Mississippi bonds. The whole nation was in a trance; it was intoxicated with the hopes and expectations of enormous gains, nay—with actual realization of great treasures. The French, however, soon woke up from their trance with a cry of distress; the Mississippi bubble burst, and thousands of speculators were ruined and reduced to poverty and misery.

In the year 1720 a fever of speculation seized on the English mind. The South Sea Company, in order to raise the value of its stock, spread fanciful rumours that all the Spanish colonies would soon be granted free trade, and then the rich product of Potosi would be poured into the lap of the English. Silver and gold would be as plentiful as iron. England would become the wealthiest country in the world, and the richest company in England would be the South Sea Company ; every hundred pounds invested in it would produce hundreds per annum.

Strange to say, people believed in all those fables, and bought shares and speculated recklessly. Business men were in a high fever of excitement. They abandoned their trades and turned to speculation. For a time it looked as if the whole nation turned stock jobbers. Exchange Alley was blocked up by crowds. Everybody came to purchase stock. "Every fool aspired to be a knave."The epidemic grew in vigour and intensity; the mania for speculation became more acute. New companies with schemes of the most extravagant and fanciful nature sprang up on all sides like mushrooms. The share lists were speedily"filled up, and the shares grew on wind and water. Business bubbles were raised on all sides, and people were sure to get rich on them.

Verily, verily, there are no bounds to human credulity and folly. People invested their fortunes in such absurd schemes that one who has never experienced the fever of modern speculation can hardly realize the state of the public mind. Thus one of the projects that received great encouragement was for the establishment of a company "to make deal boards out of sawdust."One project was more absurd than the other: "For furnishing funerals to any part of Great Britain "; "For a wheel of perpetual motion "; "For extracting silver from lead"; "For the transmutation of quicksilver into a malleable fine metal."Such were the nature of the projects. Some bold speculator started "A company for carrying on an undertaking of great advantage, but nobody to know what it is."In his prospectus the speculator stated that the required capital was half a million, in five thousand shares of one hundred pounds each; deposit, two pounds per share. Each subscriber paying his deposit would be entitled to one hundred pounds per share. "Man believes as much as he can,"says Prof. James, but as a gregarious animal man believes whatever is suggested to him.

The waves of business speculation ran higher and higher, and along with it rose the stock of the South Sea Company. The shares rose three hundred to five hundred, five hundred to five hundred and fifty, and then made a prodigious leap to eight hundred and ninety, and finally the price of the stock rose to one thousand per cent! The bubble was full blown and burst. People began to sell stock to realize profit. The stock fell. The rush for selling increased. The stock began to sink rapidly. The fall produced an alarm, a panic! The course of speculation epidemics is to rise to the highest point of heavenly bliss, and then to fall to the lowest depth of misery; to pass from a state of acute maniacal exaltation to a state of still more acute melancholic depression. The course of the speculation epoch is a kind of social folie d double forme. It is this modern social folie d double forme that clearly discloses the extreme suggestibility of gregarious man.

A chronological table will show at a glance the uninterrupted chain of European epidemics:

Pilgrimage epidemic, 1000 to 1095

Eastern and Western Crusades

109o-1270 demic Children's Crusade,)

Flagellant epidemic, 1260-1348

Black Death and Antisemitic mania, 1348

St. John's dance, 1374

St. Vitus' dance, 1418

Tarantism, 1470 ; century to the end of seventeenth century.

Tulipomania, 1634

Speculative The Mississippi Scheme, 1717

The South Sea Bubble, 1720

And business bubbles, up to our own times .

CHAPTER XXXIII.
AMERICAN MENTAL EPIDEMICS.

TURNING now to American social life, so radically different from that of the middle ages, we still find the same phenomena manifesting themselves. The social spirit runs riot in mobs, crazes, manias, pests, plagues, and epidemics.

American religious epidemics hallowed by the name of "revivalism "are notorious. A Jonathan, a Mc-Gready, a Sankey, or a Moody is stricken by the plague, falls into a delirium, and begins to rave on religion. The contagion spreads, and thousands upon thousands pray wildly in churches and chapels, rave furiously, and fall into convulsions in camp meetings. A revival epidemic has come, rages violently for some time, and then disappears as suddenly as it came. To take a few instances of the many cases of revivals:

In 1800 a wave of religious mania passed over the country and reached its acme in the famous Kentucky revivals. The first camp meeting was held at Cabin Creek. It began on the 22d of May and continued four days and three nights. The crying, the singing, the praying, the shouting, the falling in convulsions made of the place a pandemonium. Those who tried to escape were either compelled to return, as if drawn by some mysterious force, or were struck with convul -

sions on the way. The pestilence spread, raging with unabated fury. Families came in wagons from great distances to attend the meetings. The camp meetings generally continued four days, from Friday to Tuesday morning, but sometimes they lasted a week. One succeeded another in rapid succession. The woods and paths leading to the camp meeting were alive with people. "The labourer,"writes Dr. Davidson, " [46] quitted his task; age snatched his crutch; youth forgot his pastimes ; the plough was left in the furrow ; the deer enjoyed a respite upon the mountains; business of all kinds was suspended ; bold hunters and sober matrons, young men, maidens, and little children nocked to the common centre of attraction."As many as twenty thousand people were present at one of these meetings.

The general meeting at Indian Creek, Harrison County, continued about five days. The meeting was at first quiet. The suggestion, however, was not slow to come, and this time it was given by a child. A boy of twelve mounted a log and began to rave violently. He soon attracted the main body of the people. Overcome by the power of emotions, the little maniac raised his hands, and, dropping his handkerchief wet with tears and perspiration, cried out: "Thus, O sinner, shall you drop into hell unless you forsake your sins and turn to the Lord!"At that moment some fell to the ground "like those who are shot in a battle, and the work spread in a manner which human language can not describe."Thousands were wriggling, writhing, and jerking in paroxysms of religious fury. So vim-lent was the revival plague that mere indifferent lookers-on, even mockers and sceptics, were infected by it, and joined the exercises of the raving religious maniacs and fell into jerking convulsions of religious hysteria. The following case may serve as a fair example:

"A gentleman and a lady of some note in the fashionable world were attracted to the camp meeting at Cone Ridge. They indulged in many contemptuous remarks on their way about the poor infatuated creatures who rolled over screaming in the mud, and promised jestingly to stand by and assist each other in case that either should be seized with the convulsions. They had not been long looking upon the strange scene before them, when the young woman lost her consciousness and fell to the ground. Her companion, forgetting his promise of protection, instantly forsook her and ran off at the top of his speed. But flight afforded him no safety. Before he had gone two hundred yards he, too, fell down in convulsions."*

In many places the religious epidemic took the form of laughing, dancing, and barking or dog manias. Whole congregations were convulsed with hysterical laughter during holy service. In the wild delirium of religious frenzy people took to dancing, and at last to barking like dogs. They assumed the posture of dogs, "moving about on all fours, growling, snapping the teeth, and barking with such an exactness of imitation as to deceive any one whose eyes were not directed to the spot.f Nor were the people who suffered so mortifying a transformation always of the vulgar classes ; persons of the highest rank in society, on the contrary, men and women of cultivated minds and polite manners, found themselves by sympathy reduced to this degrading situation." [47] The baneful poison of religious revivalism turns its victims into packs of mad dogs. In 1815 a religious revival swept over the country, and ended in the excesses of camp meetings. In 1832 a great revival epidemic raged fiercely in this country. An excellent description of this revival is given by Mr. Albert S. Rhodes, I give his account verbatim:

"What is usually called ' the Great American Revival ' began simultaneously in New Haven and New York in 1832, and does not seem to have been set in motion by any particular individual or individuals, but to have been in a full sense a popular expression. It was in men's minds and in the atmosphere. It broke out and raged like a fire over a certain portion of the country known by the old inhabitants as the 'burnt district.' It was especially felt along the shore of Lake Ontario and in the counties of Madison and Oneida.

"The host that marched in this revival movement had many banners, but were without known chieftains. . . . The corporals and sergeants who marched with the uprising were men of mediocrity (unknown heroes of mobs). These did not make the revival, but it made them. They were of various religious colours, and formed a motley group gathered from the Wesleyan Methodists, Episcopal Methodists, Evangelists, Independents, Congregationalists, and Presbyterians.

"The characteristic signs [of revivalism] attended this spiritual tempest. Ballrooms were turned into places of prayer and theatres into churches. . . . Clergymen who reasoned logically were told that they held the sponge of vinegar to the parched lips of sinners, instead of leading them to the brook of life where they might drink to completion. They met with the treatment usual in such popular upheavals — they were pushed aside to make room for the new expounders and prophets, ignorant men full of faith and vociferation, who preached night and day the golden streets of the New Jerusalem and the wrath to come.

"The apple of Sodom grew out of this religious mania; the followers soon became incapable of sin. . . . ' [48] And when a man becomes conscious that his soul is saved,' proclaimed one of their spiritual leaders, ' the first thing that he sets about is to find his paradise and his Eve.' The leaders could not find paradises in their own homes, nor Eves in their own wives, and sought their ' affinities ' elsewhere. One of their leaders had a vision of an immense throng of men and women in heaven who wandered hither and thither in search of something necessary to their happiness with an expression of longing depicted on their faces. The men hunted for wives, as women did for men. The spirit of yearning for an incomplete joy was everywhere visible in these great hosts. The seer gave an interpretation of his vision that men and women were wrongly yoked on this earth, and that this may be remedied by a proper and spiritual union in the terrestrial sphere. The interpretation was received with favour, and even with enthusiasm. The man who saw the vision set the example by putting his legitimate wife aside and taking to his bosom the comely wife of one of his brethren. Others quickly followed the example. . . . The union was popularly designated among them as spiritual wedlock. . . . Old ties were given up. The kingdom of heaven was at hand. Old rules were no longer binding, and old obligations were set aside. Men and women, regardless of marital ties, selected their celestial companions.

"At first such unions were to be of purely spiritual character, but, of course, in the end became sexual. . . . Before long the spiritual union was found to be incomplete, and it assumed the ordinary character of that which exists between man and woman who live together in close intimacy. Men who lived with the wives of others, and women who lived with the husbands of others, produced a strange confusion. . . . Children were abandoned by their natural protectors.

"It resulted in evil still worse. Men and women discovered that they had made mistakes in their spiritual unions, and, after having lived for a certain period together, they separated to make new selections. It soon came to pass that they made new selections in comparatively short periods of time, and the doctrine of spiritual affinity thus inevitably merged into gross licentiousness.

"If the facts were not before us, some of the unions would appear incredible. These were what the French would call mariages a trois. The lawful husband and the spiritual one lived under the same roof, in some cases with the same wife, who denied all conjugal rights to the husband in law, and accorded them freely to the husband in spirit; and there are remarkable instances furnished of the husbands submitting to such a state of things as being in accordance with the divine will. And such examples of degradation, according to the annals of the time, do not appear to have been rare.

"Such were some of the results which the revival of 1832 left behind in the ' burnt district.' . . . Such was the revival in its moral aspect. It had still a physical and mental side, which was worse to contemplate, in the number of deluded people who were placed in the hospitals and insane asylums."

About the year 1840 the so-called "Miller mania"broke out. [49]

"This delusion originated in the readings, reflections, and dreams of one "William Miller, of the State of New York, who came to know about the year 1840 at what time ' the Lord was to appear in the heavens' and the end of all things to come. He soon found adherents—as will the author of any ' humbug,' however palpable—who with a zeal worthy of a better cause set themselves to proselytizing. They went abroad preaching their doctrine to all who would hear, and publishing their views to the world through periodicals and newspapers. ... At the outset they pitched not only upon the year, but the day and hour on which the ' Son of Man should come with power and great glory.' A doctrine like this, solemn and momentous beyond expression, spread abroad with all the rapidity that novelty could lend to it; the zeal of its adherents . . . soon collected around its standard throngs of men and women who hugged the delusion as the announcement of great events, and the support of raptures and glorious ecstasies.

The beggarly amount of intellect with which its deluded followers were possessed soon yielded to the farce of religious excitement, and long before 'the time drew near when they were to be received up' they forsook their respective callings, closed their shops and stores, left their families to suffer, or abandoned them to the cold charities of the world, attending meetings for prayers and exhortations, ' rendering night hideous by their screams' and by ceaseless prayers and watchings, intending to open in 'the great day of the Lord.'

The excitement, of which the above brief presentation furnishes by no means an exaggerated description, soon began to produce its effects upon both the bodies and minds of these wretched beings. A pale and haggard countenance, indicative at once of physical exhaustion and great mental solicitude, strange and erroneous views in reference to their worldly relations and affairs, together with their conduct, which showed that the controlling power of reason was swallowed up in the great maelstrom of Millerism —all indicated the shock which had been produced by the terrors of this fearful delusion. As the time for the great denouement approached meetings increased, their prayers were heard far and wide around; converts were multiplied; baptisms were celebrated, not by sprinkling, but by immersions which lasted sometimes longer than life. The gift of tongues was vouchsafed, ascension robes of snowy whiteness were made ready, property was freely given away, and on the morning of ' the great day,' with hearts prepared, and decked in robes of peerless white, they went forth to meet the ' bridegroom.' Some, not content to meet him upon earth, actually ascended trees in order first to greet his approach.

The day first announced passed off quietly...Great was the disappointment of the followers of the doctrine of Miller. Their time for weeks and months had been lost, their business broken up, and their property gone. Yet, to exhibit, as it were, still more forcibly the strength of religious fanaticism (religious suggestion) operating upon (weak) minds, they still clung to their delusion, again ' searched the Scriptures,' and happily found that they had been in error. It was on a certain day and hour of the Jewish year 18^4 on which their calculation should have been based, instead of the corresponding year of our calendar. The joyful news was spread abroad throughout the realms of Millerism, and the zeal and fervour of the followers rose higher than before.

" Meanwhile institutions for the insane were daily furnishing new proofs of the mental ravages Millerism was producing throughout the country. Miller maniacs were almost daily brought to the doors of the insane asylums. Worn out and exhausted by ceaseless religious orgies, many broke down completely and became hopelessly insane. Some were already in heaven, clothed with the new bodies provided for the saints; others, like spectres, were hastening to convert to the same faith their fellow-victims to disease; while a third class refused to eat, having no further need of other than ' angels' food.' So strictly did many of the believers adhere to the cherished passages of the sacred Scriptures that they declined to go abroad to respond to the calls of Nature, because, forsooth, we were commanded ' to become as little children,' and hence soiled their underdresses. None slept, or slept but little; al l

were waiting, waiting in obedience to a divine command. . . . Sleep, in fact, was far from their eyes in consequence of the long-continued watchfulness which had been imposed. They had passed the point of sleep ; some of them even passed the rallying point of exhausted nature, and sank to rise no more. Scores of the victims to this modern delusion (epidemic) were known by all to be the tenants of madhouses, and it was promulgated far and wide by the most respectful authorities that this was a legitimate result of their misguided views and acts, yet it fell unheeded upon the ears of those for whom in kindness it was designed.

Meanwhile the period approached when the correctness of their last reckoning was to be verified. ... If possible, a more firm conviction of the truth of Miller-ism existed in the minds of its followers generally than before; converts to it had increased, and all the elements of prodigious and extended commotion were concentrating preparatory to this event. The scenes which were enacted in view of the fulfillment of this second interpretation greatly exceeded the first. Like the first, it proved to be a baseless fabric of a vision. . . . The epidemic, however, did not abate. The Cry of November 22, 1844, announced the fact that 'our brethren and sisters are not only strong, but much stronger than ever. Our brethren are all standing fast, expecting the Lord every day.'):

Well may President -Jordan, of Stanford University, exclaim: " Whisky, cocaine, and alcohol bring temporary insanity, and so does a revival of religion — one of those religious revivals in which men lose their reason and self-control. This is simply a form of drunkenness no more worthy of respect than the drunkenness that lies in the gutter." Prof. Jordan was attacked on all sides 2 4

by the small fry of the pulpits. But Prof. Jordan was, in fact, too mild in his expression. Religious revivalism is a social bane, it is far more dangerous to the life of society than drunkenness. As a sot, man falls below the brute; as a revivalist, he sinks lower than the sot.

In 1857 a great industrial panic occurred in this country. Business was pressed to its utmost limits. The greed of gain became a veritable mania. Commercial centres, cities, towns large and small, and even villages were possessed by the demon of financial speculation. Speculation rose to a fever heat; the wildest projects were readily undertaken by the credulous business public. Finally the crash came. Social suggestion began to work the other way, and the stream of business life turned in the opposite direction. Everyone ran for his life, not so much because he perceived danger, but simply because he saw his neighbours running—a stampede, a panic, ensued.

In this morbid condition of the body politic the toxic germs of religious mania, the poisonous microbes of the revival pest, once more found a favourable soil. A fierce religious epidemic set on and spread far and wide. The religious journals of the country gloried in it. " Such a time as the present," writes triumphantly one of them,* " was never known since the .days of the apostles for revivals. Revivals now cover our very land, sweeping all before them. . . . Meetings are held for prayer, for exhortation, with the deepest interest and the most astonishing results. Not only are they held in the church and from house to house, but in the great marts of trade and centres of business. In New York there is a most astonishing interest in all the churches, seeming as if that great and populous and depraved city was enveloped in one conflagration of divine influence. . . . Prayer and conference meetings are held in retired rooms connected with large commercial houses, and with the best effects (!). The large cities and towns generally from Maine to California are sharing in this great and glorious work." [50]

A Boston journalist caught a glimpse of the true nature of this religious revival. " For the last three months," he writes, " a revival of religion has spread like an epidemic over a wide extent of the country. Prayer meetings noon and night; prayer meetings in Boston, New York, Philadelphia, Chicago; prayer meetings in Richmond, Charleston, Mobile, New Orleans ; prayer meetings in town, village, hamlet, North and South, crowded with expectant listeners and accompanied with a copious outpouring of the Divine Spirit. The whole thing is emotional contagion without principle." This religious revival then spread to Ireland, where it raged with as great a fury as in its native place, the United States, the country of the revival plague.

" I am unwilling to give the details," writes Rev. J. Llewelyn Davies, " [51] of the kinds of affection which have prevailed. They are painful, and in many cases, to speak frankly, simply disgusting. The attacks have so far the character of an epidemic that they have had a singular resemblance to one another. The prevailing symptoms have been a state of perfect physical helplessness beneath an overwhelming sense of guilt and danger; . . . sudden prostrations, shrieks and cries, cataleptic rigidity, oppression at the heart and stomach, in some cases temporary blindness, deafness, and numbness."

American society oscillates between acute financial mania and attacks of religious insanity. I^o sooner is the business fever over than the delirium acutuin of religious mania sets in. Society is thrown from Scylla into Charybdis. From the heights of financial speculation it sinks into the abyss of revivalism. American society seems to suffer from circular insanity.

The friends of revivalism are not unaware of this fact. Thus Rev. H. C. Fish, who made a text-book of revivalism, naively tells us : " It is an interesting fact that they [revivals] frequently succeed some great [public] calamity, a prevailing epidemic, or financial embarrassment." The germs of religious insanity require for their development a diseased and exhausted body politic.

Women in general, and American women in particular, are highly suggestible.* The woman's crusade.

I take here the opportunity to mention the interesting fact of revivalism among the American Jewish women. The revival of ancient Jewish customs and the separation from the Gentile world are among the aims of this religious mania. " Those who take part in this revival," a well-known rabbi informs me, " consider themselves superior to other women." This sense of superiority of those who were " saved " is a well-marked symptom of the revival plague. The germs of this epidemic seem to be very active. Although they started their career in Chicago, at the World's Fair, in the year of our Lord 1893, they have invaded nearly every city of the United States. Rich Jewish ladies form the main body of victims; they are very susceptible to this religious disease.

The interesting peculiarity of this Jewish revival plague is that it attacks only women and rabbis of 1873 may serve as a good illustration.* The crusade commenced in Hillsborough, Ohio, on a Christmas morning. After a lecture by Dr. Dio Lewis on the Potency of "Woman's Prayer in the Grogshop, the response was general. A meeting for prayer and organization was held, the women, led by a distinguished Methodist lady, the heroine of the mob, marched forth on their first visit to drug stores, hotels, and saloons. The crusade mania, like a true epidemic, spread rapidly into adjacent towns, the women visiting saloons, preaching, singing, and praying. Ladies of all denominations joined the crusade. Neither threats nor harsh treatment nor rough weather could check the fervent religious zeal of the female mobs. In many places the ladies suffered severe privations; they were oftentimes kept standing in the cold and rain; they were often offended and ill treated; but of no avail — the crusade epidemic kept on raging with unabated fury. The churches were crowded day and night. Like all things taken up by women, the enthusiasm of this crusade did not last long; it soon died out. Social suggestibility is too strong in woman to permit her to remain long under the influence of suggestions that are out of the way of commonplace life. Woman can not leave long the routine of her life, the beaten track of mediocrity; she can rarely rise above the trite ; she is a Philistine by nature.

Such were, in the main, some of the religious epidemics that befell American society for the brief space of its existence. Who can enumerate all the commercial "revivals," the "business bubbles," and the economical panics closely following in their wake ?

Who can tell of all the crazes and manias—such, for instance, as the football mania, the baseball mania, the prize-fight insanity, the Trilby craze, the bicycle frenzy, the new-woman pest—that have taken possession of the American social self ? Who can count all the industrial, political, and lynching mobs hi which the spirit of American society has manifested itself ? Their name is legion, for they are innumerable, countless.*

Sad and melancholy are the mental aberrations of the social mind, but very painful is it to find that they flow from the inmost soul of society. Society by its very nature tends to run riot in mobs and epidemics. For the gregarious, the subpersonal, uncritical social self, the mob self, and the suggestible subconscious self are identical.

While this work was in progress a great economico-political epidemic, the so-called silver movement, was raging over the country. The work was hardly completed when the excitement of the silver mania subsided, but only to give place to a different form of social malady, the speculative " gold-mining mania," the Klondike plague .

[1] The psycho-physiological state of suggestion I term suggestibility. By "suggestibility of a factor" is meant the power of the factor to induce the psycho-physiological state of suggestion of a certain degree of intensity, the suggestiveness of the factor being measured by the degree of suggestibility induced.

[2] * Mind, Oct., 1884 .

[3] Zeitschrift, Januar, 1894 .

[4] November and December, 1892 .

[5] Let me add here that the figures bring out rather the relative than the absolute suggestiveness of the factors studied .

[6] * See also his book, Les alternations de la personnalite .

[7] See Chapter III

[8] * See Chapter III

[9]

[10] Suggestive Therapeutics. Hypnotism. Die Hvpnose.

[11] * Psychology, vol. ii. f Animal Magnetism. Suggestive Therapeutics.

[12] See G. H. Lewes's Problems of Life and Mind, second series.

[13] Mind, October, 1884. P. S. P. R., December, 1884. f Ibid., January, 1884. P. S. P. R., January, 1884. 6

[14] Sphygmographic or pulse tracings Illustrate well this state of catalepsy (see diagram, Plate I).

[15] Binet, On Double Consciousness. Vide Binet, Sur les alternations de la Conscience, Revue Philosophique, v, 27, 1884 .

[16] Binet, On Double Consciousness; also, Rerue Philosophique, v, 27 .

[17] Pierre Janet, L'Automatisme Psychologique .

[18] E. Gourney. Poet-hypnotic States, Pr. S. P. R., April, 1887 .

[19] Lunatic asylum near Nancy .

[20] Unconscious Cerebration, American Journal of Psychology, November, 1892 .

[21] I am rather disposed to think that the answer in these cases is given not by the upper but by the lower consciousness of the subject.

[22] Proceedings of the American Society for Psychological Research.

[23] Braid, Neurypnology.

[24] James, Psychology, vol. ii

[25] Proceedings of the Society for Psychical Research, May, 1889 .

[26] Proceedings of the Society for Psychical Research, December, 1896 .

[27] Myers, The Subliminal Self, Proceedings of the Society for Psychical Research, vol. viii.

[28] Self is often understood by writers as equivalent to personality, while I use the terra self to designate mere consciousness .

[29] See Lloyd Morgan's Comparative Psychology, chapter Memory in Animals .

[30] See James's essay On Some Hegelisms.

[31] It is this type of consciousness that answers Prof. James's description of personality.

[32] The neuraxon is not retracted as a whole; it may remain practically stationary as far as its whole length is concerned, but the fibrillae by contracting withdraw the terminal arborizations for minute distances, and the same holds true of the dendrons .

[33] A knowledge of the hypnoleptic state is of the utmost value to therapeutics. A discussion of this state will appear in the State Hospitals' Bulletin.

[34] During the whole course of investigation and treatment of the case hypnosis was not and could not be used. The reasons will be given in the full report of the case .

[35] Myers, Some So-called Spiritualistic Phenomena, Proceedings of the Society for Psychical Research, November, 1884 .

[36] *W. Hammond, A Treatise on Insanity .

[37] Ribot, Diseases of Memory. Archiv fur Psychiatric, 1873, vol. iv .

[38] The Psychological Review, November, 1895 .

[39] I may add that in a private talk with me Prof. Royce admitted that we must look for that source to the subconscious. f Theil II, Die Paranoischen Zustiinde, 1896

[40] A Malo-Russian term for Veliko-Russians. In all anti-Jewish riots Veliko-Russians were the ringleaders.

[41] "The vast majority of persons,"writes F. Galton, "of our race have a natural tendency to shrink from the responsibility of standing and acting alone; they exalt the vox populi, even when they know it to be the utterance of a mob of nobodies, into the vox Dei. and they are willing slaves to tradition, authority, and custom."

[42] Anon. Chron. Rhythmicum, in Ranch's Rerum Austriacarum Scriptores .

[43] Phantasmata, vol. i. R. R. Madden. 33 1

[44] The repetition of the Lord's Prayer and Creed was a sure test to discover the followers of Beelzebub. No witch could do so correctly. If she missed a word, or even if she pronounced one incoherently, she was guilty. Tearlessness was also a good test. Witches can not shed more than three tears, and that only from the left eye.

[45] Charles Mackay, Memoirs.

[46] History of the Presbyterian Church in Kentucky .

[47] Gospel Herald. Prof. D. W. Yandell, Epidemic Convulsions Brain, October, 1881. McNemar .

[48] Prof. D. W. Yandell, Brain, October, 1881. Appleton's Journal, December 11, 1875 .

[49] Esquirol, Mental Maladies, English translation .

[50] H. C. Fish, Handbook of Revivals. For the use of Winners of Souls .

[51] Macmillan, vol. i, March, 1860 .

PHILISTINE AND GENIUS

Boris Sidis

New York—1911

To
The Fathers and Mothers
of
The United States

Contents:

CHAPTER I

I ADDRESS myself to you, fathers and mothers, and to you, open-minded readers. I take it for granted that your lifework is with you a serious matter and that you put forth all your efforts to do your best in the walk of life which you have chosen. I assume that you want to develop your energies to the highest efficiency and bring out the best there is in you. I assume that you earnestly wish and strive to bring out and develop to the highest efficiency the faculties not only of your children, but also those of your friends and co-workers with whom you associate in your daily vocation, and that you are deeply interested in the education of your countrymen and their children, who share with you the duties, rights and privileges of citizenship. I also assume that as men and women of liberal education you are not limited to the narrow interests of one particular subject, to the exclusion of all else. I assume that you are especially interested in the development of personality as a whole, the true aim of education. I also assume that you realize that what is requisite is not some more routine, not more desiccated, quasi-scientific methods of educational psychology, not the sawdust of college-pseudogogics and philistine, normal school-training, but more light on the problems of life. What you want is not the training of philistines, but the education of genius.

We need more light, more information on "the problems of life." Is it not too big a phrase to employ? On a second thought, however, I must say that your problems are the problems of life. For the problems of education are fundamental, they are at the bottom of all vital problems. The ancient Greeks were aware of it and paid special attention to education. In rearing his revolutionary, utopian edifice, Plato insists on education as the foundation of a new social, moral and intellectual life. Plato in his Republic makes Socrates tell his interlocutor, Adeimantus: "Then you are aware that in every work the beginning is the most important part, especially in dealing with anything young and tender? For that is the time when any impression which one may desire to communicate is most readily stamped and taken."

We may say that all man's struggles, religious, moral and economical, all the combats and conflicts that fill the history of mankind, can be traced finally to the nature and vigor of the desires, beliefs and strivings which have been cultivated by the social environment in the early life of the individual. The character of a nation is moulded by the nature of its education. The character of society depends on the early training of its constituent units. The fatalism, the submissiveness of the Oriental; the aestheticism, the independence, love of innovations and inquisitiveness of the ancient Greek; the ruggedness, sturdiness, harshness and conservatism of the ancient Roman; the emotionalism, the religious fervor of the ancient Hebrew; the commercialism, restlessness, speculation and scientific spirit of modern times, are all the results of the nature of the early education the individual gets in his respective social environment. We may say that the education of early life forms the very foundation of the social structure.

Like clay in the hands of the potter, so is man in the hands of his community. Society fashions the beliefs, the desires, the aims, the strivings, the knowledge, the ideals, the character, the minds, the very selves of its constituent units. Who has the control of this vital function of moulding minds? Fathers and mothers, the child is under your control. To your hands, to your care is entrusted the fate of young generations, the fate of the future community, which, consciously or unconsciously, you fashion according to the accepted standards and traditions with which you have been imbued in your own education.

It is related, I think, in Plutarch's Lives, of Themistocles telling with the ironical frankness characteristic of the Greek temperament that his son possessed the greatest power in Greece: "For the Athenians command the rest of Greece, I command the Athenians, his mother commands me, and he commands his mother." This bit of Greek irony is not without its significance. The mind of the growing generation controls the future of nations. The boy is father to the man, as the proverb has it; he controls the future. But who controls the boy? The home, the mother and father, the guides of the child's early life. For it is in early life that the foundation of our mental edifice is laid. All that is good, valid and solid in man's mental structure depends on the breadth, width, depth, and solidity of that foundation.

CHAPTER II

THAT the groundwork of man's character is laid in his childhood appears as a trivial platitude. I am almost ashamed to bring it before you. And yet, as I look round me and find how apt we are to forget this simple precept which is so fundamental in our life, I cannot help calling your attention to it. If we consider the matter, we can well understand the reason why its full significance is not realized. We must remember that all science begins with axioms which are apparently truisms. What is more of a truism than the axioms of Geometry and Mechanics—that the whole is greater than the part, that things which are equal to the same thing are equal to one another, or that a body remains in the same state unless an external force changes it? And yet the whole of Mathematics and Mechanics is built on those simple axioms.

The elements of science are just such obvious platitudes. What is needed is to use them as efficient tools and by their means draw the consequent effects. The same holds true in the science of education. The axiom or the law of early training is not new, it is well known, but it is unfortunately too often neglected and forgotten, and its significance is almost completely lost.

It is certainly surprising how this law of early training is so disregarded, so totally ignored in the education of the child. Not only do we neglect to lay the necessary solid basis in the early life of the child, a solid basis ready for the future structure, we do not even take care to clear the ground. In fact, we even make the child's soul a dunghill, full of vermin of superstitions, fears and prejudices, a hideous heap saturated with the spirit of credulity.

We regard the child's mind as a *tabula rasa*, a vacant lot, and empty on it all our rubbish and refuse. We labor under the delusion that stories and fairy tales, myths and deceptions about life and man are good for the child's mind. Is it a wonder that on such a foundation men can only put up shacks and shanties? We forget the simple fact that what is harmful for the adult is still more harmful to the child. Surely what is poisonous to the grown-up mind cannot be useful food to the young. If credulity in old wives' tales, lack of individuality, sheepish submissiveness, barrack-discipline, unquestioned and uncritical belief in authority, meaningless imitation of jingles and gibberish, memorization of mother-goose wisdom, repetition of incomprehensible prayers and articles of creed, unintelligent aping of good manners, silly games, prejudices and superstitions and fears of the supernormal and supernatural, are censured in adults, why 'should we approve their cultivation in the young?

At home and at school we drill into the child's mind uncritical beliefs in stories and tales, fictions and figments, fables and myths, creeds and dogmas which poison the very sources of the child's mind. At home and at school we give the child over as a prey to all sorts of fatal germs of mental diseases and moral depravity. We leave the child's mind an open field to be sown with dragon's teeth which bring forth a whole crop of pernicious tendencies,— love and admiration of successful evil, and adoration of the rule of brute force. From the dragon's teeth sown in early childhood there rises in later life a whole brood of flint-hearted men who blindly jostle and fight and mercilessly tear one another, to obtain for some greedy Jason, some witch of a Medea their coveted golden fleece.

CHAPTER III

WE regard with disapproval the bloody combats of some savage tribe; we regard with horror the sacrifice of children and prisoners to some idol of a Phoenician Moloch or Mexican Huitzlio-Potchli; we are shocked at the criminal proceedings of the infamous Torquemada with his inquisition glorying in its terrors and tortures in the name of Christ; we are sickened as we read of the religious wars in Europe; we shudder at the horrors of the night of St. Bartholomew; we are appalled by the recent slaughters of the Jews in Russia, by the wholesale massacre of the Christians in Turkey.

All such atrocities, we say, belong to barbaric ages and are only committed in semi-civilized countries. We flatter ourselves that we are different in this age of enlightenment and civilization. Are we different? Have we changed? Have we a right to fling stones at our older brothers, the savage and the barbarian? We are so used to our life that we do not notice its evils and misery. We can easily see the mote in the eye of our neighbor, but do not notice the beam in our own.

We are still savage at heart. Our civilization is mere gloss, a thin coating of paint and varnish. Our methods of inflicting pain are more refined than those of the Indian, but no less cruel, while the number of the victims sacrificed to our greed and rapacity may even exceed the numbers fallen by the sword of the barbarian or by the torch of the fanatic. The slums in our cities are foul and filthy, teeming with deadly germs of disease where the mortality of our infants and children in some cases rises to the frightful figure of 204 per thousand!

The sanitary conditions of our cities are filthy and deadly. They carry in their wake all forms of plagues, pests and diseases, among which tuberculosis is so well known to the laity. "Tuberculosis," reads a report of a Tenement House Commission, "is one of the results of our inhumane tenements; it follows in the train of our inhumane sweatshops. It comes where the hours of labor are long and the wages are small; it afflicts the children who are sent to labor when they should yet be in school."

"The Consumers' League," says Mr. John Graham Brooks, "long hesitated to lay stress upon these aspects of filth and disease, because of their alarmist and sensational nature, and of the immediate and grave risk to the consumer of the goods manufactured in the sweatshop and the tenement house. If the sweatshop spread diphtheria and scarlet fever, there is the hue and cry before personal danger. But these diseases are the very slightest elements of the real risk to the general good. It is the spoiled human life, with its deadly legacy of enfeebled mind and body, that reacts directly and indirectly on the social whole." We do not realize that we drift into national degeneracy. We fail to realize that we raise a generation of stunted lives, of physical and nervous wrecks, of mental invalids and moral cripples.

We boast of our wealth unrivalled by other countries and by former ages. We should remember the great poverty of our masses, the filthy conditions of our wealthy cities, with their loathsome city-slums, in which human beings live, breed and teem like so many worms.

We spend on barracks and prisons more than we do on schools and colleges. What is the level of a civilization in which the cost of crime and war far exceeds that of the education of its future citizens? We spend on our army and navy a quarter of a billion dollars, which is found to be insufficient, while the "total money burden of crime amounts in this country to the enormous sum of 600 million dollars a year!"

The cost of crime alone is so enormous that a representative of the Board of Charities of one of our Eastern states considers "the entire abolition of all the penal codes and the complete liberty of the criminal class." Our civilization can boast of the city-slum, the abode of misery and crime, the gift of our modern industrial progress, wealth and prosperity.

Professor James and myself were over once on a visit to a charitable institution for mentally defective. With his clear eye for the incongruities and absurdities of life, Professor James remarked to me that idiots and imbeciles were given the comforts, in fact, the luxuries of life, while healthy children, able boys and girls, had to struggle for a livelihood. Children under fourteen work in factories, work at a wage of about twenty-five cents a day, and, according to the labor bureau, the daily wage of the factory children of the South is often as low as fifteen cents and sometimes falls to nine cents. In many of our colleges many a student has to live on the verge of starvation, freeze in a summer overcoat the whole winter and warm his room by burning newspapers in the grate. We are charitable and help our mediocrities, imbeciles and idiots, while we neglect our talent and genius. We have a blind faith that genius, like murder, will out. We know of successful talent, but we do not know of the great amount of unsuccessful talent and genius that has gone to waste. We favor imbecility and slight genius.

One of the physicians of the institution overheard our conversation and attempted to justify his work by an argument commonly advanced and uncritically accepted—"Our civilization, our Christian civilization values human life." Does our civilization really value human life? The infant mortality of the slums of our large cities and the factory work of our young children do not seem to justify such a claim.

The loss of life on our railways is as large as one caused by a national war. Thus the number of persons killed on America on railways during a period of three years ending June 30, 1900, was about 22,000, while the mortality of British forces, including death from disease, during three years of the South African war amounted to 22,000. In 1901, one out of every 400 railway employees was killed and one out of every 26 was injured. In 1902, 2,969 employees were killed and 50,524 were injured.

Commenting on the statistics of railway accidents, Mr. John Graham Brooks says: "One has to read and re-read these figures before their gruesome significance is in the least clear. If we add the mining, iron and lumbering industries,—portions of which are more dangerous than the railroad,—some conception is possible of the mutilated life due to machinery as it is now run." It may also be of interest to learn that, according to the calculation made by a representative of one of the insurance companies, more than a million and a half are annually killed and injured in the United States alone.

The waste of human life is in fact greater than in any previous age. "Saul hath slain his thousands, but David his ten thousands." Think of our modern warfare, with its infernal machines of carnage, mowing down more men in a day than the warlike Assyrians and Romans, with their crude bows, arrows and catapults, could destroy in a century. And is not our country, our civilized Christian society, with its high valuation of human life, keeping on increasing its army and navy, and perfecting deadly weapons of slaughter and carnage? What about the justice dealt out by Judge Lynch? From 1882 to 1900 there were about three thousand lynchings! What about our grand imperial policy? What about our dominance over weak and ignorant tribes, treated in no gentle way by the armed fist of their civilized masters, who send to the benighted heathens their missionaries to preach religion and their soldiers to enforce the sale of narcotics and other civilizing goods?

CHAPTER IV

WE are stock-blind to our own barbarities; we do not realize the enormities of our life and consider our age and country as civilized and enlightened. We censure the faults of other societies, but do not notice our own. Thus Lecky, in describing Roman society, says: "The gladiatorial games form indeed the one feature which to a modern mind is most inconceivable in its atrocity. That not only men, but women, man advanced period of civilization,—men and women who not only professed, but very frequently acted upon a high code of morals—should have made the carnage of men their habitual amusement, that all this should have continued for centuries with scarcely a protest, is one of the most startling facts in moral history. It is, however, perfectly normal, while it opens out fields of ethical inquiry of a very deep, though painful, character."

As in modern times, our college authorities justify the brutalities of football and prize-fights, so in ancient times the great moralists of those ages justified their gladiatorial games. Thus the great orator, the moralizing philosopher, Cicero, in speaking of the gladiatorial games, tells us: "When guilty men arc compelled to fight, no better discipline against suffering and death can be presented to the eye." And it is certainly instructive for us to learn that "the very men who looked down with delight, when tile sand of the arena reddened with human blood, made the theater ring with applause when Terence in his famous line proclaimed the brotherhood of men."

One feeble protest is on record, a protest coming from the mother of civilization, from ancient Athens. "When an attempt was made to introduce the games into Athens, the philosopher Demonax appealed successfully to the better feelings of the people by exclaiming: "You must first overthrow the altar of pity!"

The philosopher Demonax had not the compromising spirit of the modern professor. Although the brutal games of our youth and populace need a Demonax, we certainly should not look for one in our colleges and universities. Our college authorities assure us that athletic prestige is indispensable to a good university. In fact, according to some official statements, football teams are supposed to express the superior intellectual activities of our foremost colleges. Like Cicero of old, we claim that "our games are good,—they train men, and no better discipline can be presented to the eye."

The fact is, man is bat-blind to the evils of the environment in which he is bred. He takes those evils as a matter of course, and even finds good reasons to justify them as edifying and elevating. In relation to his own surroundings, man is in the primitive condition of the Biblical Adam,—he is not conscious of his own moral nakedness. Six days in the week we witness and uphold the wholesale carnage, national and international, political, economical, in shops, factories, mines, railroads and on the battlefields, while on the seventh we sing hymns to the God of mercy, love and peace.

We pick up the first newspapers or popular magazines that come to our hand, and we read of wars, slaughters, murders, lynchings, crimes and outrages on life and liberty; we read of strikes, lockouts, of tales of starvation and of frightful infant mortality; we read of diseases and epidemics ravaging the homes of our working population; we read of corporation iniquities, of frauds and corruption of our legislative bodies, of the control of polities by the criminal classes of the great metropolis of our land. We read of all that evil and corruption, but forget them next moment.

Our social life is corrupt, our body politic is eaten through with cankers and sores, "the whole head is sick and the whole heart is faint. From the sole of the foot even unto the head, there is no soundness in it; but wounds, and bruises and putrefying sores, and yet we think we are a civilized people, superior to all countries and to all ages. "The voice of our brother's blood crieth unto us from the ground." How can we be so callous? How can we be so mole-blind and so stone-deaf?

The truth is, we have but a thin varnish of humaneness, glossing over a rude barbarism. With our lips we praise the God of love, but in our hearts we adore the God of force. flow much physical force is worshipped we can realize from the crowds that throng the games of base-ball, football, prize-fights and boxing exhibitions. They go into tens of thousands. flow many would be drawn by a St. Paul, an Epictetus, or a Socrates?

The newspaper, the mirror of our social life, is filled with the names and exploits of our magnates of high finance, our money-mongers and usurers. Our journals teem with deeds and scandals of our refined "smart set" set up as patterns, as ideals, after which our middle class so longingly craves. Like the Israelites of old we worship golden calves and sacred bulls. Our daughters yearn after the barbaric shimmer and glitter of the bejewelled, bespangled, empty-minded, parasitic females of "the smart set." Our college boys admire the feats of the trained athlete and scorn the work of the "grind." Our very schoolboys crave for the fame of a Jeffries and a Johnson. If in the depths of space there is some solar system inhabited by really rational beings, and if one of such beings should by some miracle happen to visit our planet, he would no doubt turn away in horror.

CHAPTER V.

We press our children into the triumphant march of our industrial juggernaut. Over 1,700,000 children under 15 years of age toil in fields, factories, mines and workshops. The slums and the factory cripple the energies of our young generation The slaughter of the innocents and the sacrifice of our children to the insatiable Moloch of industry exclude us from the rank of civilized society and place us on the level of barbaric nations.

Our educators are narrow-minded pedants. They are occupied with the dry bones of text-books, the sawdust of pedagogics and the would-be scientific experiments of educational psychology; they are ignorant of the real vital problems of human interests, a knowledge of which goes to make the truly educated man.

About the middle of the nineteenth century, Buckle made the prediction that no war was any more to occur among civilized nations. Henceforth peace was to reign supreme. "The wolf shall dwell with the lamb, and the leopard shall lie down with the kid; their young ones shall lie down together, and the lion shall eat straw like the ox. . . . Nations shall beat their swords into ploughshares and their spears into pruning hooks. Nation shall not lift lip sword against nation, nor shall they learn war anymore." This prophecy was rather hasty. We have had since the Civil war, the Franco-Prussian war, tile Spanish-American war, the Boer war, the Russo-Japanese war, not counting the ceaseless wars of extermination carried on by civilized nations among the various semi-civilized nations and primitive tribes. Civilized nations do not as yet beat their swords into ploughshares, but keep on increasing the strength of their "armed peace," and are ready to fight bloody battles in the quest of new lands and the conquest of new markets.

In spite of The Hague conference of peace convoked by the peace-loving Czar, no other age has had such large standing armies provided with such costly and efficient weapons of execution ready for instant use. The red spectre still stalks abroad claiming its victims. We still believe in the baptism of fire and redemption by blood. The dogma of blood-redemption is still at the basis of our faith and, consciously or unconsciously, we brand that sacred creed on the minds of the young generation. We are not educated to see and understand the wretchedness, the misery of our life,-the evil of the world falls on the blind spot of our eye. In the name of evolution and the survival of the fittest, we justify the grasping arm of the strong, and even glory in the extermination of the weak. The weak, we say, must be weeded out by the processes of natural selection. The strong are the best; it is right that they should survive and flourish like a green bay tree. The fact is that we are still dominated by the law of the jungle, the den and the cave. We are still wild at heart. We still harken to the call of the wild; we are ruled by the fist, the claw and the tooth.

Love, justice, gentleness, peace, reason, sympathy and pity, all humane feelings and promptings are with us sentiments of unnatural" or supernatural religion which we profess in our churches, but in which we really have no faith as good for actual life. We mistake brutishness for courage, and by fight and by war we train the beast in man.

All humane feelings are regarded as so many hindrances to progress; they favor, we claim, the survival of the weak. We are, of course, evolutionists, and believe most firmly in progress. We believe that the luxuries and vices of the strong are conducive to prosperity, and that the evils of life by the automatic grinding of that grind-organ known as the process of evolution *somehow* lead to a higher civilization.

When in the beginning of the eighteenth century Bernard de Mandeville proclaimed the apparently paradoxical principle that *Private Vices are Public Benefits* , the academic moralists were shocked at such profane brutality. Mandeville only proclaimed the leading, the guiding principle of the coming age of industrial prosperity. We now know better. Are we not evolutionists? Have we not learned that progress and evolution and the improvement of the race are brought about by the fierce struggle for existence, by the process of natural selection, by the merciless elimination of the weak and by the triumph of the strong and the fit? What is the use of being sentimental? Like Brennus, the Gaul, we throw our sword on the scales of blinded justice and shout triumphantly *"Væ victis!"*

CHAPTER VI

WE are confirmed optimists and sow optimism broadcast. We have optimistic clubs and mental scientists and Christian scientists,—all afflicted with incurable ophthalmia to surrounding evil and misery. We are scientific, we are evolutionists, we have faith in the sort of optimism taught by Leibnitz in his famous Theodicea. We are the Candides of our oracles, the Panglosses. You may possibly remember what Voltaire writes of Professor Pangloss. "Pangloss used to teach the science of metaphysico – theologo – cosmologo - noodleology. He demonstrated to admiration that there is no effect without a cause and that this is the best of all possible worlds. It has been proved, said Pangloss, that things cannot be otherwise than they are; for everything, the end for which everything is made, is necessarily the best end. Observe how noses are made to carry 'spectacles, and spectacles we have accordingly. Everything that is, is the best that could possibly be." It is such shallow optimism that now gains currency.

Verily, we are afflicted with mental cataract. "If we should bring clearly to a man's sight," says Schopenhauer, "the terrible sufferings and miseries to which his life is constantly exposed, he would be seized with horror, and if we were to conduct the confirmed optimist through the hospitals, infirmaries, and surgical operating-rooms, through prisons, asylums, torture-chambers and slave-kennels, over battlefields and places of execution; if we were to open to him all the dark abodes of misery, where it hides itself from the glance of cold curiosity, he would understand at last the nature of this best of possible worlds."

Schopenhauer is metaphysical, pessimistic, but he is certainly not blinded by a shallow optimism to the realities of life. Drunk with the spirit of optimism, we do not realize the degradation, the misery and poverty of our life. Meanwhile the human genius, the genius which all of us possess, languishes, famishes, and perishes, while the brute alone emerges in triumph. We are so overcome by the faith in the transcendent, optimistic evolution of the good, that through the misty heavenly, angelic visions, we do not discern the cloven hoof of the devil.

Professor James in a recent address told the Radcliffe graduates that the aim of a college-education is "to recognize the good man," when you see him. Thisadvice may be good for Radcliffe young ladies; but, fathers and mothers, the true education of life is the recognition of evil wherever it is met.

The Bible begins the story of man in a paradise of ignorance and finishes it with his tasting of the fruits of the forbidden tree of knowledge of good and evil. "And the eyes of them both were opened and they knew that they were naked. And the Lord God said,—Behold, the man is become as one of us to know good and evil, and now, lest he put forth his hand and take also of the tree of life and eat and live forever. Therefore, the Lord God sent him forth from the garden of Eden. So he drove out the man." We prefer the sinful, mortal, but godlike man with his knowledge of evil to the brutish philistine in the bliss of Elysium.

CHAPTER VII

IN the education of the young generation the purpose of the nation is to bring up the child as a good man, as a liberal-minded citizen, devoted soul and body to the interests of social welfare. This purpose in the education of the young citizen is of the utmost importance in every society, but it is a vital need in a democratic society. We do not want narrow-minded patriots devoted to party-factions, nor bigoted sectarians, nor greedy entrepreneurs fastening in trusts, like so many barnacles, on the body-politic. We do not want ringleaders and mobs, unscrupulous bosses and easily led voters. What we need is men having at heart the welfare of their fellow-men.

The purpose of the education provided by the nation for its young generation is the rearing of healthy, talented, broad-minded citizens. "We need, above all, good citizens, active and intelligent, with a knowledge of life and with a delicate sense of discrimination and detection of evil in all its protean forms; we need strong-minded citizens with grit and courage to resist oppression and root out evil wherever it is found. A strong sense of recognition of evil should be the social sense of every well-educated citizen as a safeguard of social and national life. The principle of recognition of evil under all its guises is at the basis of the true education of man.

Is it not strange that this vital principle of education, the recognition of evil,—a fundamental principle with the great thinkers of humanity,—should remain sosadly neglected by our educators and public instructors? Our educators are owl-wise, our teachers are pedants and all their ambition is the turning out of smooth, well-polished philistines. It is a sad case of the blind leading the blind.

It is certainly unfortunate that the favored type of superintendent of our public education should be such a hopeless philistine, possessed of all the conceit of the mediocre business man. Routine is his ideal. Originality and genius are spurned and suppressed. Our school-superintendent with his well-organized training-shop is proud of the fact that there is no place for genius in our schools.

Unfortunate and degraded is the nation that has handed over its childhood and youth to guidance and control by hide-bound mediocrity. Our school-managers are respected by the laity as great educators and are looked up to by the teachers as able business men. Their merit is routine, discipline and the hiring of cheap teaching-employees.

It is certainly a great misfortune to the nation that a good number of our would-be scientific pedagogues are such mediocrities, with so absurd an exaggeration of their importance that they are well satisfied if the mass of their pupils turn out exact reproductions of the silly pedagogue. What can be expected of a nation that entrusts the fate of its young generation to the care or carelessness of young girls, to the ire of old maids, and to pettifogging officials with their educational red tape, discipline and routine,—petty bureaucrats animated with a hatred towards talent and genius?

The goody-goody schoolma'am, the mandarin-schoolmaster, the philistine-pedagogue, the pedant-administrator with his business capacities, have proved themselves incompetent to deal with the education of the young. They stifle talent, they stupefy the intellect, they paralyze the will, they suppress genius, they benumb the faculties of our children. The educator, with his pseudo-scientific, pseudo-psychological pseudogogics, can only bring up a set of philistines with firm, set habits,—marionettes,—dolls.

Business is put above learning, administration above education, discipline and order above cultivation of genius and talent. Our schools and colleges are controlled by business men. The school-boards, the boards of trustees of almost every school and college ill the country consist mainly of, manufacturers, store-keepers, tradesmen, bulls and bears of Wall street and the market-place. What wonder that they bring with them the ideals and methods of the factory, the store, the bank and the saloon. If the saloon controls politics, the shop controls education.

Business men are no more competent to run schools and colleges than astronomers are fit to run hotels and theaters. Our whole educational system is vicious. A popular scientific journal entered a protest against the vulgarization of our colleges, the department-store trade methods of our universities, but to no avail. The popular hero, the administrative business superintendent still holds sway, and poisons the sources of our social life by debasing the very foundation of our national education.

CHAPTER VIII

FROM time to time the "educational" methods of our philistine teachers are brought to light. A girl is forced by a schoolma'am of one of our large cities to stay in a corner for hours, because she unintentionally transgressed against the barrack-discipline of the school-regulations. When the parents became afraid of the girl's health and naturally took her out of school, the little girl was dragged before the court by the truant officer. Fortunately "the judge turned to the truant officer and asked him how the girl could be a truant, if she had been suspended. He didn't believe in breaking children's wills. "

In another city a pupil of genius was excluded from school because "he did not fall in with the system" laid out by the "very able business-superintendent." A schoolmistress conceives the happy idea of converting two of her refractory pupils into pin-cushions for the edification of her class. An "educational" administrative superintendent of a large, prosperous community told a lady who brought to him her son, an extraordinarily able boy, "I shall not take your boy. into my high-school, in spite of his knowledge." When the mother asked him to listen to her, he lost patience and told her with all the force of his school-authority, "Madam, put a rope around his neck, weigh him well down with bricks!"

A principal of a high school in one of the prominent New England towns dismisses a highly talented pupil because, to quote verbatim from the original school document, "He is not amenable to the discipline of the school, as his school life has been too short to establish him in the habit' of obedience." "His intellect," the principal's official letter goes on to say, "remains a marvel to us, but we do not feel, and in this I think I speak for all, that he is in the right place." In other words, in the opinion of those remarkable pedagogues, educators and teachers, the school is not the right place for talent and genius!

A superintendent of schools in lecturing before an audience of "subordinate teachers" told them emphatically that *there was no place for genius in our schools.* Dear old fogies, one can well understand your indignation! Here we have worked out some fine methods, clever rules, beautiful systems and then comes genius and upsets the whole structure! It is a shame! Genius cannot fit into the pigeon-holes of the office desk. Choke genius, and things will move smoothly in the school and the office.

Not long ago we were informed by one of those successful college-mandarins, lionized by office-clerks, superintendents and tradesmen, that he could measure education by the foot-rule! Our Regents are supposed to raise the level of education by a vicious system of examination and coaching, a system which Professor James, in a private conversation with me, has aptly characterized as "idiotic."

Our schools brand their pupils by a system of marks, while our foremost colleges measure the knowledge and education of their students by the number of "points" passed. The student may pass either in Logic or Blacksmithing. It does not matter which, provided he makes up a certain number of "points"!

College-committees refuse admission to young students of genius, because "it is against the policy and the principles of the university." College-professors expel promising students from the lecture-room for "the good of the class as a whole," because the students "happen to handle their hats in the middle of a lecture." This, you see, interferes with class discipline. *Fiat justitia, pereat mundus.* Let genius perish, provided the system lives. Why not suppress all genius, as a disturbing element, for "the good of the classes," for the weal of the commonwealth? Education of man and cultivation of genius, indeed! This is not school policy.

We school and drill our children and youth in schoolma'am mannerism, schoolmaster mind-ankylosis, school-superintendent stiff-joint ceremonialism, factory regulations and office-discipline. We give our pupils and students artisan-inspiration and business-spirituality. Originality is suppressed. Individuality is crushed. Mediocrity is at a premium. That is why our country has such clever business men, such cunning artisans, such resourceful politicians, such adroit leaders of new cults, but no scientists, no artists, no philosophers, no statesmen, no genuine talent and no true genius.

School-teachers have in all ages been mediocre in intellect and incompetent. Leibnitz is regarded as a dullard and Newton is considered as a blockhead. Never, however, in the history of mankind have school teachers fallen to such a low level of mediocrity as in our times and in our country. For it is not the amount of knowledge that counts in true education, but originality and independence of thought that are of importance in education. But independence and originality of ,thought are just the very elements that are suppressed by our modern barrack-system of education. No wonder that military men claim that the best "education" is given in military schools.

We are not aware that the incubus of officialdom, and the succubus of bureaucracy have taken possession of our schools. The red tape of officialdom, like a poisonous weed, grows luxuriantly in our schools and chokes the life of our young generation. Instead of growing into a people of great independent thinkers, the nation is in danger of fast becoming a crowd of well-drilled, well-disciplined, commonplace individuals, with strong philistine habits and notions of hopeless mediocrity .

In levelling education to mediocrity we imagine that we uphold the democratic spirit of our institutions. Our American sensibilities a-re shocked when the president of one of our leading colleges dares to recommend to his college that it should cease catering to the average student. "We think it un-American, rank treason to our democratic spirit when a college president has the courage to proclaim the principle that "To form the mind and character of one man of marked talent, not to say genius, would be worth more to the community which he would serve than the routine training of hundreds of undergraduates."

We are optimistic, we believe in the pernicious superstition that genius needs no help, that talent will take care of itself. Our kitchen clocks and dollar timepieces need careful handling, but our chronometers and astronomical clocks can run by themselves.

The truth is, however, that the purpose of the school and the college is not to create an intellectual aristocracy, but to educate, to bring out the individuality, the originality, the latent powers of talent and genius present in what we unfortunately regard as "the average student." Follow Mill's advice. Instead of aiming at athletics, social connections, vocations and generally at the professional art of money-making, "Aim at something noble. Make your system such that a great man may be formed by it, and there will be a manhood in your little men, of which you do not dream."

Awaken in early childhood the critical spirit of man; awaken, early in the child's life, love of knowledge, love of truth, of art and literature for their own sake, and you arouse man's genius. We have average mediocre students, because we have mediocre teachers, department-store superintendents, clerkly principals and deans with bookkeepers' souls, because our schools and colleges deliberately aim at mediocrity.

Ribot in describing the degenerated Byzantine Greeks tells us that their leaders were mediocrities and their great men commonplace personalities. Is the American nation drifting in the same direction? It was the system of cultivation of independent thought that awakened the Greek mind to its highest achievements in arts, science and philosophy; it was the deadly Byzantine bureaucratic red tape with its cut-and-dried theological discipline that dried up the sources of Greek genius. We are in danger of building up a Byzantine empire with large institutions and big corporations, small minds and dwarfed individualities. Like the Byzantines we begin to value administration above individuality and official, red-tape ceremonialism above originality.

We wish even to turn our schools into practical school-shops. We shall in time become a nation of well-trained clerks and artisans. The time is at hand when hall be justified in writing over the gates of our school-shops "mediocrity made here!"

CHAPTER IX

I ASSUME that as liberal men and women you have no use for the process of cramming and stuffing of college-geese and mentally indolent, morally obtuse and religiously "cultured" prigs and philistines, but that you realize that your true vocation is to get access to the latent energies of your children, to stimulate their reserve energies and educate, bring to light, man's genius. The science of psychopathology now sets forth a fundamental principle which is not only of the utmost importance in psychotherapeutics, but also in the domain of education; it is the principle of stored up, dormant, reserve energy, the principle of potential, subconscious, reserve energy .

It is claimed on good evidence, biological, physiological and psychopathological, that man possesses large stores of unused energy which the ordinary stimuli of life are not only unable to reach, but even tend to inhibit. Unusual combinations of circumstances, however, radical changes of the environment, often unloose the inhibitions brought about by the habitual narrow range of man's interests and surroundings. Such unloosening of inhibitions helps to release fresh supplies of reserve energy. It is not the place here to discuss this fundamental principle; I can only state it in the most general way, and give its general trend in the domain of education.

You have heard the psychologizing educator advise the formation of good, fixed, stable habits in early life. Now I want to warn you against the dangers of such unrestricted advice. Fixed adaptations, stable habits, tend to raise the thresholds of mental life, tend to inhibit the liberation, the output of reserve-energy. *Avoid routine.* Do not let your pupils fall into the ruts of habits and customs. Do not let even the *best* of habits harden beyond the point of further possible modification.

Where there is a tendency towards formation of over-abundant mental cartilage, set your pupils to work under widely different circumstances. Confront them with a changed set of conditions. Keep them on the move. Surprise them by some apparently paradoxical relations and strange phenomena. Do not let them settle down to one definite set of actions or reactions. Remember that rigidity, like sclerosis, induration of tissue, means decay of originality, destruction of man's genius. With solidified and invariable habits not only does the reserve energy become entirely inaccessible, but the very individuality is extinguished.

Do not make of our children a nation of philistines. Why say, you make man in your own image? Do not make your schools machine-shops, turning out on one uniform pattern so much mediocrity per year. *Cultivate variability.* The tendency towards variability is the most precious part of a good education. Beware of the philistine with his set, stable habits.

The important principle in education is not so much *formation* of habits as the power of their *re-formation*. The power of breaking up habits is by far the more essential factor of a good education. It is in this power of breaking down habits that we can find the key for the unlocking of the otherwise inaccessible stores of subconscious reserve energy. *The cultivation of the power of habit-disintegration is what constitutes the proper education of man's genius.* *

A well known editor of one of the academic Journals on Educational Psychology writes to me as follows: "Your remarks on the avoidance of routine would be like a red rag to a bull for a number of educators who are emphasizing the importance of habit formation in education at present."

CHAPTER X

THE power of breaking down or dissolving habits depends on the amount and strength of the *aqua fortis* of the intellect. The logical and critical activities of the individual should be cultivated with special care. The critical self, as we may put it, should have control over the automatic and the subconscious. For the subconscious has been shown to form the fertile soil for the breeding of the most dangerous germs of mental disease, epidemics, plagues and pestilences in their worst forms. We should try to develop the individual's critical abilities in early childhood, not permitting the suggestible subconsciousness to predominate, and to become overrun with noxious weeds and pests.

We should be very careful with the child's critical self, as it is weak and has little resistance. We should, therefore, avoid all dominating authority and categorical imperative commands. Autocratic authority cultivates in the child the predisposition to abnormal suggestibility, to hypnotic states, and leads towards the dominance of the subconscious with its train of pernicious tendencies and deleterious results.

There is a period in the child's life between the ages of five and ten when he is very inquisitive, asking all kinds of questions. *It is the age of discussion in the child.* This inquisitiveness and discussion should by all means be encouraged and fostered. We should aid the development of the spirit ofinquisitiveness and curiosity in the child. For this is the acquisition of control over the stored-up, latent energies of man's genius.

We should not arrest the child's questioning spirit, as we are often apt to do, but should strongly encourage the apparently meddlesome and troublesome searching and prying and scrutinizing of *whatever interests the child.* Everything should be open to the child's searching interest; nothing should be suppressed and tabooed as too sacred for examination. The spirit of inquiry, the genius of man, is more sacred than any abstract belief, dogma and creed.

A rabbi came to ask my advice about the education of his little boy. My advice was: "Teach him not to be a Jew." The man of God departed and never came again. The rabbi did not care for education, but for faith. He did not wish his boy to become a man, but to be a Jew.

The most central, the most crucial part of the education of man's genius is *the knowledge, the recognition of evil* in all its protean forms and innumerable disguises, intellectual, æsthetic and moral, such as fallacies, sophisms, ugliness, deformity, prejudice, superstition, vice and depravity. Do not be afraid to discuss these matters with the child. For the knowledge, the recognition of evil does not only possess the virtue of immunization of the child's mind against all evil, but furnishes the main power for habit disintegration with consequent release and control of potential reserve energy, of manifestations of human genius. When a man becomes contented and ceases to notice the evils of life, as is done by some modern religious sects, he loses his hold on the powers of man's genius, he loses touch with the throbbing pulse of humanity, he loses hold on reality and falls into subhuman groups.

The purpose of education, of a *liberal* education, is not to live in a fool's paradise, or to go through the world in a post-hypnotic state of negative hallucinations. The true aim of a liberal education is, as the Scriptures put it, to have the *eyes opened,—to* be free from all delusions, illusions, from the *fata morgana* of life. We prize a liberal education, because it *liberates* us from subjection to superstitious fears, delivers us from the narrow bonds of prejudice, from the exalted or depressing delusions of moral paresis, intellectual dementia-praecox, and religious paranoia. A liberal education liberates us from the enslavement to the degrading influence of *all* idol-worship.

In the education of man do not play on his subconscious sense by deluding him by means of hypnotic and post-hypnotic suggestions of positive and negative hallucinations, with misty and mystic, beatific visions. Open his *eyes* to undisguised reality. Teach him, show him how to strip the real from its unessential wrappings and adornments and see things in their nakedness. *Open the eyes of your children so that they shall see, understand and face courageously the evils of life.*

Then will you do your duty as parents, then will you give your children the proper education.

CHAPTER XI

I HAVE spoken of the fundamental law of early education. The question is *"how early?"* There are, of course, children who are backward in their development. This backwardness may either be congenital or may be due to some overlooked pathological condition that may be easily remedied by proper treatment. In the large majority of children, however, the beginning of education *is between the second and third year.* It is at that time that the child begins to form his interests. It is at that critical period that we have to seize the opportunity to guide the child's formative energies in the right channels. To delay is a mistake and a wrong to the child. We can at that early period awaken a love of knowledge which will persist through life. The child will as eagerly play in the game of knowledge as he now spends the most of his energies in meaningless games and objectless silly sports.

We claim we are afraid to force the child's mind. We claim we are afraid *to strain his brain prematurely.* This is an error. In *directing* the course of the use of the child's energies we do not force the child. If *you* do not *direct* the energies in the right course, the child will *waste* them in the *wrong* direction. The same amount of mental energy used in those silly games, which we think are specially adapted for the childish mind, can be directed, with lasting benefit, to the development of his *interests in intellectual activity and love of knowledge. The child will learn to play at the game of knowledge-acquisition with the same ease, grace and interest as he is showing now in his nursery-games and physical exercises.*

CHAPTER XII

ARISTOTLE laid it down as a self-evident proposition that all Hellenes *love knowledge* . This was true of the national genius of the ancient Greeks. The love of wisdom is the pride of the ancient Greek in contradistinction to the barbarian, who does not prize knowledge. We still belong to the barbarians. Our children, our pupils, our students have no love of knowledge.

The ancient Greeks knew the value of a good education and understood its fundamental elements. They laid great stress on early education and they knew how to develop man's mental energies, without fear of injury to the brain and physical constitution. The Greeks were not afraid of thought, that it might injure the brain. 'They were strong men, great thinkers.

The love of knowledge, the love of truth for its own sake, is entirely neglected in our modern schemes of education. Instead of training men we train mechanics, artisans and shopkeepers. We turn our national schools, high schools and universities into trade-schools and machine-shops. The school, whether lower or higher, has now one purpose in view, and that is the training of the pupil in the art of money-making. Is it a wonder that the result is a low form of mediocrity, a dwarfed and crippled specimen of humanity?

Open the reports of our school superintendents and you find that the illustrations setting forth the prominent work performed by the school represent carpentry, shoe making, blacksmithing, bookkeeping, typewriting, dressmaking, millinery and cookery. One wonders whether it is the report of a factory inspector, the "scientific" advertisement of some instrument-maker or machine-shop, a booklet of some popular hotel, or an extensive circular of some large department-store. Is this what our modern education consists in? Is the aim of the nation to form at its expense vast reserve armies of skilled mechanics, great numbers of well-trained cooks and well-behaved clerks? Is the purpose of the nation to form cheap skilled labor for the manufacturer, or is the aim of society to form intelligent, educated citizens?

The high-school and college courses advised by the professors and elected by the student are with reference to the vocation in life, to business and to trade. Our schools, our high schools, our colleges and universities are all animated with the same sordid aim of giving electives for early specialization in the art of money-getting. We may say with Mill that our schools and colleges give no true education, no true culture. We drift to the status of Egypt and India with their castes of early trained mechanics, professionals and shopkeepers. Truly educated men we shall have none. We shall become a nation of narrow-minded philistines, well contented with their mediocrity. The savage compresses the skull of the infant, while we flatten the brain and cramp the mind of our young generation.

CHAPTER XIII

THE great thinker, John Stuart Mill, insists that "the great business of every rational being is the strengthening and enlarging of his own intellect and character. The empirical knowledge which the world demands, which is the stock in trade of money-getting, we would leave the world to provide for itself." We must make our system of education such "that a great man may be formed by it, and there will be a manhood in your little men of which you do not dream. We must have a system of education capable of forming great minds." Education must aim at the bringing out of the genius in man. Do we achieve such aim by the formation of philistine-specialists and young petty-minded artisans?

"The very cornerstone of an education," Mill tells us, "intended to form great minds, must be the recognition of the principle, that the object is to call forth the greatest possible quantity of intellectual power, and to inspire the intensest *love of truth; and this without a particle of regard to the results to which the exercise of that power may lead* ." With us the only love of truth is the one that leads to the shop, the bank and the counting-house.

The home controls the school and the college. As long as the home is dominated by commercial ideals, the school will turn out mediocre tradesmen.

This, however, is one of the characteristic types of the American home: the mother thinks of dresses, fashions and parties. The daughter twangs and thrums on the piano, makes violent attempts at singing that sound as "the crackling of thorns under a pot," is passionately fond of shopping, dressing and visiting. Both mother and daughter, love society, show and gossip. The father works in some business or at some trade and loves sports and games. Not a spark of refinement and culture, not a redeeming ray of love of knowledge and of art, lighting up the commonplace and frivolous life of the family. What wonder that the children of ten and eleven can hardly read and write, are little brutes and waste away their precious life of childhood in the close, dusty, overheated rooms of the early grades of some elementary school? Commercial mediocrity is raised at home and cultivated in the school.

"As a means of educating the many, the universities are absolutely null," exclaims Mill. "The attainments of any kind required for taking all the degrees conferred by these bodies are, at Cambridge, utterly contemptible." Our American schools, with their ideals of money-earning capacities, our colleges glorying in their athletics, football teams and courses for professional and business specializations would have been regarded by Mill as below contempt.

What indeed is the worth of an education that does not create even as much as an ordinary respect for learning and love of truth, and that prizes knowledge in terms of hard cash? What is the educational worth of a college or of a university which suppresses its most gifted students by putting them under the ban of disorderly behavior, because of not conforming to commonplace mannerisms? What is the educational value of a university which is but a modern edition of a gladiatorial school with a smattering of the humanities? What is the educational value of an institution of learning that expels its best students because they "attract more attention than their professors"? What is the intellectual level of a college that expels from its courses the ablest of its students for some slight infringement, and that an involuntary one, under the pretext that it is done for the sake of class-discipline, "for the general good of the class" What travesty on education is a system that suppresses genius in the interest of mediocrity? What is the cultural, the humanistic value of an education that puts a prize on mediocrity.

CHAPTER XIV

DISCIPLINE, fixed habits approved by the pedagogue are specially enforced in our schools. To this may be added some "culture" in the art of money-getting in the case of the boys, while in the case of girls the æsthetic training of millinery and dressmaking may be included. The colleges, in addition to class-discipline looked after by the professors and college-authorities, are essentially an organization of hasty-pudding clubs, football associations and athletic corporations. What is the use of a college if not for its games? Many regard the college as useful for the formation of business acquaintances in later life. Others again consider the college a good place for learning fine manners. In other words, the college and the school are for athletics, good manners, business companionship, mechanical arts and money-getting. They are for anything but education.

We have become so used to college athletics that it appears strange and possibly absurd to demand of a college the cultivation of man's genius. Who expects to find an intellectual atmosphere among the great body of our college undergraduates? Who expects of our schools and colleges true culture and the cultivation of a taste for literature, art and science? A dean, an unusually able man, of one of the prominent Eastern colleges tells me that he and his friends are very pessimistic about his students and especially about the great body of undergraduate students. Literature, art, science have no interest for the student; games and athletics fill his mental horizon.

In the training of our children, in the education of our young, we think that discipline, obedience to paternal and maternal commands, whether rational or absurd, are of the utmost importance. "We do not realize that in such a scheme of training we fail to cultivate the child's critical faculties, but only succeed in suppressing the child's individuality. We only break his will-power and originality. We also prepare the ground for future nervous and mental maladies characterized by their fears, indecisions, hesitations, diffidence, irritability, lack of individuality and absence of self-control.

We laugh at the Chinese, because they bandage the feet of their girls, we ridicule those who cripple their chest and mutilate their figure by the tight lacing of their corsets, but we fail to realize the baneful effects of submitting the young minds to the grindstone of our educational discipline. I have known good fathers and mothers who have unfortunately been so imbued with the necessity of disciplining the child that they have crushed the child's spirit in the narrow bonds of routine and custom. How can we expect to get great men and women when from infancy we train our children to conform to the philistine ways of Mrs. Grundy?

In our schools and colleges, habits, discipline and behavior are specially emphasized by our teachers, instructors and professors. Our deans and professors think more of reel tape, of "points," of discipline than of study; they think more of authoritative suggestion than of critical instruction. The pedagogue fashions the pupil after his own image. The professor, with his disciplinarian tactics, forces the student into the imbecile mummy-like mannerism of Egyptian pedantry and into the barrack-regulations of class-etiquette. Well may professors of our "war-schools" claim that the best education is given in military academies: They are right, if discipline is education. But why not the reformatory, the asylum and the prison?

We trust our unfortunate youth to the Procrustean bed of the mentally obtuse, hide-bound pedagogue. We desiccate, sterilize, petrify and embalm our youth in keeping with the rules of our Egyptian code and in accordance with the Confucian regulations of our school-clerks and college mandarins. Our children learn by rote and are guided by routine.

CHAPTER XV

BEING in a barbaric stage, we are afraid of thought. We are under the erroneous belief that thinking, study, causes nervousness and mental disorders. In my practice as physician in nervous and mental diseases, I can say without hesitation that I have not met a single case of nervous or mental trouble caused by too much thinking or over study. This is at present the opinion of the best psychopathologists. What produces nervousness is worry, emotional excitement and lack of interest in the work. But that is precisely what we do with our children. We do not take care to develop a love of knowledge in their early life for fear of brain injury, and then when it is late to acquire the interest, we force them to study, and we cram them and feed them and stuff them like geese. What you often get is fatty degeneration of the mental liver.

If, however, you do not neglect the child between the second and third year, and see to it that the brain should not be starved, should have its proper function, like the rest of the bodily organs, by developing an interest in intellectual activity and love of knowledge, no forcing of the child to study is afterwards requisite. The child will go on by himself, —he will derive intense enjoyment from his intellectual activity, as he does from his games and physical exercise. The child will be stronger, healthier, sturdier than the present average child, with its purely animal activities and total neglect of brain function. His physical and mental development will go a pace. He will not be a barbarian with animal proclivities and a strong distaste for knowledge and mental enjoyment, but he will be a strong, healthy, *thinking man.*

Besides, many a mental trouble will be prevented in adult-life. The child will acquire knowledge with the same ease as he learns to ride the bicycle or play ball. By the tenth year, without almost any effort, the child will acquire the knowledge which at present the best college-graduate obtains with infinite labor and pain. That this can be accomplished I can say with authority; I know it as a fact from my own experience with child-life.

From an economical standpoint alone, think of the saving it would ensure for society. Consider the fact that our children spend nearly eight years in the common school, studying spelling and arithmetic, and do not know them when they graduate! Think of the eight years of waste of school buildings and salaries for the teaching force. However, our real object is not economy, but the development of a strong, healthy, great race of genius.

As fathers and mothers it may interest you to learn of one of those boys who were brought up in the love and enjoyment of knowledge for its own sake. At the age of twelve, when other children of his age are hardly able to read and spell, and drag a miserable mental existence at the apron strings of some antiquated school-dame, the boy is intensely enjoying courses in the highest branches of mathematics and astronomy at one of our foremost universities. The Iliad and the Odyssey are known to him by heart, and he is deeply interested in the advanced work of Classical Philology. He is able to read Herodotus, Æschylus, Sophocles, Euripides, Aristophanes, Lucian and other Greek writers with the same zest and ease as our schoolboy reads his Robinson Crusoe or the productions of Cooper and Henty. The boy has a fair understanding of Comparative Philology and Mythology. He is well versed in Logic, Ancient History, American History and has a general insight into our politics and into the groundwork of our Constitution. At the same time he is of an extremely happy disposition, brimming over with humor and fun. His physical condition is splendid, his cheeks glow. with health. Many a girl would envy his complexion. Being above five feet four he towers above the average boy or his age. His physical constitution, weight, form and hardihood of organs, far surpasses that of the ordinary schoolboy. He looks like a boy of sixteen. He is healthy, strong and sturdy.

The philistine-pseudogogues, the self-contented school-autocrats are so imbued with the fear of intellectual activity and with the superstitious dread of early mental education, they are so obsessed with the morbid phobia of human reflective powers, they are so deluded by the belief that study causes disease that they eagerly adhere to the delusion, to quote from a school-superintendent's letter, about the boy being "in a sanitarium, old and worn-out." No doubt, the cramming, the routine, the rote, the mental and moral tyranny of the principal and school-superintendent do tend to nervous degeneracy and mental break-down. Poor old college owls, academic barn-yard-fowls and worn-out sickly school-bats, you are panic-stricken by the power of sunlight, you are in agonizing, in mortal terror of critical, reflective thought, you dread and suppress the genius of the young.

We do not appreciate the genius harbored in the average child, and we let it lie fallow. We are mentally poor, not because we lack riches, but because we do not know how to use the wealth of mines, the hidden treasures, the now inaccessible mental powers which we possess.

In speaking of our mental capacities, Francis Galton, I think, says that we are in relation to the ancient Greeks what the Bushmen and Hottentots are in relation to us. Galton and many other learned men regard the modern European races as inferior to the Hellenic race. They are wrong, and I know from experience that they are wrong. It rests in our hands either to remain inferior barbarians or to rival and even surpass in brilliancy the genius of the ancient Hellenes. We can develop into a great race by the proper education of man's genius.

CHAPTER XVI

ONE other important point claims our attention in the process of education of man's genius. We must immunize our children against mental microbes, as we vaccinate our babies against small-pox. *The cultivation of critical judgment and the knowledge of evil are two powerful constituents that form the antitoxin for the neutralization of the virulent toxins produced* by *mental microbes.* At the same time we should not neglect proper conditions of mental hygiene. "We should not people the child's mind with ghost-stories, with absurd beliefs in the supernatural, and with articles of creed charged with brimstone and pitch from the bowels of hell. *We must guard the child against all evil fears, superstitions, prejudices and credulity.*

We should counteract the baneful influences of the pathogenic, pestiferous, mental microbes which now infest our social air, since the child, not having yet formed the antitoxin of critical judgment and knowledge of evil, has not the power of resisting mental infection, and is thus very susceptible to mental contagion on account of his extreme suggestibility. The cultivation of credulity, the absence of critical judgment and of recognition of evil, with consequent increase of suggestibility, make man an easy prey to all kinds of social delusions, mental epidemics, religious crazes, financial manias, and political plagues, which have been the baleful pest of aggregate humanity in all ages.

The immunization of children, the development of resistance to mental germs whether moral, immoral or religious, can only be effected by the medical man with a psychological and psychopathological training. Just as science, philosophy and art have gradually passed out of the control of the priest, so now we find that the control of mental and moral life is gradually passing away from under the influence of the church into the hands of the medical psychopathologist.

As we look forward into the future we begin to see that the school is coming under the control of the medical man. The medical man free from superstitions and prejudices, possessed of the science of mind and body, is to assume in the future the supervision of the education of the nation.

The schoolmaster and the schoolma'am with their narrow-minded, pedantic pseudogogics are gradually losing prestige and passing away, while the medical man alone is able to cope with the serious threatening danger of national mental degeneration. Just as the medical profession now saves the nation from physical degeneration and works for the' physical regeneration of the body-politic, so will the medical profession of the future assume the duty of saving the nation from mental and moral decline, from degeneration into a people of fear-possessed, mind-racked psychopathies and neurotics, with broken wills and crushed individualities on the one hand, accompanied, on the other hand, by the still worse affliction and incurable malady of a self-contented mediocrity and a hopeless, Chinese philistinism.

There are in the United States about two hundred thousand insane, while the victims of psychopathic, mental maladies may be counted by the millions. Insanity can be greatly alleviated, but much, if not all, of that psychopathic mental misery known as functional mental disease is entirely preventable. It is the result of our pitiful, wretched, brain-starving, mind-crippling methods of education.

CHAPTER XVII

IN my work of mental and nervous diseases I become more and more convinced of the preponderant influence of early childhood in the causation of psychopathic mental maladies. *Most, in fact all, of those functional mental diseases originate in early childhood.* A couple of concrete cases will perhaps best illustrate my point:

The patient is a young man of 26. He suffers from intense melancholic depression, often amounting to agony. He is possessed by the fear of having committed the unpardonable sin. He thinks that he is damned to suffer tortures in hell for all eternity. I cannot go here into the details of the case, but an examination of dread of the unknown, from claustrophobia, fear of remaining alone, fear of darkness and numerous other fears and insistent ideas, into the details of which I cannot go here. By means of the hypnoidal state the symptoms were traced to impressions of early childhood; when at the age of five, the patient was suddenly confronted by a maniacal woman. The child was greatly frightened, and since that time she became possessed by the fear of insanity. When the patient gave birth to her child, she was afraid the child would become insane; many a time she even had a feeling that the child *was* insane. Thus the fear of insanity is traced to an experience of early childhood, an experience which, having become subconscious, is manifesting itself persistently in the patient's consciousness:

The patient's parents were very religious, and the child was brought up not only in the fear of God, but also in the fear of hell and the devil. Being sensitive and imaginative, the devils of the gospel were to her stern realities. She had a firm belief in "diabolical possessions" and "unclean spirits"; the legend of Jesus exorcising in the country of the Gadarenes unclean spirits, whose name is Legion, was to her a tangible reality. She was brought up on brimstone and pitch, with everlasting fires of the "bottomless pit" for sinners and unbelievers. In the hypnoidal state she clearly remembered the preacher, who used every Sunday to give her the horrors by his picturesque descriptions of the tortures of the "bottomless pit." She was in anguish over the unsolved question: "Do little sinner-girls go to hell?" This fear of hell made the little girl feel depressed and miserable and poisoned many a cheerful moment of her life.

What a lasting effect and what a melancholy gloom this fear of ghosts and of unclean spirits of the bottomless pit produced on this young life may be judged from the following facts: When the patient was about eleven years old, a young girl, a friend of hers, having noticed the patient's fear of ghosts, played on her one of those silly, practical jokes, the effect of which on sensitive natures is often disastrous and lasting. The girl disguised herself as a ghost, in a white sheet, and appeared to the patient, who was just on the point of falling asleep. The child shrieked in terror and fainted. Since that time the patient suffered from nightmares and was mortally afraid to sleep alone; she passed many a night in a state of excitement, frenzied with the fear of apparitions and ghosts.

When about the age of seventeen, she apparently freed herself from the belief in ghosts and unclean powers. But the fear acquired in her childhood did not lapse; it persisted subconsciously and manifested itself in the form of uncontrollable fears. She was afraid to remain alone in a room, especially in the evening. Thus, once when she had to go upstairs alone to pack her trunks, a gauzy garment called forth the experience of her ghost-fright; she had the illusion of seeing a ghost, and fell fainting to the floor. Unless specially treated, fears acquired in childhood last through life.

"Every ugly thing," says Mosso, the great Italian physiologist, "told to the child, every shock, every fright given him, will remain like minute splinters in the flesh, to torture him all his life long.

"An old soldier whom I asked what greatest fears had been, answered thus: 'I have only had one, but it pursues me still. I am nearly seventy years old, I have looked death in the face I not know how many times; I have never lost heart in any danger, but when I pass a little old church in the shades of forest, or a deserted chapel in the mountains, I always remember a neglected oratory in my native village, and I shiver and look around, as though seeking the corpse of a murdered man which I once saw carried into it when a child, and with which an old servant wanted to shut me up to make me good.'" Here, too, experiences of early childhood have persisted subconsciously throughout lifetime.

CHAPTER XVIII

I APPEAL to you, fathers and mothers, and to you, liberal-minded readers, asking you to turn your attention to the education of your children, to the training of the young generation of future citizens. I do not appeal to our official educators, to our scientific, psychological pseudogogues, to the clerks of our teaching shops,—for they are beyond all hope. From that quarter I expect nothing but attacks and abuse. We cannot possibly expect of the philistine-educator and mandarin pseudogogue the adoption of different views of education. We should not keep new wine in old goat-skins. The present school-system squanders the resources of the country and wastes the energies, the lives of our children. Like Cato our cry should be *Carthago delenda est,*— the school-system should be abolished and with it should go the present psychologizing educator, the schoolmaster and the schoolma'am.

Fathers and mothers, you keep in your hands the fate of the young generation. You are conscious of the great responsibility, of the vast, important task laid upon you by the education of your children. For, according to the character of the training and education given to the young, they may be made a sickly host of nervous wrecks and miserable wretches; or they may be formed into a narrow-minded, bigoted, mediocre crowd of self-contented "cultured" philistines, bat-blind to evil; or they may be made a *great race of genius* with powers of rational control of their latent, potential, reserve energy. The choice remains with you .

Nervous Ills: Their Causes and Cures

"The thing in the world I am most afraid of is fear."

-Montaigne.

Table of Contents

INTRODUCTION

In this volume I give a brief, popular account of some of my work in Psychopathology, or Abnormal Psychology for the last quarter of a century. I do not refer to my work on psychopathic reflexes, moment-consciousness, moment-thresholds, multiple personality and other subjects. The reader will find all these subjects in my other works. In this volume I make an attempt to simplify matters. I lay stress on the main factors and principles of that part of Abnormal Psychology that deals with the subject of nervous ills.

It is to be regretted that some physicians, and among them many neurologists of excellent standing, hesitate to accept the work accomplished in the domain of Psychopathology, confusing the latter with what parades at present under the name of psychoanalysis. Thus a well known physician writes to me:

"I think that the majority of men in general work (medical) do not separate Psychopathology from Psychoanalysis. Freud's theories and the whole trend of psychoanalysis have been so turned into channels of distorted and perverted sexual life that it has blinded people to the fact that there are many dominant phases in mental life which are not sexual. The ordinary, healthy minded, and vigorous practitioner sees a lot of motives in life that are not sexual, and when-everything is twisted and turned to one side, to one 'complex,' he becomes indignant and disgusted, and condemns the whole broad subject of Psychopathology." I think that the physician is right in his attitude.

As a matter of fact psychoanalysis, by which Freud and his adherents have baptized their sexual theories and metaphysical wish-speculations, should be regarded as savage and barbaric. Psychoanalysis is a sort of Astrology, full of superstitious symbolizations, dream vagaries, and idle interpretations, foisted on the credulous, on those obsessed by sexual inclinations, and on those suffering from sexual perversions. It is idle and credulous to search in adults for "unconscious" memories of ha!ties a few months old. Many take up psychoanalysis as a sort of mental masturbation which in the long run is sure to play havoc with their nerve and mind.

Psychoanalysis excites the curiosity of the vulgar just as for thousands of years Astrology held the interest of semi-civilized nations to the detriment of the science of Astronomy. Psychoanalysis belongs to the class of dangerous superstitions, harmful to health, both social and individual. Psychoanalysis, like Palmistry or Oneiroscopy, that is, "interpretation of dreams," imposes on the uncritical

sense of the credulous public. Freudian psychoanalysis should be openly declared as a fraud.

Lecky points out that superstitions are not destroyed by discussion. To start a discussion in an earnest way a common ground is required. What common ground is there between science and superstition? Superstition should be left alone to die of inanition. There is no common ground between psychoanalysis and psychopathology. That is why it is just as impossible to argue with a psychoanalyst as with a Mormon or a Mohammedan. Anyone who does not accept the dogmas and superstitions of psychoanalysis is accused of "resistance of hidden complexes," just as pious believers accuse sceptics of evil thoughts.

A famous professor of a well known eastern college asked me to continue my "good work" against psychoanalysis. But criticism of psychoanalysis is a thankless task. It is futile to discuss psychological and medical matters with psychoanalysts. For psychoanalysts care for nothing else but the fulfillment of sexual wishes. It is useless to argue with psychoanalysts, who as a rule possess no more critical sense than Mormon saints. Psychoanalysis is a sort of Mormonism. In the far West psychoanalysis is preached from the pulpits in elm relies. Psychoanalysis is a sex religion. One should combat it with ridicule and scorn. Psychoanalysis needs a Voltaire, a Moliere, or a Swift.

The so-called present civilized humanity, and especially our populace, lives in an age of vulgarity. Success per sc is the sole aim in life. Books by the thousands tell how to achieve "success," how to fool the nerves, or how to deceive the mind. "Efficiency" and "success" fill home and school with all sorts of lucubrations and advertisements. Mental tests arc supposed to help to success. Business suc-is the slogan. And success is only to the mediocre and the vulgar. Mediocrity writes for mediocrity, and is applauded by mobs of mediocrity. To teach the truth is a great privilege, but to deceive the ignorant and to debauch the young and inexperienced is a serious offence.

When science, literature, and art sink to the movie stage, why wonder at their triviality? When Government experts take seriously Freudian "Sublimation," why blame the credulity of the layman? When the Bureau of Education spreads far and wide pamphlets on mental tests, why wonder at the gullibility of the populace?

The tendency towards the rule of mediocrity in the twentieth century was observed by Tolstov:

"About twenty years ago Matthew Arnold wrote a beautiful article on the purpose of criticism. According to his opinion, it is the purpose of criticism to find what is most important and good in any book whatever, wherever, and whenever written, and to

direct the reader's attention to what is important and good in them.

"Such a criticism seems to me indispensable in our time of newspapers, periodicals, books, and advertisements. Such a criticism is requisite for the future of the cultured world.

"Printing has for some time served as the chief instrument for the diffusion of ignorance among the well-to-do (the middle classes, especially the so-called new women).

"Books, periodicals, especially the newspapers, have in our time become great financial undertakings for the success of which the largest possible number of purchasers is needed. The interests and tastes, however, of the largest possible number of purchasers are always low and vulgar. For the success of the press it is necessary that the productions should respond to the demands of the great majority of the purchasers, that is, that they should touch upon the low interests and correspond to the vulgar tastes. The press fully satisfies these demands, which it is quite able to do, since among the number of workers for the press there are many more people with the same low interests and vulgar tastes as the public than men with high interests and refined taste.

"The worst thing about it is that the reading of poor works corrupts the understanding and taste. Good works can no longer be appreciated.

"In proportion as newspapers, periodicals, and

books become more and more disseminated, the value of what is printed falls lower and lower, and the class of the so-called cultured public sinks more and more into a most hopeless, self-contented, incorrigible ignorance. . . .

"A striking example is that of the English prose writers. From the great Dickens we descend at first to George Eliot, then to Thackeray, to Trollope; and then begins the indifferent manufacture of a Rider Haggard, Kipling, Hall Caine, and so forth.

"Still more striking is this fall noticed in American literature. After the great galaxy, Emerson, Thoreau, Lowell, Whittier, and others, everything breaks off suddenly, and there appear beautiful editions with beautiful illustrations and with beautiful stories and novels which are impossible to read on account of absence of all meaning.

"The ignorance of the cultured crowd of our times has reached such a pass that great thinkers and writers of former times no longer satisfy the highly refined demands of new men (and new women).

"The last word of philosophy is the immoral, coarse, inflated, disconnected babbling of Nietzsche. Senseless, artificial conglomeration of words of decadent poems is regarded as poetry of the highest rank. The theatres give dramas, the meaning of which is not known to any one, not even to the author."

What would Tolstoy have said had he witnessed the full blown art of our movies ?

What the movies and literature accomplish in the world of art and letters, that is what psychoanalysis and mental tests achieve in normal and abnormal psychology.

The mediocrity of the modern man is akin to the vulgarity of the ancient freedman, so well described by Petronius in his type of Trimalchio. Both, the greedy freedman and the "efficient" freeman, have the same deleterious influence on the course of civilization.

Our age is not the age of Democracy, but of Mediocrity. It is in such an age that sensationalism, movies, and psychoanalysis are apt to flourish like green bay trees.

The reader will find that I often turn to Social Psychology. This is requisite. As I carry on my work on nervous ills I become more and more convinced that a knowledge of Social Psychology is essential to a clear comprehension of nervous ills.

The number of cases given in the volume will, I am sure, be of great help to the reader. For the concrete cases, carefully studied by me, bring out distinctly the mechanism, the factors, and the main principles of nervous ills. I address this volume to the reader who wishes to learn the truth, not to those who are in search for ever new amusements, or for the "best seller" of the year. I hope that this work will prove of value to the thoughtful physician and of interest to the cultured layman.

I further hope that my reader will not be offended by my statements about superstitions. / address myself to the liberal-minded- reader who does not care to follow the herd.

Boris Sidis Maplewood Farms, Portsmouth, New Hampshire

CHAPTER I
SELF-PRESERVATION AND FEAR

The impulse of self-preservation is at the basis of all animal life. From the simplest lump of protoplasm constituting a microbe to the highest form of life, such as man, one meets with the same primitive life tendency,—the impulse of self-preservation. Throughout all animal creation one important purpose runs, and that is the preservation of life.

When a creature is launched into the world, it is animated with one central, innate mission,—to live; and to fight for its living. For this purpose,— if purpose it really be, the creature, however small and insignificant, is provided with a rich arsenal of armour for defense and attack. When a biologist demonstrated the anatomical structure of a caterpillar, a bystander exclaimed in surprise: "Why, I always thought that a caterpillar was nothing but skin and squash!"

The simple living creatures, swarming in the waters of stagnant ponds and murky pools, the bits of living matter, inhabiting by the million the little world of a hanging drop of water, are supplied with the most complicated reactions, mechanical and more especially chemical, for the maintenance of their life existence. Simple as a cell, a minute particle of protoplasm, may appear, it is none the less a most wonderful laboratory where toxins, anti-toxins, and an infinite variety of secretions, highly poisonous and protective, are being produced, for the keeping in existence of that insignificant, microscopic bit of living matter. Self-preservation is the central aim of all life-activities.

The tendency of all organic processes is the maintenance of the life of each particular individual organism. It is this aspect that I wish to impress on the minds of my readers. Self-preservation is the nucleus of organic life. It is the mainspring of organic activities and functions. The tendency of life is not the preservation of the species, but solely the preservation of each individual organism, as long as it is in existence at all, and is able to carry on its life processes.

Every living thing, from the ultra-microscopic to the highest and most complex multicellular organism, man included, has only one fundamental tendency, the maintenance and defense of its individual existence. The claim that the individual counts for little or nothing, and that the species is everything, is not true to facts. "Nature cares not for the individual, but for the species" is a glittering generality of a metaphysical character.

It is the maintenance of its individual existence and the struggle for this individuality and its preservation, whether in defense or aggression, that form the main object of organic life in all its aspects. The aim of life activities is the individual, the species is a secondary matter. It is only when we keep this fundamental truth in mind that we begin to understand life in general, and human life in particular.

The struggle for existence of which so much is heard in modern science, theoretical or applied, means really the preservation of the individual organism, or the self-preservation of individuality. We may say that the struggle for existence in the biological, and social worlds means nothing else but the Struggle for Individuality.

Wherever the organism forms a whole as to its vitality, whether it be an amoeba or a man, the struggle is for the maintenance of that whole or of that particular individual organism. All the structures and functions go to the preservation of that individuality, or of that individual organic self, constituting the impulse of self-preservation in the total activity of the particular individual organism. The great number of physico-chemical and mechanical processes, adaptations and adjustments of inner structures and functions, as well as the different reactions to the stimuli of external environment, even in the lowest of micro-organisms, are for the whole of the individuality.

When organisms take to forms of social life the fundamental aim is still the protection or self-preservation of the individual. The community is an additional defense of the individual against a hostile environment. Thus the herds of Damara cattle, or of social aggregates of other animals, offer greater protection to each individual animal. The individual wolf running in packs has more power for attack and defense. The individual man has more forces for aggression and for protection by living in a social medium which provides the individual with more sensory organs for observation of danger and with more organs for defense and attack, than in isolated states. The herd, the pack, the horde, the society are for the self-preservation of the individual.

It has been shown on good grounds that the very sense of external reality has become intensified in the individual by his capacity of living in a social aggregate. The social aggregate strengthens each individual member of the group. The individual is not for the group, but the group is for self-preservation of the individual. Should the individual lose his self-protection, or even have his impulse of self-preservation lowered, the whole aggregate faces ultimate destruction. That is why when in a social aggregate the impulse of self-preservation becomes limited, inhibited, and lowered by tyranny of social commandments, society is sure to decline, degenerate, and finally dissolve; or fall a victim to an external invader,—the fate of tribes, communities, and nations in the past and the present. The moving power of life is self-preservation of the individual.

A close study of life in general and of animal life in particular brings one to the inevitable conclusion that life in all its forms has self-preservation as its fundamental principle. Self-preservation is the main impulse, the prime mover of life. The prime mover of life is not the impulse of species preservation, or of sex, but the impulse of self-preservation of the individual organism.

Self-preservation has two aspects, the positive and the negative. In the positive form the primitive impulse is to keep the individual alive, to keep the functions and structure in normal condition, to conduce to the full development and harmonious activity of the individual. The negative form of the preservative impulse is the preservation from injury, degeneration, destruction, and death. This negative aspect of the impulse of self-preservation expresses itself in the higher animals in the form of fear.

The fear instinct is an essential constituent of the impulse of life. We may call the fear instinct the guardian of all sentient being. Wherever there is the least scent or even the least suggestion of danger, there the instinct of fear is aroused. Fear is the companion following close on the heels of the impulse of self-preservation. Since every animal is always surrounded by enemies, and since every strange thing or strange occurrence is a menace or possible signal of danger, the fear instinct is aroused on all strange occasions. The fear instinct requires the slightest stimulus to start into function.

While most of the instincts require special conditions, and are usually periodic, the fear instinct is ever present and can be awakened on all occasions, and under any circumstances. Anything unfamiliar, —darkness, a state of exhaustion, weakness, fatigue, arouses the fear instinct, startling the animal into running, hiding, crouching, and preparation for attack or defense. The fear instinct stays with us, and watches over us day and night. It follows us closely in our active, waking life, attends us in our resting hours, and watches over us in our sleeping periods. The fear instinct is the last to fall asleep, and the first to awake. The fear instinct follows us like our shadow, with the only difference that it constantly affects our actions, hardly ever leaves us alone, and keeps steady vigilance over our life activities. The reason for this apparently strange companionship is the fact that the fear instinct is the primitive instinct of the life impulse, the impulse for self-preservation.

The overwhelming intensity of the fundamental impulse of self-preservation is well described by the great writer Dostoevsky, whose insight into the psychology of human life and especially into abnormal mental life transcends that of any other writer: "Where is it I have read that someone condemned to death says or thinks, an hour before his death, that if he had to live on some high rock, on such a narrow ledge that he had only room to stand, and the ocean, everlasting darkness, everlasting solitude, everlasting tempest around him, if he had to remain standing on a square yard of space all his life, a thousand years, eternity, it were better to live so than to die at once! Only to live, to live, and live! Life whatever it may be!"

Just as the touch and pain nerves enmesh closely our body, warning us against hurtful stimulations, so we may say that fear, through our distant receptors of sight, hearing and smell, surrounds us, warning us against enemies, or inimical, suspicious objects, and forces. Were it not for the fear instinct, directly awakened, the animal threatened with danger would not have the time and the strong impulse to get ready for defense or for escape, by running or by hiding.

The fear instinct is of the utmost importance in animal life. Looked at from this standpoint the fear instinct is as important in animal economy as the skin which covers our body, which, by pain and hurts, warns of external injurious objects, and has an important function of warding off incessant invasion of disease-bearing organisms. In nervous ills we find the same fundamental factors:— self-preservation and the fear instinct.

CHAPTER II
STAGES OF FEAR

The fear instinct in its course of development passes through three stages:

I. The Stimulating Stage

II. The Arrestive, or Inhibitory Stage

III. The Paralyzing Stage.

In its milder forms when the fear instinct is but nascent, it serves as a sort of trigger to the activities of the organism. The animal may for a moment stop whatever activities and pursuits in which it happens to be engaged, and have its interest turn in the direction of the particular new stimulus, whether it be of an auditory, visual, or olfactory character. The fear instinct is just strong enough to suspend present interests, and direct its activities to the new source of the unknown stimulus.

When the source is unfamiliar, the animal becomes prepared for action. The energies are aroused for attack, or for hiding, freezing, or running, according to the mode of defense to which the animal has been adapted in its adjustments to the stimulations of its environment. The lion, the tiger, the skunk, the snake, the bird, the rabbit, the squirrel will act differently, according to their natural disposition in response to external objects and stimuli.

While the motor system may react differently in various animals, the fear instinct is alike in all of them. This stage of the fear instinct should be regarded as the healthy physiological reaction to strange and new stimuli, and is essentially protective, inasmuch as it serves for the arousal of energy and proper reactions of self-defense, characteristic of the particular individual.

In its milder forms the fear instinct is normal, physiological, and healthy in its reactions. In fact, the absence of it is rather pathological. It is quite natural that under the influence of some danger, the organism may feel the urging of this vital instinct, the consequent of the fundamental life impulse, and feel it as a stimulus rather than as a deterrent experience, feel fear as the key for the unlocking of energies in defense or attack. Such a reaction is healthy and strictly requisite in the total economy of life.

When I advanced the theory that the fear instinct is at the bottom of functional psychosis, or of psychopathic maladies, some jumped to the conclusion that I regarded the fear instinct as abnormal, giving rise to pathological states under all conditions and circumstances. This is not correct. The fear instinct in its initial stages is perfectly normal, and is as indispensable to life as hunger and thirst. It is only in the mere advanced and extreme stages that the fear instinct becomes pathological, and is apt to give rise to psychopathic states.

In the arrestive or inhibitory state, the innervation of the voluntary and the involuntary muscular systems is arrested, or weakened. There is tremor and even convulsive contractions, the voluntary reactions are affected, and are carried out with some difficulty; there is cardiac arrhythmia, the respiration is irregular; there may be chattering of the teeth; the various bodily secretions are interfered with, and the vasomotor nerves as well as the general vascular structures are thrown into disorder. Peristalsis, intestinal secretions, and the innervation of the sympathetic nervous system may become affected, first by inhibition, and then by irregular functioning. Associative mental or cerebral activity becomes arrested, confused; memory is disturbed, and the whole personality or individuality appears in a state of dissociation, accompanied by a lack of precision and lack of exactness of neuromuscular adaptations. The delicate reactions and adaptations are specially affected.

If this stage of fear instinct does not become intensified, the organism recovers its control,—many of the disturbances pass away, and the following reaction may come with a greater release of energy, developing a greater output of activity than under normal conditions. In short, the fear instinct may still serve as a stimulation to greater effort, but the chances of such a result are far smaller than in the first stage, which is essentially of a stimulating, useful, and healthful character.

The second stage of the fear instinct is the possibility of a pathological state, and, if persistent, leads directly to the third stage with consequent paralysis and danger of destruction. The first stage of fear is fully normal, helpful, and self-defensive. The second stage is harmful, but with the possibility of recovery and restitution of normal function. The third stage leads to destruction and death.

In the third stage there is paralysis of function of most of the muscular, secretory, excretory, circulatory, intestinal, and nervous systems. The animal is petrified with fear, and falls into a state of paralysis, rigidity, cataplexy, or in a state simulating death. This last stage of the effects of the fear instinct is pathological, and instead of conducing to the good of the individual, really leads to his destruction and death. The fear instinct in its extreme cases is not a help to the organism, but is distinctly a hindrance, and is felt as such by the organism which experiences it.

The fear instinct, which originally is a stimulating agent for self-defense, when in excess becomes a danger hastening the dissolution of the animal organism into its constituent parts. The intensity of the fear instinct is the expression of the fact that the organism is in imminent danger of destruction. The fear instinct in its extreme state is decidedly to the disadvantage of the animal.

Of course, it may be claimed that the paralysis and inhibition stages might have been of service or of protective value in the lower forms of life, when mimicking death or freezing prevented the animal from being noticed. This may possibly hold true in the cases of lower forms, but in the higher forms the fear instinct in its third stage, by bringing about inhibitions and paralysis of the vital functions, is decidedly of disservice to the organism, and leads to its destruction and death.

CHAPTER III
THE PRIMACY OF FEAR

The fear instinct is intimately related to the innermost principle, characteristic of all life, namely the impulse of self-preservation. When, however, the fear instinct becomes deranged by being too intense, and especially when reaching the extreme stage, the instinct becomes pathological, and its functioning leads to degeneration, destruction, and death. Even in its initiatory stages the fear instinct may become abnormal, when associated with objects, situations, and sensorimotor reactions which are otherwise normal and beneficial, or actually requisite in the total economy of life activity of the particular organism. Under such conditions the fear instinct is decidedly pathological.

In fact we may say that the fear instinct is the main source of functional, psychopathic diseases. This also holds true of the individual in his aggregate capacity. If the impulse of self-preservation is at the basis of life, the fear instinct is its intimate companion. We may unhesitatingly assert that the fear instinct is one of the most primitive instincts of animal life. We are sometimes apt to overlook the power of fear, because our life is so well guarded by the protective agencies of civilization that we can hardly realize the full extent, depth, and overwhelming effects of the fear instinct. Fear is rooted deep in the nature of animal life, in the impulse of self-preservation.

The fear instinct is the earliest instinct to appear in child life. Preyer observed definite manifestations of the fear instinct on the twenty-third day after birth. Perez and Darwin put its appearance somewhat later. In my observations of child life I found the manifestation of the fear instinct during the first couple of weeks. Ribot and other psychologists regard the fear instinct as "the first in chronological order of appearance."

"The progress from brute to man," says James, "is characterized by nothing so much as the decrease in the frequency of the proper occasion for fear. In civilization in particular it lias at last become possible for large numbers of people to pass from the cradle to the grave without ever having had a pang of genuine fear. Many of us need an (attack of mental disease to teach us the meaning of the word. Hence the possibility of so much blindly optimistic philosophy and religion. (James refers here to the blind optimism and cheerful metaphysical mysticism handed out to the uncultured classes.) Fear is a genuine instinct, and one of the earliest shown by the human child."

The fear of the unknown, of the unfamiliar, of the mysterious, is of the utmost consequence in the life history of children, savages, and barbaric tribes, and even in the social life of civilized nations. The fear of coming mysterious, unknown evil is a source of great anxiety to the young, or to the untrained, uncultivated minds. All taboos of primitive societies, of savages, of barbarians, and also of civilized people take their origin, according to anthropological research, in the perils and salvation of the soul, or in the fear of impending evil. As an anthropologist puts it: "Men are undoubtedly more influenced by what they fear than by what they love."

The civilized nations of antiquity used to be terrorized by omens, by occurrences of an unfamiliar character, such as storms, thunders, lightnings, comets, meteors, meteorites, and eclipses. Affairs of states and wars were guided by superstitions of fear. Whole armies used to throw away their weapons and run panic-stricken at the appearance of meteorites, meteors, and especially of comets. Even the ancient Athenians were influenced by strange, meteorological phenomena. On the appearance of a solar eclipse Pericles saved his ship by throwing his mantle round the helmsman, telling him that that was all that an eclipse was, and that there was no reason to be scared by the veiling of the sun from us. The father of pragmatic history, the great Thucydides, in his history of the Peloponnesian wars, puts the appearance of comets among national disasters.

The fear of the mysterious, the unknown, and the unfamiliar is a source of anxiety and distress in the young, or in the untrained and uncultured minds. Fear may become fixed and morbid when taking place in early childhood, when not inhibited by the course of further development, and, all the more so, when kept up by further events of life.

In most people the instinct of fear is controlled, regulated by education, and inhibited by the relatively secure life led in the herd, pack, group, and society generally. The instinct of fear, however, is but dormant and requires the opportune moment such as a social, mental epidemic, a "group-panic," to become manifested in its full intensity, giving rise to a morbid state of the "group-mind," or "herd-mind."

There are again cases when even under ordinary conditions fear becomes developed in the individual from early childhood either by lack of inhibitory training or by accidents in early child life. In all such cases the fear instinct becomes morbid, giving rise in later life to various forms of mental disease known as psychopathies, or recurrent morbid states.

We can, therefore, realize the full significance of the principle laid down by one of the greatest thinkers of humanity, Plato, that to learn "What to fear and what not to fear" is of the utmost consequence to the individual, both in his private and social activities. Throughout the whole domain of the animal kingdom anything strange and unfamiliar is an occasion for the awakening of the fear instinct. The strange, the unfamiliar may be detrimental to the organism, and the animal recoils from meeting it directly. There must be exploration made before the reaction of approach can be effected. We find the same tendency in children and savages who run in terror of anything unusual.

On the whole escape is probably the safest course, since the unfamiliar may prove of great danger. The well known saying "Familiarity breeds contempt" has its significance in that the familiar does not arouse the fear instinct, and can be approached without risk. Reactions to a familiar object or known situation run in well established, habitual grooves. In man the sense of familiarity may be acquired by the use of intelligence, by observations of various forms of unfamiliar situations and strange objects. Reason, leading to the understanding of the causes of things, turns the strange and unfamiliar into the familiar and the known, and thus dispels the terrors and horrors of the fear instinct.

The function of the intellect is to conquer the world by making man at home and familiar in this "wild universe." This is the course of human progress. "The aim of knowledge," says Hegel, "is to divest the objective world of its strangeness, and to make us more at home in it." In the words of the ancient poet:

Felix qui potuit rerum cognoscere causas, Atque metus omnes, et inexorabile fatum, Subject pedibus, strepitwmque Acherontis avari. [1]

CHAPTER IV
FEAR AND SUPERSTITION

An individual limited in intelligence, leading a narrow life, is specially subject to fear suggestions which can be easily aroused. Inhibitions of the personal self are produced by stimulation of the fear instinct with consequent easy access, by means of fear suggestions, to man's subconscious fear instinct, thus inducing various forms of morbid mental life.

When a person is limited in his interests, when he is ignorant and full of prejudices and superstitions, his critical, personal sense is embryonic, and the predisposition to fear suggestions is specially pronounced. He easily falls a victim to all kinds of bizarre beliefs and absurd superstitions, such as the mysticism which obsesses uncultured classes of all ages.

The optimistic, "metaphysical" beliefs, rampant in this country, are all due to the beggarly intelligence subconsciously obsessed by innumerable fear suggestions. Neurotic adherents cling to their irrational optimism in order to assuage the pangs, caused by the fear instinct, from which they are unable to free themselves. In the embryonic personality of the child, as well as in the undeveloped or narrowed individuality of the adult, the sense of the strange, of the unknown, and of the mysterious, is apt to arouse the fear instinct. In fact, the unfamiliar arouses the fear instinct even in the more highly organized mind.

"Any new uncertainty," says Bain, "is especially the cause of terror. Such are the terrors caused by epidemics, the apprehensions from an unexperienced illness, the feeling of a recruit under fire. The mental system in infancy is highly susceptible, not merely to pain, but to shocks and surprises. Any great excitement has a perturbing effect allied to fear. After the child has contracted a familiarity with the persons and things around it, it manifests unequivocal fear on the occurrence of anything strange. The grasp of an unknown person often gives a fright. This early experience resembles the manifestations habitual to the inferior animals."

In another place Bain rightly says, "Our position in the world contains the sources of fear. The vast powers of nature dispose of our lives and happiness with irresistible might and awful aspect. Ages had elapsed ere the knowledge of law and uniformity prevailing among those powers was arrived at by the human intellect. The profound ignorance of the primitive man was the soil wherein his early conceptions and theories sprang up; and the fear inseparable from ignorance gave them their character The essence of susperstition is expressed by the definition of fear."

Compayre, in speaking of the fear of the child, says, "In his limited experience of evil, by a natural generalization, he suspects danger everywhere like a sick person whose aching body dreads in advance every motion and every contact. He feels that there is a danger everywhere, behind the things that he cannot understand, because they do not fit in with his experience.

"The observations collected by Romanes in his interesting studies on the intelligence of animals throw much light on this question; they prove that dogs, for instance, do not fear this or that, except as they are ignorant of the cause. A dog was very much terrified one day when he heard a rumbling like thunder produced by throwing apples on the floor of the garret; he seemed to understand the cause of the noise as soon as he was taken to the garret, and became as quiet and happy as ever.

"Another dog had a habit of playing with dry bones. One day Romanes attached a fine thread which could hardly be seen, to one of the bones, and while the dog was playing with it, drew it slowly towards him; the dog recoiled in terror from the bone, which seemed to be moving of its own accord. So skittish horses show fright as long as the cause of the noise that frightens them remains unknown and invisible to them.

'It is the same with the child. When in the presence of all the things around him, of which he has no idea, these sounding objects, these forms, these movements, whose cause he does not divine, he is naturally a prey to vague fears. He is just what we should be, if chance should cast us suddenly into an unexplored country before strange objects and strange beings—suspicious, always on the qui vive, disposed to see imaginary enemies behind every bush, fearing a new danger at every turn in the road."

Similarly, Sully says, "The timidity of childhood is seen in the readiness with which experience invests objects and places with a fear-exciting aspect, in its tendency to look at all that is unknown as terrifying, and in the difficulty of the educator in controlling these tendencies."

Sully is right in thinking that education tends greatly to reduce the early intensity of fear. "This it does by substituting knowledge for ignorance, and so undermining that vague terror before the unknown to which the child and the superstitious savage are a prey, an effect aided by the growth of will power and the attitude of self-confidence which this brings with it." An uncultivated personality with a limited mental horizon, with a narrow range of interests, a personality trained in the fear of mysterious agencies, is a fit subject for obsessions. In certain types of functional psychosis and neurosis the patient has an inkling of the fear instinct in his dread of objects, or of states of mind, lack of confidence, blushing, expectations of some coming misfortune and some mysterious evil, but he is not aware of the fear instinct as developed in him by the events and training of early childhood. The fears of early childhood are subconscious. At any rate, the patient does not connect them with his present mental affection.

In other types of psychopathic affections the patient is entirely unaware of the whole situation, he is engrossed by the symptoms which he regards as the sum and substance of his trouble; the fear is entirely subconscious. Frights, scares, dread of sickness, instructions associated with fear of the mysterious and unseen, injunctions with fear of punishment or failure in moral standards, enforcement of social customs with dread of failure and degradation, —all go to the cultivation of the fear instinct which in later life becomes manifested as functional psychosis or neurosis.

Functional psychosis or neurosis is an obsession, conscious and subconscious, of the fear instinct. Thus one of my patients became obsessed with fear of tuberculosis, manifesting most of the symptoms of "consumption," after a visit to a tubercular friend. Another patient was obsessed by the fear of death after visiting a sick relative of his in one of the city hospitals. Another became obsessed with the fear of syphilis after having been in contact with a friend who had been under antiluetic treatment. Still another of my patients, in addition to the fear of darkness, became obsessed with the fear of stars, and also with a fear of comets, regarded by some people as poisoning the air with noxious gases.

In all such cases anxiety and dread were present, but in none of the patients have I found an insight into the real state of the mind. In all of them the fear was traced to early childhood, to early experiences of the fear instinct, fostered and fortified by unfavorable conditions. In all of those fears there was a long history of a well-developed subconscious fear instinct. I may assert without hesitation that in all my cases of functional psychosis, I find the presence of the fear instinct to be the sole cause of the malady. Take away the fear and the psychosis or neurosis disappears.

The fear instinct arises from the impulse of self-preservation without which animal life cannot exist. The fear instinct is one of the most primitive and most fundamental of all instincts. Neither hunger, nor sex, nor maternal instinct, nor social instinct can compare with the potency of the fear instinct, rooted as it is in self-preservation,—the condition of life primordial. When the instinct of fear is at its height, it sweeps before it all other instincts. Nothing can withstand a panic. Functional psychosis in its full development is essentially a panic,—it is the emergence of the most powerful of all instincts, the fear instinct.

Functional psychosis or neurosis is a veiled form of the fear of death, of destruction, of loss of what is deemed as essential to life, of fear of some unknown, impending evil. How many times has it fallen to my share to soothe and counteract the fear instinct of panic-stricken psychopathic patients! A psychogenetic examination of every case of functional psychosis brings one invariably to the fundamental fear instinct.

Conflicts, repressions, imperfections, sex-complexes, sex-aberrations, and others do not produce psychopathic symptoms or neurotic states. It is only when mental states become associated with an exaggerated impulse of self-preservation and an intensified fear instinct that neurosis arises.

A close study of every neurotic case clearly discloses the 'primary action of those two important factors of life activity,—self-preservation and fear instinct.

CHAPTER V
THE POWER OF FEAR

The function of fear is quite clear. Fear is the guardian instinct of life. The intensity of the struggle for existence and the preservation of life of the animal are expressed in the instinct of fear. The fear instinct in its mild form, when connected with what is strange and unfamiliar, or with what is really dangerous to the animal, is of the utmost consequence to the life existence of the animal. What is strange and unfamiliar may be a menace to life, and it is a protection, if under such conditions the fear instinct is aroused.

Again, it is of the utmost importance in weak animals, such as hares or rabbits, to have the fear instinct easily aroused by the slightest, strange stimulus: the animal is defenseless, and its refuge, its safety, is in running. The unfamiliar stimulus may be a signal of danger, and it is safer to get away from it; the animal cannot take chances.

On the other hand, animals that are too timid, so that even the familiar becomes too suspicious, cannot get their food, and cannot leave a progeny,—they become eliminated by the process of natural selection. There is a certain amount of trust that nature demands even of its most defenseless and timid children.

Animals in whom the fear instinct can be aroused to a high degree become paralyzed and perish. Under such conditions the fear instinct not only ceases to be of protective value, but is the very one that brings about the destruction of the animal possessed by it. Intense fear paralyzes the animal.

"One of the most terrible effects of fear," says Mosso, "is the paralysis which allows neither of escape nor defense. Not all the phenomena of fear can be explained on the theory of natural selection. In their extreme degree they are morbid phenomena, indicating imperfection of the organism. One might almost say that nature had not been able to find a substance for brain and spinal cord which should be extremely sensitive, and yet should never, under the influence of exceptional or unusual stimuli, exceed in its reactions those physiological limits which are best adapted to the preservation of the animal." Mosso quotes Haller to the effect that "phenomena of fear common to animals are not aimed at the preservation of the timid, but at their destruction."

The fear instinct is no doubt one of the most fundamental and one of the most vital of animal instincts, but when it rises to an extreme degree, or when associated with familiar instead of strange and unfamiliar objects, then we may agree with Haller that the phenomena are not aimed at the preservation of the animal, but at its destruction; or, as Darwin puts it, are of "disservice to the animal." This is just what is found in the case of psychopathic or neurotic affections. The fear instinct, when aroused and cultivated in early childhood, becomes associated in later life with particular events, objects, and special states.

When the instinct of fear is aroused in connection with some future impending misfortune, the feeling of apprehension with all its physiological changes, muscular, respiratory, cardiac, epigastric, and intestinal, goes to form that complex feeling of anxiety so highly characteristic of the acute varieties of psychopathic maladies. When fear reaches its acme, the heart is specially affected; circulatory and respiratory changes become prominent, giving rise to that form of oppression which weighs like an incubus on the patient,—the feeling known as "precordial anxiety."

The fear instinct is the ultimate cause of functional psychosis,—it is the soil on which grow luxuriantly the infinite varieties of psychopathic disturbances. The body, sense, intellect, and will are all profoundly affected by the irresistible sweep of the fear instinct, as manifested in the overwhelming feeling of anxiet\\ The fear instinct and its offsprings—hesitation, anxiety, conflicts and repressions—weaken, dissociate, and paralyze the functions of the body and mind, producing the various symptoms of psychopathic diseases. The fear instinct keeps on gnawing at the very vitals of the psychopathic patient.

Even at his best the psychopathic patient is not free from the workings of the fear instinct, from the feeling of anxiety which, as the patients themselves put it, "hangs like a cloud on the margin or fringe of consciousness." From time to time he can hear the distant, threatening rumbling of the fear instinct. Even when the latter is apparently stilled, the pangs of anxiety torment the patient like a dull toothache.

Montaigne, writing of fear, says, "I am not so good a naturalist (as they call it) as to discern by what secret springs fear has its motion in us; but be this as it may, it is a strange passion, and such a one as the physicians say there is no other whatever that sooner dethrones our judgment from its proper seat; which is so true, that I myself have seen very many become frantic through fear; and even in those of the best settled temper, it is most certain that it begets a terrible confusion during the fit. Even among soldiers, a sort of men over whom, of all others, it ought to have the least power, how often has it converted flocks of sheep into armed squadrons, reeds and bullrushes into pikes and lances, and friends into enemies. . . .

"The thing in the world I am most afraid of is fear. That passion alone, in the trouble of it, exceeding all other accidents. Such as have been well banged in some skirmish, may yet, all wounded and bloody as they are, be brought on again the next day to the charge; but such as have once conceived a good sound fear of the enemy will never be made so much as to look the enemy in the face. Such as are in immediate fear of losing their estates, of banishment or of slavery, live in perpetual anguish, and lose all appetite and repose. And the many people who, impatient of perpetual alarms of fear, have hanged or drowned themselves, or dashed themselves to pieces, give us sufficiently to understand that fear is more importunate and insupportable than death itself."

A well known writer, who is a psychopathic sufferer, writes: "Carlyle laid his finger upon the truth, when he said that the reason why the pictures of the past were always so golden in tone, so delicate in outline, was because the quality of fear was taken from them. It is the fear of what may be and what must be that overshadows present happiness; and if fear is taken from us, we are happy. The strange thing is that we can not learn not to be afraid, even though all the darkest and saddest of our experiences have left us unscathed; and if we could but find a reason for the mingling of fear with our lives, we should have gone towards the solving of the riddle of the world."

Anxiety states of neuroses and psychoses are essentially due to the awakening of the fear instinct, normally present in every living being. The fear instinct is a fundamental one; it is only inhibited by the whole course of civilization and by the training and education of life. Like the jinn of the "Arabian Nights," it slumbers in the breast of every normal individual, and comes fully to life in the various neuroses and psychoses.

Kraepelin and his school lay special stress on the fact that "Fear is by far the most important persistent emotion in morbid conditions. . . . Fear is manifested by anxious excitement and by anxious tension." "Experience," says Kraepelin, "shows an intimate relationship between insistent psychosis and the so-called 'phobias,' the anxiety states which in such patients become associated with definite impressions, actions, and views." The states are associated with the thought of some unknown danger. Violent heart action, pallor, a feeling of anxiety, tremor, cold sweat, meteorisms, diarrhoea, polyuria, weakness in the legs, fainting spells, attack the patient, who may lose control of his limbs and occasionally suffer complete collapse.

"These states," says Kraepelin, with his usual insight into abnormal mental life, "remind one of the feeling of anxiety which in the case of healthy people may, in view of a painful situation or of a serious danger, deprive one of the calmness of judgment and confidence in his movements."

Thus, we find from different standpoints that the feeling of anxiety with its accompanying phenomena is one of the most potent manifestations of animal instincts, the fear instinct, winch is at the basis of all psychopathic, neurotic maladies.

The fear instinct, as the subtle and basic instinct of life, is well described by Kipling:—

Very softly down the glade runs a waiting, watching shade,

And the whisper spreads and widens far and near; And the sweat is on thy brow, for he passes even now—

He is Fear, O Little Hunter, he is Fear!

Ere the moon has climbed the mountain, ere the rocks are ribbed with light, When the downward dipping trails are dank and drear, Comes a breathing hard behind thee— snuffle — snuffle through the night— It is Fear, O Little Hunter, it is Fear!

On thy knees and draw the bow; bid the shrilling arrow go: In the empty, mocking thicket plunge the spear; But thy hands are loosed and weak, and the blood has left thy cheek— It is Fear, O Little Hunter, it is Fear!

When the heat-cloud sucks the tempest, when the slivered pine trees fall, When the blinding, blaring rain-squalls lash and veer; Through the war gongs of the thunder rings a voice more loud than all— It is Fear, O Little Hunter, it is Fear!

Now the spates are banked and deep; now the footless boulders leap— Now the lightning shows each littlest leaf-rib clear; But thy throat is shut and dried, and thy heart against thy side Hammers: Fear, O Little Hunter,—This is Fear!

It is interesting to learn what a practical and thoughtful surgeon, such as George Crile, has to say on the matter of fear. Dr. Crile lays stress on the facts that in his researches he finds evidence that the phenomena of fear have a physical basis similar to those morphological changes in the brain cells observed in certain stages of surgical shock and in fatigue. . . . That the brain is definitely damaged by fear may be proved by experiments.

"According to Sherrington the nervous system responds in action as a whole, and to but one stimulus at a time . . . Under the influence of fear or (fear of) injury the integration of the common path is most nearly absolute . . . Hence fear and injury (or fear of injury) drain the cup of energy to the dregs. . . .

"We can understand why it is a patient consumed by fear suffers so many bodiiy impairments, (so many functional disturbances) and diseases even. We can understand the grave digestive and metabolic disturbances under strain of fear. . . . We can understand the variations in the gastric analyses in a timid patient alarmed over his condition and afraid of the hospital. The patient is integrated by fear, and since fear takes precedence over all other impulses, no organ can function normally (under the influence of fear)" . . . Dr. Crile arrives at the conclusion that "Fear dominates the various organs and parts of the body." . . .

Dr. Crile lays special stress on the pathological character of the fear instinct: "That the brain is definitely influenced, damaged even, by fear has been proved by the following experiments: Rabbits were frightened by a dog, but were neither injured nor chased. After various periods of time the animals were killed and their brain cells compared with the brain cells of normal animals, widespread changes were seen (in the brain cells of the animals affected by fear). The principal clinical phenomena expressed by the rabbits were rapid heart, accelerated respiration, prostration, tremors, and a rise in temperature. The dog showed similar phenomena, excepting that, instead of such muscular relaxation as was shown by the rabbit, it exhibited aggressive muscular action."

Animals in which the fear instinct can be aroused to a high degree become paralyzed and perish. The animal mechanism is by no means perfect. A stab in the heart, a rip in the abdomen, a cut of the carotids, a prick in the medulla, a scratch of a needle infected with anthrax, or tetanus bacilli, a drop of hydrocyanic acid, an arrow tipped with curare, extinguish every spark of life. Organic material may be delicate and complex, but for that reason it is highly imperfect and vulnerable.

Living matter is the feeblest material in nature, and is as fragile as a delicate crystal vase. Protoplasm, or living matter, may be wonderful material, but it can be crushed with a pebble. The most beautiful colors may be displayed by a thin, delicate bubble, but it bursts at the least touch. Living matter is like a bubble, like foam on the ocean. Perhaps no better material is available for the functions of life.

Meanwhile it remains true that the flimsiness of living material makes it easily subject to decay and destruction. It is a profound error, having its root in prejudice, that nature always helps, and that the processes going on in the organism are always of benefit to the individual. Nature is as ready to destroy life as to protect it.

Preservation or destruction of a particular individual depends on the fact as to whether or no normal or pathological processes predominate in the total economy of the organism. This holds true of the fear instinct. The fear instinct is a delicate mechanism, and when its action is slightly intensified, the animal is on the way to destruction. For the cosmic forces are careless of the creatures which keep on pouring forth in generous profusion from the lap of nature.

Living matter, or protoplasm can only exist under special, restricted conditions, —the least variation means death. The more complicated, and more organized protoplasm is, the more restricted are the conditions of its existence. A rise of a couple of degrees of temperature or a fall means disease and death. The same holds true of the rise and fall of quantity and quality of bodily secretion of glands and of other organs. Protoplasm can only exist in an optimum environment. Any change spells disease and death.

The fear instinct, being at the heart of highly organized life activities, is delicately responsive to any changes and variations from the optimum, requisite for the proper functioning of the organism. Any deviation from the optimum environment, external or internal, produces corresponding changes in the fear instinct with consequent pathological changes in the organism.

The fear instinct like a delicate indicator is the first to get deranged, with harmful results to the organism as a whole. We can thus realize the importance of keeping the fear instinct in good condition. We can understand the significance of Plato's doctrine of rational guidance of the fear instinct. "What to fear and what not to fear" is at the basis of all organized life, individual and social. [1]

CHAPTER VI
FEAR AND DISEASE

If we examine closely the symptoms of fear, we invariably find the symptoms of functional psychosis or neurosis. Fear affects the muscular and sensory systems, the vasomotor system, the respiratory system, the sudorific glands, the viscera, the heart, the intestines, all organs and functions of the organism.

Bain, in describing the emotions of fear or terror, says, "Terror on the physical side shows both a loss and a transfer of nervous energy. The appearances may be distributed between the effects of relaxation and effects of tension. The relaxation is seen, as regards the muscles, in the dropping of the jaw, in the collapse overtaking all organs not specially excited, in trembling of the lips and other parts, and in the loosening of the sphincters. Next, as regards the organic processes and viscera. The digestion is everywhere weakened; the flow of saliva is checked, the gastric secretion arrested (appetite failing), the bowels deranged; the respiration is enfeebled. The heart and circulation are disturbed; there is either a flushing of the face or a deadly pallor. The skin shows symptoms—the cold sweat, the altered odor of the perspiration, the creeping action that lifts the hair. The kidneys are directly or indirectly affected. The sexual organs feel the depressing influence. The secretion of milk in the mother's breast is vitiated."

Darwin gives the following description of fear:— "The frightened man at first stands like a statue, motionless and breathless, or crouches down as if to escape observation. The heart beats quickly and violently, but it is very doubtful if it then works more efficiently than usuar so as to send a greater supply of blood to the body; for the skin instantly becomes pale, as during incipient faintness. The paleness of the surface, however, is probably in large part or is exclusively due to the vasomotor center being affected in such a manner as to cause the contraction of the small arteries of the skin. That the skin is much affected under the sense of great fear we see in the marvelous manner in which the perspiration immediately exudes from it. This exudation is all the more remarkable as the surface is then cold, and hence the term, a cold sweat; whereas the sudorofic glands are properly excited into action when the surface is heated. The hairs also on the skin stand erect, and the superficial muscles shiver. In connection with the disturbed action of the heart the breathing is hurried. The salivary glands act imperfectly; the mouth becomes dry and is often opened and shut. I have also noticed that under Blight fear there is a slight tendency to yawn. One of the best symptoms is the trembling of all the muscles of the body. From this cause and from the dryness of the mouth, the voice becomes husky or indistinct, or may altogether fail."

If we turn now to the manifestations of psychopathic maladies, we meet with the same fear symptoms :—

(a) The attacks may be muscular, involving symptoms such as trembling, shaking, paresis, paralysis, or rigidity; there may be affection of locomotion or of muscular co-ordination.

(b) There may be sensory disturbances,—anesthesia, paresthesia, analgesia, or hyperalgesia as well as affection of muscular sense and kinesthesia.

(c) There may be skin disturbances, such as arrest of perspiration or profuse perspiration, especially under the influence of emotions, worry, and fatigue; such perspiration may also occur at night, and in some cases the fear of tuberculosis may be associated with such conditions.

(d) The lungs may become affected functionally, and there may occur respiratory disturbances; coughing, hawking, apnea, dyspnea, and asthmatic troubles.

(e) The heart becomes affected, bringing about precordial pain; palpitation of the heart, bradycardia, tachycardia, and cardiac arrhythmia.

(f) The stomach and intestines become affected,

indigestion and vague fugitive soreness and pain may be experienced all over or in special regions of the abdomen; constipation or diarrhea may ensue.

(g) The renal apparatus may become affected and its activity arrested, or, as is more often the case in the milder forms of psychopathic troubles, there may be present an alteration! in the amount or frequency of micturition, such as is found in the conditions of anuria and polyuria.

(h) Menstruation becomes disturbed, and we may meet with conditions of dysmenorrhea, amenorrhea, menorrhagia, and other disturbances of the tubes, ovaries, and uterus.

(i) There are disturbances of the nervous system, such as headache and a general dull sensation of fatigue and paresis of all mental functions, with dizziness and vertigo.

On the mental side we find in the psychopathies the following disturbances:—

(a) Affections of perceptual activity,—illusions and hallucinations.

(b) Affections of intellectual activity, — argumentativeness in regard to insignificant things.

(c) Affections of the moral sense,—scrupulousness, over-conscientiousness, not living up to ideal states.

(d) Affections of religious life,—fear of commission of sins and terror of punishment.

(e) Affections of social life,—timidity, blushing, etc.

(f) Affections in regard to objects, such as astro-phobia, acmephobia, agoraphobia, claustrophobia, etc.

(g) Affections of conceptual life,—insistent ideas, (h) Affections of the attention,—aprosexia.

(i) Affections of the will,—states of aboulia, indecision, discord, conflicts, and uncontrollable impulses.

(j) Affections of the memory,—amnesic and par-amnesic states.

(k) General mental fatigue.

(1) Affections of sexual life—impotence, perversion, and inversion.

(in) Affections in regard to marital relations.

(n) Affections in regard to personal life,—diffidence, self-condemnation, self-depreciation.

(o) Affections of apparent loss of personality— feeling of self gone.

(p) Formation of new personalities,—dual and multiple personality.

In connection with all such neurotic affections we find invariably present a feeling of unrest, hesitation, doubt, conflict, discord, uneasiness, a feeling of anxiety, conscious or subconscious, feeling of some impending evil. In all such affections we find the brooding spirit of the most powerful of all animal instincts,—the fear instinct. Neurosis is a disease of self-preservation and fear.

CHAPTER VII
FORMS OF NEUROSIS

A brief outline of a classification of nervous and mental diseases, made by me in mj various works, may be of help towards a clear understanding of neurotic disturbances.

The different forms of nervous and mental diseases may be classified into Organic and Functional.

By organic affections I mean to indicate pathological modifications of the neuron and its processes taking place in the very structure (probably the cytoreticulum) of the nerve cell. Under this category come such maladies as general paresis, dementia praecox, all mental and nervous affections of a degenerative and involutionary character. Such diseases are termed by me Organopathies, or Necropathies. By functional affections I mean to indicate all neuron changes in which the functions of the neuron and its reactions to external and internal stimulations are involved in the pathological process without, however, affecting the anatomical structure of the nerve cell. The pathological changes are not permanent,—recovery of normal function is possible with the restitution of favorable conditions of nutrition and elimination.

Functional nervous and mental diseases are in turn subdivided into Neuropathies and Psychopathies. Neuropathic diseases are disturbances of functioning activity, due to defective neuron matabolism, brought about by external stimuli, and more specially by harmful internal stimuli—glandular secretions, hormones, toxic and autotoxic agencies. The pathological, neuropathic process produces few, if any anatomical, changes in the structure of the neuron. The pathology of neuropathic diseases, probably of the cytoplasm) is essentially chemico-physiological in nature.

Neuropathic diseases include maladies in which the neuron undergoes degenerative changes. At first there is an apparent increase, then an inhibition, and finally a complete suspension of neuron function, not terminating in the destruction of the neuron. Neuron restitution is possible. Such affections arc produced by mild poisons, organic, or inorganic, by autotoxic products, by hyposecretion or hypersecretion, or by absence of hormones in the economy of the organism. Here belong all the temporary, or recurrent maniacal, melancholic, delusional states, puerperal mania, epileptic insanity, the mental aberrations of adolescent and climacteric periods, periodic insanity, alternating insanities, and in general all the mental affections known under the description of manic-depressive insanity.

Where the disease depends on the interrelation of neurons in a complex group, on association of systems of neurons, the condition is psychopathic in nature. In psychopathic troubles the neuron itself may remain unaffected, may be perfectly normal and healthy. The disorder is due to association with systems of neurons which are usually not called into action by the function of that particular neuron system.

By Organopathies or Necropathies I indicate a group of psychophysiological symptoms, accompanied by structural, necrotic changes of the neuron, terminating in the ultimate death of the neuron systems, involved in the pathological process. By Neuropathies I indicate a group of psychophysiological manifestations due to pathological functional neuron modifications, capable of restitution through normal metabolism.

By Psychopathies I designate pathological phenomena of psychophysiological dissociation and disaggregation of neuron systems and their functions in clusters, the neuron itself and its special function remaining undamaged.

The psychopathies are further subdivided into

Somatopsychoses and Psyclioneuroses or Neuropsychoses.

The Somatopsychoses arc characterized by somatic symptoms, by disturbances of bodily functions, such as paralysis, contractures, convulsions, anesthesia, analgesia, hyperalgesia, and other sensory disturbances, as well as b , intestinal, cardiac, respiratory, and genito-urinary troubles.

The psyclioneuroses or Neuropsychoses are characterized by mental symptoms. The patient's whole mind is occupied with mental troubles.

Such conditions are found in obsessions, fixed ideas, imperative impulses, emotional compulsions, and other allied mental and nervous maladies.

Somatopsychoses simulate physical and organic nervous troubles. Thus, many "hysterical" forms simulate tabes, or paralysis agitans, hemiplegia, paraplegia, or epilepsy, while many of the neurasthenic, hypochondriacal, and their allied states may simulate tumor, cancer, intestinal and glandular derangements, cardiac, laryngeal, pneumonic, hepatic, splanchnic ovarian, tubal, uterine, renal, and other bodily afflictions.

The neuropsychoses or psyclioneuroses simulate all forms of mental disease, beginning with melancholia and mania, and ending with general paresis and dementia.

Psychuneurosis and somatopsychosis are diseases

of the subconscious ; in the former mental, in the latter physical symptoms predominate.

Psychopathic states should be rigidly differentiated from oilier disturbances, such as neuropathies and organopathies, or necropathies. T

CHAPTER VIII
FEAR AND THE HYPNOIDAL STATE

In my work on "Sleep'* I report a series of interesting experiments carried out by me on guinea pigs, rabbits, cats, dogs, children, and adults. I discovered one of the most important states of animal life, a state which I termed hypnoidal. The study shows that in almost every animal, from the lowest to the highest, from frog to man, a somewhat sudden change of the usual environment deprives that animal of its activities and its functions. If the change is not too intense and prolonged, the animal merges into the hypnoidal state in which the lost functions are restored. During this hypnoidal state the functions are weakened, the animal may be regarded in a state of invalidism, its reactions being enfeebled, practically speaking, paretic.

Perhaps it is advisable to approach the phenomena from their more striking aspect. In seizing a triton, salamander, or frog, and stretching it on the table, one will observe with surprise that the animal remains in the same position given it. The most uncomfortable and bizarre position may be given to the limbs, and still the animal will not move. Testing the extremities one finds them rigid and resisting. Something similar we find in the hypnotic condition, when under the suggestion that the extremities are rigid, and they cannot be moved by the subject. The same can be done with a lobster and other animals of the same type.

Everyone has heard of the experimentum mirabile made by Kirchner in the seventeenth century. A rooster or hen is seized, the legs are tied with a string and the bird is put on the ground. A piece of chalk is passed over the beak,—the chalk tracing a line from beak to some distant point on the ground. When the bird is released, it remains in the same position. Some explain that the animal is kept prisoner, because it "imagines" that it is bound by the line of chalk. The chalk, however, is unnecessary. The animal may be seized, shouted in its ear, or kept down forcibly, and the same result will happen. This state has been termed by Preyer "cataplexy." The phenomenon can also be produced in insects, in mol-lusca.

Many investigators have been interested in this phenomenon. I have devoted a good deal of work to this condition which is also found in mammals in which it is induced by the fear instinct. In mammals, however, the state of cataplexy is not neces-

sarily accompanied by rigidity, although it may be present, but there is a complete loss of voluntary activity. Horses tremble violently and become paralyzed at the sight of a beast of prey, such as a tiger or a lion. At the sight of a serpent, monkeys are known to be in such an intense state of fear that they are unable to move, and thus fall easy victims to the reptile.

Under similar conditions birds are so paralyzed by fear that they are unable to fly away from the source of danger, and fall a prey to the threatening serpent. The birds resemble very much the hypnotized subject in a state of catalepsy. Although the gibbons are the most agile of all the simians, they are easily taken by surprise, and captured without any resistance,—they are paralyzed by fear. Seals when pursued on land become so frightened that they are unable to offer any opposition to their pursuers, and let themselves easily be captured and killed.

In large cities one can often witness nervous people affected suddenly by the presence of danger; they remain immobile, in the middle of the street, becoming exposed to fatal accidents. The fear instinct paralyzes their activities, they are petrified with terror.

I was told by people who have experienced the effects of earthquakes, that during the time of the

earthquakes they were unable to move, and the same condition was observed in animals, especially in young dogs. It is hard to move cattle and horses from a burning stable, on account of the fear of fire which obsesses the animals, .so that they become paralyzed, suffocated and burnt to death. So vital is the fear instinct that the least deviation from the normal state is apt to play havoc with the safety of the individual.

The fear instinct is the most primitive, the most fundamental, and the most powerful of all instincts. When the fear instinct is let loose, the animal succumbs. We should not wonder, therefore, that with the aberration of the fear instinct, the life guardian of the individual, all orientation is lost, the animal becomes demoralized, and the organism goes to destruction. No other instinct can surpass the fear instinct in its fatal effects.

The more one studies the facts, the more one examines various psychopathic, functional maladies, without going into any speculations and without being blinded by foregone conclusions and pseudo-scientific hypotheses, the more one is driven to the conclusion that the fear instinct is at the bottom of all those nervous and mental aberrations, conscious and subconscious.

The infinite varieties of functional psychopathic diseases are the consequences of some abnormal asso-

TO Nervous Ills

ciation with the fear instinct which alone gives rise to the infirmities characteristic of functional mental maladies.

President Stanley Hall accepts my view of the subject. In a recent paper he writes: "If there be a vital principle, fear must be one of its close allies as one of the chief springs of the mind" ... In spite of his former psychoanalytic inclinations President Hall asserts now that "Freud is wrong in interpreting this most generic form of fear as rooted in sex. Sex anxieties themselves are rooted in the larger fundamental impulse of self-preservation with its concomitant instinct of fear." This is precisely the factor and the teaching which I have been expounding in all my works on Psychopathology.

So deeply convinced is Professor Stanley Hall of the primitive and fundamental character of the fear instinct, that he refers to the facts that "if the cerebrum is removed, animals, as Goltz and Bechterev have proved, manifest very intense symptoms of fear, and so do human monsters born without brains, of hemicephalic children, as Sternberg and Lotzko have demonstrated."

The fear instinct is of such vital importance that it is found in animals after decerebration, and persists in animals after spino-vago-sympathetic section. Sherrington found the fear instinct present in dogs after section of the spinal cord and also after complete section of the vago-sympathctir

nerves, thus removing all sensations coming from the viscera, muscles, and skin, below the shoulder, leaving only the sensations from the front paws, head and cerebral activity. The dog was a sort of cerebral animal. The whole body below the shoulder, skin, muscle, viscera, were all anaesthetic, and yet the fear instinct remained intact.

On the other hand, after complete ablation of the cerebral hemispheres of the dog, so that the animal became spinal, all cerebral functions being totally wiped out, Goltz invariably found that the fear instinct remained unimpaired. The fear instinct is inherent in animal life — existence. As long as there is life, there is fear.

So potent, all embracing, and all pervading is the fear instinct, that the physician must reckon with it in his private office, in the hospital, and in the surgical operating room. In a number of my cases psy-chognosis, the study and examination of mental states, clearly reveals the fact that even where the neurosis has not originated in a surgical trauma, surgical operations reinforced, developed, and fixed psychopathic conditions.

The fear instinct is one of the most primitive and most fundamental of all instincts. Neither hunger, nor sex, nor maternal instinct, nor social instinct can compare with the potency of the fear instinct, rooted as it is in the conditions of life primordial.

When the instinct of fear is at its height it sweeps

before it all other instincts. Nothing can withstand a panic. Functional psychosis in its full development is essentially a panic. A psychogenetic examination of every case of functional psychosis brings one invariably to the basic instinct of life, self preservation and the fear instinct. As Whittier puts it:

Still behind the tread I hear Of my life companion, Fear, Still a shadow, deep and vast From my westering feet is cast; Wavering, doubtful, undefined, Never shapen, nor outlined. From myself the Fear has grown, And the shadow is my own.

CHAPTER IX
HEALTH AND MORBIDITY

While health cannot be separated from disease by a sharp line, the two are relative and fluctuating. Still, on the whole, the two can be differentiated by the criterion of hurt and dissolution. Any process or state conducive to hurt, and tending to dissolution of the organism may be regarded as pathological or abnormal. The same criterion should be applied, when differentiating the healthy, normal states of instincts and emotions from abnormal and morbid states of instinctive and emotional activities. Those states that further life activities are healthy, normal; those that hinder life are morbid.

The same holds true of the fear instinct. Every form of fear which, instead of helping or furthering vigor of life, instead of stimulating living energy, instead of being a protection, becomes a hindrance, a menace to the organism, is accompanied with suffering and distress, and ultimately leads to destruction, should be regarded as essentially morbid.

The following are the chief characteristics of morbid instinctive and emotional states:

I. When they are disproportionate to the cause.

II. When they are chronic.

III. When their feeling-tone is painful, distressing.

IV. When they are non-adaptive to the stimulations.

V. When the reactions are not adjusted to the external environment.

VI. When they are uncontrollable.

VII. When coming in recurrent or periodic attacks.

VIII. When the physical and mental reactions are of great intensity.

IX. When they are dissociative.

X. When they lead to dissolution.

Fear is not a matter of belief. To regard fear as a form of belief, is fallacious, dangerous, and suicidal. It is as dangerous as to consider smallpox and cholera the result of faith. We must never forget that fear is one of the most fundamental of animal instincts having its roots deep down in animal life existence. To ignore tlus fact is suicidal.

According to the great anthropologist, Galton: "Every antelope in South Africa has to run for its life every one or two days, and the antelope starts and gallops under the influence of a false alarm many times a day. Fear is a fundamental condition of animal existence."

The fear instinct in its healthy normal state is a

protection and defense. As Ribot puts it: "The basis of fear exists in the organism, forms part of the constitution of animals and man, and helps them to live by a defensive adaptation:" In fact, we may even go to the point of affirming that the fear instinct, like all other healthy, normal instincts, is absolutely requisite in the total economy of animal and human life.

In man, however, fear should not be at the mercy of blind animal instincts and reflexes, but should be guided and controlled by reason, by reflection, by scientific, medical measures, by scientific sanitation, by physical and mental hygiene, and by the rational cultivation and development of all human functions and faculties.

One of the greatest Greek thinkers well puts it: "Imbeciles, fools, and the mad alone have no understanding of fear. True education, true reason, and true courage consist in the knowledge of what to fear and what not to fear."

Mysticism, occultism, and credulity act like virulent germs, fatal to man. "Metaphysical" cults anaesthetize the intellect, put judgment into lethargic sleep from which there is no awaking. Mysticism kills the most precious essence of man's life,—the critical sense of human personality.

Occultism, mysticism, et id genus omne declare that "fear is a false belief, an error of the mortal mind." Mystics claim the "unreality" of the mate-

rial fear instinct of which they are in "reality" in "mortal" terror. This zealous negation of fear is its strongest affirmation.

As a matter of fact, fear is one of the most stern realities of life. The neurotic in denying disease, evil, and fear is like the proverbial ostrich which on perceiving danger hides its head in the sand. The "Love" of mysticism is the Fear of death.

CHAPTER X
THE SUBCONSCIOUS 1

Man's nerve cell organization may be classified into two main systems:

(I) The inferior, the reflex, the instinctive, the automatic centers.

(II) The superior, the controlling, selective, and inhibitory brain-centers of the cortex.

The double systems of nerve-centers have correspondingly a double mental activity, or double-consciousness as it is sometimes called, the inferior, the organic, the instinctive, the automatic, the reflex consciousness, or briefly termed the sub-consciousness, consciousness below the threshold of self-consciousness ; and the superior, the choosing, the willing, the critical, the will-consciousness. This controlling will-consciousness may also be characterized as the guardian-consciousness of the individual.

From an evolutionary standpoint, we can well realize the biological function or importance of this guardian-consciousness. The external world bombards the living organism with innumerable stimuli.

1 The theory of the subconscious was first developed by me in my volume "The Psychology of Suggestion," 1898.

From all sides thousands of impressions come crowding upon the senses of the individual. Each neuron system with its appropriate receptors has its corresponding system of reactions which, if not modified or counteracted, may end in some harmful or fatal result.

It is not of advantage to an individual of a complex organization to respond with reaction to all impressions coming from the external environment. Hence, that organism will succeed best in the struggle for existence that possesses some selective, critical, inhibitory "choice and will'* centers. The more organized and the more sensitive and delicate those centers are, the better will the organism succeed in its life existence.

The guardian-consciousness wards off, so far as it is possible, the harmful blows given by the stimuli of the external environment. In man, this same guardian consciousness keeps on constructing, by a series of elimination and selection, a new environment, individual and social, which leads to an ever higher and more perfect development and realization of the inner powers of individuality and personality.

Under normal conditions man's superior and inferior centers with their corresponding upper, critical, controlling consciousness together with the inferior automatic, reflex centers and their concomitant subconscious consciousness, keep on functioning in full harmony. The upper and lower consciousness

form one organic unity, —one conscious, active personality.

Under certain abnormal conditions, however, the two systems of nerve-centers with their corresponding mental activities may become dissociated. The superior nerve-centers with their critical, controlling consciousness may become inhibited, split off from the rest of the nervous system. The reflex, automatic, instinctive, subconscious centers with their mental functions are laid bare, thus becoming directly accessible to the stimuli of the outside world; they fall a prey to the influences of external surroundings, influences termed suggestions.

The critical, controlling, guardian-consciousness, being cut off and absent, the reduced individuality lacks the rational guidance and orientation given by the upper choice- and will-centers, and becomes the helpless plaything of all sorts of suggestions, sinking into the trance states of the subconscious. It is this subconscious that forms the highway of suggestions. Suggestibility is the essential characteristic of the subconscious.

The subconscious rises to the surface of consciousness, so to say, whenever there is a weakening, paralysis, or inhibition of the upper, controlling will and choice-centers. In other words, whenever there is a disaggregation of the superior from the inferior nerve-centers, there follows an increase of ideo-sensory, ideo-motor, sensori-secretory, reflex excita-

bility; and ideationally, or rationally there is present an abnormal intensity of suggestibility. 2

8 1 object to the term "Subliminal," because it is understood in a cosmic, or metaphysical sense. The term "co-conscious" is limited and refers to independently functioning, contemporaneous personalities, or mental systems. The term "Unconscious" is misleading, because it may refer to the metaphysics of Hartmann. At best it simply means nervous processes which, as such, belong to neurology, physiology, but not to the domain of abnormal psychology.

The term "subconscious," used by me in "The Psychology of Suggestion," means tracts of mental states which mag or may not function in the total mental reaction of the individual.

CHAPTER XI
THE CONDITIONS AND LAWS OF SUGGESTION

In order to bring to the fore subconscious activities with their reflex, automatic psycho-motor reactions by removal of the upper consciousness I have found requisite, in my investigations, the following conditions:

Normal Suggestibility, — Suggestibility in the Normal, Waking State.

(1) Fixation of the Attention.

(2) Distraction of the Attention.

(3) Monotony.

(4) Limitation of Voluntary Activity.

(5) Limitation of the Field of Consciousness.

(6) Inhibition.

(7) Immediate Execution of the Suggestion. Abnormal Suggestibility, — Suggestibility in Hypnotic and Trance States:

(1) Fixation of the Attention.

(2) Monotony.

(3) Limitation of Voluntary Activity.

(4) Limitation of the Field of Consciousness.

(5) Inhibition.

The nature of abnormal suggestibility, the result of my investigations, is a disaggregation of consciousness, a cleavage of the mind, a cleft that may become ever deeper and wider, ending in a total disjunction of the waking, guiding, controlling guardian-consciousness from the automatic, reflex, subconscious consciousness. . . .

Normal suggestibility is of like nature,—it is a cleft in the mind. Only here the cleft is not so deep, not so lasting as in hypnosis or in the other subconscious trance states. The split is but momentary. The mental cleavage, or the psycho-physiological disaggregation of the superior from the inferior centers with their concomitant psychic activities is evanescent, fleeting, often disappearing at the moment of its appearance.

The following laws of suggestibility were formulated by me:

I. Normal suggestibility varies as indirect suggestion and inversely as direct suggestion.

II. Abnormal suggestibility varies as direct suggestion and inversely as indirect suggestion.

A comparison of the conditions of normal and abnormal suggestibility is valuable, since it reveals the nature of suggestibility, and discloses its fundamental law. An examination of the two sets of conditions shows that in abnormal suggestibility two conditions, distraction of attention and immediate execution are absent, otherwise the conditions are

the same. This sameness of conditions clearly indicates the fact that both normal and abnormal suggestibility flow from some one common source, that they are of like nature, and due to similar causes.

Now a previous study led us to the conclusion that the nature of abnormal suggestibility is a disaggregation of consciousness, a slit produced in the mind, a crack that may become wider and deeper, ending in a total disjunction of the waking, guiding, controlling consciousness from the reflex conciousness. Normal suggestibility is of a like nature. It is a cleft in the mind. The cleft is not so deep, not so lasting as it is in hypnosis, or in the state of abnormal suggestibility. The split is but momentary, disappearing almost at the very moment of its appearance.

This fleeting, evanescent character of the split explains why suggestion in the normal state, why normal suggestibility requires immediate execution as one of its indispensable conditions. We must take the opportunity of the momentary ebb of the controlling consciousness and hastily plant our suggestion in the soil of reflex consciousness. We must watch for this favorable moment, not let it slip by, otherwise the suggestion is a failure. Furthermore, we must be careful to keep in abeyance, for the moment, the ever active waves of the controlling consciousness. We must find for them work in some other direction, we must divert, we must distract them. That is why normal suggestibility requires

the additional conditions of distraction and immediate execution. For in the waking state the waking, controlling consciousness is always on its guard, and when enticed away, leaves its ground only for a moment.

In normal suggestibility the psychic split is but faint; the lesion, effected in the body consciousness, is superficial, transitory, fleeting. In abnormal suggestibility, on the contrary, the slit is deep and lasting,—it is a severe gash. In both cases, however, we have a removal, a dissociation of the waking from the subwaking, reflex consciousness, suggestion becoming effected only through the latter. For suggestibility is the attribute of the subwaking, reflex consciousness.

A comparison of the two laws discloses the same relation. The two laws are the reverse of each other, thus clearly indicating the presence of a controlling, inhibiting, conscious element in one case, and its absence in the other. In the normal state we must guard against the inhibitory, waking consciousness, and we have to make our suggestion as indirect as possible. In the abnormal state, on the contrary, no circumspection is needed; the controlling, inhibitory, waking consciousness is more or less absent. The subwaking, reflex consciousness is exposed to external stimuli, and our suggestions are therefore the more effective, the more direct we make them.

Suggestibility is a function of disaggregation of

consciousness, a disaggregation in which the subwaking, reflex consciousness enters into direct communication with the external world. The general law of suggestibility is:

Suggestibility varies as the amount of disaggregation, and inversely as the unification of consciousness.

CHAPTER XII
IS THE SUBCONSCIOUS A PERSONALITY?

The problem that interested me most was to come into close contact with the subwaking self. What is its fundamental nature? What are the main traits of its character? Since in hypnosis the subwaking self is freed from its chains, is untrammeled by the shackles of the upper, controlling self, since in hypnosis the underground self is more or less exposed to our view, it is plain that experimentation on the hypnotic self will introduce us into the secret life of the subwaking self. For, as we pointed out, the two are identical.

I have made all kinds of experiments, bringing subjects into catalepsy, somnambulism, giving illusions, hallucinations, post-hypnotic suggestions, etc. As a result of my work one central truth stands out clear, and that is the extraordinary plasticity of the subwaking self.

If you can only in some way or other succeed in separating the primary controlling consciousness from the lower one, the waking from the subwaking self, so that they should no longer keep company, you can do anything you please with the subwaking

self. You can make its legs, its hands, any limb you like perfectly rigid; you can make it eat pepper for sugar; you can make it drink water for wine; feel cold or warm; hear delightful stories in the absence of all sounds; feel pain or pleasure, see oranges where there is nothing; you can make it eat them and enjoy their taste. In short, you can do with the subwaking self anything you like. The subwaking consciousness is in your power, like clay in the hands of the potter. The plasticity of the subconscious is revealed by its extreme suggestibility.

I wanted to get an insight into the very nature of the subwaking self; I wished to make a personal acquaintance with it. "What is its personal character?" I asked. How surprised I was when, after a close interrogation, the answer came to me that there cannot possibly be any personal acquaintance with it,—for the subwaking xclf hicks personality.

Under certain conditions a cleavage ma} 7 occur between the two selves, and then the subwaking self may rapidly grow, develop, and attain, apparently, the plane of self-consciousness, get crystallized into a person, and give itself a name, imaginary, or borrowed from history. This accounts for the spiritualistic phenomena of personality, guides, controls, and communications by dead personalities, or spirits coming from another world, such as have been observed in the case of Mrs. Piper and other mediums of like types; it accounts for all the phenomena of

multiple personality, simulating the dead or the living, or formed anew out of the matrix of the subconscious.

All such personality metamorphoses can be easily developed, under favorable conditions in any psycho-pathological laboratory. They can be easily formed, by suggestion in trance, hypnotic, and waking states. The newly crystallized personality is, as a rule, extremely unstable, ephemeral, shadowy in its outlines, spirit-like, ghost-like, tends to become amorphous, being formed again and again under the influence of favorable conditions and suggestions, rising to the surface of consciousness, then sinking into the subconsciousness, and disappearing, only to give rise to new personality-metamorphoses, bursting like so many bubbles on the surface of the upper stream of consciousness.

There are cases when the personality of the individual is changed, or more personalities are formed. This metamorphosis may be brought about artificially, by suggestion, either direct or indirect. This is often brought about in a state of hypnosis when any number of personalities may be formed at the will of the hypnotizer who may create them deliberately ; or they may become formed by subtle indirect suggestion, coming from the hypnotizer, of which he himself is not fully conscious; or the personalities may be formed by auto-suggestions. Such

phenomena may be regarded as the artefacts of P sychopathology.

There are again cases which are no play-personalities depending on hypnotic suggestion, or suggestion in waking life, but which are really due to pathological agencies. The former, due to suggestion, are suggestion-personalities, the latter, due to pathological agencies, are pathological personalities. The formation of multiple personality by means of suggestion does not belong to our present subject.

I have discussed these facts of suggestion personalities in my volume, "The Psychology of Suggestion," and other works. The pathological multiple personalities are of immense interest from many standpoints which we need not go into just at present, since our object is rather the causation, not the nature and character of the personalities themselves. 1

The subwaking self is extremely credulous; it lacks all sense of the true and rational. "Two and two make five." "Yes." Anything is accepted, if sufficiently emphasized by the hypnotizer. The suggestibility and imitativeness of the subwaking self were discussed by me at great length. What I should like to point out here is the extreme servility and cowardliness of that self. Show hesitation, and

1 The subject of pathological multiple personalities is discussed in my work, "Multiple Personality."

it will show fight; command authoritatively, and it will obey slavishly.

The subwaking self is devoid of all morality. It will steal without the least scruple; it will poison; it will stab; it will assassinate its best friends unhesitatingly. When completely cut off from the waking person, it is precluded from conscience.

CHAPTER XIII
THE CHARACTER OF THE HYPNOIDAL STATE

In "The Psychology of Suggestion," I pointed out the conditions of normal and abnormal suggestibility. Among these conditions, monotony and the limitation of voluntary movements play an important role. Any arrangement of external circumstances, tending to produce monotony and limitation of voluntary movements, brings about a subconscious state of suggestibility in which the patient's mental life can be influenced with ease.

I find that in the subconscious hypnoidal state consciousness is vague and memory is diffused, so that experiences apparently forgotten come in bits and scraps to the foreground of consciousness. Emotional excitement is calmed, voluntary activity is somewhat passive, and suggestions meet with little resistance.

The induced subconscious hypnoidal state is a rest state, a state of physical and mental relaxation. It is a state of rest and relaxation that is specially amenable to psychotherapeutic influences. The important results obtained by me led to a closer study

of what I then thought was a peculiar mental state designated by me as the subwaking, or the hypnoidal state.

The subwaking, or the hypnoidal state is essentially an intermediary state belonging apparently to the borderland of mental life. On the one hand, the hypnoidal state touches on the waking condition; on the other it merges into sleep and hypnosis. A close study of the hypnoidal state shows that it differs from the hypnotic state proper and that it can by no means be identified with light hypnosis.

In my years of work on patients and subjects, I have observed the presence of the hypnoidal state before the development of hypnosis and also before the onset of sleep. When again the hypnotic or sleep state passes into waking, the hypnoidal state reappears. The hypnoidal state then may be regarded as an intermediate and transitional state.

A somewhat related state has been long known in psychological literature as the hypnagogic state which precedes the oncome of sleep and is rich in hallucinations known under the term of hypnagogic hallucinations. In coming out of sleep, a closely related state may be observed, a state which I have termed hypnapagogic. In both states, hypnagogic and hypnapagogic, dream-hallucinations hold sway.

The hypnagogic and hypnapagogic states do not belong to light hypnosis, as it can hardly be claimed

that men fall into light hypnosis twice, or possibly more than that, every day of their life. We do not go into light hypnosis with every nap we take. We do, however, go into the hypnoidal state when we pass into sleep or come out of sleep. Every drowsy state has the hypnoidal state as one of its constituents; every sleep state is preceded and followed by the hypnoidal state.

Hypnosis may be regarded as belonging to the abnormal mental states, while the hypnoidal state is more closely allied to waking and sleep, and belongs to the normal, physiological, mental states. At first, I regarded the hypnoidal state as peculiar, but as I proceeded with my observations and experiments I could not help coming to the conclusion that the hypnoidal state is found in all the representatives of animal life and is as normal as waking and sleep.

The hypnoidal state may be said to partake not only of the nature of waking and sleep, but also to possess some characteristics of hypnosis, namely, suggestibility. It is clear that, from the very nature of its mixed symptomatology, the hypnoidal state is variable and highly unstable. The hypnoidal state may be regarded in the light of an equivalent of sleep. Like sleep, the hypnoidal state has many levels of depth. It differs, however, from sleep in the rapidity of oscillation from level to level.

In the experiments of various investigators, the depth of sleep is found to be represented by a rap-

idly rising curve during the first couple of hours, and by a gradually descending curve during the rest of the hours of sleep. No such regularity of curve can be found in the hypnoidal state. The depth of the hypnoidal state changes very rapidly, and with it the passive condition and suggestibility of the patient.

For many years investigations of the hypnoidal state were carried out by me on subjects and patients, adults, and children. The work was entirely limited to the study of such states as found in man. Having found that during the hypnoidal state the condition of suggestibility is quite pronounced for therapeutic purposes, and having effected many cures of severe psychopathic maladies ranging throughout the whole domain of hysterical affections, neurasthenia, obsessions, drug habits, especially alcoholic ones, the hypnoidal state has become, in my practice, quite an important therapeutic agent. Other investigators have obtained some excellent results with the hypnoidal state in their treatment of various functional, psychopathic maladies.

Thus far, the work with the hypnoidal state has been confined entirely to observations and experiments on human subjects and patients, and also to the treatment of man's psychopathic ailments. I undertook a series of experiments on sleep, both from a phylogenetic and ontogenetic standpoint, following up the conditions and manifestations of sleep

in the ascending scale of animal life, from the frog and the guinea pig, through the cat, the dog, to the infant and the adult.

My experiments clearly prove that the hypnoidal state is by no means confined to man, but is also present in animals. This is important since it indubitably shows how widely spread the hypnoidal state is throughout the domain of animal life. Moreover, the experiments clearly prove that the further down we descend in the scale of animal organization, the more prominent, the more essential, does the hypnoidal state become.

The conclusion is forced upon me that the hypnoidal state is tlie primitive rest-state out of •which sleep has arisen in the later stages of evolution. We may say that sleep and hypnosis take their origin in the hypnoidal state. 1 Sleep and hypnosis are highly differentiated states; they have evolved out of the primitive, undifferentiated, hypnoidal state which is essentially a subwaking rest-state characteristic of early and lowly-organized animal life. The hypnoidal state is the primordial sleep state.

The development of the hypnoidal state into sleep has proven itself useful in the struggle for existence of the higher animals; it has, therefore, become fixed as the rest-state, characteristic of the higher representatives of animal life. Hypnosis and other

1 Prof. Ed. Clapered6 of Geneva University, Switzerland, and Anastav seem to favor some similar view.

trance-states, variations of the primitive hypnoidal rest-state, have become eliminated as useless and possibly harmful to the normal life adjustments of the higher animals and can only be induced under artificial conditions in but a fraction of the human race.

The hypnoidal state is the normal rest-state of the lower vertebrates and invertebrates. The rest or sleep state of the lower animals is a sort of passive waking state,—a subwaking state which has survived in man as the hypnoidal state. Of course, the state has been largely modified in man by the course of evolution, but it can still be clearly detected, just as the tail of the simian can be discerned in the human coccyx, or as the structure of the prehensile hand of the quadrumana can be still clearly traced in the foot of man. Waking, hypnoidal, and sleep-states may be termed normal states, while hypnosis and various other trance-states may be termed subnormal states.

The relation of the hypnoidal state to waking, sleep, hypnosis, and other subconscious states may be represented by the diagram on following page.

The hypnoidal state is normal, it is present in all representatives of animal life.

Sleep, hypnosis, and trance-states are variations of the fundamental hypnoidal state. The sleep-state has proven useful and has become normal in the higher animals, while hypnosis like animal "cataplexy" and the various forms of trance-states, like-

DIAGRAM II

wise variations of the fundamental hypnoidal state, characteristic of man, have not proven of vital value, and have fallen below the normal stream of consciousness with its concomitant adaptive reactions. The hypnoidal state is brief, variable, and unstable. They who have observed the rest-states of the lower metazoa can form a clear idea of the nature as well as of the biological significance of the hypnoidal state in the life of the lower animals. The animal is at rest for a brief period of time as long as it remains undisturbed by external conditions of its environment, or by internal conditions, such as hunger, sexual impulses, or other internal disturbances. Soon the animal begins to move, sluggishly at first, and then more quickly, and if there are no

disturbing stimulations, comes to rest, to be again disturbed from its rest-equilibrium by the varying conditions of its environment.

The resting state is brief, irregular, differing from the waking state in but slight relaxation, in comparatively slow reactions to stimulations, and in a passive condition of the muscular system. Respiration is regular, and diminished in rate. The heart beat is slightly decreased, and general katabolic activity is somewhat reduced.

The animal, however, is quite alive to what is going on. The animal rests, watching for danger.

Resting and active states alternate periodically, if possible, but usually are irregular. The resting state is but a passive condition in which the animal may be considered to hover between waking and what we describe in the case of the higher animals as sleep. Sleep, in its proper sense, does not exist among the lower representatives of animal life.

This state of hovering between waking and sleeping, the characteristic of the hypnoidal state, is no doubt of paramount importance in the life-existence of the lower animals, considering the numerous dangers to which they are continually exposed. The animal must always be on the watch, either for food or for foe. It can only rest or "sleep" with its eyes wide open. The hypnoidal "sleep" can be best characterized as a subwaking, "twilight" rest-state.

I demonstrated in my experiments that the ahi-

mal, while in the hypnoidal, subwaking rest-state, is apt to fall into a cataleptic state, especially when the movements are suddenly and forcibly inhibited. This cataleptic state, which reminds one of the hypnotic state, may be observed in the lower animals, such as the frog, the snake, the lobster, the bird, and, to a slighter degree, even in the higher animals, such as the guinea pig, the cat, the dog, especially in the young ones, such as the kitten, the puppy, and the infant.

There is little doubt that the cataleptic state into which animals fall during the hypnoidal rest-state is of some protective value in their life. The animal "freezes," "feigns death," and is thus either enabled to remain undetected by the animal on which it feeds or, what is still more important, is enabled to remain unnoticed by its enemy and thus escape certain death. The subwaking, hypnoidal state may be regarded as the fundamental rest-state of lower animals, and is characterized by a mixed symptomatology of waking, sleep, and hypnosis.

The hypnoidal state is a powerful instrument in the tracing of the past history of the growth and development of the symptoms of psychopathic or neurotic cases; and practically is of far greater value, inasmuch as the hypnoidal state has proven to be an easy agency in effecting a cure, and bringing about beneficial results in otherwise uncontrollable cases.

For the present, we can only say that the hyp-noidal state is found in man but in a rudimentary condition. It is a vestige of man's primitive, animal ancestors. The hypnoidal state is brief, variable, forming the entrance and exit of repose, —the portals of sleep. The primordial rest-state has shrunk to a transitory, momentary stage in the alternation of waking and sleep. The subwaking, hypnoidal rest-state shrinks with the increase of security of life.

CHAPTER XIV
HYPNOIDAL PSYCHOTHERAPY

Once the hypnoidal state is induced by any of the various methods of hypnoidization, we can either attempt to follow up the history of the development of the malady, or we may chiefly work for therapeutic effects. It is, however, advisable, from a purely practical, therapeutic purpose to combine the two procedures; the cure is then effective and far more stable. When the history of the origin and development of the disease can not be traced, on account of the age or unintelligence of the patient, the therapeutic effects alone of the hypnoidal states have been utilized.

The getting access to subconscious experiences, lost to the patient's personal consciousness, makes the hypnoidal state a valuable instrument in the tracing of the origin and development of the symptoms of the psychopathic malady.

From a practical standpoint, however, the therapeutic value of the hypnoidal state is most important. Our experiments have revealed to us the significant fact that the hypnoidal state is the primor-

dial rest-state; sleep is but a derivative form. In many conditions of disease it is advisable to have the patient revert to a simple and primitive mode of life. Similarly, in psychopathic diseases a reversion to a simple, primitive state proves to be of material help to the patient.

In plunging the patient into the hypnoidal state, we have him revert to a primitive rest-state with its consequent beneficial results. The suggestibility of the state, if skillfully handled, is apt to increase the therapeutic efficacy. Relaxtion of nervous strain, rest from worry, abatement of emotional excitement are known to be of great help in the treatment of nervous troubles of the neurasthenic, or of the so-called "psychoasthenic" variety. That is what we precisely observe in the treatment of psychopathic or neurotic diseases by means of the agency of the hypnoidal state, the efficacy of which is all the greater on account of the presence of the important trait of suggestibility.

The most important fact, however, is the access gained through the hypnoidal state to the patient's stores of subconscious reserve neuron energy, thus helping to bring about an association of disintegrated, dissociated mental-systems.

Dr. John Donley in his article, "The Clinical Use of Hypnoidization" (Journal of Abnormal Psychology for August-September, 1908), gives the following account of the method of hypnoidization:

"The treatment of that large group of disorders, forgotten memories, and emotions is operative in the production of mental disaggregation, but also in those numerous instances where the experience causing the obsessive idea or emotion is well known to the upper consciousness.

"In hypnoidal states they were made to reproduce their obsessive thoughts and images and then to describe them in words. When this had been accomplished and they had received further assurance and persuasion from the experimenter, although the purely intellectual content of their obsessions remained known to them, the insistent automatic character and disturbing emotional factors had disappeared. In this metamorphosis of emotional reaction we may observe one of the most interesting and useful attributes of the hypnoidal state."

Dr. Donley gives a series of cases which he treated successfully from psychognostic and ps\'chothera-peutic standpoints. The reader is referred to the original article.

"The value of hypnoidization," says Dr. T. W. Mitchell, "in the resurrection of dissociated memories is that which is perhaps best established. And this applies not only to the restoration of the forgotten experiences of ordinary amnesia, but to the recovery of dissociated memories that are of pathogenic significance . . . Sidis himself has insistently

taught that the reassociation of dissociated complexes effects a cure of psychopathic disease. . . . My own experience, so far as it goes, tends to corroborate in every respect the claims put forward by Sidis . . ."

While in the hypnoidal state the patient hovers between the conscious and the subconscious, somewhat in the same way as in the half-drowsy condition one hovers between wakefulness and sleep. The patient keeps on fluctuating from moment to moment, now falling more deeply into a subconscious condition in which outlived experiences are easily aroused, and again rising to the level of the waking state. Experiences long submerged and forgotten rise to the full light of consciousness. They come in bits, in chips, in fragments, which ma}' gradually coalesce and form a connected series of interrelated systems of experiences apparently long dead and buried. The resurrected experiences then stand out clear and distinct in the patient's mind. The recognition is fresh, vivid, and instinct with life, as if the experiences had occurred the day before.

It cannot be insisted too much that the hypnoidal state is not a slight hypnosis. The hypnoidal state is a light sleep state, a twilight state. The hypnoidal state is the anabolic state of repose, characteristic of primitive life.

The hypnoidal state is an intermediary state between waking and sleep. Subwaking is an appro-

priate descriptive term of the character of the hypnoidal state.

The subwaking hypnoidal state, like sleep and hypnosis, may be of various depth and duration; it may range from the fully waking consciousness and again may closely approach and even merge into sleep or hypnosis. The same patient may at various times reach different levels, and hence subconscious experiences which are inaccessible at one time may become revealed at some subsequent time, when the patient happens to go into a deeper hypnoidal state.

On account of the instability of the hypnoidal state, and because of the continuous fluctuation and variation of its depth, the subconscious dissociated experiences come up in bits and scraps, and often may lack the sense of familiarity and recognition. The patient often loses the train of subconscious association. There is a constant struggle to maintain this highly unstable hypnoidal state.

One has again and again to return to the same subconscious train started into activity for a brief interval of time. One must pick his way among streams of disturbing associations before the dissociated subconscious experiences can be synthesized into a whole, reproducing the original experience that has given rise to the whole train of symptoms.

The hypnoidal state may sometimes reproduce the original experience which, at first struggling up in a broken, distorted form, and finally becoming synthe-

sized, produces a full attack. The symptoms of the malady turn out to be portions, bits and chips of past experiences which have become dissociated, giving rise to a disaggregated subconsciousness.

The method of hypnoidization, and the hypnoidal states induced by it, enable us to trace the history and etiology of the symptoms, and also to effect a synthesis and a cure. The hypnoidal state may not be striking and sensational in its manifestations, but it is a powerful instrument in psychopathology and psychotherapeutics.

For many years my investigations of the hypnoidal state were carried out on subjects and patients, adults and children. Having found that during the hypnoidal state the condition of mental plasticity is quite pronounced for therapeutic purposes, and having effected many cures of severe psychopathic maladies, ranging throughout the whole domain of so-called hysterical affections, neurasthenia, obsessions, drug habits, especially alcoholic ones, the hypnoidal state has become in my practice quite an important therapeutic agent. Lately, others have obtained excellent results with the hypnoidal state in their treatment of various functional, psychopathic or neurotic maladies.

Perhaps it may be opportune here for the sake of further elucidation to give a few extracts from the Presidential address on "The Hypnoidal State

of Sidis," given by Dr. T. W. Mitchell before the Psycho-Medical Society of Great Britain, January

26, 1911.

"The history of science," says Dr. Mitchell in his address, "affords us many instances in which the neglect of residual phenomena in experimental research has led to the overlooking of important facts, and prevented investigators from making discoveries which, had they paid attention to their residues, they could hardly have missed. The great chemist, Cavendish, probably missed the discovery of argon, because in his estimate of nitrogen of the air he neglected a residue which his experiments showed him could not be more than 1-120 part of the whole. More than a hundred years afterwards this residue was accounted for by the discovery of argon.

"Now in the history of Psychotherapeutics, from its earliest beginning down to our own time, we find many cases where the circumstances under which curative results have been obtained render it difficult for us to range these results under the category of the therapeutics of suggestion.

"Such cases as these may be regarded as the residual phenomena of the therapeutics of suggestion, and just as Cavendish and his successors too readily assumed that all the so-called nitrogen of the air was the same as the nitrogen of nitre, so we may be missing some important truth, if we too readily assume

that all these therapeutic results are due solely to suggestion. The value of suggestion during hypnosis is well attested, and the possibility of effecting physiological and psychological changes by its means is supported by a large amount of experimental evidence. But evidence of this kind is lacking in regard to suggestion without hypnosis, and until it is forthcoming, we are justified in receiving with some suspicion the account of the therapeutic efficacy of suggestion in the waking state. We seem bound to consider whether some state of consciousness intermediate between waking and hypnosis may not be artificially induced and utilized for the purpose of giving therapeutic suggestion.

"The scientific investigation of states of consciousness intermediate between waking and hypnosis is a contribution to psychology and psychotherapy which we owe practically to one man—Dr. Sidis. A research into the nature of suggestibility led him to formulate certain laws and conditions of normal and abnormal suggestibility. . . .

"By keeping the patient for a short time under the conditions of normal suggestibility we induce a peculiar mental state which Sidis named Ht/pnoidal state. The process by which it is induced is what Sidis calls, hypnoidization.

"By the use of various methods a state of consciousness is induced which differs from full waking, but is not hypnosis or ordinary sleep.

"The hypnoidal state is an intermediary territory, on the borderland of waking, sleep and hypnosis. In the course of a valuable experimental investigation of sleep in man and the lower animals, Sidis discovered that the hypnoidal state is a phase of consciousness which is passed through in every transition from one of these states to another. In passing from the waking state to ordinary sleep or hypnosis, there is always a longer or shorter hypnoidal stage. In the practice of hypnoidization the patient sometimes drops into hypnosis, or he may fall asleep without touching on hypnosis. And so also in awaking from sleep or from hypnosis, the hypnoidal state has to be passed through. Sidis found that the further we descend in the scale of animal life, the more important does the hypnoidal state become in relation to bodily rest and recuperation, and he concludes that it is the primitive rest-state out of which both sleep and hypnosis have been evolved.

"The relation to each other of waking, sleep, hypnosis and the hypnoidal state, may be represented in a diagram in which the primitive hypnoidal state is represented as a nucleus from which the segments of the larger circle, waking, sleep and hypnosis, have arisen. The transition from one of these segments to another can take place through the central territory with which they each have relations. (See diagram on page 110.)

Nervous Ills

"The spontaneous occurrence of the hypnoidal state in man is as a rule merely a transitory stage in the alternation of waking and sleep. From the point of view of evolution it is a vestige derived from a long race of ancestors, a rudimentary function

DIAGRAM III

which has been superseded by the more highly specialized rest-state, sleep. But it can be artificially induced and maintained by the methods which have been described, and it can be utilized with effect in the treatment of psychopathic disorders.

"The therapeutic use of the hypnoidal state is a somewhat complex subject, for hypnoidization may

be employed as an adjunct to other methods or as a curative measure in itself.

"The full record of hypnoidization is in the account of the well known Hanna case, given in his 'Multiple Personality.' This was a case of total amnesia, following a severe injury to the head. The patient, a cultured clergyman, was reduced to the mental condition of a new-born child. All his former acquisitions and memories had entirely disappeared, and he had to start learning everything again from the beginning. When he (the patient) was put into the hypnoidal state various fragmentary experiences of his past life emerged into consciousness, demonstrating to his observers that his lost memories were merely dissociated and not destroyed. This same method (hypnoidization) was made use of in other cases of amnesia, and it was found to be of great assistance in effecting the resurrection of dissociated mental material and its reintegration in consciousness.

"With the progress of his studies in Psychopath-ology, the reintegration of consciousness became, for Sidis, the aim of all therapeutic endeavor in connection with maladies that are associated with, or produced by, mental dissociation. The recurrent psycho-motor states of functional psychosis, insistent ideas* imperative concepts, persistent, or periodically appearing emotional states, socalled psychic epilepsy, and other states of dissociation all lent

themselves to treatment by hypnoidization. By its means the dissociated complexes could be recovered, the ps}'chogenesis of the malady could be traced, a synthesis of consciousness effected, and the patient thereby cured. As his confidence in his method increased, Sidis gradually extended its employment, until at the present time he seems to use it in every kind of disorder in which psychotherapy is indicated.

"I have no doubt that Dr. Bramwell induces in his patients a state of consciousness which is identical with the hypnoidal state of Sidis.

"My own experience, so far as it goes, tends to corroborate in every respect the therapeutic claims put forward by Sidis. I have observed the good effects of the hypnoidal state apart from any other measure.

"In his later writings Sidis insistently maintains that the use of hypnoidization alone is sufficient to cure certain morbid conditions. He bases this claim on the fact that he has found the hypnoidal state effective towards this end, and he interprets his results as being due to a release of reserve energy which has been locked up in the inhibited and dissociated systems or complexes.

"The principle of reserve energy is based upon a wide generalization of facts, namely, that far less energy is utilized by the individual than is actually at his disposal. In the struggle for existence, those

forms of life which have accumulated a store of reserve energy that can be drawn upon in emergencies have the best chance for survival."

According to my experimental and clinical work the waking state, sleep, hypnosis, and the hypnoidal state, may be differentiated as follows:

(I) In the waking state the upper, controlling consciousness ■predominates over the subconscious. In other words, in the waking state the conscious is more responsive and more active than the subconscious which as a rule under such conditions may be regarded as partially dormant.

(II) In sleep both the conscious and the subconscious are reduced in activity, often even inhibited in function. Motor consciousness is arrested; motor control is paralyzed. The personality is disintegrated.

(III) In hypnosis the upper, controlling consciousness is diminished in activity, while the subconscious activities are increased in extensity and intensity. In h3 T pnosis the relationship of the conscious and subconscious is interchanged,— the conscious becomes subconscious, and vice versa. The habitual type of character may become changed by suggestion, giving rise to double and multiple personality, according to the crystillization of various association systems, while the habitual, critical attitude is reduced in intensity.

(IV) In the hypnoidal state both conscious and

subconscious functions are lowered in activity with no decrease in the intensity of critical attitude, and with no change of personality.
The hypnoidal state is therefore not a light hypnosis, but rather a light steeping state, a twilight state. The hypnoidal state is a primitive rest-state out of which sleep and hypnosis have arisen in the course of animal evolution.

CHAPTER XV
EGOTISM AND FEAR

As we have pointed out, the fear instinct is the arousal of the impulse of self-preservation. Psychopathic conditions are at bottom fear states interrelated with hypnoidal states and with an abnormal, pathological condition of the impulse of self-preservation. This is manifested in the fundamental trait of extreme selfishness characteristic of psychopathic patients. The patient is entirely absorbed in himself, and is ready to sacrifice every one to his terrors.

For many years, day after day and night after night, I lived with patients who were under my care, observation, and treatment. One trait always revealed to me the predominant characteristic under the constantly changing psychopathic symptom-complex and that is the extreme selfislwiess of the patients. There is no greater egotism to be found than in the typical cases of psychopathic disorders. This egotism runs parallel to the condition of the psychopathic state. This does not mean that every egotist is necessarity psychopathic, but every

psychopathic case is essentially egotistic.

The psychopathic patient does not hesitate a moment to sacrifice to his "affection" father, mother, brother, sister, husband, wife, lover, friend, and children. In severe cases the patient stops at nothing and only fear of suffering, sickness, evil consequences, and punishments can restrain the patient. In some extreme cases the patient is almost diabolical in his selfishness.

The constant sympathy which the patients crave from others, and which they demand, if it is not given to them immediately, is but an expression of their extreme obsession by the impulse of self-preservation. In their struggle for self-preservation they forget everything else, nothing is remembered but themselves. This condition becomes the ground character which is often expressed in a frank, brutal way. Even in the best of patients one can find glimpses into the depths of the psychopathic soul which is nothing but the immense egotism of the beast, worsted in the struggle for existence, tortured by the agonizing pangs of the fear instinct.

In the vanity, conceit, arrogance, and overbearing attitude towards others, friend or stranger, as well as in the total indifference to the suffering of his intimate friends and acquaintances, we once more find the expression of that terrible selfishness which obsesses the psychopathic patient. In order to get rid of some small inconvenience, or to obtain some slight pleasure, the patient will put others as well

as his "near and dear ones" not only to inconvenience, but to permanent pain, and even torture.

The patient lacks confidence, at least that is what he complains of, but he does not hesitate to demand of his best friends and even of total strangers all the services possible, if they are given to him, thinking that he is fully entitled to them. The patient has the conceit and vanity of his great worth in comparison with other people. The world and especially his family, physicians, attendants, friends, acquaintances, lovers, should offer their happiness and life for his comfort.

Even when the psychopathic patient does some altruistic act, it is only in so far as he himself can benefit by that deed. He is ready to drop it as soon as the work does not answer his selfish purposes. Himself first and last, that is the essence of psychopathic life.

The patient is convinced of his goodness and kindness, and of his human affections which are far superior to those of the common run. He adores himself and he is always ready to dwell in the glory of his delicacy and extraordinary sensitivity. This trait he is specially anxious to impress on his friends, on his family, and even on those whom he apparently loves. "I am the delicate being of whom you all, unappreciative, gross, insensible people should take care." That is the principle on which the psychopathic patient lives. The patient will do anything

to attract attention to this side of his personality. He will emphasize his sickness, exaggerate his symptoms, and even manufacture them for the benefit of those who dare to ignore him or who pay little attention to his condition, to his wants, needs, caprices, passing whims, and especially his fears, which underlie all his wishes and desires. There is nothing so tyrannical and merciless as the autocratic, fear-obsessed "weak" will of a psychopathic or neurotic patient.

The patient's whole attention is concentrated on himself, or more specially on the symptoms of his psychopathic malady, symptoms which obsess him for the time being. Whatever the symptoms be, permanent or changing, the patient's demand is to have others sympathize with the illness from which he suffers, to have them realize the "fearful" agonies which he undergoes. The selfishness of the patient is exacting and knows no bounds. The whole world is to serve him, and be at his command. The psychopathic patient is driven by the impulse of self-preservation and by the furies of the fear instinct.

Many of my psychopathic patients tell me that they feel sensitive as long as they witness the sufferings of other people, otherwise they do not care to know anything about them. They are anxious to have such things away from them as a nuisance. They insist on being surrounded only with pleasant things or with persons and objects that contribute

to their health and happiness. Everj'thing is absorbed by the worship of Moloch Health to whom the patients sacrifice everything. Pain, suffering, and distress of other people are looked at only from the standpoint of the possible effect they may have on the patient's "precarious health." Like Nero, who was probably a psychopathic character, the psychopathic patient is ready to burn others for his health; if necessary, to torture "health and happiness" out of his best friends.

One of my patients, who is highly intelligent, tells me frankly that he uses others to squeeze out of them strength for himself. As soon as he can no longer get it, or has obtained all he can, he is anxious to part with them, gets tired of them, and even begins to be resentful because they are in the way of his health. Another of my patients was ready to burn parks, stables, and destroy everything, if he knew that it was good for his health. Other patients of mine do not hesitate to wake up the whole house to help them in insomnia or indigestion. Many of my patients take pleasure in forming acquaintances and even friendship with people, ask for their sympathy, require their help and assistance, come to them early in the morning and late at night, disturb their sleep in the small hours of the morning, display all their symptoms of indigestion, nausea, eructation, and vomiting. The patients then turn round, abuse the person who helps them, telling him disagreeable

things, because he is no longer useful. A few hours later the patients may turn again for help to the same person, because they find that they could still make use of him.

Psychopathic patients do not hesitate, for the alleviation of their pains, of depression, of insomnia, to take a bath in the early morning and wake up all the other patients. They are entirely absorbed in themselves. Self is the only object of their regard. A clever lawyer, aptly characterized one of my most severe and typical ps\'chopathic cases as "egomaniac." "When you talk of gravity, 'I am gravity,' she claims. Talk of the Trinity: 'I am the Trinity.' ' As a matter of fact every psychopathic patient is an egomaniac.

Bacon's aphorisms about self-lovers may well apply to psychopathic patients: "And certainly it is in the nature of extreme self-lovers, as they will set a house on fire, and it were but to roast their eggs . . . That which is specially to be noted is, that those which are sui amantes sine rivali, are many times unfortunate."

Driven by the impulse of self-preservation and by the anguish of extreme fear, the psychopathic patient may be pitied as a most unfortunate, miserable wretch.

In the psychognosis of the particular condition, mental or nervous, be it object, idea, or action from which the patient suffers, the impulse of self-pres-

ervation with its instinctive emotion of fear can always be found in the background of consciousness or in the subconsciousness.

An insight into a series of cases will help best to understand the fundamental psychopathological processes that give rise to the different forms of psychoneuroses and somatopsychoses.

The inhibition of the patient's activities, produced by the most primitive impulse of self-preservation with its instinct of fear, limits the patient's life to such an extent that the interests and the activities are reduced to automatic repetition of reactions of a stereotyped character. The stimuli must be the same, otherwise the patient does not care to respond. He loses interest in his business, in reading, in his work, and games. The attention keeps on wandering. Games, pleasures, and hobbies in which he formerly used to take an interest lose their attraction for him. The life he is disposed to lead is of a vegetative existence. He is afraid of anything new. Things are done in an automatic way. Routine and automatisms are characteristic of his activities.

The psychopathic or neurotic patient talks about his humanitarian ideals, about his great abilities superior to the common run of humanity, and how with his talents he is willing and has been willing to confer benefits on poor suffering humanity in spite of the fact that he has to struggle with his poor health, physical, nervous and mental. In spite of

the overwhelming fatigue due to ill health, and in spite of the fearful ideas and impulses that have beset him day and night he still has succeeded in fighting his way through.

The patient hankers for notoriety, for praise, for appreciation by other people. He is apt to complain that the family, neighbors, acquaintances, friends cannot appreciate his good points, his good will, and his high ideals to which he conforms his life, tortured as it is with pains and suffering of poor health. The egocentric character of the psychopathic patient is bound up in his abnormally developed impulse of self-preservation and in his pathological state of the fear instinct.

Thus one patient opens his account with the phrase: "From boyhood I had a sensitive conscience."

Another patient writes: "As a child I had a keener instinct as to the real unexpressed attitude of those about me toward each other than the average child."

One of my patients, a puny being of mediocre intelligence, writes: "I have always, from the earliest childhood, felt that I was different from those about me; and I must acknowledge that it was not alone a feeling of inferiority on account of poor control, but a feeling that I understood more than they. I was, however, of a delicate constitution and suffered from ill health."

Psychopathic patients subscribe to the "cheerful" effusions of "New Thought," and plaster the walls of their rooms with elevating "Rules for Health and Happiness." Phychoanalysis and Christian Science are the rage. The victims hide behind the veil of sickly, psychopathic "Love."

The writings and accounts of the patients are full of introspection about health, and about the minutiae of their feelings in the various parts of their body. Some of the patients with a literary turn keep on writing volumes about the most minute symptoms of their troubles to which they happen at any moment to be subject. I have numbers of manuscripts, biographies, autobiographies, all telling the same old story of "blighted lives" due to ill health, drugs, and treatment, all describing with the over-scrupulous exactness of microscopic anatomy the different symptoms that plague them by night and by day. The patients tell of their talents and remarkable abilities, superior to the average run, of their ill luck and failures, due to their unfortunate state of ill health.

In quoting from some of the accounts given to me by the patients themselves I wish to attract attention to this side of the patient's mental condition, the expression of the impulse of self-preservation, manifested in the general panic of health, or fear of disease, whether nervous or physical.

A patient of mine, a clerk of mediocre intelligence,

with hardly any ability, but with plenty of selfishness, introspection, and immeasurable conceit, writes about his ideals in life:

"I would ask that this manuscript be considered in connection with my other two writings. I have already partially covered this ground in my autobiography. I should be glad to have my general outlook on life considered, and to receive suggestions relative to vocations and avocations, since my anxieties regarding these are inseparably intermingled with my thoughts of physical and mental health.

"Of course since childhood my ideals have undergone a gradual modification. First, there was the religious motive of life: I wanted to be a soldier of the cross and assist in the regeneration of souls and their preparation for the life beyond ... I began to meditate upon ethical theories ... It appears that in doing the world's work the tendency is to specialize. ... In the matter of choosing my employment my own interest is identical with the interest of society. At different times of my life I have fancied I had a liking for one calling or another . . . My lines of thought have gradually drifted into the philosophical (patient means the various occult scribblings about 'health metaphysics'). I now ask myself why I should be a lawyer, a physician, a minister, a philanthropist or any other special thing? I conceive that a man's life is largely what circumstances make it, and it may be, therefore, that I shall always be a clerk in an office, trying to be useful in a small way; but now we are talking of influencing such matters as far as we can by choice. I imagine that perhaps my field is in the line of ethics, philosophy, or whatever words may be used to signify the general principles governing human affairs. My reasons for thinking so are as follows: First, I feel a strong interest in those principles comparing to no other interest in my life. Second, I find very few people who seem to feel any such interest in such matters. Third, I believe such principles to be of supreme importance. The question is,—Is my position in regard to general truths so peculiar that I should regard it my mission to give those subjects more attention in study and expression than do other men?

"The question I want to settle is,—Do other men feel this same philosophical interest, realize the broad field of human obligation, and come down to special occupations, not because they are more interesting to them than the general field, but because they realize they must specialize in order to properly assist in carrying on the world's work? If this be so then I am mistaken in thinking I should give particular attention to general principles. But my observations have gone to show that the average physician, lawyer, merchant or politician is not interested in the broad questions of life, but only in medicine, law, business, or politics, caring little for the relation of his vocation to other vocations except as he makes his bread by it. Why then if the various departments of human activity must be correlated, and if the individuals making up those respective departments have no disposition to do the correlating,—should it not be done by those who are interested in the general field?"

It means that such work could be and should be done by the patient, by the philosophical clerk, interested in the general "metaphysics" of health. Such confessions can be easily elicited from psychopathic patients even in their best states of apparent diffidence, humility. This paranoidal aspect of self-aggrandizement is present in all psychopathic cases. In some this trait stands out more clearly and distinctly than in others. It is, however, present in all psychopathic patients, if one observes them closely and attentively. It is the expression of an intensified state of the impulse of self-preservation and fear instinct. In other words, it is a state of an exaggerated, hypertrophied egotism.

"We must appeal to a law higher than the material law," a patient writes in his account. "I worried much over it. Since that time the relation of mind and matter greatly interested me. . . . My health at this time failed, I lost appetite and strength, had hysterical symptoms. I was treated for general neurasthenia." . . . Psychopathic, philosophical and ethical speculations and interests have their sole source in fear of sickness and self-preservation.

"One of my anxieties,' another patient writes, "of my present life is connected with my business and my relationship to my partners. I am naturally conscientious and inclined to be not only earnest and sincere, but serious. My nature, instincts, and desires are not superficial. Yet my relation to the business is a superficial one. I am neither fitted by natural tastes nor by training for the indoor, rather mechanical, conventional, and routine processes upon which business and commercial success depends...

"Without the common motives of an ordinary merchant (greed) I am placed in the position of the one who lives not by the usual and conventional standards of right and wrong, but rather by a more exalted and more rigid one of his own making which, unsupported by habit, and institutions, requires a greater loyalty, a higher resolve, and a firmer will than is required of the conventional and conforming citizen. Emerson says it demands something Godlike in one who would essay such a task, not placing the same values on money, trade, commerce, and profits as the natural money maker and money lover, and not the opportunity to substitute and supplement the usual motives by and with the larger, and to me more compelling, of community betterment and employee welfare..."

This man had abandoned his wife and three children.

Another patient writes of himself, "The hypersensitive nervous system with the initial shock has inhibited the development of my highest potentialities and my highest endeavors." He summarizes his symptoms: "Dread and anxiety about being away from home and friends, self-consciousness, mental sluggishness, quick fatigue, inability for deep thought, general state of irritability."

A neurotic patient tells me that he suffers from fatigue, insomnia, dullness, inability of concentration of attention, failure in studies, slowness of comprehension, and so on; and yet he gives his opinion with papal infallibility on every conceivable subject, and hints at being an undeveloped, unappreciated genius. The psychopathic, neurotic patient rarely, if ever, suffers from a complaint of inferiority. His real fear is that his superiority may be humbled.

Obsessed by the impulse of self-preservation and fear instinct, and with utter disregard of others, the patients are convinced of their extraordinary kindness, gentleness, sympathy, martyrdom, and even saintliness. It is from this class that neurotic philanthropists are recruited. Psychopathic patients are always ready "to sacrifice themselves for the good of humanity." They talk endlessly about goodness, and may even devote themselves to charity and instruction of the "poor and degraded." A patient of mine worked for three years for the "good of the poor," had "high ideals and a sensitive conscience," according to his accounts, but abandoned readily his wife and children.

Another young woman, a typical psychopathic, full of high ideals, ran away with a married man, had a child that died of exposure. This patient was interested in modern education and improvement of humanity. In reality she never cared to do anything for anybody, and without any hesitation took advantage of others in order to satisfy the least whim that might have crossed her mind, especially those whims that relate to health. She had all kinds of directions, prescriptions, exercises, requisite for the strength and health of the body and the nerves.

One of my patients used to be anxious about my going and coming. Was it love or devotion? I found out that he was afraid that I might be killed. This fear was developed in him by an actual accident in which his brother had died, but the same fear associated with me was due to the fact that the patient was sure that my treatment was requisite for his health and welfare. He was in fear lest I might be killed, he would be unable to get his treatments, and thus lose time in getting back his health. For the sake of his "health" the patient will not stop at anything. Neurotics may well name their troubles "Health and Science." The psychopathic, neurotic patient makes of health his science and religion, because self-preservation and fear are at the bottom of the psychopathic, neurotic constitution.

CHAPTER XVI
NEUROTIC PARASITISM

The psychopathic patient may be regarded as a case of parasitism. The parasite, living on his host, gradually loses all active functions, a condition followed by atrophy of organs no longer necessary to the life existence of the organism.

According to Demoor, "Atrophy begins with function when an organ has become useless. This uselessness may arise from two causes: the function may be no longer useful to the individual or to the species, or it may be assumed by another organ." When an organism turns parasite it is an economy of nutrition and energy to save as much as possible. The tendency of parasitism is to dispense with unnecessary functions in the struggle for existence.

The loss of function is from the less useful, to the more useful, to the functions absolutely indispensable to survival; from the less essential, to the more essential, to functions absolutely essential to the life existence of the individual. The life activity of the parasite becomes more and more narrowed, circumscribed, and dwindles down to a few functions requisite to its life existence, namely self-preservation, nutrition, and reproduction. With the further increase of parasitism even the digestive and reproductive functions become simplified, the parasitic individual becomes reduced to the most fundamental of all impulses, the impulse of self-preservation and reproduction.

The penalty of parasitic life is the simplification of organic activities, the atrophy of all higher and complex life processes. This is what takes place in the case of the psychopathic individual. All higher activities, all higher interests cease. In many neurotic cases of the severe type even the sexual instinct becomes gradually atrophied. The patient's life is narrowed down to the impulse which is absolutely requisite for individual life existence, namely the impulse of self-preservation with its concomitant fear instinct.

The growth of the impulse of self-preservation with its fear instinct brings about their hypertrophy which in turn hastens the degenerative processes or atrophy of all higher and more complex activities. The psychopathic patient in the process of degeneration and atrophy falls so low that not only moral, social, intellectual, but simpler psychomotor reactions become gradually diminished and atrophied. In severe cases even the instinct of sex, requisite for the preservation of the species, is made subservient to the impulse of self-preservation and the fear instinct.

In psychopathic life all activities are narrowed down to the pettiness of individual existence. It is not sex, it is not species-interests, nor conflicts, nor self-repressions that trouble the neurotic patient. An abnormal impulse of self-preservation and fear instinct are at the bottom of all psychopathic miseries. All psychopathic, neurotic interests are reduced to the sorry life of self and fear. Lacking interest in anything but himself, terrorized by the fear of existence, the psychopathic patient lives a dreary, monotonous life out of which he seeks to escape. Monotony, ennui, indifference form the curse of his life. The patient is in a frantic condition, constantly in quest of interests which he cannot enjoy. Nothing can interest him, because he has no other interest but himself, and that is so narrow, that it can hardly fill existence.

As a matter of fact he is afraid to meet his fears, he is afraid of himself. He is afraid to come to a decision, never at peace, ever at war with himself. He is bored with himself, wearied with everything and with everybody. He is constantly eager to find new pastures and new excitements, so as to fill with some living interest his poor, narrow, mean, short existence obsessed by fear, misery, wretchedness, and brutish selfishness.

The patient is afraid to work, because it may "fatigue and exhaust" him, and may bring about a state of disease, while he looks for health. He has no interest, because he only thinks of his little self, reduced to digestion, evacuation, and sleeping. The psychopathic patient leads an inactive existence of a sluggard, a lazy, idle existence of a parasite, and still he is driven to life and activity which, from the very nature of his narrow, parasitic individuality, he can no longer enjoy. He has the ideals of a hero and lives the life of a coward. This puts the patient in a state of dissatisfaction, discontent, and ceaseless contest with himself and others. Fear and self never leave him at peace. He is ever in a state of agitation, restlessness, and anxiety.

Obsessed with the anxious fears of self-impulse, the patient avoids the terrors of life, and drags the grey, monotonous existence of a worm. Hence there is a tendency in the psychopathic patient to be on the lookout forever new energetic personalities, lean on them, suck out all the energies he possibly can, then reject his new friends unhesitatingly and brutally, and be again in search for new personalities who can disperse, for ever so brief a time, the fearful monotony and dread of his miserable, psychopathic, neurotic existence.

The neurotic patient may be characterized as a psychopathic leech, or truer still, a psychopathic vampire. For it is on the life and blood of other people that the psychopathic ogre is enabled to carry on his bewitched, accursed, narrow, selfish existence, full of terror and anguish of life.

"When the attack is on," exclaimed a psychopathic patient, affected with cardiac palpitation and intense fear, "I am too d—d scared about myself to think about her!" referring to the woman with whom he was in love. The psychopathic patient is a parasitic ogre with an hypertrophied ego.

Patients who claim to love children when the latter are well and healthy, avoid them, like a pest, when the children happen to fall sick, for fear of disease and for fear that the sick children may produce an evil influence on the patient's "sensitive" nerves. The patient is afraid to come near sickness, or even afraid to hear of evil things, such as description of misfortunes, ailments, accidents, and sufferings, because they may upset him and arouse his fears of himself.

All the patient wants is to be surrounded with cheer, joy, merriment, excitement, and happiness which he is unable to enjoy. The psychopathic patient is in constant search after happiness. Not that he is interested in the problem of happiness from a moral, philosophical, or even purely religious standpoint. His interest is of the crudest, the meanest, the most selfish kind. It is happiness for self,— for a low, mean, short, and brutish self. Psychopathic search for happiness is the anguish of the beast, cornered by terror. The patient is tortured by an unsuccessful search for happiness, ever tantalized by self and fear. Egotism, fear, ennui, restlessness, anxiety, discord are the harpies of psychopathic, neurotic life.

The love of the psychopathic patient is at bottom .self-love; it is like the love of the wolf for the lamb. Lover, husband, child, friend, father, mothor, brother, sister, are all victims to the patient's greedy self. The fear instinct has a positive and negative aspect. There is the fear of life, fear of putting forth energy in meeting the exigencies of life. The patient is afraid to participate in the struggle of life. Struggle spells to him danger, peril,—fear of the external world. Struggle means to him fear, suffering, and misery. The patient avoids society, avoids not only strangers, but even his acquaintances, friends, and sometimes his own family.

While he constantly craves forever new stimulations to his depleted nerves, he is at the same time in terror of everything that is new. The patient is afraid of life, he shirks duties, responsibilities, efforts, and joys of life struggle. Hence his love of automatism, routine, and fear-fatigue. The fear manifests itself more often in the form of the negative side of life, such as fear of sickness, weakness, incapacity, degradation, loss of vitality, and generally the fear of death. Neurotic states are due to fear of life and fear of death.

CHAPTER XVII
FUNDAMENTAL PRINCIPLES

The following principles may be regarded as fundamental in the development of psychopathic or nervous ills:

I. The Principle of Embryonic Psycho genesis

The mental states of psychopathic or nervous ills are of an infantile, child type. In this respect the mental states simulate cancerous and other malignant growths of an embryonic character. The psychopathic mental states are not only of a childish character, but they are often associated with child experiences of early life. The psychopathic condition points to some early fear-producing experience, or fear awakening shock.

II. The Principle of Recurrence

Fear experiences tend to repeat themselves in consciousness, and especially in the subconscious states of the child. This repetition or recurrence keeps alive the psychopathic fear nucleus, and fixes it in the mind. Fixed fear systems become further developed by the subsequent experiences of life. The aroused fear instinct may either become weakened or strengthened. When the conditions of life are unfavorable and adverse, tending to further cultivation of the impulse of self-preservation and the fear instinct, the outcome is a psychopathic disposition, ending in a nervous state with typical symptoms of some definite nervous trouble, formed by the latest or ultimate fear experiences.

III. The Principle of Proliferation and Complication

With the growth of the child the fear experiences increase and multiply. These experiences become associated with the original child nucleus of fear and thus a complexity of fear systems is built up. Worries, depressions, and anxieties help to increase and develop the psychopathic system of groups of fear experiences. The morbid state grows like an avalanche in its progress downwards.

IV. The Principle of Fusion or of Synthesis

All the fear experiences become associated and grouped gradually around the original child fear experience which is often of a subconscious character. The long series of fear experiences becomes fused and synthesized by the central fear instinct and impulse of self-preservation, which are fundamental in every being, but which have been specially cul-

tivated by the course of events and experiences in the neurotic patient. The experiences become fused, synthesized, and systematized, forming one complex network of closely interrelated fear obsessions with the fear instinct and impulse of self preservation in the background.

V. The Principle of Contrast

Feelings and emotions follow by contrast. Excitement is followed by depression, enjoyment by disgust, exhilaration by disappointment. This is well brought out in the changes observed in the psychopathic self and fear states.

Fear may be followed by anger, especially against those who are sure to show no opposition, or may even manifest fear. The excitement of fear in others is a way which diminishes fear in the patient and helps him to have confidence in himself, strengthening his impulse of self preservation.

The fear of the psychopathic may even resort to love so as to gain safety and protection from the tantalizing agonies of the fear instinct. That is why some physicians are deceived, and ascribe psychopathic troubles to love instead of to the real fundamental cause of all psychopathic disorders, namely self-preservation and the fear instinct.

Similarly mysticism, a psychopathic malady of a social character, has its origin in the impulse of self-preservation and the fear instinct, and takes refuge in "love" or in "union" with the Infinite which serves as a rock of protection, security, and salvation from all terrors of life. Psychopathic love is a neurotic fear delusion. There is nothing more deceptive and delusive than psychopathic love,—for it takes its origin in self and fear.

VI. The Principle of Recession

Experiences are blotted out from memory in the course of time. A very small percentage of impressions is registered by the brain, a still smaller percentage can be reproduced, and out of them a very small percentage carries recognition as memory, that is, of impressions experienced before. Forgetfulness is therefore a normal physiological function characteristic of the brain and mind.

Forgetfulness depends on at least three conditions, lack of registration, lack of reproduction, and lack of recognition. There will correspondingly be at least three forms of amnesia or forgetfulness, amnesia of registration, amnesia of reproduction, and amnesia of recognition. The real problem of Psychology is not so much the lapses of memory, but the why and how of memory, and especially of recognitive memory.

This, however, we may establish as a law that when memory in regard to definite experiences weakens in the course of time, the lapse follows from recognition to reproduction, and finally to registration. Recognition fails first, then comes the failure of memory reproduction, and finally memory registration of the special experience becomes blurred and wiped out. This may be termed the law of memory decay, or of memory regression. This is the principle of memory recession.

Some, though by no means all, child memories or infantile experiences follow this law of regression or recession. Child experiences, like all old experiences, tend to recede in their course of decay or of regression below the threshold of consciousness. The experiences are not recognized on reproduction, or are reproduced with great difficulty, or have even lost the function of being reproduced. When under such conditions, the experiences are said to have become subconscious, or have receded into the subconscious.

On the other hand some of those subconscious experiences, or subconscious memories may, under favorable conditions, once more regain their functions of reproduction and recognition, and become fully conscious. This may occur in various trance states, subconscious states, and in various psychopathic conditions.

Such states, however, rarely fix the experiences in memory, because the states are instable, temporary, and the memories lapse with the disappearance of the states. This principle of recession may be regarded as one of the fundamental facts of the Psy- chopathology of the Subconscious. In fact, subconscious states may also be termed Recessive States.

VII. The Principle of Dissociation

Recessive states, becoming marginal and subconscious, lapse from voluntary control, they cannot be recalled deliberately and consciously b} T the activities of voluntary, recognitive, associative memories, constituting the mental life of personality, and hence may be regarded as mental systems in a state of dissociation. The lapsed states are present subconsciously when not completely blurred and obliterated by the process of decay or regression.

Dissociated, subconscious states, when affected by the impulse of self-preservation and the fear instinct, tend to become parasitic, and like malignant growths may suck the life energy of the affected individual. Under such conditions we have psychopathic, subconscious, dissociated states.

VIII. The Principle of Irradiation and Diffusion

In the dormant, subconscious states the fear instinct gradually extends to other subconscious states. The fear instinct acts like a malignant growth, like a fermenting enzyme. The subconscious fear instinct gradually infiltrates, diffuses, irradiates its affective state throughout the subconscious life of the patient, finally giving rise to a psychopathic disposition with its selfishness, apparent repressions, apprehension, anxiety, anguish, terror, and panic. This may also give rise to the general psychopathic character of doubt, indecision, and conflicting states, all being determined by the underlying fear instinct.

IX. The Principle of Differentiation

With the growth of the impulse of self preservation and with the development of an exaggerated fear instinct, the individual becomes more and more neurotic and psychopathic. This general, neurotic, mental state attaches itself to various events in the life of the individual. The psychopathic disposition keeps on progressing from one event to another. Each one may be regarded as a separate fear state, or phobia. Finally the disposition may settle on the last event in the patient's life experience. This last event may often become the nucleus, or rather the apparent nucleus of the neurosis.

The last experience appears to be central. As a matter of fact there is a great number of fear states or of phobias in the neurotic patient. A few only appear to predominate in the network of fear events. The network of fears is woven into an incongruous whole by the impulse of self-preservation and the fear instinct. This network becomes differentiated into a tangle of numerous fear states.

X. The Principle of Dominance

The last fear states or Ultimate Fear States which stand out clearly and distinctly in the patient's mind become the leading, the dominant abnormal, pathological states. The patient thinks that they are the real source of all his troubles, and if they were removed he would be cured. As a matter of fact the ultimate states are not causes, but occasions. The real causes of the psychopathic constitution arc the exaggerated impulse of self-preservation and the intensified fear instinct.

XL The Principle of Dynamo gene sis

Recessive, and especially dissociated systems, being dormant subconsciously, may become invigorated, may accumulate emotion, and when the opportunity comes, may react to external stimuli with vigor and energy. The attacks may occur like epileptic fits. They often so well simulate epileptic maladies that even good clinicians have classed such attacks under the term of larval epilepsy, psychic epilepsy, hystero-epilepsy, or psychic equivalent of epilepsy. This subconscious energy manifestation may be termed Dynamogenesis.

XII. The Principle of Inhibition

Self-preservation and the fear instinct inhibit associated mental systems, producing morbid states.

Morbid mental states, however, are not produced by inhibitions, or repressions. It is only when the inhibitive factors are self and fear that a true morbid mental state, or neurosis arises. To regard self repression as a bad condition and leading to diseases is to misapprehend the nature of man, to falsify psychology, and to misrepresent the development of humanity. The self should not become hypertrophied. Self-preservation should not become overgrown. The self must be kept within limits. The self impulse should be kept under control by the individual. For true happiness is to be a law unto oneself. As the great Greek thinkers put it: Happiness is in self rule. The unruly are miserable. In fact, self-control is absolutely requisite to mental health, to sanity. Self-repression is requisite for happiness. Self-repression never leads to disease. It is only when self-repression is produced and dominated by selfishness and fear that morbid states of a psychopathic, neurotic character are sure to arise. It is not inhibitions that produce fear, but it is fear that produces inhibitions. To ascribe neurosis to self-repression and to conflict is like attributing malaria or tuberculosis to air and light.

XIII. The Principle of Mental Contest and

Discord

Mental states associated with intense emotions tend to take a dominant lead in consciousness. This, however, may be totally opposed by the general character of the individual. In such cases the whole mental set, being in opposition to the total individuality, is in contest with the character of the person who is then in state of discord. A mental set in contest with the makeup of the person is usually inhibited, becomes subconscious, and as a rule fades away from the mind, often leaving no trace even in memory, conscious or subconscious. In some cases where a compromise is possible, a reconciliation is effected. The mental set is assimilated, and disappears from consciousness as an independent, functioning state.

When, however, the opposing or contesting mental set is based on a fundamental impulse and accompanying instinct, such as the impulse of self-preservation and the fear instinct, a total inhibition is not always possible, even a compromise may not be successful, because the mental set is in association with the core of the individual,—namely self-preservation. The contesting mental set remains, in what Galton terms, "the antechamber of consciousness."* The mind is in a state of tension, in a state of anxiety, in restless, uneasy discord, due to the fear instinct, the companion of the impulse of self-preservation. The contesting mental set, charged with intense fear emotion, presses into the foreground of consciousness, and a contest, a discoid, ensues in the mind of the individual, a contest, a discord, a conflict which keeps the person in a state of indecision and lack of willpower.

The partly inhibited, contesting mental set, when not fading away , may thus remain in the mind, and act like a splinter in the flesh, giving rise to a state of discomfort. This is just what happens when the individual has not been trained to assimilate fear states, and is unable to adjust fear reactions to the welfare of total psycho-physiological life activity. In cases where the impulse of self-preservation and the fear instinct have become aroused, the contesting fear set of mental states presses again and again to the foreground of consciousness. When no compromise of the contesting states can be brought about, when the fear set cannot be assimilated, the mind is in a state of restless discord. It is not, however, the discord that produces the neurosis, it is the impulse of self-preservation and the fear instinct that constitute the cause of the psychopathic, neurotic condition.

XIV. The Principle of Diminishing Resistance

In proportion as the neurotic attacks keep on recurring the formed pathological system is gaining in energy and in ease of manifestation. The psychopathic attacks with their symptoms emerge at an ever diminishing intensity of stimulation. The resistance of healthy normal associations is ever on the decrease until a point is reached when all power of resistance is lost. The conscious and subconscious groups which enter into the psychopathic system, forming the neurosis, get control over the patient's life, and become an uncontrollable, psychopathic obsession.

XV. The Principle of Modification

The patient attempts to control or alleviate his fear state by a totally different fear state. In the long run this is a losing game. For the general fear disposition becomes ultimately reinforced. Finally he may land in the mystic regions of love or of an Infinite Love in which he expects to find safety, protection, and salvation from the miseries of exaggerated self impulse and intensified fear instinct. Such a course, however, leads to a swamp in which the patient's individuality becomes engulfed and obliterated. The end is mental suicide.

These fundamental principles of neurosis-development should be kept in mind in the examination and study of psychopathic cases. The cases adduced in this volume will help one to understand the mechanism of the main factors and principles of neurosis.

CHAPTER XVIII
ILLUSTRATIONS, NEUROTIC HISTORIES

The psychopathic character appears to be full of contradictions, "a house divided against itself." Neurotics are like "the troubled ocean which never rests." Some of my patients complain of fatigue, physical and especially intellectual, inability of concentration of attention, and yet they hint at being undeveloped, unappreciated geniuses. The patient may be said to suffer from a paradoxical state of "humble superiority."

A few of my cases may help one to form some faint idea of the intensity of the impulse of self-preservation and fear instinct which obsess the psychopathic sufferer.

M. A. Age 43, female, married; sister and brother died of tuberculosis. When young, she herself had an attack of tuberculosis from which, however, she entirely recovered. This made her, from her ver} r childhood, think of herself and of the fear of death. She suffers from headaches, backaches, indigestion, and intestinal pains. Her mind is entirely engrossed with herself. The whole world

is for her sake, and she does not scruple to utilize anyone who is willing to serve her. She takes advantage of everybody and does not care what the feeling of others might be about her extreme selfishness. If she were sure that no fine or punishment would follow, she would not hesitate to take anything that belongs to others, no matter whether it be a friend or enemy, provided it does her good, drives away some of her discomforts, fear of disease, or gives pleasure to her, even at the expense of other people's agonies. If there were a prize for selfishness, she would be sure to get it. She is sure to take advantage of people who do not know her and who practice the ordinary activities and amenities of life in regard to her. She does not get offended when people refuse her demands. She goes to look for other victims who have as yet no knowledge of her temperament and "sickness." Everything is legitimate to her in order to get well and healthy.

The patient talks of high ideals and of service to humanity, and yet she has not hesitated to lure away a man who had a wife and three children. She made him divorce his wife who was her bosom friend, and marry herself. She spends all his money on her "artistic dresses," while his former wife and his little family are allowed just enough to keep them from starvation. The patient goes around travelling, visits physicians, cures herself, keeps on being sick in various health resorts, learning all kinds of fads, modes of "healthy living."

The patient is in terror of disease and of old age. She fears even to think of such things. She carries around with her all kinds of prescriptions and directions as to how to preserve youth. I was especially instructed by her husband not to inquire for her age. Everything must be subservient to her impulse of self-preservation and instinct of fear. She has dwindled to a parasitic existence, obsessed with the lowest instincts of life. She avoids all responsibilities. She wants to get as much as she can in order to obtain for herself the highest possible benefit. When she meets people who do not know her, she is quick in taking advantage of them. Life to her has no duties but rights. Patient is a typical Nero, a Caligula. She would cheerfully sacrifice a nation to get out a mite of pleasure, comfort, and health.

V. S. Age 49, female. Married; no children. She has three sisters and two brothers who are all well. As a child she lived in great poverty. She was neglected and met with accidents and scares; suffered from sickness until her little body was emaciated from privation. She managed, however, to go through school and become a clerk in a small store; she was very careful of her appearance which meant to her a good marriage, comfortable life. She also took care of her health which was rather precarious, on account of the many colds accompanied by severe headaches. At the same time on account of the poor life led, she also suffered from some obscure troubles. After years of precarious health and quests for happiness, for marriage, she succeeded in capturing a well-to-do merchant in whose store she had worked as a clerk. Immediately after marriage she rigged up a beautiful home with "rich mahogany furniture" which the husband regarded with a gasp, settled down to a life of leisure, to complete idleness, and began to attend to her health. . . .

The patient began to find more and more troubles with her organs, from the top of her head to the pelvis and intestines. Nothing was quite right. Things could be improved. The impulse of self-preservation gained more and more control over her. Along with this impulse the fear instinct gained in strength, became more and more extensive.

The patient became full of fear which, by the principle of proliferation and diffusion, kept on growing and diffusing in ever neAV directions, and spreading to ever new associations and systems. The central fear was poverty. The patient was afraid she might become poor. This was naturally a fear from her early childhood,—the fear of suffering in poverty, a fear which persisted throughout her life. The fear became accentuated and developed with time. She was afraid to spend money, especially sums above a five dollar bill. No matter how much she tried to reason with herself this fear persisted. She was afraid to buy new things which she regarded more or less expensive. She was afraid to put on new dresses, to buy new furniture, to spend money in any way. In fact, quite often the fear was so uncontrollable that even when she had no thought of threatening poverty she was in a panic of being confronted with expensive purchases.

The fears then began to spread to other things,— such as giving away small articles or loaning books, or presenting any things or objects that might be regarded as expensive and valuable. The fears spread to other objects of importance and value. Along with it she had fears of indigestion and nutrition, nausea, vomiting, intestinal pains, discomfort, and especially an inordinate amount of distress when in a state of nervous excitement.

The patient was as obstinate as a mule, though claiming that she was doing her best and trying everything in her power to co-operate. She was doing everything in her power to frustrate the physician's directions, claiming at the same time that she was doing her best to follow scrupulously the doctor's orders. She claimed she was nice to people when she was nasty and offensive to everybody who in any way happened not to fall in with her whims and caprices. In fact, even those who went out of their way to please her and did everything in attending to her, and helping her in every way day and night, even those she treated with lack of consideration, even positive disdain and contempt. She was the in carnal ion of demoniacal obsession of psychopathic meanness and egotism.

She abused and dominated her husband by her sickness, trouble, fainting and crying spells, headaches, moans and weeping. She made him do everything she pleased. In fact, she tyrannized over her husband, and kept on claiming she loved him. She could not for a moment be without him, and complained that on account of her extreme devotion to him, "her will was broken."

She was a regular termagant, a demon incarnate. She knew how to make a scene and put the blame on her "dear ones." It was enough for her to suspect what her friends wanted her to do, she was sure out of sheer malice, to act the contrary. She was distrustful, spying on others, sneaky and lying without any scruples; and yet "no one was so mild, so ideal, so kind, so affectionate, so considerate, so calm as she was." She went around reciting poetry about ideals, health, and happiness. She persuaded herself that she was highly educated, that she was the best business woman, the best critic, appreciative of poetry and of art in general. She was a veritable Nero, an "egomaniac" devoid of all love and human sympathy. She suffered so much, because she was so unusually altruistic. A coyote in her fear, a tigress in her rage, she claimed the gentleness of the dove and the innocence of the babe.

Not for a moment could she fix her attention on anything but herself, eating, drinking, sleeping, and feeling. Nothing interested her but herself. She avoided work, however short and easy. She could, however, talk of herself, of her achievements, of her moral, intellectual qualities by the hour and by the day. Even games did not interest her, nothing but herself, and self. This was so evident that one of the attendants noticed this characteristic psychopathic trait, and described her as "egomaniac." She was the "Great I am." "The Ego-person is the reflection of the Ego-god." . . .

Whenever one spoke of a great man, she was sure to have her opinion of him. She was at any rate superior to him. She could give her opinion on any conceivable subject in literature, economics, and politics. She was as cunning as a savage, and as treacherous as a wild brute, and yet she was to all appearances a veritable saint, full of suffering for the sins of humanity, and for the faults of her husband who was "boyish and foolish, whom she had to manage," and whom she did control and handle with an iron rod.

There is no doubt, however, that she herself was driven by her intense, uncontrollable impulse of self-preservation and by the instinct of fear. What especially terrorized her was the slow but sure extension of the fear instinct to more and more objects and acts. The fear instinct kept on creeping on her, slowly choking the life sources of her being. To call the patient "egocentric" is a mild descriptive term,—"tigress," "satan," "fiend," would be more appropriate appellations. In her terror of self-preservation she tormented herself and others. She was a firebrand from hell, a firebrand fanned by the furies of self and fear.

F. W. Age 47; female, married; has no children. The patient claims to have been an invalid from childhood; that she was of extremely delicate health; she always had to take care of her health, and had to go through all kinds of diseases, especially gastrointestinal troubles. At the age of eighteen she got married and then her family felicity began. She began to complain of all kinds of infirmities. The gynecologist humored her with operations and treatments. The fear disease became strengthened, and finally she cultivated a typical pathophobia; she was in terror of some fearful malady that might possibly take possession of her.

The patient always wanted to have someone near her. This fear of remaining alone dated from childhood, when at the least discomfort, she asked and screamed in terror for help. A companion, or nurse had to be with her day and night, so as to protect her from any impending evil.

Occasionally, to relieve her feelings, in the middle of a conversation, whether for the sake of impressing her family, her husband or her physicians with the gravity of her disease, or as a vent for the rising instinct of fear, she emitted a scream, wild and weird, reminding one of the howling of a timber wolf, or of a wild whoop of an Indian. This was a habit she kept up from childhood. It was a reaction of her fears, and a protection, it was a call for help which was sure to attract attention. The family could not refuse help at hearing such an unearthly call. Later on, it was consciously and unconsciously utilized by the patient as a rod to rule the family and especially her husband, when the latter happened to become refractory. The fear reaction was thus used as a protection and as a weapon of defense.

Things had to run according to her pleasure, or else she was put in a state of nervous excitement and fear with its awful yell of which the family and the husband were in perfect terror; they yielded unconditionally. The patient literally subjugated her husband by her spells of fear, especially by the fearful acoustic performance, the aura, the harbinger of a psychopathic attack.

The patient was always discontented and grumpy. Nothing could satisfy her, nothing was good enough for her. Everybody was criticized. No matter how one tried to please her, she always found fault with the person. In fact, the fault-finding was in proportion to the eagerness one tried to serve and oblige her. The nurses are not good, the servants intolerable, and people in general are bad, mean, stupid, and vulgar. She claims she comes from an "old New England family, from good stock." Her grandfather was a fisherman, and her father a petty tradesman. The patient makes pretensions to education, poetry, art, and drawing. In reality, she is quite dull and ignorant.

G. A. Female, age 63; the patient was obsessed with pathophobia for over thirty-five years. She has been to a number of physicians, and to many sanitariums, looking for health everywhere, not finding it anywhere. The fears date to her early childhood. She was regarded as a delicate child, the fear of disease was strongly impressed on her. She went through a number of children's diseases. Although she had several sisters and brothers, the child's supposed delicate constitution was the fear and worry of the parents. This fear was communicated to the child, who for the rest of her life became a psychopathic patient with the characteristic developed impulse of self-preservation and intense fear of disease. She could not think of anybody but herself, everything had to be arranged for her,—for her food, for her sleep, and for her rest. She kept on complaining at the slightest change either in herself, in others, about the arrangements of the house, or about the weather. Everything had to be arranged just as she demanded, otherwise she was sick, or was going to become dangerously ill.

When about the age of thirty, she married a widower with two children. She trained the children to obey her commands implicitly, otherwise she resorted to the rod of sickness. The pathophobia, consciously or unconsciously, became a power which she wielded in the most tyrannical way. The children had to sacrifice themselves for the pleasure of the sick step-mother. The}' had to stay with her, and minister to all her whims and fears. The very individuality of the children became almost obliterated by the persistent, egotistic tyranny of the sick, old step-mother. She was like a regular vampire, sucking the life blood of her family.

It goes without saying that the same fear of disease tamed her husband over whom she ruled with an iron hand. The least opposition to her whims, or to her fears of possible disease made her so sick with all kinds of pains that the family and the husband were driven into submission. The woman was obese as a hippopotamus, well nourished, with a florid complexion, and with an appetite that would shame a Gargantua. The rarest, the best, and the most appetizing dainties had to be on her table. She made of her meals a form of worship, requisite to propitiate the goddess of maladies. She did not hesitate to take the best morsels from the plates of her daughter and son in order to satisfy her appetite which was supposed to be "delicate and small."

The patient was conscious of every square inch in her body; she was afraid that some form of malady may lurk there. She was a typical case of pathophobia. Fear of disease and quest of health were ever in her mind. She could not talk, or think of anything else, but herself and her symptoms. She made of her step-daughter a poor, colorless being, a day and night nurse, tyrannized over by pitiful, neurotic whimpering.

When the patient happened to wake during the night for ever so short a period of time, she did not hesitate to wake her step-daughter, tired as the latter was by constant attendance on this psychopathic shrew. The daughter had to wake up everybody who could in any way bring comfort to that "poor, old, suffering invalid." After much groaning, moaning, and bewailing her bitter lot the invalid took some medicine to appease the fear of disease, partook of some nourishing food to keep up her strength and health, and went to sleep for the rest of the night.

Years ago, the patient was under the care of Weir Mitchell who sent her to me as a last resort. Dr. Weir Mitchell characterized the patient as an "American humbug." As a matter of fact, the patient herself was convinced that she was on the verge of death, and was in terrible agony of her fears of disease, fears which made her quest for health a matter of life and death. The patient was obsessed by parasitic egotism, the quintessence of psychopathic affections.

Many times during the day she paced the room reciting elevating passages from the Bible, from "great poets,"—Emerson being her favorite writer. I have heard neurotics with their "Mortal Mind," "Sin and Error," "Disease and Nothing," recite edifying phrases such as: "The decaying flower, the blighted bud, the gnarled oak, the ferocious beast, like the discords of disease, sin, and death are unnatural" . . . "Fear is inflammation, error" . . . "Adam, a-dam, a-dam, dam-, dam" . . .

A man, thirty-eight years old, married, highly sensitive, suffers from migraine; he is irritable and restless. When about eight years old, he wandered in the woods near his house. An Italian ran after him, flourishing a big knife. The boy ran away in terror. When he reached home he dropped from exhaustion and fear. Once or twice, on account of the fear of sharp objects, he actually hurt himself while handling knives. This increased his terror and fixed his fear. The instinct of fear was still further developed and stimulated by a series of events, such as falling into a river, from which he was saved. He does not like to take baths, he is afraid to enter a river, and he is in terror of sharp objects, such as knives and razors.

The patient is extremely selfish. He insists on playing games which he likes much, irrespective of the pleasure of his friends and acquaintances. All he cares for is to have a good time, to neglect his duties to his family. In his business he is exacting of others, although he himself is rather slovenly in his work, and slow in the performance of his obligations. He always insists on having his own way. Other people's rights do not trouble him, provided his rights are carefully and scrupulously observed. He always demands services from others, especially from his friends.

The patient's mind is occupied with his health, his fears, and his ailments. The interest he takes in his friends and acquaintances is how far they may serve his purposes of pleasure, game, health, and avoidance of fear of disease. His wife and child are regarded from a personal standpoint of his own good, otherwise they are totally ignored. When they interfere with him, or arouse his fears, he becomes impatient, angry, and furious. He claims to be the most considerate and kindest of men, brimful of humanitarian ideals. He thinks that he can accomplish more than anyone else in his circumstances. Nothing is too good for him, nobody is superior to him. As a rule things are badly conducted, he finds fault with everybody and with everything. He is driven by psychopathic furies, —discord, fear, and maddening egotism.

CHAPTER XIX
HYPNOIDAL TREATMENT

Psychopathic or neurotic maladies do not depend on the abnormal action of some one organ or function, but on a general condition common to all bodily and mental functions, — the fundamental primitive fear instinct which relates to life m general.

The deranged functions, cardiac, respiratory, or sexual,—fatigue, conflict, shock, repression and others are only the occasions. To regard any of these occasions as the sources of psychopathic maladies is like regarding the weather-cock as the cause of the wind. Self-preservation and the fear instinct alone form the source of all psychopathic maladies.

I adduce here a few cases which may be taken as typical:

Mrs. M. C, aged thirty-two years. Family history good; well developed physically and mentally. A year before the present trouble set in, patient suffered from a severe attack of grippe. Menstruation, which was before painless and normal in amount, became painful and scanty, accompanied by headaches, indisposition, irritability, crying spells and backache which lasted long after the menstrual period was over. The family physician ascribed the symptoms to endometritis, mainly cervical and treated her with absolute rest, fomentations, injections, scarification and dilatation of the cervix, and finally curetted the uterus. As the patient grew worse under the treatment, she was taken to a gynecologist, who after an examination suggested an operation. The operation was duly performed, with the result that the nervous symptoms became intensified, and the attacks increased in violence and duration. The turn of the nerve specialist came next. Hysteria, neurasthenia, and the more fashionable "psychasthenia" have been diagnosed by various neurologists. A year of psychoanalysis made of the patient a complete wreck, with depression, introspection and morbid self-analysis. Patient was put by neurologist under Weir Mitchell's treatment.

When the patient came under my care, she was in mental agonies, a complete wreck. I gave up the Weir Mitchell rest treatment, sent away the nurse, released the patient from solitary bed confinement, told her to leave the sick room, to give up dieting and medicines, and to return to a normal, active life. I kept on treating her by the hypnoidal state. The patient began to improve rapidly, and finally all her physical and mental symptoms disappeared; she has continued for over six years in excellent condition of health.

A study of the case traced the fear instinct to experiences of early childhood, fears accentuated and developed into morbid states by the deleterious tendencies of the treatment, giving rise to a somatopsychosis, the physical symptoms mainly predominating.

A lady, aged fifty-nine years, suffered from kyno-phobia. When about the age of twenty-nine years she was bitten by a dog; since then she was afraid of hydrophobia. She kept on reading in the papers about cases of hydrophobia until the fear became developed to an extraordinary degree and became fixed and uncontrollable. According to the principles of evolution of psychopathic states, the fear kept on extending. The fear psychosis included all objects that might possibly carry the germ of hydrophobia. The neurosis became a mysophobia.

As in all other cases of psychopathic states the psychosis was traced to the fear instinct, the germ of which was laid in the patient's early history. The patient was a timid child, and was afraid of strange animals. In the village where she lived there were a few cases of hydrophobia which impressed her when a child. This germ was in later life developed by thirty years' cultivation.

Psychopathic or neurotic symptom complexes I observed in children whose early training was favorable to the awakening and development of the fear instinct. In children affected with fear of animals I traced the fear psychosis to the parents who were afraid of animals, on account of actual traumas in their life history, the child being influenced by imitation, by suggestion, often subconscious, by the behavior of the parents in the presence of animals. Such children are predisposed to recurrent psychopathic states.

In all such cases the etiology is easy to find, if the patient is carefully examined. In many cases the fear instinct with its symptom complex is associated with external objects, giving rise to the so-called phobias. Instead, however, of being associated with external objects, the fear instinct is frequently associated with somatic functions (pathophobia), or with mental activities (phrenophobia).

Man, aged forty-seven years; actor; family neurotic. Patient suffered from anorexia, indigestion, choking, vomiting, gagging, eructation, gas-tralgia, and occasional pains in the limbs. He led a rather gay and irregular life up to the age of thirty-two years, when he had syphilis, for which he was under treatment for two years. This scared him because he had the opportunity to see the consequences of syphilis in many of his friends. He had been under continual fear of the possibility of development of parasyphilitic diseases.

Seven years ago, at the age of forty years, he had to watch at the bedside of an intimate friend, who had been suffering from severe gastric crises of tabes dorsalis. After one specially exhausting night of vigil, worry and fear, he went to bed for a short nap and woke up with the idea of general paresis and intense fear. From that time he began to suffer, from symptoms of tabes with fear of general paresis.

The patient had been an imaginative child; he had his fear instinct cultivated from early childhood by stories of frights, scares, and horrible accidents. When ten years old, his grandfather gave Faust to him to read. Since then the patient was troubled with the fear of selling his soul to Satan. The patient was religious in his childhood, prayed much, and was possessed by the fear of committing sins. "It has now all come back," he complained. A great number of fears could be traced to his early childhood. The somatic symptoms were the manifestations of association of experiences of para-syphilitic diseases, based on the pathological state of the fear instinct, a case of pathophobia, a somatopsychosis.

A few hypnoidal treatments effected a cure. The patient returned to his occupation, free from any distressing symptoms. H. M. aged twenty-seven years, male, Canadian. Family history good; looked pale, anemic, and frail; very intelligent, sensitive, restless, and had a tendency to worry. About a year ago, he began to feel depressed, to worry about his health; thought he suffered from tuberculosis. His physician assured him that nothing was the matter, but he had an uncontrollable fear of consumption; and the idea kept on recurring. Up to the age of nineteen years he was perfectly well. He was then laid up with a sore knee for a few weeks. He had time enough to brood over the knee, and read some literature on the subject. He thought it was tuberculosis and worried much. The knee, however, got well, and gradually he forgot all about it, although the idea of tuberculosis often made him feel uncomfortable, and the idea of "water in the knee" used to flash through his mind, to pass away the next moment.

A year ago, however, he happened to lose his work, became despondent, began to worry and to brood over his financial troubles, slept restlessly, suffered from anorexia, and began to lose flesh. The idea of the knee and the fear of tuberculosis got possession of him. He could not rid himself of the idea of tuberculosis. If in the clinic the physician assured him that he was all right, he felt better for a couple of hours; but often it did not last even as long as that. The least pain, cough, heart beat, a feeling of chill or heat, and the like, brought the idea and fear of tuberculosis back to his mind with renewed energy. He was obsessed by the fear of tuberculosis and felt he was doomed to certain death, a psychosomatic pathophobia.

Hypnoidal states did good service. The patient's mental condition began to improve rapidly. He was no longer troubled with depression, insomnia, and fears; began to gain in weight, appetite improved, felt energy flowing in; began to look for work in real earnest, finally found it, and kept at it.

Man, aged forty-three years, suffered from palpitation of the heart, fainted easily, especially on physical examination by physician, or at the beginning of medical treatment. He suffered from indigestion for which he had been under treatment for a number of years by physicians who gave him medicine for his bowels and also from time to time kept on washing his stomach. He had a great fear of becoming a victim of cardiac troubles, especially of some unknown, terrible, valvular affection. When under my care he kept on asking to be taken to heart and stomach specialists, to be examined, and have some radical operation performed. Frequently under the influence of the fear states and obsession of heart and stomach trouble, especially the heart, he would collapse suddenly, be unable to walk, and be afraid that he suffered from some paralysis.

On examination the patient revealed a history full of various traumas which, from his very childhood until he came under my care, helped to bring about his psychopathic condition, and developed the fear instinct to an extraordinary degree. Physicians had the lion's share in this special case by their rearing of the fear instinct, and by their favoring the patient's phobias by their examinations, by their prescriptions, and by the diet and treatment. The patient was in such a panic that he kept on taking his pulse on the least occasion, was feeling his heart, stomach, and intestines at every opportunity. The hypertrophied growth of his morbid self and fear instinct had invaded and dominated the patient's whole personality, developed a typical psychosomatic pathophobia with its recurrent states. The patient was cured by hypnoidal states.

In the Trudi for 1913 of the University of Moscow, Russia, Doctor Ribakov made an extensive study of a series of cases of psychopathic or psychoneurotic asthma, and arrived at a conclusion similar to my own, although he was no doubt unaware of my work and publications on the same subject. He came to the same conclusion as I that the etiology of neurosis is to be found in fear, which alone forms the basis of psychopathic neurosis. All other factors, social, professional, sexual, religious, repressions, conflicts are only occasions of the disease. It is fear, and fear alone that forms the pathology of the psychopathic neurotic symptom complex.

A young lady was afflicted with ornithophobia, fear of birds, fear of chickens. The sight of a chicken set her into a panic. The patient is very timid, and this timidity can be traced to her early childhood. When at the age of six, a play-mate threw a live chicken at her in the dark. The child was terribly frightened, screamed, and fainted. The mother used to tell her fairy stories full of adventure, of ghosts, of dragons, and of monsters. This prepared the patient to react so violently to the sudden attack made by the flight, struggling, and feel of the chicken in the dark. Since that time, patient has formed an uncontrollable fear of live birds.

Another patient of mine, a lady of forty-nine years, single, suffered from potamophobia, a fear of going into rivers, or into the ocean. When about seven years old she was thrown into water by one of her elder sisters. She was nearly drowned and was half dead with fear when rescued. Since then she has been in terror of water, or rather of rivers and oceans. Several times she made conscious efforts to get rid of the fear, but the attempts were unsuccessful. In fact, the more she was forced or forced herself consciously to get into the water, the greater was the fear. This fear became all the more intensified, when some of her intimate friends were drowned in a boat. This fixed the fear which became uncontrollable.

A patient of mine, a man of thirty-five years, was afraid of going out in the dark. This was traced to early associations of fears of the dark, to superstitious beliefs in ghosts and spirits cultivated in the patient's early childhood. He was afraid to remain alone in the dark or to go down at night into cellars or other secluded places. This fear was unfortunately still more intensified by an accident. At the age of twenty-seven, one night when returning late from a visit, he was assaulted from behind by foot-pads. This accident fixed the fear of darkness.

A lady of sixty-seven years, with pronounced arteriosclerosis, had an attack of hemiplegia of the left side. She suffered from motor aphasia, but did not lose consciousness. The paralysis cleared up in a few days, but the sudden attack demoralized her. Since that time she is in terror of another attack. She watches for symptoms, and the least sensation of faintness throws her into a panic. The patient is the wife of a general and was in China during the Boxer riots, in the Spanish American war, in the Philippines, and other military engagements. The fear instinct was cultivated in her by all such conditions.

In her early childhood there were fears and frights of child character, enough to arouse the fear instinct, which was gradually developed and cultivated by the circumstances of life and by worries in the course of the various wars, of which she was a witness. Finally the fear culminated by the stroke of paralysis.

Similarly, I had patients who suffered from tuberculosis, from asthma, from heart trouble, and from all kinds of intestinal affections which specially abound in psychopathic cases. All such cases can be clearly traced to various somatic symptoms based on the fear instinct. The etiology is fear, the arousal and development of the fear instinct in respect to the special symptom complex.

A patient, aged twenty-six years, suffered from agoraphobia at various intervals. As a child of nine years, he was attacked by rough boys. He freed himself and ran in great terror. The boys threatened him with another "licking" when he appeared again on the street. He was afraid to go out for several weeks. The parents forced him to go and buy some things. Living in a rough neighborhood, on account of his father's circumstances, he had been many times subjected to knocks, blows, and assaults by rough boys, until the fear of the open street became fixed into the well known form of agoraphobia.

Another case, that of a lady of thirty-eight years, married, suffers from ailurophobia, or fear of cats. This can be traced to the patient's early childhood. When she was a child her brothers and sisters went through attacks of diphtheria, which was ascribed to infection caused or transmitted by cats. The patient was specially impressed with the danger from cats. Under such training and suggestion given in early childhood, the patient gradually formed a fear of cats. This fear was still more intensified and became a panic when she was put into a dark room and a cat was let loose on the poor victim by her mischievous companions, who knew of the patient's fear. When the patient had children of her own, she was still more affected by the fear of cats, on account of the subconscious and conscious fear of the possibility of infection transmitted by cats to her children.

All those cases were investigated and cured by hypnoidal states.

Mr. D., a young man of twenty-five years, was born in Poland. As far as can be ascertained, the parents as well as the brothers and sisters are well. A physical examination of the patient reveals nothing abnormal. There are no sensory, no motor disturbances. He complains of severe headaches, preceded by a feeling of indisposition, depression, vertigo and distress. During the attack there is hyperesthesia to touch, pressure, temperature, and to visual and auditory stimulations. The patient shivers and looks pale. The cold experienced during the attack is so intense that the patient has to wrap himself in many blankets, as if suffering from a malarial paroxysm.

Fears have strong possession of the patient's mind. He is afraid to remain in a closed place in the daytime and especially at night. When he has to remain alone at night, he is in an agony of fear, and cannot go to sleep. Every passer-by is regarded as a robber or murderer, and he quakes at the least noise. When walking in the house in the dark, he has the feeling as if someone were after him, and occasionally even experiences the hallucination of someone tugging at his coat. He is mortally afraid of the dead and shuns a funeral. The patient has also a fear of dogs, a kynophobia. The fear is irresistible, and is as involuntary as a reflex.

An investigation, by means of the hypnoidal states, brought out of the patient's subconscious life the following data: When a child of three years, the patient lived with his family in a small village near a large forest infested with wolves. In one of the intermediary states a faint memory, rather to say a vision, struggled up, a vision of wolves and dogs. Someone cried out: "Run, wolves are coming!" Crazed with fear, he ran into the hut and fell fainting on the floor. It turned out to be dogs instead of a pack of wolves. It is that fright in early childhood which has persisted in the subconscious mind, and, having become associated with subsequent experiences of attacks of dogs, has found expression in the patient's consciousness as an instinctive fear of dogs.

But why was the patient in such abject terror of dead people? This found its answer in the experiences and training of his early life. When a young child, the patient heard all kinds of ghost stories, and tales of wandering lost souls and of spirits of dead people hovering about the churchyard and burial grounds; he heard tales of ghouls and of evil spirits inhabiting deserted places, dwelling in the graves of sinners and the wicked. He listened to stories of haunted houses and of apparitions stalking about in the dark. His social and religious environment has been saturated with the belief in the supernatural, as is usually the case among the superstitious populations of Eastern Europe. We cannot wonder, then, that an impressionable child brought up under such conditions should stand in mortal fear of the supernatural, especially of the dead.

When the patient was about nine years old, his parents noticed some prominences on his right chest. It was suggested to them that the hand of a dead person possessed the property of blighting life and arresting all growth, and would, therefore, prove a "powerful medicine" for undesirable growths. It happened that an old woman in the neighborhood died. The little boy was taken into the room where the dead body was lying, and the cold hand of the corpse was put on the child's naked chest. The little fellow fainted away in terror. The fear of dead people became subconsciously fixed, and manifested itself as an insistent fear of the dead, and, in fact, of anything connected with the dead and the world of spirits.

The patient had hardly recovered from the shock of the "dead hand," when he had to pass through a still more severe experience. A party of drunken soldiers, stationed in the little town, invaded his house and beat his father unmercifully, almost crippled him: they knocked down his mother, killed a little brother of his, and he himself, in the very depth of a winter night, dressed in a little shirt and coat, made his escape to a deserted barn, where he passed the whole night. He was nearly frozen when found in the morning, crouching in a corner of the barn, shivering with fear and cold.

From that time on the headaches manifested themselves in full severity, with hyperesthesia and death-like paleness and intense cold of the body. The early cultivation of the fear instinct resulted in a neurosis with its recurrent states. Another patient is a man of thirty years; his family history is good. He is physically well developed, a well known professor of physics in one of the foremost institutions in this country. He suffers from attacks of loss of personality. The attack is of a periodical character, coming on at intervals of two weeks, occasionally disappearing for a few months, then reasserting itself with renewed energy and vigor. During the attack the patient experiences a void, a panic, which is sudden in its onset, like petit mal. The trouble was diagnosed as larval or psychic epilepsy; the man was referred to me by Dr. Morton Prince as an extremely interesting, but puzzling neurological case.

Patient feels that his "self" is gone. He can carry on a conversation or a lecture during the attack, so that no outsider can notice any change in him, but his self is gone, and all that he does and says, even the demonstration of a highly complex problem in integral calculus is gone through in an automatic way. The fury of the attack lasts a few moments, but to him it appears of long duration. He is "beside himself," as he puts it. He seems to stand beside himself and watch his body, "the other fellow," as he describes it, carry on the conversation or the lecture. He is "knocked out of his body, which carries on all those complicated mental processes." For days after he must keep on thinking of the attack, feels scared and miserable, thinking insistently, in great agony, over his awful attack, a recurrent psychoneurotic phrenophobia.

At first the patient could trace this attack only as far back as his seventh year. Later on, earlier experiences of childhood came to light, and then it became clear that the attack developed out of the primitive instinctive fear of early childhood, fear of the unfamiliar, fear of the dark, of the unknown, of the mysterious, fears to which he had been subjected in his tender years.

This state was further reinforced by the early death of his parents, it was hammered in and fixed by hard conditions of life, full of apprehension and anxiety. Life became to the child one big mysterious fear of the unknown. The fear instinct formed the pathological focus of the attack. As the patient puts it: "It is the mystical fear of the attacks which overpowers me." With the disintegration of the focus the symptom complex of the attacks disappeared. The patient is in excellent condition, he is doing brilliant work in physics and chemistry and is professor in one of the largest universities in Canada.

I present another case apparently "paranoidal," a case interesting from our standpoint. The patient is a man of twenty-seven years; his parents are neurotic, religious revivalists. As far back as the age of eight he suffered from agonizing fears of perdition and scares of tortures in hell, impressed on his sensitive, young mind during the revivals. He is very religious, obsessed with the fear of having committed an unpardonable sin. He thinks he is damned to suffer tortures in hell for all eternity.

He keeps on testing any chance combinations, and if his guesses turn out correct, he is wrought up to a pitch of excitement and panic. For to him it means a communication coming from an unseen world of unknown mysterious powers. With his condition diagnosed as "paranoidal dementia praecox," the patient was committed to an insane asylum, from which he was subsequently released.

The attack comes in pulses of brief duration, followed by long periods of brooding, depression, and worry. The primitive fear of pain, of danger and death, and the sense of the mysterious cultivated by his religious training, reached here an extraordinary degree of development. Among the earliest memories that have come up in the hypnoidal state was the memory of a Sunday school teacher, who cultivated in the patient, then but five years of age, those virulent germs which, grown on the soil of the primitive instinctive fear and the highly developed sense of the unknown and the mysterious, have brought forth poisonous fruits which now form the curse of his life. The case is a typical psychoneurotic phrenophobia with its characteristic recurrent states.

"It is difficult," the patient writes, "to place the beginning of my abnormal fear. It certainly originated from doctrines of hell which I heard in early childhood, particularly from a rather ignorant teacher who taught Sunday school. My early religious thought was chiefly concerned with the direful eternity of torture that might be awaiting me, if I was not good enough to be saved."

After a couple of years of persistent treatment by means of the hypnoidal state and by methods of association and disintegration of the active subconscious systems, the patient recovered. He entered a well known medical school and took the foremost rank among the medical students.

In the investigation or psychognosis of psychopathic cases I invariably find the psycho pathology to be a morbid condition of the fear instinct, rooted in the primordial impulse of self-preservation. The psychognosis of this underlying pathological state and disintegration of the latter are of the utmost consequence in the domain of psychopathology and psychotherapeutics.

1 A full account of the cases ifl published in my volume "The Causation and Treatment of Psychopathic Diseases."

CHAPTER XX
FEAR CONFESSIONS

A few "Confessions" made by psychopathic sufferers will help us best to understand the character, the mechanism, the factors, and principles of neurosis:

"As you are desirous of knowing more about my life and environment, I state concerning them as follows:

"You will remember that I told you that my stepfather was a liquor dealer. Throughout all the time that he was in business we either lived over the bar-room or else right in the place where the liquor was sold. My step-father was a very heavy drinker, a man of violent nature, and decidedly pugnacious. As a child I have been scared to death by drunken brawls, and many nights have been dragged out of bed by my mother who would flee with me to the house of a neighbor for safety.

"I might say that until I was seventeen years old, I lived in continual terror of something going to happen. If he was arrested by the police, as often happened, our home would be a scene of turmoil until the case was settled.

"I remember one incident very plainly, when he came home one night completely covered with blood as the result of being held up by thugs, and another time when he left the house to subdue some quarreling drunks with a pistol and returned after an exchange of shots with his hand shot through.

"As a child, I was inclined to study, and associated very little with other children. My mother tells me that I talked early, but when about three years old I began to stammer. This trouble bothered me a great deal, and I used to worry about it all the time, especially in school when I would try to recite. I might add that even now, when excited, I am troubled in the same way.

"My stepfather has been subject to nightmares nearly all his life; when asleep he would cry and moan and would be unable to move until someone would shake him out of it. He was terribly afraid of them, and I remember he used to say that he expected to die in one of them. I used to be left alone with him quite frequently, and I stood in constant fear of his dying; and if he fell asleep, as he frequently did in the daytime, I would wake him or watch his respiration to see if he was alive.

"At other times I have been awakened in the night by his cries and would assist my mother in bringing him to consciousness. It was during one of these times that I became aware of my heart palpitating, and whenever he had such a spell, I would be in a state of fear and excitement for some time after. He would have these nightmares nearly every night and sometimes four or five times in one night, and I might add that he has them even now.

"I began to have attacks of dizziness in the streets, and finally one day, I had one, and all symptoms and fears of the attack came on in school, and from that time on I have watched my respiration and suffered from dizziness, mental depression, and sadness.

"You have asked me to tell you more in detail about the attacks or nightmares to which my stepfather was subject, and which always frightened me greatly, especially when a child.

"My step-father had the habit of falling asleep quite often, even in the day time, and I have never known him to go to sleep without having an attack in some form. If one watched him asleep, as I often did, one could tell by his respiration when an attack was coming. His breathing would become slower and hardly perceptible, and finally he would begin to moan, and cry out; then, when shaken vigorously and spoken to, he would awaken in great fear and apparent suffering. If he had an attack, and we did not respond soon enough, he would be very angry and say that we cared not if he should die. We were so afraid of these attacks that we had trained ourselves to be ever on the look-out for his cries, even at night.

"It really seemed as if his life rested in our hands. I might say that sometimes these attacks lasted several minutes, before he could be awakened. He used 'to say that at such times he always dreamed someone was choking, beating, or otherwise torturing him. He had been told by some physician that he would ultimately die in such an attack.

"These attacks were sufficient to precipitate a small panic in the house. I know not a single hour of the day or night, but that I have either been called or awakened by my mother in her efforts to awaken him. With the attack over, I would be trembling all over, and my heart would be beating madly. I can remember these attacks from my earliest childhood, and it seems to me that on one occasion, at your office, I was startled just as these attacks used to make me."

While in the hypnoidal state, patient exclaimed: "I am afraid. All my life I lived under terror . . . This is just my disease,—fcar."

"I lived from infancy in a state of apprehension and fear. In my home there seemed to be always a tension. I don't know that I ever relaxed there during my waking hours. I was never at peace mentally.

This was largely brought about by my mother's chronic condition of fear. I should not have had such a large development of the fear habit had there been any neutralizing influence. But my father was a weak character, living under fear, being afraid of responsibility, so that my character was closely molded on his. He gave me no moral fiber to resist fears of mother, and so did not help me to build any character of my own. I still carry with me the state of apprehension and fear that I contracted in my early life. I had only one serious illness in my life outside of my nervous troubles. Had an attack of bowel trouble somewhere near the age of six. I was once struck in the face by a dog's teeth. I have had various cancer experiences.

"My father, when I was very young, had some irritation of the throat. A physician told him he was in danger of cancer. I can recall him anxiously looking at his throat. Later a neighbor went to a 'plaster specialist' to have a supposed cancer of the tongue removed. His wife was often at our home talking of his sufferings.

"While attending dental school I contracted some trouble. I went to a physician near where I lived. He talked to me of a possibility of syphilis. I became much frightened, and read all I could find on syphilis. The books scared me still more. At last on the advice of friends, I went to another physician who reassured me, and I lost part of my fear.

"After this I returned home for a summer vacation. This was in 1904-. That summer my tongue felt sore, I looked at it, and found it peculiar. This aroused my fears of syphilis. Upon returning to Chicago in the fall (1904) I asked my physician to recommend a specialist. He sent me to a syphil-ographer, who told me I had no syphilis, but that the condition of my tongue was caused by gallbladder trouble. He wished me to have the gall bladder operated which I refused to do. I thought no more about my tongue until I studied cancer in oral surgery. I would then occasionally worry over my condition. About this time an actor whom I knew died of cancer of the tongue. I worried over my tongue, being afraid of cancer, for several days after this. I then went along for seven or eight years without much thought of my tongue.

"One day in February 1913, after some pain in my side which brought the thoughts of gall bladder and then of the tongue, I asked advice of a physician. He looked at my tongue and said: 'I don't wish to frighten you, but you should have that tongue attended to. You might some day have a cancer there.' He sent me to a throat specialist who said the condition of my tongue was due to a back tooth. I had the tooth removed. I afterwards consulted Dr. L., a surgeon at Eau Claire, Wis., with the idea of having the gall bladder operated upon. He laughed at the gall bladder trouble, but sent me to

Battle Creek Sanitarium with the idea, I think, that the change would relieve me of my fears. At Battle Creek I was told I had a mild case of colitis, and was put under treatment for it.

"While at Battle Creek my fears grew less. I remained at Battle Creek about two months. Shortly before leaving there I was given a Wasserman test. This they told me was faintly positive. I was then given three injections of Neo-Salvarsan. I then left Battle Creek and stopped at Chicago to see Dr. P. Dr. P. said any Wasserman would be positive, taken with no more care than mine had been. That there was no reason to think there was any syphilis anyway. He then sent me to Dr. W., an internist, who said I had hyperacidity of the stomach.

"I did not feel very badly at this time, although my fears of cancer persisted. I was carrying on the work in my office. Later in the summer I went to the Mayo Clinic at Rochester, Minn., where I was given a local application for my tongue. In the fall of 1913, while in Milwaukee I consulted an oral surgeon, Dr. B. He said 'I will send you to Dr. F., a dermatologist who knows more about diseases of the tongue than any man I know.* I consulted Dr. F. who said: 'Geographical tongue, do not worry about it.* My fears were instantly relieved. I seldom thought of my tongue in the next two years.

"In the fall of 1916 I had some trouble with my stomach. This seemed to bring my fears to mind and one day my fear of cancer returned. There was a connection between my fears and the stomach and gall bladder trouble diagnosed in regard to my tongue. At least the stomach trouble would bring thoughts of the tongue condition.

"I tried to help myself out of my mental condition by reading articles on cancer. This made me worse. I went to Chicago where I was told by Dr. S., a dermatologist, that radium might remedy the condition of my tongue. I had several applications of radium. After this I still worried a great deal. I went through the spring and summer under a nervous strain, but still able to carry on my work. That fall (1917) I had such intense fear that I was attacked by acute insomnia. I was unable to sleep without Veronal. The day after my insomnia began I found myself very weak. I was pale, and my heart would pound on the least exertion. I had also a great deal of pain in my bowels. I went to Chicago and consulted Dr. E., Dean of Northwestern University Medical School. He told me such conditions usually traveled in a circle, that my nervous condition might leave me in a few months. I went through the winter in this condition.

"I began to have a great fear of the fact that it was necessary to use hypnotics. This fear of drugs was strong, and overshadowed my other fears. I read an article on hypnotics as a habit; this added to my fear of them. Before using hypnotics I noticed my sexual power was less, or rather there was no pleasure in it. This did not trouble me as I thought it a part of my nervous condition.

"In April, 1918, 1 went again to Battle Creek. I did very well there for a week, but then got into a deep depression, became weak, and was frightened to think I was no better. I remained in Battle Creek for three weeks, and then went home. A month later I went to St. Paul and consulted a neurologist. He did not know what to do for me.

"I went to Milwaukee and consulted another neurologist. I was becoming more despondent all the time. I decided to go to a sanitarium to see if I could not get rid of my drug habit. I went to Wauwatosa, Wis., and remained there three weeks, but I could see they did not know what to do for me.

"In August I entered the Rest Hospital at Minneapolis and remained there for a while under the care of Dr. J. I managed to drag along, terrorized by my condition and by the fact that I could get no relief. The drug habit was my greatest obsession at this time. I used bromides and chloral hydrate,— changed hypnotics frequently.

"In January, 1919, I saw Dr. P. of Chicago, who sent me to a sanitarium where I received no help. I then hunted through magazines for articles on nervous diseases. I read of Dr. S. and his work and came under his care at Portsmouth in May, 1919. While there I learned to control my fears. I left Portsmouth in August feeling sure of myself. I would occasionally have a depression which would not frighten me and did not remain with me long. I was looking forward to a happy future.

"During the summer of 1921 I felt tired most of the time. However, I was still sure of being able to handle myself. One day after feeling very tired my fear of cancer returned. I got into a panic and started East to see Dr. S. On arriving in Boston I found he was in the West. I went to Dr. P.'s office; was sent to Dr. W. and by him to a psychoanalyst. The psycho-analyst said I had a 'mother complex, without usual sexual features.' Psycho-analysis proved a failure, and I abandoned the treatment with disgust, as useless and silly."

The patient was under my care for five months. He is now back to his dental work. He writes to me that he is gaining rapidly in weight, and is in excellent condition.

"I am a married woman of fifty-two. All my life I have been imprisoned in the dungeon keep of fear. Fear paralyzes me in every effort. If I could once overcome m} r enemy, I would rejoice forever more.

"In childhood everything cowered me. I was bred in fear. At five or six my mother died, and I feared and distrusted a God who would so intimidate me and bereave me. I heard tales of burglars being discovered hiding under beds, and a terrified child retired nightly for years. I was in agony of fears. My fears I never told. Later I heard of the doctrines of God's foreknowledge, and, as a little rebel, I would place dishes on the pantry shelves, changing from place to place, and then giving up in despair, knowing that if foreknowledge were true, God knew that I would go through with all that performance.

"Through childhood I feared suicide. It was a world of escape that appealed to me and yet appalled me. I also heard of somnambulism, and I never saw a keen bladed knife, but I dreaded that in my sleep I might do damage to myself or to my friends in a state of unconsciousness.

"In my twenties I did attempt suicide a number of times, but somehow they proved unsuccessful. I always aimed to have it appear an accident. I dreaded to have my death appear as a stain and disgrace to my family which I loved.

"I always fear to walk at any height, on a trestle over running walls, or even to walk on a bridge without side railings. As a child I was afraid of the dark, I was afraid of going out on the street in a dark night. In fact, even a moonlight night terrified me when I remained alone. I was afraid to go into dark places, such as cellars, or into lonely places even in the daytime.

"As a child I was always shy, fearful, timid, and self-conscious to a painful degree. Even as a grownup woman I am often a sufferer from the same cause, although I have sufficient self-control to conceal it.

"I have to be careful of my state of health, as the latter is ver}' delicate. I am a chronic sufferer from indigestion and constipation, although I somehow manage to regulate these troubles.

"When I need my nerves in good control so frequently, they are in a state of utter collapse. My brain is in a state of confusion, in a state of whirl just when I need to think the clearest. My poor brain feels as if a tight band encircled and contracted it. It seems to me as if the brain has shrunken from the temples.

"My memory is unreliable. Often I read quite carefully, but I am unable to recall what I have read. Especially is this so, if called upon without previous warning. My brain goes into a panic of an extremely alarming kind.

"I was told that I was a woman of a good brain and of great talent, that all I needed was to exercise my will and determination, and that I would succeed. I lack concentration and I lack confidence.

"In my childhood hell fire was preached. Foreordination and an arbitrary God were held up to my childish comprehension. I was bred in fear, and self destruction resulted."

The following valuable account given by an eminent physician brings out well the factors and principles of neurosis expounded in this volume:

"You ask me to write about my fears. I give you a brief account.

"As a child, as far as memory carries, I had a fear of ghosts, of giants, of monsters, and of all kinds of mysterious and diabolical agencies and witchcraft of which I had heard a number of tales and stories in my early childhood. I was afraid of thieves, of robbers, and of all forms of evil agencies. The fears were stronger at daytime, but more so at night. Strange noises, unexpected voices and sounds made a cold shiver run down my back.

"I was afraid to remain alone in a closed room, or in the dark, or in a strange place. It seemed to me as if I was left and abandoned by everybody, and that something awful was going to happen to me. When I happened to be left alone under such conditions I was often in a state of helplessness, paralyzing terror. Such states of fear sweep occasionally over me even at present. I find, however, that they are far more complicated with associations of a more developed personal life. I know that in some form or other the fears are present, but are inhibited by counteracting impulses and associations. I still feel a cold shiver running down my back, when I happen to go into a dark cellar in the dead of night, or happen to remain alone in a dark, empty house. Such fears date back to my fourth year, and possibly to an earlier time of my childhood.

"As a matter of contrast-inhibitions of such fears I may either brace myself and put myself in a state of courage and exaltation, or when this does not succeed, I let my mind dwell on other fears and troubles. I find that the last method is often far more effective in the inhibition of fear states which at the moment are present with me. All I need is to press the button, so to say, and awaken some other fears, the present fears diminish in intensity, and fade away for the time being. I actually favor, and welcome, and even look for disagreeable and painful experiences so as to overcome some of my present fears. The new fears are then treated in the same way.

"As I became older, about the age of eight, I began to fear disease and death. This may be due to the infectious diseases that attacked many members of our family, about this time. In fact, I have been present at the deathbed of some of them, and the impression was one of terror, mysterious horror. I was afraid I might get diseases from which I might die. After my witnessing the last agonizing moment of death, my elders thought of removing me to a safer place; their fears and precautions still more impressed the fear of danger of disease and death. I may say that I really never freed myself from the fear of disease and death. The latter fear is always present with me in a vague form, always ready to crop up at any favorable opportunity. This fear, in so far as it is extending its tentacles in various directions, is often the bane of my life. Even at my best there is always a kind of vague fear of possible danger, lurking in various objects which may be infected or possibly poisonous.

"This fear has been spreading and has become quite extensive, involving my family, my children, my friends, my acquaintances, and my patients. Usually I ignore these fears, or get control over them by an effort of will. When, however, I happen to be fatigued, or worried over small things in the course of my work, or happen to be in low spirits by petty reversals of life, these fears may become aroused. Under such conditions I may become afraid, for instance, of drinking milk, because it may be tuberculous.

"This fear may spread and involve fear for my children and my patients; or again I may be afraid of eating oysters and other shell fish, because they may be infected with typhoid fever germs. I may refuse to eat mushrooms, because they may be poisonous. The other day I was actually taken sick with nausea and with disposition to vomiting after eating of otherwise good mushrooms. The fear seized on me that they all might be poisonous 'toadstools.' Such fears may extend to ever new reactions and to ever new associations, and are possibly the worst feature of the trouble.

"I have a fear of coming in contact with strangers, lest I get infected by them, giving me tuberculosis, influenza, scarlet fever, and so on. This mysophobia involves my children and my friends, inasmuch that I am afraid that strangers may communicate some contagious diseases. A similar fear I have in regard to animals, that they may possibly be infected with rabies, or with glanders, or with some other deadly, pathogenic micro-organism. I am afraid of mosquito bites, lest they give me malaria, or yellow fever. The fears, in the course of their extension, may become ever more intense and more insidious than the original states.

"As a child I had some bad experiences with dogs; I was attacked by dogs and badly bitten. Although this fear is no longer so intense as it was in my childhood, still I know it is present. My heart sometimes comes to a sudden standstill, when I happen to come on a strange dog. When the strange dog growls and barks, all my courage is lost, and I beat an inglorious retreat. It is only in the presence of other people that I can rise to the effort of walking along and apparently paying no attention to the dog. This is because I fear the opinion of others more even than I fear the growls of dogs. My social and moral fears are far greater than my purely physical fears.

"When I became older, about the age of eighteen to twenty, a new form of fear appeared, like a new sprout added to the main trunk, or possibly growing out of the main fear of disease and death, that is the fear of some vague, impending evil. The fear of some terrible accident to myself and more so to my family, or to any of the people of whom I happen to take care, is constantly present in the margin of my consciousness, or as you would put it, in my subconsciousness. Sometimes the fears leave me for a while, sometimes they are very mild, and sometimes again they flare up with an intensity that is truly alarming and uncontrollable. The energy with which those fears become insistent in consciousness, and the motor excitement to which they give rise are really extraordinary. The fear comes like a sudden flood. The energy with which those fears rise into consciousness is often overwhelming.

"Fear gets possession of me under circumstances in which my suspicions are, for some reason or other, aroused to activity, all the more so if the suspicions of possible impending evil are awakened suddenly. In other words, the fears arise with stimulations of associations of threatening danger to myself and to my family. I am afraid that something may happen to my children; I fear that they may fall sick suddenly ; I fear that some terrible accident may happen to them; I fear that they may fall down from some place, and be maimed or be killed, I fear that my children and other members of my family may be poisoned by people who are not well disposed towards them. I am afraid that the}' may pick up some food that was infected, or that they may be infected in school by children who happen to suffer from some infectious maladies. I am afraid that my children may be overrun by some vehicles, by automobiles, or that they may be killed in an accident, that they may be killed by streetcar, or even that the house may collapse. This latter event has actually taken place when I was a child. In fact, many, if not all of those fears have actually their origin in my experience.

"As I write you these lines, memories of such events come crowding upon my mind. Are they the noxious seeds that have been planted on the soil of fear? I am afraid sometimes that even the food I and my children as well as other people eat may give rise to toxic products and thus produce disease. Often in the dead of night, I may come to see my children in order to convince myself that they have no fever, and that they are not threatened by any terrible disease. The very words 'sickness,' 'disease,' 'not feeling well,' 'death,' arouse my feeling and sometimes throw me into a panic. I am afraid to use such words in connection with any of my children. I am afraid that the evil mentioned may actually happen.

"When a child I learned about testing and omens. If a test comes through in a certain way, it is an omen of good luck, otherwise it means bad luck. This superstitious testing and omens have remained with me, and that in spite of my liberal training and knowledge of the absurdity of such superstitions. I may test by opening the Bible at any page, or I may test by anything that might occur, according to my guesses. All of these fears I know have no meaning for me, they are senseless and absurd, but they are so rooted in my early childhood, they have been so often repeated, they have accumulated round them so much emotion of fear that they come to my mind with a force which is truly irresistible. Many of the fears have multiplied to such an extent that I cannot touch anything without rousing some slumbering fear.

"To continue with my fears; I am often afraid that the doors are not well locked, and I must try them over and over again; I go away and come back again, and try and try again, and once more. It is tiresome, but as the fear is constantly with me, and is born again and again, I cannot be satisfied, and must repeat the whole process over and over until I get tired, and give up the whole affair in sheer despair. In such cases a contrary and different fear comes in handy. One devil banishes another. I am afraid that the gas jet is left open, and I must try it over and over, and test the jets with matches. This process of testing may go on endlessly. The fear remains and the process must begin again until it is stopped by sheer effort of will as something meaningless, automatic, and absurd. The performance must be stopped and substituted by something else.

"Colds, or attacks of influenza of the mildest character have given rise to fears of pneumonia. Pain in the abdomen, or a little intestinal distress has awakened fears of possible appendicitis, or of tumor, or intestinal obstruction. The least suspicion of blood in the stools awakens the fear of possible cancer. Vomiting or even nausea brings fears of cancer of the stomach. There is no disease from which I have not suffered.

"The same fears have naturally been extended to my children, and to all those who are under my care. The least symptom is sufficient to arouse in me fears of possible terror and horrible consequences.

"I am afraid that suits may be brought against me, or that some of my own people, patients and even employees whom I discharged, may bring legal action against me in court, or blackmail me. When I leave home, I am afraid that something terrible has happened. The fear of impending evil is always with me. The fears have invaded every part of my being. It seems as if there is no resistance in my mind to those terrible fear states.

"Perhaps it may interest you to know that, although I am quite liberal, and even regarded as irreligious, still I am afraid to express any word against God, Christ, saints, martyrs of any church and denomination, be they Christian, Mohammedan, Buddhist, or pagan. I am afraid lest they may hear me and do me harm; I fear to say a word even against the devil or Satan. I am obsessed by fears. Fears pursue me as long as I am awake, and do not leave me alone in my sleep and dreams. Fears are the curse of my life, and yet I have control of them, none but you has any suspicion of them. I go about my work in a seemingly cheerful and happy way. The fears, however, are the bane of my life, and torture me by their continued presence.

"I tried to find whether or not those fears had any relation to my wishes or to my sexual experiences. I must say that I find they bear no relation whatever to wish or sex. My mental states grow on fear, take their origin in fear, and feed on fear. Fear is the seed and the soil of all those infinite individual phobias that keep on torturing me unless opposed by a supreme effort of my will.

"Truly the Biblical curse well applies to my life. The Lord will make thy plagues wonderful, and the plagues of thy seed, even great plagues, and of long continuance, and sore sickness, and of long continuance. Moreover, he will bring upon thee all the diseases of Egypt, which thou wast afraid of, and they shall cleave unto thee. And every sickness and every plague, which is not written in the book of this law, them will the law bring upon thee, until thou be destroyed. Thou shalt find no case/, neither shall the sole of thy foot have rest; but the Lord shall give thee a trembling heart, and failing of eyes, and sorrow of mind. And thy life shall hang in doubt before thee, and thou shalt fear day and night and shall have none assurance of thy life. In the morning thou shalt say, Would God it were even! and at even thou shalt say, Would God it were morning! for the fear of thine heart wherewith thou shalt fear. . . .'

"I laid bare my soul before you. I permit you to do with this document whatever you may think fit." I was bom of healthy parents; grandparents were also healthy. All lived to a ripe old age, and died of natural causes. Father is still living; I was a healthy normal child with little sickness up to the age of 16. A few years prior I belonged to a gymnasium and enjoyed superb physical strength and health, though I was from childhood somewhat of a coward. I then became associated with some youngsters who liked nightlife. This association influenced me to join them in their nightly escapades.

"Between overtaxing myself in my work and trying to keep up with the boys socially my system was drained. This was kept up for about five years. I was working for a dry cleaning establishment the owner of which did not appreciate my hard work. I gave ten hours a day service, but he required even more, so that I spent as many as fifteen and eighteen hours a day, and kept that up for about five years.

"It was in January, 1911, at the age of twenty while sitting in a restaurant eating my lunch, I felt a strange sensation coming over me, such as blood rushing to my head, followed by weakness, trembling, and fainting spells. I summoned up what will power I had left, shook my head in effort to brace up, and tried to finish my meal, but without success. I left the restaurant and coming outside felt the same sensation. I leaned against a building, and my knees gave way from under me until I was compelled to lie down. I made an attempt to get up, boarded a street car, and started for my father's store which was about a mile down the street. As I stepped on the platform I felt the same spell coming over me. Some of the men standing on the back platform saw my condition, and helped me. I arrived at the store where I collapsed.

"An ambulance was called, and I was taken to the city hospital. The interne diagnosed the case as acute indigestion. He prescribed some soda tablets, and told me to be careful with my diet. I felt relieved at what he told me, because I thought it was not so serious as I had expected. For I thought the end was near. My brother who accompanied me spoke kind and encouraging words which soothed my nerves.

"On the street car my thoughts started to go over the whole of what had occurred. I could not control myself and gave way again. When I got home I could not eat. I lay down and tried to get some sleep, but sleep was out of the question. My thoughts always wandered back to these spells, and that would bring back another spell. I took the tablets prescribed by the physician, but they did not help me any.

"The next day I tried to go to work, but could not on account of these spells. I then decided to call our family physician. He told me it was a nervous breakdown, and prescribed bromides. I kept on having these spells in spite of the bromides. I was at a loss what to do. From then on I became afraid to venture anywhere, to go to any place, for fear of these spells. My real trouble began. I was afraid to live, and afraid to die, afraid to go out, afraid to lie down, always afraid of these spells.

"I remained at home for a couple of weeks, but the spells continued. I then decided to try another doctor. This time a stomach specialist, and as might be expected he claimed my stomach was the cause of my disturbances. The news was gratifying to me. I knew that stomach troubles could be cured, and the thought helped to quiet some of the fears. I went back to work after a few weeks. The belief in the efficacy of the drug enabled me to get downtown to work, but I kept on having spells, losing weight, and feeling miserable.

"I decided to try another physician. This time a nerve specialist. After examination he diagnosed the case as nervous prostration. He gave me what he called a good nerve tonic. In addition to it he used to stripe my back with red hot instruments. I was under this doctor's care for about a year. I kept on going to work whenever I could, but the spells continued right along, at home in the night, or at work in the daytime. After a year of treatment I felt no better.

"I decided to try another nerve specialist,—his diagnosis was depletion of the nerves. He advised me to come in a couple of times a week for electric treatment. I followed instructions for a couple of months, but the spells continued just the same. One April day there was an electric storm. The lightning caused in me a great dread and fear. The wind broke some of the windows in our house. I had then the worst spell. I lost consciousness. When I awoke I was worse than ever. I was just choked up with fear of everything and everybody.

"I found I could no longer live in ('., for the last bit of life was ebbing right out of me. I started on the train for Los Angeles. No one can realize the suffering I had to endure on my trip out West. Everybody on the train talked about accidents, wrecks, and robberies. After arriving in Los Angeles I felt somewhat relieved, but the spells kept on just the same. I consulted a great nerve specialist in Los Angeles. He claimed I had neurasthenia, and that I was much run down. His method of therapy was different from the rest. He suggested renting a cottage along the oceanfront, and he would furnish a trainer whose wife was to take care of the cottage. The trainer was supposed to have some knowledge of physical culture and massage. After being in this camp for three months I saw no improvement in my condition.

"I went to another doctor who employed a different method. He would inject pig serum into my arm three times a week. After a thorough trial I found no relief. I then decided to try Christian Science for a while, but I had no relief from all my woe and misery. (When asked why he went to Christian Science while he was of Jewish faith, he replied that he was in such a state of fear that had he been ordered to be a cockroach he would have tried to become one).

"I tried another nerve doctor. After a while it was the same old story. I then tried a chiropractor. After three months' trial I found out that I had to give it up, because the manipulator aggravated my condition. Towards the end I felt such pains in my back and spine that I was compelled to lie in bed for a week before I could recover enough strength to sit up. I then tried Osteopathy. I felt no better, so I had to abandon that.

"In search for health I could not stop here, so I went to another nerve specialist who after examination claimed to have discovered something different from any other physician. He discovered I had a pair of tonsils in my mouth which did not look well to him. He ordered them removed; that meant an operation under an anesthetic. Can you imagine my feeling when he told me the news? I had a terrible time in making up my mind what to do. Bad as I felt I made up my mind that I might as well die under ether as in any other way. I consented to the operation. It is needless to go into details here of what took place after the operation. Words cannot express it. All the tortures of hell would have been paradise towards what I went through after this operation.

"I have been going since from physician to physician, each one claiming that I haven't been to the right one, and that he was the proper physician who understood my case and could cure me. No one has been able to effect a cure.

As an example of the patient's state of extreme fear the following instance may be given. One day he came to me, a picture of misery and depression. He told me he had suffered agonies for the last couple of days, on account of an "ingrowing hair.'* It turned out that the patient overheard a conversation among his gossips, that some one died of an "ingroAving hair." This news strongly impressed him, and aroused his fear instinct, since he discovered an "ingrowing hair" on his throat. I found his throat was wrapped around with cotton, and covered with adhesive plaster. On unwrapping the mess I found just an ordinary little pimple. I threw away the wrappings, and gave the patient a scolding, and ridiculed him for his silliness. He felt as he said in "paradise." A competent observer will find this trait of trivial fears, characteristic, in various degrees, of every psychopathic patient.

By a series of trance states the patient was freed from his psycholeptic fear attacks; he is now in good health, and attending successfully to his business.

CHAPTER XXI
FEAR TRANCE APPARITIONS

The following study of a psychopathic case brings out the character of the fear trance dream.

Mrs. A. is twenty-two years old; Russian; married. She suffers periodically from attacks of violent headaches, lasting several days. Family history is good. The patient was brought up in the fear of ghosts, evil spirits, magical influences, and diabolical agencies. Mrs. A. is easily frightened, and has suffered from headaches and pressure on the head for quite a long time, but the pain became exacerbated some five years ago. The attack is sudden, without any premonitor}' feelings, and lasts from eight hours to two days. The headache often sets in at night, when she is asleep, and she wakes up with frightful pain.

At the time of the first attack she was much run down. Otherwise the patient is in good condition, but complains that her memory is getting bad. Patellar reflex is exaggerated. Field of vision is normal. The eyes show slight strabismus and astigmatism, corrected by glasses which did not in the least

diminish the intensity as well as the frequency of the headaches.

Mrs. A. suffers from bad dreams and distressing nightmares, the content of which she cannot recall in her waking state. She also often has hallucinations, visions of two women wrapped in white, pointing their fingers at her and running after her. She never had any fall, nor any special worry or anxiety, never suffered from an} 7 infectious diseases.

After a persistent inquiry, however, she gave an account of an accident she met with when a child of eight. Opposite her house there lived an insane woman of whom she was mortally afraid. Once when the parents happened to be away, the insane woman entered the house, caught the child, and greatly frightened her. Another time she was sent out by her parents to buy something in a grocery store. It was night and very dark. She bought the things and on the way back she saw two women in white with hands stretched out running after her. She screamed from great fright and ran home.

Mrs. A. is afraid to remain alone, and especially in the dark. She is not so much afraid in the street as in the house. The two women appear to her now and then, and she is mortally afraid of them. The patient was put into hypnotic state. There was marked catalepsy; the eyes were firmly closed, and she could not open them when challenged. Suggestion of general well-being was given and she was awakened. On awakening, she could not remember what had taken place in the hypnotic state.

Next day she was again put into hypnosis and went into a deeper state than the day before. She was asked whether she thought of the crazy woman occasionally, she replied in the negative. The patient spoke in a low, suppressed voice, the words coming out slowly, as if with effort and with fear. It was then insisted that she should tell one of her recent dreams. After some pause, she said: "Last night I had a bad dream; I dreamt that I stood near a window and a cat came up to the same window. I saw it was crazy. I ran away, the cat ran after me and scratched me. Then I knew that I was crazy. My friends said there was no help for me.

"I dropped the baby, ran, and jumped down stairs. I remember now that when I fell asleep I saw a woman, maybe the crazy woman. I covered myself ; I knew I was only afraid, and that she was not real. Six weeks ago I saw the same woman, when falling asleep or when asleep. I ran away, and she ran after me."

Mrs. A. in relating these dreams, shivered all over and was afraid, as if actually living the dream experience over again. "It was this woman who caught me in her arms, kissed me, and embraced me, and did not let me go, until my screams brought friends and my father; they took me away from her by force."

Gradually some more dreams emerged. "I dreamt some time ago that the woman came to me and spilled hot water on me. Another time I dreamed that I was in the insane asylum; she came out, told me she was well; I was greatly frightened and ran away."

Mrs. A. then became quiet. After a while she began to relate a series of dreams. Some time ago she dreamed that the woman entered the room where her father was and ran up to him, evidently with the intention of hurting him. Her father ran away, and she hid herself in a closet in the next room. "I also dreamt that the woman was shadowing me in an alley. She wanted to get hold of me, while I was trying to get away from her. I turned round, and she gave me such a fierce look. I ran and she could not catch me. I should die, if she catches me. In one of my dreams about her, I saw people putting cold water on her, and I could hear her scream. It was awful. I dreamt I went upstairs, opened the door and met her. I was badly frightened. I jumped out of the window."

This is an extract from a letter sent to me by the patient's husband: "... She had another attack. It did not last long, and it was not severe. She dreamt several times a week. I shall try to relate them as accurately as possible. She dreamt that I left the room for a while. Our baby was asleep in the next room. All of a sudden she heard baby cry out: 'Mamma, I am afraid.' She told the baby to come to her as she herself was afraid to leave the bed. Baby came to her. The child looked frightened, her face pale with fear, exclaiming 'Mamma, a devil.' As the child cried out, my wife heard a noise in the room, something moved close by. She became scared. It seemed to her that something terrible and unknown was after her. She wanted to scream for help, but could not. A hand was stretched out after her to catch her. She woke up in great terror. Another time she dreamt that she was in a hallway. She saw a woman and became frightened. It was the same crazy woman. My wife is exceedingly nervous, and is in fear that something awful is going to happen to her or to the family."

A rich, subconscious dream-life of agonizing fears was thus revealed, a life of terrors of which the patient was unaware in her waking state. The dreams referred to the same central nucleus, the shock and fears of her early childhood. Worries about self and family kept up and intensified the present fear states.

Her selfishness has no bounds, her fears have no limits. The symptoms of the "fear set," as in all other psychopathic cases, took their origin in the impulse of self-preservation with its accompanying fundamental fear instinct.

This patient was cured after a long course of hypnotic treatment.

CHAPTER XXII
RECURRENT FEAR STATES—PSY-CHOLEPSY

There are cases in which the nature of the psychopathic states stands out more clearly and distinctly than in others. They occur periodically, appearing like epileptic states, in a sort of an explosive form, so that some authorities have mistaken them for epilepsy, and termed them psychic epilepsy. My researches have shown them to be recurrent explosions of subconscious states, which I termed psycholepsy. They really do not differ from general psychopathic states, but they may be regarded as classic pseudo-epileptic, or psycholeptic states; they are classic fear-states — states of panic.

M. L. is nineteen years of age, of a rather limited intelligence. He works as a shopboy amidst surroundings of poverty, and leads a hard life, full of privations. He is undersized and underfed, and looks as if he has never had enough to eat. Born in New York, of parents belonging to the lowest social stratum, he was treated with severity and even brutality. The patient has never been to any elementary school and can neither read nor write. His

mathematical knowledge did not extend beyond hundreds ; he can hardly accomplish a simple addition and subtraction, and has no idea of the multiplication table. The names of the President and a few Tammany politicians constitute all his knowledge of the history of the United States. Family history is not known; his parents died when the patient was very young, and he was left without kith and kin, so that no data could be obtained.

Physical examination is negative. Field of vision is normal. There are no sensory disturbances. The process of perception is normal, and so also is recognition. Memory for past and present events is good. His power of reasoning is quite limited, and the whole of his mental life is undeveloped, embryonic. His sleep is sound; dreams little. Digestion is excellent; he can digest anything in the way of eatables. He is of an easy-going, gay disposition, a New York "street-Arab."

The patient complains of "shaking spells." The attack sets in with tremor of all the extremities, and then spreads to the whole body. The tremor becomes general, and the patient is seized by a convulsion of shivering, trembling, and chattering of teeth. Sometimes he falls down, shivering, trembling, and shaking all over, in an intense state of fear, a state of panic. The seizure seems to be epileptiform, only it lasts sometimes for more than three hours. The attack may come anytime during the day, but is more frequent at night.

During the attack the patient does not lose consciousness ; he knows everything that is taking place around him, can feel everything pretty well; his teeth chatter violently, he trembles and shivers all over, and is unable to do anything. The fear instinct has complete possession of him. He is in agony of terror. There is also a feeling of chilliness, as if he is possessed by an attack of "fear ague." The seizure does not start with any numbness of the extremities, nor is there any anaesthesia or paraesthesia during the whole course of the attack. With the exception of the shivers and chills the patient claims he feels "all right."

The patient was put into a condition close to the hypnotic state. There was some catalepsy of a transient character, but no suggestibility of the hypnotic type. In this state it came to light that the patient "many years ago" was forced to sleep in a dark, damp cellar where it was bitter cold. The few nights passed in that dark, cold cellar he had to leave his bed, and shaking, trembling, and shivering with cold and fear he had to go about his work in expectation of a severe punishment in case of non-performance of his duties.

While in the intermediary, subwaking, hypnoidal state, the patient was told to think of that dark, damp, cold cellar. Suddenly the attack set in,—the patient began to shake, shiver, and tremble all over, his teeth chattering as if suffering from intense fear. The attack was thus reproduced in the hypnoidal state. "This is the way I have been," he said. During this attack no numbness, no sensory disturbance, was present. The patient was quieted, and after a little while the attack of shivering and fear disappeared.

The room in which the patient was put into the subconscious state was quite dark, and accidentally the remark was dropped that the room was too dark to see anything; immediately the attack reappeared in all its violence. It was found later that it was sufficient to mention the words, "dark, damp, and cold" to bring on an attack even in the fully waking state. We could thus reproduce the attacks at will,—those magic words had the power to release the pent-up subconscious forces and throw the patient into convulsions of shakings and shiverings, with chattering of the teeth and intense fear.

Thus the apparent epileptiform seizures, the insistent psychomotor states of seemingly unaccountable origin, were traced to subconscious fear obsessions. The following case is of similar nature. The study clearly shows the subconscious nature of such psycholeptic attacks Mr. M., aged twenty-one years, was born in Russia, and came to this country four years previously. His family history, as far as can be ascertained, is good. There is no nervous trouble of any sort in the immediate or remote members of his family.

The patient himself has always enjoyed good health. He is a young man of good habits. He was referred to me for epileptiform attacks and anaesthesia of the right half of his body. The attack is preceded by an aura consisting of headache and a general feeling of malaise. The aura lasts a few days and terminates in the attack which sets in about midnight, when the 'patient is fully awake. The attack consists of a series of spasms, rhythmic in character, and lasting about one or two minutes. After an interval of not more than thirty seconds the spasms set in again.

This condition continues uninterruptedly for a period of five or six days (a sort of status epilepticus), persisting during the time the patient is awake, and ceasing only during the short intervals, or rather moments, of sleep. Throughout the whole period of the attacks the patient is troubled with insomnia. He sleeps restlessly for only ten or fifteen minutes at a time. On one occasion he was observed to be in a state of delirium as found in post-epileptic insanity and the so-called Dammerzustande of epilepsy. This delirium was observed but once in the course of five years.

The regular attack is not accompanied by any delirious states or Dammerzustande. On the contrary, during the whole course of the attack the patient's mind remains perfectly clear.

During the period of the attack the whole right side becomes anaesthetic to all forms of sensations, kinaesthesis includcd, so that he is not even aware of the spasms unless he actually observes the affected limbs. The affected limbs, previously normal, also become paretic. After the attack has subsided, the paresis and anaesthesia persist (as sometimes happens in true idiopathic epilepsy) for a few days, after which the patient's condition remains normal until the next attack. After his last attack, however, the anaesthesia and paresis continued for about three weeks.

He has had every year one attack which, curiously, sets in about the same time, namely, about the month of January or February. The attacks have of late increased in frequency, so that the patient has had four, at intervals of about three or four months. On different occasions he was in the Boston City Hospital for the attacks. There was a profound right hcmianaesthesia including the right half of the tongue, with a marked hypoaesthesia of the right side of the pharynx. All the senses of the right side were involved. The field of vision of the right eye was much limited. The ticking of a watch could not be heard more than three inches away from the right ear. Taste and smell were likewise involved on the right side. The muscular and kinaesthetic sensations on the right side were much impaired.

The patient's mental condition was good. He states that he has few dreams and these are insignificant, concerned as they are with the ordinary matters of daily life. Occasionally he dreams that he is falling, but there is no definite content to the dream. These findings were indicative of functional rather than organic disease. The previous history of the case was significant. The first attack came on after peculiar circumstances, when the patient was sixteen years of age and living in Russia. After returning from a ball one night, he was sent back to look for a ring which the lady, whom he escorted, had lost on the way. It was after midnight, and his way lay on a lonely road which led by a cemetery. When near the cemetery he was suddenly overcome by a great fright, thinking that somebody was running after him. He fell, struck his right side, and lost consciousness. The patient did not remember this last event. It was told by him when in a hypnotic state.

The patient was a Polish Jew, densely ignorant, terrorized by superstitious fears of evil powers working in the dead of night. By the time he was brought home he regained consciousness, but there existed a spasmodic shaking of the right side, involving the arm, leg, and head. The spasm persisted for one week. During this time he could not voluntarily move his right arm or leg, and the right half of his body felt numb. There was also apparently a loss of muscular sense, for he stated that he was unaware of the shaking of his arm or leg, unless he looked and saw the movements. In other words, there was right hemiplegia, anaesthesia, and spasms.

For one week after the cessation of the spasms his right arm and leg remained weak, but he was soon able to resume his work, and he felt as well as ever. Since then every year, as already stated, about the same month the patient has an attack similar in every respect to the original attack, with the only exception that there is no loss of consciousness. Otherwise the subsequent yearly attacks are photographic pictures, close repetitions, recurrences of the original attack.

A series of experiments accordingly was undertaken. First, as to the anaesthesia. If the anaesthesia were functional, sensory impressions ought to be felt, even though the patient was unconscious of them, and we ought to be able to get sensory reactions. Experiments made to determine the nature of the anaesthesia produced interesting results. These experiments show that the anaesthesia is not a true one, but that impressions from the anaesthetic parts which seem not to be felt are really perceived subconsciously.

Different tests showed that the subconscious reactions to impressions from the anaesthetic hand were more delicately plastic and responsive than the conscious reactions to impressions from the normal hand. We have the so-called "psychopathic paradox" that functional anaesthesia is a subconscious hyperesthesia.

It is evident then that there could be no inhibition of the sensory centres, or suppression of their activity, or whatever else it may be called. In spite of the apparent, profound anaesthesia, the pin pricks were felt and perceived. Stimulations gave rise to perception, cognition, to a sort of pseudo-hallucinations that showed the pin pricks were counted and localized in the hand. The results of these tests demonstrate that in psychopathic patients all sensory impressions received from anaesthetic parts, while they do not reach the personal consciousness are perceived subconsciously.

Inasmuch as the sensations are perceived, the failure of the subject to be conscious of them must be due to a failure in association. The perception of the sensation is dissociated from the personal consciousness. More than this, these dissociated sensations are capable of a certain amount of independent functioning; hence the pseudo-hallucinations, and hence the failure of psychopathic patients to be incommoded by their anaesthesia. This condition of dissociation underlies psychopathic states.

For the purpose of studying the attacks, the patient was hypnotized. He went into a deep somnambulic condition, in which, however, the anaesthesia still persisted. This showed that the dissociation of the sensory impressions was unchanged. In hypnosis he related again the history of the onset of the trouble. His memory became broader, and he was able to give the additional information, which he could not do in his waking state, that at the time he was badly frightened, he fell on his right side. Moreover, he recalled what he did not remember when awake, that throughout the period of his attacks when he fell asleep, he had vivid dreams of an intense hallucinatory character, all relating to terror and fall.

In these dreams he lived over and over again the experience which was the beginning of his trouble. He again finds himself in his little native town, on a lonely road; he thinks someone is running after him; he becomes frightened, calls for help, falls, and then wakes up with a start, and the whole dream is forgotten. After he wakes he knows nothing of all this; there is no more fear or any emotional disturbance; he is then simply distressed hy the spasms.

While testing the anaesthesia during hypnosis, an attack developed, his right arm and leg began to shake, first mildly and then with increasing intensity and frequency. His head also spasmodically turned to the right side. The movements soon became rhythmic. Arm and leg were abducted and adducted in a slow rhythmic way at the rate of about thirty-six times per minute. With the same rate and rhythm, the head turned to the right side, with chin pointing upward. The right side of the face was distorted by spasm, as if in great pain. The left side of the face was unaffected. Pressure over his right side (where he struck when he fell) elicited evidences of great pain. Respiration became deep and labored, and was synchronous with each spasm. The whole symptom-complex simulated Jacksonian epilepsy.

Consciousness persisted unimpaired, but showed a curious and unexpected alteration. When asked what was the matter, he replied in his native dialect, "I do not understand what you say.' It was found that he had lost all understanding of English, so that it was necessary to speak to him in his native dialect. His answers to our questions made it apparent that during the attack, as in his dreams, he was living through the experience which had originally excited his trouble.

The attack was hypnoidic, a fear attack, hallucinatory in character. He said that he was sixteen years old, that he was in Rovno (Russia), that he had just fallen, because he was frightened, that he was lying on the roadside near the cemetery, which in the popular superstitious fear is inhabited by ghosts. At that hour of the night the dead arise from their graves and attack the living who happen to be near.

The hypnoidic state developed further, the patient living through, as in a dream, the whole experience that had taken place at that period. He was in a carriage, though he did not know who put him there. Then in a few moments he was again home, in his house, with his parents attending on him as in the onset of his first epileptiform seizures. The attack terminated at this point, and thereupon he became perfectly passive, and when spoken to answered again in English. Now he was again twenty-one years old, was conscious of where he was, and was in absolute ignorance of what had just taken place.

It was found that an attack could regularly and artificially be induced, if the patient in hypnosis was taken back by suggestion to the period when the accident happened. The experimenter was now taking him back to a period antedating the first attack. He was told that he was fifteen years old, that is, a year before the accident occurred. He could no longer speak or understand English, he was again in Rovno, engaged as a salesman in a little store, had never been in America, and did not know who we were. Testing sensation, it was found that it had spontaneously returned to the hand. There was not a trace of the anaesthesia left. The hands which did not feel deep pin pricks before now reacted to the slightest stimulation. Spontaneous synthesis of the dissociated sensory impressions had occurred. Just as formerly before the accident, sensation was in normal association with the rest of his mental processes, so now this association was re-established with the memories of that period to winch the patient was artificially reduced.

The patient was now (while still believing himself to be fifteen years old) taken a year forward to the day on which the accident occurred. He says he is going to the ball tonight. He is now at the ball; he returned home; he is sent back to look for a ring. Like a magic formula, it calls forth an attack in which again he lives through the accident,—the terror and the spasms. It was thus possible to reproduce an attack at any time with clock-like precision by taking him back to the period of the accident, and reproducing all its details in a hypnoidic state. Each time the fear and the physical manifestations of the attack (spasms, paresis, and anaesthesia) developed. These induced attacks were identical with the spontaneous attacks, one of which we had occasion to observe later.

At periodic intervals, as under the stress of fear, the dormant activity is awakened and, though still unknown to the patient, gives rise to the same sensorimotor disturbances which characterized the original experience. These subconscious dissociated states are so much more intense in their manifestations by the very fact of their dissociation from the inhibitory influences of the normal mental life. The psychognosis of such cases reveals on the one hand a dissociation of mental processes, and on the other hand an independent and automatic activity of subconscious psychic states, under the disaggregating, paralyzing influence of the fear instinct.

A patient under my treatment for four months during the year of 1922 presents interesting traits. I regard the case as classic as far as the fundamental factors of neurosis are concerned. Patient, male, age 32, married, has two children. He lives in an atmosphere of fear and apprehension about himself. He comes from a large, but healthy family. The patient is of a rather cowardly disposition especially in regard to his health. He worked hard in a store during the day, and led a life of dissipation at night. One day, after a night of unusual dissipation, or orgy, when on his way to his work, he felt weak, he was dizzy, he became frightened about himself; he thought he had an attack of apoplexy, and that he was going to die. His heart was affected, it began to beat violently, and he trembled and shivered in an "ague" of intense fear. The palpitation of the heart was so great, the trembling was so violent, and the terror was so overwhelming that he collapsed in a heap. He was taken to his father's store in a state of "fainting spell." A physician was called in who treated the patient for an attack of acute indigestion.

For a short time he felt better, but the attacks of terror, trembling, shivering, weakness, pallor, fainting, palpitation of the heart and general collapse kept on recurring. He then began to suffer from insomnia, from fatigue, and is specially obsessed by fear fatigue. He is in terror over the fact that his energy is exhausted; physical, mental, nervous, sexual impotence. This was largely developed by physicians who treated him for epilepsy, putting him on a bromide treatment; others treated and diagnosed the case as cardiac affection, kidney trouble, dementia praecox, and one physician operated on the poor fellow for tonsillitis. The patient was terrorized. He was on a diet for toxaemia, he was starved. He took all sorts of medicine for his insomnia.

The patient became a chronic invalid for ten years. He was in terror, scared with the horrors of sleepless nights. He has been to neurologists, to psychoanalysts, and he tried Christian Science, New Thought, Naturopathy, and Osteopathy, but of no avail. The condition persisted. The attacks came on from time to time like thunderstorms. There were trembling, shivering, chattering of teeth, palpitation of the heart, weakness, fainting, and overwhelming, uncontrollable terror.

The first time I tried to put the patient into a hypnoidal state was nine at night. I put out the electric light, lighted a candle, and proceeded to put him into a hypnoidal condition. The patient began to shiver, to tremble, to breathe fast and heavily, the pulse rose to over 125, while the heart began to thump violently, as if it were going to jump out. He was like one paralyzed, the muscles of the chest labored hard, and under my pressure the muscle fibers hardened, crackled, became rigid, and he could not reply when spoken to. It took me some time to quieten him. He was clearly in a state of great panic. I opened his eyelids and found the eyeball turned up. The whole body was easily put in a state of catalepsy. Clearly the patient was not in a hypnoidal state, he was in a state of hypnosis.

Night after night he fell into states of hypnosis
with all the symptoms of intense fear attacks. When
the fear attacks subsided the depths of the hypnotic
state proportionately diminished.

In my various clinical and laboratory experimental work, covering a period of a quarter of a century, I have gradually come to the conclusion that fear and hypnosis are interrelated. In fact I am disposed to think that the hypnotic state is an ancient state, a state of fear cataplexy, or rather trance obedience. While the hypnoidal state is a primitive sleep state, the hypnotic condition is a primitive, fear condition, still present in lowly formed organisms.

After some time the general fear instinct becomes alleviated. The patient goes by habit into a trance hypnotic state under the influence of the hypnotizer in whom he gains more confidence. The patient gets into a state of trance obedience to the hypnotizer of whom he is in awe, and who can control the patient's fear instinct.

Man obeys the commands, "the suggestions" of the hypnotizer, of the master whom he subconsciously fears, and who inspires him with awe, with "confidence-fear". The crowd, the community, "public opinion," the mob, the leader, the priest, the magician, the medicine man, are just such forces, such authorities to procure the slavish obedience of the subconscious described as hypnosis. Soldiers and slaves fall most easily into such states.

Man has been trained in fear for milleniums, in fear of society, custom, fashion, belief, and the authority of crowd and mob. He fears to stand alone, he must go with the crowd. Man is a social being, a hypnotized, somnambulic creature. He walks and acts like a hypnotized slave. Man is a social somnambulist who believes, dreams, and acts at the order of the mob or of its leader. Man belongs to those somnambulists who become artificial, suggested, automatic personalities with their eyes fully open, seeing and observing nothing but what is suggested to them.

The hypnoidic states, observed and described by me in the classical Hanna case, belong to the same category. The hypnoidic states are essentially fear cataleptic states of a vivid character, closely related to hypnotic conditions of primitive life.

CHAPTER XXIII
APHONIA, STAMMERING, AND CATALEPSY

S. R. Age 25. Russian Jewess ; married ; has four children. Patient was brought to me in a state of helplessness. She could not walk, and was unable to utter a word. When spoken to she replied in gestures. When challenged to walk, she made unsuccessful attempts. The step was awkward, the gait reeling, the body finally collapsing in a heap on the floor. When I shut her eyelids, the eyeballs began to roll upwards, the lids soon became cataleptic, and the patient was unable to open them. When I insisted that she should open the lids, she strained hard,—the muscles of the upper part of the body became painfully tense,—wrinkled her forehead, and contorted violently her face. After long insistence on her replying to my questions, and after long vain efforts to comply with my request, she at last succeeded in replying in a barety audible voice. When whispering she kept on making incoordinate movements with jaws and lips, began to shut her eyelids, rolled up the eye-balls, forced the tongue against the teeth, stammered badly on consonants, uttering them with great difficulty after long hesitation, the sound finally coming out with explosive force.

I insisted that she must stand up, she raised herself slowly and with effort, took a couple of steps, and sat down at once on the chair. During the period of effort there was marked tremor in her left arm. When she sat down, she threw her head backward, rolled up her eyeballs, and began gradually to close her eyelids. She remained in this position for a couple of minutes, and then began spasmodically to open and shut the eyelids. When taken to her room, the patient walked up, though with some difficulty, three flights of stairs without the nurse's support.

The patient was greatly emaciated,—she lived in extreme poverty. She was married five years, and had given birth to four children. Patient was suffering from severe headaches which set in soon after the birth of the second child. At first the headaches came at intervals of a few weeks, and lasted about a day, then with the birth of the other children the headaches grew more severe and more frequent, and finally became continuous. From time to time the attacks were specially exacerbated in violence, she then complained of violent pains in the head, excruciating agony toward the vertex. The face was deadly pale, the hands and feet were ice-cold, the pulse weak and sluggish. During the attack the head had to be raised, since in an} r other position the pain was unbearable. The pain was originally unilateral, starting on the left side of the head. Of late the pain spread from left to right. The whole head felt sore, like a boil, the scalp was highly sensitive. The intense attacks, sweeping over the patient unawares, were accompanied by twitchings of the eyelids, rolling of the eyeballs, dizziness, sparks before the eyes, pains in the left side of the chest, and by numbness and hypoaesthesia of the face, arms and legs. The patellar reflex was markedly exaggerated, no clonus was present; the pupils reacted well to light and accommodation.

The patient was admitted to a local hospital, and was allowed to nurse her one year old baby. Three days after admission, while nursing her baby, she was seized with a violent attack of headache and pain in the left side. The arms felt numb and "gone." The patient was seized with a panic that the child might fall; hugging the baby to her left breast she screamed for help in agony and terror. Immediately following this seizure the patient lost her voice, speech, and power of walking.

After staying in the hospital for two weeks, the patient was put under my care. The patient was an extremely timid creature. She lived in Russia in a small town where the religious persecutions of the neighbors were persistent and unremittent. To this were joined the petty annoyances by the village police, the representatives of which acted with all the cruel tyranny characteristic of the old Russian regime. The patient's family was in constant terror. In childhood the patient has undergone all the horrors of the pogromi with all the terrors of inquisitorial tortures. A highly sensitized impulse of self-preservation and intense easily stimulated fear instinct were the essence of the patient's life. She was afraid of everything, of her very shadow, of anything strange, more so in the dark, and at night. With this morbid self-preservation and intensified fear instinct there were associated superstitions to which her mind was exposed in early childhood, and in her later life. The patient lived at home in the fear of the most savage superstitions and prejudices, characteristic of the poor ignorant classes of Eastern European countries, and outside the house she was in fear of her life. The patient was brought up on fear and nourished on fear. No wonder when she was run down, and met with a fear shock, that the fear instinct seized on her and gave rise to the symptoms of physical and mental paralysis.

To this life of terror we may add the extreme poverty in which the patient lived in Russia and afterwards in this country. The hard work in a sweat-shop and the ill nutrition ran down the patient and further predisposed her to disability and disease. Patient lived in constant dread of actual starvation, with fear of having no shelter, with fear of no roof over her head. She was so timid that she was scared by any sudden movement, or by a severe, harsh, threatening voice. She was extremely suggestible, imitative, and credulous. She was like a haunted animal, like a scared bird in the claws of a cat. Fear often threw her into a state of rigidity.

The patient suffered from a fear of fatigue, from fear of exhaustion, from fear of disability, from fear of paralysis, pain, sickness, and death, fear of the negative aspect of the most primitive, and most fundamental of all impulses, the impulse of self-preservation. The fear psychosis, based on an abnormally developed fear instinct which formed the main structure of her symptom complex, had a real foundation in the psycho-physiological condition of her organism. The patient actually suffered from fatigue due to exhaustion, underfeeding, and overworking.

Married at the age of twenty, she bore four children in succession. This was a drain on the poor woman, and further weakened her feeble constitution. Her husband was a poor tailor working in a sweatshop, making but a few dollars a week. The family was practically kept in a state of chronic starvation. The wolf was hardly kept away from the door. The family was in constant dread of "slack time" with its loss of employment and consequent privations and suffering.

The husband was a hard worker, did not drink, but the long hours of work, the low wages, the poor nutrition, the vicious air, and the no less vicious environment, cheerless and monotonous, sometimes gave rise to moods, discontent, anger, and quarrels, of which the patient with her timidity stood in utter terror.

The patient's dream life was strongly colored by a general underlying mood of apprehension. The fear instinct of self-preservation formed the soil of the whole emotional tone of the psychosis, waking, subwaking, dreaming, conscious, and subconscious. Again and again did the nurses and attendants report to me that, although the patient was aphonic and it was hard to elicit from her a sound, in her sleep she quite often cried out, sometimes using phrases and words which were hard to comprehend, because they were indistinct, and because the}' were sometimes in her native language. When awakened immediately, it was sometimes possible to elicit from her shreds of dreams in regard to scares and frights about herself, about her children, about her husband, relatives, and friends. When she came under my care the patient often used to wake up in the morning in a state of depression due to some horrible hallucinatory dreams in which she lived over again in a distorted form, due to incoordination of content and to lack of active, guiding attention, dreams in which the dreadful experience of her miserable life kept on recurring under various forms of fragmentary association and vague synthesis, brought about by accidental, external and internal stimulations.

The patient was taken to her room in the evening, and put to bed. During the night she was somewhat restless, kept on waking up, but on the whole, according to the nurse's account, she slept quite well. In the morning the patient had a hearty breakfast, and felt better than the day before when she was brought to me. The voice improved somewhat in strength and volume. During the day she rested, felt well, and enjoyed her meals. Speech was still in a whisper barely audible, but there was no stammering, no muscular incoordination, no twitchings of the face. About four in the afternoon patient sat up in bed, her voice became somewhat stronger, though speech was still in a whisper. This improvement lasted but a few minutes. When her arms were raised, the left hand manifested considerable tremor and weakness as compared with the right arm. After having made a few remarks which apparently cost her considerable effort, she had a relapse, she again lost her voice, and was unable to whisper. I insisted that she should reply to my questions; she had to make a great effort, straining her muscles and bringing them into a state of convulsive incoordination before she could bring out a few sounds in reply. A little later, about ten or fifteen minutes after I left the room, the nurse came in and quietly asked her a question, the patient answered in a whisper, with little strain and difficulty. An hour later the patient regained her speech for a short period of a few minutes. These changes went on during the patient's waking period. Once towards evening the patient regained her voice and speech to such an extent that she could talk with no difficulty and little impediment; the voice was so resonant and strong that it could be heard in the hall adjoining the room. This however lasted but a few moments.

After having had a good night's sleep the patient woke up in good condition; appetite was good. Voice was clear, though low. She was in a state of lassitude and relaxation. I attempted to examine her and kept testing her condition, physical and mental. I was anxious to make a prognosis of the patient's case. The tests and the questions strained her nervous system by requiring to hold her attention, and by keeping her in a state of nervous and mental agitation. She looked scared, anxious,—the scared, haunted look in her face reappeared. The patient was no more than about twenty to twenty-five minutes under experimentation when a severe headache of the vertex and of the left side of the head set in. The eyeballs began to roll up, eyelids were half closed; lids and eyeballs were quivering and twitching. The hands were relaxed and looked paralyzed. When raised they fell down by her side in an almost lifeless condition. There was marked hypoaesthesia to pain and heat sensations. The anaesthesia was more marked on the left than on the right side. The left arm when raised and kept for a few seconds showed marked tremor as compared with the right arm. This is to be explained by the fact that the exacerbations oi* the headache, of pain, and the general cataleptic seizures set in usually during or after the nursing periods. The infant while nursing was kept by the mother on the left arm, the left side thus bearing the pressure, weight, and strain, —it was with the left side that fear became mainly associated.

During the height of the attack the patient was quietened, her fears allayed, and a five-grain tablet of phenacetine was given her with the authoritative remark that the drug was sure to help her. As soon as she swallowed the tablet the patient opened her eyes, and said she felt better. About an hour later, when another attempt at an examination was made, patient had an attack of headache, cried, said she was afraid, but she answered in a whisper when spoken to. She talked slowly, in a sort of staccato way. I insisted that she should talk a little faster and pronounce the words distinctly. She made violent attempts to carry out my command, but. got scared, began to hesitate, and stammer, her voice and speech rapidly deteriorating with her efforts, ending in complete mutism.

During the day I tried from time to time to keep up the experiment of insisting that the patient should speak, and every time with the same result of bringing about an attack. The patient began to stammer and stutter, becoming more and more frightened the more the nurse and myself insisted that she should make an effort and reply to our questions. Still, When the patient's attention became distracted, when she was handled gently, when her fears were allayed, the speech and sound improved in quality and in loudness, and at times her sentences were quite fluent, her enunciation quite distinct.

This state of instability lasted for several days until the patient became somewhat familiar with the surroundings. In one of her better moments the patient told me that she thought her stammering began with a definite event. One evening when she was fatigued with the labors of the day for her family, a stammerer came in to see her. The stammering made a strong impression on her. She felt the strain of the stammerer; she could not control the sympathy and the strain, and involuntarily began to imitate stammering. She began to fear that she might continue to stammer and be unable to enunciate sounds and words. The more she feared the harder it was for her to speak or even to use her voice.

A few days later the patient began to improve, she began to adapt herself to her surroundings, and did not get so easily scared. About eight days after the first examination the patient woke up one morning in a state of depression; she cried a good deal. She did not sleep well the night before, dreamt and worried on account of her children. She was afraid that something might have happened to them in her absence, perhaps they were sick, perhaps the husband could not take good care of them. She talked in a whisper, her eyes were shut. When I insisted on opening the eyelids, she opened them, but did it with difficulty. I put her into a hypnotic state. In about a minute her eyes rolled up, and the eyelids shut spasmodically. There was present a slight degree of catalepsy. Mutism was strongly marked. Upon sudden and unexpected application of an electric current, the patient opened her eyes, cried out, but soon relapsed into a state of lethargy. Gradually patient was brought out of the lethargic state.

A couple of hours later, after she had a good rest a few more experiments as to her sensorimotor life were attempted. I asked her to raise objects, tested her sensitivity to various stimulations, her concentration of attention, asked her questions about her life, about her family, took again her field of vision. All that was a great effort to her. While I was taking her field of vision the patient's eyes began to close, and it took about twenty seconds before she could open them. She opened them with effort, but shut them again. This time it took her about 45 seconds before she could open the lids. Fatigue, or rather fear fatigue, set in sooner with each repetition of experiment and test, and lasted a longer time.

For several days the patient kept on improving slowly. She then had another relapse. She slept well the night before, but woke up early about six in the morning; she began to worry about her family, and complained of headache. About half past eight the headache became severe, there was again pain in the left side, the left hand began to tremble, and felt anaesthetic, the eyelids closed, and could not open, aphonia returned, in fact she fell into a state of mutism. About ten o'clock patient opened her e}'es, but she was unable to talk. After long insistence on her reply to my question as to how she was, she finally replied in a whisper: "Well," then added "I have a bad headache." She had great difficulty in replying to my questions, moved her jaws impotently before she was able to emit a sound, her muscles were strained, the face was set, tense, and drawn, the brow was corrugated, the eyeballs rolled up, and the eyelids shut tightly. The patient was unable to raise her hands, they lay powerless at her side. When raised the arms were found to be lethargic, fell to her side, only the left hand manifested light, fibrillary twitchings and a gross tremor. When insisted upon that she must raise her arms, she became agitated, scared, began to moan and cry. Claimed severe pain in head, in chest, in heart. "Pain in heart, in head, I am afraid," she moaned in a whisper. There was loss of kin-aesthetic sensibility, patient complained that she did not feel her arms, "they are not mine. She had to look at the arm in order to find it. There was also present anaesthsia to other sensations such as pain, touch, heat, and cold. After a couple of hours' rest the sensibility returned. The sensibility was affected more on the left side than on the right, and also returned earlier on the right side.

When the fatigue and the scare subsided the patient was tested again. This time the reactions to sensory stimulations were normal. The patient was touched, pinched, and pricked, she reacted to each stimulus separately, and was able to synthesize them and give a full account of their number. Kinaesthetic sensibility was good,—she was fully able to appreciate the various movements and positions in which her limbs and fingers were put. The patient was left to rest, quietened, treated carefully, avoiding sudden stimulations, allaying her fears and suspiciousness of danger, lurking in the background of her mind. After a few hours she sat up, made an attempt to raise herself from bed, got up with some effort, and sat down in an easy rocking chair next to her. Her eyes were wide open. Asked how she was, she replied in a whisper that she felt quite well. The effort however fatigued her, her head began to drop, eyelids began to close, and the eyeballs began to roll up. Twitchings were observed in the eyelids, and tremors in the left arm. She was again put to bed and given a rest of a few hours. She opened her eyes, and told me that she was weak. This statement she herself volunteered. I found that she could move her hands easily, and that the numbness was completely gone.

For a whole week the patient kept on growing in health and in strength, her sensorimotor reactions improved, she walked round the room for a few minutes, talked in a low voice for a quarter of an hour at a time without manifesting her symptoms of fatigue; her appetite and sleep improved accordingly. At the end of the week there was again a relapse,—she did not sleep well the night before, dreamt of being hunted and tortured, woke up depressed, had no appetite for breakfast, complained of headache, pains, worries, and fears. The headaches have abated in their virulence during last week, but now they seemed to have reappeared in their former vigor. When I began to examine her she looked frightened, her eyeballs rolled up, her eyelids closed. The aphonia was severe, patient lost speech and voice. When spoken to she could not answer. Asked if she heard me, she nodded her head affirmatively. There were slight twitchings of her left hand and also of the muscles of her face. When attention was attracted to the arm the twitchings increased in violence and rapidity. With the distraction of the attention the twitchings disappeared. When the left hand was put in the patient's field of vision, thus making her attention concentrate on that limb, the tremors increased again, becoming finally convulsive in character.

I insisted she should try to open her mouth, and sajr something,—she made fruitless efforts, moving incoordinately the muscles of the face and of the forehead, but she could not utter a sound. She could not move her arms on command, could hardly wriggle the fingers of her hand. She appeared like a little bird paralyzed by fear. When the arm was raised passively it fell down slowly being in a cataleptic state. I allayed the patient's fear. I strongly impressed her with the groundlessness of her fears, and also with the fact that everything was well with the children, and that her husband will be good and gentle with her. The patient was permitted to see her family. The husband was made to realize that he must treat her with more consideration.

He came often to visit her, and learned to treat her well. He soon found a better position, was advised to remove to a healthy locality and to more cheerful surroundings. The children were well cared for. The patient found deep satisfaction in the midst of this family happiness. The fear state abated,—the patient became more confident, more hopeful for the future, and began to improve. The infant was weaned so that the strain of nursing was removed. The patient's appetite began to improve; she gained several pounds in a few days. Long periods of examination and investigation of her nervous and mental state no longer exhausted or terrified her. Her concentration of attention could be kept up from a quarter to half an hour at a stretch without giving rise to fatigue, headache, or to a seizure with its consequent psychomotor effects. The haunted look of fear disappeared, and along with it were also gone the fatigue and dread of physical and mental exercise or work. She could work and walk with ease the whole length of the room and of the hall. She began to take more and more interest in her appearance and in dress. For many minutes at a time she looked out on the street taking an interest in all that was done and what was going on.

The case was discharged, and was sent home. She continued to stay well.

CHAPTER XXIV
SUGGESTED HALLUCINATIONS

The servility, the state of fear of the subconscious, the source of neurosis, in its relation to the master hypnotizer is well brought out in the mechanism of hypnotic and post-hypnotic hallucinations.

Before we proceed with our discussion it may be well to give an analysis, however brief, of the normal percept, of the abnormal percept or hallucination, and then compare them with hypnotic and posthypnotic hallucinations. The understanding of perception, normal and abnormal, is, in fact, at the basis of normal and abnormal psychology.

We may begin with the percept and its elements. In looking at the vase before me I see its beautiful tints, its rounded shape, its heavy pedestal with its rough curves, its solidity, weight, brittleness, and other experiences which go to make up the perception of the vase. The visual elements are given directly by the visual perceptive experience; but whence come the seemingly direct experiences of weight, heaviness, roughness, smoothness, and others of the like kind? They are evidently derived from other senses. The whole perceptive experience is of a visual character. We take in the whole with our eye. In the organic structure of the percept then, besides the experiences directly given by the stimulated sense-organ, there are other experiences, sensory in character, indirectly given, and coming from other sense organs which are not directly stimulated.

The percept is a complicated dynamic product, and its elementary processes are never derived from one isolated domain of sensory experience. The activities of all the sensory domains co-operate in the total result of an apparently simple percept. Along with sensory processes directly stimulated, a mass of other sensory processes becomes organized and helps to contribute to the total result. The direct sensory elements are termed by me primary sensory elements; the indirectly given experiences are termed secondary sensory elements. The secondary sensory elements may be figuratively said to cluster round the primary sensory elements as their nucleus.

The whole perceptual experience is tinged by the character of the primary elements which constitute the guiding nucleus, so to say. Thus, where the primary sensory elements are visual, the whole mass, no matter from what domain the sensory experiences are derived, appears under the form of the visual sense, and the percept is a visual percept. While the primary sensory elements form, so to say, the dynamic center of the total perceptual experience, the secondary sensory elements mainly constitute its content. Both primary and secondary elements are sensory and are induced peripherally; the primary directly, the secondary indirectly. The percept then is sensory and is constituted by primary sensory elements, or primary sensations, and by secondary sensory elements, or secondary sensations.

The character of the secondary sensory elements stands out clear and independent in the phenomena of synaesthesia, of secondary sensations. In the phenomena of synaesthesia we have a sensation of one sense organ followed, without an intermediary direct stimulation, by a sensation coming from another sense organ. Thus, when a sensation of light instead of giving rise to a subsequent idea gives rise to a sensation of sound, for instance, we have the phenomenon of secondary sensation. Here the secondary sensations stand out free and distinct, but they are really always present in our ordinary perceptive experiences as bound up secondary sensory elements, as secondary sensations grouped round primary sensations.

When the phenomena of synaesthesia were first brought to the notice of the scientific world, they were regarded as abnormal and exceptional, and only present in special pathological cases. Soon, however, their field became widened, and they were found not only in the insane and degenerate, but in many persons otherwise perfectly normal. We find now that we must further widen the field of secondary sensory elements, and instead of regarding them as a freak of nature existing under highly artificial conditions, we must put them at the very foundation of the process of perception.

Secondary sensations are at the basis of perception. We have become so accustomed to them that we simply disregard them. When, however, the conditions change, when the secondary sensations stand out by themselves, isolated from the primary nuclear elements with which they are usually organically synthesized into a whole, into a percept, when they become dissociated, it is only then that we become conscious of them directly and declare them as abnormal.

Secondary sensations are always present in every act of perception; in fact, they form the main content of our perceptual activity, only we are not conscious of them, and it requires a special analysis to reveal them. Secondary sensations per se are not something abnormal—just as hydrogen present in the water we drink or the oxygen present in the air we breathe are not newly created elements, —it only requires an analysis to discover them. If there be any abnormality about secondary sensations, it is not in the elements themselves, but rathe in the fact of their dissociation from the primary nuclear elements.

When the secondary sensory elements come to the foreground and stand out clearly in consciousness, a full-fledged hallucination arises. In the phenomena of synaesthesia we have hallucinations in the simplest form, inasmuch as only isolated secondary sensory elements dissociated from their active primary central elements stand out in the foreground of consciousness. This very simplification, however, of hallucinations reveals their inner character. The most complex hallucinations are only complex compounds, so to say, of secondary sensory elements. Hallucinations are not anything mysterious, different from what we find in the normal ordinary processes of perception; they are of the same character and have the same elements in their constitution as those of perception. Both hallucinations and percepts have the same secondary as well as primary elements. The difference between hallucinations and percepts is only one of relationship, of rearrangement of elements, primary and secondary. When secondary sensory elements become under conditions of dissociation dynamically active in the focus of consciousness we have hallucinations.

From this standpoint we can well understand why a hallucination, like a percept, has all the attributes of external reality. A hallucination is not any more mysterious and wonderful than a percept is.

We do not recognize the humdrum percept, when it appears in the guise of a hallucination, and we regard it as some strange visitant coming from a central, or from some supersensory universe. Hallucinations, like percepts, are constituted of primary and especially of secondary sensory elements, and like percepts, hallucinations too are induced peripherally. How is it with suggested or hypnotic hallucinations? Do we find in hypnotic or suggested hallucinations, as in the case of hallucinations in general, the requisite primary and secondary sensory elements directly and indirectly induced? Binet makes an attempt to establish a peripheral stimulus in the case of hypnotic hallucinations, claiming that there is a point de repere, a kind of a peg, on which the hypnotic hallucination is hung. It is questionable whether Binet himself continued to maintain this position. However the case may be, this position is hardly tenable when confronted with facts. Hypnotic hallucinations may develop without any peg and prop.

Furthermore, granted even that now and then such a peg could be discovered, and that the alleged hypnotic hallucination develops more easily when such a peg is furnished, still the fact remains that even in such cases the peg is altogether insignificant, that it is altogether out of proportion and relation to the suggested hallucination, and that on the same peg all kinds of hallucinations can be hung, and that finally it can be fully dispensed with. All this would go to show that the peg, as such, is of no consequence, and is really more of the nature of an emphatic suggestion for the development of the alleged hypnotic or post-hypnotic hallucinations.

The arbitrariness of the hypnotic hallucinations, showing that the whole thing is simply a matter of representations, or of what the patient happens to think at that particular moment, is well brought out in the following experiments: Mr. F. is put into a hypnotic state, and a post-hypnotic suggestion is given to him that he shall see a watch. The eyeball is then displaced, the watch is also displaced ; now when the eyeball returns to its normal condition we should expect that the hallucinatory watch would return to its former place; but no, the watch is not perceived in its previous place,—it appears in a displaced position. The hallucinatory watch could thus be displaced any distance from its original position. The patient evidently did not see anything, but simply supplied from his stock of knowledge as to how a seen watch would appear under such conditions, and he omitted to observe the fact that with the normal position of the eye the watch should once more return to its former

More intelligent and better informed patients would reason out the matter differently, and would give different results. If the subject knows of contrast colors and if a color is suggested to him he will without fail see such contrast colors. If his eyes have been fixed on some hallucinatory color, such as red, for instance, he will even give you a detailed account of the green he sees, but if he does not know anything of the effects of contrast colors no amount of fixation on hallucinatory colors will bring out the least contrast effects. The reason is the patient does not know anything about it and cannot think of it.

We tried to mix by suggestion different hallucinatory colors, and as long as he knew nothing of the real results his replies were uniformly wrong; no sooner did he find out what the right mixture should be than he gave correct results. The hypnotic subject really does not perceive anything; he tells what he believes the master wants him to see under the given conditions. The subconscious fear instinct makes the hypnotized subject obey and please the hypnotizer, as the dog obeys his master.

CHAPTER XXV
TRANCE SERVILITY

Dr. C, a known psychoanalyst, on whom I carried on a series of experiments, goes into a deep somnambulistic state. He is an excellent visualizer and takes readily visual hallucinations. Being a physician and psychiatrist the subject's account is all the more valuable. Now Dr. C. describes his hypnotic hallucinations as "mental pictures," as "auditory memories," which "lack exteriority, are not located in space." He aptly characterizes his hallucinations, visual, auditory, and others, as "fixed ideas."

Mr. M. goes into deep hypnosis. When in one of the deep trance-states a suggestion is given to him that on awakening he shall see a watch. When awake he claims he sees a watch. He was asked: "Do you really see it?" He replied, "Yes." The interesting point here was the fact that the subject did not even look in the direction where the suggested hallucinatory watch was supposed to be placed and where he himself claimed that the watch was located. When tested by automatic writing the hand wrote: "Yes, I see the watch." The subconscious then was also under the influence of the suggested hallucination. It is well to bear in mind this point.

Re-hypnotized, and suggested that on awakening he would see two watches. One was a real silver watch and the other was suggested hallucinatory. The subject claimed he saw both, but he only handled the hallucinatory one, and when asked which of the two he would prefer he pointed to the hallucinatory watch. When asked why, he replied that the suggested watch was bigger. He was really indifferent to the chosen watch and paid no further attention to it, as if it did not exist for him. He tried to please the master hypnotizer of whom he was subconsciously in awe.

He was again put into the hypnotic state and was suggested to see a flower. On awakening he claimed he saw a flower and smelled it in an indifferent, perfunctory fashion. The subconscious was then tested by automatic writing and the writing was to the effect that he saw it. "I see a flower." The subconscious then had also the same hallucination. A series of similar experiments was carried out with the same results. The subconscious claimed in automatic writing that the suggested hallucination was real.

The subject was again put into hypnosis and was given the suggestion that he would see a watch on awakening, but here I made some modification. "When you wake up you will be sure to see a watch," I said, emphatically. "Look here; I want you to write what you really see and not what you do not see." When awake he saw a watch, but he immediately wrote: "I do not see anything." Here the subconscious disclaimed the suggested hallucinations which it had claimed and insisted on before.

Re-hypnotized, and was given the suggestion that on awakening he would see three watches. He was awakened and a real silver watch was put before him; the other two were suggested hallucinatory. He claimed he saw all three. Meanwhile, in automatic writing he wrote: "One silver watch, real, the others golden, not real; nothing there." A series of similar experiments was made and with the same results. The automatic writing disclaimed the hallucinations, although before, under the same conditions, it most emphatically insisted on their reality.

The subject was put into hypnosis and a posthypnotic suggestion was given to him that he would see his wife and child. When awake, he began to smile. When asked why he smiled he said: "I see my wife and child"; but he wrote "I see nobody." When put again in hypnosis he still continued to smile and said: "I see my wife and child"; but he wrote (in hypnotic state): "I really do not see them; I see nothing; I see my child, but I really see nothing." That was when the psychopathic patient got the inkling that I wished to know the truth rather than to be misled by his slavish obedience and fears by complying with my orders. "What do you mean," I asked, "by 'I see my child, but I really see nothing?' " To which he, replied in automatic writing: "I mean that I see my child in my mind only, but I don't see anything."

I then gave him a post-hypnotic suggestion to see a snake. He claimed on awaking that he saw a snake. He manifested little fear. He certainly did not behave as if he really saw a snake and instead wrote "I see a snake. I see it in my mind." A great number of similar experiments were carried out by me, varying the suggestions, and all with the same results. I shall not burden the reader with a detailed account, as they all gave identical results.

At first the automatic writing claimed emphatically the presence of the hallucinatory object and when the truth of the automatic writing was insisted on, the writing disclaimed fully the perception of the hallucinatory object. Finally we came on the real character of the suggested hallucination; "I see my child, but honestly, I do not see anything; I see my child in my mind only, I don't see anything." In other words, if we take the facts plainly and do not play hide and seek with the subconscious, we come to the conclusion that in the suggested hallucinations the subject does not perceive anything as is the case in an actual hallucination. He does not perceive, but he simply thinks of the suggested hallucination.

As long then as the automatic writing was regarded by the subject as independent, for which he was not responsible, as long as the suggestion of the hallucination was not taken as directly addressed to it, the subject himself frankly acknowledged the fact that he did not see anything. When this truth of automatic writing was brought home to the subject he was bound by suggestion to claim that he actually saw the suggested hallucination, although he really did not see anything at all.

This clearly shows that the hypnotic consciousness, from the very nature of its heightened suggestibility, clings most anxiously to the given suggestion, and insists on the reality of its fulfillment. We must, therefore, be on our guard and not trust the subject's introspective account, unless it is well sifted by good circumstantial evidence. It is because such precautions have not been taken in the close interrogation of the subject's actual state of mind, and because of the deep-rooted psychological fallacy as to the relation of ideational and perceptual activities, that the prevalent belief in the validity of suggested hallucinations has passed unchallenged. If not for those factors, it would have been quite evident that the hypnotic and post-hypnotic suggested hallucinations are not genuine, but are essentially spurious. Hypnotic hallucinations, unlike actual hallucinations, are not really experienced. Hypnotically suggested hallucinations are only forms of delusions, attempts to appease the master hypnotizer of whom the subconscious stands in awe and fear.

The state of hypnotic subconsciousness is a state based on the will to conform to the master hypnotizer's commands. At bottom the subconscious trance-will is one of slavish obedience to the authoritative, fear-inspiring will of the master hypnotizer, whom the hypnotic subconscious attempts to please and obey slavishly. The hypnotic state is a fear state of a primitive type. It is the fear state of the Damara ox obeying the herd, or the leader of the herd.

Man is hypnotizable, because he is gregarious, because he is easily controlled by self-fear, because he easily falls into a self-less state of complacent servility. Man, subconscious man, is servile, in fear of his Lord. The independent, free man is yet to come.

CHAPTER XXVI
THE HYPNOIDAL STATE AND SUPERSTITIONS

The hypnoidal state into which man is apt to fall so easily, is well adapted to fear suggestions, since the fear instinct and the impulse of self-preservation are present in the subconsciousness, exposed during trance states to all sorts of fear suggestions and superstitions. It is during these brief periods of primitive hypnoidal states that the animal is exposed to attacks of enemies whose senses become sharpened to detect the weak spots in the armor of their victims, immersed in the momentary rest of the hypnoidal state.

During these periods of repose and passivity or of sleep stage, the animal can only protect itself by all kinds of subterfuges, such as hiding in various inaccessible places, or taking its rest-periods in shady nooks and corners, or in the darkness of the night. Each hypnoidal period closely corresponds to the larval stage of the insect, reposing in its cocoon,—the most critical time of the insect organism, most exposed to the depredations of its enemies. And still the hypnoidal state is requisite to the animal in order to restitute its living matter and energy which have been wasted during the active moments of its life activities. Hence the weakness of the animal depends on the very constitution of its organism.

The hypnoidal state, although absolutely necessary in the process of matabolism, is also the moment of its greatest danger, and the fear instinct is specially intense at the onset of that hypnoidal moment, the lowest point of the weakness of the organism. The animal, after taking all precautions, is finally paralyzed into temporary immobility at the risk of its own existence.

The fear instinct determines the nature and character of rest and sleep. The lower the animal, the scantier are its means of defense in the ceaseless struggle for its preservation. The simpler the animal, the greater and more numerous are the dangers menacing it with total extinction,—hence it must be constantly on its guard. A state of sleep such as found in the higher animals is rendered impossible. The sleep must be light, and in snatches, rapidly passing from rest into waking,—the characteristic of the hypnoidal state. The fear instinct is the controlling factor of sleep and rest. When we are in danger the sleep is light and in snatches, and we thus once more revert to an ancient form of rest and sleep.

The insomnia found in cases of neurosis is a re-

version to primitive rest-states, found in the lower animals. The insomnia is due to the fear instinct which keeps dominating the conscious and subconscious mental activities, a state which lias prevailed in the early stages of animal life. That is why the sleep of neurotics is unrefreshing and full of dreams of dangers and accidents, and peopled with visions of a terrorizing nature. Hence the neurotic fear of insomnia which is itself the consequence of the obsession, conscious and subconscious, of the fear instinct.

In my work on sleep I was greatly impressed with the place fear holds in animal life existence. From the lowest representative, such as the insect to the highest, such as man, fear rules with an iron hand. Every animal is subject to cataplexy of fear and to the hypnoidal state itself, the consequence of fear-adaptations to the external conditions of a hostile environment. Cataplexy and the consequent hypnoidal state which paralyze the animal, depriving it of all defense, are grounded in the imperfections of living protoplasm.

Man is subject to the hypnoidal periods of primitive life. It is during those periods that the shafts of suggestion are most apt to strike his subconsciousness, divorced as it is during those moments from the nodding self consciousness. During these nodding moments of his life he is exposed to harmful suggestions, since they are apt to arouse the fear instinct, the most sensitive of all human instincts. It seems as if the fear instinct is never fully asleep, and is the easiest to arouse. It seems to be watchful or semi-watchful during the most critical moments of man's helplessness.

Fear of darkness and fear of invisible foes are specially strong in man, because of the deeply rooted fear instinct, but also because of his memories of accidents and dangers that have befallen him, and which may befall him. Man's fears hang round dark places, gloomy corners and nooks, caves and forests, and more especially during the darkness and shades of night, appearing as treacherous visions and specters of lurking dangers. And still from the very nature of his being man must rest and sleep, hence the association of terrors with night time. He can only overcome his night terrors by living and sleeping in more or less secure corners, in the neighborhood of his fellow-beings who by the mere fact of numbers multiply not only the means of defense, but actually increase susceptibility for the scent of danger and possible speedy defense. In the society of his fellows the sense organs of the individual are increased by the presence of others who are in various stages of vigilance, and hence there is greater protection against dangers and invisible foes that lurk in the darkness of night, foes of which primitive man is in terror of his life.

The fear of the unknown, the mysterious, and the dark, peoples the mind of primitive man with all sorts of terrible spectres, ghosts, spirits, goblins, ghouls, shades, witches, and evil powers, all bent on mischief, destruction and death. Primitive man suffers from chronic demonophobia. Fear states are specially emphasized at night when the "demons" have the full power for evil, and man is helpless on account of darkness and sleep which paralyze him. Hence the terrors of the night, especially when man is alone, and defenseless.

The fear of solitude comes out strongly in the intense fear that obsesses man in the gloomy darkness of the night horrors. Fire and fellow-beings can alone relieve his night terrors. The fear of foes, of demons, of evil powers does not abate in the day, only it is relieved by reason of light, of association, and of wakefulness. Man, more than any other animal, is the victim of the fear instinct. Many tribes, many races of men perished, due to superstitions and fear obsessions.

The Homo sapiens is rare. We may agree with Tarde that Homo somnambtdis would be a proper definition of the true mental condition of most specimens of the human race. For the human race is still actuated by the principle of "Credo, quia absurdum est." I need not go far to substantiate the fact that this principle still guides the life of the average specimen of civilized humanity. Spiritualism, theosophy, telepathy, ghost hunting, astrology, oneiromancy, cheiromancy, Christian Science, psychoanalytic oneiroscopy employed in events and situations of individual and social life, and many other magical practices whose name is legion, based on the mysteries of communication with ghosts, spirits, demons, and unknown fearsome powers, still haunt the credulous mind, obsessed with conscious and subconscious horrors of the terrible, invisible spirit world.

Against the fears of diseases, the scares of the day and terrors of night, civilized man still uses the magic arts and mysterious, miraculous powers of the magician, the wizard, the witch, the mental healer, the shaman, the medicine man, the miracle man, and the psychoanalyst. Just at present under my own eyes I witness the pitiful credulity of man, driven by the terrors and horrors of the fear instinct. In San Jose, San Diego, in Los Angeles, and in many other Western "culture" centers mystic cults hold high carnival, swaying the minds of fear-crazed, deluded humanity. As typical specimens of superstitious fears and absurd beliefs, due to the fear instinct, we may take as illustrations the following occurrences in the centers of the far West, obsessed by the aberrations of the fear instinct (I quote from Los Angeles papers) :

"Faith Healer at Los Angeles, Venice, California, after several wonder cures, orders sun's rays to be darkened. 'Brother Isaiah,' called by thousands the 'Miracle Man,' claimed to have repeated the marvel of dimming the sun at Venice yesterday evening.

"At 6 o'clock the disciple of healing by faith raised his hands and announced that as evidence of his power he would blot out the brilliant solar rays. He gazed at the dazzling red ball above the waters of the Pacific, and his lips moved in low murmurs.

" 'It is done,' he said. 'I have clouded the sun. All those who have seen this miracle raise your hands.' Hundreds of hands waved in the air.

"The first time 'Brother Isaiah' claimed to have dimmed the sun's rays was at Miracle Hill, when he had been in Los Angeles but a few days.

"Brother Isaiah stepped to one side of his wooden platform on the Venice Beach yesterday. He placed a silver police whistle to his lips and blew. The piercing crescendo sent a shiver through the tense mass of humanity which stretched from the sand back to the ocean walk." Similar miracles and cures were carried on by Mrs. Amy McPherson in San Diego, San Jose, and all along the Pacific coast.

The self-impulse and the fear instinct, in their intensified forms, are the bane of deluded, neurotic humanity.

CHAPTER XXVII
NEUROSIS AND HEREDITY

The following discussion in the form of questions and answers may prove of interest to the physician and to the intelligent layman. The discussion occurred in the course of correspondence. A friend of mine thought the subject of sufficient importance to have it brought to the attention of the cultured public.

The questions are as follows:

"Are not all neuropathic conditions the results of a morbid, unstable nervous organism, the basis of which lies in a faulty heredity?

"Are not weak nerves the cause of hysterical, neurasthenic and neuropathic affections in general?

"Is not all neurosis due to defective parent stock?

"If the occasions for fear, as some psychopathologists claim, were more frequent in primitive times than now, then the cave men must have had more psychopathic affections than civilized man."

To these questions the following answers are given:

Psychopathic diseases are not hereditary—they are acquired characteristics, having their origin in the abnormal, hypertrophied growth of the fear instinct which is at the root of the primal impulse of self-preservation. This is proved by psycho-pathological studies of clinical cases; and it can be further demonstrated by experimental work in the laboratory even in the case of animals. "Weak nerves," "a run down, exhausted nervous system," whatever the terms may mean, may overlap psychopathic conditions, but the two are by no means equivalent, much less identical. Psychopathic, psychoneurotic states are not "weak nerves" or "fatigued nerves." Above all, there is no need to obscure the matter and resort to the much abused, mystical and mystifying factor of heredity. It is easy to shift all blame on former generations, when, in most cases, the fault is close at hand, namely, a debased environment, a defective training, and a vicious education.

There is good reason to believe that primitive man had a far greater tendency to dissociation, to subconscious psychopathic states than modern man. Even the Middle Ages teem with psychopathic mental epidemics of the most puerile type. In the course of evolution, social and individual, this neurotic, psychopathic tendency has gradually diminished, but has never been completely eliminated. Increase of knowledge, better education, the increase of social safeguards, sanitary and hygienic conditions with consequent increase of safety from dangers, have all helped materially in decreasing the occasions for the cultivation of the fear instinct.

Under the rigorous conditions of primitive life individuals who have been unfortunate and have become affected with mental troubles and emotional afflictions of the fear instinct are mercilessly exterminated by the process of tribal and social selection. Each generation weeds out the individuals who have been unfortunate enough to fall under unfavorable circumstances and have become mentally sick, suffering from acquired psychopathic disturbances. In primitive life the crippled, the maimed, the wounded, the sick fall by the way, and are left to perish a miserable death. In fact, the less fortunate, the wounded and the stricken in the battle of life, are attacked by their own companions,— they are destroyed by the ruthless, social brute. The gregarious brute has no sympathy with the pains and sufferings of the injured and the wounded. The faint and the ailing are destroyed by the herd.

Civilization, on the other hand, tends more and more towards the preservation of psychopathic individuals. We no longer kill our sick and our weak, nor do we abandon them to a miserable, painful death,—we take care of them, and cure them. Moreover, we prevent pathogenic factors from exercising a harmful, malign social selection of the "fit." We do our best to free ourselves from the blind, merciless, purposeless selection, produced by pathogenic microorganisms and by other noxious agencies. We learn to improve the external environment.

We do not condemn people to death because they are infected with smallpox, typhus, typhoid bacilli, or because of an infected appendix. We no longer regard them as sinful, unclean, accursed, and tabooed. We vaccinate, inoculate, operate, (and attempt to cure them. By sanitary and prophylactic measures we attempt to prevent the very occurrence of epidemics. Our valuation of individuals is along lines widely different from those of the stone age and cavemen. We value a Pascal, a Galileo, a Newton, a Darwin, a Pasteur, and a Helmholtz far above a Milo of Croton or an African Johnson.

Civilization is in need of refined, delicate and sensitive organizations, just as it is in need of galvanometers, chronometers, telephones, wireless apparatuses, and various chemical reagents of a highly delicate character. We are beginning to appreciate delicate mechanisms and sensitive organizations. We shall also learn to train and guard our sensitive natures until they are strong and resistant to the incident forces of an unfavorable environment. The recognition, the diagnosis, and the preservation of psychopathic individuals account for the apparent increase of neurotics in civilized communities.

It may be well to add that, although occasions for sudden, intense, overwhelming fears are not so prevalent in civilized societies as they are in primitive savage communities, the worries, the anxieties, the various forms of slow grinding fears of a vague, marginal, subconscious character present in commercial and industrial nations, are even more effective in the production of psychopathic states than are the isolated occasions of intense frights in the primitive man of the paleolithic or neolithic periods.

CHAPTER XXVIII
NEUROSIS AND EUGENICS

In my work on Psychopathology I lay special stress on the fact that the psychopathic individual has a predisposition to dissociative states. Early experiences and training in childhood enter largely into the formation of such a predisposition. Still, there is no doubt that a sensitive nervous system is required—a brain susceptible to special stimuli of the external environment. This, of course, does not mean that the individual must suffer from stigmata of degeneration. On the contrary, it is quite possible, and in many patients we actually find it to be so, that the psychopathic individual may be even of a superior organization. It is the sensitivity and the delicacy of nervous organization that make the system susceptible to injurious stimulations, to which a lower form of organization could be subjected with impunity.

An ordinary clock can be handled roughly without disturbance of its internal workings, but the delicate and complicated mechanism of a chronometer requires careful handling and special, favorable conditions for its normal functioning. Unfavorable conditions are more apt to affect a highly complex mechanism than a roughly made instrument. It is quite probable that it is the superior minds and more highly complex mental and nervous organizations that are subject to psychopathic states or states of dissociation. Of course, unstable minds are also subject to dissociative states, but we must never forget the fact that highly organized brains, on account of their very complexity, are apt to become unstable under unfavorable conditions. A predisposition to dissociation may occur either in degenerative minds or in minds superior to the average. Functional psychosis requires a long history of dissociated, subconscious shocks, suffered by a highly or lowly organized nervous system, a long history dating back to early childhood.

As Mosso puts it: "The vivid impression of a strong emotion may produce the same effect as a blow on the head or some physical shock." We may, however, say that no functional psychosis, whether somatopsychosis or psychoneurosis, can ever be produced simply by physical shocks. In all functional psychoses there must be a mental background, and it is the mental background alone that produces tJie psychosis and determines the character of the psychopathic state.

Fear is an important factor in the etiology of psychopathic affections which include somatopsychoses and psychoneuroses. To regard fear as "error," as do some sectarians, is absurd, and is certainly unscientific. Abnormal fear which is the basis of all functional nervous or psychopathic maladies, is essentially a pathological process affecting the organs in general and the nervous system in particular in as definite a way as the invasion and infection of the organism by various species of bacteria, bacilli, and other microorganisms which attack the individual during his lifetime.

Like infectious diseases, the deviations, abnormalities, and excesses of the fear instinct are acquired by the individual in the course of his relations with the external environment, and are as real and substantial as are syphilis, smallpox, diphtheria, cholera, and the bubonic plague. To regard them as imaginary or to relegate them to the action of Providence or to heredity is theoretically a misconception, and practically a great danger to humanity.

There is nowadays a veritable craze for heredity and eugenics. Biology is misconceived, misinterpreted, and misapplied to social problems, and to individual needs and ailments. Everything is ascribed to heredity, from folly and crime to scratches and sneezes. The goddess Heredity is invoked at each flea-bite— in morsu pulicis Deum invocare. Even war is supposed to be due to the omnipotent deity of Heredity. Superior races by theirpatriotism and loyalty destroy the weak and the helpless, and relentlessly exterminate all peaceful tribes. Such warlike stock comes of superior clay. The dominant races have some miraculous germ-plasm, special "'unit characters," wonderful dominant "units" which, like a precious heritage, these races transmit unsullied and untarnished to their descendants.

Wars, carnage, butcheries make for progress, culture, and evolution. Our boasted civilization with its "scientific" business thoroughness and its ideal of "efficiency" attempts to carry into effect this quasi-evolutionary doctrine—this apotheosis of brute force under the aegis of science. The eugenic belief is really a recrudescence of the ancient savage superstition of the magic virtues of noble blood and of divine king stock.

All nervous, mental, neuropathic, and psychopathic maladies are supposed to be a matter of heredity. If people are poor, ignorant, superstitious, stupid, degraded, brutal, and sick, the eugenists unhesitatingly put it all down to poor stock.

The eugenic remedy is as simple as it is believed to be efficacious: Introduce by legislation "efficient" laws favoring "eugenic" marriage, and teach the masses control of births. The select and chosen stock alone should multiply—the millennium is then bound to come. Such is the doctrine of our medico-biological sages.

"Scientific" farmers and breeders of vegetables, fruits, and cattle are regarded as competent judges of human "breeders." Agriculturists and horticulturists set themselves up as advisers in "the business of raising good crops of efficient children." Bachelors, spinsters, and the childless generally, are specially versed in eugenic wisdom and pedagogics.

All social ils and individual complaints are referred to one main source—heredity. With the introduction of eugenic legislation, with the sterilization of the socially unfit, among whom the greatest men and women may be included, with the breeding of good "orthodox, common stock," and with eugenic Malthusian control of births, all evil and diseases on earth will cease, while the Philistine "superman" will reign supreme forevermore.

In the Middle Ages all diseases and epidemics, all wars, all social and private misfortunes were considered as visitations of Divine wrath. The fear instinct held sway, terrorizing poor, deluded humanity. In modern times our would-be eugenic science refers all ills of the flesh and woes of the mind to an outraged Heredity. The dark ages had resort to prayers, fasts, and penitence, while our age childishly pins its faith to the miraculous virtues and rejuvenating, regenerative powers of legislative eugenic measures, and to the eugenic Malthusian control of births.

Our scientists in eugenics gather hosts of facts, showing by elaborate statistical figures that the family history of neurotics reveals stigmata of degeneration in the various members of the family. The eugenic inquirers do not stop for a moment to think over the fact that the same sort of evidence can be easily brought in the case of most people. In fact, the eugenists themselves, when inquiring into the pedigree of talent and genius, invariably find somewhere in the family some form of disease or degeneration. This sort of "scientific" evidence leads some eugenic speculators, without their noticing the reductio ad absurdum, to the curious conclusion or generalization that degeneration is present in the family history of the best and the worst representatives of the human race.

The so-called scientific method of the eugenists is faulty, in spite of the rich display of colored plates, stained tablets, glittering biological speculations, brilliant mathematical formulae, and complicated statistical calculations. The eugenists pile Ossa on Pelion of facts bjr the simple method of enumeration which Bacon and the thinkers coming after him have long ago condemned as puerile and futile. From the savage's belief in sympathetic, imitative magic with its consequent superstitions, omens, and taboos down to the articles of faith and dogmas of the eugenists, we find the same faulty, primitive thought, guided by the puerile, imbecile method of simple enumeration, and controlled by the wisdom of the logical post hoc, ergo propter hoc.

What would we say of the medical man who should claim that measles, mumps, cholera, typhoid fever, yellow fever, malaria, tetanus, and various other infectious diseases are hereditary by quoting learnedly long tables of statistics to the effect that for several generations members of the same family suffered from the same infectious diseases? What would we say of the medical advice forbidding marriage to individuals whose family history reveals the presence of exanthemata? We stamp out epidemics not by eugenic measures, but by the cleansing of infectious filth, and by the extermination of pathogenic micro-organisms.

Every human being has a predisposition to smallpox, cholera, tetanus, bubonic plague, typhus fever, malaria, and to like infectious diseases, but there is no inherent necessity for everyone to fall a victim to the action of pathogenic organisms, if the preventive and sanitary conditions are good and proper. No one is immune against the action of bullets, cannon balls, shells, and torpedoes, or to the action of various poisons, organic and inorganic, but one is not doomed by fate to be killed by them, if one does not expose himself to their deadly action.

Every living organism is, by the very nature of its cellular tissues, predisposed to wounding by sharp instruments, or to the burning action of fire, but this does not mean an inherent organic weakness to which the organism must necessarily submit and perish. We are all of us predisposed to get injured and possibly killed, when we fall down from a high place, or when we are run over by an automobile or by a locomotive, but there is no fatalistic necessity about such accidents, if care is taken that they should not occur.

We may be predisposed to neurosis by the very nature of complexity, delicacy, and sensitivity inherent in the structure of a highly organized nervous system, and still we may remain healthy and strong all our life long, provided we know how to keep away from noxious agencies. The creed of the inevitable fatality of neurosis is as much of a superstition as the Oriental belief in the fatalism of infectious diseases, plagues, and accidents of all kinds. Such fatalistic superstitions are dangerous, fatal, because they distract the attention from the actual cause and from the requisite prophylactic measures.

We go far afield in search for the remote source of our troubles, when the cause is close at hand. We need only open our eyes to see the filth of our towns, the foul, loathsome slums of our cities, the miserable training, the wretched education given to our children, in order to realize at a glance the source of our ills and ailments. We should have the guilt at the door of our social order. We starve our young. We starve our children physically and mentally- We piously sacrifice our tender children and the flower of our youth to the greedy, industrial Moloch of a military, despotic, rapacious plutocracy.

Witness semi-civilized Europe with its lauded culture brutally shedding the blood of its youth and manhood on the altar of commercial patriotism! It is not heredity, it is the vicious conditions of life that stunt the physical, nervous, and mental growth of our young generation. When we are confronted with the miserable, degraded, crippled forms of our life, we fall back cheerfully on some remote grandparent, and credulously take refuge in the magic panacea of eugenics.

The practical aspect is clear. Psychopathic neurosis in its two varieties, somatopsychosis and psychoneurosis, is not hereditary, but acquired. We should not shift the blame on former generations and have resort to eugenics, but we must look to the improvement of mental hygienic conditions of early childhood, and to the proper education of the individual. It is easy to put the blame on grandparents,— they are dead and cannot defend themselves. Could they arise from their graves, they could tell some bitter truths to their descendants who are ready to shift responsibility to other people's shoulders. It is about time to face the truth fairly and squarely, a truth which is brought out by recent investigations in psychopathology, that no matter where the fons et origo of neurosis be, whether in self-preservation and its accompanying fear instinct, the condition of life primordial, or in the other forms of self-preservation, the formation of psychopathic neurosis with all its characteristic protean symptoms is not hereditary, but acquired. Neurosis arises wthm the life cycle of the individual; it is due to faulty training and harmful experience of early child life.

Future medicine will be largely prophylactic, preventive, sanitary, hygienic, dietetic. What holds true of medicine in general holds true of that particular branch of it that deals with neurosis. The treatment will become largely prophylactic, preventive, educational, or pedagogic. It is time that the medical and teaching profession should realize that functional neurosis is not congenital, not inborn, not hereditary, but is the result of a defective, fear-inspiring education in early child life.

The psychopathic diathesis can be overcome by dispelling the darkness of ignorance and credulity with their false fears and deceptive hopes, above all, by fortifying the critical, controlling, guiding consciousness. Let in sun and air into the obscure cobwebbed regions of the child and man. The gloom and the ghosts of the fear instinct are dispersed by the light of reason.

As the great Roman poet, Lucretius, well puts it:

"Hunc igitur terrorem animi tenebrasque necessest Non radii sobs neque lucida tela diei Discutiant, sed natura species ratioque." [2]

CHAPTER XXIX
PRIMITIVE FEARS

Various authorities in Ethnology and Anthropology concur in their description and testimony as to the superstitious fears that obsess primitive man.

Professor Baldwin Spencer, the anthropologist, writes of the Australian aborigines that they have "an intense belief in evil magic. The natives have no idea of disease or pain as being due to anything but evil magic, except that which is caused by an actual accident which they can see. . . . Anything they do not understand they associate with evil magic. . . . You have only to tell a native that he is the victim of evil magic, and he succumbs at once, and can only be cared by the exercise of counter magic.

"The number of supernatural beings feared by aborigines of Australia is exceedingly great. For not only are the heavens peopled with such, but the whole face of the country swarms with them; every thicket, most watering places abound with evil spirits. In like manner, every natural phenomenon is believed to be the work of demons, none of which seem to be of a benign nature, one and all apparently striving to do all imaginable mischief to the poor black fellow."

The same is true of the negro. "The negro is wont to regard the whole world around him as peopled with envious beings, to whom he imputes every misfortune that happens to him, and from whose harmful influence he seeks to protect himself by all kinds of magic means." "The religion of the Bolok (of the Upper Congo River)," writes an observer, "has its basis in their fear of those numerous invisible spirits which surround them on every side, and are constantly trying to compass them in their sickness, misfortune and death; and the Boloki's sole object in practising their religion is to cajole, or appease, cheat or conquer or kill those spirits that trouble them, by their Nganga (medicine men), their rites, their ceremonies, and their charms. If there were no evil spirits to circumvent there would be no need of medicine men and their charms. . . . The Boloki folk believe that they are surrounded by spirits which try to thwart them at every twist and turn, and to harm them every hour of day and night. ... I never met among them a man daring enough to go at night through the forest that divided Monsembe from the upper villages even though a large reward was offered. Their invariable reply was:

'There are too many spirits in the bush and forest.' The spirits whom the people dread so much are the mingoli, or disembodied souls of the dead; the life of the Boloki is described as 'one long drawn out fear of what the mingoli may next do to them.' Those dangerous beings dwell everywhere, land and water are full of them; they are ever ready to pounce on the living and carry them away, or to smite them with disease, and kill them. . . . The belief in witchcraft affects their lives in a vast number of ways. It regulates their actions, modifies their mode of thought and speech, controls their conduct towards each other, causes cruelty and callousness in a people not naturally cruel, and sets the various members of a family against each other. . . . Belief in witches is interwoven into the very fiber of every Bantu speaking man and woman; and the person who does not believe in them is a monster, a witch to be killed."

The fear of evil spirits, the fear of witchcraft, and the fear of malicious spiritual agencies have been the pests of credulous, fear-obsessed humanity in all the ages of its existence. The crusades, and religious wars have shown us the blight suffered by humanity, obsessed by the impulse of self-preservation and the fear instinct. Fear or pretended Love of the great spirit, under whatever name, is used for the avoidance of fears and evils.

Sir E. F. im Thurn describes the Indian of Guiana as haunted by the omnipresence of malicious ghosts and spirits. "The whole world of the Indian swarms with these beings. If by a mental effort, we could for a moment revert to a similar mental position, we should find ourselves surrounded everywhere by a host of harmful beings. ... It is not therefore, wonderful that the Indian fears to move beyond the light of his camp-fire after dark . . . nor is it wonderful that occasionally the air round the settlement seems to the Indian to grow so full of beings, that a sorcerer is employed."

The Indians of Paraguay "live in constant dread of supernatural beings and if nothing else contributed to make their life miserable, this ever present dread would be in itself quite sufficient to rob it of most of its joys."

Professor Powell writes of the Indians: "The Indians believed that diseases were caused by unseen evil beings and by witchcraft, and every cough, every toothache, every headache, every fever, every boil and every wound, in fact all their ailments were attributed to such a cause. Their so called medical practice was a horrible system of sorcery and to such superstition human life was sacrificed on an enormous scale. . . ." Similarly, the malignant spirits of the Maori are "so numerous as to surround the living in crowds. The Maori claims: "the spirits throng like mosquitoes, ever watching to inflict harm." The Melanesian "sees himself surrounded at every step by evil spirits and their influences."

The Papuans "people land and sea with mysterious, malignant powers which take up their abode in stones and trees or in men, and cause all kinds of misfortunes, especially sickness and death." The Bakua of New Guinea are in constant fear of spirits. . . . "Of forest spirits the number is infinite; for it is above all in the mysterious darkness, the tangled wilderness of the virgin forests that the spirits love to dwell. . . . The spirits are never bent on good, they live in evil places. At night-fall the native hears the voices of the spirits, they make inroads into human habitations, and drive man crazy."

In Java, the people are firmly convinced that "the number of spirits is innumerable, they are a source of fear and anxiety." The natives of Sumatra are possessed of "fear of unknown powers. . . . Every misfortune bespeaks the ill-will of hostile spirits. The whole world is a meeting place of demons." The Batakas "live in perpetual fear of evil spirits."

Professor M. Williams writes of the Hindoos: "The great majority of the inhabitants of India are, from the cradle to the burning ground, victims of a form of mental disease which is best explained by the term demo no phobia. They are haunted and oppressed by a perpetual dread of demons. They are firmly convinced that evil spirits of all kinds, from malignant fiends to mischievous imps and elves, are ever on the watch to harm, harass and torment them, to cause plague, sickness, famine, and disaster, to impede, injure and mar every good work. The worship of at least ninety per cent of the people of India in the present day is a worship of fear. The simple truth is that evil of all kinds, difficulties, dangers and disasters, famines, diseases, pestilences and death, are thought by an ordinary Hindoo to proceed from demons, or more properly speaking, from devils, and from devils alone." "The underlying principle (of the religion of the Kacharis of Assam) is characteristically one of fear or dread."

"The Thibetans," writes an observer, "are thorough-going demon worshippers. In every nook, path, big tree, rock, spring, waterfall and lake there lurks a devil, —for which reason few individuals will venture out alone after dark. The sky, the ground, the house, the field, the country, have each their special demons; and sickness is always attributed to malign demoniacal influence."

The Burmese, the Laosians of Siam, the Thay of Indo-China are in all their activities controlled by the fear instinct which is at the bottom of all their beliefs. "The Thay cannot take a single step without meeting a demon on the path. . . . Spirits watch him, ready to punish negligence, and he is afraid. Fear is not only for him the beginning of wisdom, it is the whole of his wisdom."

The Koreans may be regarded as the most superstitious people among the Orientals. Before me lies a Korean book full of superstitions which can only be matched in their absurdities with those of Australian aborigines who, in their savage culture belong to the paleolithic period. The whole course of the Korean's life is controlled to the very minutiae by the terrors and horrors of demoniacal, invisible, deadly, malignant powers of demons, spirits, ghosts, hobgoblins, specters, and witches. According to the Korean belief the earth is a pandemonium in which witches and evil spirits hold high carnival. J. M. de Groot writes "In Korean belief, earth, air, and sea are peopled by demons. They haunt every umbrageous tree, shady ravine, spring and mountain crest. . . . They make a sport of human destinies. They are on every roof, ceiling, oven and beam. They fill the chimney, shed, the living room, the kitchen, they are on every shelf and jar. In thousands they waylay the traveler as he leaves his home, beside him, behind him, dancing in front of him, whirring over his head, crying out upon him from air, earth, and water. They are numbered by thousands of billions, and it has been well said that their ubiquity is an unholy travesty of Divine Omnipresence. This belief, and it seems to be the only one he possesses, keeps the Korean in a perpetual state of nervous apprehension, it surrounds him with indefinite terrors, and it may be truly said of him that he passes the time of his sojourning here in fear. . . . The spirits keep the Korean in bondage from birth to death."

Im Bang, a Korean writer on Korean beliefs, has a characteristic story of a poor relative of some Korean dignitary. This poor relative of the hi^h official once a year gathered hundreds of thousands of spirits whom he checked off, so as to keep their malignant disposition under control. And this gentleman was but one of the many clerks; he was but one census man of the vast bureaucratic spiritistic machinery for the regulation and control of evil demons. The same holds true of the other tribes in Asia. Thus the Gyliaks think that all the places on earth are filled with malicious demoniacal agencies. Similarly, the Koryaks on the Amoor are terrorized by the malignancy of evil spirits that dog their steps. W. Jochelson tells of the Koryaks that "when visiting the houses to cause diseases and to kill people, they (the spirits or demons) enter from under the ground. . . . They are invisible to human beings, they are sometimes so numerous in houses that they sit on the people, and fill up all corners. . . . With hammers and axes they knock people over their heads and cause headache. They bite, and cause swellings. They shoot invisible arrows which stick in the body causing death. The demons tear out pieces of flesh from people, thus causing sores and wounds to form on the body." The same spirit of fear of the invisible and of the mysterious, fear of evil powers, controlling the fate of man, constitutes the central belief of almost every primitive tribe, semi-civilized, ancient, as well as modern nation. They are all controlled by the fundamental instinct of life—the fear instinct.

The Semitic scholar, R. H. Harper, writes of the Assyrians and Babylonians as follows: "There is no place in the universe where evil spirits can not penetrate. Every manner of evil and disaster is ascribed to them, from pestilence, fever, and the scorching wind of the desert, down to the trifles of life,—a quarrel, a headache, a broken dish, or a bad dream. They walk the street, slip into the door, get into the food, in short, are everywhere, and the danger from their presence is always imminent. . . . Corresponding to a widespread belief in demons was a similar belief in witchcraft. It was not at all strange that the demons, who worked in ever}' possible corner of the universe, should take possession of human beings..."

The tablets excavated in the imperial library of Ashurbanipal show the spirit of the people even of the highest classes debased with delusions and religious hallucinations due to self-preservation and fear instinct, so dominant in man who, when common-sense departs from him, may be regarded as the irrational animal par excellence. We may give the following illustration taken from one of the many tablets of the Shurpu series:

"The evil spirits like grass have covered the earth. To the four winds they spread brilliancy like fire, they send forth flames. The people living in dwellings they torment, their bodies they afflict. In city and country they bring moaning, small and great they make to lament. Man and woman they put in bonds, and fill with cries of woe. Man they fall upon and cover him like a garment. In heaven and earth like a tempest they rain; they rush on in pursuit. They fill him with poison, his hands they bind, his sides they crush."

According to the ancient rabbis, a man should not drink water by night, for thus he exposes himself to the Shavriri, demons of blindness. What then should he do if he is thirsty? If there be another man with him, let him rouse him up and say: "I am thirsty," but if he be alone, let him tap upon the lid of the jug (to make the demon fancy there is someone with him), and addressing him by his own name, let him say: "Thy mother bid thee beware of the Shavriri, vriri, riri, ri." Rashi, a mediaeval commentator, says that by this incantation the demon gradually contracts and vanishes as the sound of the word Shavriri decreases.

The ancient rabbis instruct that "no one should venture out at night time on Wednesday or Saturday, for Agrath, the daughter of the demon Machloth, roams about accompanied by eighteen myriads of evil demons, each one of which has power to destroy." The rabbis claim that the air, land and sea are full of demons, all bent on evil and destruction of man. In this respect the learned rabbis differ but little from the superstitious Koreans and Australian savages. The rabbis warn the pious Jew that "should he forget to fold his prayer cover, he is to shake it thoroughly next morning, in order to get rid of the evil spirits that have harbored there during the night." The evil spirits are infinite in number. Thus the Talmudic authorities are in full accord with the ancient Babylonians, Assyrians, and with the lowest savages, ancient and modern, obsessed by the fear of spirits, by Demonophobia.

One cannot help agreeing with the English anthropologist, Frazer, who after his study of the subject, arrives at the following conclusion: "In India from the earliest times down to the present day the real religion of the common folk appears always to have been a belief in a vast multitude of spirits of whom many, if not most, are mischievous and harmful. As in Europe beneath a superficial layer of Christianity a faith in magic and witchcraft, in ghosts and goblins has always survived and even flourished among the weak and the ignorant (and apparently cultivated) so it has been and so it is in the East (and we may say also in the West). Brahmanism, Buddhism, Islam may come and go, but the belief in magic and demons remains unshaken through them all, and, if we may judge of the future from the past, it is likely to survive the rise and fall of other historical religions. For the great faiths of the world, just in so far as they are the outcome of superior intelligence, of extraordinary fervor of aspiration after the ideal, fail to touch and move the common man. They make claims upon his intellect and his heart, to which neither the one nor the other is capable of responding. With the common herd who compose the great bulk of every people, the new religion is accepted only in outward show. . . . They yield a dull assent to it with their lips, but in their heart they never abandon their old superstitions (and fears of evil and mysterious miraculous agencies) ; in these they cherish a faith such as they can never repose in the creed which they nominally profess; and to these, in the trials and emergencies of life, they have recourse as to infallible remedies."

And he quotes Maxwell to the effect that "The Buddhists in Ceylon, in times of sickness and danger . . . turn to demons, feared and reverenced in the same way as do 'the Burmese, Talaings, and Malays.' " The Jews firmly believed in demoniacal agencies. "When the even was become, they brought unto Him many that were possessed with devils; and He cast out the spirits with His word, and healed all that were sick." "And in the synagogue there was a man which had a spirit of an unclean devil; and he cried out with a loud voice." "And devils also came out of many . . ., and He rebuking them suffered them not to speak." "And there was a herd of many swine feeding on the mountains . . . Then went the devils out of the man, and entered into the swine, and the herd ran violently down a steep place, and were choked." "Casting out devils" was a sure proof of divine mission.

Perhaps a quotation from the Talmud will make clear the fear of demons which possesses the Jew: Abba Benjamin says, "if the eye were permitted to see the malignant spirits that beset us, we could not rest on account of them." Abai, another sage, says: "They outnumber us, they surround us as the heaped up soil in our garden plots." Rav Hunna says: "Every one has a thousand on his left side and ten thousand on his right." Rava claims: "The crowding at the schools is caused by their (demons) pushing in; they cause the weariness which the rabbis experience in their knees, and even tear their clothes by hustling against them. If one would discover traces of their presence, let him sift some ashes upon the floor at his bedside, and next morning he will see their footmarks as of fowls on the surface. But if one would see the demons themselves, he must burn to ashes the after-birth of a first born black kitten, the offspring of a first-born black cat, and then put a little of the ashes into his eyes, and he will not fail to see the demons."

In the words of Lord Avebury, the archaeologist, "the savage is a prey to constant fears...Savages never know but what they may be placing themselves in the power of these terrible enemies (the demons); and it is not too much to say that the horrible dread of unknown evil hangs like a thick cloud over savage life and embitters every pleasure.'*

In our modern times the preachers, the revivalists, the pulpit, appeal to fear and to hell in order to keep their flock in the fold. Fear of eternal damnation for infidels is the war cry of religion. Professor Dreslar elicited from 875 California normal school students four-fifths of whom were young women, 3225 confessions of belief in superstitions. . . . "How thin is the veneer of culture over that great mass of irrational predisposition which in the hour of fear and excitement resumes control of the popular mind, and leads on to folly and ruin!" (Ross).

Buckle is right in pointing out the significant fact that superstition is found in any walk of life in which risk or danger predominates. Sailors are more superstitious than landsmen, while farmers and business people, especially gamblers and speculators, are more superstitious than industrial workers. Similarly Cumont is right in ascribing the superstitions of soldiers as due to risks and dangers of war.

After the great world war one notices the rise of all sorts of superstitions. Superstitions and fear are close companions. A modern historian does not hesitate to declare that "Europe is held in hate, because the nations fear each other . . . What sentiment has dug the ditch separating Russia from the rest of the world? It is fear. The states of Western Europe, which the Soviets regard as their persecutors, think themselves menaced in their turn by the Soviet republic." The Great War was produced by self-preservation and fear. The world is still in the grip of the fear instinct. The Bible claims: Fear of the Lord is the beginning of wisdom. The Latin poet declares: Primus in orbe deos fecit timor. The real state of things is: Self and fear are the Lords of life, individual and social.

Bacon in his essay "On the Wisdom of the Ancients," with his clear insight has stated the matter succinctly: "In the Panic terrors there is set forth a very wise doctrine; for by the nature of things all living creatures are endued with a certain fear and dread, the office of which is to preserve their life and existence, and to avoid or repel approaching mischief. But the same nature knows not how to keep just measure,—but together with salutary fears ever mingles vain and empty ones; insomuch that all things (if one could see into the heart of them) are quite full of Panic terrors; human things most of all; so infinitely tossed and troubled as they are with superstition (which is in truth nothing but a Panic terror), especially in seasons of hardship, anxiety, and adversity.'

CHAPTER XXX
THE HERD AND THE SUBCONSCIOUS

Superstitious terrors are by no means confined to race; they are common to all races. For example, among the aborigines of Australia a native will die after the infliction of even the most superficial wound, if he is scared by the suggestion that the weapon which inflicted the wound has been sung over, and thus endowed with magical virtue. He simply lies down, refuses food, and pines away.

Similarly among some of the Indian tribes of Brazil, if the medicine-man predicted the death of anyone who had offended him, "the wretch took to his hammock instantly in such full expectation of dying, that he would neither eat nor drink, and the prediction was effectually executed."

Speaking of certain African races Major Leonard observes: "I have seen more than one hardened old Haussa soldier dying steadily and by inches, because he believed himself to be bewitched; so that no nourishment or medicines that were given to him had the slightest effect either to check the mischief or to improve his condition in any way, and nothing was able to divert him from a fate which he considered inevitable.

"In the same way, and under very similar conditions, I have seen Kru-men and others die, in spite of every effort that was made to save them, simply because they had made up their minds, not (as we thought at the time) to die, but that being in the clutch of malignant demons they were bound to die."

The gregarious individual must obey the master leader on pain of death. In gregarious life the whole pack attacks the disobedient individual for challenging the chief, king, priest, the god-man, the lord of the horde. Obedience is a virtue, disobedience is a mortal sin, affecting the whole horde, hence a horrible death of the sinner is the sole punishment. The independent personality}' is inhibited, the individual falls into a state of social somnambulism, and the will-less, self-less subconscious, a semblance of personality, charged with self-preservation and fear instinct, obeys the commands of the master leader who is often a brutal type, a Nero, a Domitian, a Caracalla, a Caligula, a John the Terrible.

In a society where the socio-static press is always at work, where political pressure is far stronger than even in the ancient despotic monarchies, where a class government is in possession of all modern improvements, where gray uniformity and drowsy monotony reign supreme, obedience must be the rule. Blind, stupid obedience, that slavish obedience which is peculiar to somnambulic subjects, characterizes such societies.

Servility is well illustrated by the following historical incident: Prince Sougorsky, ambassador to Germany in 1576, fell sick en route in Courland. The duke of the province often inquired as to his health. The reply was always the same: "My health matters nothing, provided the sovereign's prospers." The duke, surprised, said, "How can you serve a tyrant with so much zeal?" He replied, "We Russians are always devoted to our Czars, good or cruel. My master (Ivan the Terrible) impaled a man of mark for a slight fault, who for twenty-four hours, in his dying agonies, talked with his family, and without ceasing kept repeating, 'Great God, protect the Czar!'"

The same is true of modern class societies where the Demos is the despot. God preserve the Demos! When the business demon of the Demos requires sacrifice, self immolation, anticipate his order. Pray for the Demos; Great God, protect the greedy Demos! The Demos is my Lord, to him is due my servile loyalty.

It is interesting to observe that the superstitious, the savage, the negro, and the soldier are excellent subjects for hypnotic purposes. Soldiers as experiments show, have a strong predisposition to hypnotic states. I was told by Professor Munsterberg that the hypnotic predisposition was strongly developed in the German soldier. M. Liebault experimented on ten hundred and twelve persons, and found only twenty-seven refractory. Berenheim remarks on this that "It is necessary to take into account the fact that M. Liebault operates chiefly upon the common people."

The great pressure exerted on the lower social strata, and especially on soldiers, the dull monotony of their life, the habit of strict obedience to command, predisposes them to social subconscious automatisms,—to the formation of mobs, clubs, unions, lodges, associations, parties, clans, sects, mobocracies. In all such organizations there is present the same servile spirit—the impersonal self and the gregarious fear instinct—the basis of subconscious, social somnambulism.

Man is a social somnambulist, he lives, dreams, and obeys with his eyes open. Whenever the impulse of self-preservation gets a special grip on the gregarious individual, when he becomes wild with terror in the bosom of the herd, then he may be regarded as a psychopathic victim.

The historian of the future will represent our age as dark, barbaric, savage, an age of the cruel Napoleonic wars, of commercial crises, financial panics, religious revivals, vicious, brutal, savage world wars, —mobs, crazes, plagues, social pests of all sorts and description. . A herd of sheep stand packed close together, looking stupidly into space. . . . Frighten them,— and if one begins to run, frantic with terror, the rest are sure to follow,—a stampede ensues, each sheep scrupulously reproduces the identical movements of the one in front of it. This susceptibility to imitation is but what we, in relation to man, term suggestibility, which consists in the impressing on the person of an idea, image, movement, however absurd and senseless, which the person in his hypnotized state reproduces like an automaton,—although he or she thinks it is done quite voluntarily. Suggestibility is natural to man as a social animal. Under specially favorable conditions this suggestibility which is always present in human beings may increase to an extraordinary degree, and the result is a stampede, a mob, an epidemic.

It is sometimes claimed that somnambulic persons are asleep. Sleep and somnambulism have been identified. This is a misuse of words since there are a whole series of subconscious states in which not one symptom of sleep appears. Extreme susceptibility to suggestions and mental automatisms are the chief traits of the subconscious. Gregarious men and women carry within themselves the germs of the possible mob, or of mental epidemics. As social creatures men and women are naturally suggestible. When this susceptibility or sensitivity to suggestions becomes abnormally intense, we may say that they are thrown into a social subconscious, somnambulic state.

We know by psychological and psychopathological experiments that limitation of voluntary movements and inhibition of free activities induce a sub-conscious state. This subconscious state is characterized by inhibition of the will power,— memory remains unaffected; consciousness appears intact; the subject is aware of all that goes on. Keeping this in mind, we can understand social life, and especially morbid, social movements, mob life of all ages.

A subconscious state is induced in the organized individual by the great limitation of his voluntary activities and by the inhibition of his free critical thought. Bound fast by the strings of tradition and authority, social men and women are reduced to subconscious automata. The subconscious rises with the growth of organized civilization, while the critical, independent powers of the individual correspondingly fall. Hence the apparent social paradox that the growth of society tends to destroy the mental forces which helped to build up civilization.

In such societies the individual staggers under the burden of laws and taboos. Individuality is stifled under the endless massive excretions of legislators. Recently even the lawgivers or law manufacturers .began to object to the labor involved in the work on the ever growing mass of bills introduced into the legislature of one state alone. Thus a senator of a Western state complained that in one year over 1700 bills passed through the mill of his Legislature. Multiply that figure by the number of states, add the municipal edicts, and the endless laws turned out by the Federal Government, and one can form some faint idea of the vast burden laid on the shoulders of the individual citizen.

The Los Angeles Times, which no one will accuse of radicalism, pointedly remarks: "The State has just issued a reference index to the laws of California since 1850—it is of itself a bulky volume of more than 1300 pages. When it takes a book of that size merely as an index it would seem that the lawmakers had about done their worst." Overproduction of laws is one of the great evils of modern civilization. Civilized society is apt to be obsessed by a state of law-mania which is a danger and a menace to the free development of the individual citizen.

The Roman legal thinkers left us two significant sayings: Ex Scnatus consultis et plebiscitis, crimina execrentur, — (Senatorial decisions and popular decrees give rise to crimes) and: Ut olim vitiis, sic nunc legibus laboramus, —(As we formerly suffered from vices and crimes so we suffer at present from laws and legislation) . . .

In describing the gregariousness of the Damara oxen Francis Galton writes: "Although the ox has so little affection for, or interest in, his fellows, he cannot endure even a momentary severance from his herd. If he be separated from it by stratagem or force, he exhibits every sign of mental agony; he strives with all liis might to get back again, and when he succeeds, he plunges into the middle to bathe his whole body with the comfort of closest companionship. This passionate terror is a convenience to the herdsman." . . . When an animal accustomed to a gregarious life is isolated from the herd, it is agitated with extreme terror. The same holds true of man who is a social animal. Man must go with the herd or with the pack, and he is terrified to stand alone, away from the crowd,—and still more terrorized when the crowd disapproves of him. Man is gregarious, and as such he must go with the mass, with the crowd. He is in mortal fear of social taboo. As a gregarious animal man lives in fear of external danger, and is in terror of social authority.

As Galton writes: "The vast majority of persons of our race have a natural tendencv to shrink from the responsibility of standing and acting alone; they exalt the vox popull, even when they know it to be the utterance of a mob of nobodies, into the vox Dei; they are willing slaves to tradition, authority and custom. The intellectual deficiencies corresponding to these moral flaws are shown by the rareness of free and original thought as compared with the frequency and readiness with which men accept the opinions of those in authority as binding on their judgment." This slavish obedience is intimately bound up with one of the most fundamental of all instincts,—the fear instinct.

The individual is so effectively trained by the pressure of taboo based on self and fear, that he comes to love the yoke that weighs him down to earth. Chained to his bench like a criminal galley slave, he comes to love his gyves and manacles. The iron collar put around his neck becomes a mark of respectability, an ornament of civilization. Tarde finds that society is based on respect, a sort of an alloy of fear and love, fear that is loved. A respectable citizen is he who is fond of his bonds, stocks, and shekels, and comes to love his bonds, stocks, and shackles of fears and taboos.

Human institutions depend for their existence and stability on the impulse of self-preservation and its close associate,—the fear instinct.

CHAPTER XXXI
MYSTICISM, PRAYER, CONVERSION, AND METAPHYSICS

The psychology of mysticism and conversion is a fascinating subject. This is not the place to go into detail or even adequately cover the subject which is as extensive as it is important. I can only touch the matter in a superficial way—enough to answer the present purpose. The state of mysticism is essentially a hypnoidal trance state, and its traits are the characteristics of the hypnoidal consciousness. Like the hypnoidal state, that of the mystic state may pass into waking, sleep, or into the hypnotic condition.

James marks off mystic states, by the traits of Ineffability, Transciency, Passivity, and Noetic Quality. These traits are just the ones found in the deeper states of the hypnoidal consciousness, especially the ones which approximate and pass into the hypnotic condition. In the mystical state, as in the hypnoidal state, there is a delicious languor, a lack of tension to the stimulation of the external environment which retreats in the distance; there is the instability of the hypnoidal consciousness which soon passes into the other forms such as sleep, hypnosis, or waking. There is also present the refreshing, invigorating condition of the whole individuality on emerging from those peculiar subconscious states. The lethargic and cataleptic states often present in states of ecstasy, in which the mystics fall, depend entirely on states of the hypnoido-hypnotic trance.

The mystic consciousness and the hypnoidal one are not identical. The mystic consciousness is a species of the hypnoidal consciousness. What are then its special features? In the first place, the mystic consciousness has a negative and a positive aspect, depression and exaltation. In the second place, mysticism expresses a definite reaction of the individual to the conditions of his external environment. This reaction is one of retraction from the miseries and fears of life.

If we examine closely the type of consciousness characteristic of the state preceding the onset of the mystic condition, we find that it is essentially that of suffering, of misery, of disappointment, of despair, of inability to meet fairly, squarely, and courageously the experiences of life. There is a strong feeling of insecurity, a feeling of anxiety as to self and the world. A feeling of intense anguish seizes on the individual that he and the world are going to perdition, that on such terms life is not worth living. The instinct of fear penetrates every pore of his being, and inspires the individual with dread, horror, and terror. Terrorized by the wild evils of life, the personality becomes benumbed and paralyzed, and ready to succumb. This state of intense depression is not simply related to fear, it is fear. It is the status melancholicus often preceding states of exaltation. The individual reaches a critical condition where life becomes impossible. The whole universe holds for him nothing but terrors and horrors.

Carlyle expresses this attitude when he makes Teufelsdrockh say: "I live in a continual, indefinite, pining fear; tremulous, pusillanimous, apprehensive of I know not what: it seems as if things, all things in the heavens above and the earth beneath would hurt me; as if the heavens and the earth were but boundless jaws of a devouring monster, wherein I, palpitating, lie waiting to be devoured." In this state of agony of fear, the individual looks for salvation in fleeing from the terrors of the world to the arms of the divinity.

In his terror the individual passes through a second stage, he becomes "converted," he turns with prayers to the divine power to which he looks for shelter from the dangers of life. He appeals to the divinity for protection from the evils of the day and from the terrors of the night. This second stage is often preceded by a period of subconscious incubation which sometimes gives rise to sudden conscious explosions, conscious conversions, or sudden onset of mystic state of ecstasy.

"O Goddess, in the anguish of my heart have I raised cries of anguish to thee; declare forgiveness. May thy heart be at rest. May thy liver be pacified. The sin which I have committed I know not. The Lord in the anger of his heart hath looked upon me. The goddess hath become angry and hath stricken me grievously. I sought for help, but no one taketh my hand. I wept, but no one cometh to my side. I utter cries, but no one harkens to me. I am afflicted, I am overcome. Unto my merciful god I turn. I kiss the feet of my goddess. How long, known and unknown god, until the anger of thy heart be pacified? How long, known and unknown goddess, until thy unfriendly heart be pacified? Mankind is perverted, and has no judgment, Of all men who are alive, who knows anything? They do not know whether they do good or evil. O Lord, do not cast aside thy servant! He is cast into the mire; take his hand. The sin which I have sinned turn to mercy ! Known and unknown goddess, my sins are seven. times seven; Forgive my sins! Forgive my sins, and I will humble myself before thee. May thy heart, as the heart of a mother who hath borne children, be glad! As a father who hath begotten them, may it be glad!"

In this respect we agree with Ribot. "Depression," says Ribot, "is related to fear. . . . Does not the worshipper entering a venerated sanctuary show all the symptoms of pallor, trembling, cold sweat, inability to speak—all that the ancients so justly called sacer horror? The self abasement, the humility of the worshipper before the deity supposed to be possessed of magic power, is essentially one of fear." With the anthropologist we may refer this awe or fear to the terror which the savage mind feels in the presence of the magician, the witch, the medicine man, the man-god, and the woman-deity.

The Mithraic religion, which for some time has been the great rival of Christianity for the salvation of the individual from the terrors of the world, played a great role in the mystic ceremonies of the cult. In fact, the dying and the resurrection of a god-man for the salvation of the worshippers constituted a cardinal principle in the actual practices or rites of barbarous nations and savage tribes. The man-god or woman-deity had to die, had to be sacrificed by the community. The sins of the savages were redeemed by the divine flesh and blood of "the man-god."

In describing the life and theological doctrines of St. Paul, Professor Pfleiderer says: "Perhaps Paul was influenced by the popular idea of the god who dies and returns to life, dominant at that time in the Adonis, Attis, and Osiris cults of Hither Asia (with various names and customs, everywhere much alike). At Antioch, the Syrian capital, in which Paul had been active for a considerable period, the main celebration of the Adonis feast took place in the springtime. On the first day, the death of "Adonis," the Lord, was celebrated, while on the following day, amid the wild songs of lamentations sung by the women, the burial of his corpse (represented by an image) was enacted. On the next day (in the Osiris celebration it was the third day after death, while in the Attis celebration it was the fourth day) proclamation was made that the god lived and he (his image) was made to rise in the air. It is noteworthy that the Greek Church has preserved a similar ceremony in its Easter celebration down to our own day.

"During the joyous feast of the resurrection of the god in the closely related Attis celebration, the priest anointed the mouths of the mourners with oil, and repeated the formula:

'Good cheer, ye pious! As our god is saved, So shall we, too, be saved in our distress.'

"The rescue of the god from death is the guarantee of a like rescue for the adherents of his cult. In the mysteries of Attis, Isis, and Mithra, the fact that the worshippers partook of the god's life by the mystical participation in his death, was visualized by such rites, which employed symbols showing the death of the initiate, his descent into Hades, and his return. Hence, this ceremony was called the 'rebirth to a career of new salvation,' a 'holy birthday.' In one Mithra liturgy, the newly initiated pray: 'Lord, reborn, I depart; in that I am lifted up, I die; born by that birth which produces life, I will be saved in death, and go the way which thou hast established, according to thy law and the sacrament which thou hast created.' "

In all those mysteries the central note is the salvation of the worshipper from the "perils of the soul. In some cases the terrorized individual is driven to the mystic state. He falls into a sort of trance. The world of fears becomes veiled from him, and recedes in a mist, and even completely disappears from his view. He finds repose in his god. This is the positive stage of mental exaltation, of ecstasy; it figures as "the union" of the worshipper with his god or goddess. It is this oblivion in the depths of the hypnoidal and the hypnotic states, it is this relapse into the regions of the subconscious that brings about relief from all fears of life. The bliss felt in these dim regions of mental life refreshes and invigorates the wearied soul. The coming in contact with new vast stores of subconscious reserve energy may once more vitalize and supply with new energy the fear stricken personality. This is the inspiration of those who have experienced the mystical power of "conversion."

In a later chapter I take up the subject of subconscious reserve energy advanced by James and myself, independently. Meanwhile, we may say that the phenomena of prayer, conversion, and especially of mysticism belong fundamentally to the manifestations of self-preservation and the fear instinct on the one side and to subconscious reserve energy on the other. Of course, we must add the fact that certain historical and social conditions are apt to give rise to phenomena of mysticism, the conditions of social unrest being especially favorable. When social life begins to decay, when the protection of society is weakened, and the individual is set loose, and left to stand alone, something that especially terrorizes the social brute, then nothing is left to the individual bereft of his social stays and social stimulants, but to turn inward and upward, that is to turn mystic. In his states of desolation and fear-obsession the individual is inclined to turn to the stimulating, narcotizing influence of the deity which puts the soul in a state of transcendental bliss, thus hiding the terrorized soul in a misty and mystic cloud, so that he no longer sees the terrors and horrors of life.

Such mystic states are found in periods of social and moral decay. Instance the decaying Roman empire, the Hellenistic period, the Middle Ages, and in fact, any period in which security, safety, and social stability are on the ebb, while fears and perils are on the increase. Mysticism, Salvation of the soul, under all their guises, are interrelated with the primordial fear instinct which dominates the hunted beast and the terror-stricken neurotic patient.

If we turn to philosophical and metaphysical speculations, we find, on examination from a pragmatic point of view, that their essential differences revolve on the security and safety of the world scheme. From Plato and Aristotle to Seneca, Epictetus, Marcus Aurelius, down to Schopenhauer, Hegel, and our American thinkers Royce and James, as well as from the Bible to Brahmanism and Buddhism, we find the same valuation of world safety, based on the vital impulse of self-preservation and its fundamental fear instinct. The Salvation of the World and the Individual is the fundamental keynote of theological metaphysics and metaphysical religion.

Professor Royce, the representative of transcendental, monistic idealism in America, thus summarizes his philosophical and religious attitude: "It is God's true and eternal triumph that speaks to us 'In this world ye shall have tribulations. But fear not; I have overcome the world." This reminds one of the ancient Assyrian cuneiform oracles addressed to the Assyrian kings: "To Esarhaddon, king of countries, Fear not! I am Ishtar of Arbela. Thine enemies I will cut off, fear not!" "Fear not, Esarhaddon, I, Bel, am speaking with thee. The beams of thy heart I will support." "Fear not, you are saved by Faith. Fear thy Lord only, He is your Rock and Salvation," says the Bible. "Fear not!" teaches the Buddhist, "Nirvana, the Absolute, is your refuge."

Professor James in his inimitable way summarizes the difference between his pluralism and idealistic monism: "What do believers in the Absolute mean by saying that their belief affords them comfort? They mean that since in the Absolute finite evil is 'overruled' already, we may, therefore, whenever we wish, treat the temporal as if it were potentially the eternal, be sure that we can trust its outcome, and, without sin, dismiss our fear and drop the worry of our finite responsibility. . . . The universe is a system of which the individual members may relax their anxieties . . ." James contrasts his empirical, pragmatic pluralism with the idealistic monism:

In another place James says: "Suppose that the world's author put the case before you before creating, saying: 'I am going to make a world not certain to be saved, a world, the perfections of which shall be conditioned merely, the condition being that each several agent "does his level best." I offer you the chance of taking part in such a world. Its safety, you see, is unwarranted. It is a real adventure, with real danger, yet it may win through . . . Will you join the procession? Will you trust yourself and trust the other agents enough to face the risk?' Should you in all seriousness, if participation in such a world were proposed to you, feel bound to reject it as not safe enough? Would you say that rather than be part and parcel of so fundamentally pluralistic and irrational a universe, you preferred to relapse into the slumber of nonentity from which you had been aroused by the tempter's voice?

"Of course, if you are normally constituted, you would do nothing of the sort. There is a healthy-minded buoyancy in most of us which such a universe would exactly fit. . . . The world proposed would seem 'rational' to us in the most living- way.

"Most of us, I say, would, therefore, welcome the proposition, and add our fiat to the fiat of the creator. Yet perhaps some would not; for there are morbid minds in every human collection, and to them the prospect of a universe with only a fighting chance of safety would probably not appeal. There are moments of discouragement in us all, when we are sick of self, and tired of vainly striving. Our own life breaks down, and we fall into the attitude of the prodigal son. We mistrust the chance of things. We want a universe where we can just give up, fall on our father's neck, and be absorbed into the absolute life as a drop of water melts into the river or the sea.

"The peace and rest, the security desiderated at such moments is security against the bewildering accidents of so much finite experience. Nirvana means safety from this everlasting round of adventure of which the world of sense consists. The Hindoo and the Buddhist, for this is essentially their attitude, are simply afraid, *afraid* of more experience, afraid of life. . . .Pluralistic moralism simply makes their teeth chatter, it refrigerates the very heart within their breast."

Thus we find that at the bottom of philosophical, metaphysical, and religious speculations there are present the same primitive impulse of self-preservation and fear instinct. While there are some other important factors in that theological and metaphysical problem which has agitated humanity for ages, a problem which I expect to discuss some other time in another place, there is no doubt that James with his great psychological genius has laid his finger on fundamental factors of human life,—self-preservation and the fear instinct.

CHAPTER XXXII
FEAR SUGGESTIONS

In my psychopathological and clinical work of the various manifestations and symptoms of psychopathic and functional diseases I come to the conclusion that the principal cause of all those morbid affections is the fear instinct, rooted in the very impulse of life, the impulse of self preservation. Fears are not secondary effects, they are due to one of the most fundamental of all instincts, the instinct of fear which is primary and elemental.

Anything which arouses the fear instinct in the inhibitory or paralyzing stages will necessarily give rise to psychopathic functional psychosis or neurosis. The fear instinct and the impulse of self-preservation, inherent in all life, are the alpha and omega of psychopathic maladies. The fear instinct is usually cultivated by a long history of events of a fearsome character so that fear instinct and the impulse of self-preservation become easily aroused on various occasions of external stimulation, producing general fear,

mental or emotional, and often accompanied by sensory, motor, and intestinal derangements of various organs with their secretions and hormones, as well as with general morbid, functional changes of the central nervous system, sympathetic and parasympathetic systems. This in its turn gradually cultivates a disposition to formation of hypnoidal states, that is, the brief momentary formation of trance states, in which the subconscious becomes through dissociation exposed to fear suggestions or fear stimulations, which arouse in the morbidly cultivated subconscious morbid fear symptoms, motor, sensory, intestinal, emotional in their various combinations and associations.

The cultivated predisposition to lapses into hypnoidal states is a prerequisite of psychopathic disturbances. We may, therefore, say that the three factors, namely, Self-preservation, Fear instinct, Hypnoidal states form the triumvirate of psychopathic, functional neurosis. Charcot with his sharp eye for observation as well as his long clinical experience observed, in what he termed hystericals, a brooding period which precedes the manifestations of the hysterical attacks and symptom complex of the hysterical manifestations. These brooding periods are of the utmost consequence, although Charcot and his disciples as well as the psychopathologists generally, hardly paid any attention to this important phenomenon.

These brooding periods preceding the onset of the malady afterwards recur regularly before each attack of the malady, only the period is brief, and is hardly noticeable except by the one who looks searchingly. Psychopathologists pass this important stage without noticing its full significance. The period appears as a sort of a psychic aura, a sort of momentary attack of epileptic petit mat. This brooding state is a modification of the hypnoidal state.

It is during such hypnoidal states, when the conditions which I have shown to be requisite for the induction of trance or .subconscious states, happen to be specially strong and the hypnoidal state is prolonged, that the unprotected subconscious becomes subject to fear suggestions or to stimuli arousing the fear instinct and the impulse of self-preservation.

"Many patients," says the famous physiologist and physician, Mosso, "die in the hospital from fear and depression who would probably have recovered had they been tended in their own homes. ... In their morning round the physicians find that the serious cases have grown worse, while those who are better beg to be dismissed. . . . The physician, who has the night watch must walk up and down the whole night, and is kept busy preventing convulsive attacks, or fainting fits.

"Fear attacks nullify every effort of the will. . . . Even Alexander of Macedon had to count with fear in his courageous army of select Macedonians. In order to insure victory he offered sacrifices to Fear before he joined battle."

Physical maladies become worse during the night, and especially during the early morning hours when the energy of the body is at its lowest level,—conscious and subconscious fears reaching their highest intensity. This holds specially true of nervous cases, and particularly of psychopathic patients, who are dominated by the impulse of self-preservation and the fear instinct. The fears and worries keep the patient awake, and the subconscious fears become emphasized by concentration of attention, monotony, limitation of field of consciousness, limitation of voluntary movements, and other factors favorable to dissociation and the induction of the hypnoidal state, in which the patient becomes sensitive to the awakening of the fear instinct, with all its horrible fear suggestions.

The symptoms of the disease which are more or less under his control during the day become often so intensified in the dark, that the patients become demoralized with fear, suffering as they do the anxiety and anguish induced by the terrors of the night. Even medical men, professors of medical colleges, who have come under my care, have confessed to me that, when in a state of insomnia, the terrors of the night are so intense that they had to resort to morphine to still the anguish of the fear instinct.

For years I lived in close relation with neurotic, psychopathic patients. I watched them day and night. I have been called by patients for medical aid in the late hours of the night, and more so during the vigil hours of the darkness of the night. I had to relieve and soothe the fears, the terrors of the night. It is in the night, when in a low state of neuron energy that patients feel the grip of horrors oppressing them with nightmares of the relentless and merciless instinct, the fear instinct. To be relieved of the night terrors many patients are willing to risk anything, even the consequence of deadly narcotics, the plagues of mental healers, and the sexual phantasms of Psychoanalysis.

The hypnoidal state is induced artificially, often brought about by intoxication, as in the case of holy Soma drink among the Hindoos, or by fasting, as among the American Indians during the initiation periods, or by dancing, such as the corrobboree among the aborigines of Australia, or by singing, or by praying. All the conditions of disjunction of consciousness with the manifestations of subconscious activities are brought into play, in order to come in contact with demons, spirits, totems, and find among them guides and protectors.

In prolonged hypnoidal states, the fear instinct and the impulse of self-preservation are calmed under appropriate conditions. Illusions and hallucinations which easily appeared in the twilight states of hypnoidal subconscious states became manifested as beneficent spirits, as agents favorable to the life existence of the individual, the spirit appearing as the totem, the guardian of the individual. Prayer and singing, which are the most successful of all the methods of inducing subconscious subwaking, twilight states, have survived to our present day.

Of all the methods of utilization of subconscious subwaking, twilight states the most effective is prayer, especially-, the individual form of prayer. Prayer admirably fulfills the conditions requisite for the induction of the hypnoidal state and for the getting access to the subconscious activities, the formation of subconscious personalities, subconscious illusions and hallucinations. Such subconscious states have been shown, on experimental evidence, to be not of a sensory, but of a purely delusional character, strong enough to affect the individual with an intense belief in its external reality.

The deluded human mind in its craven fear of the unseen and the mysterious spirit-forces helps itself to any soporific or anaesthetic, narcotic stimulant, to bring about a scission of the conscious self from the subconscious activities. The induction of the hypnoidal state is brought about by all kinds of intoxicants, narcotics, fasting, dancing, self-mortification, sex excesses which exhaust the devotee, and leave him in a state of trance. All such practices and rites seek blindly for some trance-state to still the morbid fear instinct.

The psychoanalysis of Freud, Jung, Adler, Stoekel, with their sexual love, belongs to this category of narcotic sexual religions which inhibit the critical self. [3] "Die Theorie behauptet mit ausschliessender Sicherheit (?), das es nur sexuelle Wiinschregungen aus dem Infantilen sein konnen, welche in den Entwicklungsperioden der Kindheit die Verdrangung (Affectverwandlung) erfahren haben, in spateren Entwicklungsperioden dann einer Erneuerung fahig sind, sei es in folge der sexuelle Konstitution, die sich ja aus der ursprunglichen Bisexualitat herausbildet, sei es in folge un-giinstiger Einflusse des sexuellen Lebens, und die somit die Triebkrafte fiir alle psychoneurotische Symptombildung ab geben." (S. Freud, 'Die Traumdeutung," p. 376, zweite Auflage 1909.) In other words, slippery and mutable as Freud's statements are, he clearly declares in his magnum opus the far-reaching generalization that neurosis is based on infantile sexual wishes, either due to bisexuality or to unfavorable influences of sexual life. Suppression of sexual experiences can be easily observed (by competent observers, of course), in infants a few months old. If you miss the process of suppression in the baby, you can easily trace it by means of psychoanalysis lo the early recollections of tender infancy. It is certainly lack of comprehension that induces Ziehen to dub Freud's speculations as Unsinn (nonsense). Freud's admirers with a metaphysical proclivity delight over the theory of repressed wishes. The wish is fundamental and prior to all mental states. This piece of metaphysical psychologism is supposed to be based on clinical experience. If wishes were horses, beggars would ride. The Freudist manages to ride such horses.

The following specidation of Jung's well represents the metaphysico-religious character of psychoanalysis: "By entering again into the mother's womb he (Christ) redeems ir death the sin of life of the primitive man, Adam, in order symbolically through his deed to procure for the innermost and most hidden meaning of the religious libido its highest satisfaction and most pronounced expression ... In the Christian mysteries the resurrected one becomes a supermundane spirit, and the invisible kingdom of God, with its mysterious gifts are obtained by his believers through the sacrifice of himself on his mother. In psychoanalysis the infantile personality is deprived of its libido fixations in a rational manner. The libido which is thus set free serves for the building up of a personality matured and adapted to reality, a personality that does willingly and without complaint everything required by necessity. (It is, so to speak, the chief endeavor of the infantile personality to struggle against all necessities, and to create coercions for itself where none exist in reality.)" Such metaphysico-religious lucubrations parade under the term psychoanalysis.

"Man," says James, "believes as much as he can," but the credulity of the psychoanalyst is limitless. The psychoanalyst with his allegories, symbolism, sublimation, incest phantasies, bi-sexuality, sexual suppression, mother complexes, Oedipus and Electra phantasms, and all the other complex psychoanalytic instrumentalities is an excellent example of sex obsessed, delusional dementia praecox. Psychoanalysis is a sort of sexual mysticism. All mental life is reduced by psychoanalysis to "creation" or "procreation."

CHAPTER XXXIII
LIFE ENERGY AND THE NEUROTIC

The subject of fear may be considered from a somewhat different point of view, namely from a purely physiological and biological aspect. The cell in general, the nerve cell, or neuron, is a reservoir of energy. In fact the great biologist Sachs proposed to term the cell, energid.

For we must look at the organism as a store of energy which is used up in the course of the adjustments of the individual to his environment. The organism stores up energy and uses the energy during the course of its life activity. Life energy is physiological, bio-chemical, electrical, mechanical, etc. The mental and emotional activities are intimately related with the expenditure of energy accumulated by the cells of the organism, which discharge that energy in response to the various stimulations of the external world. In its activities the organism keeps on taking in energy, and once more discharging energy in its life reactions. The storing up of energy falls under the anabolic or building up processes, while the discharging or liberating processes of the amount of the stored up energy are classed under the catabolic processes.

The total cycle of energy from the start of storage to the end of liberation of energy, starting once more with the storing of energy, may be regarded as the cycles of organic functional activity which is classified under metabolism. We deal here with a reservoir of vital energy whose life activities or reactions depend on the amount of energy contained in the cell or the neuron, and whose functioning and reactions vary with the level of energy in the reservoir.

The neuron is but a highly differentiated cell or reservoir for the intake and outgo of energy. In this respect the nerve cell is entirely like other cells of humbler function. Every cell is a storage cell, accumulating energy and then liberating it at an appropriate occasion of a given stimulus, all cells working for the preservation of the organism as a whole. The rise and fall of the level of energy in the reservoir regulate the various manifestations, sensory, motor, emotional, mental which the individual displays to the various stimulations coming from his environment.

Within certain limits the fall of energy is normal, —when it reaches a certain level the organism once more replenishes the store and once more the level of energy rises. This energy is Dynamic under certain conditions. However, the discharge of energy must go on, and the organism must draw further on its store of energy, on the accumulated store of energy put away for safety and emergency. This stored up energy is Reserve Energy. [4]

The late Charles S. Minot, the American histologist, points out this reserve energy present in the organism, a reserve energy of growth called forth under special emergencies of life. By a striking series of instructive facts, Dr. Meltzer points out that "all organs of the body are built on the plan of superabundance of structure and energy." Like Minot, Meltzer refers to the significant fact that most of our active organs possess a great surplus of functioning cells. This surplus is requisite for the safety of the individual.

If, however, the drain of energy still goes on without replenishing the total store, the energy drawn on the region of the danger zone is entered. This energy is Static. The concomitant symptoms are various psychomotor and psycho-secretory disturbances of a psychopathic or psycho-neurotic character. This energy is drawn from the upper levels of energy. Under such conditions restitution of the total amount of energy to its normal level is still possible. Should the process of liberation of energy go on further without restitution, the energy drawn is taken from the lower levels of static energy, and the symptoms are functional, neuropathic. The lowermost levels of static energy are the last the cell can dispense with to save itself from total destruction. With further increase of discharge of energy the cell must give its very life activity, the energy is drawn from the breaking up of cell tissue; this energy is organic or necrotic.

Thus the total energy of the nerve cell or the neuron may be divided into normal dynamic energy, reserve energy, static energy, and organic or necrotic energy. The various nervous and mental diseases may thus be correlated with the flow and ebb of neuron energy, with the physiological and pathological processes that take place in the neuron in the course of its activity and reactions to the stimuli of the external and internal environment.

The various levels of neuron energy may be represented by the diagram on page 336.

Static energy is indicated by the diagram NWFI. By organic energy is meant that energy contained in the very structure of the tissues of the neuron, not as yet decomposed into their inorganic constituents. This is indicated by diagram IFGH.

These phases of neuron energy are not different kinds of energy, in the sense of being distinct entities ; they merely represent progressive phases or stages of the same process of neuron activity. Liberation of neuron energy is correlative with active psychic and physical manifestations. Hence states of the nervous system corresponding to liberations of energy are designated as waking states. Restitution of expended energy or arrest of liberation of neuron energy goes hand in hand with passive conditions of the nervous system; hence states of restitution or arrest of energy are termed collectively sleeping states.

The ascending arrow, indicating the process of restitution of energy, corresponds to the ascending arrow on the right, indicating the parallel psychomotor sleeping states. The descending arrows indicate physiological and pathological processes of liberation of energy, and also their concomitant psychomotor waking states. "Ascending" and "descending" mean the rise and fall of the amount of neuron energy, taking the upper level of dynamic energy as the starting point. Briefly stated, descent means liberation of energy with its concomitant, psychomotor, waking states. Ascent means restitution of energy with its parallel sleeping states.

The cycles in dynamic energy correspond to the physiological manifestations of the nervous system in the activity and rest of the individual in normal daily life. Concomitant with the expenditure of dynamic energy of the neurons, the individual passes through the active normal waking state, and hand in hand with the restitution of this expended energy, he passes through the sleeping states of normal daily life.

When, however, in the expenditure of energy, the border line or margin is crossed, dynamic and reserve energies are used up. In crossing KA the ordinary normal energies of everyday life are exhausted, and reserve energy has to be drawn upon. If this reserve energy is not accessible, the static energy is used, or in case the reserve energy is exhausted, then once more the static energy has to be drawn upon; in either case the individual enters the domain of the abnormal, of the pathological.

When the upper levels of static energy are used, the symptoms are of a psychopathic or neurotic character. When the use of energy reaches the lower levels of static energy, affecting the very nutrition of the neuron, neuropathic manifestations are the result. When the neuron itself is affected, that is the organic structure is being dissolved, then organopathies result. It means the death of the nerve cell.

CHAPTER XXXIV
DYNAMIC ENERGY

Whenever the dynamic energy is exhausted and the levels of reserve energy are reached, the individual affected begins to feel restless, and if there is no access to the levels of reserve energy, the individual gets scared. The fear instinct becomes awakened, giving rise, after repeated unavailing attempts, to the states of psychopathic neurosis. In states of depression, such as hypochondria and more especially in states of melancholia, the fear instinct is potent. The fear instinct is brought about in the darkness of the night, when the individual is fatigued from his day's labor, when the external stimuli are at a minimum, and reserve energy is not available. The fear instinct rises from the subconscious regions to the surface of conscious activities.

Convalescent states as well as exhaustion from pain and disease, such as fever or a shock from some accident, war-shock, shell-shock, surgical shock predispose to the manifestation of the fear instinct. Hence the caution of surgeons in the preparation of the patient for a serious operation. For the result may be a shock to the system due to the subconscious activities of the fear instinct present in subconscious mental life, no longer protected by the guardianship of the upper consciousness. And it may also be shown, both by experiment and observation, that during the subconscious states when the lower strata of dynamic energy are reached, such as hypnoidal, hypnoid states, and sleep, that the individual is more subject to fear than during the waking states. We know how a sudden noise, a flash of light during drowsy states or sleep startles one, and the same holds true of any stimulus. I have observed the same condition of fright during hypnoidal states.

We must agree with the French psychologist, Ribot, when he comes to the conclusion that "every lowering of vitality, whether permanent or temporary, predisposes to fear; the physiological conditions which engender or accompany it, are all ready; in a weakened organism fear is always in a nascent condition. "

The fear instinct becomes morbid when the individual has to draw on his reserve energy, and finds he is unable to do it. The cure consists in the release of the reserve energy which has become inaccessible. This can be done by various methods, but the best is the method of induction of the hypnoidal state under the control of a competent psychopathologist. The whole process consists in the restitution of the levels of dynamic energy and the building up of the patient's active personality.

From our point of view, fear is not necessarily due to pain previously experienced, it may be purely instinctive. The fear instinct may be aroused directly, such for instance is the fear of young children who have never before experienced a fall. In fact we claim that the fear instinct and the restlessness which expresses it antedate and precede pain. The fear of pain is but one of the forms under which the fear instinct is manifested. The fear instinct appears long before pain and pleasure come into existence. This holds true not only of the lower animal life, but also of the vague fear found in many a case of neurasthenia and functional neurosis and psychosis. Ribot also calls attention to pantophobia. "This is a state in which the patient fears everything, where anxiety instead of being riveted on one object, floats as a dream, and onl} r becomes fixed for an instant at a time, passing from one object to another, as circumstances may determine."

It is probably best to classify fears as antecedent and subsequent to experience, or fears as undifferentiated and differentiated. When the dynamic energy is used up in the course of life adaptations, and reserve energy is drawn upon, there may be danger that the energy may be used up until the static energy is reached, and neuropathic conditions are manifested. These conditions are preceded by psychopathic disturbances. Associative life becomes disturbed, and emotional reactions become morbid. There is a degeneration or reversion to earlier and lower forms of mental activity, and to lower instinctive life. The primitive instincts, the impulse of self-preservation and the fear instinct, come to the foreground, giving rise to the various forms of psychopathic affections.

This process of degeneration and simplification is characteristic of all forms of psychopathic conditions, though it may be more prominent in some cases than in others. The type of mental life becomes lowered and there is a reversion, a sort of atavism, to simpler and more childish experiences, memories, reactions of earlier and less complex forms of mental life. I have laid special stress on this feature of psychopathic reactions in all my works on the subject. What I emphasize in my present work is the fact that psychopathic reactions are dominated by self and fear, which are laid bare by the process of degeneration.

The patient in psychopathic states is tortured by his fears, he is obsessed by wishes which are entirely due to his fear and deranged impulse of self-preservation. As the static energy is reached, and with lack of functional energy of the dynamic character, the energy habitually used in the ordinary relations of life, the patient experiences a monotony, a void in his life activity. He has a feeling of distress, as if something is haunting him, and possibly something terrible is going to happen to him or his family. He may have a feeling of some depression, and may suffer from a constant unquenchable craving for new stimulations, run after new impressions and excitements which pale in a short time on his fagged mind. He is restless, demanding new amusements and distractions. He is distracted with fear, conscious and more often subconscious, —which he is unable to dispel or shake off. He seems to stand over a fearful precipice, and he is often ready to do anything to avoid this terrible gap in his life. Life is empty, devoid of all interest; he talks of ennui and even of suicide; he is of a pessimistic, gloomy disposition, his state of mind approaching a state of melancholia. He asks for new sensations, new pleasures, new enjoyments which soon tire him. He is in the condition of a leaking barrel which never can be filled.

Psychopathic individuals are in a state of the wicked "who are like the ocean which never rests." This misery of ever forming wishes and attempting to assuage the inner suffering, this craving for new pleasures and excitements, in order to still uneasiness, distress, and the pangs of the fear instinct with its gnawing, agonizing anxieties, brings the patient to a state in which he is ready to drink and use narcotics. The patient seeks ways to relieve his misery. The patient has used up all his available dynamic energy, and being unable to reach the stores of reserve energy looks for a key or stimulant to release his locked up reserve energies. The patient is unable to respond to the stimuli of life, so he attempts then the use of his static energy. This can only result in producing psychopathic and neuropathic symptoms.

The patient needs to be lifted out of the misery of monotony and ennui of life, he needs to be raised from his low level of vitality, to be saved from the listlessness into which he has fallen. The low level of energy makes him feel like a physical, nervous, and mental bankrupt. This bankruptcy is unbearable to him. He is in a state of distraction, distracted with the agony of fear. Something must be done to free himself from the depression of low spirits and from the low level of energy which keeps him in a state devoid of all interest in life, accompanied by physical, mental and moral fatigue. He is like a prisoner doomed to a life long term.

This constant craving for stimulation of energy, this reaction to the anxiety of the morbid fear instinct is the expression of exhaustion of available dynamic energy for the purpose of normal life activity. The patient attempts to draw on his latent reserve energy. Since this form of energy is not accessible to the stimulations of common life, he tries to release the energy by means of artificial stimulations, be it morphine, alcohol, mysticism, Freudism, sexual and religious "at-one-ments" or by other stimuli of exciting character. Unable to release energy by fair means the patient is driven to the employment of foul means for the stimulation of new sources of energy. The psychopathic patient is driven by fear, by fears of life and death.

The morbid fear instinct in all cases is brought about by exhaustion of energy, whether sudden or gradual. Fear is due to exhaustion of lower levels of dynamic energy and to the inability of liberation of stored up reserve energy. The more intense this incapacity of utilization of reserve stores of energy be, the more intense is the fear. When this condition is prolonged the psychopathic symptoms become unendurable. The experienced, thinking surgeon has learned the danger of this condition in his operating room. Thus it is told of Porta, the great surgeon of Pavia, when his patients died under an operation, he used to throw his knife and instruments contemptuously to the ground, and shout in a tone of reproach to the corpse: "Cowards die of fear."

The great physiologist Mosso gives a graphic description of the effects of fear in a pathetic case that has come under his personal observation: "As army surgeon, I had once to be present at the execution of some brigands. It was a summary judg- ment. A major of the besaglicri put a few questions to one or two, then turning to the captain said simpty: 'Shoot them.' I remember one lad, of scarcely twenty years of age, who mumbled replies to a few questions, then remained silent, in the position of a man warding off a fatal blow, with lifted arms, extended palms, the neck drawn between the shoulders, the head held sideways, the body bent and drawn backwards. When he heard the dreadful words he emitted a shrill, heart-rending cry of despair, looked around him, as though eagerly seeking something, then turned to flee, and rushed with outspread arms against a wall of the court, writhing and scratching it as though trying to force an entrance between the stones, like a polyp clinging to a rock. After a few screams and contortions, he suddenly sank to the ground, powerless and helpless like a log. He was pale and trembled as I have never seen anyone tremble since. It seemed as though the muscles had been turned to a jelly which was shaken in all directions."

CHAPTER XXXV
FEAR VARIETIES

The great psychologist Ribot classifies fears into pain fears, and disgust fears. To quote from Ribot: "'I propose to reduce them (fears) to two groups. The first is directly connected with fear and includes all manifestations, implying in any degree whatever the fear of pain, from that of a fall or the prick of a needle, to that of illness or death. The second is directly connected with disgust, and seems to me to include the forms which have sometimes been called pseudophobia (Gelineau). Such are the fear of contact, the horror of blood and of innocuous animals, and many strange and causeless aversions. Let us remark furthermore that fear and disgust have a common basis, being both instruments of protection or defense. The first is the defensive-conservative instinct of relative life, the second the defensive-conservative instinct of organic life. As both have a common basis of aversion, they show themselves in equivalent ways: fear of withdrawal, departure, flight, disgust by vomiting and nausea:

The reflexes of disgust are the succedanea of flight; the organism cannot escape by movement in space from the repugnant object which it has taken into itself, and goes through a movement of expulsion instead."

I hesitate to accept Ribot's classification, inasmuch as we have pointed out that fear is prior to pain. In most lower animals it is hardly probable that not having representations that there is present a fear of pain in advance of the pain itself. Fear under such conditions can only be awakened by an actual sensory experience whether it be painful or not. In fact Ribot himself agrees to the fact that "There is a primary, instinctive, unreasoning fear preceding all individual experience, a hereditary fear."

Perhaps a word may be said in regard to the factor of disgust as having a common basis with fear. It is only by a stretch of imagination, if not by a stretch of words, that fear and disgust can be identified. There may be fear where there is no disgust, and there may be disgust where there is no fear. The two are independent variables, and can hardly be referred to as one and the same fundamental reaction, such as withdrawal and flight. The object of disgust does not preclude approach. The avoidance or aversion, the nausea and vomiting are all subsequent phenomena. Disgust may even follow after an abuse of food, of pleasant or necessary objects of nutrition, such as satiety.

The reactions of the fear instinct run the contrary way, approach is precluded from the very start. Fear is not associated with useful objects or events, unless it be in morbid states of fear. And still fear and disgust may become intimately associated when disgust and its objects awaken the fear instinct, and the fear becomes the fear of disgust or of the disgusting object. Disgust is more of a specialized character, and is associated with particular events or specific objects, while fear, in its primitive form at least, is more of a generalized character.

In the higher forms of life disgust may be so intimately related to fear that the two become synthesized, so to say, and are felt like one emotional state, the state becoming one of fear disgust. In such cases the fear instinct, fear disgust, is a determining factor of the morbid state. This is confirmed by clinical experience of the various cases of psychopathic functional neurosis and psychosis. In the various morbid states of the depressive types fear is awakened long before any pain is actually suffered, or any particular cause is found by the patient to account for the terror that dominates his mental life. The fear comes first while the representative cause is assigned by the sufferer as the cause of the fear.

Similarly in the functional psychosis and neurosis the object, experience, event, may be quite ordinary without any suggestion of pain or distress in it. In fact, the experience may be indifferent or even pleasant, but when associated with the fear instinct may become the nucleus of a very distressing pathological state. The experience is the occasion, while the fear instinct, the intimate companion of the impulse of self-preservation, is the only cause of functional psychopathic maladies.

The fear instinct in its primitive state is anterior to all experiences of danger, pain, and suffering, as is the case in most of the lower animals. In the higher animals where memory is developed, the fear instinct is associated with some form of representation, however vague, and then fear becomes posterior to experience. In man both forms of fear are present. The anterior form is specially found in children, while in adults the posterior form is, under normal conditions, predominating. The primitive anterior type of the fear instinct is by no means absent, in fact, it is more overpowering, its effects are overwhelming when it comes forth from the subconscious regions to which it is confined, and is manifested under conditions of lowered vitality.

When the strata of dynamic energies are passed and the strata of reserve energies are reached, the reserve energy not being accessible, the fear instinct is elemental, fundamental, while the fear of pain and of some definite representation of danger, or of suffering is a secondary consequence. People may suffer from pain, disease, and even danger, and still have no fear, while others may have never experienced the pain or disease, and still be obsessed by intense pangs of fear. Fear is sui generis, it is at the foundation of animal life.

The fear instinct may be awakened directly by a sensory stimulus, when, for instance, one finds himself in darkness and feels some creeping, slimy thing, or when attacked suddenly with a club or a knife. The fear instinct may again be aroused by an expectation, by something to which his dynamic energies cannot respond adequately, while the reserve energies are in abeyanace, such for instance as the expectation of some threatening event either to himself or to the objects bound up with his life existence. When one is threatened with some misfortune, with torture, death, or with a mortal disease, or with a serious operation, or when confronted with great danger against which his energies prove inadequate, in such cases the fear is ideational. These types of fear may in turn be either conscious or subconscious.

We may thus classify the fears as follows:

Conscious

I. Sensory

II. Ideational

Subconscious Conscious

Subconscious

The fear of the etherized or chloroformed patient is entirely of the subconscious type. It is the arousing of subconscious fear which, from the nature of the case, cannot be reached and alleviated that gives rise to functional psychosis and neurosis. From this standpoint it may be said that psychopathic diseases are subconscious fear states, in other words functional psychosis or neurosis is essentially a disease of subconscious activities. This is, in fact, confirmed by my clinical experience and by my psychopathological research work.

Dr. L. J. Pollock, professor of nervous diseases at Northwestern University Medical School, made an extremely interesting "Analysis of a Number of Cases of War Neurosis." This analysis fully conforms to the results obtained by me in my work on functional psychosis and neurosis carried on for a great number of years. It fully confirms the results of my studies, clinical and psychopathological, that the causation, or etiology of functional psychopathic states depends on fluctuations of the levels of neuron energy, or physical exhaustion, fatigue, hunger and thirst, or shock to the system, and more especially on the ravages of the fear instinct, aroused during the dangers and horrors of war.

"Of several hundred cases which I observed in base hospitals in France, copies of about 350 records were available. From these 200 of the more detailed ones were selected to determine the relative frequency of some of the factors. . . . From the numerical group has been excluded cases of emotional instability, timorousness, hospital neuroses occurring as an aftermath of an illness or a wound, the phobic reactions of gassed patients and constitutional neuroses, and those not directly related to the war.

"Heredity as a factor plays but a small part, and the incidence of neuropathic taint constituted little over 4 per cent.

"Of these 43 per cent followed shell fire, 36 percent after concussion as described by the soldier. . . . A definite history of fatigue and hunger was obtained in 30.5 per cent. Both probably occurred in a greater percentage, but were frequently masked by other symptoms which occupied the patient's attention to a greater extent. Fatigue and hunger are important factors, not only because they prepare the ground for an ensuing neurosis by breaking down the defensive reactions, but also in that when the patient is more sensitive and impressionable, the natural physical consequences of fatigue are misinterpreted by him as an evidence of an illness, and give rise to apprehension and fear.

"As frequently as fear is seen in some form or other in the neuroses of civil life, so does it manifest itself in the war neuroses. Fifty per cent of the cases admitted considerable fear under shell fire. Concussion was the immediate precipitating cause of the neuroses in 31 percent of the cases. The symptoms of the neuroses could be divided into those of the reactions of fear and fatigue."

These results corroborate my work on neurosis as due to exhaustion of Neuron Energy and Self-Fear. In fact, in one of my works written at the beginning of the war, I predicted the wide occurrence of what is known as shell shock, war shock or war neurosis. The prediction was fully corroborated by the facts.

Fear, Self, Reserve Energy, and Fatigue are the main factors in the formation of the psychopathic or neurotic condition. Janet, in a recent article of his, lays stress on the fear states in psychopathic affections and refers these conditions to the levels of vital energy. There is no doubt that Janet lays his finger on the very heart of the psychopathic diathesis. In my work I come to a similar conclusion only I lay more stress on the fear states, being referred to the fundamental instinct present in all animal life as a primordial condition of existence. This instinct is intensified and extended in the psychopathic diathesis.

The level of energy and the fear instinct are vitally interdependent. A low level of energy, especially a dissociation or inhibition of the store of reserve energy, arouses an excess of reaction of the fear instinct, and vice versa the excessive reaction of the fear instinct locks up the stores of reserve energy, thus intensifying and extending the psychopathic states with their fear-fatigue conditions. Janet refers indirectly to the impulse of self-preservation which is of the utmost consequence in psychopathic affections. On the whole, I may say that my work and clinical experience are in accord with that of the great French psychopathologist.

Where the fear instinct, self, and inhibition of reserve energy are present, then any emotion, even that of love, and devotion, will give rise to psychopathic states. This psychopathic state is not produced, because of the intensity or repression of the emotion, but because of the underlying subconscious predisposition to fear-instinct, self-preservation, and inhibition of reserve energy.

The feelings of inhibited reserve energy produced by fear and self, make the individual hesitate in decision, in action, and finally demoralize and terrorize him. These conditions take away from him all assurance and security of life and action, and hold him in a perpetual state of anxiety until he becomes completely incapacitated for all kinds of action and reaction. Events that threaten the impulse of self-preservation of the individual, such as misfortunes, shocks, losses, tend to bring about psychopathic states, on account of the aroused fear instinct, on account of the impulse of self-preservation, and sudden inhibition of the stores of reserve energy. Events that may lead to dissolution of personality are, hence, attended with intense anxiety.

As we have seen, an intense state of fear, conscious or subconscious, produces a state of abulia, a state of indecision, a state of incompletion of action, a state of insufficiency, a paralysis of will power, and a sense of unreality, all of which are intimately interrelated. For the fear instinct, when intense, inhibits and arrests the will and paralyzes action. The patient fears, not because he is inactive, but he is inactive, because he fears. The impulse of self-preservation, the fear instinct, and the principle of subconscious reserve energy give an insight into the multiform symptomatology of the psychopathic diathesis.

The following classes of people are subject to psychopathic affections:

(I) Childless people.

(II) People who had been afflicted with various diseases in childhood.

(III) Children of sickly, nervous, psychopathic parents who have kept their progeny in a constant state of anxiety, full of terrors and troubles of life.

(IV) People who had been affected by a series of shocks and fears in childhood and routh.

(V) People whose parents suffered long from various systemic diseases, especially cardiac and tubercular troubles.

(VI) In a large family of children the first, or last child, or sickly child of psychopathic parents.

(VII) The only child, or sickly child, especially of a widowed parent who is of a psychopathic diathesis.

In all these cases the psychopathic state is due to early cultivation of the fear instinct, self-impulse, and low level or dissociated state of vital reserve energy.

CHAPTER XXXVI
CONTROL OF THE NEUROTIC

The first thing in the examination and treatment of neurosis is the elimination of any physical trouble. It is only after such an elimination that one should resort to psychotherapeutic treatment. In psychopathic or neurotic diseases one should take into consideration the fact that the patients are characterized by the tendency of formation of habits which are hard to break. The patients are apt to ask that the same thing be done again and again for the simple reason that it has been done several times before. In other words, psychopathic neurosis is characterized by automatism and routine. This tendency to recurrence is characteristic of all forms of primitive life as well as of mental activities which are on the decline,—it is the easiest way to get along.

Effort is abhorrent to the patient. He is afraid of change in the same way as the savage is afraid of any novelty or of any change in custom. Tradition is holy, and in a double sense, because it has been handed down by former generations, regarded as divine and superior, and because the new is strange and, therefore, may prove dangerous and of evil consequence. What has not been tried may prove harmful, pernicious, and even deadly. The old has been tried and approved by generations and the consequences are known, while the new may be in alliance with evil powers. This holds true in all cases obsessed by the impulse of self-preservation and the fear instinct. What the patients have tried several times and what has proved good and pleasant is demanded by the patient to be repeated; the new is not known and may be risky, dangerous. I have great difficulty in making changes in the life of advanced psychopathic cases, because of the fear of the new, neophobia. Once the change is made, and the patient becomes adapted to the new way, then the old way is shunned. In short, neophobia is an essential trait of psychopathic patients.

The physician must take this trait of neophobia into account, and as the patient begins to improve, lie must gradually and slowly wean the patient of this phobia, inherent in the very nature of the malady. The patient must learn to do new things, and not simply follow mechanically a regime, laid out by the physician.

The patient's life must become personal. The patient should be made to change many of his ways, and above all he should learn to follow reason, rather than habit and routine. Everything, as much as possible, should be reasoned out,—he should be able to give a rational account of his habits and actions. Whatever appears to be a matter of routine, irrational and unaccountable habit, simply a matter of recurrence, of repetition of action, should be discarded, should be changed to actions and adaptations for which the patient could give a rational account.

We must remember that the patient lives in the condition of recurrent mental states, that his mental activity, as I have pointed out, follows the laws of recurrence, characteristic of the type of t recurrent moment consciousness. It is, therefore, the physician's object to lift the patient out of this low form of mental activity to the higher types of rational, personal life in which the patient can rise above the perturbations of life, above the pettiness of existence with its worries and fears. This procedure is essential.

We can realize how pernicious are those schemes which physicians and many people in sanitariums lay out for the patients just to keep them busy for the time of their stay under special care. As soon as the patients leave, they are in the same predicament as before. The patients wish to have their lives conducted in the same mechanical, automatic routine. In this way they are really on the same low plane of mental life, on the plane of recurrent moment consciousness, a type which forms the pathological web and woof of the patient's life.

Unless the patient is lifted out of this low, mean, and animal form of conscious activity, he cannot be regarded as cured. Instead of having the patient's life saturated and controlled by the recurrent automatisms of the fear instinct, he should learn to be controlled by the light of reason. "A free man is he," says Spinoza, "who lives under the guidance of reason, who is not led by fear." Epicurus and the ancient Epicureans laid special stress on the necessity of getting rid of fear through reason, enlightenment, and education. Thus the great poet Lucretius:

"The whole of life is a struggle in the dark. For even as children are flurried and dread all things in the thick darkness, thus we in the daylight fear things not a whit more to be dreaded than those which the children shudder at in the dark and fancy future evils. This terror, therefore, and darkness of mind must be dispelled not by the rays of the sun and glittering shafts of day, but by knowledge of the aspect and law of nature."

As Carlyle tersely puts it: "The first duty of a man is still that of subduing Fear. We must get rid of Fear; we cannot act at all till then. A man's acts are slavish, not true but specious (we may add psychopathic) ; his very thoughts arc false, he thinks too as a slave and coward, till he has got Fear under feet. . . . Now and always, the completeness of his victory over Fear will determine how much of a man he is."

The patient complains of lack of confidence. This is a pathognomonic symptom of psychopathic states. At the same time there is confidence iA the symptom complex which is often described by him with microscopic minuteness. The patient has no doubt about that. He is in search of someone who can overcome this symptom complex in a way which he specially approves. The patient matches his morbid self-will against the physician's control. The physician is not to be subdued by the authority of the diseased personality, he should not let himself be controlled by the ruling symptoms of the patient's life. Either the physician meets with opposition, and after some time, must give up the treatment of the case, or he is victimized by the patient's demands, and must comply with them. In the latter case the patient may stick to the physician for some time. In both cases the patient is not really cured. It is only when the diseased self becomes subdued and falls under the physician's control, it is only then that a cure is really possible, it is only then that the normal healthy self may come to the foreground.

The first and foremost characteristic of psychopathic states is the narrowing down of the patient's life interests. He begins to lose interest in abstract problems, then in that of his own profession or occupation, then he loses interest in the welfare of his party or his country, and finally, in his family, wife, and children. Even in the case of love, the psychopathic patient seeks to utilize the person he loves for his own, neurotic benefit, namely, his neurotic comfort and health. He loves the person as a glutton likes his meal, or as a drunkard his liquor. The self becomes narrowed down to health, the key to his supposed spiritual life. Self-preservation and fear permeate the patient's life.

We notice that the patient's life activity, especially his mental functions, becomes narrowed down. His attention becomes circumscribed to a few subjects and objects. This is the limitation of the extent of attention. There is afterward a limitation of the temporal span of attention. The patient cannot keep his attention on any subject for any length of time. This span of attention becomes more and more limited with the growth and severity of the psychopathic malady. If the patient is educated and has had an interest in various subjects, the latter become more and more limited in scope. Finally the patient becomes reduced to the least amount of effort of the attention, and that only for a brief period of time. When the trouble reaches its climax, the patient loses all interest and capacity of reading and of studying. He cannot think, he becomes less and less original in his thoughts, he becomes even incapable of thinking. The patient's whole mind becomes limited to himself and to the symptoms of his disease.

Along with it the fear instinct grows in power, inhibiting all other activities. There is a limitation of the patient's personal self. The personality becomes reduced to the lowest levels of existence, caring for his own selfish pains and small pleasures, which are exaggerated and magnified to an extraordinary degree. In other words, the personal life of the patient becomes more and more limited as the pathological process goes on. It becomes harder and harder for the patient to take an active interest in life.

It is clear that under such conditions the tendency of the patient is to rest and brood about himself, and keep indulging his limited interests, which get still more narrowed as the pathological process becomes more extensive and intensive. Under% such conditions it is suicidal to indulge the patient and suggest to him a rest cure, a cure which lies along the line of the disease process, thus tending to intensify the disease. What the patient needs is to change his environment, and be put under conditions in which his interests of life can be aroused. His life activities should be stimulated to functioning on the right lines, laid out by physicians who understand the patient's condition. Rest is harmful to the neurotic. What the patient needs is work, work, and work

What we must remember in the treatment of psychopathic patients is the fact that we deal here with the aberrations of the impulse of self-preservation, the most powerful, the most fundamental, and the least controllable of animal impulses, accompanied with the fear instinct, which is the most primitive of all animal instincts. This morbid state of the impulse of self-preservation must be fully realized before any treatment is begun. The physician must also see and study closely the line on which the self-preservation impulse is tending, and comprehend the associations along which the impulse takes its course in the history of the patient and in the symptom complex.

What one must especially look after is the elusive feeling of self-pity which manifests itself under various garbs, and hides itself under all kinds of forms. As long as the patient is introspective and has the emotional side of self-pity present, so long is his condition psychopathic. The extreme selfishness and the uniqueness with which psychopathic patients regard their own condition should be eradicated from their mind. It must be impressed on them that their case is quite common, and that there is nothing exceptional about

them. It must be made clear to them that the whole trouble is a matter of maladjustment, that they have developed inordinately the impulse of self-preservation and the fear instinct until their mental life has become morbid and twisted. The whole personality has to be readjusted. It is the special tendency of psychopathic patients to regard themselves as unique, privileged above all other patients, they are a kind of geniuses among the afflicted, possibly on account of the special endowments possessed by them, gifts of quite exceptional and mysterious a character. "Have you ever met with a case like mine?" is the stereotyped phrase of the psychopathic, neurotic patient. As long as the patient entertains that conception of nobility, the impulse of self must still be regarded as morbid.

The neurotic must be made to understand clearly that there is no aristocracy in disease, and that there is no nobility of the specially elect in the world of morbid affections, any more than there is in the domain of physical maladies. The egocentric character of the psychopathic patient puts him in the position of the savage who takes an animistic, a personal view of the world and of the objects that surround him. Natural forces are regarded as dealing with man and his fate, often conspiring against man.

Magic is the remedy by which the savage tries to defend himself, and even to control the inimical or friendly natural forces or objects, animate and inanimate, with which he comes in contact. This same attitude, animistic and personal, of the primitive man is present in the psychopathic patient. The patient is afraid that something fearful may happen to him. Against such accidents he takes measures often of a defensive character which differ but little from the magic of the savage and the barbarian. That is why these patients are the victims of all kinds of fakes, schemes, panaceas of the wildest type, unscrupulous patent medicines, absurd regimes, mental and religious, whose silliness and absurdity are patent to the unprejudiced observer. The mental state of the psychopathic or neurotic patient is that of the savage with his anthropomorphic view of nature, with his fears based on the impulse of self-preservation. The psychopathic patient is in a state of primitive fear and of savage credulity with its faith in magic.

The emotional side of the impulse of self-preservation and of the fear instinct should always be kept in mind by the physician who undertakes the treatment of psychopathic cases. The physician must remember that the emotions in such cases are essentially of the instinctive type, that they therefore lie beyond the ken of the patient's immediate control and action of the personal will. The physician should not, therefore, be impatient, but while protecting the invalid against the fears that assail the latter, he should gradually and slowly undermine the violence of the impulse of self-preservation and the anxiety of the fear instinct. For in all psychopathic maladies the main factors are the impulse of self-preservation and the fear instinct.

CHAPTER XXXVII
REGAINED ENERGY AND MENTAL HEALTH

The principle of reserve energy, developed independently by Professor James and myself, is of the utmost importance to abnormal psychology. The principle is based on a broad generalization of facts —psychological, physiological and biological— namely, that far less energy is utilized by the individual than there is actually at his disposal. A comparatively small fraction of the total amount of energy, possessed by the organism, is used in its relation with the ordinary stimuli of its environment.

The energy in use may be regarded as kinetic or circulating energy, while the energy stored away is reserve energy. There must always be a supply of reserve energy requisite for unusual reactions in emergency cases. Those organisms survive which have the greatest amount of reserve energy, just as those countries are strong and victorious which possess the largest amount of reserve capital to draw upon in critical periods.

As life becomes more complex, inhibitions increase; the thresholds of stimulations of a complex system rise in proportion to its complexity. With the rise of evolution there is a tendency to increase of inhibitions, with a consequent lock-up of energy which becomes reserve. Now there are occasions in the life of the individual, under the influence of training and emotional trauma, when the inhibitions become unusually intense, tending to smother the personality, which becomes weakened, impoverished in its reactions, and is unable to respond freely to the stimuli of its environment. The inhibited system becomes inactive and may be regarded as dissociated from the cycle of life.

In case of an emotional trauma there is often a breach in the continuity of association. The affected system becomes dissociated from the rest of the personality, and is like a splinter in the flesh of the individuality. Its own threshold, when tapped, may be very low, but it is not directly accessible through the mediacy of other systems;_ hence its threshold appears unusually or pathologically high. When the inhibitions are very high they must be removed. This removal of inhibitions brings about an access to the accumulated energy of the inhibited systems. In case of disjunction or break of continuity we must stimulate the dormant reserve energy of the systems, and thus assist the process of repair and bridge the breach of associative continuity. A new, fresh, active life opens to the patient. He becomes a "reformed" personality, free and cheerful, with an overflow of energy.

The hypnoidal state is essentially a rest-state characterized by anabolic activity. There is a restitution of spent energy; inhibitions become removed, and access is gained to "dormant" systems or complexes. The awakened "dormant" complex systems bring with them a new feeling-tone, a fresh emotional energy resulting in an almost complete transformation of personality.

As an illustration of the transformation effected I take at random the following extracts from some of the letters written to me by patients who have experienced this welling up of reserve energy: "Indeed, were I to fill this entire sheet with expressions of the gratitude which wells up from my inmost heart it would be only a beginning of what I feel. Surely the darkness of the world has been dispelled since this new light has illuminated my soul, and / feel that this wondrous light will never fail me. It were vain to attempt to thank you for this wonderful transformation."

A letter from a patient reads: "You will be glad to know that all is well with me. Life is one happy day. I am a marvel to my friends in the way of happiness and cheer. I have to confess that I feel almost wicked to be so happy." Another letter runs as follows: "Next to the gladness in my own restoration, I am rejoiced at the wonderful transformation that has come to my dear friend T from your treatment. She writes most enthusiastically of her steady and sure progress toward the goal of perfect health, of her strength to take up the home duties which had been so burdensome, and she now finds a delight in the doing of them, and of her husband's and friends' joy in the transformation that has been wrought in her."

A patient writes: "Your treatments cut a deep channel in my subconscious life, one from which if I do happen to wander astray is for only a short time; then I am carried right back in the trend. In fact, there exists a deep indelible, happy and cheerful impression incorporated in my subconscious life that it is impossible to eradicate. . . . You have laid a concrete foundation upon which I am building, little by little, a structure that someday you will be proud of, and for which words are insufficient to express my profound gratitude."

Another patient writes: "The big result of your treatment was restoring my faith and arousing my ambitions. I never think of suicide. I only want to live and work and redeem myself. I have never been so happy and I have never worked harder . . . I feel the most extraordinary eagerness; a strange, irrepressible enthusiasm; and an absolute conviction of the truth and beauty of work, of my work. I dare not think of failure, and yet success as I conceive it is too wonderful ever to come. The brave will of life in me permitting, I shall some day approximate my prayer, my dream, my vision; and then I must let the earth know you are responsible."

The following extract of a letter, written to me by a patient, an experienced English surgeon, now in charge of a hospital in England, whose case was severe and chronic, dating from early childhood, is valuable, both on account of his medical training and his mental abilities which make him an excellent judge as to the fundamental change and cure effected:

"It is now exactly two years since I was undergoing treatment at your kindly and sympathetic hands. I remember that you once told me that the seed sown by you would probably take this length of time to come to fruition. Therefore, it may not be without interest to you to receive a supplement to many other letters in which I will endeavor to summarize my progress—for the last time.

"I have no longer even the least lingering doubt that you can count me among your most brilliantly successful cures. I say this after many—too many —heart searchings which are probably characteristic of my somewhat doubting temperament. At first, I was disappointed with the whole business: I suppose I looked for strange and dramatic events to occur which would change my whole personality and temperament in a short time. Nothing so exciting happened; I left Portsmouth still feeling that I owned the same name, and very much the same 'ego' that I arrived with. I was unaware that any profound psychological operation had taken place. To be candid, I did not think it had—the beginnings, no doubt, were there—but no more. But now when I carry my mind back to the type of obsession which used to assail me— is there any change? Good God! I behold a miracle, although it has come about so silently that I can only realize the difference by comparing the present with the past. In conclusion I can only send you my undying gratitude. You have saved me from what, I honestly believe, would have one day resulted in deliberate suicide which I often contemplated as the one solution of my trouble. . . ."

These extracts are typical of many others, and clearly show the enjoyment of new strength and powers until now unknown to the patient. Fresh reservoirs of reserve energy have been tapped and have become available in an hour of dire need. The patient has light and strength where there were darkness and depression. We are confronted here with the important phenomenon of liberation of dormant reserve energy. The patient feels the flood of fresh energies as a "marvelous transformation," as a "new light," as a "new life," as "a something worth more than life itself."

The hypnoidal state helps us to reach the inaccessible regions of dormant, reserve energy, helps to break down inhibitions, to liberate reserve energies and to repair the breaches or dissociation of mental life. The painful systems become dissociated, disintegrated and again transformed, reformed, and reintegrated into new systems, full of energy and joy of life. The banishment of credulity, the cultivation of the upper, critical consciousness, the rational control of the subconscious, the moderation of the self-impulse, the regulation of the fear-instinct, and the access to the vast stores of subconscious reserve energy, all go to the formation of a strong, healthy-minded personality, free from fear and psychopathic maladies.

[1] Happy is he who knows the causes of things, who can trample on fear, inexorable fate, and the horrors of death.

[2] Darkness and terror of the soul are not dispelled by the rays of the sun and glittering shafts of the day, but by the rational aspect of nature.

[3] The popular novelists try to disclose "the secrets of the heart" by means of Freudian sex phantasies, psychoanalytic mother complexes, and Jungian mystic sex libido.

[4] The principle of reserve energy was developed independently by my friend, William James, and myself.

THE THEORY OF THE MOMENT CONSCIOUSNESS

Boris Sidis
(1867-1923)

Boston—Toronto
1914

To the Memory of My Master and Friend
WILLIAM JAMES

Who, being the foremost pioneer in the vast domain of
the human mind, has generously encouraged others
in their efforts at clearing fresh trails, leading
to an ever more comprehensive view of
the rich varieties of mental life.

Contents:

Chapter XIII.
Desultory Consciousness

Chapter XIV.
The Synthetic Moment and its Reproduction

Chapter XV.
The Accumulative Character of the Synthetic Moment

Chapter XVI.
The Simple and Compound Synthetic Moment

Chapter XVII.
The Desultory Type in Pathological States

Chapter XVIII.
Presentations and Representations

Chapter XIX.
Representations and The Laws of Their Combinations

Chapter XX.
Representation and Recognition

Chapter XXI.
The Recognitive Moment and Its Reproduction

CHAPTER I
THE MOMENT CONSCIOUSNESS

WE must try to realize the precise meaning of the "moment consciousness," as a clear comprehension of it is of the utmost importance to psychology in general and to psychopathology in particular.

In a former work I pointed out that "consciousness is not uniform, that of the infant differs from that of the adult; the consciousness of the brute differs from that of the man, and still they all belong to the genus consciousness." I also insisted on the fact that there is a confusion in the use of the term "consciousness," a confusion which almost amounts to what I may term as "the psychologist's fallacy." The fully developed type of consciousness characteristic of the adult human mind, namely, self-consciousness, is substituted for the lower forms, or for types of consciousness characteristic of the lower animals. The psychologist, and, especially the physiologist, when writing on psychological matters is apt, to substitute, either on account of the introspective method used or on account of lack of discrimination, the type of consciousness of the observer, namely, self-consciousness.

No biologist, not even Loeb, will accept unrestrictedly the Cartesian view that consciousness, or the soul, or mind is the privilege of man alone, while all other animals have no soul, no mind, no consciousness, they are complex reflex mechanisms, highly developed automata with no psychic life to them. We must allow the fact that other animals lower than man in the rungs of development possess some form of psychic life. The horse, the dog, the cat, the cow, the ant, the bee, and other animals have some form, however varied, of psycho-physiological activity, some form of mental life, however different in type from that of man. Abnormal psychology discloses to us dissolving views of human consciousness, such as found in the various forms of insanity and in the various manifestations of psychopathic states, presenting conditions of all stages of dissociation and disaggregation of consciousness. Psychic life is by no means uniform, there are many types of consciousness.

We have pointed out above that synthetic unity is the essence of consciousness. Consciousness is not an association of independently existing ideas, images, feelings, and sensations. Mental events must form a unity, a synthesis in the total psychic life of some psycho-biological organization. Disconnected words of a sentence thought by a series of thinkers do not give rise to that unified mental process which goes to form the psychic experience of the meaning of the sentence. The words must be cognized by the consciousness of *one* psychobiological organism. Ideas, images, feelings, emotions, volitions do not meet on independent ground, associate, fuse and go to form a unity, a new idea or feeling. Experiences in different minds do not combine and associate to form a new synthesis. Even the associationist tacitly implies that the various associations of ideas and feelings take place in some *one mind.*

In order to get some form of cognizance or some form of experience of sensations and ideas there must be someone organic consciousness that experiences or lives through the psychic events. Thoughts, feelings, ideas, images, and sensations are occurrences in some one psychic individuality, a psycho-biological or psycho-physiological organism, an organism which possesses the living synthetic unity of consciousness. From a purely psychological standpoint we may term this living organic unity of consciousness—a subject. I use the term "moment-consciousness," or simply "moment" to indicate this synthetic unity of consciousness which constitutes the characteristic of the subject having the synthesis of mental experiences. This holds true of all psychic life, from the very lowest representative of mental life to the very highest, such as the self-consciousness of man.

The subject, or the unity of the psycho-physiological individuality cannot be represented by a series, whether temporal or spatial, as a series ceases to be a unity, or a synthesis. For a series of independent events remains a series, while the synthesis or unity of the series is a superadded event. A series of psychic events must exist *in* and *for* some psychic unity or individuality which stands for the organic unity of consciousness, or for the synthesis of consciousness, no matter what the type of consciousness is, low or high, animal or human. This synthetic unity of consciousness, no longer a series, is indicated by the term "moment" or "moment consciousness." There are various types of moment consciousness, according as there are various forms or types of synthesis.

Psychic contents or states of consciousness are always found in connection with some individuality. That piece of bread lying yonder may awaken hundreds of mental states under different conditions and in various organizations. My friend sitting by my side sees it, so do I, and so does the child, so does the bird in the cage, so does the dog, and so possibly does the fly flitting around the table. The states awakened are no doubt different, but they are of a psychic character none the less. My friend and I may be conscious of the personal element along with it. We may think it in the form of ownership; "It is who thinks, who has the thought of the bread;" but this is only one of the many forms under which the perception or thought of the bread may appear. One thing, however, is essential to all the states, different as they may be in their content, and that is the fact that they belong to someone individuality which under certain special conditions may also be of the nature of a personality. The individuality may be of a high or of a very low type, it may be that of a man or it may be that of a fly, but it must be some*one* conscious being that synthetizes the psychic state. It is this *one* synthetizing consciousness that constitutes the essence of what we term "moment consciousness."

The moment consciousness is the subject, the psychobiological individuality, requisite in all psychic activity. The psychic individuality cannot be regarded as a series of independent physical events. For it may be asked, for whom does that series exist and to whom is it presented? A synthetizing moment consciousness, both subject and content, is a fundamental assumption of psychology, just as space is that of geometry, and matter and force that of physics and chemistry. This necessity of assuming a synthetizing moment consciousness becomes clearly manifested in the highest form of psychic activity, such as self-consciousness. For if self-consciousness be reduced to a series, it may be pertinently asked with John Stuart Mill, "How can a series be aware of itself as a series?"

A moment consciousness must not be considered as something apart from its content; it does not exist by itself; it exists wherever and whenever psychic states are synthetized; it is the synthetized psychic material; mere synthesis without material is meaningless. On the whole, we may say that the moment consciousness is like an organism, it forms a whole of many constituent parts.

In the moment consciousness we find psychic material synthetized round one inmost central event which in its turn may have a central point. It reminds one strongly of the cell; although it branches out in all directions, it has always its inmost central point, its nucleus, nucleolus, and nucleolinus. While I am sitting here writing, I take in the many impressions coming to me: The sunshine pouring through the window, the table, the ticking of the clock, the chair, the bookcase, and many other things in the room; all of them are formed and synthetized into one, and as such they form a moment consciousness.

They are not, however, indifferently grouped; their unity is an organized whole with a center, with a vital point, so to say. At the heart of the synthetized whole there is a central point, the grouping around which constitutes the individuality of the particular moment consciousness. In my own case, the central interesting point is the paper on which I write the sentence just formulated, and is the inmost point, the principal idea under discussion which forms the nucleolinus, so to say, of the whole moment consciousness. The most interesting or the most important experience forms the center of the moment.

The same object which seemingly gives the same experience assumes different meanings and is therefore really quite a different experience, according to the moment consciousness in which the perception or knowledge of that object is synthetized. These presently experienced states, synthetized within the moment, form the matter, or what we may term the content of the moment consciousness. The moment of consciousness will change with the changes of the synthetized content. As an official, I am now in my office doing my work, and the different experiences form one whole, an association of experiences, systematized and synthetized into an organic unity. As a family man, I am at home enjoying the company of my wife, children, and friends, and once more the experiences are organized into the unity of a moment consciousness. Now I am climbing mountains and stand on the slippery edge of a precipice, now T enjoy a conversation with the child I love, now T take part in the excitement of the political arena, now T sit on the bench of the jury listening gravely to the cross examination of witnesses in a murder case; all these are nuclei for the formation of different moments. All of these depend on the different central experiences that form the kernel for the moment consciousness.

The central experience, round which all other experiences are grouped and synthetized, forms, so to say, the very essence of the given moment consciousness, and as long as this central experience remains unchanged in its position the new experiences are assimilated within the same moment consciousness. The moment consciousness, therefore, does not vary with the change of the content, if only the assimilating nucleus remains invariable. Should, however, the content vary so that the central experience is transposed and some other one occupies its place, then the moment consciousness itself is changed. In fact, we may have the content of the moment consciousness entirely unchanged; but if the central experience alone is displaced from its position, then the moment consciousness itself becomes changed in its nature. Thus, if as a traveller I climb the mountains chiefly for the sake of pleasure, and keep the scientific and aesthetic aspects in the background, the moment consciousness will be entirely different from the one where the scientific or aesthetic aspects are in the foreground, and all other considerations in the background. *The moment consciousness, we may say, is entirely determined by the leading central experience.*

The content of the moment consciousness, however, is not confined to the presently experienced psychic states only; it embraces the past, it includes memory, that is, it synthetizes outlived moments. In my present capacity of physician and working in the office, I may also include the experiences as traveller, as juror, as teacher, as companion, and as lover, but still the tone of this particular moment consciousness is given by the duties of my present occupation. The most vivid, interesting, and leading experiences form in this synthesis the nucleus round which all other experiences are crystallized and synthetized into one organic whole. We have here a series of moments, all of them being coordinated and contained in one synthesis of one moment consciousness.

The members of this synthetized series are not of equal value nor are they qualitatively the same. The leading experience that constitutes the assimilating element of the given moment has reality, interest, and value, while others are only so much material support for the principal central experience. This central experience differs also from the other experiences synthetized in the moment consciousness by the fact that it alone, that is, the nucleus only, has the most vivid psychic states, sensational and perceptual elements, while the others may totally lack them. Other subsidiary synthetized moments are rather of an ideational character; they are what is called "reproductions," ideal representatives of formerly experienced, outlived moments.

The moment consciousness may contain moments that happened to emerge by the dynamic process of association, such as contiguity, similarity, or contrast. Each moment consciousness may become content for the next. Each successive moment consciousness may synthetize the preceding ones, contain them in an abridged ideational form, and may, moreover, recognize and claim them as belonging to itself, and as being one with them. There may, in short, be various forms of mental unification, but one thing stands out clear and that is the nature of the moment consciousness. The essence of the moment consciousness is *mental synthesis.*

If we take a cross section of the moment consciousness, and try to fixate it with our mental eye, we find a central psychic element round which other psychic elements are crystallized. This central psychic element is prominent, vivid, forms, so to say, the vital point of all the states and gives the tone to the rest, forming a whole, one organized experience. The psychic matter that surrounds the luminous central point does not stand in a free, more or less disconnected relation to the latter, it is intimately related to the centre, and cannot be separated without destroying the moment as a whole and even the life existence of each particular constituent. The whole moment seems to form an organic network in which the other elements take their place, according to a plan.

The structure of the moment may in this respect be compared to that of the cell. In the cell we discriminate the nucleus round which the protoplasm is grouped. The protoplasm is connected with the nucleus by a network, a cytoreticulum. The destruction of the nucleus affects the protoplasm and the destruction of the protoplasm affects the nucleus. The two are intimately, organically interrelated by the common network, the general plan of their organization.

A concrete example will perhaps best answer our purpose. Suppose the moment is perceptual and consists only of one percept. Now in the percept we find a central sensory element surrounded by other elements. This central element stands out prominently in the given psychic state, while the other elements are subordinate. Not that those elements are unimportant for the percept, on the contrary they are of the highest consequence and moment, they only lie outside the focus of the psychosis. Along with the focus those elements form one organized whole. The intensity of the psychic state proceeds from the periphery to the centre. The elements can as little be separated from the central element as the area of the circle from its centre. By removing the centre the circle will be destroyed and the centre will cease to be what it is. All the elements of the percept form one texture having the central sensory element as its nucleus.

Integrated as all those elements are they are not, however, of equal value and importance for the life existence of the whole. The central sensory element is of the utmost consequence, it is the vital point of the whole experience. While the change or destruction of one or some of the subordinate elements may still leave the total moment unchanged, or but slightly modified, a change of the central sensory element or of the nucleus will profoundly modify all the other elements and their interrelation; and a destruction of the nucleus will destroy the total moment. Like their neuron counterparts, the moments may be regarded as being organized into groups, systems, communities and constellations, aggregates of greater and greater complexity.

CHAPTER II
TYPES OF MOMENTS AND MOMENT-THRESHOLD

WE may discriminate the following types of moment-consciousness:

I. The Desultory Moment,

(a) The Absolute,

(b) The Relative, or Reflex Moment.

II. The Synthetic Moment.

(a) The Simple Accumulative,

(b) The Compound Accumulative.

III. The Recognitive Moment.

(a) The Synthetic, or Generic Recognitive,

(b) The Specific, the Reflective, or the Synthetic Moment of Self-consciousness.

The chief characteristic of the desultory moment is the lack of interconnection of the links of the psychic series. Each pulse of psychosis stands out as an isolated fact without "before" and "after." A moment of such a character has no reproduction, no recognition, no memory, and certainly no personality. The lower stages of this moment, the absolute desultory moment-consciousness are mere moment-content devoid of all organization and substance. The higher forms of the desultory moment, those of the reflex moment-consciousness, have an elementary organization, but of such a fixed character that the series of manifestations, or of functioning remain completely isolated. Reproductions appear here for the first time in an elementary form, inasmuch as the recurrences of the moment leave the latter unmodified; it is reproduction only on account of the modifications produced in a higher observing moment.

This moment has the germs of reproduction, but no recognition and hence no memory, no self-consciousness. The moment of the absolute desultory type may possibly be found in unorganized protoplasm and in the lowest forms of the protozoa. The higher forms of moment of the desultory type, the reflex moment, may be found in the lower forms of lowly organized life and in the lower structures of the higher metazoa.

The moment-consciousness of the synthetic type has its series of links interconnected. In each link the preceding ones are synthetized. The recurrence of this type of moment, unlike the moment of relative desultory consciousness, is embodied in the structure and function of the moment. It is in this type of moment that reproduction is for the first time clearly and fully manifested. The moment is modified with each reproduction; it accumulates more content with each recurrence and, as such, the synthetic moment may also be characterized as *accumulative*.

This type of moment has reproduction, and the reproduction is not only for the external observer, but is present and inherent through changes in the organization, structure and function of the moment itself. Memory first appears in this type, but it is rather organic, not recognitive in nature.

The more elementary form of this type of moment shows accumulations only along single lines of development. The lines remain disconnected. Sensory nuclei surrounded by secondary sensory elements do not occur, and perceptual psychosis characteristic of the higher forms is absent in this stage of the synthetic moment, which is therefore termed *the simple accumulative moment of synthetic consciousness*. It is only in the higher forms of synthetic consciousness, in the *compound synthetic moment* that perceptual life may be said to arise.

In the compound synthetic moment, series along diverse lines become severally compounded and sensory nuclei with secondary sensory elements make their appearance. But even here recognition is not present and hence memory may from a subjective standpoint be regarded as absent. The synthetic moment even in its highest phase of development lacks ideational life and is entirely devoid of self-consciousness. The higher invertebrates and the lower vertebrates probably do not rise in their psychological development above the higher form of synthetic consciousness, the compound synthetic moment.

In the recognitive moment the series of reproductions are intimately connected as we find the case to be in the synthetic moment. The moment becomes modified with each occurring reproduction, containing in an abridged form the history of previous modifications. The mode of reproduction of the recognitive moment, however, differs widely from that of the synthetic moment. The content of the previous occurrence need not be actually reproduced, but only represented and any psychic element may fulfill this function of representation. It is through such representation that the reproduction of this type of moment is effected. Through representation the moment reproduces form and content, and cognizes over again immediately what it has just experienced, in short, it *re-cognizes*.

Recognition is the function of representation and is the essential characteristic of this type of moment-consciousness. Ideational psychosis germinates and develops with the growth of the recognitive moment. For the very function of the idea is the cognition over again of what has been cognized in perception, in short, recognition is the essence of the idea.

In generic recognition the time element is absent or but vaguely present. In perceiving the table yonder we also recognize it as table by classing the percept table with representations derived from previously perceived tables, but hardly does any time-element enter into this form of recognition, the idea of having generic recognition does not refer to any percept experienced at some definite point of time. The recognitive moment uses the idea as a means to reproduce its former experience without actually living them over again. The representation in the lower form of moment is so bound up with the percept that the function of recognition is but implicit, and becomes explicit in the higher forms, when the ideational or representative elements become completely free and appear in mental trains, or in series of associated ideas.

In its specific form, however, the recognitive moment also includes the time element. The moment-content or object generically recognized is classed or combined with a definite representation generically referring to perceptual experience; specifically recognized, the content or object is placed in a definite point of the objective schema of the flowing time series. The particular rose thought of now is the particular rose seen before, say yesterday. The idea of the rose substitutes and represents the percept and has the function of the percept as reproduced, thus referring to the same object. That is why the qualitatively different representation is identified with the actual perception. What is common to the two is their reference to the same object, in all else they really differ widely. The recognitive moment that lacks the time-element is termed *generic,* while the moment that has time element included in the process of its recognition is termed *specific recognitive moment-consciousness.*

In the lower and simpler stages of the recognitive moment the generic form predominates, in the higher and more complex stages the specific form of recognition arises and attains its full development. From a biological standpoint one can understand the importance and immense advantage in the struggle for existence of those organisms whose moment-consciousness has varied in the direction of representation and has begun to reproduce after the mode of the recognitive type. To effect a modification and new adaptation to changes in the environment the moments of the desultory type have no other mode of modification but by the slowly working factors of spontaneous variations and natural selection, a process of adaptation and useful modification prolonged throughout the course of generations. The adaptations of the different forms of the synthetic type are greatly facilitated, and the course of the process is so much foreshortened that it becomes reduced to the life-existence of the given individual organisms. The adaptations are brought about by the slow process of chance success and error, and the whole series of modifications must be fully and directly undergone by the organism.

The recognitive moments have reduced the time-elements of adaptations to changes of conditions in the external environment almost to a *minimum.* the series of reactions in the growth to most perfect adaptations is effected in representation, saving itself the necessity of actually undergoing a series of intervening modifications. Representative elements, being free, can enter into different modes of combinations, and thus form adjustments and adaptations with an ease of which the primary and secondary sensory elements of the lower moments do not admit. This freedom of movement in the formation of new representative combinations is an important factor in organic life, as it gives the organism that possesses this variation an advantage in the struggle for existence. Adaptation can be made for the future from the experiences of the past.

In those forms of the recognitive moment in which the time-element plays a part in the determination of the whole there is always present a specific time-localization of the given psychic or moment content. Where the form of recognition is specific the representation or idea is regarded as actual and localized in some definite point in the stream of past time, where the recognition is generic the representation or idea is referred to no definite point in the stream of objective time, and when present in the highest types of moments, is regarded as belonging to what is termed imagination. Recognition determines the place of the given experience in the series of events.

In the lower stages of the recognitive moment no time element is present, in the higher stages some vague reference to time may be present in the forms of specific recognition, but definite localization appears only with the rise of the recognitive moment of self-consciousness. With the appearance of the conceptual schema of objective time the specific form of recognition refers not only to a definite point on the scale of objective time, but to a definite mental synthesis localized on that objective time-schema; in other words, the self-concept is involved in specific recognition, which therefore belongs to the highest form of the recognitive moment, namely, the moment of self-consciousness or of personality.

In specific recognition the present self projects the bit of representative experience into the past self which is felt to be identical with the former in the series of selves to which the reproduction of the moment gives rise. The highest recognitive moment, or moment of self-consciousness may be represented as a series of selves projected in the time schema the preceding selves being synthetized by each succeeding self. From this standpoint we may regard such a moment as synthetic and term it *the synthetic moment of self-consciousness.*

Should this series of reproductions constituting the history of the moment become dissociated and isolated through mental degradation and degeneration, then the form of consciousness becomes analogous to the desultory consciousness and may therefore be termed *the desultory moment of self-consciousness.*

The functioning moments of a highly organized psychic being, at any point of time, present a hierarchy of moments differing not only in degree of consciousness, but also in the type of structure and function. Moments-consciousness from the lowest to the highest, from the simplest to the most complex, from the desultory type to the recognitive type of self-consciousness all are present in the adult stage of

the most highly organized psychic life. Now in the series of moments going to form such a highly complex being, those that are of the recognitive type can become focal, while those that belong to the lower types can never enter the focus. The lower types of moment-consciousness, belonging to the groups and systems of reflex and instinctive activity, cannot, from their very nature, reach that level of consciousness and that degree of psychosis as to become qualified to enter into the focus of the moment of self-consciousness.

From this standpoint, then, the subconscious may be divided into two regions, the one including all the moments belonging to that of the recognitive type, the other comprising all the moments belonging to the lower types. Within the subconscious, then, there is a threshold which the lower types of moments cannot pass. This threshold may be termed *the threshold of recognitive consciousness.*

The moments lying above the threshold of recognitive consciousness may change in psychic intensity, may pass through all degrees of sensory intensity and representative vividness ranging from *minimum* to *maximum;* they may sink and rise gradually or suddenly, but they do not and cannot fall, without becoming degenerated, below the recognitive threshold. Those moments that lie below the recognitive threshold cannot rise above it, they are condemned to remain in the obscure regions of the subconscious; their fate is never to enter the strong light of the upper world of consciousness. At the same time their psychic intensity does not suffer any change, they do not shift forwards and backwards in the field of consciousness like the moments of the recognitive type lying above the threshold, they remain unalterable, they are fixed.

In a certain sense the moments lying below the threshold of recognitive consciousness may be considered as dissociated from the upper regions, inasmuch as they lie outside the field of the upper consciousness. From the standpoint of activity, however, they stand in intimate relation to the upper level of consciousness. The highly organized moment uses the lower ones as instruments to carry out its purpose, and through them it also enters into relation with the external environment. Stimuli are received by the lower moments, and motor responses are once more given by these moments. In other words, the lower types of moments are in service of the higher moments.

From a teleological standpoint one can understand the importance of it for the life-existence of the individual. In order to save time and energy any activity that can be carried out by the lower aggregates is directly responded to by the less complex and more fixed moments. The lowermost moments are the easiest to gain access to by the external stimuli, and in case the adaptation is simple the response immediately follows without any reference to higher aggregates. Should, however, the stimulus be under conditions where more complex adaptations are requisite then the next higher aggregate is set into activity. The ascending degree of complexity of aggregates set into activity grows in accordance with the need of complexity of adaptation, until the most complex of all aggregates is reached, the one representing the complete organization of sensori-motor adaptations of the organism as a whole.

At the same time it must be pointed out that there is a series of moments almost independent of this organized hierarchy of moments, never falling under the sway, or but indirectly and casually being affected by the principal complex moment-consciousness; such are the moments that go along with functions, directly subservient to the internal needs of the organism. This complex aggregate of moments from its very nature is withdrawn from the general control of the other aggregates, inasmuch as it need not adapt itself to the varying conditions and different stimulations of the external environment. The set of stimuli this aggregate responds to remains almost unchanged, hence their activity is of a low order, belonging to the character of the reflex moments.

CHAPTER III
MODIFICATIONS OF MOMENTS IN THE ORGANIZED AGGREGATE

IN pointing out the parallel in the series of moments as they appear in ontogenesis and phylogenesis, we must make some restrictions. The series of the subordinate-moments in the organization of a highly evolved and complex moment may be homologous to the phylogenetic series, but still the two greatly differ in character. Each moment in the series subordinate to the principal moment is greatly modified in its activity and, as such, differs in nature from the moment of the corresponding stage in the phylogenetic series. A complicated act after a series of repetitions sinks into the subconscious, becomes degraded in character and falls to the level of the so-called "secondary automatic" acts. This does not mean that in the phylogenetic or even in the ontogenetic evolution the moment occupying a parallel stage is of a secondary automatic character, as it appears in the moment of higher organization.

When the sensori-motor series going to constitute the secondary automatic act becomes well organized, the links in the series fall to a *minimum* of psychic intensity, but the moment consciousness occupying a corresponding position in the scale of evolution has a higher psychic intensity than the one characteristic of the secondary automatic stage. The psychosis of a dog, horse, mouse, rabbit is hardly of the same order of intensity characteristic, for instance, of the act with which one buttons his coat, opens his door, walks in the street, or simply maintains his equilibrium. The consciousness of the dog, rabbit or mouse may be and surely is of a lower order than that of a man, but its intensity is not necessarily of the same level with the automatic activity of man.

The greater differentiation of elements in the highly constituted being is also their greater simplification. The lower a moment is in the scale of a highly organized being, the more differentiated it is, and the more simplified is its function in the organic whole. Quite different is it in the case of the lower type of moment in the phylogenetic series, there the differentiation has not proceeded far, and although it may be low in type and structure, the very lack of differentiation of function makes that lowly moment more complex as to function. A low moment of a high type of organization is lower than a high moment in a lower type of organization. A moment occupying a low stage in a statically established hierarchy is really lower than a corresponding stage in either the phylogenetic or ontogenetic series. The highest moment-consciousness of a fish is homologous with a very low moment in man, but the latter lacks the intensity to which the former attains.

The moment by entering as a unit in an organized hierarchy becomes degraded and loses much of its psychic activity by becoming differentiated and confined to one mode of reaction, though reaching its acme of perfection in that direction. The number of functions present, though in an imperfect, undeveloped, sketchy way, in the representatives of the low type of moment becomes narrowed down, even limited to one function, highly developed and intensified in the lower representatives of moments belonging to a hierarchy organized on the plan of a higher type.

If $a, b, c, d, e \ldots$ etc., represent the functioning modes of a low type of moment, then the total of functioning modes of the moment may be represented by the sum $(a^1 + b^1 + c^1 rd^1 + e^1 + \ldots)$, each function is in its first degree, that is, it is present in a primitive undeveloped form. The low moment, however, forming a part of a highly developed organic hierarchy, becomes highly differentiated in the process of evolution of the whole and is finally reduced to the exercise of one function only, fully developed and intensified to its highest pitch. The number of functions then present in a primitive form in the moment of low type is in the course of evolution gradually sundered into its units, each unit reaching a high stage of perfection in the low moment belonging to a high type of moment hierarchy.

If a function in its primitive form is represented by a quantity, then the same or analogous function highly developed may be represented by the same or similar quantity raised to (n^{th}) degree. Now let a^n stand for the primitive function, then a^n will stand for the fully developed function. The number of the moment's functions is limited, but highly developed. The moment's functioning activities may be represented by the formula: $a^n + b^n$. The highest moment of the low type has a richer and more variable content than the lower moment belonging to the higher type. This truth can be still further realized by having recourse to the higher guiding moment-consciousness, the lower moments are shown there to work with an almost mechanical-like activity. Man, dog, or monkey with their spinal or medullary ganglia only fall lower than a fully developed fish or a full grown lobster.

If we come to consider the moment of corresponding stages in the ontogenetic and phylogenetic series, we once more meet with resemblance, but at the same time with one of fundamental difference. The moment of high type that passes ontogenetically the stages of phylogenetic evolution does it in a general, and, so to say, sketchy form, each stage of ontogenesis in reality fundamentally differing from that of the parallel stage in phylogenesis. Just as the human embryo in the course of its growth and passing the stages that reflect phylogenesis is not necessarily once a worm, then a fish, then a bird, but only approaches these types in a most general form, so also is it in the case of the moment in the different stages of its growth; it *approaches* the lower types of activity in a most general and sketchy form.

The moment in phylogenesis is independent and is fully developed, while the corresponding stage in ontogenesis is but a stage in the growth of another and higher moment, and as such is certainly different in nature from the phylogenetic moment. The embryo in the first state, though provided with gills, is still not a fish and could not live in water. The consciousness of the infant in passing through stages running parallel to the lower moments-consciousness does not temporarily become that particular low moment-consciousness. It is simply a general outline of the type of moment-consciousness that the higher moment is passing or a stage in the course of its ontogenetic development.

The infant in the growth of its psychic life does not actually turn butterfly, fish, bird, monkey, savage, he does not really pass those modes of psychic states, but he passes through stages which in a general outline remotely resemble the lower grades of animal psychosis. All the stages are determined by the principal type of moment-consciousness, and, in reality, are not a series of low moments ending in a high type, but stages of growth of one high type of moment-consciousness. The stages through which the infant and child pass are the evolution of *man*. The moments of the low form develop on the type of $a^n + b^n + c^n +$, while the moments of the highest forms develop on the type of $(a+b+c+c+)^n$, a far more complex organization.

CHAPTER IV
MENTAL ORGANIZATION

MOMENTS of the same type form aggregations in an ascending series of complexity, groups, systems, communities, clusters, constellations. Isolated moments are organized into groups, groups into systems, systems into communities and communities into constellations. Groups are the simplest, while constellations are the highest and most complex of the aggregates. The firmness, the stability of organization stands in direct relation to complexity, the more complex an aggregation the less stable it is.

The order of complexity also represents the order of development, so that the more complex is also the latest to appear in the course of evolution. Evolution and stability stand thus in inverse relation. What appears early in the course of development is less firmly organized than what appears later on. The whole tendency of evolution is from stability to instability. The order of growth and instability is in the ascending scale —from groups, through systems, communities, to clusters, and constellations. The simpler sensori-motor reactions are, both ontogenetically and phylogenetically, the first to appear in the course of evolution and they are also more stable than the more complex sensori-motor reactions. We can possibly best realize the relation of instability to complexity of structure, if we regard life, including both physiological and psychic processes, as an ascending organization of sensori-motor reactions to the influences of the external environment.

The sensori-motor reactions represent a hierarchy of organized aggregations beginning in the lowest reflexes and culminating in the highest activity.

An illustration of the lower reflexes may be taken, such as the knee-jerk, the action of the bladder, persistaltic movements of the intestines, respiratory movements, heart-beats, and other organic activities. Association among these various reflexes may be taken as higher aggregates. The complex coordination of orientation and space adjustment, such as the maintenance of equilibrium, walking, running, jumping, flying, swimming, etc., represent more complex activity. A still higher aggregate is to be found in the association of groups and systems of sensori-motor reactions within the sphere of a sense-organ with the complex coordination of motor adjustment of the whole body. The highest aggregates are to be found in the association of all the motor reactions organized within the different spheres of sense-organs with the complex motor coordination of body-adjustments.

Simple sensori-motor reflexes, complex reflexes, sensori-motor coordinations, instinctive adaptations and intelligent adjustments, statically regarded, correspond to the classification of psycho-motor aggregates into groups, systems, communities, clusters, and constellations. In other words, the study of the sensori-motor constitution of the higher organized beings in their adult stages, reveals the presence and interrelation of moments. We find that the history of the use and growth of aggregates is in the order of their complexity. In ontogenesis we find that the simple reflexes appear first, then the association, the more complex sensori-motor coordination, later on the so-called instinctive adaptations begin to appear, while the intelligent adaptations appear late in the course of development.

The child at its birth is a purely reflex being; the different reflexes are not even associated, it is the medulla and the spinal cord that are principally active; the pupils react to light, the legs and hands react to more or less intense sensory stimuli, such as tickling, and sensori-motor reflexes to taste-stimuli are present. All of those reactions are isolated, incoordinated; they are so many simple groups of sensori-motor reflexes, even the sucking activity of the infant is largely of the sensori-motor reflex type; the child at its birth is a spinal being, and its moment consciousness is desultory, consisting of the desultory activities of isolated functioning sensori-motor groups.

Later on the reflex activity such as of the hands, legs, eyes become associated through the development of sight and kinaesthetic sensations; the eyes can follow an object, the hands become adapted to the seizing movements. Movements and body coordination then begin to appear, such as turning the body to right or left, then sitting up, then creeping, standing, then walking, then talking, all involving more and more coordination of muscles and kinaesthetic sensations, aided by the association of sensations and sensori-motor reactions from different sense-organs. It is late in its history of development that the child begins to gain full control of its actions and adjustment to the stimuli coming from the external environment.

The history of phylogenesis runs a parallel course. The lower organisms are purely reflex in their sensori-motor reactions, and as such, they belong to the type of the desultory moment-consciousness, such for instance as may be found in the lower form of the Mollusca as the class Tunicata. In the higher forms of Mollusca association of sensori-motor reflexes begins to appear. These associations become more and more complex with the rise and growth of differentiation of sense-organs in the higher forms of Mollusca and the lower Arthropodes, giving rise to groups, systems, communities, reaching the cluster-stage, in the higher Arthropodes and the lower Mammalia, finally culminating in the complex functions characteristic of the constellation-stage, such as found in the sensori-motor reactions of man in his adaptation to physical and social surroundings.

Each highly organized moment represents a hierarchy of many moments, but of lower types. The highest constellation has at its command lower types of psychic aggregates, and had it not been for these lower moments, the higher type would have lacked matter and activity for carrying on its own work.

The lower forms of moments, however, are subordinate to the higher type which constitutes the centre, the nucleus of the total psychosis. The other constituent moments, from the simplest to the most complex, are in the service of the highest type of moments, though the former lie outside the central focus of the principal controlling moment-consciousness. These lower forms are by no means to be ignored, since they form the main factors that determine indirectly the moment's activity; they constitute the storehouse from which the central moment draws its material. Without the lower moments the principal, controlling moment could not have received stimulations from the external environment, nor would it have been enabled to make proper motor responses. In fact we may say that without the lower forms of moments, the moment-nucleus would have lost its vitality and even its meaning.

The perception of an object and the proper adjustments to it depend not so much on what is directly present in the focus of consciousness, but on the wealth of accumulated material lying outside the moment focus. In reading a book, for instance, the handling of it, the motor adjustments in keeping it, the perception of the letters, of the words, of the phrases lie outside the focus of consciousness, and still it is this mass of perceptions that forms the matter of the controlling moment. The inventor in working on his particular invention has a mass of accumulated material and experience indispensable for the development of the invention, subconscious material lying in the background of his consciousness. Similarly the mathematician in solving his problem which forms the focus of his consciousness possesses a body of knowledge or a mass of material which, though it lies on the margin of his consciousness, forms the main stay of his particular investigation.

There is more in consciousness than is actually directly present in the focus of the moment. While I am writing these last phrases my consciousness is occupied with them alone, but they are supported by a body of subconscious thought. All our perception is largely determined by the results of our previous experience which falls outside the central point of consciousness. Many perceptual illusions find their explanation in habit. An otherwise novel experience surrounds itself with familiar experience which disguises the novelty and transforms the percept by substituting what is otherwise familiar and habitual.

This mass of familiar experience is not present in the focus of the moment-consciousness, it lies outside the centre and is often submerged in regard to the direct introspective scrutiny; it has, however, a powerful influence on the activity of the moment. The submerged moments, though lying outside the direct group of the main focus, still exercise a great influence on the course of the moment's growth and development. The conscious controls the material supplied by the subconscious, while the subconscious by the quantity and quality of the mass of its material, in its turn modifies and determines the course of conscious activity.

CHAPTER V
THE GROWTH AND FUNCTION OF THE MOMENT

WE may turn now to the study of the moment's functions. This can be best investigated in following up its history, in watching the growth and development of the most elementary moment-consciousness. In its perceptual stage the moment-consciousness may become modified in its subordinate psychic elements only, indirectly reacting on the nuclear sensory elements, giving a further determination of the total moment without changing its fundamental character. The moment may express then only more distinctly the final aim to which it is striving. The changes brought about in the moment are of such a nature that the latter in its whole tendency becomes adapted for reaction to the external environment, a reaction for which it primarily maintains itself in being.

The moment as percept may have at first an inadequate content which brings about a reaction inadequate for the purpose of the given psychic moment. The reaction brings more content, both primary and secondary. The new content enriches the moment and gives rise to a modification resulting in a reaction which in its turn further enriches the content, until a reaction results fully adequate to the purpose of the moment. The moment reaches for the time being its full maturity. To give a concrete example. A small puff-fish is thrown into a tank containing a hungry tautog. The tautog perceives the puff-fish and comes up to seize it; the puff-fish begins to swell. The sudden swelling of the little fish frightens the tautog away. The tautog's reaction has proved unsuccessful. Some modification is being produced in the tautog's state relating to the puff-fish yonder. Another reaction may then follow, a sudden pounce and bite, the puff-fish swelling in the tautog's mouth. The tautog's reaction is once more a failure, the puff fish is dropped, but considerably hurt. A series of similar reactions with a series of similar modifications finally result in a totally different reaction. The fish by a series of sudden pounces and bites succeeds in debilitating the puff-fish, paralyzing its power of swelling and finally devouring it. A series of such repetitions of experiences determine the general procedure of the tautog to the puff-fish. The tendency to a series of sensori-motor reactions may thus become organized.

The chick emerging from the egg sees an object, say a caterpillar, and attacking the caterpillar misses it at first. This procedure enriches the chick's psycho-motor life and modifies its next reactions in relation to the caterpillar, until the whole moment of pecking at edible objects when presented to the eye consists of successful reactions, as the result of their repetition, finally ending in perfect organization. The infant in seeing an object makes at first fruitless attempts at seizing it. These futile attempts further determine his activity and finally he reaches a state when the adaptation is complete. The psycho-motor reaction becomes adequate to the stimulus.

In all these cases there is no need that the growth and improvement of adaptation should be brought by explicit processes of judgments and associations of free ideas. The fish, the chick, the infant have no distinct consciousness of what sort of psychic process is going on, nor do they deliberately after weighing the *pros* and *cons* of their actions, finally decide on one which is consciously to be rejected on trial and so on, at length hitting on the right solution of the problem. Such is not the state of their mind. To ascribe to them conscious thought, cunning, knowledge, is to ascribe modes and forms of adult human consciousness to a lower stage where all this is absent. Their psychic processes are far simpler. The growth of the moment-consciousness in the stage under consideration is altogether different in nature from that of the adult stage.

In the moment-consciousness under consideration each sensory response to a given stimulus along with its resulting motor reaction brings about a modification of the total moment. Each new modification brings the moment nearer in its sensory and motor elements, to a more perfect adaptation to the specific conditions of the external environment; this modification is reproduced on the recurrence of the moment.

Let a be the moment and b, b_1, b_2, b_3, the successive modifications, then the modified moment at each stage of its growth may be represented as follows: a, $ab, abb_1, abb_1b_2, abb_1b_3$, etc. The reproduced successive modifications do not emerge singly. The reactions of the moment do not occur in repetition of the order in which they have primarily followed each other. In other words, the reactions are not gone through in the order in which they have taken place. The series is not literally repeated. Each subsequent modification is super-imposed on the previous ones and modifying them becomes synthetized in a single complex reaction. The last successful reaction is the only one that emerges in the occurrence of the particular stimulus under a given set

of conditions.

All the intermediate, unsuccessful reactions, although they have gone to determine the last state of the moment with its particular reactions and are implicitly contained in it, gradually drop out, and only the last forms of reaction occur. The last moment-consciousness at each birth generated by a given stimulus under appropriate conditions possesses in a vague outline the history of its previous stages. Most of the stages seem to drop out, only the ones that are indispensable remain.

The moment-consciousness in its growth and development expands into a series of moments, each subsequent moment being an expansion of the preceding one. In this expanded series each succeeding moment is richer in content than the one that has passed away, and is more adapted to the original end for which the moment as a whole subsists and maintains itself in the struggle for life. The last moment is an epitome of the preceding series, an epitome in which by adaptive selection many links have dropped out, and in which the ones that survive appear not in their bare isolation, but in a synthesis of organic unity.

In respect to synthesis the moment may be compared to the percept in which the moment-elements are not in a free state and cannot be separately reinstated. In the moment as in the percept the elements are firmly bound together, and in this bondage they are reproduced. In the psychic moment itself the previous stages are not discriminated, since the whole moment emerges as one compound in which the elements are firmly held together in a form of "mental-chemistry" by a process of cumulation, a process which, as we have pointed out, is essentially different from the process of association of ideas in which the ideal elements are free.

A moment-consciousness lacking free elements in its constituents cannot know its own history; in other words, it cannot recognize the identity or similarity of its elements with the ones that have been present in a previous state. The recognitive element is entirely wanting in such a type of moment-consciousness. A moment-consciousness of such a nature may be termed *reproductive*. *A reproductive moment-consciousness reproduces its contents, but lacks the element of recognition.*

CHAPTER VI
THE RELATION OF THE MOMENT TO THE ENVIRONMENT

IF we inspect closely the reproductive moment-consciousness, we can discover in it definite traits specially characteristic of it. From the very character of its organization the moment-consciousness is of such a nature as to be accessible to and at the same time affected by definite stimuli of the external environment. The moment-consciousness itself is formed through the influence of stimuli coming from its environment. The psychic states that go to make up the nucleus-content of the moment-consciousness are primarily sensory in character, due entirely to incoming stimulations proceeding from some external source. This is fundamentally true not only of the lowest and simplest, but also of the highest psychic moment. The infinite wealth of our experiences is of an incoming character derived entirely from stimulations coming from the periphery, or from the outside world. Even where the moment is ideal in character it is still originally derived from sensation.

The nature and primary function of the moment is to be sensitive to stimuli. The origin of the moment takes its rise in sensory responsiveness, and its growth is due to the formation of successive layers of sensory elements. The sensory characteristic is still further brought out in the fact of adaptation and possibility of further modification of the moment. Psychic modification under the influence of external stimuli clearly demonstrates the important characteristics of sensitivity. We may say that sensitivity, meaning by it psychic processes aroused by stimuli, is a fundamental character of the moment-consciousness, however elementary.

The moment-consciousness is not only sensory, but also motor in character. The whole purpose of the moment's being is adaptation to external conditions. These adaptations, however, are brought about not by *the mere sensitivity,* but by motor reactions. If the moment shows sensitivity towards the play of definite external stimuli, it shows itself still more ready to give vent to its activity in definite sets of motor reactions. In fact we may say that primarily sensitivity is readiness for reaction. The stimulus that irritates the naked protoplasm of the amoeba results in movement of its pseudopodium. The irritation of the nerve endings of the ascidian or of the medusa results in the contractions of the muscular coat. In the more highly organized animals the excitation of the peripheral sense-organ results in contraction and relaxation of muscles or secretions of glands.

This is clearly manifested in the life-phenomena of invertebrates and lower vertebrates. The fly, the bee, the ant, the butterfly, the fish, the frog react immediately as soon as they are acted upon by influences of their external medium. In this respect they almost resemble highly complicated mechanisms that manifest definite sets of movements when acted on different parts of structure. Especially is this manifested in the lower centres.

The fly, the ant, the bee, the butterfly, without their higher central ganglia are pure automata. Thus if the fly is deprived of its frontal ganglia, or head, it remains quiet as if dead, until it is stimulated, when a motor reaction immediately follows. If such a "headless" fly is turned on its back, it rights itself, or flies some distance, alighting on its legs, and again remaining in the same state until a new stimulus brings it out of its torpor. If the thorax is stimulated, the front legs pass through the wiping movement. If the delicate hair on the lower part of the abdomen are irritated, the hind legs react. If the side hair are stimulated, the side legs respond, and so on. In short, the stimulus is followed by immediate reaction of the stimulated organ.

With the central ganglion present, the fly differs but little as a reactive being, only the reactions are more complicated, more co-ordinate, more adaptive; they do not occur in a uniform and automatic fashion in the directly stimulated organ, but in some other organs distant from the stimulus directly applied and in a series of co-ordinate movements, responding to the stimulus in a form advantageous to its needs, or preservative of its life.

In the frog we meet once more with the same state of things. Without its brain the frog is an automaton responding to external stimuli immediately with some simple set of movements. With its brain present the response differs only in the fact that it is more complex and more adaptive. The same holds true in the case of the higher vertebrates, in the bird, in the rabbit, in the dog, in the monkey, and also in man. When deprived of the brain they are automata immediately responding to stimuli with simple movements of but little adaptation. With their brain in full and healthy function they are, biologically regarded, highly organized beings responding to external stimulations with complex movements of more or less perfect adaptation.

Should we like further illustration and evidence we can find it not only in phylogenesis, but also in ontogenesis. Young animals react to any passing stimulus; their life is full of movement and activity. The movements are not adaptive to the special conditions of the environment; in fact these reactions may often be of such a nature as to hurt and even endanger the life of the young animal. External stimuli simply liberate pent-up energy in centres which are but little co-ordinated. In this respect of lack of co-ordination and adaptation young animals resemble vertebrates or invertebrates deprived of their frontal ganglia.

The restlessness of children and of infants is notorious; in an infant under my observation, I have observed kicking of legs as many as 25-35 per minute, and this was kept up for a quarter of an hour, sometimes for half an hour at a time; each kick of the leg served as a stimulus for another one, until fatigue was induced. An external stimulus at once calls forth a reaction in the child or the infant. The reaction is usually not adaptive, purposeless, and frequently hurtful.

There are also purposeful reactions, reactions that are of a purely instinctive character, useful for the life and growth of the animal. These reactions, however, are, physiologically regarded, of a more complex reflex character. Given a definite stimulus and a certain set of conditions, a series of reactions immediately follows in a certain order and succession. Thus the aphis secretes its limpid drops of sweet juice, when its abdomen is tickled by the antennae of the ant only. No other delicate tickling stimulations can bring about the reaction of secretion. The ant on seeing the aphis runs at once up to it and begins to play with its antennae on the abdomen of the aphis, and the latter on feeling the particular stimulations reacts in lifting up its abdomen and secreting the viscid juice.

The white butterfly lays her eggs as soon as it comes in contact with stimuli coming from cabbage leaves. As soon as the change of temperature occurs, the migration instinct of birds is awakened. Young pointers are sometimes known to point the first time they are taken out. Young chicks disperse and show fright as soon as they hear an intense sound. In an infant of two days old I have observed protective grasping movements; the infant when immersed in the bath tub for the first time got hold and clasped firmly with his little finger the hand of the person that bathed him. Furthermore, the whole body assumed strained and rounded positions, lifting itself out of the water with which it came in contact; the infant was clinging with all its little strength to the hand that bathed him.

The character of instinctive reaction is perhaps more closely manifested in the following interesting experiment performed by me on a very young infant. The infant was not more than three hours old, he was put to the breast and the nipple put to the mouth. The stimulus of the nipple in the mouth at once excited the physiological arrangement for sucking movement, an arrangement which the infant brings with him in a more or less ready state, on his coming into the world. When the infant had enough, the sucking movements ceased. The nipple was then withdrawn, and then put again into his mouth, the sudden fresh stimulus once more awakened the mechanism to activity, and the sucking movements began only to stop soon. This was repeated a few times, every time as soon as the stimulus was supplied the sucking movement began.

The experiment was then slightly modified, the baby after ceasing its sucking movements was left keeping the nipple in its mouth, and instead of taking away the nipple and putting it back, thus enforcing the stimulus directly, some other stimuli were employed. The infant's legs were tickled, the skin of the body was rubbed, pricked in different places, and every time as the stimulus was applied the sucking movements were started.

A few hours later when the baby became sensitive to sound, I tried the same experiments with sound stimuli, and obtained the same results. Sensory stimulations followed by motor reactions are the elements out of which moment-consciousness from the lowest to the highest is formed. If one aspect of the moment-consciousness is sensory, the other aspect is motor. The two aspects are inseparable, correlative.

The sensori-motor relation is observed not only in the lowest forms of psychic life, but also in the highest. In the highest form of mental life we still meet with the same factor of motor reactions. Mental activity tends to pass into action. Psychic processes, motor and glandular reactions are interrelated. All along the course of mental activity reaction is present as its invariable concomitant. Some muscles are in a state of tension, others in a condition of relaxation. According to the flow and content of ideas, representation is now retarded, now accelerated. The functioning activity of the glands, of the vaso-motor system is influenced, the circulation of blood is affected, more blood rushing to the brain.

This reaction aspect of mental life, and especially of affective, emotional life, can easily be demonstrated by appropriate instruments. By aid of the sphygmograph, the tromograph, the pneumograph, the plethysmograph, the automatograph, the galvanometer, and other instruments registering physiological results, it can clearly be shown that mental activity with its affective tone results in some end effect, muscular or glandular reaction. With a very delicate automatograph, or swinging pendulum, it can even be shown that the movements manifested often express the content of consciousness.

This is especially striking in case of different forms of automatisms—in people who are of the motor type. When the subject's hand is put on the automatograph, and the subject begins to think, the pen of the automatograph begins to move and write. When the person thinks of the left side of the room the movements swing to the left; when the subject thinks of a series of definite movements, movements of a similar order and character are followed out by the pen of the automatograph. Subjects who are of a pronounced motor type when their attention is distracted write with the automatographic pen the ideas of which they happen to think at that moment. The remarkable experiments made by Pavlov and his pupils are here to the point. The experiments clearly prove the close interrelation of mental activity and glandular function.

The reaction character of mental life is still more distinctly manifested in the various forms of mental dissociation, such as are to be found in the psychopathic and neuropathic diseases and in the states of hypnosis, and in fact in all the phenomena belonging to the order known as the subconscious. Many of the most important methods in psychology and psychopathology are based on this reaction aspect of the moment-consciousness.

CHAPTER VII
THE ASSIMILATION OF THE MOMENT IN NORMAL STATES

THE fact that the moment-consciousness expands, grows, and develops in its organization until it reaches a point of perfect adaptation to external conditions clearly shows that the moment is capable of working new psychic material into its constitution. The material which it gets is of such a nature as to help to perpetuate the psychic life of the moment. The moment cannot possibly go on growing without having such material at hand. If the moment comes in contact with any psychic element or experience that can further its content, the experience is at once seized on and synthetized in the moment. The psychic element is not simply taken in and associated or annexed to the rest of the content, it is actually transformed in this process.

When the moment is stimulated to activity by an external object, the sensory stimulations of the present time-moment are new. Just these particular stimulations and sensory processes awakened have not occurred as yet in the life history of the animal, and still the object meets with its appropriate sensory response and motor reaction. The moment that has more or less like content to the given new psychic experience aroused appropriates the new states, works them into its own psychic content, and sends out its characteristic reaction in response to the stimuli. The moment that gets hold of new psychic material is ordinarily the one which is in the process of activity at the given time when the stimulations occur. The new material is absorbed by the moment as a whole, and is then assimilated by the functioning nucleus. The primary sensory elements of the nucleus become strengthened.

At the same time the new sensory material absorbed awakens some new secondary sensory elements which are assimilated by the secondary sensory elements constituting the so-called protoplasm of the moment. In this absorption of new material the moment does not and cannot possibly remain exactly the same, it is modified in a degree, although the internal relations of its constituents may practically remain unaltered. Readjustments may occur and usually do so, but they are made as nearly as possible to the old plan, and are assimilated to the old content.

In the perceptual moment of the tautog that which constitutes its content may be the perception, say of a little fish yonder; soon, however, a new feature may arise in the course of experience, namely, change in color for instance in the case of the squid, or swelling in the case of the puff-fish. If the fish usually reacts in making attacks when receiving perceptive stimuli coming from small fish, and if the new experience is somewhat unusual in its ordinary life experience, and at the same time not so striking as to call forth the reaction of fear, the fish will still carry out its ordinary reaction of aggressive movement, slightly modified by the new incoming experience.

The chick in seeing a cinnabar caterpillar has the new experience of the different color from that of the caterpillar on which it usually feeds, but the reaction is still the same which caterpillars call out in chicks, namely, seizing and pecking. The new experience of taste got through the reaction may further modify the reaction of the chicks when confronted with cinnabar caterpillar.

The young infant pushes indiscriminately everything in its mouth, everything is for sucking, and only by experience it learns gradually to modify its reaction towards objects. On seeing a lemon, a child that is only acquainted with oranges will take it as an orange. The child will perceive the new visual experiences given by the lemon, as different from orange, but they will be assimilated to his sensory orange experience. The special visual experiences will give rise in the child's mind to some qualification of the percept "orange," the object being a kind of orange, a bad orange. The reaction in relation to the lemon will then be of the kind relating to orange in general. This reaction will be of course modified by repeated experiences resulting from a series of reactions in relation to the lemon.

Savages confronted for the first time with the horse or the ox, consider them a species of pig, an animal with which they are well acquainted, and they expect from the horse, or the ox similar manifestations. Their reactions towards those new species of animals will be of the same kind, as if those animals were pigs.

The same relation is still better illustrated in cases of young children with a definite moment-consciousness, which for convenience sake may be characterized as the family-moment. The child's moment-content of life-relationship consists of his experience gotten from his relation with his papa and mamma. Baby, papa, and mamma and their various relations go to make up the total moment of the child's family life experiences. When the child is confronted with young animals, the latter are regarded in the light of "babies," they are also babies, they have their papas and mammas who give them cookies, tea, and oatmeal, undress them, and put them to bed.

A young child of about three years and a half asked me whether the baby-calf's mamma gave it pie to eat. Another time the same child on seeing a young kitten inquired after its mamma and papa, and when the baby kitty was going to have its tea and put to bed. In one child of less than three years old, young animals, plants, such as young trees and flowers, and even little stars were so many "baby Willies." Their lives were fully assimilated to his own, they were eating oatmeal, drinking milk and were having tea, sugar, and biscuits for their supper. The same child was greatly surprised and partly even horrified at finding that baby-Willie-flowers had no papa and no mamma. The moment-consciousness is awakened by definite specific traits in the object, by familiar experience sense-data constituting the content of the moment; the rest and differential traits of the object are worked into the general plan and character of the functioning moment.

The assimilative power of the moment is clearly revealed in the very character of perception. That pitted object yonder is perceived as an orange with all its attributes of color, shape, size, weight, fragrance, and taste. The synthesis of so many sensory elements corresponding to such a complex of stimuli was gradually effected in the course of ontogenetic development, and no doubt determined by inherited disposition of phylogenetic evolution.

Suppose the orange turns out to be a new species never met before by the individual; it feels differently when touched, it has different weight, special taste, and fragrance. When such sense data are experienced repeatedly, the percept orange is modified by assimilation of the new sense data. On seeing another time such a sort of an orange all the previously separately experienced sense-data appear together in one synthetized percept. The moment-consciousness which we, for illustration sake, have assumed as consisting only of experiences relating to oranges and with corresponding psycho-physiological reactions, has enlarged its content, has increased, and modified its adaptation to external conditions.

The assimilative power of the moment-consciousness is well brought out in the activity of the higher form of consciousness. The desire to go to the post-office to get my mail forms the central point of my present moment-consciousness. Round it as a focus are grouped ideas, feelings, and sensations, all more or less tending in the same direction. The actual walking to the postoffice gives a series of new motor sensations which are subconsciously assimilated by the moment as a whole. The tactual and motor sensations coming from each step are assimilated by the moment, leading in their turn to new series of reactions. Each new step is followed by new sensations that give rise to new reactions and so on, until the end of the moment is reached and the purpose accomplished.

The whole sensori-motor series is guided by the nuclear elements of the moment, although the successive stages of the series are assimilated subconsciously. In reading a book the successive stages are guided by the central general idea. The perception of the letters, words, and their isolated meaning is assimilated subconsciously, all of them being incorporated into the guiding moment-consciousness which is growing and developing, becoming enriched with more and more content. In writing a letter or an article on a certain subject we find the same fact of assimilation by the moment-consciousness of the sense-data coming in the successive steps of the whole experience. The handling of the pen, the dipping it into ink, its guiding by the hand, its gliding over the paper, the drawing of the letters, the formation of letters into words, and of the words into lines and sentences, all follow in successive stages and are assimilated partly subconsciously and partly consciously. All are guided by the principal moment which grows richer in content with each successive step made, with each succeeding link of the series. In fact we may say that all those successive steps are stages in the growth and development of the one moment-consciousness.

The growth and development of the moment-consciousness is through its assimilation of fresh psychic material. In the man of science a favorite theory exercises such an assimilative power over facts otherwise disconnected. The moment-consciousness having the given theory as its nucleus absorbs more and more material, and with the assimilation of new material the content and strength of the internal organization grows in a corresponding degree. The assimilation is guided by the intense interest aroused by the nucleus of the total moment, and is in its turn aided by the active process of assimilation, especially by the influence of submerged, subconscious moments which have reached the *minimum* of consciousness, or lie on the margin of the sphere of waking consciousness.

The influence of the subconscious is in proportion to the duration and intensity of the activity of the mental process. We are well acquainted with the fact that an action requiring at first great stress of attention, finally, with its repetition, drops out of the focus of consciousness and becomes, as it is called, automatic or unconscious. They who have observed a child striving to stand by himself or beginning to walk realize how such seemingly automatic acts as standing or walking are at first accompanied with intense attention. The child, when standing up all by himself, does it hesitatingly; he shakes and trembles, as if occupying unsafe ground, or doing a difficult act; he looks around for support, stretches out his hands, asking the help of his parents or nurse, and if he does not get aid in time, begins to cry from fear and drops on all-fours. It is a difficult feat for him. Withdraw his attention from his performance, and in the first stages of his series of trials he drops helplessly to the ground.

The same holds true in the case of walking. The child in beginning to walk, does it with great hesitation and fear. It can only be compared to the attempt of an adult in learning to walk a rope, or a narrow board on a high place. Each step requires intense attention. The least distraction of attention and the baby falls down in a heap. The least change in the touch, muscular and kinaesthetic sensations arrests the successful attempt at standing or walking. Thus in the case of my baby of fourteen months after the first two days of more or less successful trials at walking, a new pair of shoes was put on. This arrested the walking. When the baby became accustomed to the new sensations which fell in the background of his consciousness, he once more started a series of trials, and with such success that after two days' practice he walked almost a whole mile.

After a period of long practice the complex muscular adjustments, required in the acts of standing and walking, gradually retreat to the background of consciousness and become automatic. Not that consciousness in those acts is lost: it has simply reached its necessary *minimum,* leaving the focus of consciousness free for other new and unaccustomed adjustments, which in their turn retreat from the centre to the periphery and fall into the subconscious. The usual movement of mental processes is *from the conscious to the subconscious.*

Experiences, however, may first be perceived by submerged subconscious moments and then transmitted to the focus of consciousness, the movement of the process thus taking a direction opposite to the usual one, from the subconscious to the conscious. Experiences, for instance, lived through in hypnotic states, in trance states or in dreams, may come to the surface as hypnoidal states and then become synthetized in the upper waking consciousness, or they may be lighted up in hypnosis, and then permanently synthetized in the centre of attentive consciousness.

Similarly experiences first lived through in the subconscious states induced by alcoholic intoxication or by anaesthetics may be brought by hypnoidal states or by hypnosis into the focus of consciousness. Hypnoidal states are uprushes of the subconscious, and by means of them many a hidden and obscure region of the subconscious may be discovered. Thus the Hanna case was largely marked by hypnoidal states. In many of my cases hypnoidal states are the means by which subconscious experiences become completely revealed. In cases of amnesia the hypnoidal states give glimpses into subconscious regions which even deep hypnosis can not reveal.

The method of guesses is valuable in showing the reverse process of mental activity, the passage of r subconscious state into the focus of consciousness.

If the anaesthetic spot of a psychopathic case is stimulated, the patient is unaware of such stimulation; should he, however, be asked to guess, or to tell anything that happens to come into his mind, he is often found to give correct answers. The patient perceives *subconsciously.* This perception, often in a slightly modified form, is transmitted to the upper consciousness, or to what for the present constitutes the patient's principal moment consciousness, or personality.

If, for instance, the anaesthetic spot of the patient is pricked a number of times, the patient remains quiet and is seemingly insensible. Should we now ask the patient to tell anything that comes into his mind, he will say, "pricking" and will be unable to tell why he happened to think of "pricking" at all. Should we now ask him to give any number that may enter his mind, he will give the correct number, once more not being able to give the reason why this particular number happened to enter his mind, considering it a mere "chance number." The subconscious sensations experienced are transmitted as abstract ideas to the focus of consciousness.

Often instead of the particular idea being transmitted, only the general aspect of it reaches the focus. Thus the patient is not able to guess the particular nature of the stimulus, but he may give the character of the unfelt stimuli. This reveals the reverse movement from the subconscious to the conscious.

This reverse movement of the psychic state, from the originally subconscious to the upper consciousness, is well manifested in psychopathic cases of visual anesthesia as well as hypnotically induced anesthesia. The patient's field of vision is limited. If objects are inserted in any place of the zone extending from the periphery of the narrowed field to the utmost boundary of the normal field, the patient can guess correctly the names of the inserted objects invisible to him. General guesses are correct on the periphery of that "subconscious" zone. Some of the phenomena of paramnesia can be explained by this principle of reverse movement, when subconscious experiences transmitted to central consciousness appear under the form of "familiar" memories.

A lighting up of the subconscious regions bringing about a reverse movement from the subconscious to the conscious can also be brought about by the use of toxic drugs. Pent-up neuron energies become liberated from lower and lower-most moment consciousness, long forgotten experiences well up to the centre of consciousness; outlived moments are resurrected and come to the focus of consciousness with all the vividness of a present perceptual experience. Thus De Quincey, in his "Confessions of an English Opium-Eater," tells us that "the minutest incidents of childhood or forgotten scenes of later years were often revived. I could not be said to recollect them, for if I had been told of them when waking, I should not have been able to acknowledge them as my past experience. But placed as they were before me in dreams like intuitions and clothed in all their evanescent circumstances and accompanying feelings, I recognized them instantaneously."

Hypnoidic states reveal the wealth and extent of psychic experience hidden in the subconscious regions. Glimpses into the subconscious are also given in hypnoidal states which are induced by the process of hypnoidization. The patient is asked to close his eyes and keep as quiet as possible without, however, making any special effort to put himself into such a state. He is then asked to tell anything that comes into his mind. The patient may also be asked to attend to some stimuli, such as reading or writing or the buzzing of an electrical current, and he is then to tell the ideas, thoughts, images, phrases, no matter how disconnected, that happen to flitter through his mind.

This same condition of hypnoidization is sometimes better accomplished through mental relaxation with concentration of attention in a definite direction. The patient is put into a quiet condition, and with his eyes closed and the experimenter's hand on the patient's forehead, the latter is urged to mental effort and strain, and, if necessary, given some hints. Experiences seemingly inaccessible flash lightning-like on the upper regions of self-consciousness. In all such cases the active moment-consciousness seizes on and assimilates any cognate experience, conscious or subconscious.

CHAPTER VIII
ABNORMAL MOMENTS

THE power of the moment's assimilation is well brought in the activity of abnormal moments. Distressing thoughts, gloomy ideas, painful sensations, and feelings of depression form a nucleus round which other mental states become firmly organized. A delusion arises which constitutes the moment-consciousness of the melancholiac. This moment assimilates all other cognate experiences. Everything that takes place is seized on by the moment and assimilated. The patient who believes that he has no intestines, or that he is made of glass and is transparent and hence hides himself from people, as his functions are open to the sight of outsiders, such a patient will make all experiences confirm and strengthen the delusion. The delusion constituting the predominant moment-consciousness in the patient's life absorbs and assimilates most, if not all of the material that gains access to the patient's psychic life. The moment like a cancerous growth expands, grows, and develops at the expense of other moments, starves them by cutting off their mental food supply. What cannot be used by the moment is rejected as waste material.

A similar state of affairs we meet with in paranoia, as well as in many paranoidal states of a purely psychopathic character. A moment-consciousness is formed of high organizing and assimilating power. Any experience relevant and irrelevant entering consciousness is greedily absorbed and assimilated. Any flitting thought, any passing impression is worked in and organized into the moment. All other moments fall a prey to this dominant all-absorbing moment.

In some cases the assimilating capacity of the moment seems to be limitless. In fact, the more it assimilates, the greater grows its craving and capacity for getting more material. The most trivial facts, the slightest sense-impressions all are pressed into the service of the despotically ruling moment. The insignificant becomes significant and points to the central delusion.

In other cases the limit of the process of assimilation soon reaches its maximum point, more psychic material is rejected by the moment. Such conditions are to be found in various states of dissociation manifested in different forms of psychopathic diseases. The moment's capacity for assimilating new material is of limited range, soon reaches its utmost bounds and loses for the time being all capacity for further assimilation. Such states may be found in amnesia. The moment is then said to be dissociated from the main current of psychic life-activity. Specific stimuli under definite conditions are requisite to resuscitate the moment and arouse its power of assimilation.

It is certainly interesting and instructive to study the fluctuations of the moment's power of assimilation in abnormal mental states. In some forms of mental diseases and general psychic derangements the moment may be of ephemeral and unstable character; it may dissolve soon after its birth. Such conditions are to be found in various forms of maniacal states and in the initial stages of many cases of general paresis.

In psychomotor manifestations of a psychopathic character moments-consciousness are often formed and dissolved like soap-bubbles. The investigation of them is of the utmost interest and value. In hypnosis moments of such a nature may be experimentally induced and studied. The whole process can thus be followed through all the stages of evolution and dissolution.

A greater condition of stability is to be found in the various automatisms preceding or following epileptic seizures, or in the so-called "psychic equivalents of epilepsy." The pure "psychic epilepsies" are essentially hypnoidic states, moments of stable character. This can be demonstrated both by observation and experiment.

The principle of selection is fundamental in the life-history of the moment. The whole tendency of the moment is to select material conducive to the furtherance of its activity and to reject all material that thwarts its functions and growth. This process of selection is from a biological standpoint essential for the survival and development of the moment.

The development of the moment may become arrested on some one stage of ontogenesis, and then the moment, belonging to a higher type resembles in its psychic activity that of a lower type; although it has many vestiges of the higher type, it is greatly modified in nature and as such really differs from the healthy normal representative of the corresponding low type. Still we may affirm that the arrested high type has virtually become a moment of low type. The state of psychosis of the imbecile, or idiot, may be taken as a good illustration. The mental activity of the idiot resembles the lower types of animal psychosis. Although as we have already pointed out, the consciousness of the idiot and that of the animal are by no means identical, still both belong to a low type of moment, and as such, they may be put on the same level.

In pathological cases where mental degeneration sets in we also have a similar course. The moment of the higher type becomes degraded and falls to the level of lower and lowermost types, according to the advance of the process of degeneration. Such states are to be found in the degenerative psychosis characteristic of secondary dementia. When the pathological process is wide, intense, persistent, and lasting, then secondary dementia results in most cases of mental degeneration. Should, however, the process become arrested then the moment simply falls to the level of a relatively lower type.

CHAPTER IX
MENTAL CONTINUITY AND THE PSYCHIC GAP

THE activity of the moment-consciousness is continuous, without break and interruption. Should the activity become arrested and the break be seemingly absolute, continuity is still present with the resumption of activity. The thread is taken up where it was dropped, the moment appears as a whole without any break. *There is no lesion in the moment consciousness, at least as far as the moment itself is concerned.* In going to sleep and waking up again we may be indirectly conscious of the interruption, but the activity of the moment is still continuous, the moment begins its activity at the point where it has left off. In fainting, in coma, in hypnosis, or somnambulism the periods of unconsciousness are immediately bridged over by the awakening activity of the moment.

Objectively considered, we have the moment's activity, then break, or absence of that activity, and then the resumption; subjectively, however, the moment's activity is felt as one and continuous without a break and gap. In consciousness the psychic content and activity preceding the break along with present cognizance of the break are synthetized into a unified continuity; the present consciousness of the break is taken into the synthesis, the very gap thus forming the bridge for unity.

The cognizance of the break may, however, be completely absent, and the edges of the mental wound may become closed, healed, and united with the functioning activity of the moment, the moment, without even the least consciousness of the intervening gap, resuming its line of work precisely at the place where it had been arrested. From the moment's own standpoint, the gap is as if non-existent, there is no break in the moment's psychic life-activity.

The break formed by the interruption of the moment's functioning activity, objectively regarded, may present an actual gap in which, for all intents and purposes, it may be supposed that no mental activity is taking place. Such cases are found in the state of deep sleep, undisturbed by dreams, or in the states of unconsciousness produced by toxic and narcotic agencies, in states of deep coma, in the attacks of typical epilepsy, *petit* or *grand mal,* in *status epilepticus,* in the states of unconsciousness produced by intense mechanical stimuli, such as a blow, or a fall, or a strong electrical current. In all such cases we often find a state that may, for all intents and purposes, be characterized as unconsciousness. No other moment comes to the surface, even temporarily, to fill the mental gap caused by the interruption of the moment's functional activity. The gap presents a mental blank.

To the important question: "How, then are we to explain amnesia where consciousness is indicated?" Ribot answers "By the extreme weakness of the conscious state." This explanation is inadequate. For first of all, what is the meaning of a weak state of consciousness? Is it a state felt as being weak? If so, the explanation is obviously wrong. We may far better retain in memory the whisper of a dear friend than the striking of the tower clock or the explosion of a gun. Does he mean by a weak state of consciousness a confused indistinct state? Once more he is wrong. A confused and indistinct state of mind is often clearly remembered. I am dizzy, everything is confused and indistinct, I am unable to tell in detail what I have seen and heard, but I can clearly and distinctly remember the state of dizziness and confusion, and very often far better than any other less confused mental state. This, however, is not the case in the states of amnesia under discussion.

In amnesia there is no memory at all of the experienced mental states and what the subject or the patient remembers is the last link of the state preceding the amnesia. The state preceding the amnesia and the one succeeding it are joined together, the intermediary is left out, as if it had never been in existence. Evidently the theory is that the state of consciousness is so weak that it leaves no "trace," no memory behind. But if this be the case, then the explanation is a tautology. The problem is, why is there no memory in certain states of consciousness? To this the reply is that the states of consciousness leave no memory behind. It is obvious that this explanation is vague and when one tries to give to it a definite meaning, it is either wrong or turns out to be a reasoning in a circle.

Granted, however, that a weak state of consciousness is something definite, that by it is meant to indicate confusion, indistinctness of consciousness, and granted furthermore, that such a state leaves no memory behind, how then shall we explain amnesia of mental states when consciousness was intense, clear and distinct, as in the case of hypnosis or of artificial somnambulism? In these states the senses are almost hyperaesthetic, the sense of discrimination is extremely acute and memory is in a state of exaltation. Why is it then that amnesia can be enforced in the case of almost any experience immediately after the trance is over, or even during the very state of hypnosis? *The state of consciousness is intense and still there is amnesia.*

How is it in cases of double consciousness or of multiple personality? Surely the explanation of "weakness" of the states of consciousness cannot be advanced by anyone who has a personal knowledge of these phenomena. How is it in psychopathic cases where the amnesia is brought about by an intense painful state of consciousness, such as fright, fear or great grief? On the theory of weakness of consciousness all these phenomena are mysterious, incomprehensible. On our theory of moment-consciousness, however, the phenomena presented could not possibly be otherwise, in fact, we should expect them *a priori,* if our theory be correct.

A psychic blank, however, is not the only possible consequence of the moment's lapse of function. The moment's activity is interrupted, but only, what is more often the case, to give rise to activity of another moment. The break produced in the moment's life is not a real gap; for the gap is filled in with the functioning activity of another moment which is usually of a lower, though sometimes it may even be of a higher type. From the standpoint of the arrested moment, however, there is a distinct gap, not that the moment itself is cognizant of the gap, but it is so for the external observer that takes that moment for his standpoint. The gap exists *in* the moment, though not *for* the moment.

Such states may be found in hypnosis especially in that stage of it known as somnambulism. When the subject falls into a deep hypnotic state, it is possible to make him pass through a series of complicated actions, changes of personalities without the least awareness on awakening. The whole series of his waking consciousness it is as non-existent, in short, it is a gap.

This gap however, is far from being a mere mental blank. On the contrary there may have been intense psychic activity, but only that of another moment which in the waking state has become submerged. This submerged moment may be brought up in the waking state by suggestions or by means of hypnoidization and be synthetized in the upper consciousness. Sometimes glimpses of the submerged moment may come up in dreams, in reveries, in sudden flashes during the waking state, or in spontaneous hypnoidal states, the subject doubting whether they refer to something actual or are simply mere whims and fancies.

In the cases of the so-called "psychic epilepsy" which are really amnesia of a psychopathic character, one meets with psychic states in which the gap is not absolute, but relative, being filled with the activity of another moment. Thus, M. carried on conversations, arguments, and discussions while in the abnormal subconscious state and could not remember anything of it when emerging from it and returning to the normal condition. Similarly F. in his subconscious state travelled a distance, sold horses and returned, but knew nothing of what had taken place from the beginning to the end of his journey.

In the H. case the gaps formed in the secondary state by the manifestations of the primary state were as if nonexistent for this secondary consciousness. The same held good of the primary consciousness: the two were working independently of each other, each synthetizing its own experience, each beginning at the place where it had left off. Neither of them knew of and felt subjectively the gap. There was a gap, only it was filled in by another moment consciousness of which the present functioning moment was not aware.

In cases of typical epilepsy subconscious states are sometimes found, states that constitute gaps in the activity of the normally working moment-consciousness. Thus in some cases of idiopathic epilepsy under my observation, the patients in the stuporous states succeeding the epileptic attack answer questions, but do not recognize me, nor do they know the nurse who takes care of them, although they can remember and recognize other names mentioned to them. In their normal state, however, they neither know of their attacks nor do they remember anything of the conversations and experimentations during the stuporous post-epileptic state. In other severe cases of epilepsy with frequent attacks of *grand mat* and *petit mal,* the patients during the periods of their stuporous post-epileptic states answer questions often mistaking persons and environment, referring to events and incidents of their early childhood. On emerging from their abnormal states, the patients are completely unaware of what had taken place, the epileptic attack with stuporous post-epileptic state forming a gap in the functional activity of his principal or upper moment-consciousness.

If we look at the moment from its subjective standpoint there may be consciousness of the gap bridging over the edges of the mental lesion, or such consciousness may be altogether lacking, the psychic edges of the mental lesion being closely unified in the synthetic activity of the temporarily arrested, but now once more functioning moment-consciousness. If we look at the objective side of the gap, we find that there may be total absence of all mental activity, no other moment coming up to fill the place of the one that has ceased functioning, or another moment may take the place of the one arrested in function, seemingly fill up the mental gap, and become submerged with the restitution of the arrested moment's activity. Not that the gap is really filled up objectively or subjectively; it is like the close successive manifestations of different individualities. The close observer can easily detect the arrest, the gap, the filling up of the gap with another moment's activity, and finally the restitution of the original temporarily arrested moment-consciousness. What is presented to cursory observation is apparent continuity of mental activity.

Mental gaps may be classified as follows:

When the principal moment becomes arrested in its activity and a new dominating moment takes it place in the formed gap, the type of the new moment is usually of a lower grade. The conditions that bring about an aggregation of moments are of such a nature as to allow of the activity of a high type of moment Not appearing in the mental synthesis of the organization of moments characteristic of consciousness in the normal state, the moment is poor in content and simple in nature. Falling as it does outside the complex normal aggregate of moments, the moment lacks the harmony and balance in its psychomotor and psycho-physiological reactions, since the counteracting balancing and hence regulative psychomotor tendencies of other systems of moments are wanting.

A moment that enters into a highly complex aggregation of moments, when stimulated to activity, sets also other moments into functioning, moments that are closely associated with it and often of different and even contrary psychomotor and psycho-physiological reactions. Strengthening other systems against the lines of its own activity the moment is thus controlled, inhibited, and regulated in the very act of awakening to functioning activity. For it must be clearly understood that there is no special controlling agency somewhere in the mind sending out orders, mandates, inhibitions, like a despotically ruling autocrat, like a psycho-analytic censor, or like an omniscient, omnipotent, omnipresent, invisible deity. *The regulative, inhibiting control to which a moment is subject is in the mutual interrelation, balance, and harmony of the systems and constellations of moments, entering into an aggregate, and forming the organized activity of a highly complex moment-consciousness.*

When a moment becomes dissociated and isolated from other systems of moments, it loses its balance and being freed from control, manifests its psychomotor reactions in the full force of its original powers. The lack of control and the moment's energy of manifestations are just in proportion to the depth and extent of dissociation or of disaggregation of moments. *Dissociation and over-action are co-related.*

The intimate relation of dissociation and over-action is clearly seen in cases of so-called "psychic epilepsy." The dissociated subconscious states manifest themselves with an over-powering activity, with an energy that can neither be resisted nor controlled, they come like irresistible, uncontrollable, imperative impulses, which are closely related to them in nature. If, however, these states are brought out from the hidden subconscious depth from which they make invasions; if they are brought to light before the court of the upper consciousness one by one in hypnoidal states, and are forced to become associated with and synthetized into the principal moment-consciousness, the impetuosity and energy of their manifestations are gone. All my cases of dissociation give experimental confirmation of this law of dynamagenesis of dissociation.

The dissociated cluster, although inaccessible through the ordinary channels of intercommunications, on account of the disaggregation of the aggregate into which it enters as a constituent part, may still be reached through other channels, coming from other moment-aggregates. For a moment, or a combination of them forms a constituent part not only of one aggregate, but of many other aggregates. Loss of communication through a certain channel does not necessarily exclude loss of all communications. If the lost channel is habitual, the activity of the seemingly lost moments may be awakened through unhabitual channels.

If the moment cannot be set into activity by the organization of constellations constituting the conscious personality, on account of disaggregating processes, the moment may still be set into functioning activity through aggregates falling outside the focus of personality, but which work with that focus in close co-operation, namely the subconscious. In other words, in the process of disaggregation, conscious, or rather self-conscious experiences fall into the region of subconscious life; what is absent in personal thought may be present in impersonal, subconscious states. All psychopathic functional disturbances consist just in such an interrelation of mental aggregates; in the process of disaggregation of the self-conscious personality aggregates of moments drop out and fall into the domain of the subconscious. What disappears from attentive consciousness may fall into subconsciousness. The disaggregated moment, ceasing to enter into relations with the upper personal consciousness of the highly complex constellation, may still form a component of the lower aggregates of the subconscious.

CHAPTER X
THE MOMENT-THRESHOLD

TAKING an initial stimulus with its concomitant sensory effect as the starting point we add by degrees small unperceived stimuli until a point is reached when a barely perceptible change of the external stimulation is effected in consciousness. The sum of the differential stimuli up to the point where the perceptible change is produced is found out, and brought into relation with the quantity of the initial stimulus. Working with this method of least observable differences Weber succeeded in expressing the relation of the differential stimulus to sensation in the formula known as "Weber's law." Within certain limits, no matter what the absolute value of the stimulus be, the differential stimulus, or what is the same the barely sensible addition to the initial total stimulus, must bear the same proportion to the total stimulus. By many experiments Weber found that in the case of weight, for instance, the relation is one-third. Thus if the first weight be nine pounds the barely sensible addition will be one-third of nine, or three pounds; in twelve pounds the increment is one-third of twelve, or four pounds; in fifteen pounds the barely sensible increment is again one-third of the total stimulus that is one-third of fifteen, or five pounds, and so on.

Further investigations have shown that, within certain limits, there is for all the senses which admit of exact measurement a constantly uniform quantitative relation between the stimulus and the just noticeable stimulus-difference. Experimentation by different investigators have confirmed "Weber's law" for the different senses by showing that, within a certain range of intensities of stimuli, there is a more or less constant ratio between the increase of the stimulus necessary to produce a just noticeable difference of sensation and the total stimulus intensity. Thus, it has been shown that noise stimuli must increase by one-third; pressure stimuli by one-fortieth; stimuli of muscular sensations, such as lifting weights, by one-fortieth; achromatic light stimuli by one-hundredth. Weber in his paper *De Tactu* expressed his law as follows: *"In observando discrimine rerum inter se comparalarum non differentiam rerum, sed rationem differentiæ ad magnitudinem rerum inter se comparatarum percipimus."*

Gustav Theodor Fechner, the founder of psychophysics and its methods, starting with Weber's law worked out a general formula for the quantitative relation between physical stimuli and sensations. Assuming that the just noticeable differences of sensation given by ascending or descending series of different stimuli to be equal units, he finds by means of different psychophysical methods, first elaborated by him, the threshold of sensations or that stimulus which is just near the limit of giving rise to a sensory effect, but which is still not sufficient to awaken a sensation; in short, he finds the stimulus the correlating sensation of which is zero.

The *minimum* perceptible or stimulus-threshold is found by measurements of the different senses. Thus two parallel lines are for most people barely distinguishable when the distance between them subtends an angle of less than 60 seconds. In the sense of hearing the vibrations recurring between 30-35 per second are barely distinguishable. Below 16 vibrations per second no sensation of sound can be produced.

Thresholds have been similarly determined for all other sensations. Thus the sense of touch, when tested by the aesthesiometer, an unsatisfactory instrument, gives the average for the tip of the forefinger about 1.65 mm., on the back of the hand about 16.0 mm., Sensibility to pain as tested by the algeometer varies from 10 to 15 degrees. Sensitivity to smell varies with different substances; thus for smell of garlic sensitivity varies in detecting 1 part in 44,000 parts of water to one part in 57,000 parts of water; for oil of lemon from 1 to 116,000 to 1 to 280,000. Taste can detect the bitterness of quinine in a solution of 1 part quinine to about 400,000 to 459,000 of water; the sweetness of sugar can be detected in a solution of 1 part sugar to 200 of water; the taste of salt can be detected in a solution of 1 part salt to about 2,000 parts of water.

After discovering the zero point of sensation and the *minimum* perceptible he finds the constant ratio for the just noticeable difference. The *minimum* perceptible forms the unit of sensation. Each increase of the stimulus giving a just noticeable difference is counted as an additional sensation-unit to the total sum of sensations.

Let A be the threshold giving sensation zero, and let r be the constant ratio of increase then we have the following series of stimuli and their corresponding sensations:

Sensation o is given by stimulus A

Thus we find that while the stimulus increases in a geometrical ratio, the sensation grows in an arithmetical ratio. The sensations stand therefore in the same relation as the logarithms to their numbers. Hence we may say that *sensation increases as the logarithm of the stimulus.* If S be the sensation, R the stimulus and C the magnitude of the constant ratio, then we have the following formulae:

$$S = C \log. R.$$

This formula is known as "Fechner's law."

Fechner's expression of Weber's law is rather questionable. Fechner assumes that the just noticeable difference of different stimuli are qualitatively and quantitatively equal,—a dubious assumption. A third of an ounce added to an ounce does not feel the same as a third of eighteen pounds added to the same number of pounds, or as nine pounds added to twenty-seven pounds. These units even, if they have a quantitative expression, do not stand in a simple quantitative relation and are rather incommensurable.

Furthermore, it may even be considered that Fechner's assumption is fundamentally wrong and unpsychological. In opposition to the first elementary principle of psychology Fechner tacitly postulates that sensations can be measured and that one sensation or a complex sensation is a multiple of another. Now the peculiar trait of the phenomena of mental life is essentially their qualitative character. Sensations are not quantities to be measured, but are essentially qualities. A strong sensation is not a weak sensation many times over, but its very strength, its intensity is its own separate individual quality constituting the essence of that particular sensation. An intense sensation of pure white is not a multiple of a weak sensation of grey just as the thought "nation" is not the thought "man" raised to the nth degree.

In psychological investigations one must be careful not to confound the nature of the physical stimulus with that of the sensation. A physical stimulus can be measured quantitatively, but a sensation does not consist of quantitative units, and hence, is not measurable. The only relation that can be measured and expressed quantitatively is that between stimulus and physiological process, the physical concomitant of psychic states.

Whether or not we accept Fechner's statement of Weber's law we may safely assume that the threshold rises with successive stimulations. This law holds true of all life processes, from the life of an ameba to the life activity of a highly organized moment-consciousness. In the sphere of sensation we find such a rise of threshold. We are all acquainted with the fact that an additional candle or lamp, for instance, in a well lighted room does not produce the same sensory effect as when brought into a more or less dark room. An electric light in the sun is scarcely perceptible. An additional ounce to a lifted pound does not feel as heavy as when raised by itself. A sound added to another sound or noise, sounds less loud than when appearing isolated, or when the same sound is breaking upon silence. The same relation holds true in the case of other senses.

This same truth is still more clearly brought out in the fact that, if we take a certain stimulus as a unit, giving rise to a definite sensation, then as we progressively ascend and add more and more units of the same stimulus, the intensity of stimulation is far from rising proportionately. If we take, for instance, the weight of an ounce as our unit of stimulation, then the successive moments of unit stimulations, that is, of ounces, will not give rise to as distinct and similar sensations as the initial sensation. The second ounce will give a sensation fainter than the first one, and the third fainter than the second, and so on until a point is reached when the sensation of an additional ounce will not at all be appreciated, will dwindle away and almost reach the zero point.

In the same way, if the pressure of a gramme is excited in the hand, successive increments of grammes will not in equal degree increase the sensory effect; the additional increments of grammes, though they are equal units of stimulation, give rise to fainter and fainter sensations, until finally all sensory appreciation of the added unit fades away and disappears. If the hand is immersed in water, say at the freezing point, an addition of ten degrees will be perceptibly appreciated, while successive increments of ten degrees each will be felt less and less, and finally will not be noticed and will be difficult to detect. In short, the threshold rises with the process stimulation.

To bring about a sensory response of an already stimulated sense-organ the intensity of the stimulus must be relatively increased. This is what constitutes Weber's law. The continuous progressive sensory response of a sense-organ requires a constant increase of stimulations which, within certain limits, bears a constant ratio to the total stimulus. This law is sometimes summed up by psychologists in the statement that "the increase of the stimulus necessary to produce an increase of the sensation bears a constant ratio to the total stimulus." Activity raises the threshold; it is the beginning of fatigue.

The rise of threshold after stimulation holds true in the whole domain of biological activity. If the gastrocnemius muscle of a frog, for instance, is stimulated by an electric current, the muscle, with each successive stimulation, responds less readily with a contraction, and this becomes more evident with the onset of fatigue. Pffefer, in a series of extremely interesting experiments, has shown that spermatozoids of ferns are attracted by malic acid, the progressive response of attraction of the cell requiring a constant increase of the degree of concentration of the acid, the increment of stimulations, as in the case of sensation, bearing, within certain limits, a constant ratio to the total stimulus. The threshold rises with each successive stimulation.

The rise of thresholds increases with intensity and duration of stimulation as we approach the state of fatigue. Through the influence of exhaustion, fatigue, or the influence of toxic, autotoxic, emotional, and other stimulations, the thresholds of certain moments have been raised so that ordinary or even maximal stimuli can no longer call out any response. When such a rise of thresholds is present the moments with raised thresholds can no longer enter into association with systems of moments with which they are usually associated, and the result is dissociation, giving rite to the great multitude of phenomena of functional psychosis with a subconscious background, the extent of which depends on the number of raised thresholds, on the extent of the dissociation effected.

When a moment or aggregate of moments begins to function, it radiates stimulation to other moments or aggregates of moments. All the aggregates which these radiated stimulations reach do not equally begin to function. It will depend largely on the state of the aggregate and its threshold. If the radiated stimuli be minimal, the many aggregates that have a high threshold will not be effected at all. Furthermore, many aggregates whose arousal could otherwise be easily effected by the given stimulus may temporarily be in a condition in which their thresholds have become raised and thus fall outside the sphere of activity of the functioning aggregate. On the other hand, aggregates that are usually inaccessible to those minimal stimuli may under certain conditions be set into activity by minimal stimuli, if there is a lowering of the threshold of the total aggregate. Thus the aggregates set into activity by the functioning aggregate are conditioned by the rise and fall of their thresholds.

In case where the threshold of an aggregate is raised the radiated minimal stimuli coming from a particular functioning aggregate may become efficient and reach the threshold, when another aggregate begins to function simultaneously. This holds true even in the case when the minimal stimuli, coming from two different aggregates are just below the threshold-stimulus. Thus, under certain conditions, when visual stimuli are barely or not at all discernible, they can become intensified by re-enforcing them with auditory stimuli. This is commonly found in the mode of recovery of some forgotten name, or of some lapsed experience. We try to find the name and seek to come to it in one line of thought, but of no avail; new lines are attempted, and finally the combined activity of the systems reaches the lapsed aggregate whose threshold has become temporarily raised.

We find the same law further exemplified in the case of the infant under my observation. When with the nipple in his mouth the infant ceased nursing, the sucking movements could be induced again by stimulating some other sense-organ. The tactile, pressure, temperature, and taste stimuli coming from the nipple in the infant's mouth became insufficient to stimulate to activity the functioning aggregate of sucking movements, on account of its raised threshold; only additional stimulation could bring about a further functioning of the lapsed aggregate. This, of course, could also be effected by making the tactual and pressure stimuli more intense, such, for instance, as shaking the nipple while the infant kept it in its mouth. This increase of intensity, however, mainly indicates that the stimuli were no longer effective, and an additional stimulus was requisite, a stimulus that might come either from the same aggregate or from a totally different aggregate.

In the many cases of post-hypnotic amnesia, we find the same truth further illustrated. In the deeper stages of hypnosis, from which the subject awakens with no remembrance of what had occurred during the state the lapsed memories can be brought into the upper consciousness by plying the subject with many questions. During the trance or during the intermediate stages, with subsequent trance and suggested amnesia, the subject is made to perform a certain action,—to light and extinguish the gas four times in succession, or to open and close the door a certain number of times. The subject is then awakened from his trance; he remembers nothing of what has taken place. If he is asked point-blank whether he remembers any incidents of his hypnotic state, he answers with an emphatic negative. If now the subject is asked whether he knows how much two times two are or his attention is incidentally directed to the gas or to the door, he at once becomes reflective, the subconscious memories are on the way to surge up, and a few further indirect questions, the number depending on the depth of hypnosis, finally bring out the lost memories. The threshold that has risen at the end of the trance is stepped over by the combined effect of the many stimulations coming from different directions, and the subconsciously submerged moment or aggregate of moments surges up to the focus or nucleus of the upper consciousness.

Once a particular moment is stimulated in its appropriate way, it may go on developing, and usually does so by stimulating and setting into activity aggregates of moments associated with it, or may form new combinations of aggregates. The solution of a problem may present great difficulties, but once started on the appropriate line, the whole series of combination goes on unfolding, stimulating other moments and aggregates and forming more and more complex combinations. Thus, Archimedes, as the story runs, while in the bath, made the discovery of the law of specific gravity. According to the popular account Newton was led to his discovery of universal gravitation by the accidental fall of an apple. Hughes was started by the idea of symmetry in his discovery of the laws of crystallography. Goethe was led to his conception of metamorphosis and evolution by a skull on the plains of Italy. Darwin by reading Malthus' economical treatise on population was inspired to work out the great principles of the struggle for existence and natural selection. Myers was led by the greater redness of blood in the blood-vessels of tropical patients to his grand conceptions of transformation, equivalence, and conservation of energy. All these examples illustrate the fact that once a moment has been started it goes on developing by stimulating other cognate moments and aggregates to functioning activity.

The same condition is also found in psychopathic borderland states, such as dreams. In dreams a peripheral stimulus gives rise to sensations that start the activities of moments, which in turn give rise to phantastic combinations of different aggregates. This phantastic combination of aggregates, giving rise to the functioning of otherwise unusual, or what may be termed abnormal constellations, is largely due to the fact, of redistribution of thresholds in the dream state.

The dream state is characterized by a rise of the thresholds of moments and their aggregates that have been functioning during the waking states, the thresholds of these aggregates having been raised through activity. In the sleep state moments that have their thresholds relatively or absolutely lowered through inactivity, moments or aggregates that are unusual or have not been in use during the waking state, become aroused, and begin to function. Hence the arousal of hypnotic dream states reproducing long lapsed moments of child-life, hence the phantasms of the world of dreams.

CHAPTER XI
THE PROCESS OF MOMENT DISAGGREGATION

EACH stimulation leaves after it some moment-disaggregation, a condition that makes further disaggregation more difficult. The more intense the stimulation is, the more extensive and deeper is the disaggregation, and hence, the more difficult further disaggregation becomes. If the stimulation is continued or made highly intense, a point is soon reached beyond which no stimulation can pass without giving rise to disaggregation having as its manifestation the different forms of *pathological* mental dissociation. The pathological process underlying the phenomena of abnormal mental life is not essentially different from the one taking place in normal states. If difference there be, it is not certainly one of a quality, but of degree.

The more intense a stimulation is, the more extensive is the process of disaggregation, the higher mounts the moment-threshold giving rise to the different phenomenon of psycho-physiological and psychomotor dissociation. As expressed in a former work: "The process of disaggregation setting in under the action of strong and hurtful stimuli is not something new and different in kind from the usual; it is a continuation of the process of association and dissociation normally going on within the function and structure of higher constellations. The one process gradually passes into the other with the intensity of duration of the stimulus."

The process of disaggregation is a descending one, it proceeds from constellations to groups. Under the influence of strong stimulation such as mechanical and chemical agencies, and psychic affections, such as intense emotions of fear, anger, grief, anxiety, or worry, the degenerative process of disaggregation sets in, affecting first the higher aggregates and then with the continuity and intensity of the stimulations the process descends deeper and deeper affecting less complex aggregates, finally reaching the simplest aggregates of moments. The higher types of moments degenerate and fall to lower and lower stages of consciousness.

The law of disaggregation as that of degeneration in general is from the complex to the simple. The lower moments, on account of the simplicity of their organization, are more stable, and are in a better condition to resist the disaggregating action of hurtful stimulations. Furthermore, the lower and simpler an aggregate of moments is, the older it is, either phylogenetically or ontogenetically, and its stability is therefore more firmly assured by selection and adaptation. In the course of the life-existence of the individual and the species lower types of moments have come more often into activity, since the higher an aggregate is the later does it rise in the history of evolution. Hence moments that are not working smoothly and with little friction are continually weeded out.

This same process is going on not only in the history of the species by the eliminating action of natural selection, but also by the special adaptations brought about in the life experience of the individual. In phylogenesis the best and most firmly organized instincts survive, while in ontogenesis those habits are consciously or unconsciously selected which are most firmly established and are best adapted to the given end. At the same time the older an instinct is, the more thoroughly organized it becomes, the more is it enabled to withstand the onslaught of external hurtful stimuli. The same holds true in the case of habits. A habit of long standing is well organized, and it is often extremely difficult, if not impossible, to control.

Food instincts, sex instincts, social instincts, and personal moral life from an ascending series both as to time of appearance in the history of the species as well as complexity of structure and function. Food instincts in time and simplicity precede sex instincts, and sex instincts in their turn precede social instincts which antecede personal, moral life. Now we find that the instability is in the same ascending line. Food instincts are more stable than sex instincts, sex instincts are more stable than social instincts which are more firmly organized than a highly unified personal life, guided by a moral ideal. The structure and functions of the system of alimentation remain unchanged for ages; the sex instincts may become slightly modified for some period of time; the functions relating to social life vary from generation to generation, while the moral life guided by the moral ideal is highly individualized and personal.

In the downward course of mental disease-processes the degeneration is from the complex to the simple, from the stable to the unstable, from the highly organized to the lowly organized. In the different forms of mental diseases first the moral life, then the social instincts become affected, the patient becomes selfish, introspective, morally selfish, then loses all regard for others, becomes careless, wasteful and negligent of his vocations, life-work, and duties; his whole thought becomes concentrated on himself. In certain forms of mental alienation, such as melancholia and paranoia, the patient becomes suspicious of others, of his near and dear ones, becomes cruel and revengeful, sometimes ending by attacking his own friends and near relatives, and committing homicide. When the deterioration of personal moral life and social instincts is well under way, degeneration of other functions sets in,—the patient gives himself over to excesses, to all kinds of debauches, and indulges in the different forms of abnormal sexual practices. Only very late in the course of the disease are the food instincts in any way affected.

Even in the lighter forms of psychic degenerative forms that lie on the borderland of mental alienation, such, for instance, as are present in the various forms of psychopathic maladies we still find that the same relation holds good. Moral life is the first to be affected. Social instincts, follow, while disturbances of sex and food instincts set in very late in the course of the pathological process of disaggregation and degeneration.

In the mentally defective, such as in imbeciles, idiots, and cretins we once more find that our law holds good. The depth of the congenital mental degeneration is from moral to social, then to sex, and last to food instincts. In the imbecile, only the moral, social, and intellectual activities are affected, the imbecility being according to the depth of the degeneration, the other instincts are more or less normal. In the idiot and cretin the process of degeneration has gone still deeper and sex and food instincts with their psycho-physiological functions and psychomotor adjustments become affected, the idiocy being in proportion to the gravity of the affection.

The phenomena manifested under the action of narcosis go further to confirm the same point of view. Moral, personal life is the first to succumb, other activities follow in the order of their complexity and duration of function. In other words, the law of disaggregation or that of degeneration is from the complex to the simple, from the highly organized to the lowly organized, from the least stable to the most stable. This stability is proportionate to the complexity of moment aggregates, and the frequency and duration of their associative activity.

In habits, formed within the life time of the individual, the same law holds true. Old habits become inveterate, habits formed in childhood and perpetuated can hardly be eradicated, while those that are formed later in life become more easily dissolved. Complex habits formed in late life, relating to moral life and social intercourse, become dissolved at the first onset of the process of mental degeneration, while habits formed early in life, such as handling spoons, fork, and plate or dressing and buttoning the coat long resist the degenerative process. Paretics and patients of secondary dementia in general, though far advanced on the downward path of degeneration, are still for some time able to attend to the simpler functions of life activity, such as dressing and feeding. Once more we are confronted with facts pointing to the same law that the process of degeneration of which disaggregation constitutes a stage is from the highly to the lowly organized, from the complex to the simple.

If we observe more closely the history and stages of disaggregation, we find that, although the process itself is going on within the centre or nucleus of the aggregate, the course of the process is inverse, from the periphery to the centre. This law is really a corollary of the first law of degeneration. For the nucleus of the moment aggregate usually consists of moments that have early become organized, and round which more moments gather from all sides, the aggregate finally attaining a high grade of organization. The further away from the centre or from the nucleus, the newer is the formation of the strata of moments, and the more unstable is their structural and functional relationship within the total aggregate. Hence, when the process of degeneration sets in affecting the controlling nucleus, the associative ties of moments within the aggregate become lowered, and the newest strata, the most remote from the nucleus are the first to be affected, the process passing from newer to older strata. In other words, the process of degeneration is from periphery to centre.

In the building up of a moment-aggregate the early deposits are less complex than the later deposits which are not as yet well organized by use and adaptation. The child under my observation learned early that the shining point yonder in the "ky" (sky) is "venu(s) the (s) tar," and when absent it is "hidden by a c(l)oud." This knowledge is certainly extremely meagre, but still it forms the nucleus round which gradually more knowledge will become formed and organized. The child will learn the dimensions of the planet, its distance from the earth, its orbit, its relation as a member within the solar system, relations that may be extended endlessly, making the whole moment-aggregate more and more highly complex and unstable

If we turn to motor adaptations, we find a similar course of development. It took the infant time before out of the aimless series of spontaneous motor reaction? some definite adaptations emerged relative to external visual stimuli, so that he learned to grasp the object yonder. These grasping motor reactions are at firs crude and inexact. The distance of objects is often mistaken, and the child stretches his hand to fetch distant objects, while small objects cannot be picked up; the hand often goes in the wrong direction and objects are often dropped, because the reactions are not exact and steady. Still these grasping movements form the nucleus for the formation of new and more complex strata of motor reactions. He learns the delicate adaptation; of grasping small objects and the fine adjustments of producing a series of highly complex and extremely delicate motor reactions, such for instance as one finds in the handling of instruments, reading, writing in the execution of musical pieces, in singing, and piano playing. All these motor reactions as they become more complex and delicate are further and further removed from the organized nucleus.

What happens now in the descending process of dissolution? The reverse process takes place. The more complex the psycho-motor structure is, and the further it is removed from the original nucleus, the more easily does it become disintegrated in the downward course of the process of degeneration. In the different forms of mental diseases, such as the various types of mania melancholia, paranoia, general paresis, primary dementia, dementia praecox, senile dementia, and in all those chronic forms that end in secondary dementia, adaptations and acquisitions further removed from the original nucleus, constituting the simple relations of things acquired in early youth and childhood, gradually become disintegrated. The more remote the stratum is from the central nucleus the earlier does dissolution set in.

With the setting in of the process of dissolution the scientist, the professor, the student loses by degrees the lately acquired wealth of knowledge, the complex and delicately balanced conceptual structure of scientific relationship; the more remotely related to the original nucleus of sense experience is the first to become shaken and tumble down. When the degenerative process has gone far enough, the original meagre nucleus of sense-experience becomes disintegrated in its turn.

With the onset of the process of degeneration the banker, the business man, the speculator, gradually begin to lose the understanding of those speculative aspects of business adaptations and adjustments that are remotely related to the original nucleus of self-preservation. With the further advance of the process of disintegration, more stable strata, more nearly related to the original nucleus become affected, until finally the nucleus itself is reached and its constituents are affected, the patient is unable to take care of himself.

In motor reactions we find that the same law holds true. The finer, the more complex a given activity is, the more remote it is from the primary nucleus of motor adaptations, the easier and sooner does it become disintegrated in the course of the pathological process. The musician, the virtuoso loses the power of infusing harmony, life, and emotion into the play; the painter loses control over his brush, the singer over his voice; the watchmaker, or the mechanician is unable to regulate the fine movements of the spring, the wheels of the delicate mechanism, and the mechanic is unable to handle his instruments. Drawing deteriorates, writing is impaired and defective. The liquid "r" a sound which children acquire late becomes difficult, if not impossible to pronounce. The speech test of general paralysis is well known. The patient is unable to repeat such a simple formula as "round about the rugged rock the ragged rascal ran,", or "truly rural."

With the further advance of the process, such simple actions as picking up a pin, or threading a needle are executed with great difficulty, and much hesitation. To produce a straight line or to draw a circle becomes impossible. Involuntary tremor is predominant, a tremor, the rhythmical regularity of which becomes fully manifested in senile degeneration, and which is also observed, though without its rhythmical regularity, on the very eve of mental life, in infancy.

CHAPTER XII
REPRODUCTION AND THE REFLEX MOMENT

WE have described the moment-consciousness as being stimulated to activity, as emerging, as assimilating new material, as growing and developing, as passing through many stages in the history of its individual evolution and dissolution. All this tacitly implies another characteristic besides the ones found as belonging to the nature of the moment. The moment-consciousness has the function of reproduction. We have incidentally discussed reproduction of the moment-consciousness, but we have not studied this character more closely from the standpoint of the moment's general nature.

A close inspection of the moment-consciousness reveals the fact that every moment-consciousness can be reproduced as long as it is not destroyed, as long as it is not dissolved into its constituent elements. For as long as the moment exists, each time when it is stimulated to activity the manifestation of its content, both sensory and motor, is *ipso facto* the moment's reproduction. What remains for us to investigate is the various modes and forms of reproduction, and also the conditions under which they occur.

The simplest case we may suppose is a moment-consciousness set into activity by an appropriate stimulus. This activity runs a certain course and comes to an end; it ceases when the purpose of the moment is accomplished. A second stimulus will call forth a repetition of the activity, a recurrence of the phenomena: a third, a fourth, a fifth stimulus of the same kind will each time call to life the moment-consciousness; the moment will be *produced* again, will be *reproduced.* A repetition of the specific appropriate stimulus will be followed by a reproduction of the moment.

The reappearance of the moment presents a series of moments situated at a distance of different time intervals. The members of this series are disconnected, inasmuch as each member does not contain the fact of its previous appearance. The present functioning activity is not felt in the moment by some modification effected in the content, it is not cognized as a reappearance. This is impossible from the very character of this form of reproduction, since the emerging moment is supposed to appear with an unchanged content, while modifications, feeling, and cognition of previous appearances require something added to the moment which makes it different in content. The members in such a series are disconnected and do not enter into relation. Each moment presents a separate beat of consciousness. The previous appearances of the moment are not represented in its subsequent appearances; each one stands by itself. No modification is produced in the organization of the moment by the previous history of its life activity, no "trace" is left by and of former experience. On each occasion the same psychic content is reproduced.

Since the form of consciousness, now under consideration, is of such a nature as to have no modification left by each separate beat of the moment, no connections are formed by the fact of functioning. Only that connection exists which is given in the organic constitution. In other words, we may say that a being with such a type of moment-consciousness does not profit by individual experience; it does not, and cannot get any acquired characters during its individual life existence. It lives only by what has been obtained by the process of natural selection, during the life history of the species.

Primary sensory elements are certainly present, but secondary sensory elements may be absent as it depends entirely as to whether such connections requisite for secondary sensory elements have been established by variation and natural selection in the phylogenetic history of the moment. We may possibly say that while such connections are absent in a lower stage of the moment, they are present in a higher stage. Both stages, however, lack the formation of acquired characters during their individual history.

Such states of the moment consciousness may be largely hypothetical, but they are probably present in the very lowest representatives in the scale of evolution. The throwing out of pseudopodia in the amoeba are as perfect in the daughter amoeba as in the mother before fusion has taken place. The young vorticella is just as efficient as its parent in its sudden spring-like reactions of contracture and expansion, both of its body and of its long attached thread-like fibre. What is present is in all probability some primitive primary psycho-biological element, a germ out of which the elements of the higher forms of psychic life have differentiated.

The structure and functions of the higher forms of life have become differentiated out of the homogeneous activity of lower forms. The sensory nerve cell, the recipient of the stimulation, like the muscle cell, the reagent to stimuli, has evolved from the primitive cell by greater and greater differentiation, both of structure and function. In the crustaceans, invertebrates, and lower vertebrates where motor reactions to stimuli are more or less complex and varied, the sensory aspect of the moment is probably correspondingly complicated,—organic connections are present giving rise to secondary sensory elements, constituting the material of perceptual life.

The soft-bodied hermit crab as soon as he hatches out from the egg looks for a shell to fit his body in, to protect it from danger, and does the fitting and measuring of the shell with as delicate a nicety and circumspection as his seemingly more experienced older relatives. As a matter of fact, experience does not count here,—a baby hermit-crab is as learned as its parent. Not even organic modifications are acquired, the organization or mechanism is ready, and the first appropriate stimulus sets into activity reactions to external conditions in the most perfect way of which this organization is capable The butterfly, the ant, the bee on emerging from their chrysalis are as perfect in their reactions as any of the adult individuals. Acquired characters count for nothing, inherited organization is everything.

In the lower vertebrates such as fishes, acquired characters, modifications formed during the life time of the individual begin to appear, but this is only in its germ; here too inherited organization is everything. The mechanism is ready and perfect as soon as it comes into life, and enters into relation with the condition of the external environment. The moment-consciousness concomitant with such a type of organization is perfect from the start and has reached its maturity at birth. The contents of the moment cannot be enriched, the internal relations cannot be improved,—no modifications can be brought about in its sensory response and motor reactions. External stimuli set the organization into activity with an unvaried psychic content, with an unalterable psycho-physiological structure and motor manifestations. The content of such a moment is fixed and unalterable. This low stage differs but little from reflex activity; in fact, such a type of psychosis may be termed *reflex moment-consciousness.*

CHAPTER XIII
REPRODUCTION AND THE REFLEX MOMENT

WE have described the moment-consciousness as being stimulated to activity, as emerging, as assimilating new material, as growing and developing, as passing through many stages in the history of its individual evolution and dissolution. All this tacitly implies another characteristic besides the ones found as belonging to the nature of the moment. The moment-consciousness has the function of reproduction. We have incidentally discussed reproduction of the moment-consciousness, but we have not studied this character more closely from the standpoint of the moment's general nature.

A close inspection of the moment-consciousness reveals the fact that every moment-consciousness can be reproduced as long as it is not destroyed, as long as it is not dissolved into its constituent elements. For as long as the moment exists, each time when it is stimulated to activity the manifestation of its content, both sensory and motor, is *ipso facto* the moment's reproduction. What remains for us to investigate is the various modes and forms of reproduction, and also the conditions under which they occur.

The simplest case we may suppose is a moment-consciousness set into activity by an appropriate stimulus. This activity runs a certain course and comes to an end; it ceases when the purpose of the moment is accomplished. A second stimulus will call forth a repetition of the activity, a recurrence of the phenomena: a third, a fourth, a fifth stimulus of the same kind will each time call to life the moment-consciousness; the moment will be *produced* again, will be *reproduced.* A repetition of the specific appropriate stimulus will be followed by a reproduction of the moment.

The reappearance of the moment presents a series of moments situated at a distance of different time intervals. The members of this series are disconnected, inasmuch as each member does not contain the fact of its previous appearance. The present functioning activity is not felt in the moment by some modification effected in the content, it is not cognized as a reappearance. This is impossible from the very character of this form of reproduction, since the emerging moment is supposed to appear with an unchanged content, while modifications, feeling, and cognition of previous appearances require something added to the moment which makes it different in content. The members in such a series are disconnected and do not enter into relation. Each moment presents a separate beat of consciousness. The previous appearances of the moment are not represented in its subsequent appearances; each one stands by itself. No modification is produced in the organization of the moment by the previous history of its life activity, no "trace" is left by and of former experience. On each occasion the same psychic content is reproduced.

Since the form of consciousness, now under consideration, is of such a nature as to have no modification left by each separate beat of the moment, no connections are formed by the fact of functioning. Only that connection exists which is given in the organic constitution. In other words, we may say that a being with such a type of moment-consciousness does not profit by individual experience; it does not, and cannot get any acquired characters during its individual life existence. It lives only by what has been obtained by the process of natural selection, during the life history of the species.

Primary sensory elements are certainly present, but secondary sensory elements may be absent as it depends entirely as to whether such connections requisite for secondary sensory elements have been established by variation and natural selection in the phylogenetic history of the moment. We may possibly say that while such connections are absent in a lower stage of the moment, they are present in a higher stage. Both stages, however, lack the formation of acquired characters during their individual history.

Such states of the moment consciousness may be largely hypothetical, but they are probably present in the very lowest representatives in the scale of evolution. The throwing out of pseudopodia in the amoeba are as perfect in the daughter amoeba as in the mother before fusion has taken place. The young vorticella is just as efficient as its parent in its sudden spring-like reactions of contracture and expansion, both of its body and of its long attached thread-like fibre. What is present is in all probability some primitive primary psycho-biological element, a germ out of which the elements of the higher forms of psychic life have differentiated.

The structure and functions of the higher forms of life have become differentiated out of the homogeneous activity of lower forms. The sensory nerve cell, the recipient of the stimulation, like the muscle cell, the reagent to stimuli, has evolved from the primitive cell by greater and greater differentiation, both of structure and function. In the crustaceans, invertebrates, and lower vertebrates where motor reactions to stimuli are more or less complex and varied, the sensory aspect of the moment is probably correspondingly complicated,—organic connections are present giving rise to secondary sensory elements, constituting the material of perceptual life.

The soft-bodied hermit crab as soon as he hatches out from the egg looks for a shell to fit his body in, to protect it from danger, and does the fitting and measuring of the shell with as delicate a nicety and circumspection as his seemingly more experienced older relatives. As a matter of fact, experience does not count here,—a baby hermit-crab is as learned as its parent. Not even organic modifications are acquired, the organization or mechanism is ready, and the first appropriate stimulus sets into activity reactions to external conditions in the most perfect way of which this organization is capable The butterfly, the ant, the bee on emerging from their chrysalis are as perfect in their reactions as any of the adult individuals. Acquired characters count for nothing, inherited organization is everything.

In the lower vertebrates such as fishes, acquired characters, modifications formed during the life time of the individual begin to appear, but this is only in its germ; here too inherited organization is everything. The mechanism is ready and perfect as soon as it comes into life, and enters into relation with the condition of the external environment. The moment-consciousness concomitant with such a type of organization is perfect from the start and has reached its maturity at birth. The contents of the moment cannot be enriched, the internal relations cannot be improved,—no modifications can be brought about in its sensory response and motor reactions. External stimuli set the organization into activity with an unvaried psychic content, with an unalterable psycho-physiological structure and motor manifestations. The content of such a moment is fixed and unalterable. This low stage differs but little from reflex activity; in fact, such a type of psychosis may be termed *reflex moment-consciousness.*

CHAPTER XIV
THE SYNTHETIC MOMENT AND ITS REPRODUCTION

IN our last analysis we have examined the trait of reproduction in the lowest types of psychic life, such as the different forms of desultory moment-consciousness. We may now turn to the higher types of moments and show that in them, too, the same fundamental character is present, only of course, becoming more complicated and more differentiated with the progress of psychic life. The moment which we have thus far studied is one in which growth is impossible as the reproduction of the moment does not embody the previous manifestations of the moment. In other words, the type examined is of such a character as only to synthetize content within the occurring moment, but it lacks synthesis of moments themselves. The reproduction is of inherited content, it is phylogenetic in nature. We turn now to higher types of moments in which content and moments are synthetized alike. Such a type of psychic activity may be termed *synthetic consciousness,* and its moment the *synthetic moment-consciousness.*

The reproduction of the synthetic moment-consciousness is not isolated, it stands in relation to the antecedent and subsequent moments. Each reproduction modifies the next one to a certain degree, however, slight that may be. The moment is essentially modifiable and capable of improvement up to a certain point of which its internal organization permits. The reproduction of the synthetic type bears in its organization the stamp of its previous life history. *We may say that just as the moment of the desultory type is an epitome of phylogenetic evolution, so is the moment of the synthetic type an epitome of ontogenetic development.*

In its lowest form the synthetic moment undergoes modification by the fact of previous functioning activity. The synthetic moment in its reproduction may be represented in a series of moments, each reproduced moment is modified by the preceding moment and in its turn modifies the succeeding moment. The series is interrelated and interconnected. Each link in the series includes the previous link, and is in its turn included by the succeeding link. Each member in the series possesses itself of the wealth and being of its predecessor, and is itself inherited by its successor. The whole series is really a history of the continued growth and development of the one moment-consciousness passing through various stages in the way of reaching maturity, both in structure and function.

It is true that once the synthetic moment has reached its maturity it may go on reproducing in the same way as the desultory moment, but the element of modification is still present, although it cannot be so clearly seen by a superficial examination. To detect this element of modifying influence of one reproduction on the succeeding one, we must watch the moment closely and, if possible, experiment on it. As long as the content of the moment remains relatively unchanged, no change is observed in its reproductions after having reached the acme of development. Should, however, some change be introduced during the functioning of the moment, at once this modification reappears on the reproduction of the moment

A change may be introduced in the moment in 1 somewhat different way, namely, by letting it rest for a time longer than requisite for its restitution by arresting its activity. This introduces a change in the internal constitution of the moment, weakening the intensity of its activity, or loosening the co-ordination of its internal relationship. The co-ordination and activity of the psychic elements synthetized in the moment become shaken; the stability of the moment is interfered with; its equilibrium gained in growth and development by the successive series of modifications is partially overthrown; the moment becomes unstable, its structure and function regress and fall back a few steps lower in the course of its adaptation to the conditions of the external environment, adaptations acquired during the life history of its individual development. The mere arrest of the moment's function for a shorter or longer period at once tells on the subsequent reproduction of the moment. The function of the moment succeeding the period of arrest is less perfect; the moment is less adapted in its reactions to external stimuli. These facts, it seems, clearly indicate that in reaching maturity the moment has not lost its capacity for adaptability and modification.

Furthermore, the fact of arrest with subsequent modification and degradation of function shows that the adaptation reached by the moment in its mature state is really kept in stable equilibrium by its more or less continued reproduction. Each reproduction of the moment is indispensable to the existence of the next one, and manifests its influence by maintaining the succeeding moment in the stage of maturity reached by the long series of modifications.

The moment of the synthetic type profits by experience, the moment of the desultory type does not. We realize now the difference between the moment of the desultory type and the moment of the synthetic type. The desultory reproductive moment is highly stable in its organization, formed by variations and the iron hand of natural selection; it is crystalized in character, function does not effect its organization. The reproductive moment of the synthetic type, however, while having on the one hand as its basis a functioning apparatus, formed in the course of phylogenesis, has on the other hand a large capacity for modification, and is mainly built up by function; it is profoundly modified by its own functioning activity. In other words, while the moment of the desultory type is entirely *organic* in its nature, the moment of the synthetic type is mainly of a *functional* character. The contrast between the two types of moment may be summarized in the one phrase: "function vs. structure." The aphorism "function maketh structure" holds good only of the synthetic moment.

In speaking of the fact that the synthetic moment profits by its experience, while the desultory moment does not, we must be guarded against the term 'experience.' For it implies a psychic state belonging to a higher type of moment-consciousness, and it is misleading, unless the term be qualified, when used for a lower type of psychic life. Experience would imply that the moment under consideration has an idea of its state and remembering it takes on another occasion advantage of its acquired knowledge. Nothing of the kind occurs in the synthetic type. The synthetic moment has no knowledge of what is taking place in its psychic activity, it is not conscious of the states it is living through. The only knowledge the synthetic moment possesses is the one characteristic of sensory life in general,—it is somewhat like what some writers term knowledge of acquaintance. The content of the synthetic moment only approaches to this form of knowledge, which is really different in nature, inasmuch as "knowledge of acquaintance" is only a lower stage of mental activity characteristic of a higher type of moment than the one under investigation. Knowledge of acquaintance implies a sensation also the free image and free idea of that sensation. The synthetic type on the contrary has only the sensation, the free image and idea are totally wanting.

The psychic life of the infant is probably the nearest that comes up to the nature of knowledge or experience characteristic of the synthetic moment. I say that the infant's psychic life comes nearest to that of the synthetic moment, but still the two are not exactly the same. In the infant's consciousness, however young, free images and ideas are potential and on the way to germinate, while the synthetic moment lacks this potentiality, inasmuch as the synthetic moment reaches its full development without giving rise to free psychic elements. The consciousness of the infant is a low stage of a high type of moment-consciousness; while the synthetic consciousness is a high stage of a low type of moment-consciousness. The high stage of a low type and the low stage of a high type may be respectively illustrated by the algebraic formulae:

$(a+b)^n$ and $(a+b+c+d+e+f+ \ldots)^1$ where $a, b, c, d \ldots$ are the functions of the moment and n the degree of development of the moment.

The consciousness of the young infant as closely resembles the synthetic moment as the fish stage of the human embryo resembles the fish itself. Still the analogy is useful as it gives a closer insight into the constitution and relations of the two types of moment-consciousness. The infant in its psychic growth no doubt passes through the inferior types of moment-consciousness, but in a most general and sketchy form. The ontogenesis of psychic life is probably as much an epitome of its phylogenesis as the ontogenesis of biosis is an epitome of its phylogenesis. Both give a most generalized epitome modified by adaptations and by the specific type of organization in which the ontogenetic evolution is taking place.

CHAPTER XV
THE ACCUMULATIVE CHARACTER OF THE SYNTHETIC MOMENT

THE experience of the synthetic moment means not consciousness of the presented content, but simply modification of psychic function. The experience of the functioning moment influences the content on its next reproduction. If A is the original functioning synthetic moment and b_1, b_2, b_3, b_4 its modifications due to the functioning activity, then the successive reproductions of the moment may be represented by the following formula: A, $A_1 b_1$, $A_2 b_2$, $A_3 b_3$, $A_4 b_4$, $A_5 b_5$ until it reaches its maturity or state of stable equilibrium, say $A_n b_n$. The whole series may be represented by the formula: A, $A_1 b_1$, $A_2 b_2$, $A_3 b_3 - A_n b_n$. Each member of the series reproduces in an epitomized form all the members that preceded it and the last one, the mature moment in its state of equilibrium, representing an epitome of the whole series. The series in its successive stages represents the life history of the growth and development of the synthetic moment.

Concrete examples may help to make the matter clearer. The fish in making repeated attacks on another fish contained in the same tank and meeting repeatedly with failures will finally desist from its attempts. The fish that has been snapped at many times and has escaped will keep away from the dangerous place. This does not mean that the fish remembers its experiences, that it is conscious of its failures, of the futility of its attacks, or that it knows that yonder is a dangerous place which is to be avoided. The whole matter is far simpler. Each repeated failure modifies the moment-consciousness so that the content slightly changes, the unsuccessful motor reactions diminish and finally disappear, while in their place others are substituted. Thus the fish on perceiving its prey may either avoid it and swim away, or it may keep quiet simply following the prey with its eye.

The chick on emerging from the egg may peck at its excrements a few times, but each time the disgust experienced modifies the moment. The reaction of the next moment, when confronted with the same stimulus, becomes less vigorous and finally with the reproductions of the moment, the adaptation becomes so perfect that the mere sight of the disagreeable object suffices to repel the chick and make it turn aside. Here once more it is not that the chick remembers the disgust, and as soon as it is confronted with its excrements, its straightway remembers the disgust it has experienced. This is to ascribe a high form of consciousness to a moment of a low type. The process that has taken place is simpler. The disgust experienced has so modified the sensory motor reactions of the moment that finally different reactions result in response to definite stimulations under definite conditions.

The same holds true of the cat, and the dog. The first weeks of their life kittens or puppies are unable to walk well, they seem to pick their way continuously; gradually they learn to walk and run; the dog soon begins to race and the cat becomes graceful and nimble in its movements. It will certainly be agreed that young puppies or young kittens do not actually remember the steps of their experiences. What happens is that the activity of the organs, along with the growth of the corresponding motor cells, so modifies the function that the walking becomes more and more perfect until it reaches perfect adaptation.

The same thing occurs in the training of brutes. It is not that the brute remembers the steps of the process, and knows how improvement has taken place by a given way of action. In the process of training modifications are brought about by each successive reproduction of the moments in response to the action of external stimuli. Modifications due to successful chance action, being more satisfactory to the brute, are stronger and modify the moment in their own direction, while unsuccessful reactions tend to drop out and thus adaptation, improvement is brought about. The cat in scratching for the door to open it scratches at first aimlessly and does not open,—the actions are unsuccessful. Should the cat happen to scratch the handle and open the door, which certainly is probable, considering the activity of the cat's paw, the result is satisfactory. The repetitions of such chance actions will gradually so modify the cat's scratching that it will become more and more definite. The successful actions alone will be repeated, the unsuccessful will drop out. Finally the adaptation will become so perfect that the sight of the closed door will at once result in the reaction of scratching the handle and opening the door.

The young bird is brought in the world in a rather helpless condition as to movement of co-ordination, especially flying movements. The apparatus for flying is undeveloped, but it soon reaches its perfect adaptation through activity, exercise, practice, that modify both structure and function. The bird does not remember the steps of its acquisitions and profits by its failures so as to make consciously better and more adaptive movements. The process that takes place is far more simple: Each act of functioning produces and reproduces modifications, both in structure and function, until the apparatus and its activity reach perfect adaptation. The total moment is modified on each reproduction until a point is reached where further growth and development ceases and maturity of function is established.

The same holds true in the case of the child. The child on learning to sit is doing it in a very clumsy fashion, tumbles over every time; it must be supported by pillows to keep it in the same position and also to prevent it from being hurt. The structure works imperfectly. The exercise of the apparatus, along with its further growth, brings about a more perfect adaptation, and the child finally learns to maintain its equilibrium when in the sitting posture. The standing upright passes through a similar history. When the coordinating apparatus for walking begins to appear, it works at first in a very awkward manner. The child first walks by holding on to some objects, such as chairs, or the wall, or the hand of his parent and nurse. When he makes a step all by himself, he is almost frightened, and when left alone often cries.

Practice and growth of the walking apparatus becomes more and more perfect. The child makes two or three steps hesitatingly, stops, asks for help and support. Gradually his movements become more certain, and more steps are taken until finally the child learns to walk, still imperfectly, in the waddling fashion characteristic of young age. The walking apparatus grows and keeps on functioning. The function reacts on the further growth making the movements more and more perfect. Each attempt makes the next Ok easier. Adaptations develop not only by the men growth of the apparatus, but also by function. In fact function largely determines the growth of the apparatus.

It must, however, be pointed out that the example taken from baby life may be used only as an illustration of the way the synthetic moment grows by function or reproduction. The child's growth does not exactly follow the same lines as those of the synthetic moment, since the psychic life of man develops on 1 higher level belonging to a higher type of moment, h the efforts of the baby to walk some germs of deliberation and reflection may be observed, but it is hardly probable that these elements are present in the fin: attempts of the cat to walk or of the bird to fly. The moment of the synthetic type grows by simple modifications of its function brought about by its repeated reproductions.

The modifications, however, of the moment's function are not mere chance modifications. The function, is modified on a definite line in the direction of more perfect adaptation.

Reactions to stimuli coming from the external environment become more defined until a definite set of reactions is established. This involves the selective activity of the moment. Certain fit reactions are selected and assimilated by the moment, while others, unfit are rejected. This, however, is a trait which is characteristic not only of the synthetic moment, but of the moment-consciousness in general.

CHAPTER XVI
THE SIMPLE AND COMPOUND SYNTHETIC MOMENT

A FURTHER examination of the synthetic moment reveals two stages, a lower and a higher. The moment may consist of a nucleus having only one kind of sensory elements and of a net-work of subsidiary relations belonging to the domain of the same sensory elements. The animal may trace its food or its prey by the sense of smell alone. This act becomes more perfect with further function. The modifications accumulate in the domain of the same sense-element and the adaptations occur in a relatively simple one-sided sensori-motor apparatus. Modifications of such a character occur phylogenetically in the sensory apparatus of the lower invertebrates, such as Crustacea, arthropodes, and possibly also in the lower forms of vertebrates. Such a phylogenetic accumulation in these low types of moments is formed only by variation and natural selection, while in the case of the synthetic moment the accumulation is formed during the life history of the particular individual. The one is *racial acquisition,* the other is *individual experience.* Both, however, may agree in the general character of the modification effected. The modifications are in one sensory organ, and the psychic moment-content consists of similar sense-elements. Such a stage of psychic activity may be termed *simple accumulative synthetic moment-consciousness.*

If A represents the first occurrence of the moment, the first functioning of the simple sensori-motor apparatus as given by phylogenesis, and if a be the modification effected, then the accumulative process may be represented by the powers of $a;$ thus the first will be A, the next is $A_1 a^1$, the following is $A_2 a^2$, then $A_3 a$ and so on. The total process to the point of maturity may be represented by the following formula: $A, A_1 a^1, A_2 a^2, A_3 a^3, A_4 a^4 \ldots A_n a^n$. $A_n a^n$ represents the highest stage of perfection reached by the simple accumulative synthetic moment.

The synthetic moment may also have a higher stage where many different sensori-motor elements are synthetized, the accumulative modifications occur along different lines of sensory responses and motor reactions. The moment reaches here the highest form of consciousness as mere perceptual in character. The fish perceives its prey not only by smell, but also by sight along with muscular and touch sensations; all of them go to form the percept of the prey yonder, as far as perception of fish space is concerned.

The American flounder of the Atlantic coast may be taken as an illustration. Although the flounder is perfectly quiet, almost lying motionless at the bottom of the tank, only occasionally moving his small protruding eye, no sooner is some small fly thrown into the tank, than the flounder at once darts in that direction, and attacks its prey with a snap. I wanted to find out how far visual perception is concerned in the tracing of the prey, and how far sense of smell and touch are important in this particular fish at least. The flounder was deprived of its organs of sight, and after having been given about twenty-four hours time to recover from the effects of the operation, it was thrown into a tank teeming with little fishes on which it feeds.

The flounder settled to the bottom, but in about a few minutes raised itself in the attitude of attack, so highly characteristic of this species, either smelling the little ones or feeling the vibrations made in the water by the swimming movements of the little fish; it made a dart in the direction of a whole mass of them, but missed. This has been repeated many times over, the flounder failing every time and only snapping water or air bubbles. The little folk soon became emboldened and avoiding his front they came from behind pecking at his blind eye. The flounder could not reach these little fellows.

Moreover, the bottom of the tank where the blind flounder was lying was full of small sea-robins which like to walk on the bottom with their highly sensitive leg-feelers. The blind flounder did not attack them, although with his eyes in good order, he would have instantly attacked the sea-robins. It appears then that the flounder tracks its prey by the sense of sight mainly, while the other senses are indefinite guides. Still the other senses seem to take an active part in tracing the prey, as the blind flounder was most of the time in an attitude of attack. Evidently he was smelling the prey or feeling its movements all the time and was aware of its presence, though the senses without sight could not give him the definite direction in which the prey was to be found. In other words, the other senses awaken only the sensations of presence of the food, but do not give its direction and location.

It is highly probable, then, as far as we can infer from this experiment as to the psychic state of the fish, that the flounder does not get a definite percept, unless many different sensory elements are combined in a synthesis giving rise to a well defined motor reaction of more or less perfect adaptation. The synthetic moment, then, in this particular species at least, seems to be of a highly complex character, inasmuch as many different sense-elements go to make up its content

Similarly it is affirmed of the sea-robin that, if its delicate leg-feelers are cut off, the fish is unable to feed. If that be true, then the touch sensation is important here and enters as a determining element in the moment along with other elements coming from other sense-organs. In the dog smell is mainly the determining factor, but the functioning of other senses are requisite to form secondary sensory elements; here too the moment is made up of many series of various sense-elements. In the bird, in the ape, in the man, sight is the chief element in perception, but the percept arises not from visual elements alone, but from a synthesis of a multitude of elements coming from other sense-organs the visual elements often taking the lead.

From a purely biological standpoint we can understand the importance of the leading part played by the visual elements in the psychic life of the higher vertebrates and especially of that of man. It is of the greatest advantage in the struggle for existence to develop a sense organ that admits of the most delicate objective discrimination. No other senses, not even that of hearing, are so free from the general organic sensation as the sense of sight. Hence the sensory elements coming from the sense organs other than sight are *confused* and lack the objective clearness characteristic of the sense of sight. The visual sense further is of the highest sensitivity to extremely low and distant stimulations such as are produced by ether waves. An animal therefore that will by natural selection have its moment consciousness organized round a nucleus of highest sensitivity such as that of visual sense elements will have better chances to survive and succeed in the struggle for existence. Still, even in man the elements coming from other sense organs may become predominating in the nucleus and give rise to various mental types, such as audiles, motiles, and so on. This holds specially true of the higher representative elements. A moment-consciousness that has a varied content of many different sensory-elements synthetized in one compound, accompanied on the motor side with a complex of motor reactions may be termed *compound synthetic moment-consciousness.*

The compound synthetic moment-consciousness is characterized in its series of accumulations in the same way as is the simple synthetic moment, the only difference being the complexity of the lines of accumulations. The accumulated sensori-elements of the same kind or of the same sense-organ form primary compounds among themselves and secondary or double and treble compounds with other compounded series of sensory elements. If V represents the original primary visual sensory element, T tactual, A auditory, O olfactory, and M muscular sensory elements, then the series for the development of the highly adapted A aspect of the moment may be represented by the formula already given, in our analysis, namely: $A, A_1 b^1, A_2 a^2, A_3 a^3, A_4 a^4 .... A_n a^n$. The V aspect of the moment similarly gives $V, V_1 v^1, V_2 v^2, V_3 v^3, V_4 v^4 .... V_n v^n$.

The T, O, and M series will give respectively the following formulae:

$T, T_1 t, T_2 T^2, T_3 t^3, T_4 t^4 ..... T_{20} t^{20} \qquad T_n t^n$

$O, O_1 o, O_2 o^2, O_3 o^3, O_4 o^4 ..... O_{20} o^{20} \qquad O_n o^n$

$M, M_1 m, M_2 m^2, M_3 m^3, M_4 m^4 ..... M_{20} m^{20} \qquad M_n m^n .$

The process of composition begins not at the first members of the series, but rather further on. Some accumulations must be made first in each series separately before combinations of the different series can take place. For simplicity sake we may postulate that the process of composition of all lines begins in each alike, although this may not be the case; let us assume that such a process begins in the tenth stage of the series. Before that, say in the third stage compositions may be found only on two or three lines, such as $V_s\ v^s\ T_s\ t^s$ or still further $V_s\ v^s\ T_s\ t^s\ M_s\ m^s$, or $V_s\ v^s\ T_s\ t^s\ O_s\ o^s\ M_s\ m^s$. The V precedes in the formula indicating its primary importance in the case of the moment where the visual sensory elements are mainly the guide for sensori-motor reactions, the visual sensations constituting the leading and central elements of the compound. In a moment of the same type but with a differently related content O or A may be the main elements of the compound, an element round which other sense-elements become grouped. The formula may then be $O_s\ o^s\ T_s\ t^s\ M_s\ m^s$, or in the case where A is predominant $A_s\ a^s\ T_s\ t^s\ M_s\ m^s$, etc. The synthetic moment will from its starting point, say $V_{20}\ v^{20}\ T_{20}\ t^{20}\ O_{20}\ o^{20}\ A_{20}\ a^{20}\ M_{20}\ m^{20}$ proceed onward, reaching its height of development and adaptation in the compound $V^n\ v_n\ T^n\ t_n\ O^n\ o_n\ A^n\ a_n\ M^n\ m_n$. This last stage of the moment has at its disposal the accumulations of all the previous synthetic moments both simple and compound. The compound synthetic moment is the heir of all previous acquisitions and accumulations, and, as such, may be characterized as the *compound, accumulative, synthetic moment.*

Although the simple synthetic moment and the compound moment differ in character and complexity of content, they still agree in one general trait characteristic of the synthetic moment, namely, *fixed* synthesis. The series of sensory elements, both primary and secondary, that enter into the content of the moment are firmly combined. The elements of such compounds cannot get disengaged and do not therefore exist in a free state, they form *stable* compounds.

The form of reproduction common to all the moments thus far examined is that of *reinstatement*. The sensori-motor elements of the moment are reinstated in all their reality. The moment in its successive stages of reproduction is brought to life by impressions coming from external stimuli. Primary and secondary sense-elements enter into the moment's constitution whenever it reappears. In both forms of the synthetic type, the moment with the recurrence of the reproductions, becomes enriched in sensory elements, primary and secondary; but these elements must be *present,* and, from the very nature of the types of moments under consideration, no other elements can possibly be present. The series in which the successive steps of the moment, desultory or synthetic, manifests itself is composed entirely of sensory elements, most or all of which vary but little from one beat of the moment to the other.

The fact of the simple reinstatement is especially clear in the case of the desultory moment. Each reinstated moment induced by external stimuli is an exact copy of its predecessor. In the synthetic moment the content of two adjoining stages is a little varied, still the sensory elements constituting the content of the preceding moment is reinstated in the succeeding one It is true that even the desultory moment is not absolutely smooth in its course of repetitions or reinstatements. Interruptions of functions due to unfavorable stimuli often occur within the series, interruptions. which may be brought about by artificial conditions and in which different psycho-motor responses are interpolated, but these responses do not enter into the content of the moment when the favorable conditions are restored,—the responses do not become habitual. Thus the rhythmical pulsations of the vorticella may be temporarily arrested by the evaporation of the liquid in which it is contained, but no number of evaporations will change the series of rhythmical pulsations by having stages of arrests interpolated into the series. Similarly it is highly questionable whether a fly, beetle, o: cockroach could contract any habits.

Some eminent psychologists go to the length of affirming that even the lowest representative animal life. the protozoa (possibly bacteria, bacilli), possess ideational and volitional processes, that the lower stages of mental life manifest association, reproduction, memory, cognition, and recognition. Other psychologists are more moderate, they regard the acquisition of knowledge as adaptation through habit, characteristic of the lowest representative of animal life. Thus one psychologist propounds the question, "How is it that we or the brute *learn* to do anything?" Does the amoeba *learn* at all? What belongs to our type of consciousness is assumed as being true of all types—the old psychological fallacy. "Learning," habits are biological variations characteristic of the higher types of consciousness and are not present in the lower forms of mental activity.

It is highly questionable whether the formation of habits is possible even in the highest representatives of the invertebrata, such as the bee and the ant. The ant is probably largely guided by the sense of smell, while the bee is prompted in its activity both by smell and sight. The activities of these animals, though highly complex, are still fixed in their character becoming manifested with the recurrence of definite sensory stimulations. The individual acquires nothing by experience and forms no habits; everything is formed by the species. Spontaneous variation and natural selection are the only agencies of the relatively high organization and complex psycho-motor life-activity of the higher types of the synthetic moment.

Habit is a character that does not belong to the desultory moment, it comes only with the birth of the synthetic moment. The fixed character of the desultory moment admitting of no modifications precludes the formation of any habits; the moment's reproduction therefore is reinstatement *par excellence,* —each reproduced moment being an exact copy of its original. The individual presents only the history of the species. The reproductions of the synthetic moment begin to show the history of the modification which have appeared in the course of the moment's life activity. Each recurrent reproduction of the synthetic moment is an epitome of its individual life-history, an epitome of its ontogenetic psychogenesis.

CHAPTER XVII
THE DESULTORY TYPE IN PATHOLOGICAL STATES.

A FORM of reproduction analogous to the ones present in the desultory moment is to be found in various psychopathological states. The nature of reproductions of the hypnoidic states comes very near to the simple form of reinstatement characteristic of the desultory moment. The main feature of this pathological state is its recurrent sensory character isolated from the rest of the individual's psychic life. Experiences emerging in this state are actually lived over again. The hypnoidic state is desultory, it forms no connected relations in its various reproductions, it does not become modified by its many occurrences, and the first stage is as rich in psychic content as the last stage. The hypnoidic state is relatively fixed. Of course, between the desultory moment and the hypnoidic state there is only an analogy in the nature of functioning, otherwise the states are actually different, inasmuch as they belong to altogether different types of moments.

The nature of reinstatement characteristic of the reproductions of the synthetic moment is clearly revealed in the way modifications are effected and non-adaptive reactions are eliminated. Sensory responses and motor reactions that have met with failure and evil consequences are modified by degrees, in portions so to say. The law that regulates the succession of the modifications effected is the order of the degree of harm consequent on the reactions to which the sensory responses lead. If then the most harmful reactions belong to the middle of the series of motor reactions constituting the motor aspect of the moment, these are modified by being gradually dropped out and others substituted. The rest, the more or less indifferent reactions of the series are gone through, although they bear no longer any relation to the sensori-motor reactions that have immediately preceded them. To an external observer such reactions are ridiculous and unintelligible, since they cannot be understood with reference to their immediate antecedents; their nature can only be made clear from the history of the moment.

Such traces in the organization of the synthetic moment are vestiges of previous useful functions, of a series of adaptive reactions; they are like rudimentary organs in the economy of the organism. Thus a chick may peck repeatedly at his waste products or at a burning match and repeatedly wipe his bill; finally a marked modification is brought about in its sensory responses and reactions. When the chick is confronted with those objects, it comes up to them, looks at them, does not peck, but wipes its bill. To an external observer to whom the history of the chick's experience is unknown, the wiping of the bill would have been entirely unintelligible.

Reinstatement can be similarly observed in cases where conditions have changed, but the modification has not yet been effected within the content of the moment. Thus the story of the actions of the hen that brought her brood of chicks to the river and urged them to swim would have appeared strange, possibly mysterious, if not for our knowledge of the hen's former experience with a brood of ducklings. The mode of reproduction of the synthetic moment is * series of successive phases of more and more modified reinstatements which can only become intelligible or following up more or less closely the history of the moment's development.

The forms of reinstatement characteristic of the synthetic and desultory moments are to be found in higher types of moments. When undergoing the process of dissolution, secondary dementia, the terminus of chronic insanity offers a wealth of facts at our disposal. The mental states of secondary dementia are like the ruins of great castles, like fossils of former growth or vegetation and animal life. The active living moments are disintegrated, decomposed and only some of the constituents are left to function. These constituents remnants of former life-activity, are simply reinstated. One who has not known the history of the case will hardly comprehend the actions of the patient. Thus one dement may keep on covering himself with a blanket, or hiding himself into corners. He who is ignorant of the history of the case would regard the action as capricious and meaningless, he would hardy guess from the patient's actions that the latter when in a state of chronic melancholia labored under the delusion that he was made of glass, and that people could see the actions of his guts. The synthetized and systematized delusion itself was swept away in the general ruin and decomposition, only some remnants were left, a few sensori-motor elements remained. These elements are now being reinstated in the same fashion as the simple types of the synthetic and desultory moments. Similarly it would be hard to guess from the frequent mumbling of the words 'Alexander,' that the dement in his early stages of mental alienation was under the delusion that he was the deceased Russian czar come to life. The word 'Alexander' is simply a chip of a former highly systematized moment, the chip now reproducing itself after the simple fashion of the desultory moment.

The phenomena of imperative concepts, insistent or fixed ideas, uncontrollable impulses all grow and develop along the general lines of the synthetic moment. They are *reinstatements* of portions of dissociated moments buried in the subconscious and growing by the process of modification with each recurrent reinstatement.

Hypnoidal states described by me bear evidence to the same truth of reinstatement of psychic elements. In the hypnoidal states fractions of dissociated moments present in the subconscious come up like bubbles to the surface of the patient's consciousness, burst, disappear, and vanish never to come again. The fragments are reinstated chips of highly organized moments, now in a state of disaggregation. The hypnoidal chips sometimes manifest themselves in their reproduction after the mode of simple or elementary desultory consciousness, mental states appear and disappear, leaving no traces behind them.

In the phenomena of automatic writing, crystal gazing, shell-hearing and so on, reinstatement of moments in different degrees and stages of organization takes place. Finally in the phenomena of hypnosis we meet with similar conditions, the states are induced artificially in the otherwise healthy and normally functioning individuality. Such are the phenomena of personality metamorphosis and of post-hypnotic or hypnonergic states. In these states moments are artificially formed in the dissociated subconscious moments which rise to the surface of consciousness with all the energy supplied to them by the subconscious. They reproduce and perpetuate themselves after the mode of the synthetic moment until their end is achieved, when they gradually fade away, or, what is still more often the case, vanish in the same sudden and abrupt way as they come.

The artificially induced post-hypnotic or hypnonergic states studied from the standpoint of the moment-consciousness are found to be analogous to many psychopathic conditions. The main character of these states is their dissociation and reproduction, or rather reinstatement on the basis of lower types of moment-consciousness.

In psychopathic functional states not only does disintegration of content occur, but there is also present functional degradation of the type of the moment. The function of the moment reverts to lower types of psychic activity, while the content consists of constituents formed on higher lines of psychic life. Hence the lack of adaptation, the conflict in psychopathic states between function and content. It is like the formation of a barbaric society out of the remnants of a ruined civilization.

We may then affirm that the characteristic mode of reproduction, both of the desultory and synthetic moment, is *reinstatement*. The difference between the two moments being that while *the moment of the desultory type reproduces by reinstatement only, that of the synthetic type reproduces by both reinstatement and modification.*

CHAPTER XVIII
PRESENTATIONS AND REPRESENTATIONS

IN the course of our analysis of the lower types of moments it has been shown that the psychic elements entering into their synthetized content occur not in a free independent state, but in fixed accumulations and stable compounds, having reinstatement as the mode of their reproduction. There is, however, a higher type of moment in which psychic elements occur in a free independent state, having accordingly a mode of reproduction different from that of the types we have just examined. Let us see now what the nature of these free elements is, how they come to arise and what is the peculiar mode of their reproduction.

If we look at the tree yonder and then close our eyes, we can represent to ourselves the tree in its general outlines at least. We see its trunk, its branches, and its green foliage. After our friend's departure we continue to see him in our mind's eye. We live over mentally, in our imagination, all our relations, our mutual enjoyments. We seem to watch him act and hear him talk. The representative elements cannot possibly be identified with or derived from afterimages. For after images are really *after-sensations* and consist of sensory elements. The elements involved in the state of representative psychic life are freed from all immediate coexistence with sensory elements, primary or secondary; in fact, they appear when the sensory elements disappear.

The two sets of psychic elements, the presentative and representative, stand in inverse relation to each other. When the one is at its *maximum* the other is at its *minimum*. When sensory elements appear the free elements become faint. This faintness is in proportion to the intensity of the sensory element. It is hard for us to look at a color and imagine it at the same time; and the more intense and brilliant the color is, the harder it is for us to have the color, at the same time, represented. Look at an object, say the lighted lamp, take in well its sensory elements and you will find that it is almost impossible to represent it to yourself at the same time. Try hard to *represent* to yourself the object and you will find that its sensory elements will begin to vacillate and become faint, or less vivid. When absorbed in our ideas we often do not notice even very intense stimuli. The two series of elements, the sensory or, presentative, and the free ones, the representative, cannot run together without interfering with each other, nay, without arresting each other.

Representative elements bring with them a new fundamental departure in the mental activity of the moment, they may keep up its activity when flagging, may intensify it, but may also deflect it, or distract it, giving rise to another conflicting moment. Thus on the one hand my continuous thought about a certain scientific proposition constituting the substance of the present active moment may begin to flag, but it is soon kept up by new observations and experiments; on the other hand, the occasional glance at the morning newspaper may tend to deflect mental activity to quite a different channel by awakening the activity of quite a different moment-consciousness conflicting with the train of thought on scientific matter.

Presentative elements have a permanency and stability which representative elements totally lack; they can be kept up in their full strength by keeping up the same intensity of stimulation, as by maintaining the object before the particular sense organ that forms the nucleus of the percept. Thus the pricking of the needle is perceived as long as the stimulation is continued, and the chair yonder is seen as long as it is kept before the eyes. Representative elements on the contrary, are extremely unstable and fluctuating, and are aptly characterized as being very much like "the flare and flicker of a gas flame blown by the wind." When representative elements become permanent, stable, the state of the moment acquires a pathological character manifested in the phenomena of insistent thoughts and fixed ideas.

Presentative psychic elements are always firmly bound up with an external object and with stimulations of peripheral sense-organs; they can never free themselves from the bondage to the external environment. Not so the representative elements, although appearing at first in connection with sensory elements and peripheral stimulations, they finally end by freeing themselves from this bondage. The representative elements involved in the representation zebra do not originally arise without some presentative elements. Once however, the given representation has definitely arisen we may imagine the zebra without actually perceiving it. In the midst of a conversation, or in the midst of an engaging study, the image of a tiger, or of a palm seen in some distant country may rise clearly and vividly before the mind's eye, and temporarily interrupt the course and trend of our thought.

While I am writing these lines a fleeing copperhead, a pulsating vorticella, a fish's tail, a cow's head and a putting steam engine have flashed across my mental field and gone. They may be ultimately traced to some sensory stimulus and positive after images, but these are far in the background of consciousness and remain unnoticed. Representative elements come and go in consciousness, they appear independently of all other elements, they are essentially free elements. We call this coming and going of these independent elements the "free play of the imagination."

Where sensory elements appear in synthetized compounds, or in the precept, they cannot be separated, they are firmly bound together. It is only in representation that the corresponding representative elements free themselves from the bonds of union which the sensory elements cannot throw off. The orange yonder is a synthetized compound of many sensory elements, primary and secondary, but as long as they remain sensory the elements are kept in union and cannot be dissociated. Such a dissociation, however, is fully possible with the representative elements entering into the representation of the orange. We can think of its color, size, shape, weight, smell and taste separately.

The freedom of the representative elements is dearly brought out in the so-called free play of the imagination. Sensory elements are synthetized in the compound in definite relations which cannot possibly be severed unless the stimuli are rearranged, and in many cases the sensory elements do not admit even of that procedure. The sensory elements in the perception of a particular object, say a house, have definite relations which cannot be modified without first changing the color, structure, shape, size, of the house and rearranging its relative parts. In imagination or representation, however, all that is done in less than no time, without in the least interfering with the external stimuli.

Representative elements manifest even more freedom. In many cases a modification of certain relations in the sensory elements cannot possibly be effected, because the relations of the external stimuli constituting what may be termed the external object do not admit of a rearrangement. Thus we cannot have the mouth of the horse on his back, horns growing out of his sides, the mane on his hind parts and the tail on his brow. We can, however, easily accomplish such a rearrangement in our imagination. Furthermore, in representation psychic elements appear in combinations of which sensory elements do not admit. Pegasus, a horse with wings; mermaid, a being half woman half fish: centaurus, a being half man and half horse, and other combinations of the most impossible character, as far as sensory elements are concerned, may be formed in representation.

At first representative elements are started by sensations and are thus far bound up with them, but they gradually free themselves from it. Thus in a baby under my close observation, the representative element never came unless the object was present. If the object was taken away, he soon forgot it. In the uneducated mind even of a high type of moment-consciousness representations are still bound up with presentations. The gossip can keep on talking as long *u* the thought is fixed on the concrete. Persons who lack scientific, conceptual thought cannot grasp an abstract general proposition without having it first expressed in concrete terms, or fixed in sensory pictures. The savage gets a headache when his thought is forced to flow in a stream of representation. In the imbecile, in the idiot we find the same thing manifested. They can only think in concrete sensory terms. In mental asthenia which approaches the state of the higher stages of imbecility and also in secondary dementia. states consequent on psychic degeneration, we find the same truth illustrated. The patient's mental activity falls many stages nearer to the level of presentative life. It is only in the higher forms of psychic life that representative elements become free, independent, and are freely and easily associated and dissociated.

If looked at from the standpoint of control, we find *that sensory elements,* on account of their fixed relations in the combinations and compounds in which they enter, *are uncontrollable.* The compound with all its sensory elements, primary and secondary, is given, and cannot directly be controlled; it is highly stable, it resists attempts at decomposition. The combinations, however, formed of the free representative elements are of unstable equilibrium, the elements can be easily shifted, displaced, rearranged, easily dissociated, and new combinations formed. The mode of function of the representative element is *free association.*

Even when entering into the associative play the representative elements do not blend and fuse so as not to be discriminated. Representative elements certainly do not float about without entering with others into some form of association, but in the very association and combination they still manage to preserve relatively their freedom and independence. The sensory elements in the compound are so blended and fused that they cannot be discriminated in the compound without some effort and under special artificial conditions. Oculo-motor sensations, the estimation of the visual angle, of the size of the image thrown on the retina are not so very evident in the direct perception of the external object. Tactual and muscular sensations are not so very clear in our perception of space, nor are our rhythmical, respiratory and kinaesthetic sensations quite obvious in our estimation of time. The free associations, however, into which representative elements enter give full scope to their components. The elements are combined without at the same time losing their individuality; they remain clearly defined in their nature and outlines in relation to the other elements with which they form combinations.

Representations, however, presuppose presentative life, they constitute the intermediate stages of which presentations form the termini. *Representations begin and end with presentations.* At the same time it should be clearly held in mind that while representation refers to presentation, it is by no means true that representations can be analyzed into sensory elements in the same way as a living organism can be analyzed into elementary cells. The living organism is made up, is constituted by elementary cells; cells form the organism. Representations, however, are not formed out of presentative elements, sensory elements, sensation elements. Sensory processes do not enter into the make-up of a representation. Just as the sensation black is not black, so is the idea or representation of black not a sensation 'black.'

CHAPTER XIX
REPRESENTATIONS AND THE LAWS OF THEIR COMBINATIONS

REPRESENTATIVE elements form what may be characterized as mental trains. The elements of a mental train are connected by relations of contiguity, resemblance, and contrast. Association by contiguity depends on the frequency, recency with which the elements have been associated, while resemblance and contrast may be regarded as two or more mental trains of representative elements associated by contiguity, crossing and intersecting in a few points, in other words having some element in common. From this standpoint associations by resemblance and contrast are often regarded as cases of contiguity which is therefore considered as the mode of association characteristic of representative elements. From another standpoint, however, resemblance may equally be considered as fundamental. It is nearer to the truth to regard both contiguity and resemblance or similarity as fundamental modes of association of representative elements.

Association by contiguity may be expressed in the following general proposition: Ideas or images which have frequently followed one another tend to recur in the same order. If a, b, c, d, e be images or ideas that have frequently followed each other in a definite order of succession, then the tendency is that the ideas or images will occur in the same order, if the initial idea or image is awakened. Thus if $a, b, c, d, e,$ be that order, then if a is awaken the rest, $b, c, d, e,$ tend to emerge in the same order in which they have followed each other previously.

The formula for association by contiguity may be expressed as follows:
$a+b+c+d+e+$ ....

Representative elements, however, as we have pointed out are derivative, they are functions of sensory compounds, and vary concomitantly with the wealth and differentiation of sensory life-experience. Blind people have no visual images, nor can deaf persons form any idea of a sound. Although representative elements are essentially different in nature from sensory elements and their compounds, still it remains true that sensory experience is the soil from which the rich variety of representative life grows up. Sensory elements and their compounds are prerequisites of representations of their combination and organization.

The course of associative relations of representations may be determined by the course of sensory series. If a series of sensations and perceptions have frequently followed each other pretty uniformly, then their corresponding representations will tend to recur in the same uniform order. Let A, B, C, D, E. . . . be the order of succession of the sensory series, then the order of the series of representations will be: *a, b, c, d, e.* . . . When sensation A with its corresponding representation *a* are awakened, or if a alone occurs, then the rest of the series of representations tend to emerge. The formula for association of contiguity may be somewhat modified and represented as follows:

$A+a+(b+c+d+e)$, or simply $a+(b+c+d+e)$ ....

$B+b+(c+d+e)$, or simply $b+(c+d+e)$

We have shown that ideas and images are associated with motor and physical reactions, hence muscular movements or rather kinaesthetic sensations and their representations also enter the circle of the associative series. The series of representations gives rise to movements which in their turn give rise to kinaesthetic sensations, and these in turn may either give rise to another series of representations, or may maintain the same series. Hartley, the father of English associationism, who reduced all association to contiguity, states his doctrine of association in the following general proposition:

"If any sensation A, idea B or muscular motion C, be associated for a sufficient number of times with any other sensation D, idea E, or muscular motion F, it will at last excite *d*, the simple idea belonging to the sensation D, the very idea E or the very muscular motion F."

Turning now to association by similarity we find that the relations of the elements are somewhat more complex than in that of contiguity. Where mental life is complex and where there are present many different trains of ideas and images, there will be a tendency for them to cross and intersect at many points. The course of a given train of ideas and images instead of running in its habitual line will tend to become deflected along other lines and give rise to that particular form of association of representative elements known as association by similarity and contrasts.

Let a, b, c, d, e, f, be one series and let p, b, g, r, m, another series, q, r, k, l, n, a third series and s, l, x, y, z a fourth series and so on. The course of association instead of running along one line of habitual association determined by contiguity will tend to run on new lines. The course may be represented as follows:

Let each series be represented by a row of squares formed into a rectangle and let each crossing series be represented by a similar rectangle intersecting the preceding one at right angles, then the course of association by similarity may be diagrammatically represented as follows:

The course of the mental train of ideas is changed and deflected along lines which are otherwise unhabitual for the particular mental train. In association by similarity the mental train ever corruscates along new lines.

Association by similarity may be expressed in the general proposition: *like states often follow each other.* What that likeness consists in we have already seen,— it is some common characters, some representative elements which two or more crossing trains of contiguous representations possess in common. The crossing of one train by another at a point where the representations have common features is purely accidental, as far as the crossed train is concerned; it is the play of the imagination. As an illustration of such a crossing of trains we may take the example when one, from a series of images and ideas about the recent Americo-Spanish war, is led to think of the Anglo-Spanish war in the 16th Century, the common representation being the destruction of the Spanish fleet; and from the mental train on the Anglo-Spanish war to the Franco-Prussian war the common representation being invasion, and from this to the Napoleonic war, then to the political affairs of France, and thence, to the peace conference of European powers. The course of the trains of ideas is every time deflected along new channels. The deflection depends largely on the complexity and number of the trains and their activity.

The relation of likeness is present not only in trains of representations, but also in presentations or in what is termed by us psychic compounds. Thus twins we say look alike, so do eggs, so do animals of the same species; a picture say of a landscape looks like the actual landscape, and a portrait or statue resembles the original. In all these examples the likeness is constituted by the sensory elements common to the presented psychic compound. Not that the sensory elements are exactly the same; subjectively considered, they may be totally different in their psychic stuff, in the psychic relations that cluster about them, as no two sensations, no two psychic compounds, are really the same, as far as the mental state is concerned, but *they refer to the same characters in the external object.* It is this common reference to the same traits or characters in the external object that constitutes the bond of association of likeness in sensory element or psychic compound. On the same grounds may be explained the likeness between the representations and the psychic compound, the percept, which it represents.

CHAPTER XX
REPRESENTATION AND RECOGNITION

IF from the general consideration on the modes of combinations or free association characteristic of representations, we turn to analyse the nature of the moment with representative elements as content, we find that it differs essentially from the synthetic and desultory moments. A close inspection of the character of representations reveals the fact of its difference from presentation-elements. A representative element is neither of the nature of the primary nor of the secondary sensory elements, it differs from both in the character of its psychic "stuff." The difference consists in the fact that a representative element is *not cognitive, but recognitive.*

As far as the cognitive aspect is concerned the chief characteristic of the synthetic and desultory moments, having sensory elements only as their content, is the *direct* reference to the object, to the relations of the external environment, while the characteristic feature of the moment, having mainly representative elements as its constituent, is the *indirect* reference to external relations. In other words, the sensory elements of the synthetic and desultory moments have *immediate* cognition, while the representative elements of the moment now under consideration has *mediate* cognition, or *recognition.* I see the book lying on my table, I close my eyes and represent to myself the whole thing over again. As I look out of the window I see a house, a horse and carriage standing nearby; I close my eyes and imagine the whole situation over again. We say then, incorrectly though, that the representation is a copy of the presentation. Evidently the representation is regarded as not being the same as the presentation just as a copy is really not the same as the original. The psychic elements of representation have the function of cognizing again, or what is more correct to say the function of *re-cognition* which constitutes the very essence of representation. In representation events are lived over again without the actual recurrence of those experiences. In representation the moment becomes independent of the present, it becomes free from its immediate environment.

In order that a representation be a true "copy" of its original, it must be cognized as a "copy," that is, it must be cognized as something already cognized, in other words, it must be *recognized.* This function of recognition is the *sine qua non* of representation. The image, representation, or idea of a table is not itself a table, nor is it a synthetized sensory compound referring to the object, table, it is a psychic element referring to the sensory compound on its objective aspect. The representation of the table does not refer directly to the table as it is the case in the sensory compound, but to the table as *perceived.* The image or representation refers not to the object immediately, but mediately, to the object as object of the sensory compound. Hence the object is cognized over in representation, in other words, is recognized.

This recognition may be of a general or of a specific character. The function of recognition in its general aspect is manifested in the idea. The idea possesses this function of general recognition. The idea "man" recognizes its content in a general way, it refers to man in general, but does not identify its content with any particular individual. I may represent to myself an object recognized as a table, not as any particular table, and I may also represent this particular table on which I am writing. The representation I have of my friend John refers specifically to John not to anyone else. As in my imagination I scrutinize the features of my friend's face, I all along recognize that it is my friend's countenance. Recognition, general as well as particular, is involved in the very function of representation.

In immediate perception itself there is no recognition present. It is not true to fact to say that in the perception of a horse we recognize the object by perceiving it as horse and not as anything else. The fact that I perceive the object as it is depends entirely on the sensory compound which has cognition as the function of its psychic character. The sensory component, the percept horse, is the cognition of the object "horse."

Some psychologists attempt to find the origin of recognition in the feeling of familiarity. Familiarity, however, is not a primary state out of which recognition develops, but on the contrary recognition is the primary state and familiarity is derivative only. Familiarity is simply the feeling of vague, marginal, or subconscious recognition. Of course, if by the term familiarity is meant not that psychic state observed in the adult consciousness, both abnormal and normal, but that primary state of recognition out of which more definite recognition develops, then it may be admitted that familiarity is the germ of recognition, but then it is only the giving of a special term "familiarity" to an elementary form of recognition. The definite form of recognition develops out of the indefinite form of recognition, recognition must be a primary element. Recognition then is an irreducible mode of psychic activity characteristic of representative mental life.

Some psychologists regard familiarity as a pure 'feeling of at homeness' or as Fouillée puts it in the decrease of the inward shock of surprise. This is however to put the cart before the horse. It is not the feeling of familiarity that gives rise to recognition, but it is vague, indistinct, marginal, or subconscious recognition that gives rise to the feeling of familiarity. When a person, a scene, an event, or situation is familiar, the psychic state is one of having gone through the same experience before. We cannot localize its date in our scheme of time on which we project our past experiences. We have experienced the same before, but we ask ourselves,—where and when have we seen that person, the scene or the situation before? Often we succeed in forming a complete association with the past, we localize the given familiar experience, and then complete recognition ensues. *Familiarity is incomplete, vague, indefinite recognition.*

The peculiar experience of a present novel situation as having experienced or lived through the same before has been mystically referred to a previous existence, the theory of Platonic reminiscence. The explanation, however, of this phenomenon is quite simple, inasmuch that it can be shown that in such cases some similar experience had been gone through before. The subject cannot close the circuit, so to say, and effect a connection with his previous life experiences, he cannot associate fully the present experience with his former experience and localize it in his past. Other cases of such familiarity are brought about by states of dissociation. The patient perceives, goes through experiences in one state and vaguely remembers them in another. Such states of familiarity or imperfect recognition can be found in pre-epileptic states, in post-hypnotic conditions, in hypnoidal twilight states, and other subconscious dissociative states.

In regard to this phenomenon of general familiarity almost amounting to recognition without attaining it James makes the following pertinent remarks which fully bears out the fact that recognition is primary and is at the basis of what we term the sense of familiarity. "There is a curious experience" says James "which everyone seems to have had—the feeling that the present moment in its completeness has been experienced before—we were saying just the thing, in just this place, to just these people, etc. This 'sense of pre-existence' has been treated as a great mystery and occasioned much speculation I must confess that the quality of mystery seems to me a little strained. I have over and over again in my own case succeeded in resolving the phenomenon into a case of memory, so indistinct that while some past circumstances are presented again, the others are not. The dissimilar portions of the past do not arise completely enough for the date to be identified. All we get is the present scene with a general suggestion of pastness about it." I may say the same thing in my own case. Whenever I find in myself the presence of some obscure form of familiarity, I can invariably trace it to some vague, indistinct memory of an experience lived through some time before. The same holds true in the case of patients, as well as of my experiments carried out on subjects in subconscious states, hypnotic post-hypnotic, hypnoidal, and others.

When an experience enters into a number of systems, or as James would put it into a number of "settings," then the special character of the "setting" becomes confused or even obliterated. The experience present calls forth so many different systems or "settings" that the recognition element lapses and reverts to the psychic state characteristic of the lower forms of moment consciousness, passing through the more elementary forms of recognition to cognition. When the recognitive moment reproduces itself so that it becomes habitual and automatic, it falls in the scale of psychic life and reverts to the type of a lower moment.

A psychic state which recurs under a great number of conditions and circumstances loses all special and local psychic Color, so to say, and hence becomes degraded in the type of its mental activity. All ordinary experiences which have been recognized over and over again, all sorts and conditions of mental life, under different and opposite tendencies, feelings and emotions, under various settings and conflicting systems cease to be surrounded by a nimbus of pastness and become cognitive in character. When too often repeated the experience becomes so much worn by use, if we may use such an expression, that it can no longer be reproduced voluntarily in consciousness. Thus a strange face seen a few times or only once can be clearly represented, but the faces of familiar people with whom we are in constant intercourse can no longer be clearly reproduced and represented. Such a reproduction can only be brought about by a perceptual state, or by various subconscious states, such as dreams, hypnosis, or hypnoidal state. In such cases there is present a feeling of familiarity due to the series of recognitions and cognitions. Familiarity here is lapsed recognition.

James brings it out clearly: "If a phenomenon is met with, however, too often, and with too great a variety of contexts, although its image is retained and reproduced with correspondingly great facility, it fails to come up with any one particular setting and the projection of it backwards to a particular past date consequently does not come about. We recognize but do not remember it—its associates form too confused a cloud." In other words, recognition does not reach its full development. There is recognition of the phenomenon as such, but not as having had the experience in the past. The halo of pastness is gone. James quotes Spencer "To ask a man whether he remembers that the sun shines, that fire burns, that iron is hard, would be a misuse of language. Even the almost fortuitous connections among our experiences cease to be classed as memories, when they have become thoroughly familiar. Though on hearing the voice of some unseen person slightly known to us, we say we recollect to whom the voice belongs, we do not use the same expression respecting the voices of those with whom we live. The meanings of words which in childhood have to be consciously recalled seem in adult life to be immediately present.

"James then goes on saying": "These are the cases where too many paths, leading to too diverse associates, block each other's way, and all that the mind gets along with its object is a fringe of felt familiarity or sense that there *are* associates. A similar result comes about when a definite setting is only nascently aroused. We then feel that we have seen the object already, bet when or where we cannot say, though we may seem to j ourselves to be on the brink of saying it. That nascent cerebral excitation can affect consciousness with a sort of sense of the imminence of that which stronger excitations would make us definitely feel, is obvious from what happens when we seek to remember a name. It tingles, it trembles on the verge, but does not come. Just such a tingling and trembling of unrecovered associates is the penumbra of recognition that may surround any experience and make it seem familiar, though we know not why." In other words, imperfect, diffused recognition with no special system, or setting to come in live contact with and be localized in a mental series of an individual moment consciousness fails to give that mental synthesis which is the essential characteristic of the fully developed moment-consciousness. Recognition of an experience lived through in the past is the basis of what is known as the sense of familiarity.

Perhaps we may refer to the Bergsonian view of recognition, namely that recognition is interrelated with and based on special motor adaptations. "Every perception" says Bergson "has its organized motor accompaniment, the ordinary feeling of recognition has its roots in the consciousness of this organization." While it is true that recognition deals with the use of objects and with special adaptations to the external environment, as far as such recognition is expressed in motor adjustments, it can hardly be said that this view holds true of recognition in general. In the process of recognition it is not the motor accompaniment, it is the feeling of sameness of experience, the feeling of pastness with its localization in a series of "settings" or of systems that go to form the main elements.

I must say that the motor accompaniments have been too much overworked in our psychological theories. We have carried over into our philosophy, such as pragmatism, and into our psychology of recent years too much of the haste and whirl of the exchange and the shop. Everything is motor and everything is practical. This is a reflection of our present industrial age in the domain of the mind. Perhaps it expresses well the tendency of the modern philosophical and psychological trend of transmuting everything into motion when psychologists describe themselves as being "motor men on the psychological car."

Recognition is not motion at least from a psychological standpoint, unless like Bergson we resort to the metaphysical, pan-psychistic argument of reducing motion to independent objective images as constituting the nature of external reality. Barring such metaphysical speculations that, as we have pointed out, have no place in psychology which must keep strictly to the difference between the external and internal, to the opposition of the objective reality of the material world and of the subjective reality of the mental world, different spheres of phenomena which should not be reduced one to the other, we cannot help realizing the fact that there is far more of the character of recognition in mental states in which the motor element is insignificant or *nil,* such as sensations, ideas, memories, thought reasoning and so on than there is in the automatic reflex reactions of behavior and motor adjustments. When we see color green and recognize that we have seen it the day before we can hardly speak of a motor element present in recognition. When I think of the Bergsonian theory of memory, or recognition and remember of my thinking; about it the night before and disagreeing with it, the motor element can only enter by a great strain of imagination. If there are any motor elements they hardly play any significant part in the process of memory and recognition. We must deny emphatically the significance and importance of the motor element in recognition. The essential element in recognition is not the motor, but the psychic elements.

Bergson himself is driven to take this aspect of recognition when he develops his theory of pure memory with no action in contradistinction to the memory which inserts itself edgewise into the flux of sensori-motor adaptations. Bergson not without some contradiction strongly contrasts the true pure memory with the memory image sharply inserted into the plane of action. If we grant Bergson that such pure unadulterated memories are present, memories free from all motor reactions, then we must necessarily agree to the fact that remembrance, recollection, and hence recognition can exist without any motor accompaniments. In other words, recognition cannot be resolved into action, into motor accompaniments, into behavior and reactions. Recognition is a psychic *quale sui generis.*

Each set of particular representative elements carries along, as James terms it, its special "setting" or as I describe it "system." It is this special setting that helps the process of recognition in having the particular experience projected in the past, in having it oriented among many other systems of associations and having it localized in its particular past. Recognition then arises when the present experience calls forth its special system, or setting in a series of mental events. The present experience must close with the past experience and form a circuit. At the same time the experience must not be short-circuited, because in such a case we have a state of dissociation. The present experience must form a circuit with its system or setting and with the personality as a whole. Recognition thus requires a special setting in the complex web and woof of the present total moment consciousness constituting the individuality of the subject.

In the higher forms of mental life *where self-consciousness is developed, the experience forms a live circuit, so to say, with the whole personality.* The higher states of recognition appear in the form of the "I" consciousness. "It is I who experienced all that in my past. It is I who remembers that this bit of experience has taken place in 'my' experience some time ago." There *is the my present self thinking of the experience as lived through by my past self.*

In the lower forms of recognition where the self is not present, as in the higher vertebrates and possibly in infants, there exists the present cognition of the experience and the re-cognition of it in the shape of a vague memory that it had been experienced before. The present experience of an already experienced event floats in a cloud of pastness. It is this psychic state of pastness in a present experience that makes it felt to the subject who experiences it—as recurrent and recognitive. Of course, not every recurrent experience, even of the higher types of moments is recognitive, as there are psychopathic recurrent states which, like the lower forms of moment-consciousness, recur and reproduce themselves with no element of recognition present. *We can, however, fully assert that every recognitive experience is recurrent.* Recognition requires former or past experience.

CHAPTER XXI
THE RECOGNITIVE MOMENT AND ITS REPRODUCTION

RECOGNITION is one of the essential attributes of representative life. The faintest and most obscure representation requires the presence of recognition in the background We may say that without recognition representation becomes an impossibility. Recognition is the function of representative elements. Just as cognition is the function of sensory, presentative elements so recognition, or *secondary cognition* is the function of representative elements. Now that moment consciousness which has representative elements among the constituents of its content may be termed *recognitive moment-consciousness.*

The recognitive moment is of a higher type than the synthetic moment. Like the synthetic moment, material or psychic content of the recognitive moment is assimilated in a synthetized form; like the synthetic moment, it goes on reproducing not on the desultory, but on the accumulative type; and moreover, it approaches more the compound, accumulative type. Unlike the synthetic moment, the recognitive moment is possessed of representative elements having recognition as their function. Representative elements with their function of recognition, present in the recognitive moment, but absent in the other lower moments, make a fundamental difference in the nature of reproduction.

The reproduction of the recognitive moment is totally different in character from that of the desultory and synthetic moments. In the desultory and synthetic moments reproduction is effected by means of presentative elements, and actual recurrence of former experience is indispensable; in the recognitive moment nothing of the kind is required. The reproduction of the recognitive moment is effected only in *representation*. The moment with its sensory elements is not reproduced as recurrence, but only *symbolized,* or truer to say *substituted* in meaning or in function by the representative elements. The representative element, the image, the idea is recognized as functioning as a substitute, as standing for the presence of the actual experience of the original moment with its nuclear primary and secondary sensory elements. In the higher stages of the moment this recognition may become detached, and the act of recognition may become duplicated and emphasized in another subsequent representation. In reality, however, both in the lower and higher forms of the recognitive moment, the fact of recognition belongs directly to the representation itself; for as we have pointed out recognition is an essential function of representation.

Just as sensory elements express, or present the qualities of the external object, so do representative elements mirror the psychic objects as presented to sense-experience. This relation may be expressed in a proportional form: *as presentation is to the external object so is representation to the presented object.* In the higher forms of the recognitive moment the representation can be once more represented and this latter is represented in its turn, each subsequent reproduction representing, substituting and mirroring the preceding one. Thus I may see the child yonder playing with its ball, I may represent to myself the whole scene, and may further represent to myself the fact of representation itself which in its turn may be once more represented, and so on. The content of the recognitive moment in this mode of reproduction, becomes more and more modified, more and more different as it proceeds along this line, becomes further and further removed from the original experienced moment with its sensory elements.

In the more prevalent forms of the recognitive moment the process of reproduction does not proceed in this way; reproduction keeps nearer to the lower types, to the content of the types of the synthetic moments, or, in other words, it keeps nearer to sense-experience. The representation has a direct reference to the object as presented in sense-experience, and in its reproduction this direct reference is more or less preserved throughout.

The recognitive moment is every time reproduced in representation, and although having different representative elements with each successive reproduction, it still refers to the same object as presented. The modifications that occur in the moment take place only in the representative elements. Adaptations, instead of taking place by means of changes in the sensory elements due to successive modification effected by the direct influence of stimuli from external environment, are now freed from the direct influence of external conditions, and may be effected within the representative elements of the moment itself, without having recourse to the modifying influence of stimuli.

We have already shown that the characteristic trait of representative elements is their freedom from the bondage in accumulations or compounds in which sensory elements are kept; representative elements can be easily transposed, they can enter into new free associations without requiring special external stimuli to break the stable compound. The free associations of representative elements may be dissolved by other representations. The stick lying nearby may be kicked away by my foot, but may also be represented as a support; it may be imaged as a means of defense and attack, and finally the representation may be changed in another direction, the stick may be used as an instrument for bringing down apples from a tree. Adaptation is effected within the process of representation before any changes are introduced into actual, presentative life.

From a teleological standpoint one can realize the great gain in the economy of life reactions by a mode of reproduction independent of and free from the direct influence of external stimuli with their consequent sensory responses and motor reactions, resulting in further and further modifications of the original moment. The recognitive moment in its growth and development by a series of internal representative modifications spares itself ill adapted sensory responses and motor reactions. This is an immense gain to life, a great aid and powerful weapon in the struggle for existence.

Regarded from this standpoint of modification the moment-consciousness may be said to pass through important stages in the course of its development. *The stage of non-mo disability of content, then the stage of modifiability of the sensori-motor content, and finally modifiability in representation.* The special importance of the recognitive moment for the being possessing it is the greater freedom from the dominion of the external environment. External conditions are not so literally, so slavishly reflected in the moment. Changes may occur in sensori-motor reactions and adaptations due to representations alone, without any previous material changes in the external conditions. The recognitive moment carries its external world in itself, in its representation, and by affecting changes there, may bring about changes in the environment, thus controlling external conditions, instead of being controlled by them. Instead of being driven by external forces into blind obedience, into unintelligent adaptations, the moment is on the point, even in its lowest forms, to acquire some intelligent character in seeing ahead, by living over its former experiences in the states of representation, the sensori-motor reactions being accordingly modified.

The reproduction of the recognitive moment is not induced by external stimuli only, but mainly by the course of other representations. Without actually being confronted with the object the representation of it may any time arise in the mind and call forth new adaptations to the external environment.

The representation by which the recognitive moment effects its reproduction is not at all a mode of reinstatement, partial or complete, a mode characteristic of the lower types of moments. What the moment reproduces is altogether different in nature and content from what has been experienced, or directly presented. What is presented is sensory material, what is reproduced is imagery, ideal "stuff." Imagery, ideal stuff as it is, it still mirrors, substitutes, represents the "material" certainty of sensory experience.

From the very nature of the moment and mode of its reproduction the original emotional tone of the experience is not reproduced by the recognitive moment. The emotional tone like the rest of the psychic content is represented in recognitive reproduction, but not *actually* reproduced. The great gain of it from a biological standpoint is momentous, since the moment's reaction can be better adapted to the changing conditions of its environment. The representative elements entering into the idea or image of an object change from reproduction to reproduction but they always mirror, refer to the same sensory elements and compounds; they recognize their object.

The recognition of an object or an event, however vague, means some experience that has been lived through before. In other words, the representation, although experienced, as a present psychic element, must have a glow of pastness about it. *Representation is a present experience referring to a past life,* to an event that is passing or that has passed away. Representation with its function of recognition is a reference to the past.

This reference to the past may range from the indefinite to the highly definite localization of experience referred to the time past. This depends on the development of the moment, of its place in the scale of evolution. The higher the moment the more definite, the lower the less definite the localization is. The dog in recognizing his master, Ulysses, hardly knew the length of time the hero had been away in his battles and wanderings, although the dog possibly had a dim feeling of pastness, revealing it by the great joy manifested at seeing his master, as if his long delayed expectations have been finally fulfilled. If dogs are capable of recognition at all, some vague feeling of pastness is present in the recognitive moment, however low it may stand in the scale of development.

In the child we find that the time localization is quite indefinite. In very young children the future and the past such as yesterday and to-morrow have no definite meaning. Thus in children of three years that have come under my observation the apprehension of the past and future, such as yesterday and to-morrow is still wanting. When the child is told that something took place, he referred it to a "yesterday" indefinitely localized in the past. The day before, a week ago, a month ago, years past are equally projected into the vague past. The same holds true of the child-sense of the future. "When is to-morrow?" is a question I have been often asked by intelligent children of three, four and even five years old. The child recognizes his old friend after a departure of several months, but he localizes this event far off in time, say "yesterday."

The reference to the past becomes more and more definitely localized in time, the higher the recognitive moment rises in the scale of evolution. This process of localization of the recognized event in the past depends entirely on the time-sense becoming fully definite with the more or less greater perfection of the conceptual time scheme. Thus savages and the ignorant classes of even civilized societies have an imperfect form of time localization. The definiteness of localization, however, is not of material consequence as far as our point of view is concerned. For all we know Ulysses' dog, the ape and the infant have no time-localization at all, what is enough to state from our psychological standpoint is the fact that recognition involves some form of pastness belonging to the implicated representative element, a pastness which in a higher stage becomes time-localization.

Under the influence of toxic matter, of narcotics, and in some forms of mental diseases, this time-sense may swell, thus giving rise to the projection of experience on a larger scale of objective time. Such states are to be found under the influence of opium or cannabis, also in some mental diseases when the patient claims that he is many centuries old. This function of recognition with its aspect of pastness is certainly present in the passing recognitive moment. The process becomes more complicated and also more objectified in the higher types of moment-consciousness. In short, the recognitive moment-consciousness in addition to its reproduction involves some form of awareness of its being a reproduction by its reference to a past experience. Being freed from its bondage to the present circumstances, living in the by-gone past the recognitive moment gets a glimpse of the not yet born future into which the free representative elements are projected.

Printed in Great Britain
by Amazon